THE REVOLT OF THE
CATALANS

All Catalonia's rights have suffered shipwreck in the gulf of malice.

F. MARTÍ, *Noticia Universal de Cataluña* (1641)

The worst enemies of Catalonia are the Catalans themselves.

ALEJANDRO DE ROS, *Cataluña Desengañada* (1646)

Really, the Catalans ought to see more of the world than Catalonia.

OLIVARES to the COUNT OF SANTA COLOMA, 29 February 1640

THE CONDE DUQUE DE OLIVARES

THE REVOLT OF THE

CATALANS

A Study in the Decline of Spain

(1598-1640)

BY

J. H. ELLIOTT

Fellow of Trinity College
and Lecturer in History in the
University of Cambridge

CAMBRIDGE

AT THE UNIVERSITY PRESS

1963

PUBLISHED BY

THE SYNDICS OF THE CAMBRIDGE UNIVERSITY PRESS

Bentley House, 200 Euston Road, London, N.W.1
American Branch: 32 East 57th Street, New York 22, N.Y.
West African Office: P.O. Box 33, Ibadan, Nigeria

©

CAMBRIDGE UNIVERSITY PRESS

1963

Printed in Great Britain at the University Press, Cambridge
(Brooke Crutchley, University Printer)

TO
MY FATHER AND
MOTHER

CONTENTS

LIST OF ILLUSTRATIONS

PLATES

TEXT FIGURES

MAPS

PREFACE

This book began its life as a study of the political career of the favourite and chief minister of Philip IV of Spain, the Conde Duque de Olivares. But the disappearance or destruction of the bulk of Olivares's papers[1] forced me to modify my original plans, and I found that the best, and perhaps indeed the only accessible, approach to the policies of the Conde Duque was by way of an episode of outstanding importance for seventeenth-century Spanish history: the revolution of Catalonia in 1640.

The extent to which Olivares was personally responsible for the outbreak of the Catalan Revolution was a subject for debate even among his contemporaries. It was known that he was anxious to destroy the liberties of Catalonia, and an insurrection in the Principality would provide him with a useful pretext. Nineteenth-century Catalan historians like Víctor Balaguer were convinced that this was the explanation of the revolt. 'Everything induces us to believe', he wrote, 'that it was the intention of Olivares to provoke a revolution in Catalonia in order to have a justification for falling upon it and finishing for once and all with its liberties.'[2] This interpretation of the origins of the revolution, which accorded well with Catalan nationalist preconceptions, found wide acceptance. Nearly forty years later, another Catalan historian wrote: 'It is perfectly clear that the disorders and the revolt of the year 1640 were provoked by the Court and the royal authorities in Catalonia.'[3]

This explanation, even if correct—and it scarcely seemed to have been proved—appeared to me to raise certain problems. In particular, it left unasked an obvious question: why should the king of Spain's chief minister choose to provoke a revolution in a frontier province at the very moment when the war with France was approaching its climax? This question surely deserved some attention. At the very least, it suggested the need for further investigation into the circumstances which could have driven Olivares to so drastic a decision. This required an examination of the relationship between the Spanish Court and the

[1] See Appendix VI (Sources).
[2] *Historia de Cataluña* (2nd ed., Madrid, 1886), vol. VII, p. 358.
[3] A. Rovira i Virgili, *Pau Claris* (Barcelona, 1922), p. 21.

Preface

Principality of Catalonia in the years preceding the revolution, and inevitably I found that this relationship could not be understood without some knowledge of the social, political and economic conditions inside Catalonia under the government of the Habsburgs.

In beginning this inquiry, I did not find earlier studies very helpful. As far as the revolution itself was concerned, Catalan historians tended to repeat a common version of the story, which was clearly nationalist in its inspiration, and was based on a restricted range of documents; and foreign historians followed them at a distance. The Catalan Revolution was one of R. B. Merriman's 'six contemporaneous revolutions' of the mid-seventeenth century, but the few pages he devotes to it are derivative and pallid.[1] The social, economic and administrative history of Catalonia in the years preceding the revolution proved to be in even worse shape. The sixteenth and seventeenth centuries were traditionally a period of 'decadence' in Catalan history, and had not attracted the interest of native historians. I therefore found myself starting out with scarcely a single signpost along the road, but I was fortunate in that a small group of younger historians at Barcelona, under the leadership of Professor Vicens Vives, was at this moment turning its attention to similar problems in this and other periods of Catalan history. I benefited greatly from their encouragement and co-operation.

The archives, both central and local, proved to be extraordinarily rich, and as a result it has been possible to present a much fuller portrait of seventeenth-century Catalonia than was previously available. Inevitably, though, the portrait must still be very rough. Our knowledge, in particular, of Catalonia's economic history is still in its very earliest stages, and it is not yet even clear what kinds of material, and in what quantities, exist for its elucidation. The pages in this book devoted to social and economic questions must therefore be regarded as extremely tentative, and designed primarily to raise a number of problems which, it is hoped, will stimulate others to further study.

A seventeenth-century Catalan, referring to another revolution, wrote that 'it is necessary, in order to discover the causes of a popular movement or commotion, to take the narration a long way back, since experience has shown that this does not occur without being preceded

[1] *Six Contemporaneous Revolutions* (Oxford, 1938), pp. 1–10, 115–19 and 135–8.

by many preliminary events which move men to stir up trouble'.[1] In studying the Catalan Revolution I have found this to be true; and inevitably it has led to the production of a book much larger than I had originally intended. The only extenuating circumstances I can plead are that 'Spain in decline', while much discussed, has been little studied, and that the study of even one region of the Spanish peninsula in the first half of the seventeenth century can do something to explain why the greatest power in the world in the sixteenth century failed to maintain its position in the seventeenth. Moreover, beyond its implications for the career of Olivares and for the declining fortunes of the Spanish Monarchy, the Catalan Revolution has a still wider relevance, for it can stand as a case-history of that great struggle between the centralizing aspirations of monarchs and the traditional rights and liberties of their subjects, which was raging all over sixteenth and seventeenth-century Europe, and out of which the modern State emerged.

A few words seem necessary about some of the terminology used in this book. The Spaniards referred to their empire as the Monarchy, and I have used this expression throughout to denote the entirety of the territories owing allegiance to the king of Spain. The individual status of these territories varied: some were kingdoms, some were duchies, and Catalonia was a principality. In spite of its modern connotations, it seems simplest to refer to them as 'provinces', especially as 'province' was a word they sometimes used of themselves, without apparently seeing it as in any way prejudicial to their traditional rights and privileged status.

The problem of whether to use Castilian or Catalan terms has caused me much difficulty. It may appear pedantic to write Lleida for a town known to English readers by its Castilian form of Lérida, but it seemed reasonable that Catalan towns should keep, in the body of the text, the names by which they are known to their inhabitants (including Perpinyà for Perpignan, as being formerly Catalan territory), even if their use is at present officially prohibited. I have also felt it right that the names of institutions and official posts in seventeenth-century Catalonia should be given their Catalan form, and have provided a glossary of Catalan, together with a few Castilian, terms at the end of the

[1] Francesc de Gilabert in his 'Respuesta hecha al tratado...que Antonio de Herrera hace de los sucesos de Aragón...', printed in Conde de Luna, *Comentarios de los Sucesos de Aragón en los años 1591 y 1592* (ed. Duque de Villahermosa, Madrid, 1888), p. 481.

book. Personal names were even more of a problem, since seventeenth-century Catalans appear to have been indiscriminate in the use of Castilian or Catalan versions of their names. Again I have opted for the modern Catalan form, hoping that English readers will not be taken too much aback to read Joan, where they would be better acquainted with Juan. I have, however, made two exceptions. The Governor of Catalonia, Don Alexos de Marimón, bore a Christian name known neither to Castilian nor to Catalan, and it would seem wrong to deprive him of it; and the general notoriety of the duke of Lerma's Catalan favourite, whose public career belonged entirely to the world of the Court, would make it ridiculous to call him anything other than Don Pedro Franqueza. I have also left a name in its Castilian form when its owner used it in publishing a book.

I cannot end without expressing my deep gratitude for all the help and encouragement I have received from many friends both in Spain and in England, during the years that have gone to the preparation of this book. Special difficulties confront any historian rash enough to explore the past of a country other than his own, and if I have managed to overcome any of these difficulties, it is entirely because of the kindness and forbearance of a large number of Catalans, who have done everything possible to make me feel at home in their country. If some of my findings seem a poor repayment for their fine generosity, they will, I hope, know me well enough to realize that these were not reached without much thought and a careful examination of all the existing evidence. And nothing would give me greater pleasure than that they should be prompted by my more controversial assertions to unearth further evidence which will effectively confute them.

My greatest debt inside Spain is to the late Professor Vicens Vives. His death in 1960 at the age of only fifty was a calamity for modern historical scholarship. Single-handed he set in train a complete reappraisal of the traditional dogmas of Spanish and Catalan history, and his stature, already great in his lifetime, will continue to grow. Among his closest disciples I must single out for special mention Dr Joan Reglà, now Professor of Modern History at Valencia University; and Drs Jordi Nadal and Emili Giralt, who have shown me innumerable kindnesses, both personal and professional, and whose combined work on Catalan social and economic problems promises to transform our understanding of sixteenth and seventeenth-century Catalonia. I am also deeply indebted to Dr Ferran Soldevila, the doyen of Catalan historians, for his untiring interest and his most helpful criticisms; to Mossèn Josep Sanabre, the constant partner of my incursions into the Catalonia of the seventeenth century; and to Dr Don Gonçal Lloveras, who, more than anyone else, helped me to become acquainted with the Catalonia of the twentieth.

The archivists who gave me assistance and encouragement are too many to be mentioned individually, although exceptions must be made for Don Ricardo Magdaleno, Director of the Simancas Archives; Dr Martínez Ferrando, Director of the Archive of the Crown of Aragon; Sr Serra Rosselló, of the Barcelona City archives; Mossèn Junyent of Vic, and the late Mossèn Pere Pujol of the Seu d'Urgell.

I am also deeply indebted to M. Pierre Vilar, of Paris, who put his remarkable knowledge of Catalan history unreservedly at my disposal, and generously let me read part of the typescript of his forthcoming work on eighteenth-century Catalonia.

In this country, I owe much to my historical colleagues in Trinity College, Cambridge, who listened patiently while I expatiated on matters Catalan, and were generous with encouragement and advice; and it would be wrong to omit all mention of those of my pupils in Trinity whose questions and comments on a wide variety of historical topics constantly forced me to re-examine my conclusions in the light of general European and English developments. I am profoundly indebted to the Master and Fellows of Trinity for electing me to be one of their number on the strength of my original dissertation, and for enabling me to spend two years researching in Spain. I am also grateful to the Electors to the Prince Consort Prize for awarding an earlier draft of this book the Prince Consort Prize and Seeley Medal for 1956, and for allowing me to publish it in an extended form.

Dr Batista i Roca of Emmanuel College, Cambridge, Sir George Clark, Mr H. O. Evennett of Trinity College, Cambridge, the late Professor González-Llubera, Mr David Joslin of Pembroke College, Cambridge, Professor H. Koenigsberger of Nottingham University, Mrs Jean Lindsay, formerly of Girton College, and Dr R. Robson of Trinity College have read part or all of the text at some stage of its life, and have been extremely generous in their criticisms and advice. In particular, Professor Koenigsberger and Dr Batista i Roca devoted much time to the final draft of the typescript, and made numerous valuable suggestions which I have endeavoured to follow. But my most considerable debt is to Professor H. Butterfield, who guided my first steps in historical research, and whose perceptiveness and encouragement have been of the very greatest value to me over the course of the years.

Dr Robson generously offered to read the proofs, and has laboured to save me both from infelicities of style and inexactitude of expression.

Finally, my wife has been an unfailing support during the writing of the book, and has dedicated herself with patience and good humour to the ungrateful task of preparing the index.   J. H. E.

TRINITY COLLEGE, CAMBRIDGE
23 June 1962

KEY TO ABBREVIATIONS[1]

I. ARCHIVES AND LIBRARIES[2]

AAE	Archives du Ministère des Affaires Étrangères (Paris)
AAT	Archivo Arzobispal de Tarragona
AAW	Archive of the Archbishopric of Westminster
ABL	Academia de Buenas Letras (Barcelona)
ACA	Archivo de la Corona de Aragón (Barcelona)
ACG	Archivo Capitular de Gerona
ACT	Archivo Capitular de Tarragona
ACU	Archivo Capitular de la Seo de Urgel
ACV	Archivo Capitular de Vich
ADP	Archives Départementales des Pyrénées-Orientales (Perpignan)
AGS	Archivo General de Simancas
AHB	Archivo Histórico de Barcelona
AHC	Archivo Histórico de Cervera
AHM	Archivo Histórico de Manresa
AHN	Archivo Histórico Nacional (Madrid)
AMG	Archivo Municipal de Gerona
AMP	Archives Municipales de Perpignan
AMU	Archivo Municipal de la Seo de Urgel
AMV	Archivo Municipal de Vich
APB	Archivo de Protocolos (Barcelona)
APL	Archivo de la Pahería de Lérida
BC	Biblioteca Central (Barcelona)
BM	British Museum
BN	Biblioteca Nacional (Madrid)
BN (Paris)	Bibliothèque Nationale (Paris)
BUB	Biblioteca de la Universidad de Barcelona
PRO	Public Record Office (London)
RAH	Real Academia de la Historia (Madrid)

[1] I have put the actual name of a Council in the footnotes if the series does not correspond to it. Thus ACA: CA, leg. 200, consulta, 1 Feb. 1640 = consulta of the Council of Aragon. If, however, there is in this series a consulta of the Consejo de Estado, the reference will read: ACA: CA, leg. 200, Consejo de Estado, 10 March 1640.

[2] Names of Catalan archives and collections have been given in the Castilian form by which they are at present known.

Key to Abbreviations

Add.	Additional MSS
CA	Consejo de Aragón
CCO	Cartes Comunes Originals
Codoin	*Colección de Documentos Inéditos para la Historia de España* (Madrid, 1842–1915)
Cons.	Consejos
CR	Cartes Rebudes
Delibs.	Deliberaciones
Eg.	Egerton MSS
Est.	Estado
G	Generalitat
GA	Guerra Antigua
LC	Lletres Closes
leg.	legajo
lib.	libro
LT	Lletres Trameses
MHE	*Memorial Histórico Español* (Madrid, from 1851)
R	Registro

CHAPTER I

CASTILE AND ARAGON

A seventeenth-century Spaniard could well quote with pride from the Psalms: 'Their line is gone out through all the earth, and their words to the end of the world.'[1] His countrymen had discovered and colonized a New World, and had carried the Gospel to the farthest corners of the earth. They had built for themselves an empire greater than any the world had known. They had won a unique place in the annals of mankind by the prowess of their arms, the skill of their diplomats, the brilliance of their civilization, and the incomparable wealth (now perhaps a little tarnished) of their king. Who could doubt that they had found special favour in the eyes of the Lord, and were ordained to further His purposes?

The miraculous character of Spain's rise to greatness was confirmed by the extraordinary speed with which it had been achieved. Little more than a hundred years before, Spain itself could scarcely be said to have existed. 'Hispania' was the map-maker's name for the jagged corner of Europe which jutted out into an unexplored ocean; it was the historian's name for a famous province whose unity had not long survived the downfall of the Roman empire; it was the shadow of what once had been, and one day might be again, but was still no more than a shadow. Throughout the Middle Ages, the Hispania of the cartographers gave a certain factitious unity to a complex of Crowns and kingdoms—Castile and León, Navarre, Aragon, Portugal and the Moorish kingdom of Granada. Each had its own history, its own institutions and its own ways, and in so far as the Christian kingdoms preserved any semblance of the unity of [Roman times, it lay only in the feeling that all were brothers in the crusade against Islam.

The history of this fragmented peninsula was decisively changed in 1469 by the marriage of Ferdinand of Aragon and Isabella of Castile, which united the dynasties of two of the three Crowns of Christian

---

[1] Quoted by Dr Carlos García (1617). See M. Herrero García, *Ideas de los Españoles del Siglo XVII* (Madrid, 1928), p. 14.

Spain. The central and eastern blocs of the peninsula now shared a common ruling house, and only the isolation of the third kingdom, Portugal, and the continued presence of the Granada Moors, stood between the House of Trastámara and the reunion of the territories of Spain beneath a single monarch. In the course of just over a hundred years their dream of unity was to be realized; the kingdom of Granada was destroyed in 1492; Navarre was to be incorporated into the Crown of Castile in 1515;[1] and Portugal to be united to the Crowns of Castile and Aragon in 1580. But, even before the conquest of Granada and the annexation of Portugal, it seemed to contemporaries that Hispania had been revived. The marriage of Ferdinand and Isabella in 1469 and their joint rule over Castile and Aragon from 1479 signalized to the world at large the emergence of a new European nation, the birth of Spain.

The union of the Crowns of Castile and Aragon in the late fifteenth century was therefore the first in that chain of almost miraculous events which would carry the name and reputation of Spain to the farthest ends of the earth. Without it, the triumphs of the sixteenth century would have been unthinkable. The vigour and endurance of the Castilians alone made possible the discovery and conquest of a vast overseas empire, but it was the techniques of government and administration inherited from the Aragonese which ensured its organization and survival. In that sense, the Spanish empire of the sixteenth century was the outcome of the union of the two Crowns, and proof of the indispensability of one to the other. But the peculiar development of the Spanish empire was shaped not only by the fact of this union, but also by its particular characteristics. Its most important features were, first, that it was not a union of equal partners, and, second, that, as a union, it was no more than dynastic.

When Ferdinand and Isabella brought together the two territories of Castile and Aragon, these were at very different stages of development. Castile for centuries had lived in a world of its own, remote from the rest of Europe, its gaze turned inwards upon itself, and its energies directed towards the recovering of its lands from the Infidel. Castile's pastoral, nomadic society was a society organized for war, and in

---

[1] While incorporated into the Crown of Castile, Navarre preserved its Cortes and other institutions.

particular for a crusading war. Its heroes and its ideals were martial and religious; the pattern of its life was largely determined by those who fought and those who prayed. By the fifteenth century, however, the pattern was gradually beginning to change and to acquire certain elements of sophistication, as Castile moved into closer contact with the outside world. The age-old crusade against the Granada Moors seemed at last to be moving towards a triumphant conclusion. Its ending would mean the release of energies previously absorbed in the struggle with Islam; and it was to be expected that the crusading warrior would look around him for new worlds to conquer, rather than content himself with hanging his arms on the wall. At the same time, Castile's wool trade with northern Europe was expanding fast, and a vigorous urban society had grown up in Cantabria, living on the wealth, and acquainting itself with the ideas, which were flowing into the country from Flanders and the North.

The late fifteenth century therefore found Castile ready for a fresh challenge and new opportunities. The prosperity of the wool trade had brought it vast new riches. The ending of the *Reconquista* had freed it from internal wars. The discovery of the New World, and the European wars undertaken by Ferdinand in defence of Aragonese interests, would provide an ideal opportunity for canalizing the immense energies of a proud and triumphant nation, which found itself for the first time with the occasion, the resources and the incentive to turn outwards, towards Europe and a wider world.

Unfortunately, this great upsurge of national vitality in late fifteenth-century Castile was matched by no comparable upsurge in the Crown of Aragon to which it now found itself united. The Crown of Aragon's medieval history was quite the reverse of that of Castile. In dividing by a mountain barrier the eastern kingdoms of the Spanish peninsula from the central Castilian plateau, geography had brought about a different rhythm of historical advance. While the Castilians were still engaged in dynastic struggles, and their crusade against the Moors was far from complete, the inhabitants of the eastern regions had already expelled the Arabs and were laying the foundations for one of the most imposing States in medieval Europe. The Iberian portion of their creation, the Crown of Aragon, consisted of three territories, each with its own institutions but governed by a single dynasty; the kingdoms of

1-2

Aragon and Valencia, and the Principality of Catalonia.[1] In this great Catalan-Aragonese federation, with its rich seaboard and arid Aragonese hinterland, the Catalans were the leaders. Their initiative and energy turned Barcelona into one of the great ports of the western Mediterranean; their enterprise created for the federation a maritime empire which stretched from Majorca to Athens; and their remarkable organizing ability endowed it with institutions which embodied their belief that the correct relationship between a king and his subjects was contractual, with mutual obligations upon ruler and subject to serve and obey.

The thirteenth and fourteenth centuries were the great age of the Catalan-Aragonese empire. The fifteenth century was for Catalonia, the predominant partner in the federation, a century of commercial, social and political crisis. The origins of this crisis are traditionally ascribed to the change of dynasty after the extinction in 1410 of the native line of Catalan kings, which was replaced on the throne by the Castilian house of Trastámara. Recent investigations, however, suggest that the crisis was far more complex than a simple upheaval caused by the introduction of an alien dynasty which found itself out of sympathy with Catalan aspirations and ways of thought.[2] Catalonia was affected by the general economic depression of the Mediterranean world during the last decades of the fourteenth century. Its cloth trade with Italy, Sicily and the Eastern Mediterranean was disrupted by war and piracy and foreign competition. Its traditional agrarian organization was dealt a severe blow by the Black Death and its aftermath. In the countryside, the peasantry was beginning to demand from the landowners a legal status consonant with its improved economic condition. In the towns, the artisans were struggling to break the oligarchy's hold over municipal government. The political structure of the Catalan State, which for so long had made the Principality a model of order and good

[1] To avoid confusion, 'Aragon' is used throughout this book (except in the title of this chapter) only of the kingdom of Aragon, and 'the Crown of Aragon' or 'the States of the Crown of Aragon' is used to describe the Levantine territories as a unit. There is no alternative to using 'Aragonese' both for the natives of all the territories of the Crown and for the inhabitants of the kingdom of Aragon alone, but the context should make clear the sense in which the word is used.

[2] For this, and the remarks that follow, see J. Vicens Vives, *Evolución de la Economía catalana durante la primera mitad del siglo XV* (Palma de Mallorca, 1955), an admirably clear account of the present state of knowledge, read at the fourth Historical Congress of the Crown of Aragon. See also the brilliant analysis by Pierre Vilar, 'Le déclin catalan du Bas Moyen Age. Hypothèses sur sa chronologie', *Estudios de Historia Moderna*, vol. VI (Barcelona, 1956–9), pp. 1–68.

government, proved a frail barrier against the mounting tide of sub-
version. The mercantile oligarchy, clinging to this traditional structure, and to the contractual relationship between the king and his
subjects, attempted to set limits to the royal authority; the lower urban
classes, in their hatred of the oligarchy, sided with the king; the nobles,
beleaguered by their peasants, threw in their lot with an oligarchy
whose aims and interests they increasingly shared.

The resulting alignment of king, peasants and artisans against a
nobility and merchant oligarchy which controlled the Principality's
traditional institutions, plunged into civil war a country which had
already been weakened by economic crisis and by the vast effort of
commercial and military expansion in the preceding centuries. From
1462 to 1481 hostilities continued, punctuated by short-lived truces.
The Catalonia that emerged from these struggles was a battered and
exhausted country, with its spiritual and economic impetus lost. The
extent to which it could recover its former vigour and enterprise would
depend very largely on the way in which it was pacified and reorganized. This was to be the work of Ferdinand, who came to the
throne on the death of his father, John II, in 1479. He conceived his
duties along conservative lines. While accepting the existence of the
new social realities, of a prosperous class of peasantry, and of an urban
class with a right to participate in the administration of the towns, he
attempted to incorporate them into an institutional structure which
would retain all that was best and most valuable in the achievements of
the past.[1] Instead of laying in Catalonia the foundations of absolute
royal power, such as the monarchs of Castile were beginning to enjoy,
he took pains to resurrect and reinvigorate the old contractual State,
and those of its institutions which protected the subject against the
abuse of royal power. Rejecting the opportunity provided by the
Catalan civil war to bring the Principality into conformity with the
autocratic political model of Castile, he restored it to conformity with
its fellow-States of Aragon and Valencia, which had escaped the civil
strife so ruinous to Catalonia. By this means, he hoped to provide the
necessary conditions for the Principality's economic recovery, and so
to revive the ancient splendours of the Crown of Aragon.

[1] The new interpretation of Ferdinand's work is given in J. Vicens Vives, *Política del Rey
Católico en Cataluña* (Barcelona, 1940).

The gradual revival of Catalan economic life in the first years of the sixteenth century held out the hope that Ferdinand's policy would be crowned with eventual success. But this partial Catalan recovery, even when combined with the increased prosperity of Valencia, could not succeed in making the Crown of Aragon a partner equal in strength and resources to the Crown of Castile. Where Castile was entering a period of economic and military expansion, the Crown of Aragon, after centuries of expansion followed by a period of decay, was entering on a new age which, at the best, was likely to be no more than one of consolidation and slow recovery.

If Castile now surpassed the States of the Crown of Aragon in vigour and energy, it also surpassed them in size of population. With an area three times as great, it had a population which, at the beginning of the sixteenth century, may have totalled about $6\frac{1}{2}$ million; the population of the Crown of Aragon, for which the figure is more certain, was just over one million. A similar disproportion is to be found in the figures for the relative densities of population:[1]

	Extent	Density
Castile	378,000 sq. km.	22 per sq. km.
Crown of Aragon	100,000 ,,	13.6 ,,

Today it seems remarkable that Castile, with its great desert wastes, should ever have been more densely populated than the combined territories of the Crown of Aragon, but the existence of this surprising disparity is one clue to Castilian predominance in the new Spain of Ferdinand and Isabella.

The union of the two Crowns was therefore a union of very unequal partners. It was also the union of two very different partners. The Catalan-Aragonese federation, orientated towards the Mediterranean, commercial in spirit, cosmopolitan in outlook, had little in common with a Castile whose social organization was geared to the needs of crusading warfare and whose mental horizons had been limited by centuries of political and cultural isolation. The gulf between the two was made still wider by their differing political traditions and institutions. Each, it was true, possessed parliamentary institutions, or

[1] Javier Ruiz Almansa, 'La población española en el siglo XVI', *Revista Internacional de Sociología*, vol III, no. 4 (1943), p. 120. The figures for Castile are for 1594, those for Aragon and Valencia 1609, and for Catalonia 1553.

Cortes, but the Cortes of Castile, which had never attained legislating power, emerged from the Middle Ages isolated and weak, and with little prospect of curbing an energetic monarch. Those of Valencia, Catalonia and Aragon, on the other hand, shared the legislative power with the Crown and were well buttressed by laws and institutions which derived from a long tradition of political liberty. The king's powers in the States of the Crown of Aragon for the administering of justice, the exacting of tributes or the raising of armies were hedged about with legal restrictions. At every turn, a ruler would find himself limited by the *fueros*, the laws and liberties he had sworn to observe, and each of the territories possessed a standing body, like the Catalan *Diputació*, whose specific function was to defend the national liberties against the arbitrary power of the Crown. This traditional concern for political freedom differentiated the Catalans and the Aragonese, at least in their own eyes, very sharply from the inhabitants of Castile. 'Queen, queen,' the Aragonese King Alfonso IV had said to his Castilian wife, 'our people are free and not subjugated like the people of Castile; for they look on us as their lord, and we on them as good vassals and companions.'[1]

Differing in their histories and traditions, Castile and the Crown of Aragon were now joined by a union that was purely dynastic. Other than the marriage contract of Ferdinand and Isabella, there was no formal document of union, and no attempt was made at the time of the marriage to bring the two territories into closer harmony with each other. Apart from sharing common sovereigns, neither Castile nor the Crown of Aragon underwent any radical institutional alteration which might begin the slow process of merging them into a single State. Each retained unaltered its own laws and institutions; each its own coinage; and the customs barriers between the two stood as a perpetual reminder that the union of two royal houses was very far from being a union of the peoples they ruled.

The nature of this union, as much as the unequal strength of the two partners, played its part in determining the course taken by the Spanish empire during the sixteenth century. It set the pattern for the acquisition of further territories by the kings of Spain. Each new territory acquired through marriage or inheritance, like the great Habsburg in-

[1] *Crónica del Rey d'Aragó En Pere IV lo Ceremoniós* (Barcelona, 1885), p. 46.

heritance of 1504, was added as the Crown of Aragon had been added, with the retention of its own laws and privileges; and fresh conquests remained the possession of the conqueror, and not the common property of all. America fell, not to Spain, but to Castile alone. Since the New World was the conquest, and therefore the property, of the Crown of Castile, the king's Aragonese subjects would take no significant part in its colonization and development. This was perfectly logical, on the assumption that each of the king's territories was an isolated unit. But it was a tragedy for the future development of the Spanish empire. In reserving America to Castile, Ferdinand and Isabella not only tipped the scales still more heavily in Castile's favour, but also missed a unique opportunity for merging their different peoples in a common imperial adventure.[1]

An empire of territories brought together under a single ruler as the result of dynastic arrangements and accidents, and retaining their institutions and forms of government just as though these had never occurred, naturally lacked a homogeneous character. The various provinces were linked only by the fortuitous sharing of a single monarch, whose powers and functions varied greatly from one to another, since 'the kingdoms must be ruled and governed as if the king who holds them all together were king only of each one of them'.[2] Almost an absolute monarch in Castile, he was a ruler with very limited powers in Valencia or the Netherlands. What he could do in an official capacity in Mexico, governed by the laws of Castile, he could not possibly do in Aragon or Sicily. The ruler of the Spanish empire, the most powerful monarch in the world, was first and foremost king of Castile and king of Aragon, count of Flanders, lord of Vizcaya and duke of Milan. For each of these territories their sovereign's possession of the others was incidental; a cause for pride, no doubt, but otherwise of no immediate concern. His empire was, and remained throughout the sixteenth century, an agglomeration of unrelated States, with scarcely a trace of imperial unity or of an imperial mystique common to all.

[1] The exact legal status of the Aragonese in America, and the degree to which discrimination was practised against them, remain very obscure. See Richard Konetzke, 'La legislación sobre inmigración de extranjeros en América...,' in *Charles-Quint et son Temps* (Colloques internationaux du Centre Nationale de la Recherche Scientifique, Paris, 1959), pp. 96–7.

[2] Juan de Solórzano Pereira, *Política Indiana* (Madrid, 1647, reprinted Madrid, 1930), book IV, ch. XIX, §37.

Castile and Aragon

The constitutional pattern of the Spanish empire, as a group of individual States owing allegiance to a common ruler, raised problems of government and organization which, to some extent at least, were solved by the development of the famous conciliar system. Here again, the union of the Crown of Aragon with Castile paved the way for all later administrative developments in the empire. The king might be king of Aragon and Valencia no less than king of Castile, but it was physically impossible for him to be in more than one of his kingdoms at a time. This meant that most of his territories were likely to suffer from long periods of royal absenteeism, and the absence of the king was a serious matter in a world where the administering of justice, and the conferring of honours and rewards depended on a very close personal relationship between the king and his subjects.

An institutional answer was found in the development of vice-royalties, and of a Council of Aragon out of what had once been the royal Council of the kings of Aragon. Formally established by Ferdinand in 1494, the Council of Aragon remained in attendance on the person of a monarch who for long periods had to be absent from his Aragonese territories. It consisted of a Treasurer-General, a Vice-Chancellor, and five *Regentes*.[1] All of these except the Treasurer-General were natives, and they were drawn from the ranks of the *letrados*—that great class of lawyers on whom Ferdinand and Isabella relied for the administrative organization of their dominions. While the day-to-day administration of the various provinces of the Crown of Aragon was in the hands of viceroys, the Council of Aragon closely controlled their activities, and acted as the link between the viceroys and the king. It would receive the reports of the viceroys, advise the king on general matters of policy, and despatch the king's orders to the various provinces under its jurisdiction. By this method of having a council of natives about his person, and a viceroy in each kingdom, the king managed to keep a general oversight over territories he was unable to visit, and maintain some measure of contact with their inhabitants.

As the kings of Spain in the sixteenth century added to their territories, they took the Aragonese system as their model, and new councils were established on the lines of the Council of Aragon. The

[1] There is a short account of the composition and duties of the Council of Aragon in Carlos Riba y García, *El Consejo Supremo de Aragón en el Reinado de Felipe II* (Valencia, 1914).

9

principle which lay behind these councils was clearly recognized by Olivares in a memorandum on the government of the Spanish Monarchy which he prepared for Philip IV. 'As the king is represented in different ways, being king of different kingdoms which have been incorporated into the Crown while preserving their separate identities, it is necessary to have in the Court a Council for each one. Your Majesty is thus considered to be present in each kingdom....'[1] In fact, the Councils of Aragon and Flanders, Italy and Portugal were a convenient means of maintaining the fiction on which the government of the Spanish empire rested: the fiction that the king of all was exclusively the king of each. But the fiction, while useful, could not be carried to extremes. If the king was the king of each, he was also the king of all. In recognition of this, there were also various councils dealing with questions of common interest to all the king's subjects. There was the Council of the Inquisition, for matters of faith; the Council of War; and the *Consejo de Estado*—the Council of State.[2] The powers of this last council varied greatly according to the times. Under Philip II, who did his own work, they were small. Under Philip III they were rather greater. But ideally the Council of State was the coping-stone of the system. A riot in Valencia or in Palermo, while it would be discussed in the Councils of Aragon and Italy respectively, would also come within the province of the Council of State, since riots were matters of general concern, affecting the well-being of the Spanish Monarchy as a whole.

It was by means of this dual structure of individual and general councils that the dual nature of the Spanish empire was instinctively recognized: an empire of independent States which yet owed allegiance to the same sovereign. The advantages of the system were obvious, but it also had its drawbacks. While the institutional recognition of the independent identity of the various territories made the rule of an absentee monarch at least tolerable, if not palatable, to their inhabitants, it did nothing to further a closer association between the various parts of the empire. A native of Flanders was not made to feel that he had anything in common with a native of Valencia—as indeed he had not, apart from a common king—nor that he was moving with him

[1] BM: Eg. MSS 347, memorandum on government (1625), fo. 270.

[2] For a rapid but useful sketch of the councils, see the foreword by J. M. Batista i Roca to H. G. Koenigsberger, *The Government of Sicily under Philip II* (London, 1951).

towards a single goal. No serious effort was made to establish uniform systems of government, to strengthen commercial ties between the various provinces, or to introduce any form of economic reciprocity. The individual interests of each province took precedence over any measure that, in return for immediate sacrifices, might one day redound to the advantage of all. It may be that, in the circumstances of the sixteenth century, any real form of association between the provinces was out of the question, but if this was true of the Fleming and the Valencian, it was slightly less true of the Castilian and the Aragonese, and the gravamen of the charge against this system of government must be that it did nothing to foster mutual co-operation, or break down the barriers between the different peoples.

This failure of the original union to prove itself anything more than a mere dynastic union became increasingly serious as the sixteenth century advanced. Beneath a fixed constitutional formula which froze the relationship between the provinces of the Monarchy into an apparently permanent form, their real relationship was all the time being changed by new political and economic circumstances. In theory, the Crowns of Castile and Aragon were united on equal terms; the natives of each had an equal right to attention from their king. In practice, the equality did not long survive the death of Ferdinand the Catholic. The most striking feature in the development of the sixteenth-century Spanish Monarchy is the widening gap between Castile and all the other territories, including the States of the Crown of Aragon. Everything conspired to give Castile an overwhelming, and increasing, predominance. Castile had begun with greater reserves of power than the Crown of Aragon. It had increased its lead by the acquisition and exclusive possession of all the wealth and resources of America. Charles V's empire was universal, rather than Spanish, but, as the resources of Flanders and Italy became increasingly inadequate to meet the imperial expenses, the emperor was driven back on the resources of Castile and of Castile's overseas possessions. Castile's Cortes were weaker than those of the Crown of Aragon, and could therefore be induced more easily to vote the taxes and subsidies which the Habsburg monarchs required for their ambitious imperial adventures. Castile produced more soldiers than the other kingdoms. Its monopoly of trade with America ensured a constant stream of silver for the royal exchequer. By the 1550's all these considerations had conferred upon Castile a unique position among the dominions of the Spanish Habsburgs.

Philip II's departure from Flanders in 1559 and his decision to settle the capital of his empire in the very heart of Castile,[1] constituted a tacit recognition of Castile's indispensability to the Crown, and of its primacy within the Spanish empire. This recognition was bound to have repercussions, both on the character of the imperial government, and on the attitude of the other provinces towards it. An administration established in Madrid, at the centre of the harsh Castilian table-land, could hardly fail to succumb to the influence of its stridently Castilian environment. Castile was everywhere, the rest of the Monarchy—even the Crown of Aragon—far away; Barcelona was four days distance by post, and several weeks away for the more leisurely travels of king or ambassador. That the king and his ministers should come to think more and more in specifically Castilian terms was unavoidable. Castile had become their world.

The increasingly Castilian aspect of the government in Madrid did not pass unnoticed by the other realms of the Monarchy. In 1555 the Catalans and Aragonese were deeply disturbed when the government of Italy, a traditional possession of the Crown of Aragon, was taken out of the hands of the Council of Aragon, and a special new Council of Italy was established. The purpose of the change was probably administrative convenience, but to the Aragonese it appeared a deliberate conspiracy to defraud them of their own possessions. Already the Castilians enjoyed all the lucrative offices in the government of the New World; it now seemed that in the Old World they planned to wrench away from the Crown of Aragon the land that belonged to it by right of conquest. Gradually, the Aragonese developed their own embittered version of the history of the Spanish empire.

The Emperor Don Carlos spent more time in Castile than in Aragon, out of necessity, or for other reasons that are easily guessed. As a result, the great families of Castile further strengthened their position, since they enjoyed the light of the sun, which they had close at hand, and which gave warmth to induce them to serve and follow him. King Philip the Prudent took things further by choosing to govern the world from a chair, and so the families of

[1] For Philip's departure from Flanders and its significance, see Fernand Braudel, *La Méditerranée et le Monde méditerranéen à l'époque de Philippe II* (Paris, 1949), especially p. 523 and pp. 772-7.

Castile finished by aggrandizing themselves and their kingdom, and took a liking to foreign travels. Meanwhile, the inhabitants of the other kingdoms, with no one to give them a helping hand, have withdrawn from foreign enterprises, and do not leave their own lands as once they did; and all this comes from not having a king of their own nation, but only one who knows them by report, for a service is always more highly esteemed if it is done in the sight of him who gives the reward.[1]

The complaint was no doubt exaggerated. The divorce between the king of Spain and his subjects of the Crown of Aragon was far from complete when Catalans fought at Lepanto and helped to crush the revolt of the Granada Moriscos in 1570.[2] Without a list of office-holders in the Spanish empire, and of their province of origin, it is impossible to determine how far non-Castilians were justified in their complaint that Castile was building up a monopoly of offices and honours. Yet, whether their grievance was well-founded or not, it was important that the Catalans, the Aragonese and the Valencians should have entertained this impression; that they felt themselves being gradually and irrevocably elbowed out of the many lucrative offices in the Monarchy, in the Court and in the royal households. This belief inevitably helped to increase the resentment they felt towards the Castilians, who, they declared, 'want to be so absolute, and put so high a value on their own achievements and so low a value on everyone else's, that they give the impression that they alone are descended from heaven, and the rest of mankind are mud'.[3]

Only frequent journeys by the king to his various dominions would convince them that he had their interests at heart as much as those of the overbearing Castilians. But royal journeys were very expensive, and could not be lightly undertaken. For the inhabitants of the Crown of Aragon, a royal visit was simply an occasion on which they could show their traditional loyalty to their king, and bask in the sunshine of his favour. The king himself could not be expected to see things in quite the same way. Anxious as he may have been to show himself to

---

[1] BM: Add. MS 13,997, fos. 17–19, *Discurso de quan poco útil sea, en la forma que se pretende, la unión de Castilla y Aragón* (1626).

[2] Joan Reglà, *Felip II i Catalunya* (Barcelona, 1956), p. 61.

[3] Cristòfol Despuig, *Los col·loquis de la insigne ciutat de Tortosa*, ed. Fidel Fita (Barcelona, 1877), p. 46. These imaginary dialogues, first published in 1557, are extraordinarily interesting for the light they throw both on the Catalan mentality of the period, and on the general attitude to Castile.

his loyal Aragonese subjects, he was still more anxious that they should open their purse-strings to him. This could only be done by their Cortes, which it was impossible to hold unless he were personally present. But the Cortes of the States of the Crown of Aragon, unlike those of Castile, were difficult and fractious. Supplies could only be granted after the redress of grievances, and, since the list of grievances was always long, the obtaining of a subsidy from the Cortes could be extremely expensive in terms of political and administrative concessions. It was therefore not surprising that Philip II and his successors visited the Crown of Aragon at very infrequent intervals. To have travelled there more often would simply have added to the hardship and expense of the king's life without bringing commensurate advantages, either financial or political.

The consequent neglect of those territories of the peninsula other than Castile, naturally rankled in the minds of the Catalans and the Aragonese. They scarcely ever saw their king, and they felt themselves deprived of all the advantages which the royal presence could bring. This was one of the motives behind the Aragonese revolt of 1591–2. 'Our kingdom,' complained the Aragonese, 'which is the leader of many others, and a nation which for more than seven hundred years has enjoyed the presence, government, and largesse of its own native kings and princes, together with the best posts and offices in the various kingdoms and in the royal household, is now deprived of all these favours and advantages.'[1]

While this neglect of the Crown of Aragon can probably be explained in terms of administrative and financial difficulties, it was only natural that the king's Aragonese subjects should see it in a more sinister light. It came to be interpreted as part of a grand design by the Castilians to dominate and control the Spanish empire. Castile had captured the person of the king, and so was depriving his other dominions of the benefits to be derived from his presence. Might it not also be planning to subvert the various kingdoms of Spain, and reduce them to mere provinces of Castile? The behaviour of the sixteenth-century Castilian did much to foment this suspicion. His pride, his firm consciousness of being the chosen of the Lord, did not smooth his relations

---

[1] Conde de Luna, *Comentarios de los Sucesos de Aragón en los años 1591 y 1592*, p. 22. Letter from the Diputados of Aragon to the King, Sept. 1587.

with the Catalans or the Aragonese, who were deeply sensitive to the contrast between the present status of their Crown and its former glory. He naturally assumed the superiority of all things Castilian, and tended to make Castile the model to which the other provinces should conform. He had an irritating habit of identifying Castile with the entire peninsula: 'almost all the Castilian historians fall into the same error of writing Castile when they mean all Spain', complained a sixteenth-century Catalan.[1] The logical outcome of this assumption that Castile alone represented the true Spain, was an instinctive wish to hispanicize, which in reality meant to castilianize, the other provinces of the peninsula and empire, and this meant nothing less than the abolition of their individual laws and liberties, of the contractual framework of their government, and the consequent reduction of those provinces to the legal status of Castile.

How far this was simply an attitude of mind, and how far a coherent policy pursued from one generation to the next, it is impossible to say. There is no doubt that the temperament of the sixteenth-century Castilian, drunk with world conquest, inclined more towards domination than towards co-operation with others. There was some reason to suspect that successive rulers of Spain viewed this attitude with sympathy. It was natural enough for monarchs accustomed to their almost unlimited powers in Castile to chafe at the interminable obstacles, the tedious delays, created by the laws and institutions of their Levantine provinces. 'It would be better to reduce the Aragonese by force than to suffer the arrogance of their Cortes', complained Isabella.[2] But outbursts of this nature are in themselves no adequate proof of any consistently pursued royal policy to undermine the independent status of the Aragonese Crown. On the contrary, Charles V took special pains to warn his son of the need for extreme care in the government of those provinces, 'as it is easier to go wrong in this government than in that of Castile, both because of the nature of their *fueros* and constitutions, and because their passions run no less high than those of other people...and there are fewer ways of being able to investigate and punish them'.[3] Philip himself, always the devoted son of his father,

[1] Despuig, *Col·loquis*, p. 53.
[2] Vicens Vives, *Política del Rey Católico*, pp. 26–7.
[3] From clause 4 of the confidential instructions from the emperor to his son, dated 4 May 1543, printed in José M. March, *Niñez y juventud de Felipe II* (Madrid, 1941–2), vol. II, pp. 12–22.

adhered to this policy of observing the *fueros* after crushing the Aragonese revolt of 1591. This might have been an opportunity to destroy
Aragonese independence and reduce the kingdom to conformity with
Castile, but Philip limited himself to a convocation of the Cortes and the
amendment or abolition of only a limited number of laws that seemed to
him particularly obnoxious. 'My intention', he declared, 'is simply to
protect their *fueros*, and prevent them from being broken by those who,
while claiming to protect them, are those who most infringe them.'[1]

The available evidence about the relationship between Charles V and
Philip II and the provinces of the Crown of Aragon does not confirm
any deliberate intention on their part to castilianize, but it does show
that, in the government of those provinces, they were confronted with
problems which might lead them in the direction of eventual castilianization. It is all too easy to contrast a 'free' Crown of Aragon with an
'enslaved' Castile, as liberal and romantic historians have done. It is
true that the legal and political institutions of the Crown of Aragon
afforded a better protection from arbitrary royal government or taxation than was afforded by the laws of Castile. But the Crown was not
the only potential oppressor. Against the possible danger of political
oppression must be set the reality of social oppression, for, with the
king far away, it was not difficult for the nobles of the States of the
Crown of Aragon to turn the *fueros* to their own advantage, and to
harass their vassals at will. This could, and did, lead to grave disorders which demanded royal intervention—an intervention that was
bound to conflict with many of the narrow interpretations placed upon
the traditional laws. It was perfectly possible for the king to give the
impression to an Aragonese noble that he intended to subvert the constitution of Aragon while at the same moment the Aragonese peasant
hailed him as his saviour from an oppressive landlord. The true contrast
is not between a 'free' Crown of Aragon and an 'enslaved' Castile; it
is a more subtle contrast between a Castile which enjoyed justice and
good government, but had little defence against the arbitrary fiscal
demands of the Crown, and a Crown of Aragon well protected against
arbitrary taxation and royal absolutism, but possessed of a constitution
easily abused by an irresponsible aristocracy.

[1] Marqués de Pidal, *Historia de las Alteraciones de Aragón en el Reinado de Felipe II* (Madrid,
1862–3), vol II, p. 116.

If there was no prepared plan on the part of the monarchy during the sixteenth century to abolish the legal and political institutions of the Crown of Aragon, this does not necessarily exclude the possibility that abolition was the eventual aim. Although sixteenth-century rulers thought in terms of co-operation with their Estates more frequently than has been allowed by later generations, who have seen only the perpetual conflicts, it was none the less natural that they should find many of the prerogatives of their Estates irksome, and attempt to whittle them away. If the Spanish Habsburgs made so little progress in this direction in the States of the Crown of Aragon during the sixteenth century, one obvious reason for this was the need for caution. There was always a danger that excessively harsh treatment of Aragon in 1592 might provoke serious repercussions in its sister provinces of Catalonia and Valencia. Nor could a king of Spain afford to forget that France and the Crown of Aragon were neighbours, and that it would be uncomfortably easy, in the event of trouble, for the Aragonese to turn to the French for help.[1]

Among the Castilian aristocracy, there was less need for such caution. Certain Castilian nobles did nothing to conceal their contempt and dislike for the Crown of Aragon and its privileges, and seem to have spoken openly of their intention of destroying the *fueros*. Ever since the revolt of the Comuneros in 1520 one section of the higher Castilian aristocracy, represented in particular by the families of Alba and Zapata,[2] had stood for militant Castilian nationalist ideals. It is not clear whether this group of intransigent grandees had developed any firm programme of castilianization, but it was likely to support any action on the part of the Crown that tended to undermine the independence of the other provinces.

The very existence of such a group added to the anxiety felt in the Crown of Aragon about Castile's intentions. Every injudicious remark by a rabidly Castilian grandee hinted at a sinister conspiracy against the *fueros*; every action of an over-zealous royal official appeared to be one more step along the road to their destruction. It was not easy to put any more charitable construction upon such incidents when the Aragonese knew the Castilian temperament so well. A whole chain of

[1] *Relazioni degli Stati Europei*, ed. N. Barozzi and G. Berchet, serie i, 'Spagna', vol. i (Venice, 1856), p. 42.
[2] G. Marañón, *Antonio Pérez* (3rd ed., Madrid, 1951), vol. i, pp. 126 ff.

events had led them to believe that the Castilians 'do not imagine that there can be any form of government other than the type which they know and like'.[1] It was therefore natural to assume the existence of a plan to castilianize the Monarchy, and no less natural to take all possible precautions against the success of any such scheme. Terrified of what the future held in store for them, the Catalans, Aragonese and Valencians of the later sixteenth century began to barricade themselves behind the laws and institutions which alone stood between them and assimilation to Castile. Every move by the Crown was scrutinized for the minutest infringement of the laws that the king had sworn to observe. Every action of the viceregal government was observed with suspicion. Sinister motives could be found behind every untoward incident. When there was a clash between the king and the Catalan *Corts* of 1563–4, the incident was blamed on the viceroy, Don García de Toledo, 'who, according to report, was responsible for what happened because he disliked Catalonia and the Catalan nobility, and wanted all their privileges to be broken'.[2] The suspicion may have been justified; or it may simply have reflected the mounting hysteria in the States of the Crown of Aragon over the presumed aims and intentions of Castile.

However justified the Aragonese distrust of Castile may have been, its consequences were very unhappy. At the very time when the Castilians were starting to monopolize offices in the king's possessions and the royal household, the natives of Aragon, Catalonia and Valencia were assisting the process by mentally shutting themselves off from any possibility of future co-operation with the Crown. Increasingly parochial in their outlook, they even began to derive a perverse satisfaction from ruminating upon the neglect and the injuries they suffered. If the king would not honour and reward them as a king should, then he was not deserving of their services. And if they were accused of disloyalty, they could lay the blame on Castile.

Their attitude was hardly conducive to constructive discussion about the future development of the Spanish empire, such as was becoming more necessary every year. Already by the beginning of Philip II's reign, it was becoming clear that political developments had outstripped constitutional growth. The constitutional formula derived from the

[1] Conde de Luna, *Comentarios*, p. 15.

[2] BC: MS 501, fos. 157–71, *Memòries pera sempre* (the diary of a Catalan noble, Perot de Vilanova), fo. 161.

union of the Crowns of Castile and Aragon and applied to each new territory in turn, seemed to be losing its validity in an empire increasingly dominated by Castile. Was the Spanish empire to become, as it looked like becoming, a specifically Castilian empire, ruled by Castilian laws and staffed by Castilian officials, or was it to continue along the original federalist lines drawn by the union of the Crowns, and perhaps slightly amended to meet new circumstances?

This became a question of burning importance when the Netherlands revolted against the government of Philip II in the 1560's. The revolt of the Netherlands touched off the inevitable debate about the future character of the Spanish empire—a debate conducted principally at the Court in Madrid, but anxiously followed by all the provinces of the Monarchy from Aragon to Flanders. While it centred on the proper treatment of the rebels in the Low Countries, a decision in favour either of repression or of conciliation raised the whole issue of the relationship of the various parts of the Monarchy. If the duke of Alba and the Castilian extremists won the day for repression, then provinces like Aragon and Catalonia might well have reason to fear that sooner or later they would suffer the fate of the Dutch. The views of the Alba faction were, however, contested by another party at Court, led first by Ruy Gómez, prince of Eboli, and after his death by Antonio Pérez. While the Alba-Eboli struggle was primarily a struggle for power, the very composition and origins of the two factions made it also, to some extent, a struggle of rival ideologies. Where Alba and his friends were drawn from old Castilian families, Eboli was Portuguese and Pérez Aragonese, and Pérez himself had close contacts with the rebellious Dutch nobility.[1] The Eboli faction seems to have favoured some kind of federal solution to the problem of the Spanish empire, such as that suggested by the Valencian Furió Ceriol, who, as early as 1559, published in Flanders a political treatise along federalist lines.[2] This in effect entailed a continuation of the old constitutional formula established by the union of Castile and Aragon, with the continued employment of non-Castilian councillors, and careful attention to be given to the interests of the non-Castilian provinces.

Although Philip II chose to solve the problem of the Netherlands by

---

[1] Marañón, *Antonio Pérez*, vol. I, p. 254.
[2] F. Furió Ceriol, *El Concejo y Consejeros del Príncipe* (Antwerp, 1559), p. 66v.

force of arms, he was too hesitant, and perhaps too mindful of his father's counsels, to commit himself irrevocably into the hands of any faction. It was clear from his moderate treatment of the Aragonese after their revolt of 1591–2 that the Castilian extremists had not won control at Madrid; and even though the arrest of Antonio Pérez in 1579 had destroyed the original Eboli faction, its federalist views were still aired, and were to acquire further publicity from the political tracts written by Pérez himself after his escape from Spain.[1] At the time of Philip II's death in 1598, therefore, no final decision had been reached on the future course to be taken by those who steered the fortunes of the Spanish Monarchy. All that could be said of his reign was that it had seen a distinct bias in favour of Castile, largely because the king now lived there and depended on it more than on any other of his dominions. 'The king is Castilian and nothing else, and that is how he appears to the other kingdoms', remarked one of the principal ministers of Philip III early in the new reign.[2] But it remained to be seen whether the increasingly Castilian character of the Court would eventually lead to the adoption of a specific programme for the castilianization of the empire.

For the moment, then, the future of the Spanish Monarchy remained an open question. But it could not indefinitely be left unanswered. The reign of Philip III opened a new and difficult period in the history of Habsburg Spain. On one side there was Castile, increasingly dominant in the life of the Spanish empire, but yet dissatisfied with its position. The king's Castilian ministers found themselves hampered in their government of the Monarchy by the laws and liberties of the other provinces; and at the same time, Castile was being overwhelmed by an economic crisis of such magnitude that sooner or later it was bound to look towards those other provinces for fiscal relief. On the other side there were the provinces, especially those within the Iberian peninsula. These also were increasingly dissatisfied. They complained of neglect by an absentee king; of the infringement of their laws by Castilian viceroys; and of exclusion from all the benefits they might have expected to receive from a monarch who ruled the largest empire the world had ever seen.

[1] Marañón, *op. cit.* vol. II, p. 738.
[2] AGS: Cámara de Castilla, leg. 2796, Pieza 9, Inquisición, fo. 329. Don Pedro Franqueza to Dr Fadrique Cornet, 22 Jan. 1605.

Castile and Aragon

The history of the reigns of Philip III and IV is played out within the context of this rising tide of dissatisfaction among Castilians and non-Castilians alike: a tide that was to reach its highest point in the year 1640. The study of one particular province in the years before that point was reached may help to chart the course of the angry waters. Alone of the mainland provinces of the Crown of Aragon, the Principality of Catalonia had remained politically quiescent under the government of the first Habsburgs. After its reorganization by Ferdinand the Catholic at the end of the fifteenth century, it had shown signs of recovering at least some of its former prosperity. How had it fared in the century or so since the union of Castile and Aragon, and the accession of the House of Austria? What was the state of its social and political life a hundred years after Ferdinand's reforms, and what kind of relations did it enjoy with Castile and with the Court of Spain? The answers to these questions are of more than local concern, since the problems of Catalonia mirror those of the Monarchy at large.

CHAPTER II

THE ORDERED SOCIETY

'The Principality of Catalonia and Counties of Rosellón and Cerdaña constitute, in one province, a little world'—so began a seventeenth-century description of Catalonia.[1] This 'little world' can momentarily be glimpsed through the eyes of a priest of Puigcerdà called Joan Trigall, who possessed three maps of the Principality, 'one by Paolo Forlani, Veronese, printed in Italy in 1570; the second by Joan Baptista Vrient (Vrintius), Fleming, printed at Antwerp in 1586, and the third by Guillaume Postell, French, printed in Paris and undated'.[2] These maps portrayed a roughly triangular territory, wedged somewhat uneasily between France, Aragon and the sea. The northern side of the triangle was formed by the line of the Pyrenees; the western side by the plateaux that ran southwards from the Pyrenees, and by the river Ebro; its base, by the long coastline of the Mediterranean. Inside this triangle, of some fourteen thousand square miles, lay the Principality of Catalonia and the Counties—the Comtats—of Rosselló and Cerdanya.

In Trigall's company it is possible to reach a vantage-point from which to look down upon the territory depicted in his maps.

Curious to discover if the mountains of Cerdanya are the highest and coldest in Catalonia...on the eighth of October (1610) I climbed the Pyrenees on the French side, choosing the mountain which seemed to me from Puigcerdà to be the highest. I began to climb before dawn in the clear moonlight, so that, as the sun rose, I was already out of the woodland and in the open; and, constantly climbing, I arrived at a point which seemed to me higher than the others, at ten o'clock on a calm and clear day.[3]

While mist hid Languedoc, Provence, and the lower-lying areas of Catalonia and Aragon, the immediate surroundings were clearly to be seen.

Once I was there, many things filled me with wonder; above all, to see that great range of mountains competing with each other as to which can rise

[1] B.D.A.V.Y.M.F.D.P.N. (F. Martí i Viladamor), *Noticia Universal de Cataluña* (Lisbon, 1641), p. 4.
[2] BN (Paris): Baluze 238, fo. 271, Joan Trigall to Jeroni Pujades, 20 Nov. 1610.
[3] *Ibid.*

highest, and looking like innumerable loaves of sugar or points of a diamond, and all so inaccessible, and apparently threatening the heavens.... It fills one with contentment to see the variety of barren land, which serves only as a field for the winds, and land of snow and frost and storms, and to consider the greatness and wisdom of God omnipotent.

The peaks which rose around him did not then form, as they do now, the barrier between Spain and France. Beyond them lay part of the Comtats of Rosselló and Cerdanya, the original homeland of the Catalans. In 1276 the Comtats had been separated from Catalonia by James I to create, with the Balearics, a new kingdom for his second son. Reunited to Catalonia in 1343, they passed into the hands of the French in 1463, and finally, after many vicissitudes, were ceded by France to Ferdinand in 1493. Now an integral part of Catalonia, sharing the institutions and the government of the Principality, they none the less seemed something of an anomaly to minds that were groping towards the concept of natural frontiers. Good seventeenth-century cosmographers held that Rosselló was 'outside the limits of Spain, which are the Pyrenean mountains'.[1] This academic opinion was not likely to disturb the inhabitants of the Comtats, whose relations with their fellow-Catalans were close. Their concern lay not with barriers but with the ways of access, the mountain passes and the sea. A constant traffic passed along the road that linked Perpinyà, the capital of Rosselló, to Barcelona in the south. This route was one of the life-lines of Catalonia. Along it travelled Frenchmen, in search of work over the border; corn from the south of France and the plain of Rosselló, to feed the Catalan towns; and sheep—a particularly destructive flock in the winter of 1624[2]—to supply Barcelona with meat. The sea-route linking the Comtats and the Principality was equally frequented. From the harbours of Rosselló, notably Canet, were shipped the grain and iron produced by the Comtats, and in return came Catalan products, and foreign goods, re-routed from Barcelona.[3]

The mountain region, the 'land of snow and frost and storms' which divided the corn-growing plain of Rosselló from Catalonia, and stretched westwards through Cerdanya to the valleys of Andorra, was

---

[1] ACA: CA, leg. 274, no. 1, paper by Salvador Fontanet, Feb. 1627.

[2] AHB (Deposit): Administración de Carnes, documentos sueltos, lawsuit dated 24 Dec. 1624.

[3] J. Nadal and E. Giralt, *Los Seguros Marítimos y el Comercio de Barcelona, 1630–1665* (unpublished thesis), pp. 60–1.

a world on its own, nominally part of the Principality and Comtats, but different in character from both. This wild country of jagged mountain peaks and harsh escarpments, of mountain torrents flecking the barren rocks with foam, had always been a law unto itself; a land little amenable to authority, and controlled, in so far as it was controlled at all, by feudal barons like Joan Cadell, Senyor of Arsèguel, all but inaccessible in his mountain stronghold. This was a world dominated by faction, by family rivalries transmitted from one generation to the next. Wrapped in its own life, owing only the most distant allegiance to a power that was far away, it provided shelter indiscriminately to those who had fallen foul of the royal authorities in France and Spain; and they, in return for refuge, helped to swell the bandit gangs which harried the surrounding country.

Catalan authors, who rightly praised the beauty of their land, tended to ignore conditions such as these, which made the mountainous border country a place of fear and danger. No bandit casts his shadow across the smiling countryside portrayed by Father Gil in his descriptive geography of Catalonia, written in 1600.[1] His Pyrenees were memorable only for their height and loveliness: 'they are all covered with pines, firs,...heather, box and other plants and trees of an extraordinary beauty'.[2] Their foothills led southwards to gentler, less ruthless landscapes, where Gil could dwell at length on the richness of the soil and the abundance of the fruits. Only along the western side of the Catalan triangle did the landscape become so rugged and desolate that it seemed as if part of neighbouring Aragon had strayed across the border. This barren western region had played an important part in Catalan history by isolating the Principality from Aragon, and, farther away, the central Castilian plateau, thus forcing the Catalans to turn their eyes eastwards, towards the sea. Their empire had been a Mediterranean empire, and upon the Mediterranean they depended for their life and commerce. Catalan civilization faced the sea, and almost all the towns of the Principality were either on the coast itself, or in the pre-littoral depression: Barcelona, Vilafranca del Penedès, Valls, Tarragona, Reus, Tortosa. Even a town like Girona, relatively far inland, was dependent on the sea for the bulk of its supplies. The corn bought by its agents in Aragon

---

[1] See *Pere Gil, S.I. (1551–1622) i la seva Geografia de Catalunya*, an admirable edition by Josep Iglésies (Barcelona, 1949).   [2] *Ibid.* p. 191.

or the plain of Urgell would be transported to the southern coast, perhaps to Tarragona, and then shipped to the northern port of Sant Feliu de Guíxols, from where it was carried overland on the last lap of its journey to Girona.[1]

The long coastline of sandy beach alternating with stubborn rocks; the fishing villages sheltering in coves, and, behind them, the steep, pine-covered slopes dominated by a castle, where the villagers took refuge when the sails of Algiers pirates were sighted—this was maritime Catalonia. Behind it lay another Catalonia: 'land for the most part rough, broken, mountainous, full of forests, dense woods and thickets, a land of few big towns, sprinkled with small houses and villages and the solitary dwellings of people of the mountain or the plain'.[2] This was the central belt, the heart of Catalonia, a country of alternating valleys, mountains and plains that stretched from the foothills of the Pyrenees, southwards through Empordà, Girona, la Selva, the Vallès and the plain of Vic, to Penedès and the Camp de Tarragona.

This rough country, rather than the smoother maritime regions, or the high mountainous areas of the north, was the real Catalonia. Rocky and densely wooded, it was the kind of terrain most common in the Principality, and had done much to determine the pattern of Catalan life. In spite of Father Gil's glowing description, the soil was not exceptionally fertile. With regional variations, it produced cereals, vines and olives, but the ground needed hard and constant working. Only in the west of the Principality was the soil rich, but the land was poorly irrigated, and drought frequently ruined what would otherwise have been an abundant harvest. This western region, the plain of Urgell, was the granary of Catalonia. It was claimed that one abundant harvest in the plain of Urgell could keep all Catalonia fed for three years,[3] but in practice the lack of rain and the remoteness of the region greatly reduced its potential value to the Principality, and from the later sixteenth century Catalonia usually found itself heavily dependent on Rosselló, Aragon and Sicily for its supplies of corn.

Apart from corn, Catalonia could meet most of its basic needs from

---

[1] AMG: Corresp. N–Z, Benet Anglasell to Jurats of Girona, 24 Aug. 1619.

[2] Jeroni Pujades, *Discurso sobre la justa asistencia de los Conselleres de la fidelísima Ciudad de Barcelona...* (Barcelona, 1621), § VIII.

[3] Francisco de Gilabert, *Discursos sobre la calidad del Principado de Cataluña* (Lérida, 1616), Discurso 2, fo. 21 v.

its own resources, and there was no lack of labour, although this was by no means exclusively Catalan in origin. The great mortalities of the late fourteenth and fifteenth centuries had torn a gaping hole in Catalonia's population. Between 1347 and 1497 the Principality had lost 37 per cent of its inhabitants,[1] and was reduced to a population of something like 300,000. The first half of the sixteenth century saw a gradual recovery: the *fogatge* or tax census of 1553 would suggest a population for Catalonia and Rosselló of some 360,000.[2] This was still well below the probable figures for medieval Catalonia before the Black Death, but in the reigns of Philip II and Philip III the Catalan countryside made a spectacular demographic recovery. Some of this recovery was accounted for by a natural increase only momentarily checked by the plague of 1589–92, but it was also caused by a vast influx of French immigrants, many of whom made their homes in Catalonia. These immigrants, who continued to cross into Spain right up to the 1620's in the expectation of finding better opportunities than in France, did much to revitalize Catalan rural life and to make good the demographic losses sustained in the preceding century. Between 1570 and 1620 they are believed to have constituted between 10 and 20 per cent of the total male population of Catalonia, and it would be reasonable to assume that their presence helped to bring the Principality's population to around 400,000 by the beginning of the seventeenth century.[3]

For ecclesiastical purposes, the Principality formed the province of Tarragona. After the creation of a new bishopric of Solsona in 1593, it was divided into nine dioceses (see the table at the top of p. 27).

In the wake of the Tridentine reforms had come not only the new bishopric of Solsona, but also new religious houses: the Jesuits (4), the Capuchins (20), the Servites (7), the Discalced Carmelites (10), together with a number of houses of lesser Orders.[4] There were also fourteen abbeys.

---

[1] J. Nadal and E. Giralt, *La Population Catalane de 1553 à 1717* (Paris, 1960), p. 117,

[2] Iglésies, *Pere Gil*, p. 121.

[3] The subject of French immigration into Catalonia, hitherto virtually unknown, has been recovered from oblivion by Nadal and Giralt in *La Population Catalane*. Catalan population problems are complicated by the lack of any census between 1553 and 1717, but the groundwork for further studies has been prepared both by this book and by the same authors' 'Ensayo metodológico para el estudio de la población Catalana de 1553 a 1717', *Estudios de Historia Moderna*, vol. III (1953), pp. 239–84.

[4] F. Carreras y Candi, *Geografia General de Catalunya* (Barcelona, n.d.), p. 1066. The figures show new foundations up to 1640.

Diocese	Revenue[1]	Canonries[2]	Parishes[2]
Tarragona	20,000 *escuts*	24	160
Lleida	18,000	24	346
Tortosa	16,000	20	134
Girona	6,000	36	348
Barcelona	10,000	24	221
Solsona	5,000	12	115
Urgell	6,000	24	231
Vic	5,000	22	220
Elna	4,000	21	180
		207	1955

The new foundations helped to swell the already large ecclesiastical element in the Catalan population. The census of 1553 suggests that this was high even for Spain. The people were traditionally divided into three *estaments* or Estates. In 1553, 6 per cent of all the houses in the Principality belonged to the ecclesiastical Estate, and 0·8 per cent to the nobility and gentry (the *estament militar*)—a low figure by Spanish standards. The remaining 93·2 per cent were the households of the third Estate, the *estament reial*, which was represented in the Catalan Corts by the syndics of thirty-one towns.[3]

Although only the urban population was represented in the Corts, it is not easy to tell where rural population ends and urban population begins. The city of Barcelona, the capital of the Principality, had between 30,000 and 40,000 inhabitants (approaching 10 per cent of the total population). No other town reached anything near this figure. The 1553 census shows that only eight other towns in the Principality and Comtats had more than 2500 inhabitants:[4]

Perpinyà	8775	Tortosa	4940	Vic	2990
Girona	6620	Tarragona	4270	Reus	2700
Lleida	5545	Valls	3325		

[1] This list is taken from *MHE*, vol. XXI, doc. no. 334, and was prepared by Father Ferrand, Richelieu's confidential agent in Catalonia. I have preferred these to the figures taken from Núñez de Salcedo's well-known compilation of revenues in late sixteenth-century Spain and reproduced in Joan Reglà, *Els Virreis de Catalunya* (Barcelona, 1956), p. 21, since Núñez does not include all the Catalan bishoprics and one figure (that for Urgell) is patently absurd. When they can be checked, from returns for certain individual bishoprics for 1638–9 (ACA: CA, legajos 388 and 390), Ferrand's figures seem generally reliable. They do not, however, take into account the charges on bishoprics: e.g. a return for Tarragona, 24 Dec. 1639 (ACA: CA, leg. 390) gives an income of 20,070 *lliures* p.a. and expenses and pensions totalling 8,682 *lliures*.

[2] See Esteban de Corbera, *Cataluña Illustrada* (Naples, 1678), pp. 100 ff. Corbera lived from 1563 to 1635 and his book was published posthumously.

[3] *Pere Gil*, p. 123, for the 1553 figures.   [4] *Ibid.* p. 119.

These eight towns between them accounted for another 40,000 inhabitants, so that, if Barcelona is included, some 20 per cent of the Catalan population lived in towns containing more than 500 houses. But many town-dwellers were as rural in their pursuits as those who lived outside the town walls. The registers of a small town like Cervera, with a population of 2380 in 1553, include many citizens who are simply classified as peasants. Andreu Bonanat of Cervera, a peasant, owned:

One house in the street of San Francesc, with two doors, value	50 *lliures*
Three pieces of land planted with vines	180
One piece of cultivated land	15
	245

Townsmen who pursued a trade also had their plot of land outside the walls. There was Antoni Martell, a tailor, who owned one house with orchard (40 *lliures*) and one piece of land planted with vines (30 *lliures*), and the same holds good for the more prosperous citizens of Cervera, the merchants, doctors and drapers. Each had his plot of land, planted with vines or corn.[1]

With so many citizens absorbed wholly or partly in agricultural pursuits, most of the towns seem rather an extension of the countryside than separate entities on their own. This was an overwhelmingly agrarian society—a fact easily confirmed by anyone who left the coastal regions for the interior. Big settlements were out of the question here, for it was a country of small isolated valleys linked to each other only by mule-tracks winding precariously up the stony mountainside. That was why 'the centres of population are all villages, and very small ones, most of them consisting of single houses separated one from another'.[2] These single houses, 'which in this Principality are infinite',[3] were Catalonia's principal characteristic, and the hallmark of its individuality; isolated farmsteads or *masies*, as they were called, they would stand in a clearing surrounded by land that had been worked by generations of *masovers*—peasant farmers.

---

[1] AHC: Manifest de 1640. This was once a complete register, compiled for fiscal purposes, of all the property of the inhabitants of Cervera. Unfortunately, it was at some time much slashed about, and so many pages are missing that a proper analysis of the town's social composition, which would have been of great interest, is no longer possible.

[2] AGS: GA, leg. 1328, Don Ramon de Calders to the Count of Santa Coloma, 13 May 1640.

[3] ACA: CA, leg. 362, Duke of Alcalá to King, 28 Sept. 1619.

This class of peasant farmers, either owning the *mas* and the surrounding land, or holding it by a secure tenure, has been the backbone of Catalan society from the end of the fifteenth century almost to the present day; and more than anything else it was responsible for the fundamental stability of Catalan rural life in the sixteenth and seventeenth centuries. It had won its secure status as the result of Ferdinand the Catholic's measures for the pacification of the Catalan countryside after the social struggles of the fifteenth century. In his famous *Sentència de Guadalupe* of 1486 Ferdinand gave Catalonia a rural charter which was to last for centuries.[1] While constituting a victory for the peasantry, the terms of this charter, like all Ferdinand's measures, were essentially moderate. The *remença* peasants, who had been tied to the land, were freed; the six 'evil customs' exacted by the lords were abolished in return for monetary compensation; and the peasants remained in effective possession of the *masies*, which they could now leave, or dispose of, without having to obtain permission from their feudal lord. The lord, on the other hand, remained legally the 'direct' lord of the land. His vassals rendered him homage and paid him a *cens*, or ground-rent, and various feudal dues: the vassals of the seventeenth-century noble, Don Rafael de Biure, paid him a *cens* of 2d. for every 'quarter of sown ground', together with one-sixth of their fruits.[2]

The settlement of Guadalupe removed the principal cause of agrarian unrest in Catalonia—the humiliating dependence of the peasant on his lord—and gave the peasant security of tenure. The results of this new-found security were soon to be seen in the improvements to the farmsteads; in the Gothic windows and the shields over the doorways, eloquent witnesses to the pride of peasant families which had won legal emancipation and ownership of their house and land in all but name.[3] These peasant farmers, many of them very wealthy, became the new rural aristocracy. Profiting from the land-hunger of the early sixteenth century, many of them would lease the lands attached to the *mas* to other, less fortunate peasants, demanding from them a higher ground-rent than they were themselves paying to the real owner of the

[1] The text of the *Sentència* is printed in Appendix II of J. Vicens Vives, *Historia de los Remensas en el siglo XV* (Barcelona, 1945), which is indispensable for the whole question of the Catalan agrarian movement in the fifteenth century, as are also his *Política del Rey Católico en Cataluña* and *Els Trastàmares* (Barcelona, 1956). [2] AHB: Archivo Patrimonial (Biure papers), III–16
[3] José Pella y Forgas, *Historia del Ampurdán* (Barcelona, 1883), p. 700.

land.[1] The Catalan Corts of 1520 legislated against such abuses, stepping in to protect the lesser peasantry, the *menestrals*, from exploitation by peasant proprietors who had begun to assume many of the characteristics of the feudal lords from whom they themselves had only recently gained their freedom. From 1520, therefore, Catalan rural society became regularized in a hierarchical structure. At the top of the pyramid were nobles or wealthy bourgeois, absentee owners of lands and *masies* leased for certain agreed dues in cash and kind; in the middle were the *masovers*—peasant farmers who held the lease and occupied the *masia*, but who often found their property too large to work by themselves; they in turn would hand over a parcel of their lands to *menestrals*, poor peasants who would build themselves some sort of cottage on the land they had rented; and below them again at the base of the pyramid, were the landless—rural labourers who worked for the *masovers*, living with them in the *masia*, or who provided casual labour when there was heavy work to be done on the land.

The *masovers* were the most solidly entrenched rural class in sixteenth and seventeenth-century Catalonia, and their way of life reveals something of the attitude of Catalan society as a whole to the land, the house and the family. Their home, the *masia*, is the 'typical' Catalan house, the one that has most helped to shape the pattern of Catalan life over the centuries. The *masia* was generally set alone, on a hillside or in a clearing, where corn would be grown, and perhaps also vines and olives. Built of stone, it served originally as a stronghold as well as a farmstead. *Masies* constructed during the Middle Ages, and even later when situated in dangerous coastal regions, often had a fortified tower adjoining them. There were naturally several types of *masia*, but from the end of the fifteenth century perhaps the most common consisted of two stories and was covered by a sloping roof. On the ground floor would be the entrance hall, running the full length of the house, and containing agricultural implements and anything else in use about the farm. To the left of the hall would be the stable and cellar and, to the right, the kitchen, the most frequented room in the house. At the back of the hall a staircase led to the main floor, which consisted of a large room known as the *sala*, occupying the area immediately above the entrance hall, together with bedrooms leading from it. Sometimes

[1] *Constitutions y altres drets de Cathalunya* (Barcelona, 1704), vol. I, p. 345.

there would be attics above, but there was always ample storage space, as every *masia* had its outhouses, often including a lean-to shed against the side of the *masia* itself, where the crops would be dried and stored.[1]

The compact building was well suited to the needs of an agrarian society. It housed the farm animals and the farm produce as well as the family. The very distribution of rooms within the *masia*, in particular the presence of a stable and a main hall devoted to carts and tools, again emphasized the close ties linking the *masia* to the land on which it stood. In a sense the *masia*, the solid symbol of the family's property and status, was more important than any of its occupants. One generation of *masovers* succeeded another, but the *masia* remained, solid and

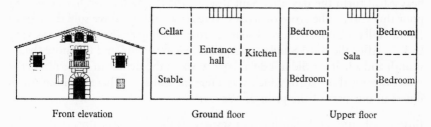

Front elevation   Ground floor   Upper floor

Fig. 1. The masia.

immutable, an entity in its own right. In the last resort, all personal considerations were sacrificed to the interest of the *masia*. The *masia* was the family—the family to which it had often given its own name. A small stream called Exercavins near the town of Rubí had given its name to the family of Xercavins in a nearby farmstead, the *mas Xercavins*, as early as the twelfth century; in 1645 the house was inherited by a Mariana Xercavins, having remained throughout the centuries in the same family, although passing on occasion through heiresses whose husbands took the name of Xercavins on marriage.[2]

The kitchen, on the ground floor to the right, was the centre of family life. Here it would congregate after the day's work. At the

[1] Many *masies* are still to be seen in Catalonia. J. Gilbert, *La Masia Catalana, Origen, Esplendor i Decadència* (Barcelona, 1947), has only a slight text but useful illustrations. Joaquim de Camps i Arboix, *La Masia Catalana* (Barcelona, 1959), is much more informative, but there is still room for a more intensive study. I am greatly indebted to Sr Serra Roselló of the municipal archive at Barcelona for conversations on the *masia*.

[2] José Serra Roselló, 'Can Xercavins, ocho siglos de dinastía rural', *Senderos* (Revista de la Unión Excursionista de Cataluña), vol. VII (1955), pp. 203–4.

long, narrow table it would eat its supper of bread, wine and the traditional *olla*, a stew of boiled meat and soup, and then sit by the fire with its great sloping chimney, possibly passing the time weaving, for 'in winter when the nights are long', the peasants 'occupy themselves in weaving as many cloths as they can'.[1]

Life inevitably was dominated by the routine of the seasons and the endless struggle against wind, rain and drought. A few extracts from the diary of a *masover* in the plain of Vic tell their own story.

1634—this year has begun well, and in particular there has been water in abundance, thanks to great downpours of rain at the end of Lent....The yield of corn has been quite good. On our land, we have harvested 93 *quarteres* of corn...but the other crops have been cruelly poor because there was a heavy hailstorm the day after Sant Roc....1635—the harvest has been very poor this year...the crops of acorns were reasonable, and we sold the pigs to Jaume Villa for 6 *lliures* less $2\frac{1}{2}$ *sous*....1636—this year the harvest was very bad....After the third Sunday in April it began to rain, and for more than a month and a half we did not do a day's work in the fields. In some places the water drowned the corn, which was a terrible sight....There has been much illness in our part of the plain of Vic....[2]

Illness, plague and famine constantly stalked the countryside. The citizens of Cervera, after suffering from bad harvests in 1627, 1628 and 1629 were struck in 1630 by an epidemic, possibly associated with the plague then raging in the south of France. The surrounding countryside was particularly hard hit, and for many days people were 'eating nothing but grass, and they arrived here all black or pallid and defunct, so that it caused pity to see them....They suffered terribly in the countryside, so much so that most of them lived on carob beans.... God grant in His infinite goodness and pity that His Christian people do not suffer such afflictions.'[3]

'God grant...'; but against God was ranged the devil, and 'it is certain that today the devil is very powerful, and does his utmost to see that no one shall be saved, seeing that the day of judgment is close at hand'.[4] Everyone knew that the stones struck by the plough, the sudden death of cattle, the heavy fogs, were all to be ascribed to the

[1] *Pere Gil*, p. 234.
[2] From the diary of Joan Guardia of Corcó. See Appendix VI, section D.
[3] AHC: Extract from the *Llibre vert de les notes*, fos. 149–51.
[4] From a speech by a noble in the Catalan Corts of 1599. AHB: R. 1052, fos. 700–700 v.

devil, or to the devil's agents, the witches;[1] everyone, that is, except the Inquisition, which thought that all the reports of witches were 'dreams and illusions and not true reality'.[2] But not even the Inquisition could prevent a great witch-hunt in the early 1620's.

The struggle against the forces of darkness demanded vigilance, and the faithful observance of the rites of the Church. The bell ringing through the valley and summoning the faithful to vespers and matins, the solid, spacious parish church, often embellished with a large fifteenth-century altar-piece depicting the saints in a profusion of gold paint, helped to give the faithful some sense of security in a harsh and hostile world. Here was the promise of ultimate salvation, and proof that the devil would not for ever triumph. Those who attended to the teachings of the Church, and venerated the relics of the saints, might hope for an answer to their prayers. Often their patience would be tried to the limit. Day after day they would pray for rain, and no rain would come. But at other times the miracle occurred, as in 1628, after the bishop of Barcelona had solemnly cursed the land because of the theft of the church silver from the church of Santa Maria del Mar, and all the growing crops were ruined, from the Castell de la Roca in Vallès to the plain of Urgell. On that occasion, the bishop's censures were suspended by a more merciful colleague, and his benediction was

followed by the mercy of the Lord, for the next day it rained a little, and although this rain was not very useful as it came too late to save the crops, two things have been divinely shown to us: one, the faith of the citizens of Barcelona, and the other the power of the Church, which closes and opens the heavens like another Elijah, since God sends rain only when the priests are willing....[3]

Prayers for rain, solemn processions to invoke the divine aid or to give thanks for the harvest, were a natural part of Catalan life. The powers of the priest in this society were great. The ordinary parish priest, separated by a great gulf from the Catalan hierarchy, was the

[1] ACA: CA, leg. 368, memorandum addressed to bishops of Catalonia, Dec. 1621.
[2] ACA: CA, leg. 368, Bishop of Vic to King, 22 Jan. 1622. This was in keeping with the general attitude of the Spanish Inquisition, which on the whole used its influence to discourage witch-hunters. Cf. H. C. Lea, *A History of the Inquisition of Spain* (New York, 1907), vol. IV, book VIII, ch. IX.
[3] BUB: MS 975, diary of Jeroni Pujades, 4, fo. 23. Pujades was a lawyer, an antiquarian and an historian. For this diary see Appendix VI, section D.

spiritual guide of his parish, the intimate friend and confidant of the local families, and the repository of the village secrets. He was generally poor. The standard of his learning, and sometimes of his morals, was not very high. But being close to his parishioners, and in many ways very like them, he could often wield considerable influence in a society which lived beneath the shadow of the Church. When Catalonia revolted in 1640 the clergy were to show their power in the pulpit. In less inflammatory times, their influence was still all-pervasive, and no doubt many of them worked hard for their parishioners and enjoyed their friendship. The 'one used parasol' among the possessions of one priest[1] conjures up a picture—perhaps not entirely fanciful—of his toiling up the steep paths in the heat of the midday sun to visit some isolated *masia* in his parish.

Only one other person outside the family circle enjoyed as much authority in it as the parish priest, and that was the notary. The priest and the notary; religion and the law. These were the twin supporters of the Catalan family structure, and it was fitting that the *sala*—the grandest room in the *masia*—should usually be reserved for occasions on which one or other of them was present. The family lived ordinarily in the kitchen, and the *sala* remained unused for most of the year. It was an imposing, and perhaps rather bleak room, with its 'two sideboards of walnut, almost new; three good armchairs; three ordinary chairs, worn; one big picture of the Magdalene, poor condition; one picture of St Peter, poor condition; two very bad arquebuses and a powder-flask; two halberds and a lance, old'.[2] The family would congregate amidst these rather oppressive possessions on the great days of the year—the days of baptisms and marriages and funerals, or the days when the notary would attend to help in the drawing up of the will or of the marriage contract.

Catalan society was ordered within the framework of the family and the community, and it is the marriage contract which can tell us most about the basic element in society—the family. Thousands of volumes of marriage contracts still stand on the shelves of the notarial archives in many Catalan towns, constituting a unique register of the fluctuating

[1] APB: A. J. Fita, lib. 2, d'inventaris, inventory of the possessions of Pere Modolell, 30 Oct. 1618.
[2] APB: A. J. Fita, lib. 2, d'inventaris, inventory of possessions of Bartolomeu Modolell, 29 Oct. 1618.

fortunes of the Catalan family over many generations.[1] It was no accident that the one seventeenth-century Catalan lawyer to achieve a European reputation was Joan Pere Fontanella, the author of *De Pactis Nuptialibus*,[2] for the Catalan legal profession had acquired a formidable mastery of the laws of marriage and inheritance, and in the marriage contract it had evolved a document perfectly epitomizing the aims and aspirations of the family.

'By the grace of the Holy Spirit, *A*, the son of *B* and *C* (living or deceased) has contracted a marriage with *D*, the daughter of *E* and *F* (living or deceased).' So the contract began. The grace of the Holy Spirit was not generally left to operate entirely on its own, for the marriage contract was the culmination of a long series of family manoeuvres, and of untiring diplomacy. After much consultation among the various members of the family, a possible match would be agreed on for the heir, and agents would be chosen to press his suit. On 12 April 1565, for example, a match was finally negotiated between a young Catalan noble, Perot de Vilanova, and a certain Hipòlita Quintana, 'with the intervention on my behalf of the Senyor de Ribelles, Don Gispert de Pons, and on her behalf of Mossèn Martí de Vergós...and Mossèn Galceran Cahors of Perpinyà'. The preliminaries had been arduous. The representatives of the lady had refused to go beyond 3500 *lliures* for her dowry, and Vilanova's agents had stood out for more. But they eventually withdrew their objections, and the contract was signed. Vilanova was then allowed to visit her: 'they gave me permission to kiss her and touch her' and the marriage was celebrated on 17 April.[3]

After the opening clause of the contract came the articles of settlement. The first article was a statement of the property promised by the parents to the son; the second, the property made over to the daughter by her parents; the third, the property brought by the daughter to her future husband, and the fourth, the sum added by the bridegroom's parents to the bride's dowry, with a promise to surrender both this and the dowry to the bride's family, if the occasion should arise.

---

[1] See Appendix VI, section B, Archivo de Protocolos.
[2] First published in two volumes in Barcelona, 1612, and republished in Cologne, Geneva and Venice during the course of the century.
[3] BC: MS 501, fos. 157–71, *Memòries pera sempre*, fo. 164v. See Appendix VI, section D.

In Catalonia, as all over sixteenth and seventeenth-century Europe, the interests of the individual were ruthlessly subordinated to those of the family. Because the family was the primary unit of society, everything possible was done to concentrate the family's estate in the hands of a single person, and then to subject him to such strict control that he would not be allowed to disperse it out of personal caprice. This person was the single, absolute heir, the *hereu universal*. For many centuries, Catalan society has been organized round the person of the *hereu*. He is the son, usually but not always the eldest son,[1] who inherits the bulk of the family's property. As the heir, he is marked out as the head of the family, and symbolizes the family's determination to survive as a unit, preserving its substance intact. For this very reason, great care was taken to prevent him from squandering his inheritance. The parents of Don Jaume Falcó made over all their property to him on his marriage, but they had no intention of allowing him to escape from the grasp of the family. The contract stipulated that they should remain for the rest of their lives the *majors poderosos y usufructuaris* of the property: they were to keep absolute control over it. They did, however, promise that 'out of the said usufruct and dowry...they will keep the married couple and their family in everything they need for their sustenance...so long as the said married couple live and cohabit with them, all sharing a common table and honouring each other as parents and children respectively'. If living together should prove impossible, Don Jaume's parents would hand over to him his wife's dowry, together with 500 *lliures* in cash, furniture to the value of 1500 *lliures*, and an annual income of 300 *lliures*.[2]

Falcó was a noble, but the formula was the same at every level of society. The heir had no control over his inheritance during his father's lifetime, and he and his wife were generally expected to live in the parental home. If his father died, his mother would often remain in control of the estate for the rest of her life. If she did not feel equal to administering the estate, and handed on the charge to her son, she was still looked upon as the head of the household. A Barcelona notary said in his last will, in which his nephew was named as his heir:

[1] Primogeniture, while customary, was not compulsory. See, for example, the will of Don Rafael de Biure, 1 Aug. 1633 (AHB: Archivo Patrimonial, leg. III–14).

[2] APB: A. J. Fita, lib. 8, cap. mat., marriage contract of Don Jaume Falcó and Maria Costa, 11 July 1626.

Because in previous wills I left to the said Senyora Massiana, my very dear wife, all the use of my estate and inheritance...and she has told me that now her indisposition and poor health and old age make the administration of the estate too heavy a burden for her....I desire that she shall be maintained in my house or that of my heir for all the days of her life, and be properly supplied with food and drink, clothes and shoes, in health and in sickness... and that she shall be the effective mistress of the house and have the keys to all the chests....[1]

Often, of course, there was no son, and the property passed to the daughter. The heiress, known as the *pubilla*, was as typical a figure in Catalan life as the *hereu*. Like him, she inherited the entire estate, and her parents would do what they could to ensure that the family's name, as well as its property, was passed on to her children. Where possible, her husband, perhaps a younger son, would be induced to adopt her name, or that of the *masia*, if this were a peasant family. Thus, if a man called Pere Arnau married the heiress to the *masia* Gironella, he would call himself Pere Arnau alias Gironella of the *masia* Gironella.[2] His children would take not their father's name but their mother's, so that the family name associated with the *masia* would not be lost.

If the heir, whether male or female, were an only child it was advisable to arrange an early marriage, to save the line from extinction. The legal age of majority in Catalonia was twenty-five, and the usual marrying age seems to have been over eighteen and under twenty-five,[3] but there were frequent exceptions. The guardians of the *pubilla* Mariana Xercavins, orphaned at six months, saw to it that she was married before the age of thirteen, and by the time she was twenty she was already married to her third husband, having been left childless by the first two.[4]

The desperate determination of this society to perpetuate the family's name and wealth, inevitably involved heavy personal sacrifices. The heir might have to forgo his personal wishes for the sake of an advantageous match, but at least he acquired the estate. His brothers and sisters, on the other hand, often acquired little or nothing. Following Roman law, it was the traditional practice in most parts of Catalonia

[1] APB: A. J. Fita, lib. 7, de testaments, fos. 89–94v, will of Rafael Vich, 5 Feb. 1643.

[2] Pelayo Negre Pastell and Enrique Mirambell Belloc, 'Sentencia Arbitral...', *Anales del Instituto de Estudios Gerundenses*, vol. v (1950), p. 238.

[3] For example, in the marriage of Joan Baptista de Olzinellas and María de Reguer, 26 March 1622 (APB: A. J. Fita, lib. 6, cap. mat.).   [4] Serra Roselló, 'Can Xercavins' (*op. cit.*).

to give each of the younger children a share, known as the *legítima*, in the third part of the estate. But in sixteenth-century Catalonia, as in sixteenth-century Castile, the desire to concentrate and consolidate the family's property was, if anything, growing, and the Corts of Monzón of 1585 reduced the *legítima* from a third to a quarter of the estate of the deceased.[1]

The reduction of the *legítima* had important social consequences. Three-quarters of the estate was now tied up in the hands of a single heir, and this may have been a minimum rather than a maximum, for the *legítima* could consist either of property or of cash, and there was an increasing tendency to pay it in cash in order to keep the estate intact.[2] The head of the family would therefore try to scrape up money to provide dowries for his daughters and settlements for his sons, rather than lay hands on his estate. If there was not enough money for a dowry, the daughter could be put into a convent. Don Josep de Pons laid it down in his will that, in the event of his leaving any daughters, one of them was to receive a dowry of 5000 *lliures* and the rest 1000 *lliures* apiece as their *legítima*, payable as and when they took the veil. His three younger sons, who were to be brought up in the heir's house and educated at his expense, were also to receive 1000 *lliures* as their *legítima* on reaching the age of twenty, 'or earlier in the event of marriage'.[3] A lump sum of 1000 *lliures* could not be expected to carry a man of noble birth very far.

By making it more difficult for second and third sons to live on inherited wealth, the law of 1585 played its part in creating another of the stock characters in Catalan family life—the so-called *fadristern* or *cabaler*, the younger brother who leaves the family home in search of his fortune. While the elder brother, by remaining at home to tend his estate, has helped to give Catalan society its fundamental stability, the younger brother, forced to fend for himself, has injected into it a dynamic element. Catalonia's vigorous industrialization in the eighteenth and nineteenth centuries can in large measure be attributed to the energy and acumen of younger sons, compelled to earn their living. But in the sixteenth and seventeenth centuries there is another, more

[1] See J. Coroleu y J. Pella y Forgas, *Los Fueros de Cataluña* (Barcelona, 1878), pp. 266 ff. and *Constitutions y altres drets de Cathalunya*, vol. I, p. 358.

[2] Coroleu y Pella, p. 269.

[3] APB: A. J. Fita, lib. 7, de testaments, fos. 95–98 v, will of Don Josep de Pons, 24 June 1639.

sombre, side to the story of the *fadristern*. His chances depended not only on his own flair and enterprise, but also on forces outside his control, like the opportunities available for profitable employment, and the attitude of the society at large to trade and manual labour and considerations of social status. If he were denied outlets and opportunities, he could easily become a burden on his family and a menace to society, hanging around his home and living at his elder brother's expense. Some of the most serious causes of social tension in sixteenth and seventeenth-century Catalonia may be traced to a family code and an inheritance system which dispossessed younger sons and then threw them out into a world which could not employ them.

The restlessness of the younger son, however, may not have been an excessive price to pay for the fundamental stability of the family as a unit. It was this stability that kept Catalan society on an even keel. The Catalan family was powerful, and solid, and anchored at some point firmly to the land. The nucleus of the family lived on the family estate, perhaps in a *masia*. It consisted of the *hereu* who had come into his inheritance, together with his wife and children and probably his widowed mother; of any younger brothers and sisters still at home; and of the domestic servants and the farm-hands, who were regarded as part of the family group and lived with it in the *masia*. The group to which they all belonged was closely knit, and essentially patriarchal, with the *hereu* as head and master of them all. But the family in the widest sense extended far beyond this nucleus. Younger sons who had left home and had families of their own would still maintain their link with the family home, and acknowledge the primacy of the *hereu*. Any success they may have achieved was regarded by themselves and their relatives not as an individual success but as a success for the family. When Don Pedro Franqueza, the younger son of an impecunious family of Catalan gentry, reached the pinnacle of his spectacular career at Court as the favourite of the duke of Lerma by acquiring a title of nobility, he wrote to his elder brother: 'His Majesty has honoured me with the title of count of Villalonga, on which I send you my congratulations, since everything redounds to your authority and that of your house, of which you are the head and I the feet.'[1] It was the

[1] AGS: Cámara de Castilla, leg. 2796, fo. 355 v, Don Pedro Franqueza to Don Jaume Franqueza, 20 Aug. 1603.

favourite Catalan success story. Another *fadristern* had made good, and in so doing had added to the glory and the honour of the family.

With every individual as part of a family, Catalan society was a society of interlocking families, rising in a pyramid at the summit of which stood a patriarchal king. '*Hijos míos*', 'my children', was the phrase with which Philip IV addressed the Catalans in the Corts of 1626.[1] Down from the king ran the ties of dependence, linking family to family to the very bottom of the social scale.

The character of these ties was determined in the first place by ordinary family relationship. Any Catalan with the name of Icart or Queralt would automatically gravitate into the orbit of the most distinguished bearer of those names, the count of Santa Coloma. As the head of the family, he was expected to provide help and protection, shielding even the most humble of his kinsmen beneath the capacious mantle of his patronage. When Santa Coloma became viceroy of Catalonia and headed his list of recommendations for the vacant archdeaconry of Besòs with the name of Don Joan de Icart, his cousin,[2] he was doing no more than was expected of him. A man's prestige in this society was measured by the size of his personal following and the degree to which he could offer satisfaction to his relatives and dependants. If he should be fortunate enough to bask in the sunlight of royal favour, then he was expected to deflect the rays of the sun on to his loyal kinsmen.

A man's following, however, was not limited to his relations in the strictest sense of the word. Just as the servants in the *masia* were regarded as part of the 'family', so a noble's vassals and dependants were also regarded as part of his 'family'. Blood relationship was here replaced by a reciprocal bond of obligation. While the feudal relationship based on land still existed, it had lost much of its meaning as the need for physical protection diminished, and homage had been transformed into little more than a vestigial symbol, setting the seal on what was purely a financial transaction. But a new kind of lordship had developed, better suited to the needs of a more secure, and more bureaucratic, age. In the sixteenth century men had need not so much of physical protection as of jobs and favours and pensions, and this was the

---

[1] ACA: G, R. 1057, fo. 181, King's speech of 18 April 1626.
[2] ACA: CA, leg. 394, Santa Coloma to King, 12 Jan. 1640.

need which the new style of lordship was designed to meet. The Court was the fountain of office and honour. The lord who stood well at Court was uniquely placed to see that some of the offices and some of the honours came the way of his own dependants. His part of the contract with his dependants was therefore to secure for them such favours as he could; their part was to render him any services he required.

'Service' and 'favour', or, in Castilian, *servicio* and *merced*. These complementary words appear over and over again in Spanish documents of the sixteenth and seventeenth centuries. Between them, service and favour constituted the two halves of the reciprocal bond of obligation uniting the lord and his dependant. In some ways they were vague expressions, for the nature of 'services' rendered was often hard to define, and 'favour' proved more often to be smooth promises than concrete benefits. But the conventions must be observed, for society was held together by unquestioning respect for the mutual obligations of a lord and his dependants. That was why Dr Pujades burst out in anger at a report that Philip III had refused to receive an embassy from the Principality: 'it is manifest injustice and barbarous unreasonableness to deny audience to peaceful vassals who come to demand justice of their lord'.[1] In flouting an elementary principle of lordship, the king's behaviour undermined the very foundations of society. It also explains the ecstatic character of the greeting which Dr Pujades prepared for his own patrons, the duke and duchess of Cardona, on their first visit to their town of Castelló d'Empúries:[2]

De ver mis señores	Crecen mis amores
Cumplióse el deseo.	Por cada momento.
Alegre les veo,	Ay que me desmayo
Y espero favores.	De gozo y contento....

What more natural than that the grateful duke should distribute largesse among faithful vassals long deprived of his company?

Family relationship and patronage cemented together the stones of the social pyramid, but it would be a mistake to assume that they always did their work effectively. There were dangers as well as ad-

[1] ABL: Diary of Pujades, 1, fo. 44, 5 June 1601.

[2] Pujades, 4, fo. 36v, 26 July 1628. It is impossible to convey the delicious flavour of the original. 'My desire to see my lords has been fulfilled. Happy am I to see them and I await their favours. Every moment my love for them grows. Ah, how I swoon with joy and contentment.'

vantages in the system. In so far as family allegiances tied the various layers of the social hierarchy together, they played an enormously important part in making society well-ordered and coherent. But if the interests of one family were pressed with excessive enthusiasm, they were likely to come into conflict with those of another family. The Venetian Navagero in 1525 referred to the factions among the Catalans,[1] and the theme of rival bands is constantly recurring in descriptions of sixteenth and seventeenth-century Catalonia. Rivalry and faction were the price that had to be paid for the vertical linking of different social groups through patronage and family relationships. All too often, the pyramid was split into separate segments running from top to bottom. How far the whole edifice was in danger of falling apart depended on the degree of harmony that could be achieved between the sense of family and the sense of something larger than the family—the entire community.

If Catalan society could be broken down into a vast number of family units, those units when put together again formed a national community. It was true that a Catalan's first territorial loyalty was to his own region, and that there were wide variations between one region and another. Dwellers in the coastal regions were notoriously more easy-going than the brusque, rugged inhabitants of the interior. Local accents varied from the soft-spoken Catalan of Girona to the harsh tones of the Segarra. People were acutely conscious of these differences, and there was a tendency to regard anyone even from the next valley as a *foraster*, a foreigner, just as *pàtria* in the first instance meant one's home town or village. After spending four years in the not very distant county of Empúries, Pujades rejoiced at the thought of returning to his '*pàtria* and dear city of Barcelona'.[2]

Yet if the *pàtria* was the home town, the word was also used of the Principality at large. In spite of a Catalan's intense local loyalties, he was also conscious of belonging to a wider community. Catalonia was his fatherland, and it was a *nation*; the phrase *la nació catalana* was already in use in the fourteenth century.[3] Sixteenth and seventeenth-

[1] *Viaje a España de Andrès Navagero*, ed. José María Alonso Gamo (Valencia, 1951), p. 38.
[2] Pujades, 2, fo. 157, 17 March 1609.
[3] Francisco Elias de Tejada, *Las Doctrinas Políticas en la Cataluña Medieval* (Barcelona, 1950), p. 21. The author claims that Catalonia may have been the first country in which the word *nation* was used 'in the modern sense of a separate political body, and not simply to describe a group enjoying common ethnographical origins'.

century Catalans wrote of the Principality indifferently as the *nació*, the *pàtria* or the *provincia*, this last word implying no thought of dependence or subordination. While these words may have conveyed different shades of meaning in different contexts, they also helped to express a strong feeling that Catalonia was a distinctive national community, whose inhabitants were united by ties of language, culture and history.

This sense of being part of a national community naturally appeared at its strongest in the Catalan's relations with the outside world. But there were various gradations in the classification of outsiders. The Catalans tended to look upon their Aragonese and Valencian neighbours as closely akin to themselves. The Valencians talked a variety of the same language, and both Aragon and Valencia had been their associates in the great medieval federation, and formed part of the Crown of Aragon to which Catalonia belonged. After the union of the Crowns of Castile and Aragon, there had, however, been some slackening of these ties, and it is significant that, for all the protestations of *germandat* or brotherhood in the letters that passed between the representatives of the three States, not one showed a real sense of brotherhood in time of urgent need. Valencia revolted in 1520, Aragon in 1591 and Catalonia in 1640, and each revolted alone.

Past differences and recent history made sixteenth-century Catalonia's relations with Castile a good deal less cordial than its relations with Valencia and Aragon. The gulf between the two countries was widened by the considerable difference in the languages they spoke. Although Catalan was now being permeated by Castilian expressions, and some members of the Catalan aristocracy in the early seventeenth century were writing at least some of their letters in Castilian, the language of Castile was still met with incomprehension or downright hostility. This was not surprising, since Castilians themselves were few and far between. If towns on the main roads, like 'Tortosa, Girona and Lleida see a Castilian only every second or third day, and then fleetingly, what of Manresa, Solsona, Vic and Urgell, where, if they ever see a Castilian, it is only by a miracle?'[1]

Although Castilians were unpopular, they were at least Spaniards, and the Catalans did think of themselves, even if rather vaguely, as

---

[1] BC: Fullet Bonsoms 9967, *Memorial en defensa de la lengua catalana*, by Dr Diego Cisteller (Tarragona, 1636).

part of Spain. The other two nations with which the Catalans came into contact—the Genoese and the French—possessed no such redeeming features. Of the Genoese, there was nothing good to be said. 'White Moors', Dr Pujades called them.[1] This hostility can probably be traced to the commercial struggles of the Middle Ages between Catalonia and Genoa, but it had been fanned in the sixteenth century into smouldering hatred by the success of the Genoese in capturing Catalonia's traditional trading empire in the western Mediterranean, and in worming their way into a favoured position as bankers to the kings of Spain. Relations with the French were, if anything, worse. Centuries of enmity with France had made the Catalans violently francophobe, and although the Principality had assimilated French settlers with surprising speed (perhaps because, being from the south of France, they spoke languages very similar to Catalan), the wave of French immigration into Catalonia in the sixteenth century had not softened the Catalans' feelings. The common word for a Frenchman—a *gavatx*—was one of the worst insults one Catalan could hurl at another.

If the Catalans held these opinions of foreigners, what opinions did they hold of themselves? What was the Catalan nation to which their first allegiance lay? Physically, it was a country abundantly blessed by the bountiful hand of God, who had given it a temperate climate, a fertile soil and refreshing streams; not to mention 'the abundance of fruits, the variety of flowers and animals, the pleasing temper of the inhabitants...their zeal in the Faith, their obedience to the law, the rectitude of their politics, the beauty of their buildings...and, above all, the inestimable possession of so many marvellous bodies of the saints'.[2] But it was above all the constitutional structure of the Principality which filled at least the more politically minded Catalans with pride. This, more than anything else, differentiated their nation from all others.

[1] Pujades, I, fo. 135, 1 Dec. 1602.
[2] F. Martí, *Noticia universal de Cataluña* (*op. cit.*), p. 4. Foreigners had a rather less high opinion of the Catalans and their country. 'Although they are no better than other Catholic nations, they show themselves great lovers of religious ceremonies, from which ecclesiastics and monks enjoy great credit among them....They are very slow and indolent in all their affairs, and content themselves with working their lands only to keep themselves alive, without bothering with commerce outside their own neighbourhood....They are almost all ignorant, and show little capacity for business....They are very fond of women, and very revengeful....Their principal vices are idleness and avarice, wanting to profit from everything and do nothing...' [*Mémoires de Du Plessis-Besançon*, ed. le Comte Horric de Beaucaire (Paris, 1892), pp. 192–3].

The basis of their constitutional system was its contractual character. 'Between Your Majesty and his vassals there is a reciprocal obligation, whereby as they must obey and serve Your Majesty as their king and lord, so Your Majesty must observe their laws and privileges.'[1] Catalonia, in fact, was a free country, whose freedom was emphasized by the voluntary election of its prince.

The affairs of the Principality of Catalonia are not to be judged by reference to those of other kingdoms and provinces, where the kings and lords are sovereign lords, with such power that they make and unmake laws and rule their vassals as they will; and where, after making laws, they themselves are not bound by them....In Catalonia, the supreme power and jurisdiction over the province belongs not to His Majesty alone, but to His Majesty and the three estates of the province, which together possess supreme and absolute power to make and unmake laws, and to alter the machinery and government of the province....These laws we have in Catalonia are laws compacted between the king and the land, and the prince can no more exempt himself from them than he can exempt himself from a contract....[2]

The laws by which the Principality was governed were agreed upon between the prince and his subjects at meetings of the Corts or parliament of Catalonia, which could only be held when the prince was present in person. These laws were known as the *Constitucions* of Catalonia,[3] and each king on his accession would swear that they should be inviolably observed by himself and his officials. When put together, the constitutions added up to a fundamental charter of Catalonia's liberties. They made arbitrary taxation by the Crown impossible; they protected the Catalan against the abuses of royal justice; they guaranteed him his property unless he were guilty of human or divine *lèse-majesté* in the first degree; they determined the size, the character and the powers of the royal administration.[4]

Within the area bounded by its constitutions, Catalonia could claim to enjoy unrivalled liberty. The powers of the prince were extraordinarily small, and could only be effectively exercised in conformity

[1] BC: Fullet Bonsoms, no. 15, *Discurso y memorial...por Fr Francisco de Copons* (Barcelona, 1622), fos. 8 and 9.

[2] BC: Fullet Bonsoms, no. 12, *Per los Diputats del General de Catalunya* (Barcelona, 1622), fo. 2.

[3] Compiled in three volumes in Barcelona (1588) under the title of *Constitutions y altres drets de Cathalunya*. References in this book are to the 1704 edition.

[4] Corbera, *Cataluña Illustrada*, pp. 77–85.

with the will of the community. It expressed its will at intervals in sessions of the Corts, and, when the Corts were not sitting, by means of a remarkable institution known as the Diputació. This was a standing committee of the Corts consisting of six men, two from each Estate. Three were known as *Diputats*, one from each Estate, and the other three as *Oidors*. They held office for a period of three years, and were always presided over by the Diputat Eclesiàstic.

The Diputació represented the interests of the *Generalitat*—the entire Catalan community—and was often known as the Generalitat itself. Its principal function was to represent the Catalan nation in its dealings with its prince. The Diputats and Oidors were intended to be the argus-eyed guardians of Catalonia's cherished laws and liberties. When a royal official was alleged to have infringed a constitution, it was they who made the necessary investigations and ensured redress from the king. It was they, also, who had sole responsibility for the levying of taxes in the Principality and for the raising of the subsidies conceded to the king by the Corts.[1]

In common with other Catalan institutions, the Diputació had fallen on evil times in the fifteenth century, and had ceased to represent anything more than the interests of a small clique. But Ferdinand the Catholic had introduced a new system for the election of officers, known as *insaculació*, whereby the names of eligible persons were drawn at random out of a silver basin by a child under eight years of age. This reform, it was hoped, would restore to the Diputació its original character as the impartial arbiter of the nation's destinies, and the mouthpiece of its aspirations. For the Diputació was intended to serve as a symbol—the symbol of the historic free community of the Catalans.

The sense of belonging to this free community was very strong. The Catalans had been taught to venerate the laws, the liberties and the institutions won for them by the heroic actions of their forefathers, and their own highest duty was to ensure that they handed on their precious heritage intact to their descendants. The feeling of obligation to the community therefore represented a natural counterbalance to the feeling of obligation to the family, and it was around the axis of family and community that Catalan life revolved. But the civil wars of the fif-

[1] See Jaime Carrera Pujal, *Historia Política y Económica de Cataluña* (Barcelona, 1947), vol. I, pp. 14–15. There is no adequate study of the Catalan Diputació in this period. See below, pp. 130ff.

teenth century had shown that everything did not automatically function as it should. There were obvious elements of stability in Catalan society: the land, the family, the bonds of kinship and the ties of obligation, and a deep devotion to an idealized historical community. But the ordered society would only remain an ordered society if every part of the machinery fulfilled neither more nor less than its allotted function, and this required constant adjustments. Allow one part of the mechanism to get out of control, and the whole delicate instrument was upset. If family loyalty turned into family vendettas, if partisan interests were allowed to prevail over the corporate interests of the nation, the ordered society was lost.

Ferdinand the Catholic had done everything possible to ensure the smooth running of the machine. He had overhauled Catalonia's legal and administrative institutions and readjusted the social balance, so that the Catalonia of the sixteenth century might approximate as nearly as possible to the Catalonia of the High Middle Ages; to that magnificently ordered society, with its noble laws, liberties and institutions, which had built for itself a great Mediterranean empire. But there was one possible flaw in Ferdinand's work. He had not created a new Catalonia, but had done what he could to restore the old, and he had restored it to a world that had profoundly changed.

The signs of change were all around. Catalonia was no longer the head of an empire, but only a semi-autonomous province in the empire of Castile. Its prince no longer held Court in Barcelona, but in a distant Madrid. This itself implied a profound transformation. The person of the king seemed to be an integral component of traditional Catalan society, based as it was on a hierarchically organized scheme of reciprocal obligations. The king was bound to his subjects personally in his natural role as patriarchal father; he was bound to them juridically as a principal party to the constitutional contract. Yet right through the sixteenth century the Catalans saw almost nothing of their king. This was unavoidable in view of his other commitments, and its very unavoidability suggested the kind of dilemma with which the Catalans were confronted.

'The ancient laws and ordinances of a republic should not be preserved simply because of their antiquity, but only in so far as they are adapted to the conditions of the age and of men....' So wrote a citizen of Barcelona who served as Diputat Reial from 1602 to 1605.[1] Ferdinand had restored the 'ancient laws and ordinances' of medieval Catalonia, but how far were these 'adapted' to the conditions of a more modern age? And if they were not properly adapted, how long could the Principality hope to remain the ideally ordered society of Ferdinand's dreams? These were not questions which seemed to worry the Catalans unduly when the new king, Philip III, paid his first, and last, visit to the Principality in 1599.[2]

[1] Joaquín Setanti, *Centellas de varios conceptos*, no. 453. A series of aphorisms first published in Barcelona in 1614, and reprinted in *Biblioteca de Autores Españoles*, vol. LXV (Madrid, 1873).

[2] There is a delightful description of Catalonia in 1599, on the eve of the king's visit, by a young Swiss, Thomas Platter, in *Félix et Thomas Platter à Montpellier* (Montpellier, 1892), pp. 395–461.

CHAPTER III

THE DISORDERED SOCIETY

When Philip III came to the Principality in 1599 he came to see, and to be seen by, his Catalan subjects and to hold a session of the Corts. The outcome of these Corts was hailed by the Catalans as a national triumph. 'His Majesty has granted everything that was requested of him', noted a Catalan gentleman in his journal, 'and in such a manner that nothing more could have been desired.'[1] His Majesty in fact had very little alternative. The main concern of Philip III and his favourite, the duke of Lerma, was money, and to get money they were prepared to make large concessions. The privileges of the aristocracy were confirmed; the towns were discharged of all arrears of taxes payable to the Crown up to 1599; permission was granted for the Catalans to build and maintain four armed galleys of their own—a concession which, it was believed, would be 'of great help to all the second sons in Catalonia' and would 'revive the memory of all the glorious naval achievements of the Catalans in times gone by'.[2] To crown the various political and administrative favours, the king ended the seven-week session of the Corts with a lavish distribution of honours. There were sixty new creations of *militars* and eighty-one of nobles, and eight nobles or viscounts were raised to the rank of count.[3]

Lerma and the king reaped the reward for their bribes and favours in a subsidy of unprecedented magnitude—1,100,000 *lliures*.[4] The Cata-

---

[1] BC: MS 510, fo. 105. From the journal of Don Federic Despalau. The proceedings of the Corts are recorded in ACA: G, Cortes, 1051–3; and the acts and constitutions passed in this session were printed at Barcelona in 1603 under the title of *Constitutions fetes per la SCR Magestat del Rey...1599*.   [2] Despalau, *ibid.*

[3] ACA: CA, leg. 358, *Certificación auténtica de los caballeros y nobles que se hizieron por SM en las Cortes de 1599.*

[4] For purposes of comparison, the following is a list of subsidies voted by the Catalan Corts since the beginning of the reign of Charles V. (Figures as given in Manuel Danvila y Collado, *El Poder Civil en España*, vol. II, Madrid, 1885.) The list also shows the striking decline in the frequency of sessions under Philip II.

1519	250,000 *lliures*	1547	235,000 *lliures*
1529	250,000	1552	201,000
1533	250,000	1563	300,000
1537	210,000	1585	500,000
1542	200,000	1599	1,100,000

49

lans, for their part, could hardly grudge money so well spent. The Corts, 'worthy to be acclaimed by future ages as unique, and for ever deserving of eternal veneration',[1] had set the seal of perfection on the well-ordered and well-governed community that was Catalonia. 'There was a delectable and perfect harmony in the government of the state.'[2]

The harmony, however, was neither as perfect nor as permanent as king and Catalans affected to believe. In so far as it depended on the maintenance of good relations between the Principality and the Court, these were rudely shaken by an unfortunate incident arising immediately out of the Corts. It was customary after a session of the Corts for the Diputats to have the new laws and constitutions printed. But on this occasion the printing was postponed from one day to the next, because of disagreement over five of the constitutions, which dealt with such important topics as the right of the viceroy to issue proclamations and of nobles and their servants to carry prohibited weapons.[3] A number of nobles, led by Don Nofre d'Alentorn and Don Gispert de Guimerà,[4] were determined that these constitutions should not become law and managed to persuade three of the six members of the Diputació to oppose their publication. Hoping perhaps to exploit the divisions within the Catalan ruling class and to reassert a royal authority which he considered dangerously undermined by the recent Corts, the viceroy, the duke of Feria,[5] decided to act. On 2 March 1602, while the attention of the Barcelona populace was distracted by a vast procession making its way to the cathedral to pray for rain, he arrested one Diputat, Don Joan de Vilanova, and one Oidor, Don Josep de Castellvell.[6]

There had been no such open conflict between the royal authorities and the supreme representatives of the Catalan nation since 1569, when,

[1] BUB: MS 115, fo. 3 v, *Historia General del Principado de Cataluña...1598–1640*. This bears the name of an eighteenth-century writer, Serra i Postius, but another MS copy in the BN (Paris), Espagne 114, shows it to be the work of a seventeenth-century Catalan, Dr Sevillà (see Appendix VI, section D).

[2] *Ibid.* fo. 4 v.

[3] Diary of Pujades, I, fo. 57.

[4] ACA: CA, leg. 267, no. 4, consulta, 31 July 1601.

[5] Don Lorenzo Suárez de Figueroa, second duke of Feria, was half English. His mother was Jane Dormer, confidante and lady-in-waiting of Mary Tudor, who met her future husband when he came to England with Philip of Spain. After her marriage she moved with her husband to Spain, where she lived on, an indomitable old lady, well into the reign of Philip III (see Henry Clifford, *The Life of Jane Dormer*, Quarterly Series, vol. LXII, London, 1887).

[6] Pujades, I, fo. 90 v.

in the course of a bitter dispute between Diputació and Inquisition, Philip II had ordered the arrest of Diputats and Oidors.[1] But Philip III had neither the strength nor the will of his father, and the duke of Lerma was anxious only for peace. The over-energetic duke of Feria was transferred to the government of Sicily, and his successor, the archbishop of Tarragona, negotiated a compromise, whereby the two prisoners were released, and the Diputats agreed to print the constitutions on the understanding that the obnoxious five should remain a dead letter. The storm died down as swiftly as it had arisen, and 'harmony' was restored.

The dispute over the printing of the constitutions showed how easily the delicate relationship between the Catalans and the Court could be upset; but it also suggested that, as long as Lerma remained in power, there was little danger of a sustained attack on the Principality's laws and privileges. Politically, at least, the prospects seemed good. But Catalonia's vaunted 'harmony' was not solely determined by the state of its relations with the Court. It implied also the satisfactory ordering of society within Catalonia itself. It was in the very years after 1603, when its outstanding political problems had at least momentarily receded, that the Principality's social problems grew more intense; so much so, indeed, that they would come to jeopardize once again the whole political relationship of king and Catalans. This growing social unrest took various forms, but the most significant of them was the spread of banditry.

In Castile, the reign of Philip III was the age of the *pícaro*. In Catalonia, it was the age of the bandit—of Roca Guinarda, who robbed the rich to give to the poor, and whose iron discipline over his gang filled Sancho Panza with terror and admiration.[2] Fundamentally, bandit and *pícaro* were the products of similar phenomena, of hunger and misery and unemployment, but they differed both in their character and in the nature of their response to misfortune. Where the *pícaro* accepted conditions as they were, and simply attempted to turn them to his own advantage, the bandit was protesting against them, or at least was believed to be so by all those members of society who felt themselves oppressed. Moreover, where *picardía* was essentially an urban pheno-

[1] Reglà, *Felip II i Catalunya*, p. 189.
[2] Miguel de Cervantes, *Don Quijote de la Mancha*, vol. II, ch. LX. There is a well-documented biography of Roca Guinarda by Lluís M.ª Soler y Terol *Perot Roca Guinarda* (Manresa, 1909).

menon, banditry was a manifestation of rural and of aristocratic discontent.

There was nothing new about banditry in Catalonia.[1] The rugged nature of the land, the closeness of the French frontier and the power and independence of the barons made it ideal bandit country. But if banditry in Catalonia can be traced back at least to the middle of the fourteenth century, it seems to have acquired both new characteristics and a new intensity during the course of the sixteenth.[2] The Wars of Religion in France brought French recruits to the gangs, many of them believed to be suspect in the Faith. At the same time, the opportunities for plunder were greatly enhanced when piracy and war closed the traditional routes to Flanders, and Philip II began during the 1570's to send his consignments of silver to Genoa by way of Barcelona, and thence up the famous *camino del Imperio* to the Netherlands.[3]

By all accounts, public order was deteriorating in the later years of Philip II. The corporation of Lleida complained in 1587 that people were afraid to leave their homes because of the danger from gangs which included Huguenots from across the frontier.[4] A virtual civil war raged in the diocese of Urgell during the 1590's,[5] and Philip II sent troops to besiege and destroy the castle of Joan Cadell at Arsèguel, which served as the headquarters of one of the bandit factions.[6] It was, however, between the ending of the Corts in 1599 and the death in office of the viceroy, the marquis of Almazán, in 1615, that the situation became acute, and the Principality seemed to contemporaries to be on the edge of anarchy. This decline of public order partly reflected a failure of government,[7] but it was also indicative of difficult economic and social conditions, especially in the countryside, and of deep-rooted aristocratic discontent.

---

[1] For the early stages of Catalan banditry, see Antonio Borrás, S.I., 'Contribución a los origines del bandolerismo en Cataluña', *Estudios de Historia Moderna*, vol. III (1953), and J. Reglà, *Felip II i Catalunya*.

[2] This would appear to be true of the whole Mediterranean region. Cf. Braudel, *La Méditerranée*, pp. 657 ff.

[3] Frank Spooner, *L'Economie mondiale et les frappes monétaires en France 1493–1680* (Paris, 1956), p. 25.

[4] ACA: CA, leg. 265, no. 26, consulta, 28 Sept. 1587.

[5] ACA: CA, leg. 343, Bishop of Urgell to King, 12 June 1592.

[6] Pere Pujol i Tubau, *Sant Josep de Calassanç, Oficial del Capítol d'Urgell* (Barcelona, 1921), p. 22. Arsèguel is a few miles from the Seu d'Urgell.

[7] See below, ch. IV.

At the heart of Catalonia's social difficulties in the early seventeenth century was the rapid growth of population in a country with a more or less static economy. Medieval Catalonia had derived its wealth from its trade. The social and political troubles of the fifteenth century had gravely injured the country's commercial prospects, but the administrative reforms of Ferdinand the Catholic offered hopes of a commercial revival, which were indeed partly realized in the opening years of the sixteenth century.[1] But the revival remained only modest, and it was not accompanied by any radical new departures from the pattern of the Principality's medieval trade. To some extent this was the result of circumstances beyond Catalonia's control. The alliance between Charles V and Genoa gave the Genoese a favoured position in Catalonia's traditional Mediterranean markets;[2] and the legal exclusion of Catalans from direct trade with the New World made it difficult for them to enter valuable new markets which might have made up for losses in the old. During the first half of the sixteenth century they petitioned on several occasions for the right to install consuls in Seville and Cadiz, and to enjoy certain privileges in the American trade.[3] But these efforts met with no success, and do not seem to have been pursued into the reign of Philip II. Somehow, events in the New World contrived to pass Catalonia by, and it was not until the 1640's, when their economy was threatened with disaster, that the Catalans turned their eyes again in the direction of America.[4]

During the sixteenth century, however, they did benefit from the American trade at second hand. By the middle of the century, the Principality had found a flourishing market for its cloths in the great fairs of Castile. According to a report of 1553, three-quarters of these were bought for sale to the Indies and to the overseas possessions of Portugal, and only one-quarter remained in Castile itself.[5] In return, Catalonia could obtain, again at second hand, the products of the New World. This intensified trade with Castile compensated for the loss of Catalonia's traditional markets in Barbary and the Levant, and supple-

[1] Catalan trade in the sixteenth century has still to be properly studied, but much uncoordinated information on the subject can be found in Carrera Pujal, *Historia de Cataluña*, vol. I, ch. II.

[2] Roberto S. López, 'Il predominio economico dei Genovesi nella Monarchia spagnola', *Giornale storico e letterario della Liguria*, vol. XI (1936).

[3] Carrera Pujal, vol. I, p. 322.   [4] See below, p. 538.

[5] Carrera Pujal, vol. I, p. 324.

mented its normal commercial relations with Sicily and Italy; but unfortunately the increase proved to be ephemeral. When the fairs of Medina del Campo declined in the last decades of the sixteenth century, Catalonia's cloth exports to Castile declined with them.[1]

It was true that the last years of the century saw a spectacular commercial recovery, at least for the city of Barcelona. When the Barcelona-Genoa route acquired its new importance, the city found itself once again part of the great world, an indispensable stage on the network of silver-routes that bound together the scattered possessions of the kings of Spain. There is an undeniable air of affluence about the Barcelona of Philip III, with its luxurious municipal life and its ostentatious ceremonial. Yet the basis of the recovery remained precarious, and it was to be ascribed less to the efforts of Catalan merchants than to unexpectedly favourable international conditions, always liable to sudden change.

The merchants played safe. There were admittedly one or two attempts at a revival of the Levant trade, and as late as 1630 a ship returned to Barcelona from Alexandria with a cargo of cotton and spices to the value of 40,000 *escuts*.[2] Wine, silk and Aragonese wool were brought from the ports of Valencia, sugar and American produce from those of Andalusia, and spices from Lisbon.[3] Much of Barcelona's trade, however, was simply a coastal trade with other parts of the Principality and with Rosselló. Only with Sicily, Sardinia and with Italy was there a really considerable overseas trade. Catalan ships would carry home-produced cloths to Sicily, and return laden with Sicilian corn, or with manufactures and luxury articles acquired when they put in at Marseilles, now the great depot of western Mediterranean trade.

Markets were therefore limited, and, although there does not seem to have been any considerable contraction of trade until the great economic recession of the Mediterranean world in the 1620's and 1630's, temporary dislocations, such as that caused by the Sicilian famine of 1603,[4] could have unpleasant repercussions on the Principality's economic life.

[1] Carrera Pujal, vol. I, p. 348.   [2] Pujades, 4, fo. 172.

[3] For information on the character of Catalan trade, I have relied on the excellent unpublished thesis of J. Nadal and E. Giralt, *Los seguros marítimos y el comercio de Barcelona, 1630–1665*, which they kindly placed at my disposal.

[4] Reported by Dr Pujades, 1, fo. 163, 28 April 1603.

The range of exports was also limited, and it was ominous that raw materials and natural products—unworked wool, leather, iron and corn —were taking an increasingly large share of the export trade. The traditional mainstay of Catalonia's foreign trade was, however, cloth, and sixteenth-century Catalonia was as dependent as sixteenth-century England on the prosperity of its cloth industry. By the early seventeenth century there were signs of trouble. In 1606 Barcelona was complaining that 'cloths are not going from this city to Castile. Instead, a great many Castilian cloths are actually being imported, of better quality than those manufactured in Catalonia.'[1] In 1630 it was reported that the number of clothworkers in Girona had sunk from five hundred to one hundred.[2]

Complaints from the traditional cloth centres do not necessarily provide a reliable index to the fortunes of the textile industry as a whole, since there are indications that it was in process of being reorganized at the expense of traditional sections of the industry. The first years of the seventeenth century were years of conflict between certain of the *paraires*, or wool-dressers, and the guild of weavers (*teixidors*). Some of the *paraires* had become large-scale dealers who went personally to Castile and Aragon to purchase wool,[3] which they then distributed to the *teixidors* for weaving. But very often they avoided the towns, where the weavers were organized into powerful guilds, and turned instead to the countryside in search of cheaper labour. In 1628, for example, the women clothworkers of Barcelona rioted, 'crying that the *paraires* were taking wool out of the city for carding and spinning'.[4] The alleged decline of the cloth industry may therefore be no more than the decline of the old clothing centres as the industry migrated to the countryside.

Yet the increasingly strong demand for protectionist legislation in the 1620's does suggest both an over-all decline in the export of finished cloths and an increase in the export of unworked wools. The Corts of 1626 asserted that the 'export of wool from Catalonia is destroying the

[1] Carrera Pujal, vol. I, pp. 363–4.
[2] BC: Fullet Bonsoms 5404, *Parer de Jaume Damians* (1630).
[3] Iglésies, *Pere Gil*, p. 233.
[4] Quoted from AHB: Delibs, 1628, fos. 49 v–50, by Pierre Vilar, in his unpublished thesis on eighteenth-century Catalonia, p. 501. I am deeply indebted to M. Vilar for his great generosity in allowing me to see, and quote from, the section of his thesis which deals with the Catalan economy in the seventeenth century, as also for all his help on Catalan economic problems.

Principality and Comtats', and drafted a constitution forbidding the export of unworked wool and skins.[1] The Barcelona merchant Jaume Damians wrote in 1630 of the large quantity of foreign textiles being purchased by the Catalans, and calculated that each year everyone spent a minimum of one *escut*, and wealthy citizens as much as a hundred *escuts*, on clothes made abroad. Only rigorous protectionism, he believed, could save Catalan industry.[2]

Not only did the Principality fail to open up new markets which would help to employ its expanding population, but it also failed to develop its agriculture sufficiently to feed it. This was the consequence both of natural conditions and of economic policies which blocked the way to agrarian expansion.

During the course of the sixteenth century, the Mediterranean world ran increasingly short of food.[3] Everywhere populations were growing faster than the capacity of the land to feed them, and famine and dearth were becoming frequent occurrences. Catalonia was no exception. While the population grew, the yield of the crops was limited by the primitive nature of agricultural techniques,[4] and perhaps also by a deterioration in climatic conditions, for the viceroy in 1576 reported that '*in our time* there has been such an increase in dearth and in the scarcity of water in the plain of Urgell and the Ribera de Sió that many houses have been deserted and towns and villages ruined'.[5] Even when harvests were good, overland transport costs were such that it was often cheaper to buy foreign corn, imported by sea, than to buy from western Catalonia. In 1567, for example, when corn stood at 48s. to 50s. the quarter in Barcelona, it was well worth importing Sicilian corn at 24s., even when an additional 12s. 9d. was payable for transport.[6]

The inadequacy of the corn supply and the considerable fluctuations in prices,[7] kept the town councillors of Catalonia in a state of perpetual anxiety. Everyone knew that 'the stomach brooks no delay',[8] and

[1] ACA: G, 1058, fo. 244, const. no. 41.
[2] *Parer de Jaume Damians.*   [3] Braudel, *La Méditerranée*, p. 461.
[4] Emilio Giralt Raventós, 'En torno al precio del trigo en Barcelona durante el siglo XVI', *Hispania*, vol. XVIII (1958), pp. 38–61.
[5] Quoted by Joan Reglà, *Els Virreis de Catalunya* (Barcelona, 1956), p. 39 (my italics).
[6] Giralt, 'Precio del trigo', p. 45.
[7] See the table of corn prices for the college of Sant Guillèm in Barcelona (Appendix II).
[8] AMG: Jeroni de Real, *Varias Noticias*, fo. 32.

municipal authorities were haunted by the fear of bread riots, like the one in Barcelona in December 1604, when 'many poor people, especially women, went down to the corn-exchange to buy corn, and, failing to find any, marched to the town hall' and set fire to the house of one of the town councillors of the previous year.[1] The larger towns, desperately trying to fill their granaries, would find themselves engaged in fierce competition with each other while corn-growers and profiteers steadily pushed up prices.[2] At the same time, private interests were liable to cut across any sense of obligation to the municipality. In 1603, for example, Barcelona bought 6000 quarters of poor-quality corn from Rosselló at 33s. or 34s. the quarter, at a time when it could have bought elsewhere at 28s. or 29s., simply because one of the town councillors had a brother engaged in the Rosselló corn trade.[3]

While speculators profited from a shortage which derived naturally from conditions of the soil and the climate, there is reason to believe that the shortage was more considerable than it need have been, as a result of the attitude of a powerful group among the merchants and landowners. The principal obstacle to the increase of Catalonia's grain supply was the shortage of water. The plain of Urgell in particular was potentially rich corn-growing land, but it suffered from lack of rain. Suggestions were made at various times for the irrigation of the plain, and indeed careful plans were prepared for an irrigation scheme in 1575, but these came to nothing. The scheme appears to have been sabotaged by Barcelona merchants who alone could finance the project, but who were afraid that it would damage their commercial interests. Dependent as they were on the Sicilian market for the sale of cloths, in return for which they bought Sicilian corn for the provisioning of Catalonia, they saw an increased yield of Catalan corn as a serious threat to their lucrative two-way trade.[4]

The merchants were joined in their opposition to irrigation schemes in the plain of Urgell by the nobles of the Segarra and of other poor regions, who feared the effects of competition from the landowners in

[1] Pujades, I, fo. 245.
[2] AMG: Corresp. N–Z, Benet Anglasell to Jurats of Girona, 31 Aug. 1619.
[3] Pujades, I, fo. 176v.
[4] BN (Paris): Baluze 238, fos. 352–67. Printed and MS papers (apparently in the hand of Dr Pujades) on the irrigation of the plain of Urgell. In the second of his *Discursos* Gilabert makes a similar attack on the corn policy of the Barcelona authorities, which prejudiced the interests of landowners in western Catalonia like himself.

a potentially more fertile Catalan West.[1] They stood to gain from the chronic corn shortage. So also did all those proprietors in regions where the hazards of drought were not abnormally high, and where communications with the towns were reasonably good. Conditions in this respect were especially favourable for farmers in eastern Catalonia and the Camp de Tarragona. In years of dearth, such corn as they managed to grow would command exceptionally high prices, and in good years the greater accessibility of their grain gave them an important advantage over the landowners of the West. It is not, then, surprising that the first years of the seventeenth century should be a time of prosperity for the *masies* of the East; a prosperity reflected in the intense construction of farmhouses throughout the region of Vic[2] and the adornment of its churches with rich and ornate altar-pieces.

The prosperity of the East contrasted strikingly with conditions in the West. A western landowner, Don Alexandre d'Alentorn, the son of the Don Nofre d'Alentorn who played a leading part in the controversy of 1601–3 over the printing of the constitutions, found on his father's death in 1606 that he had succeeded to an impoverished estate. His entire income came from the corn and barley grown on his lands, 'and the soil of Urgell is so uncertain that many years the crops cannot be harvested, and when they can be, it is extremely difficult to sell them'.[3] His only hope of escape seemed to lie in obtaining a licence to export his corn. The export of grain from Catalonia was generally forbidden, but viceroys were empowered to give export licences to merchants and landowners when they considered them justified. This naturally led to favouritism and abuse. Where an Alentorn might be refused a licence, some rival landowner might well obtain one through friendship or relationship with a royal official. The arbitrary character of the licensing system, which led to much personal bitterness, also produced curious anomalies. In 1588, for instance, 150,000 quarters of grain were said to have been exported from Catalonia, contrary to the viceroy's proclamations but by virtue of licences which he himself had issued;[4] and it was by no means unusual to find that, at a time when

[1] *Ibid.*
[2] Gonçal de Reparaz, *La Plana de Vic* (Barcelona, 1928), p. 131.
[3] ACA: CA, leg. 269, petition of Alentorn, 18 March 1614.
[4] Giralt, 'Precio del trigo', p. 49.

Catalonia was driven by the shortage of corn to make large purchases in Rosselló, France, Aragon and Sicily, Catalan corn-growers were themselves selling their produce outside the Principality.

The contradictory corn policies pursued in Catalonia, the conflicts between mercantile and agrarian interests, between the towns' need of cheap corn and the producers' desire for high prices, only served to increase the price fluctuations which annual harvest variations themselves rendered inevitable. These fluctuations could have serious consequences for wage-earners. In a normal year of the decade 1570–80 a master artisan with a daily wage of 5s. required six days of work to buy a quarter of corn. In years of dearth like 1572, 1578, 1579 and 1580, he needed ten working days to buy the same quantity.[1]

Details of wages and prices are at present so scanty that it is impossible to reconstruct the course of real wages during the sixteenth and early seventeenth centuries.[2] Corn prices in Catalonia, which probably rose more slowly than in other parts of Europe,[3] nearly trebled during the course of the century.[4] On the other hand, agricultural wages at Bagà —the only available example—remained the same for a hundred years. A ploughman at Bagà in 1484 who used his own oxen, earned 5s. a day and expenses; a ploughman who used his master's oxen earned 1s. 6d. a day. It was only in the 1590's that their wages were raised, and then by no more than 1s.[5] Nor is there any indication of a general rise in wages between 1600 and 1640. Between these years, the wages of master-masons, carpenters and ordinary workmen at Manresa ranged from 4s. to 6s. a day according to their skills.[6] This tallies with figures that have been collected for expenditure on building works on the palace of the Generalitat in Barcelona:[7]

---

[1] Giralt, p. 53. Prices are given in *sous* and *diners*. See note on coinage, Appendix I.
[2] For some notes on wages and prices, see Appendix II.
[3] Nadal and Giralt, *La Population Catalane*, p. 124, n. 3.
[4] Giralt, p. 56, gives the following corn prices for Barcelona, with base 100, 1493–8:

1501–10	109	1551–60	174
1511–20	101	1561–70	174
1521–30	143	1571–80	244
1531–40	151	1581–90	261
1541–50	153	1591–1600	290

[5] Joan Serra Vilaró, *Les Baronies de Pinós i Mataplana*, vol. II (Barcelona, 1947), p. 309.
[6] AHM: leg. 942 and leg. 965, scattered details on expenditure on public works.
[7] Reglà, *Els Virreis de Catalunya*, p. 48.

Year	Masons' labourers	Carpenters
1570	3–3·5 *sous* per day	4 *sous* per day
1575	3·5	5
1582	3	5
1596	4	5–6
1600	4	6
1610	4	5–6
1626	4	5
1644	5	7–8

If normal Barcelona corn prices ranged between 40s. and 50s. during the first three decades of the seventeenth century,[1] a mason's labourer needed eleven or twelve days' wages to buy a quarter of corn—perhaps a little more than he had needed in the early 1570's when the price was around 30s. But there is no indication of how this compared with conditions before the 1570's, and how far a workman's wages covered his needs.[2]

If there was a general increase in wages in the last years of the sixteenth century, this would seem to have been in response to a price rise which had suddenly become acute. The clergy complained in 1602 of the 'notorious' alteration in prices, some of which were double or treble what they had been a few years before.[3] Barcelona corn prices certainly rose spectacularly between 1570 and 1600. The decade 1571–80 showed a 40 per cent increase on the preceding decade;[4] years of drought, preceding and following the plague of 1589, culminated in the crisis of 1591–2, when the average price of corn reached 54s. 5d.—the highest for the entire century.[5] While special climatic conditions were partly responsible for the misery and hunger of these years, the increase in prices no doubt also reflects the pressure of a rapidly growing population on the Principality's limited food resources; and it is also probable that there was a connection between the price-rise and the new importance of Barcelona as a staging-post on the silver-route to Italy.

[1] See table of corn prices for the college of Sant Guillèm (Appendix II).

[2] At one of the discussions at the conference held in Paris in 1958 to commemorate the four-hundredth anniversary of the death of Charles V, Professor Vicens Vives said that the maximum disparity between wages and prices in sixteenth-century Catalonia occurred in the decade 1530–40, but I do not know on what evidence he based this assertion (*Charles-Quint et son Temps*, p. 187).

[3] AAT: Concilio Provincial 1602, lib. 24, fo. 141. They demanded a minimum mass-offering of 3s. to help compensate for the fall in their incomes.

[4] Giralt, 'Precio del trigo', p. 57. [5] *Ibid.* p. 55.

While Barcelona was no more than a port of transit for the consignments of American silver which the king despatched regularly to Genoa from the 1570's, it would be surprising if a certain amount of silver did not remain in the Principality for purposes connected with the royal service. There was more work to be done in the dockyards; there were supplies to be bought and officials to be paid. Any silver released to pay for these supplies and services might well push up prices, as also might the silver spent by the Genoese merchant colony in Barcelona on Catalan cloths and other products.[1] The reorganization of Barcelona's fairs of exchange in 1592 is symptomatic of the city's increased commercial activity and financial importance.[2] Its abundance of money had given it a new significance in the world of international finance.

The price to be paid for all this was a spate of monetary speculation. The lack of documentation and the absence of studies of the Catalan economy make it impossible to trace in detail the course of the recurrent monetary troubles of 1599–1617, but, on the evidence at present available, the story would seem to run roughly as follows.[3] The Principality's balance of trade, while favourable with both Castile and Italy, was unfavourable with France,[4] from which it bought meat, corn and fine-quality cloths.[5] The Catalans appear to have been concerned about the over-all balance of payments, and their concern must have been increased by the fact that some of their coins were of a higher standard than those of Castile, and the differences offered tempting possibilities to speculators. There were three types of currency in the Principality—gold, silver and *vellón* (silver with a large admixture of copper).[6] With the circulation in Catalonia of Castilian silver and *vellón* coins of a lower standard than Catalan coins of a similar character, the latter tended to disappear from circulation.[7] In face of the competi-

---

[1] Giralt, 'Precio del trigo', p. 57.   [2] Braudel, *La Méditerranée*, pp. 392–3.

[3] The lack of material unfortunately prevented Professor Hamilton from extending his investigations into Spanish price-history to cover Catalonia. For the necessarily sketchy account that follows, I have made use of pp. 508–28 of M. Vilar's thesis, and of A. P. Usher, *The Early History of Deposit Banking in Mediterranean Europe* (Cambridge, Mass., 1943). I have also benefited greatly from the advice of Professor H. Koenigsberger and Mr D. M. Joslin, who have laboured hard to save me from falling into the more obvious traps.

[4] Carrera Pujal, *Historia de Cataluña*, vol. II, p. 69, n. 1.

[5] See E. Giralt, 'La colonia mercantil francesa de Barcelona a mediados del siglo XVII', *Estudios de Historia Moderna*, vol. VI (1956–9), pp. 217–78.

[6] See Appendix I.   [7] Usher, p. 434.

tion from lower-grade *vellón* coins of foreign origin, the Barcelona authorities found themselves powerless to maintain the standard of the *vellón* coinage. They had no monopoly over the minting of coins, for some of the larger towns possessed—by royal permission—mints of their own, and Girona, for one, seized the opportunity to reduce its debts by minting low-grade *vellón* coins in considerable quantities.[1] Meanwhile, counterfeit money, known as *boscatera*, was being forged in charcoal-burners' huts in the woods.

The resulting influx of poor-quality coins naturally led to a serious inflation of prices in *vellón* currency, and attempts in 1604 and 1605 to check inflation by prohibiting the use of foreign coin and by limiting the legal tender quality of *vellón* proved unsuccessful.[2] At the same time, monetary confusion had been increased as the result of the issue in 1599 of a new gold coin, the *trentí*, of a value of 60s.[3] This rating turned out to be ill-considered, and left the older gold currency under-valued.[4]

The first decade of the seventeenth century was therefore a period of acute monetary difficulties, although Catalan prices were never to oscillate so violently as those of seventeenth-century Castile. The gold–silver ratio had been disturbed; the Catalan currency was endangered by the rather lower Castilian standard for silver and *vellón*; and Barcelona's powerful private bankers were threatening the reserves of the *Taula de Canvi* (Barcelona's Bank of Deposit, which was obliged by the terms of its charter to pay out only in good coin). Although from 1602 they were not allowed to hold accounts in the Bank of Deposit,[5] there were various subterfuges open to them. They could, for instance, offer credit facilities to the men who supplied Barcelona with its meat and corn, and, in return, the city's suppliers would see that, when the city made its payments of some 200,000 ducats annually, these would be paid by the Taula into the private banks.[6]

In October 1609, in an attempt to counter the threat to the Taula from the private banks, the Barcelona city council founded a new city bank. This was the year which saw also the founding of the Bank

[1] ACA: CA, leg. 347, Duke of Feria to King, 4 Feb. 1601.
[2] Usher, p. 435. An ordinance of 6 June 1605 restricted *vellón* to payments not exceeding 11*d*. This was raised to 23*d*. on 22 Sept.
[3] *Ibid.* p. 434.   [4] *Ibid.* p. 456.   [5] *Ibid.* pp. 444–5.
[6] ACA: CA, leg. 355, Almazán to King, 15 Nov. 1614.

of Amsterdam,[1] and Barcelona's new bank, like that of Amsterdam, was allowed to accept current coins 'even though they may be a little short of the full weight',[2] and also to exchange cheques with the private banks.[3] But, unlike the Bank of Amsterdam, it was not allowed to credit full-weight coin for light-weight coin, even with a premium.[4] Nor was it, apparently, a *giro* bank; it was, rather, considered simply as an extension of the Bank of Deposit, made necessary by the depreciated coinage, and has been described as a 'highly sophisticated device for giving limited recognition to the coins in actual circulation, without accepting them as a really satisfactory or legal currency'.[5]

If it was hoped that the establishment of a city bank would materially help to solve the problem of bad money, this hope was to be disappointed. The only really effective method of striking at the currency speculators was to lower the standard of silver in Catalan coins, but any scheme for devaluation was likely to face heavy resistance. It would naturally have serious consequences for those living on fixed incomes, and there were many *rentiers* in the Principality's ruling class. Moreover, devaluation required royal permission, and the Court would hardly be enthusiastic about a measure which would make Castile's balance of payments with Catalonia more unfavourable than it already was.

While the Barcelona city council for long hesitated whether to appeal to Madrid for permission to devalue, it did decide in 1611 to exclude clipped silver from circulation and to authorize a new coinage,[6] but this had immediate consequences that were very unfortunate. 'Within a day the province was drained of half the money that had been circulating in it',[7] and the dearth of coins was to persist for several years. Good coins were promptly exported, and poor ones remained the only circulating medium.

It was probably no coincidence that the three or four years after 1611 —years of severe scarcity of small coins—saw banditry and lawlessness at their most acute. The marquis of Almazán, whose misfortune it was to be viceroy at the time, saw indeed a direct relationship between the

---

[1] See J. G. Van Dillen, 'The Bank of Amsterdam', *History of the Principal Public Banks*, ed. Van Dillen (The Hague, 1934), pp. 79–116.

[2] Usher, p. 442.

[3] Usher, 'Deposit Banking in Barcelona, 1300–1700', *Journal of Economic and Business History*, vol. IV (1931–2), p. 154.

[4] Usher, *Early History of Deposit Banking*, p. 443.   [5] *Ibid.* pp. 445–6.

[6] *Ibid.* p. 457.   [7] ACA: CA, leg. 356, Almazán to King, 25 Jan. 1614.

two phenomena. The recoinage of 1611 had, he considered, put many counterfeiters out of business, and compelled them to have recourse to highway robbery to make up for the loss.[1] While this would seem at best only a partial explanation, the monetary instability and price fluctuation of the first fifteen years of the seventeenth century must have played an important part in adding to the causes of social discontent.

It was a symptom of the change in the economic climate around the turn of the century that the stream of French immigrants, who had done so much to repopulate rural Catalonia, began at this moment to falter.[2] The point had obviously been reached at which the disastrous population losses of the fourteenth and fifteenth centuries had been made good. Those who could secure for themselves a fixed place in rural society as *masovers* and *menestrals* had already done so. The rest had to fend for themselves as best they could, and the existence of an intense labour crisis in the plain of Vic by the end of the sixteenth century suggests that this was becoming increasingly difficult.[3] There was, admittedly, a heavy seasonal demand for casual labour, and the rural unemployed would hire themselves out at harvest-time as *segadors*, or reapers, working their way northwards from Barcelona during June and July;[4] but during much of the year there was little or nothing to do, and the attractions of more dubious ways of making a living were correspondingly increased.

In Catalonia, as in Naples, Sicily and the Papal States during the same period,[5] there were nobles prepared to exploit the discontents of this underemployed rural population. 'There are in Catalonia many unemployed vagabonds', complained the town council of Cervera, 'and as they have no occupation to earn them a living, they take service with the gentry (*cavallers*)...and go out to rob and kill.'[6] Catalan banditry conformed to the general pattern of Mediterranean banditry in that it enjoyed aristocratic connivance and support.[7]

---

[1] *Ibid.*   [2] Nadal and Giralt, *La Population Catalane*, p. 82.

[3] Reparaz, *La Plana de Vic*, p. 211.

[4] AMV: CR, 8, Cònsols of Puigcerdà to Consellers of Vic, 8 July 1613.

[5] Cf. Giuseppe Coniglio, *Il Viceregno di Napoli nel Sec. XVII* (Rome, 1955), pp. 17–19; Koenigsberger, *The Government of Sicily*, p. 117; Jean Delumeau, *Vie Economique et Sociale de Rome dans la seconde moitié du XVIe Siècle*, vol. II (Paris, 1959), p. 543,

[6] AHC: folder of *varia*. Instructions for Cervera's syndic to Corts of 1626.

[7] Braudel, *La Méditerranée*, p. 655.

The readiness of important sections of the Catalan aristocracy to countenance acts of banditry derived from the strains and stresses within a social group which had somehow lost its bearings. The *estament militar*, as the aristocracy was called, consisted of three grades of nobility.[1] The lowest rank was that known as *cavaller*, *donzell* or *militar*, roughly equivalent to the English knight. Above the *cavallers* or gentry were the nobles proper, recognizable by the prefix Don, which in Catalonia, unlike Castile, was still reserved exclusively to those who possessed privileges of nobility. This prefix was inherited by *all* the sons of a noble, just as all the sons of a *cavaller* enjoyed their father's rank. The highest class within the aristocracy was the titled nobility of viscounts, counts, marquises and dukes, the title passing only to the eldest son and the others being treated as ordinary nobles. This titled nobility was numerically of little importance. The greater Catalan families, like the Requesens, had moved to Castile during the sixteenth century and become assimilated into the Castilian aristocracy. Of the titled nobility that remained in the Principality, there were only the eight counts whose titles dated from the royal visit of 1599, and one viscount (Joc), although the duke of Cardona, the owner of vast Catalan estates, kept in close touch with the Principality's affairs, and came back to reside in it during the 1620's.

The aristocracy proper, therefore, was almost entirely a 'country' as distinct from a 'court' aristocracy, and most of its members—nobles as well as *cavallers*—would count by contemporary European standards as mere gentry. As a class, they were not wealthy: 'there are not two *caballeros* in the province who, when their debts are paid, have an income of 6000 ducats', wrote a scornful observer.[2] An income of 2000

[1] There is no study of the Catalan aristocracy, and the following pages represent no more than first soundings. No family papers or accounts have so far appeared, but Catalan nobles, like nobles in other parts of the Monarchy, reveal a good deal about themselves in the petitions for *mercedes* or favours that they addressed to the king. Although the documentation of all the Councils includes innumerable such petitions, they have not been systematically used by historians. A proper examination of them might provide a most illuminating commentary on the government and society of the Spanish Monarchy under the House of Austria.

[2] Alexandro de Ros, *Cataluña Desengañada* (Naples, 1646), p. 181. Ros was the most objectionable type of castilianized Catalan, but, partly for this reason, some of his observations on Catalan life are most revealing. 6000 ducats was a minute sum by the standards of many of the Castilian titled aristocracy, although a few had an income of only 8000 or 10,000 ducats p.a. The duke of Cardona, by contrast, is said to have had an annual income of 120,000 ducats, although I do not know the extent of his debts. See the list of nobles given in James Wadsworth, *The Present Estate of Spayne* (London, 1630).

ducats a year would appear to have been very respectable for a noble,[1] and it would not be surprising to find that many of the gentry were worth scarcely 500 ducats or *lliures*.

From the point of view of rank, as well as of income, there was not much to choose between nobles and *cavallers*. Outside Barcelona, which excluded nobles, but not *cavallers*, from its government until as late as 1621, there was little practical distinction between the two groups, and intermarriage was persistent. Together they attended the frequent meetings of their Estate—the *braç militar*—held in Barcelona whenever points of common concern arose, and together they indulged in tournaments and other knightly pursuits on days of festivity.[2] The numbers of both nobles and gentry had increased considerably since the Habsburgs had ruled in Spain; particularly the nobles. The surviving lists of members of the *estament militar* summoned to the Corts of 1518 and 1626 allow the following classification:[3]

Date	Nobles	Cavallers	Total
1518	37	451	488
1626	254	526	780

The proportionately greater increase in the number of nobles can be attributed to the upgrading of *cavallers* over the course of the century as a reward for their services (of which the most valuable was held to be a spirit of acquiescence in meetings of the Corts), and to the flood of new creations by Philip III in 1599: only 60 *cavallers* to 81 nobles.

As the new creations indicate, the aristocracy was far from being a closed caste: both the relative ease with which titles of nobility could be acquired, and the existence of a system whereby leading burgesses ranked as members of the *estament militar*, helped to keep it open. Titles of nobility could be conferred only by the king. Mass creations were reserved for his infrequent visits to the Principality and the success-

[1] This can be deduced from the petition of Joan Francesc Brossa of Vic, who in 1626 supported his request for a title of nobility (ACA: CA, leg. 500) with the statement that he kept a coach and horses and had an income of 2000 ducats p.a. See also Appendix II, section 3.

[2] Tournaments were very popular in the early seventeenth century. See, for example, the book of the Confraria of Sant Jordi in Barcelona, ACA: G, 65/2. It is interesting to find another underemployed aristocracy, the Sicilian, distracting itself in a similar way (Koenigsberger, *Sicily*, p. 89).

[3] ACA: Cancillería, R. 3896, fos. 25–33 (Corts of 1518) and R. 5515, fo. 217 (Corts of 1626). Neither of these lists can be accepted as completely accurate, especially that of 1518 which contains many repetitions, and probably also omissions.

ful conclusion of the Corts, but individual creations were relatively common in the intervening periods. The customary practice was for an aspirant to nobility to draw up a petition briefly relating his family background and details of his own career and social standing, and enumerating those services which he felt entitled him to some reward, or *merced* (favour). This petition would be sent to Madrid, where it would be considered by the Council of Aragon, which might or might not take into account the views of the viceroy. It would then be placed before the king, accompanied by the Council of Aragon's comments, to be either rejected or approved.

In theory at least, any *merced* like a title of nobility still remained the reward for a *servicio*—a specific service to the king—but by the seventeenth century the whole traditional concept of services and rewards, which belonged essentially to the age of close personal relationship between a king and his vassals, was beginning to wear very thin. It was not difficult for someone with money and influence to work his way into the aristocracy (although the sale of titles seems to have become flagrant only in the reign of Philip IV),[1] but for form's sake he would continue to cast his petition in the shape of a plea for the reward of services. When Francisco Berardo, a merchant of Italian origins long resident in Barcelona, applied to be granted the rank of *cavaller*, Philip IV wrote on the *consulta* of the Council of Aragon: 'Let the Council take note that these titles should be given for services, and those that are listed here seem to come into the ordinary run of a merchant's business.' But he granted the privilege.[2]

There were two obvious ways of entry into the aristocracy for a man of humble origins. One was service in the viceregal administration. Royal officials and judges of the *Audiència* would usually at some stage in their careers be rewarded with a title, but since posts in the administration were few, and competition fierce, the prospects were poor. The other way was to make money and buy one's way up the municipal hierarchy, like Canoves and Morgades, two notoriously wealthy

---

[1] In 1629, when potential buyers of privileges were being sought, a certain Joan Jeroni Alemany became a *militar* on payment of 1000 *lliures* and costs (ACA: CA, leg. 378, Don Guerau de Guardiola to Juan Lorenzo de Villanueva, 21 April 1629). Even at this moment, however, the sale of titles tended to be restricted by the authorities' fear of adding more potentially dissentient voices to the Corts.

[2] ACA: CA, leg. 272, no. 25, consulta, 16 Aug. 1622.

merchants, 'natives of Vic living in Barcelona, who the day before yesterday were peasants, yesterday merchants, and today *cavallers* engaged in commerce—and all in the space of thirty years'.[1] Municipal office in particular was a useful stepping-stone on the path to aristocratic status. This was especially true in Catalonia because Barcelona and one or two other towns contained a group of distinguished citizens known as *ciutadans honrats*. A *ciutadà honrat* was automatically a member of the *estament militar* and enjoyed all the privileges of the aristocracy except the right to a seat in the *braç militar* in sessions of the Corts. The title of *ciutadà honrat*, a hereditary one, could be conferred by special royal grant, but the majority of Barcelona's distinguished citizens, or their ancestors, had been elected at one of the meetings, held annually on 1 May, of those of their fellow-citizens who already held the privilege.[2] The right of election meant that it was possible for any distinguished burgess to enter the ranks of the aristocracy, whether or not the Court approved.

The existence of a class of distinguished citizens enjoying the privileges of aristocracy was of crucial importance for the development of aristocratic life in the Principality. Constant intermarriage between the old nobility and these bourgeois families, and the consequent acquisition of municipal properties, helped to facilitate the process by which, since the civil wars of the fifteenth century, many nobles abandoned their remote castles for the comforts of a town house and became an urbanized aristocracy.[3] In 1639, 174 nobles and *cavallers*, or rather under a quarter of the entire aristocracy, were listed as resident in Barcelona,[4] and to these must be added many who, without being officially resident in the city, passed much of their time there. Not a few of the smaller towns, and all the larger ones—Girona, Lleida, Perpinyà, Tarragona, Vic—also had their resident nobles, whose presence is still commemorated by a 'street of the *cavallers*,' lined by spacious, well-appointed houses. These nobles kept their estates and country castles, to which they might retreat during the hot summer months, but the majority of them seem to have shown little interest in the direct ex-

[1] Pujades, 3, fo. 164v.
[2] Fontanella, *De Pactis Nuptialibus*, Clausula III, glosa II, § 77.
[3] Joaquín Pla Cargol, 'Proceso de Idesarrollo urbano de Gerona a través de los tiempos', *Anales del Instituto de Estudios Gerundenses*, vol. II (1947), p. 218.
[4] ACA: G, caja 26, list of aristocracy resident in Barcelona, 3 Dec. 1639.

ploitation of their lands, and were content to administer them through a *procurador*, or more generally to lease them for a fixed annual rental.[1] Their interests had become those of townsmen, and it is symptomatic of the change that they became increasingly insistent that they should be allowed to participate in municipal government, from which they were traditionally excluded by their rank.[2]

The development of an urbanized aristocracy helped to create serious strains within the ranks of the nobility, for there was a sharp distinction between the town-dwelling and the rural noble in seventeenth-century Catalonia. An urban noble had adopted urban manners, and probably also urban standards of expenditure. His sons might be sent to the aristocratic college of Cordelles in Barcelona, founded in the reign of Charles V,[3] and then perhaps go on to study law at Lleida, or even in a Castilian university, though this was very rare.[4] The results were not very impressive. With one or two exceptions, like Don Galcerán Albanell, 'a great rhetorician, Greek scholar and humanist'[5] appointed tutor to the future Philip IV in 1610, the Catalan nobility was singularly lacking in intellectual distinction. Yet at least these town-dwelling nobles had a smattering of culture, went to the theatre,[6] knew something of the works of the latest Castilian dramatists, and had a nodding acquaintance with events in the outside world. This could not be said of most of their rural brethren.

The rural aristocracy, primitive and barbarous in its habits, gives the impression of being in retreat from the Catalonia that had been remodelled by Ferdinand the Catholic. According to one seventeenth-century writer, many gentlemen found that, as a result of Ferdinand's municipal reforms, 'they could not command in the cities with reputation and authority and so retired to the mountains abashed'.[7] It is

[1] The most striking exception to this is a Lleida noble, Don Francesc de Gilabert, who, after some years in the army and at Court, felt remorse at the neglect of his lands, took to farming them himself, and wrote a book about his experiences, *Agricultura Prática* (Barcelona, 1626), in the hope of persuading others to follow suit.   [2] See below, pp. 125-6.

[3] Alexandre Galí, *Rafel d'Amat i de Cortada, Baró de Maldà* (Barcelona, 1953), p. 141.

[4] For the year 1599-1600 I can find in the list of law-students at Salamanca no more than a dozen Catalans, of whom only one, Don Guillèm de Rocabertí, is a noble (Archivo de la Universidad de Salamanca, *Matrícula, 1599-1600*).

[5] Pujades, 2, fo. 223.

[6] Barcelona was unique in having a covered theatre, the Teatre de la Santa Creu, founded in 1596—the only one in Spain till the building of the royal theatre of the Buen Retiro in the reign of Philip IV (Galí, *Rafel d'Amat*, pp. 197-8).

[7] *Súplica de...Tortosa* (Tortosa, 1640), fo. 30.

doubtful whether others had ever emerged for any length of time from their rural strongholds, partly because they could not afford to do so. Among the gentry in particular there were 'many who are very poor'.[1] Bored, resentful, jealous of the greater wealth of the urban aristocracy, these country gentry tended to make up for the deficiences of their position by making the most of their influence in the countryside—by exploiting their feudal rights to the limit, by oppressing their vassals, or swaggering through the village streets with a group of armed ruffians. A Flemish traveller passing through a village near Lleida in 1585 noted that, as frequently happened in Catalonia, it lived in fear and trembling of its lord, 'a *caballero* of Barcelona...who generally lives in his derelict castle to the west of the town'.[2] Villages naturally made strenuous if largely unsuccessful efforts to exchange baronial for royal jurisdiction. Government by royal officials was much to be preferred to government by 'little lords and barons who usually tyrannize them and gnaw them right down to the bone with unjust taxes...'.[3]

Some of the pressures which drove this rural aristocracy to acts of banditry are suggested by the history of the house of Alentorn, hereditary lords of the village of Seró, whose income was so dependent on the yield of the harvest in the unirrigated plain of Urgell.[4] Don Nofre d'Alentorn and his son, Don Alexandre, displayed more political acumen that many of their colleagues in organizing resistance to the viceregal administration through the Diputació in Barcelona,[5] but they also found an outlet for their ambitions and discontents by becoming deeply involved in the activities of bandit gangs. Their family troubles make them sound like typical 'declining gentry'. Don Nofre, in his last will, set aside his eldest son, Don Jeroni, in favour of his second, Don Alexandre.[6] As might have been expected, this gave rise to immediate litigation, and a third brother begged the viceroy to mediate 'to prevent so ancient a house from being destroyed by suits'.[7] With

[1] BUB: MS 1189, *Verdad defendida...*, ch. x, § 3. An exaggerated but revealing attack on the habits of the Catalan aristocracy (1632), by Nofre de Selma i de Salavert.

[2] *Las Tierras de Lérida en el siglo XVI*. Narración de un viaje efectuado en 1585 por el holandés Enrique Cock, ed. J. A. Tarragó Pleyán (Lérida, 1944), p. 25.

[3] AAE: Corresp. Espagne, Supplément no. 3, fo. 265, *Advertissement donné au Roy par un sien très humble serviteur...* (1643).

[4] See above, p. 58.

[5] ACA: CA, leg. 346, Archbishop of Tarragona to Vice-Chancellor, 9 Oct. 1602.

[6] ACA: CA, leg. 484, petition of Don Alexandre d'Alentorn (1610).

[7] ACA: CA, leg. 483, petition of Don Nofre d'Alentorn (1608).

the brothers being 'such litigious persons',[1] it was no doubt fortunate that Don Jeroni should have died shortly afterwards of paralysis he had contracted during his military service in Flanders. But if Don Alexandre now found himself in uncontested possession of the estate, he also found himself saddled with its encumbrances. The first of these was the obligation to restore the dowry of his sister-in-law, Don Jeroni's widow. The others consisted of debts to the tune of 30,000 *escuts* (which may have been fifteen or twenty times the annual income of the estate) and the punctual payment of interest on all the *censals* by which the family had raised loans.[2]

These troubles were all the more galling because in 1599 the king had granted an annual pension of 532 *lliures* to Don Nofre,[3] probably to keep him quiet in the Corts, and, as so often happened, the pension had never been paid. Disappointed expectations, the expenses of litigation and dowries—these were the stock in trade of the Catalan aristocracy as of all aristocracies in sixteenth and seventeenth-century Europe. Younger sons in particular were a constant problem. As the principal victims of an inheritance system which aimed at the preservation of the House by the concentration of the estate in the hands of a single universal heir,[4] their prospects were not hopeful. Sometimes money would be available from their mother's side of the family,[5] but generally they would have to make their own way in the world. It was here that a pension from the Crown could be particularly useful. Don Miquel Calders, a noble of the Segarra, had 'many sons to settle' and petitioned the king for an ecclesiastical pension for one of them, so that he might continue his studies and make his way in the Church.[6] The brothers Felip and Josep Sorribes explained that their father was 'a poor caballero who cannot pay for their studies because he has other children to maintain' and made a similar plea for assistance.[7] But these pensions had to come either from the revenues of one of the Catalan bishoprics or from those of the royal estates or the royal administration in the

---

[1] ACU: Cartes 1600–29, Canon Coll to Chapter of Urgell, 16 June 1608.
[2] ACA: CA, leg. 269, petition of Don Alexandre d'Alentorn, 18 March 1614.
[3] ACA: CA, leg. 482, petition of Don Nofre d'Alentorn (1600).
[4] See above, p. 36.
[5] E.g. for Don Francesc Desbach. APB: A. J. Fita, lib. 7, cap. mat., property settlement by Dona Maria Descallar i Desbach, 28 June 1623.
[6] ACA: CA, leg. 487, petition of Carles Calders (1614).
[7] ACA: CA, leg. 484, petition (1609).

Crown of Aragon; and their number was strictly limited, especially as a hard-pressed Crown gave them also to natives of other provinces.

A noble's chances of gainful employment within the Principality were not good. There was the Church, where there was a chance of canonries and even abbacies, but bishoprics were distressingly liable to be given to outsiders. There was trade, and some nobles and gentlemen certainly engaged in this,[1] but the stigma attached to trade still remained strong in the seventeenth century. A request was made to the Corts of 1626 that nobles should be allowed 'to have a share in shops and in every other kind of trade and business without losing anything of their status as *militars*',[2] but, as a result of the failure of the Corts, nothing came of this demand.

Of the various types of offices available in the Principality, municipal offices were only just beginning to be thrown open to nobles in the early seventeenth century. The Diputació could provide the two really influential posts of Diputat Militar and Oidor Militar, a number of lucrative administrative offices in Barcelona, and several local posts as agents of the Diputació, for which the salaries were small, though there may have been opportunities for a little private profit. There was not much here to occupy an aristocracy eight hundred strong, and the same was also unfortunately true of the viceregal administration.

As far as local offices in the viceregal administration were concerned, salaries were so derisory that 'no one wants the offices except those who are unsuitable for them'.[3] The aristocracy therefore played virtually no part in local government.[4] The command of one of the thirteen castles which guarded the frontier was a more interesting proposition, although it was not well paid, but the aristocracy's main interest was directed towards posts in the central administration at Barcelona. Some of these posts were highly desirable, but the administration was extremely small, and the majority of the posts went to trained

---

[1] Cristòfol Despuig, in his *Col·loquis* of 1557 (p. 93), takes it for granted that this was common practice: 'as we all know, in this country we all have to be horses with a double saddle'. But there is no evidence that it was anything like as common as he suggests.

[2] BC: MS 979, fos. 66–70, *Diversos discursos sobre las cosas tocantes al servey de Deu, del Rey y del bé comù de Catalunya* (1626), fo. 68v.

[3] ACA: CA, leg. 344, Duke of Feria to Marquis of Denia, 28 Dec. 1598.

[4] Their lack of interest in local government in the royal service may perhaps also be attributable to the fact that baronial jurisdiction was so widespread and powerful as to reduce local government by the Crown to a very subordinate position.

lawyers—the hated *letrados*.[1] As a result, it is doubtful whether the central administration contained more than a dozen posts all told for members of the aristocracy.

With so few opportunities within the Principality, the Catalan aristocracy might have been expected to seek outlets and opportunities beyond the borders of its own country. Some nobles did indeed serve with the royal armies in Flanders or Italy. Don Felip d'Alentorn and two of his three sons spent their lives in military service in Italy and the Palatinate,[2] and doubtless in this way obtained some relief from the many troubles which beset that unfortunate family. But although statistics are lacking, it does not seem that more than a very small section of the aristocracy followed their example, and it would appear to be more a question of a military tradition running in certain families than of any general custom.

The alternative to military service outside the Principality was a post at Court or in the administration of the empire. Here, however, the Catalan nobles, like those of the other peripheral provinces of the peninsula, found the path to preferment blocked by the Castilians. There were exceptions. The Catalan adventurer, Don Pedro Franqueza, became for a few spectacular years one of the most prominent figures in the Spain of Philip III; a Catalan noble, Don Guillèm de Sant Climent, was ambassador in Prague during part of Philip III's reign; and another, the count of Erill, served as viceroy of Sardinia, winning thereby neither profit for himself nor honour for his nation.[3] Two posts were traditionally set aside for Catalan regents in the chancellery of Naples, and, when the question of appointing to one of them arose in 1616, the king wrote on the *consulta* in his own hand: 'As long as there are Catalan subjects with the necessary qualifications for these posts, I will see that their claims are taken into consideration, as is only proper in view of the loyalty and love with which the natives of the Principality serve me.'[4] Yet even if the king was sincere, the real problem of employment for the Catalan aristocracy was scarcely touched. Perhaps a dozen posts—how could this hope to satisfy the needs of an aristocracy

---

[1] For the viceregal administration, see ch. IV below. The aristocracy's hatred of the lawyers, so universal in the Europe of this time, is vigorously expressed in Gilabert's *Discursos*, no. 1, fos. 11–12.

[2] ACA: CA, leg. 382, relation sent by the Duke of Cardona, 6 Sept. 1631.

[3] Pujades, 3, fo. 149.   [4] ACA: CA, leg. 270, no. 52, consulta, 31 May 1616.

of eight hundred? The truth of the matter was that it remained a provincial aristocracy, whose services were simply not required by a king who lived in Castile. The best proof of this is to be found in the figures for the membership of the military orders, nominally open to natives of any province subject to the king of Spain. In 1625 the membership was as follows:[1]

Order	Total membership	Catalans
Alcántara	197	2
Calatrava	306	2
Santiago	949	10
	1452	14

In so far as there was a 'Spanish' aristocracy, the Catalans were not of its number.

The virtual exclusion of Catalan nobles and gentry from offices of profit and honour under the Spanish Crown inevitably had far-reaching consequences. These were partly financial—the lack of a useful supplementary source of income. But they were also psychological. At a time when the whole idea of service and rewards was still conceived of in personal terms, the absence of a king who could encourage or admonish his vassals, recognize their abilities and reward their services, was of enormous importance. No lines of communication between the viceroy in Barcelona and the Council of Aragon in Madrid, however smooth or efficient, could quite make up for this loss of personal contact. In the seventeenth century, although kings were increasingly isolated from personal contact with their subjects, a Principality without a prince still remained an anomaly. Royal absenteeism in a monarchical society demanded psychological adjustments which would take time, and as yet the Catalan aristocracy had scarcely begun to accept the necessity for such absenteeism, let alone to come to terms with its consequences. As a result, it suffered from a deep-seated *malaise*—the *malaise* of a class which had lost the reason for its existence.

Deprived of the presence of their king, lacking outlets for their energies and ambitions, and held by the conventions of an increasingly outmoded social ideal, the nobles and gentry—town-dwelling as well

[1] AGS: Hacienda, leg. 618, *Memoria de los comendadores y caballeros....*

as rural—reacted in an entirely predictable manner. They devoted their energies to feuds and vendettas.

Shooting affrays between groups of nobles were common occurrences, and royal justice was powerless to prevent them. When Don Jaume Senmenat lost his life in one such affray in the streets of Barcelona, the viceroy reported that neither side would agree to a reconciliation, nor bring a charge, 'preferring to keep their feud to the grave, in the usual manner of the nobility of this country'.[1] In such circumstances it became indispensable to maintain an armed retinue. This practice drew from the marquis of Almazán, a Castilian noble, a most revealing comment. 'They say that the *caballeros* here are free', he wrote. 'But in my opinion they are more oppressed than those of Castile, because they cannot go out of town without a large number of men, whereas I could travel from Madrid to Almazán alone, or with a single servant, without being afraid of anybody. That is what I call freedom, and not what passes for freedom in Catalonia.'[2]

Inevitably the country as a whole was drawn into the aristocracy's feuds. The wastrels and the unemployed took service with the gentry, and a bandit gang would put itself at a noble's disposal in return for the refuge afforded by his castle. But in the chaos of conflicting allegiances there was none the less a certain coherence, for the entire Principality was broadly divided into two opposing factions, known as the *nyerros* and the *cadells*.

These names had a long history behind them. Their beginnings are mysterious, although it seems probable that they originated in the feuds of two aristocratic families in the mountain regions of the north: the Cadells, *senyors* of Arsèguel, and the Banyuls, *senyors* of Anyer, both of them families which had survived into the seventeenth century.[3] Since *cadell* meant a small dog in Catalan, and *nyerro* a pig, the partisans of the two factions were provided with ready-made emblems which they sported on their sword-belts.[4] It is difficult to determine whether, behind the differing names and insignia, there lurked also differing

---

[1] ACA: CA, leg. 355, Almazán to King, 9 Aug. 1614.

[2] Jaime Villanueva, *Viage Literario a las Iglesias de España* (Valencia, 1821), vol. VII, pp. 130–4, Almazán to Council of Tarragona, 1613.

[3] Alternatively, they may have originated in the thirteenth-century feud between Bernat de Cadell and Gilabert de Neros. Cf. F. Soldevila, *Història de Catalunya* (Barcelona, 1934), vol. I, p. 328, n. 4.

[4] Selma i de Salavert, *Verdad defendida*, ch. x, § 3.

attitudes and ideologies. Many ingenious suggestions have been made: that the *nyerros* had French affiliations, or that they defended seigneurial rights against the *cadells* who championed the rights of the towns.[1] Yet such affiliations as can be discovered for seventeenth-century Catalans do not lend much support to these theories. If Roca Guinarda and his friend, Don Alexandre d'Alentorn, were *nyerros*,[2] and hence the defenders of seigneurial rights, there does not seem to be any very good reason for their inveterate hostility to Don Rafael de Biure, the most aggressively 'feudal' of nobles. It would seem more probable that allegiance to a particular faction was simply a family tradition passed from generation to generation, and that if the rivalry had ever been anything more than the rivalry of two feuding families, the original causes of dispute had long since been forgotten. Local circumstances, like the presence of many French inhabitants, may here and there have injected a new meaning into the old feuds, but it is doubtful if there was anything to choose between the two factions. 'One and the other are the ruin of this land.'[3]

As in Sicily at the same time,[4] the division of the country into rival factions coloured every aspect of its life. A network of allegiances covered the Principality, with extensions that reached even to the Court at Madrid. *Nyerros* and *cadells* would attempt to get their own partisans appointed to the judiciary and the viceregal administration, as in 1597 when a great effort was made by the *nyerros* to obtain the appointment as *Regent la Tresoreria* of Don Federic Cornet, 'an intimate friend of the Senyor of Seró [Alentorn] and all that faction', by means of their alliance with the secretary Franqueza at Court.[5] Royal officials would pursue bandit gangs of a different persuasion from their own with the utmost zeal, while being unaccountably unsuccessful in their operations against bandits of their own faction; and judges of the Audiència like Dr Rubí, 'protector of the *cadell* faction and open enemy of the *nyerros*',[6] would blandly ignore the crimes of their own partisans. Everywhere,

[1] See Soler y Terol, *Perot Roca Guinarda*, p. 444.   [2] *Ibid.* p. 33.

[3] Pujades, 1, fo. 165, 6 May 1603.

[4] Koenigsberger, *The Government of Sicily*, p. 99.

[5] AAW: MS E2 (letter-book of Thomas Fitzherbert), fo. 32, Viceroy (duke of Feria) to King, 29 May 1597. Thomas Fitzherbert, the well-known English recusant, was for a time in the service of the duke of Feria, for whose connection with England see above (p. 50, n. 5). His letter-book contains several letters written by the duke on Catalan affairs.

[6] ACA: CA, leg. 269, no. 25, consulta, 18 June 1614.

local and personal quarrels had a way of merging into the wider struggle of *nyerros* against *cadells*. The diocese of Vic was kept in a state of turmoil during the first years of the century by the disputes between the bishop, Don Francesc Robuster, and his canons. Each party called the bandit gangs to its assistance. 'The *nyerros* help the canons, the *cadells* the bishop.'[1]

The Principality's alleged 'harmony' was therefore a good deal less than perfect. Aristocratic faction and agrarian unrest both threatened the stability of the ordered society. Yet nobles had always had their feuds, and aristocratic life was no more, and no less, lacking in purpose in the reign of Philip III than in that of Philip II. Admittedly the agrarian situation had deteriorated in the closing years of the sixteenth century, but even in the last years of Philip II disorder had always been contained. This suggests that the ultimate causes of the Catalan crisis in the reign of Philip III must be sought beyond the specific troubles of the aristocracy or of any other social group, and related to the tone and character of the royal administration, which was nominally responsible for the maintenance of order. Here there were obvious signs of collapse. In 1599 Philip III had come to a Principality which was moderately peaceful, and which had greeted him with expressions of loyal enthusiasm. Within fifteen years of his visit, law and authority were gone, justice was overthrown, and his ministers were held in universal contempt. The Catalan crisis more than anything else reflected a failure of government, of which the origins were to be traced to both Barcelona and Madrid.

[1] Pujades, I, fo. 132v, 16 Nov. 1602; and see the article on the Vic disturbances by J. M. Madurell in *Analecta Sacra Tarraconensia*, vol. XXIV (1951).

CHAPTER IV

THE FAILURE OF GOVERNMENT

One of the greatest achievements of the Spanish Monarchy in the sixteenth century was the establishment of an administrative system which effectively subordinated to one central government, in Madrid, States as far apart from each other as Naples and Peru. In America, the kings of Spain were able to impose from the start their own conception of royal autocracy and to build up an elaborate organization for the government of their newly discovered territories.[1] In Naples, Sicily and Milan they had first to overcome the often fierce resistance of old-established and powerful institutions, and of strongly entrenched social groups.[2] Spanish government remained there, as everywhere, a system of checks and balances, with competing tribunals and authorities jockeying for position and bringing pressure to bear upon the councils in Madrid. But even in so intractable a province as Sicily an increasing measure of bureaucratic control was established during the course of the sixteenth century— sufficient at least to provide a solid basis of power for the Spanish Crown.[3]

It would seem that, on the whole, less progress was made towards centralized bureaucratic government in the peripheral provinces of the Spanish peninsula during the sixteenth century than in Spain's overseas territories.[4] Catalonia in particular remained curiously untouched. Admittedly, it was now governed from Madrid; but the sixteenth century had not seen, as it had in Spain's Italian possessions, a parallel concentration and centralization of power in the hands of the Crown's local agents. There was one very simple reason for this. The limits of royal power were clearly defined by the Catalan constitutions, and these constitutions were extremely specific as to the size and character of the viceregal administration. They forbade the creation of new offices without the consent of the Corts,[5] and they stipulated that all offices except

[1] C. H. Haring, *The Spanish Empire in America* (New York, 1947), p. 6.
[2] R. B. Merriman, *The Rise of the Spanish Empire* (New York, 1934), vol. IV, pp. 467 ff.
[3] Koenigsberger, *The Government of Sicily*, pp. 104–5.
[4] There is a great need for studies of the royal administration and its effectiveness in various parts of sixteenth-century Spain, as a basis for an eventual comparative history.
[5] *Constitutions de Cathalunya*, lib. I, tit. LXXI.

the viceroyalty itself must be held by native Catalans.[1] These provisions, which the king had sworn to uphold, stood in the way of any gradual transformation of the viceregal government into a more effective instrument of royal, and Castilian, control. Instead, it limped along as best it could, generally having the worst of every world; criticized on one side by the Catalans for excessive subservience to Madrid, and on the other by Madrid for its weakness when confronted by Catalan resistance. Much depended on the circumstances of the moment and on the character and abilities of the viceroy, but the administration at all times presented an easy target for attack, its weaknesses glaringly obvious, its virtues so modest as to be easily overlooked.

At the head of the administration in Barcelona stood the viceroy, or *Lloctinent General*, initially appointed for a three-year term of office which was sometimes prolonged.[2] The viceroyalty of Catalonia was considered the senior viceroyalty in the peninsula (superior to Aragon, Valencia and Majorca) and any incumbent who was promoted still further would probably move on either to Sicily or to Naples.[3] As the post was open to non-Catalans, it would generally go to a Castilian grandee, although a local bishop, Catalan or non-Catalan, was sometimes appointed instead, usually as an interim measure. A foreign origin gave a viceroy a certain detachment among the internecine feuds of the Catalans, but this advantage would be cancelled out by the distrust he was liable to incur as a foreigner, and by his ignorance of the ways of the Principality. His best hope of winning the sympathy of the province he governed was to show himself, whenever possible, relatively independent of Madrid.

Nominally, at least, he did enjoy considerable independence. As the king's *alter ego* he was entrusted with the supreme charge of civil and military administration in the Principality, although unfortunately he

[1] *Constitutions*, lib. I, tit. LXVIII. In Naples the best government posts went to Spaniards (Leopold Ranke, *The Ottoman and the Spanish Empires in the Sixteenth and Seventeenth Centuries*, trans. W. K. Kelly (London, 1843), p. 71); in Sicily local privileges were stronger, but Spaniards could legally hold a few offices (Koenigsberger, p. 101).

[2] The viceroyalty was itself, in origin, a Catalan institution. It made its first appearance in the Catalan duchy of Athens in the fourteenth century, the duke appointing a *vicarius generalis* or *viceregens* (cf. Kenneth M. Setton, *Catalan Domination of Athens, 1311–1388*, Cambridge, Mass., 1948, p. 18). A term of three years as a normal term for a viceroy was agreed upon in the Corts of Sardinia in the same century.

[3] Antonio de Capmany, *Memorias Históricas sobre la Marina, Comercio, y Artes de la Antigua Ciudad de Barcelona* (Madrid, 1792), vol. IV, appendix, p. 123.

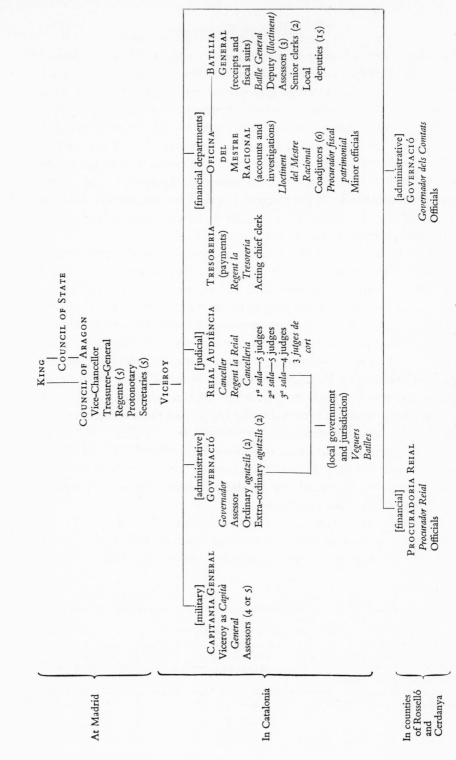

Fig. 2. The Government of Catalonia.

lacked one vital attribute of kingship which helped to make government palatable—the right to confer *mercedes,* or favours. During the sixteenth century he had, it is true, been allowed to grant certain minor favours, known as *cosas de gracia,* such as rights of legitimation or privileges enabling towns to levy new duties, but this power was to be withdrawn during the disastrous viceroyalty of the marquis of Almazán; an action which was intended to punish the Catalans but which in fact only served to undermine the viceroy's authority.[1]

The viceroy's orders came from Madrid. His despatches, addressed to the king, would be considered in Madrid by the Council of Aragon, which would embody its recommendations in a *consulta* sent up to the king for approval. When the king had reached a decision, on the advice of the Council of State or of his favourite, the Catalan secretary of the Council of Aragon would draft the letter of reply to be sent to Barcelona. All this took time, especially when the royal favourite was someone as dilatory as the duke of Lerma. But at least there was not the additional delay of a long wait between the despatch and receipt of letters, such as the overseas viceroyalties had to endure. A letter from Madrid to Barcelona took about four days, as against many months between Madrid and Lima in Peru.

The relative closeness of Madrid meant that the viceroy of Catalonia did not have the freedom of movement which his overseas colleagues enjoyed merely by virtue of their distance from the Court. But although theoretically he could not initiate a new line of policy even on relatively minor matters without first consulting Madrid, a Catalan viceroy in the reign of Philip III was less likely to feel himself cramped by his instructions from Madrid than by the laws and customs of the Principality he governed. Where the viceroy of Sicily enjoyed, at least by repute, the powers of an absolute ruler,[2] the viceroy of Catalonia found himself hemmed in at every turn. He could neither convoke and dissolve parliament, like the viceroy of Sicily, nor ask for new taxation. In all his activities he moved within a well-defined framework of law which it was difficult or impossible for him to evade. The most binding of all laws were the constitutions, the laws compacted between king and country in past sessions of the Corts. After these in

---

[1] ACA: CA, leg. 365, Alcalá to King, 29 Jan. 1622.
[2] Koenigsberger, *The Government of Sicily,* p. 98.

order of precedence came *pragmàtiques*, which were ordinances made by the king outside the Corts, and which had the force of law in so far as they did not conflict with the constitutions.[1] Finally, the viceroy himself had the right to issue *crides* (edicts or proclamations) on matters affecting the common weal.[2]

It seems that viceroys in the later sixteenth century had been making increasing use of proclamations for purposes of government, for the Corts of 1599 made a constitution which commented on their abuse, and decreed that in future no proclamations should be issued that ran contrary to the constitutions.[3] This gave the Diputats some control over the legislative activities of the viceroy, since there was no great difficulty in discovering reasons why a proclamation generally regarded as obnoxious was also unconstitutional. Thus the viceroy found himself still further restricted. There remained only one slight loophole. The viceroyalty was usually coupled with another office: that of captaincy-general. In his role as captain-general, the viceroy, assisted by a special tribunal, dealt with all questions relating to the military and naval defence of the Principality. The combination of offices in a single person offered certain political advantages, 'because what the constitutions prevent him from doing as captain-general he can do as viceroy, and each of the two posts comes to the aid of the other'.[4] But in whatever capacity he acted, he could never for long escape into those Elysian fields where the constitutions had no force.

The instructions issued to a viceroy on assuming office insisted on his duty to maintain good justice and government.[5] This was no empty phrase. He had a direct personal responsibility for the administration of justice which was not fully shared by his colleagues in the American viceroyalties. In America there was, nominally at least, a clear separation between government and judicature, the first being entrusted to the viceroy and the second to the Audiencia, with the king acting as arbiter over them. Viceroys in the Crown of Aragon, on the other hand, were regarded as the king's deputies in all his functions, including the judicial. The viceroy of Catalonia therefore not only presided

---

[1] Andreu Bosch, *Summari, Index o Epítome...dels Títols de Honor de Cathalunya* (Perpignan, 1628), p. 527.   [2] *Ibid.* p. 529.   [3] *Constitutions fetes...1599*, const. IX.
[4] ACA: CA, leg. 273, no. 28, consulta, 26 June 1625.
[5] ACA: Varias de Cancillería, R. 332, *Instrucciones públicas y secretas de SM para el Duque de Segorbe y de Cardona* (1630), nos. 1. and 2.

nominally over the Audiència but sat in its criminal chamber. All sentences were pronounced in his name, and he enjoyed the casting vote when there was no majority among the judges.[1]

The injunction to the viceroy to maintain good government was not easily obeyed, for the few instruments available to him for this purpose were hardly equal to the immensity of the task. His two immediate subordinates were known as the *Governadors*. One, the *Governador dels Comtats*, ruled the counties of Rosselló and Cerdanya from Perpinyà. The other, the Governador of Catalonia, acted as the viceroy's deputy in the government of the Principality. Since the viceroy spent most of his time in Barcelona, the governor of Catalonia was obliged, by a constitution of 1564, to travel round the Principality, never spending more than four months in the same district.[2] It was his responsibility to supervise the conduct of civil and criminal cases in the localities; to disperse, and, if possible, forestall, riots; and generally to see that order was preserved and justice done. He was liable to entrust the more unpleasant of these duties to his immediate assistants, two ordinary, and two extraordinary, *agutzils* (the Castilian *alguacil*). These in turn were relieved of their more menial duties by a crowd of parasites, the *porters*, the 'basest men in the republic',[3] who were empowered to arrest *in flagrante delicto*, and the *comissaris*, who were sent to collect information against suspected delinquents outside the city of Barcelona, and could make arrests when armed with a warrant.

One Governador and four agutzils was not much for the policing of a province as large and disorderly as Catalonia, but they did not act alone, for as agents of the central government they were supposed to co-operate with the royal officials who formed the local government in the Principality. For purposes of local government, Catalonia was divided into seventeen districts known as *vegueries*, each of which was administered by a *veguer* sometimes assisted by a *sotsveguer*. The *vegueries* themselves were subdivided into a number of smaller administrative units—*batllies*—headed by *batlles*. Local officials of the Crown, of whom there were 152 in the Principality, and 35 in the *Comtats*,[4] were

---

[1] Jesús Lalinde Abadía, 'Los virreyes de Cataluña bajo los Austrias', *Estudios de Historia Moderna*, vol. VI (1956–9), pp. 176–7.　　　　　[2] *Instrucciones*, no. 46.

[3] ACA: CA, leg. 273, no. 14, Bishop of Urgell to King, 31 Oct. 1626.

[4] ACA: CA, leg. 373, memorial of salaries of royal officials in Catalonia, sent to the King by the Viceroy, 1 June 1624.

selected by the king from lists of names sent to Madrid triennially by the viceroy. Apart from a number of privileged towns, which were allowed to pick three nominees of their own, from whom the king chose one as *batlle*, the viceroy prepared the list himself, with the assistance of his advisers. His difficulty was not so much to keep out undesirables, as to find anyone, undesirable or not, who would be willing to serve. The salaries of these local officials were ridiculously low. A *veguer* might earn 100 *lliures* a year, a *batlle* not usually more than 25 *lliures*, and often as little as 10.[1] This meant that suitable applicants were few and it was difficult to avoid unfortunate appointments. When Baltasar Claramunt applied for the post of *veguer* of Lleida and his name was placed by the viceroy at the top of the list, the Council of Aragon and the king naturally approved the appointment. It only transpired later that Claramunt was 'the most pernicious man in the republic, a poor man without a house or home of his own, living with a married woman and separated from his wife for over twelve years...an intimate friend and protector of bandits, and enjoying the worst possible reputation'.[2] With a number of Claramunts holding office in the local administration, there is no reason to be surprised if the royal government could command little respect in the Principality.

The possibilities for mischief by irresponsible *veguers* and *batlles* were particularly great because they enjoyed powers of jurisdiction as well as of administration. So-called 'ordinary' jurisdiction was exercised in the first instance by the local courts, those of the *veguer* and the *batlle*, and of the baronial officials in the large areas which remained in private, rather than royal, hands. From these local courts, which dealt with criminal as well as civil cases, appeal could be made to the main judicial tribunal in the Principality, the Audiència. The Audiència, which sat in Barcelona, was the most substantial, and the most effective, part of the viceregal administration. Since no cases could be carried on appeal outside the borders of the Principality, its judicial functions were of the very highest importance. It took direct cognizance of civil suits involving more than 300 *lliures*; of conflicts of jurisdiction; of criminal

---

[1] Memorial of Salaries, 1624.

[2] ACA: CA, leg. 269, no. 36, consulta, 9 March 1612. Twenty-five years earlier, when the town councillors of Lleida had sent a complaint about violence and brigandage in the neighbourhood, the name of Claramunt already figured prominently, as one link in a chain stretching back to the castle of Joan Cadell at Arsèguel (ACA: CA, leg. 265, no. 26, consulta, 28 Sept. 1587).

cases involving nobles or ecclesiastics, and of particularly heinous crimes, known as *regalies*, such as counterfeiting coins, or robbery on the royal highway.[1] And it dealt, in the second instance, with civil and criminal suits first brought before the local courts, whether royal or baronial, in which an appeal had been lodged.

After 1599 the Audiència, consisting of seventeen judges, was permanently divided into three *sales* or chambers, the first two of which heard civil suits and criminal appeals.[2] These two chambers, each of them consisting of five judges, were presided over respectively by the *Canceller* and the *Regent la Reial Cancelleria*. While the Regent was an ordinary lawyer who had usually risen from the ranks of the Audiència, the Canceller was a distinguished cleric. The most important royal official in Catalonia after the viceroy, he possessed the casting vote in the first chamber, and acted as supreme arbiter in contentions between clerics and laymen on points of jurisdiction.[3] If an appeal were made from a decision in a civil suit, either from his chamber or from that of the Regent, it came before the newest chamber in the Audiència, the *tercera sala*, which had originally been established in 1585 and was reorganized on a more permanent basis along lines laid down by the Corts of 1599.[4] This chamber had come to play a very important part in the judicial life of the country. Presided over by the Regent la Reial Cancelleria, and composed of four ordinary judges and three special *jutges de cort*, it had originally been set up in order to reduce the interminable delays in the Audiència's judicial proceedings. It functioned not only as a court of final appeal from decisions on civil cases in the other two chambers, but also as a criminal court. As such, its activities were by no means welcome to all the aristocracy. A noble in the Corts of 1599 complained that it was unjust

to give encouragement and opportunity to baronial vassals to lose respect for their lords, and to incite vassals to think up points of dispute with their lords, as the creation of this third chamber has done. And in any case the chamber is unnecessary, since throughout the Principality justice is administered with the utmost equity and rectitude by every baron, and vassals are treated with the greatest love and solicitude.[5]

---

[1] AAE: Corresp. Espagne, Sup. no. 3, fos. 267–71, *Preheminencias y tribunales que Su Magd. tiene en Cathaluña.*   [2] Instructions for the Duke of Cardona, nos. 1 and 2.

[3] RAH: Salazar K. 40, consulta of Council of Aragon, 20 May 1615.

[4] *Constitutions fetes...1599*, cap. 2.   [5] ACA: G, R. 1052, fo. 532v.

In spite of this outburst, the usefulness of the new chamber was sufficiently recognized for the Corts to agree to its continuation.

If the seventeen judges of the Audiència had been confined solely to their judicial activities, they would already have been playing an extremely important part in the life of the Principality. Catalan society, like other contemporary societies, was very litigious, and the Audiència was kept fully occupied by the innumerable disputes that were always arising over questions of jurisdiction and territorial boundaries and contested wills: disputes that were settled on the basis of case law, and, where this was silent, by canon law and Roman law.[1] A proper legal training was therefore essential. But with the passage of time, the scope of the Audiència's activities had come to extend far beyond its purely judicial functions, and its members required something more than mere legal erudition. The nature of these additional activities is suggested by the Audiència's alternative title of Royal Council (*Reial Consell*), for its members had come to be regarded as councillors as well as judges. This was a very natural development. When the old Royal Council of the kings of Aragon followed Ferdinand the Catholic to Castile and was transformed into the Council of Aragon, it was logical that the gap left by its departure from Barcelona should come to be filled by the Audiència. An alien viceroy, unaccustomed to the laws and traditions of the Catalans, would naturally turn for advice to the judges, both as natives of the Principality and as experts in its laws. As a result, the Audiència became an essential organ of government as well as of justice; to such an extent, indeed, that viceroys were increasingly compelled not only to take it into consultation but also to act on its recommendations.[2] In this way it came to advise on all matters of policy, and it would also provide the viceroy with names of candidates for vacant posts, which he would forward to Madrid for discussion in the Council of Aragon and eventual selection by the king.[3]

Their duty to advise the viceroy increased the burdens, as well as the powers, of the judges, but on occasions they were called upon to undertake yet more. The police arm of the administration—the Governador and the local officials—was so weak that it was always liable to be overwhelmed in an emergency. When this occurred, there was no

[1] F. Maspons i Anglasell, *Tractat dels pactes nupcials*...(Barcelona, 1916), vol. I, p. 8.
[2] Lalinde Abadía, 'Los virreyes bajo los Austrias', p. 188.
[3] Instructions for the Duke of Cardona, no. 39.

alternative but to have recourse to the Audiència. In 1614, for example, as lawlessness was reaching its peak, the marquis of Amazán prorogued the civil Audiència for two months and sent the judges out to different parts of the Principality to take command of operations against the bandits.[1] The judges were thus royal ministers in the fullest sense of the term. Not only were they part of the royal administration, but the weakness of its other parts meant that, to all intents and purposes, they *were* the royal administration.

The close association of the Catalan judiciary with policy-making and administration suggests a relationship with the Crown into which the most sinister interpretations can be read. Since Catalonia was governed from Madrid, and the Audiència was the most effective organ of royal government in the Principality, it was not difficult for nineteenth-century Catalan historians to see in it the agency whereby Castile planned to impose absolutism on Catalonia. But such an interpretation does not square with available information either about the policies of Madrid or about the character of the Audiència; nor does it receive support from contemporary attitudes to the tribunal. Situations naturally arose, as in the dispute over the printing of the constitutions between 1600 and 1603, when there was an open conflict between the Catalans and the Court. On these occasions, the Audiència was placed in a difficult position; the judges were at once under obligation to serve the king and obey the constitutions. Their natural sentiments as Catalans would make them side with their country, while their fear of incurring the royal displeasure could well prevent them from committing themselves to any line of action unpopular with the Court. How they behaved in such situations depended largely on their personal character and on their reading of the constitutions. They were not all sycophants. Recording the death in 1601 of Dr Oliva of the *tercera sala*, Dr Pujades wrote: 'He was a very good Catalan, a defender of the country's liberty. He refused to sign the *regalia* by which the viceroy, on the advice of the Regent, Dr Don Josep Mur, wanted to proceed against the Diputats in the dispute over the constitutions. He will be greatly missed, for there are few prepared to tell the truth.'[2] But until the 1630's, when pressure from the Court became much more insistent

[1] ACA: Canc., R. 5214, fo. 69, Almazán to Governador of Rosselló, 25 Oct. 1614.
[2] Pujades, I, fo. 66.

and the Audiència was called upon to pronounce judgment on a number of decrees from Madrid of dubious legality, occasions like the dispute of 1600, in which the Audiència found itself faced with an acute conflict of interests, were comparatively rare.

Since seventeenth-century Catalans, when considering their form of government, would naturally think in terms of co-operation rather than of conflict with their sovereign, the acceptance of a post in the royal administration did not in any way imply a 'betrayal' of Catalonia. On the contrary, posts were sought with an extreme eagerness. All lawyers, for instance, aspired to a post in the Audiència. This can hardly have been because of the salary. Most of the judges received 1000 *lliures* a year, though the three *jutges de cort* earned only 500;[1] yet Dr Joan Magarola accepted a post as *jutge de cort* although he had been earning over 1000 *lliures* annually in private practice.[2] No doubt perquisites did much to supplement these very moderate salaries, but the principal attractions of office were other than the narrowly financial. A post in the Audiència might eventually lead to the most coveted post of all, a seat in the Council of Aragon at Madrid. It provided opportunities for influencing appointments and for helping friends and family; it was often rewarded with a title of nobility, and it put a lawyer of humble origins on terms of equality with the aristocracy. The social advantages of a post can be gauged from the frequency of marriages between noble families and those of the judges. In the small, closed society of the Principality, office in the Audiència offered every kind of opportunity for the use and abuse of power.

Contemporary allusions make it clear that the judges were not generally slow in making the most of their opportunities. There was little love lost between them and a population which regarded them as corrupt and arrogant. In a famous satire of the time, a Catalan peasant, Pere Porter, descends into hell, where he meets a variety of well-known personages, including various judges of the Audiència, 'whom he had known very well, and among others Dr Ubach, Dr Puig, Dr Benach and many others, who used to say in their lifetimes that they were gods on earth'.[3] In order to curb the activities of the royal ministers and

[1] Memorial of salaries, 1624.
[2] ACA: CA, leg. 483, petition of Dr Joan Magarola.
[3] 'Relació y memòria y espantós viatje que feu Pere Porter...als 23 de Agost de 1608...', *La Renaixensa*, año VII, vol. I (1877), pp. 83–4.

investigate charges against them, the Corts of 1599 decreed that a *visita*, or inquiry, conducted by an independent outsider, should be held in the Principality every six years at the expense of the Generalitat.[1] But after 1614 the regular *visita* was quietly allowed to lapse. It involved the Diputació in enormous expenses, and it was regarded by viceroys of Catalonia both as prejudicial to the authority of the king's ministers, never at any time very great,[2] and as useless in fulfilling its original purpose, since the marriage of judges of the Audiència into aristocratic families meant that charges would be brought only against the upright—and the unconnected.[3]

With the *visita* inadequate or inoperative, there was always a ground-swell of resentment against the Audiència, and the royal administration in general. This was natural. Royal ministers were the agents of authority, and authority in all its forms was suspect. There were many counts on which the Audiència could more justifiably be criticized. In the atmosphere of intrigue, of family feuds and of the rivalries between *nyerros* and *cadells* which poisoned Catalan life in the opening years of the new century, it is as impossible to doubt as to substantiate the frequent charges of favouritism and corruption brought against the judges. Matters may well have improved in the following decades. The only surviving notes of a *visita*—that of 1633—suggest a reasonably conscientious body of men, dispensing adequate justice. They had their defects, of course. Dr Roca was mad; Dr Astor was too old at seventy-four; Dr Carreras was a 'vulgar, ridiculous man'; and the Regent, Dr Sala, was under the baneful influence of his wife. But several of them were good lawyers—one or two were outstanding—and nothing very serious had emerged about bribery and corruption, although there was always a good deal of bargaining and negotiation when vacancies in the administration had to be filled.[4]

The one charge that could be consistently and very reasonably upheld against the Audiència was its appalling slowness. This was partly because there were not enough judges to conduct the vast amount of business, and because Madrid was usually slow in filling vacancies, so

---

[1] *Constitutions fetes...1599*, caps. 5 and 6.
[2] ACA: CA, leg. 380, Duke of Feria to President of Council of Aragon, 3 Aug. 1630.
[3] ACA: CA, leg. 235, no. 19, Duke of Alcalá to Vice-Chancellor, 3 Oct. 1623.
[4] ACA: CA, leg. 224, no. 13, Fontanet to Cardenal Infante, 30 Jan. 1633, and rough notes on the character of ministers, dated 6 March 1633.

that the tribunal was often not working at full strength for long periods at a time. But it can also be attributed to the variety of subterfuges made possible by skilful exploitation of the legal intricacies of the Catalan constitutions. Well-timed appeals, or the rejection of one judge after another on grounds of a lack of impartiality, could delay the settlement of a case for years. The suit between the marquis of Aytona and Don Francisco de Lanuza over the barony of Llagostera had begun in 1539, been settled in favour of Aytona in 1572, and the appeal was still being heard in 1624.[1] In the 1620's the Cardona–Montagut case, begun in 1575, still occupied every Wednesday in the Sala del Regent.

It is hard to see in this slow-moving tribunal, absorbed in the niceties of legal procedure and cocooned in the web of the Catalan constitutions, even the embryo of despotic government. If Madrid had indeed been planning the castilianization of Catalonia, the Audiència would at best have been a blunt instrument for the task. The background of the judges, their ties of friendship and relationship with the aristocracy, made them unreliable agents of the Crown. Successive viceroys were perfectly aware of this. One of them complained in 1626 that

All those of the Audiència, some more than others, are too favourably inclined to the liberties of the land, even though, as beneficiaries of His Majesty, they conceal this a little better than the other provincials....Those of the criminal Audiència give me most cause for concern, as I consider them partial, and too closely allied to their relatives, and to the *caballeros*, whom they favour when the opportunity arises....This leads to lack of secrecy about proceedings in court, with the delinquents knowing everything beforehand....'

Still worse, 'all the ministers, from the big ones to the small, have within them the original sin of being *cadells* or *nyerros*, so that members of one faction cannot be entrusted with anything that conflicts with its interests'.[2]

More than one viceroy on first setting foot in Catalonia must have felt himself a Daniel in the den of lions. No doubt the majority of royal ministers were conscious of their obligations to the king and to the administration in which they served, and the hope of promotion was always an inducement to good behaviour, but their first loyalty

---

[1] ACA: CA, leg. 372, relation of cases pending in the Sala del Regent.
[2] ACA: CA, leg. 273, no. 14, Bishop of Urgell (Viceroy) to King, 31 Oct. 1626.

was to their families, their faction and their province. This meant that the best hope of making the administration a reasonably efficient and impartial instrument of government was for the viceroy to take the ministers into his confidence and show himself more concerned to work for the good of the Principality than for the satisfaction of Madrid: objects that were often far from compatible. But even with the best will in the world, there were some obstacles that no viceroy could hope to overcome. With so few royal ministers in the central administration at Barcelona, one bad appointment could do much to hamstring the workings of government and multiply the troubles of a whole succession of viceroys. The weakest link in the government of the Principality for a considerable part of the reigns of Philip III and IV was Don Alexos de Marimón, the Governador of Catalonia from 1613 to 1639. The post of Governador had become a life appointment, and in 1613 it was unexpectedly given to Marimón, then governor of the castle of Salces, partly because of his assistance in the expulsion of the Moriscos from Spain,[1] and partly because he had a private income.[2] Marimón's appointment proved to be a disaster. During the 1620's and 1630's one viceroy after another complained of his behaviour. Wherever he went, he stirred up trouble; his relations with the bandits he was supposed to be pursuing were often suspiciously close; he had a genius for being at the farthest imaginable distance from the scene of any crime, although he was quick to assume all the credit for any success, and in his later years it was almost impossible to get him to move out of Barcelona.[3] Although his crimes of omission and commission made effective government almost impossible, there was nothing to be done. Marimón's marriage to Dona Anna de Pinós, sister of the count of Vallfogona, had given him an impregnable social position, and through his relations he enjoyed the protection of influential personages at Court, where a grandee kept him informed of any moves undertaken by his enemies.[4]

[1] AGS: Est. leg. 2640, consulta, 2 Oct. 1610. Perhaps because of his success in dealing with the Moriscos of the Crown of Aragon, he was chosen as one of the three commissioners sent to Andalusia in 1611 to liquidate the few Morisco communities which still remained there. [See Henri Lapeyre, *Géographie de l'Espagne Morisque* (Paris, 1959), pp. 179–80.]

[2] ACA: CA, leg. 272, no. 51, consulta, 9 Dec. 1613.

[3] See the complaints of the bishop of Solsona, 7 Aug. and 4 Dec. 1627 (ACA: CA, leg. 375), and of the duke of Cardona in a letter to J. L. de Villanueva, 26 June 1636 (ACA: CA, leg. 386).

[4] ACA: CA, leg. 390, Bishop of Vic to Cardinal Borja, 2 Aug. 1638.

Although the presence of a Marimón in the administration did much to hamper the work of government, a more important cause of the Crown's weakness in Catalonia was impersonal—the permanent shortage of money. The fiscal foundations of royal authority in the Principality were exceptionally precarious. All secular taxation was in the hands of the Diputació, which maintained officials through the Principality to collect the import and export duties and the tax on cloths, which accounted for most of its revenues.[1] A small proportion of these revenues went to supplement the salaries of certain officials in the royal administration, and the remainder, after the needs of the Diputació itself had been met, was supposed to provide a reserve from which the Principality could pay the king the subsidy it voted him in the Corts. In practice, however, things worked rather differently. The Diputació had a great facility for spending money, and when the Corts met once more there was usually no reserve, and new taxes had to be imposed. The Crown, therefore, benefited only very marginally from all the money that passed into the coffers of the Diputació.

The Crown's major source of revenue in the Principality was ecclesiastical. There were in Catalonia, as in all the king of Spain's dominions, three sources of regular taxation deriving from papal concessions. The *cruzada* was the revenue from the annual sale of bulls of indulgence, which almost everyone would buy at 2 *reals* apiece;[2] the *subsidi* or *quarta* was a proportion of the Church's revenues handed over to the Crown for the defence of the Faith; and the *excusado*, the most recent of the papal concessions, came from the payment to the Crown, instead of to the Church, of the tithe of the principal house in every parish.[3]

---

[1] See below, pp. 134–5. The Crown's financial situation was very different in Sicily, where it could count on regular parliamentary grants, and where the revenues 'were sufficient to cover all normal demands' (Koenigsberger, *The Government of Sicily*, p. 128). Sicily also contributed to the expenses of the Monarchy in a way that Catalonia did not.

[2] *Preheminencias y tribunales (op. cit.).*

[3] The introduction of the *excusado* into Catalonia in 1572 had provoked strong aristocratic resistance, in which Don Nofre d'Alentorn played a leading part (BC: MS 510, Despalau's diary, fo. 79 v). Many parish churches were apparently dependent on a single wealthy house for their tithes, and the new system would leave them denuded of income. The dispute was resolved by a *concordia* or agreement reached at the provincial council of Tarragona in 1573, by which the king would receive a lump sum from the Church of 7000 *lliures* a year (Bosch, *Títols de Honor*, p. 131). In Catalonia, as in England, more tithes seem to have gone to the aristocracy than to the clergy (cf. the memorandum on the poverty of the Church in AAT: Concilio Provincial 1613, lib. 27, fo. 62), and this may help to explain aristocratic resistance to the *excusado*.

These three taxes brought in between them 85,500 *lliures* a year:

Quarta	16,500[1]
Excusado	7,000[1]
Cruzada	62,000[2]
	85,500

This was a large sum, but it was of no benefit to the viceregal administration. All these taxes were farmed by the Crown to its bankers who had agents to collect them in each province of Spain. Their yield was either appropriated to meet specific royal obligations, like payment for the construction of ships in the Barcelona dockyards, or was absorbed into the Crown's general revenues, which went to the bankers in return for their loans to the king.

Where, then, did the royal government in Catalonia find its money? The question is best answered by a survey of its financial organs, whose number and complexity can hardly be said to have been justified by the revenues they managed to produce between them. There were four separate financial departments: the office of *Mestre Racional*, the *Batllia General* and its equivalent in the Comtats, the *Procuradoria Reial*, and the *Tresoreria*. The Mestre Racional was a hereditary office in the family of the marquis of Aytona, and was run, in the hereditary absence of the family from the Principality, by a *lloctinent* or deputy, a Catalan gentleman. While his office itself collected no dues, his duty, in company with his assistants, was to see that all royal rents and dues in the Principality were properly collected.[3] It was in fact an office for accounting and investigation, and it would check the accounts both of the local officials of the Crown—the *veguers* and *batlles*—and of those towns in the Principality, which, by virtue of certain conditions in their charters, paid a *quint* or fifth of their annual dues to the Crown.[4] It had an income of its own, drawn from various sources and amounting to 3000–4000 *lliures* a year,[5] but it needed all this money to pay the salaries of its own officials and the pensions granted by over-generous kings.

The Batllia General, unlike the office of Mestre Racional, was actively engaged in collecting money, but its functions were judicial as well as

---

[1] ACA: CA, leg. 280, no. 38, memorandum of Feb. 1636.
[2] ACA: CA, leg. 383, relation by Don Guerau de Guardiola, 18 Dec. 1632.
[3] ACA: CA, leg. 381, *Papeles del Dr Francisco Marçal . . .* (1630).
[4] For the *quints*, see below, pp. 144 ff.   [5] Guardiola's relation.

administrative. It was at once the office and the court of the Crown as a landowner. The cases that came before it as a court were feudal and patrimonial, with an upper limit of 400 *lliures*, above which the case came before the Audiència.[1] The Batlle General and his assessors saw that fief-holders of the Crown recognized their obligations; that the king's debtors paid their debts; that roads and bridges were properly maintained, that the royal mills were in working order, and that the royal patrimony in the Principality was suitably looked after, and, where possible, augmented.

It was one of the major misfortunes of the viceregal administration that this patrimony was, by 1600, exceptionally small. In some parts of Spain, such as Valencia, the king was still a landowner on a considerable scale, but in Catalonia it was different. Over the centuries, a succession of penurious kings had alienated so much of the Crown's property in the Principality that by now very little of the original patrimony of the kings of Aragon remained. With a large part of Catalonia in the hands of the duke of Cardona, and most of the remainder distributed between the Church and the barons, many of whom had a nagging fear that the Crown might one day resume its alienated estates, the royal patrimony in Catalonia was only the ghost of a patrimony. This meant that there was no solid financial basis for royal government in the Principality, such as a firm phalanx of Crown lands would have provided. Instead, the Crown possessed a mill here, and a number of hereditary dues there, but no substantial nucleus of property. And it is very doubtful whether it was getting full benefit even from such slender rights as it possessed. Nominally, these rights were protected by fifteen deputies or *lloctinents* of the Batllia General, posted at different points through the Principality. It was their task to lease the Crown's property and rents in their locality, and remit the money to the Batllia General.[2] But since they had many friends, and drew paltry salaries of between 6 *lliures* and 25 *lliures* a year,[3] they could not be described as over-zealous in their concern for the royal patrimony.[4] More than one viceroy in the early seventeenth century tried to do something to remedy these abuses. It was believed that many towns and villages which properly belonged to the Crown had been

[1] ACA: CA, leg. 372, Viceroy to King, 13 Jan. 1624.   [2] Dr Marçal's paper.
[3] ACA: CA, leg. 384, report of Don Lluís Monsuar (Batlle General), 1630.
[4] Dr Marçal's paper.

lost to it through sheer neglect, and it was hoped that the appointment of a special *procurador fiscal patrimonial* would make it possible to begin a systematic survey of charters. But nothing very much came of all this. Even when a case of dubious ownership was suspected, proceedings in the Audiència were liable to drag on indefinitely. It was symptomatic of the difficulties—and incidentally a proof of how far the Audiència was from being a mere subservient tool of the Crown—that for the entire year 1629 not one case carried from the Batllia General into the Audiència was decided in the Crown's favour.[1]

As a result of the scantiness of the royal patrimony and of a long period of inadequate administration, the revenues entering the Batllia General were small. In 1610 it had an income of 5111 *lliures*, and since 5157 *lliures* were needed for its own running expenses, there was no surplus on which a viceroy could draw. Indeed, it had become a positive liability, because the Crown had actually added to its charges by granting a number of pensions payable out of its revenues. It was supposed to provide pensions for the heirs of Don Nofre d'Alentorn and eighteen other pensioners, all drawing between 100 and 500 *lliures* a year. Arrears were naturally heavy, and by 1610 the Batllia General was in debt to the tune of 17,992 *lliures*.[2]

If either the Batllia General or the office of Mestre Racional had ever had any surplus revenues, these would have gone to the other financial department, the Tresoreria, which acted as the administration's pay office. The Regent in charge of the Treasury—usually a member of the aristocracy, like the Batlle General and the Lloctinent del Mestre Racional—was described by one viceroy as 'the principal or sole agent through whom we viceroys of Your Majesty have to govern....the hands and feet of the viceroy'.[3] The importance of his department fully entitled him to this description. Not only was the department responsible for the prompt payment of all royal officials; it was also the office of receipt for the bulk of the royal revenues. If there had been more Crown property in Catalonia, the Batllia General would presumably have ranked as at least equal in importance with the Treasury as a source of income for the royal administration. As it was, the principal dues, not being patrimonial or feudal, were paid directly into the

[1] ACA: CA, leg. 381, report of Don Lluís Monsuar, dated 7 Sept. 1630.
[2] ACA: CA, leg. 352, Count of Erill to King, 28 Feb. 1610.
[3] AAW: MS E2, Duke of Feria to King, 29 May 1597, fos. 32 and 41.

Treasury. These dues consisted of the *quints*, paid by certain towns, and worth some 12,000 to 13,000 *lliures* a year; compositions for crimes (3000 or 4000 *lliures*) and money from bail (2000 *lliures*).

Thanks to the receipts of the Treasury, the total annual income of the viceregal administration approached the figure of 40,000 *lliures*:[1]

Tresoreria	19,000 *lliures*
Mestre Racional	4,000
Batllia General	7,000
Procuradoria Reial dels Comtats	7,000
	37,000

This figure means that the Crown's income from all secular sources was less than half the annual income of the city of Barcelona alone, and only a quarter of the income enjoyed by the Diputació. There could be no better commentary on the king of Spain's weakness in his Principality of Catalonia.

An income of 37,000 *lliures* was quite insufficient for effective government. Although the Diputació provided almost 10,000 *lliures* a year towards the salaries of royal officials and judges of the Audiència,[2] the Crown still had to find another 13,000 *lliures* to make up the balance,[3] and this figure excluded the viceroy's salary of 6000 ducats. This had to be found out of the income of the Crown's estates in Valencia,[4] a striking reflection on the miserable state of the Crown's finances in the Principality. Once the salaries of royal officials had been paid and the ordinary running expenses of the royal tribunals met, very little of the original 37,000 *lliures* remained for actual government—for chasing bandits or keeping order. In 1626, when the number of bandits had considerably decreased, the duke of Maqueda made it a condition of his accepting the viceroyalty that he should receive 20,000 ducats— more than the entire income of the Tresoreria—simply for the purpose of anti-bandit operations.[5] A much larger sum would have been required in the first years of the seventeenth century, when banditry was

---

[1] Guardiola's relation.

[2] ACA: CA, leg. 376, relation of salaries paid by the Diputació (1625?).

[3] Calculated from the list of officials and their salaries in ACA: CA, leg. 373, Viceroy to King, 1 June 1624.

[4] ACA: CA, leg. 364, Alcalá to King, 25 July 1620.

[5] ACA: CA, leg. 275, no. 55, consulta, 17 Oct. 1626.

at its height. But the money was simply not available; and, as every viceroy—and every bandit—knew, the royal administration, without a penny in the treasury, was doomed to impotence.

Ideally the government needed troops for the reassertion of its authority, but here again it lacked sufficient funds. Although the privileges of Barcelona forbade the maintenance of royal troops within the city, the king did have troops stationed in the castles which protected the Principality's frontier with France, and indeed the marquis of Almazán drew twelve cavalrymen and thirty infantrymen from these garrisons to join in hunting bandits.[1] But the withdrawal of this small force from the garrisons could ill be afforded, for such was the Crown's penury that during the reign of Philip III the Principality's frontier defences had almost ceased to exist. In 1621, after no pay had been received for three years, it was found that of the 700 men in Perpinyà— the principal bastion against a French attack—only twenty-five remained. The garrisons of Roses, Salces, Ópol and Cotlliure had similarly evaporated, and such men as were left had signed on as agricultural labourers to keep themselves alive.[2]

In addition to its own internal deficiencies and its perennial shortage of cash, the viceregal administration also found itself hampered by the private immunities and privileges which in Catalonia, as all over Europe, prevented the full assertion of royal power. Royal, baronial, ecclesiastical and mixed jurisdictions all existed side by side, splitting the Principality into an archipelago of private islands. Many of these islands were large and valuable. The duke of Cardona owned vast areas of the country; so also did Catalonia's fourteen abbeys, of which the wealthiest, Ripoll, had more than 6000 vassals.[3]

The most complete type of private jurisdiction was known as *mer i mixt imperi*—full civil and criminal jurisdiction, including the right to sentence to death, grimly symbolized by the gallows on the lands of many a baron. This kind of jurisdiction was widely coveted, and sometimes usurped. Nobles who shared jurisdiction with the Crown would petition the king for criminal as well as civil jurisdiction, as a reward for their pretended services. Alternatively, they would seek to

[1] AAT: Concilio Provincial 1613, lib. 27, fo. 141 v, Almazán to Provincial Council.
[2] AGS: GA, leg. 864, Alcalá to King, 24 April 1621.
[3] ACA: CA, leg. 485, petition from the town of Ripoll (1610).

appropriate it by covert methods, like the majority of the barons round the town of Cervera, who already possessed civil jurisdiction and wanted *mer i mixt imperi*.[1] This was a matter of acute concern to the inhabitants, who would fight desperate rearguard actions to save the neighbouring countryside from falling by default under the complete control of the local aristocracy. Although it was legally possible to appeal from a baronial court to the Audiència, many vassals can hardly have been in a position to take advantage of this right; and the *batlles* and other officials of a resident baron were much more real than the courts of the king in far-away Barcelona.

Nothing shows the limitations on royal power in the Principality better than an analysis of the ownership of areas of jurisdiction. Counting each shared jurisdiction as a half, the towns, villages and smaller administrative units (*llocs*) in the Principality can be apportioned as follows:

Baronial jurisdiction	1114½ (of which the duke of Cardona held 238½)
Royal jurisdiction	681
Ecclesiastical jurisdiction	589½
	2385

If these figures are correct—and it is possible that they are over-generous to the Crown—71 per cent of all jurisdictions in the Principality were in non-royal hands.[2]

This makes it easier to understand the lack of success of royal officials against the bandits. However efficiently he was chased by a royal *batlle*, a bandit could always slip over the border into a private barony where royal officials could not touch him. Royal authority in the countryside therefore depended on close co-operation between baronial and royal officials. This was not easily achieved. Nobles themselves were often deeply involved with the bandits, and more inclined to assist than pursue them; many barons were non-resident, and had no control over their vassals;[3] even their deputies, the governors of their

[1] AHC: Lletres missives 1609–27, fo. 141v. Pahers of Cervera to Duke of Alburquerque, 26 Jan. 1618.
[2] This list is based on the information provided in Don Luys de Peguera, *Pràctica, Forma y Estil de Celebrar Corts Generals en Cathalunya...*(Barcelona, 1701), part III. (First published in 1632.)
[3] ACA: CA, leg. 260, no. 2, Don Alexos de Marimón to Duke of Cardona, 25 March 1626.

estates, preferred a quiet urban life to the rural rigours of bandit-chasing,[1] and their subordinates, as often as not, were in league with the bandits.

Where territorial immunities did not interfere with the activities of royal officials, the course of justice was often impeded by the immunities of privileged sections of the community. Of the ecclesiastical immunities the most prejudicial were probably those enjoyed by familiars of the Inquisition. With its claim to exclusive competence in all cases involving those connected with it and their dependants, the Inquisition was as great a trial to the authorities in Catalonia as in the other dominions of the king of Spain.[2] Although there was a long history of Catalan resistance to the establishment of Ferdinand the Catholic's new-style Inquisition,[3] and the three Inquisitors who headed the tribunal in Barcelona were not natives, it does not seem that the Inquisition can be regarded as an agency for the domination of the Principality by Castile. In Catalonia, as everywhere else, it was, rather, an independent State within the State, as liable to come into conflict with the viceroy and the Audiència as with the Corts and the Diputació.

Because of the rugged nature of the land and the nearness of a heresy-ridden France, it was the practice of the Inquisition to appoint one familiar in Catalonia for every fifty houses.[4] This figure was considered by the Catalans to be excessive, and every Corts protested against the number of familiars and the immunities they enjoyed. The Corts of 1599 drew up a whole series of articles limiting the powers of the Inquisition and reducing the number of familiars,[5] but although the king gave his formal assent, their enforcement was made dependent on papal approval, and this was carefully withheld.[6] An earlier Corts however, had achieved one important victory over the Inquisition which profoundly modified its character and differentiated it from the Inquisition in the king's other dominions. By an act of 1585 familiars were declared ineligible for public office, and, as a result, few people of any social standing were prepared to accept appointment as familiars.[7]

---

[1] Serra i Vilaró, *Baronies de Pinós i Mataplana*, vol. II, pp. 33–4.
[2] See H. C. Lea, *A History of the Inquisition of Spain*, vol. I (New York, 1906), book II, ch. 4, 'Conflicting Jurisdictions'. [3] Lea, vol. I, pp. 260 ff.
[4] AHN: Inquis., leg. 1594, fo. 12, *Respuesta a los capítulos dados a SM en las Cortes comenzadas en el año 1626*.
[5] *Constitutions fetes...1599*, cap. 23. [6] Lea, vol. I, pp. 471–2.
[7] AGS: Est., leg. 2651, instructions for Cardenal Infante (1632). Familiars were eligible for public office in Castile, Aragon and Valencia (Lea, vol. I, p. 419).

This contrasted strikingly with Sicily, where many nobles became familiars to escape from royal jurisdiction and where the Inquisition was correspondingly more powerful because it enjoyed aristocratic support.[1]

Much of the hostility of the Corts to the Inquisition was therefore inspired by nobles who resented the fact that their own vassals could secure exemption from their jurisdiction by accepting appointment as familiars. The very words of the form of appointment show the extent of the threat to seigneurial as well as royal jurisdiction: 'Trusting in you, Sebastian Parets, labourer of the said village of Fonalleras, as a person worthy of entire confidence...we name and appoint you Familiar of the Holy Office...and exhort and require all officers of justice... to regard you as such, and observe all the exemptions, privileges and liberties appertaining to familiars, and we grant you licence to carry offensive and defensive weapons by day and night....' Any official who molested him did so under penalty of excommunication.[2]

In these circumstances it is not surprising that many who became familiars were primarily concerned either to escape from baronial oppression or to seek a cloak, in service for the Inquisition, for their own nefarious practices. The names of familiars figure prominently among those accused of befriending and protecting bandits,[3] but the influence enjoyed by the Holy Office at Court meant that the Crown would never do anything to reduce the powers of the Inquisition's agents.

In other respects also ecclesiastical immunities were a source of constant trouble to the viceregal administration. It was always possible for a criminal to evade capture by taking refuge in a church. Don Carles de Alemany, a noble with a criminal record stretching back to 1594, and the most notorious counterfeiter of coins in the Principality, escaped justice for twenty years by living in houses that adjoined churches, into which he could disappear whenever pursuit became too hot.[4] It was only in 1625 that the Spanish ambassador in Rome was able to obtain a modification of these rights of sanctuary.[5] Until then they proved of inestimable value to delinquents, especially as the Principality's con-

[1] Koenigsberger, *The Government of Sicily*, p. 163.
[2] Archivo Notarial, Gerona: not. no. 6, Miquel Mascord, 1622–6 (no folio number).
[3] E.g. Vicens Soldevila of Manresa (AHM: leg. 1088, instructions of 5 Sept. 1610 for Jeroni Soler Ferran).
[4] ACA: CA, leg. 370, Viceroy to King, 24 June 1623.
[5] ACA: CA, leg. 373, Duke of Pastrana to King, 21 Nov. 1625.

stitutions added the extra refinement that if the criminal, on emerging from the church, were found innocent of the crime for which he had taken refuge, he was automatically pardoned any previous offence he might have committed.

But of all the privileges and immunities that existed in Catalonia, the most troublesome to the royal administration were the privileges of the aristocracy. A noble or gentleman in Catalonia, as in other parts of Spain, could not be tortured nor could he be imprisoned for debt; moreover, he could be arraigned only before the Audiència, and be proceeded against only if the aggrieved party brought a charge.[1] This last provision was the best possible guarantee of aristocratic immunity. It meant that, except when he had committed a crime that came within the province of the Crown's *regalies*, an offending noble could never be brought to justice unless the injured party or his relatives referred the case in writing to the king's ministers. This rarely occurred.

The privileges enjoyed by the aristocracy show clearly how the constitutions tied the hands of the viceroy and his officials. It was this that made them sacrosanct to the Catalan governing class, although one or two people may have felt uneasy about the degree of licence they allowed. Even so doughty a defender of Catalonia's laws as the eminent lawyer Dr Fontanella thought that some aristocratic privileges were excessive and unjust,[2] and a study of Catalan society in the seventeenth century makes it difficult to avoid the impression that many of the constitutions were being exploited in the interests of the select few. The Diputació, controlled by a few influential nobles and by the Barcelona oligarchy, could be counted on to raise shrill cries of protest against real or pretended infringements of the constitutions whenever aristocratic interests were at stake. Whether it would act so vigorously when the rights of other sections of the community were threatened, was very much an open question. According to the town government of Cervera, it would not: 'Experience has shown that, in the event of an infringement of the constitutions, the Diputats at once come out in their defence if the interests of ecclesiastics and *militars* are involved; but they refuse to take action when towns or members of the *braç reial* bring forward complaints.'[3] The Diputació, once the bastion of Catalan

[1] Fontanella, *De Pactis Nuptialibus*, vol. I, clausula III, glosa 3, §§ 11 and 38.
[2] *Ibid.* §§ 26–8.
[3] AHC: Carpeta Capítols de Corts, M-XL-87, instructions to syndics (1632).

liberties, had fallen victim to sectional interests, and now appeared little more than a bastion of aristocratic privilege.

Between them, aristocracy and Diputació enjoyed a commanding position in the Principality. It was they who held the initiative, and every Corts held in the province added to their power, since the king, in the last resort, was more interested in securing a handsome subsidy than in strengthening the hand of his government in Catalonia. By a natural process, therefore, the Crown's power in the Principality was gradually whittled away over the course of the sixteenth century. After every Corts, the aristocracy was a little stronger than it had been before, and the constitutions encroached that much further into the dwindling area still occupied by the viceregal administration. This process reached its climax in the Corts of 1599. These were the Corts which had instituted the unfortunate *visita* of royal officials,[1] reaffirmed all the privileges of the *militars*,[2] stipulated that the Regent la Reial Tresoreria was in future to be a noble,[3] and ordered that all appeals from baronial courts that failed in the Audiència were to be returned to the barons.[4] It was concessions such as these which prompted the then viceroy, the duke of Feria, to write to his secretary:

There is little use keeping me in this province any longer because, thanks to these Cortes, no governor, however good, can keep the province in order, and no governor, however bad, can bring it to a worse pass than that to which it has already been brought by its own laws....This is the most wretched province in the whole world.[5]

In a sense, Feria's gloom was justifiable. Catalonia was ungovernable —or at least it was ungovernable by the royal administration alone. A handful of underpaid officials, most of them too closely associated with one faction or the other to be either effective or impartial, had little hope of preserving order single-handed. Yet this had always been true, and the Corts of 1599, however unfortunate, had done no more than remove one or two coping-stones from an already shaky edifice. No government in seventeenth-century Europe was capable of maintaining order solely through the efforts of its own officials. Ultimately, its success depended on the co-operation of the aristocracy and on the

[1] See above, p. 89.   [2] *Constitutions fetes...1599*, cap. 50.
[3] *Ibid.* cap. 8.   [4] *Ibid.* const. 57.
[5] AAW: MS E2, fo. 132v, Feria to Fitzherbert, 4 Feb. 1600.

acquiescence, if not the positive assistance, of the mass of the population. Catalonia was no exception.

In relatively normal times, it was possible to take for granted at least a sullen acquiescence among the local populace. When a criminal was thought to be lurking in the area, there would be a hue and cry, known as the *sometent*, and the *batlle* would call out the populace in pursuit. The *sometent* was, however, unpopular with the towns, which resented the trouble and expense of turning out while the vassals of barons remained idly at home;[1] and it usually produced a vast amount of commotion with very little to show for it at the end.[2] An attempt to improve on this procedure had been made in 1565 and was again tried from 1605 to 1611 to meet the growing challenge from the bandits. This was the *unió*, a kind of glorified *sometent*, which banded the inhabitants of an entire region under specially appointed captains for the purpose of tracking down bandits, and placed all the signatories under an obligation to indemnify anyone who had suffered from a bandit attack.[3]

The *unió* seems at first to have met with a certain success. At least, poems and pamphlets were published in its honour, and the praises of the viceroy were sung.[4] But it suffered from defects similar to those of the *sometent* and scarcely touched the fringe of the formidable problems involved in hunting bandits in a country that was mountainous and densely wooded. When the whereabouts of a gang had eventually been established, sufficient officers of the law collected, and the local villages called out, the bandits still enjoyed the advantage of greater mobility and superior weapons. Their chosen firearm was the *pedrenyal*, which, with its flintlock mechanism, enjoyed general popularity among the Catalans. In an attempt to reduce the death-rate in the Principality, the viceroy issued a proclamation in May 1602, forbidding the carrying of *pedrenyals* less than four *pams* in length, on the grounds that short *pedrenyals* were more easily concealed and were consequently a greater menace.[5]

---

[1] AHC: Lletres missives 1609–27, fos. 177–80, letter of instructions from Pahers of Cervera, 14 May 1624. [2] ACA: CA, leg. 379, Viceroy to King, 22 Aug. 1629.

[3] J. Reglà, *Felip II i Catalunya*, p. 150.

[4] Cf. *Resposta a un amich de Vich*... (Spanish Chap-books, BM: 11,450 e. 25). I owe this reference to the courtesy of Professor E. M. Wilson of Emmanuel College, Cambridge.

[5] ACA: CA, leg. 346, Viceroy to King, 5 Oct. 1602. Four *pams* were 36 inches of barrel (cf. Lea, *Inquisition*, vol. I, p. 402). A minimum length of three *pams* (27 inches) had been prescribed in the Corts of 1585 (*Constitutions*, lib. IX, tit. XIX, cap. IV) to the great annoyance of the aristocracy, which tried unsuccessfully in 1599 to secure exemption from this law (*Constitutions fetes*.... 1599, cap. 78).

Apart from provoking great discontent among the nobles and gentry, who relied on the short *pedrenyal* for self-defence and acts of revenge, the edict had singularly little effect. The bandits naturally continued to use the forbidden weapon, while royal officials and the more law-abiding citizens now lacked a good weapon with which to defend themselves. When pursuing bandits, they were obliged to have recourse to arquebuses or to long *pedrenyals* which had every conceivable disadvantage when used for this particular purpose. They were too cumbersome to be carried on foot through thick undergrowth or to be fired with one hand from horseback, and they emitted such quantities of smoke and flame that all chance of surprise was thrown away.[1]

Quite apart from the technical difficulties and the problems of effective organization, neither the *sometent* nor the *unió* could hope to be of much use against organized banditry, because they depended for their success on the co-operation of those who were little inclined to co-operate. A village might be prepared to turn out against an ordinary thief, or to recover cattle carried off by a neighbouring landowner, but banditry was a different matter. The bandits could count on the sympathy of many of their countrymen, who perhaps saw them as protectors of the poor against the rich, or as their champions against some royal official who had made himself hated throughout the region. And even if a peasant had no love for the bandits, a Roca Guinarda was a much more real and formidable person to him than some shadowy minister in Barcelona. If he did not give the bandits food and drink, and keep quiet about their whereabouts, his straw would be burnt and his animals killed.[2] Terrified by what might happen to them if they informed on the bandits, and perhaps secretly admiring their boldness and bravery, the mass of the population preferred to say, and do, nothing. 'In this country', wrote a viceroy, 'we are always ruined by lack of proof.'[3] Those who knew kept quiet.

There was, of course, nothing new about this. Philip II's ministers in the Principality had been faced with exactly the same problems as those which so baffled the ministers of Philip III. Yet, on the whole, they had managed to keep banditry in check. It is possible that their task was a little easier: that economic and social conditions were rather less

[1] ACA: CA, leg. 362, Alcalá to King, 28 Sept. 1619.
[2] AHB: Corts 1626, fos. 471–4, const. no. 5.
[3] ACA: CA, leg. 373, Viceroy to King, 19 April 1625.

favourable to the rapid spread of banditry than they later became. But if, as the social and administrative structure of the country suggests, the preservation of order ultimately depended on the willingness of the aristocracy to co-operate with the royal administration, the key to the disorders of Philip III's reign should be found in a change of aristocratic attitude towards the central government.

However much their traditional ties of loyalty had been weakened during the sixteenth century, Catalan nobles could at least feel a healthy respect for the authority of a king who sent an army into Aragon in 1591 and who used his troops to besiege and destroy the castle of one of their number, Joan Cadell.[1] But Philip II's successor could not even command their respect. They had seen something of him and his advisers when they came to the Principality in 1599, and the letters of Catalans who visited the Court only served to confirm their first impressions.[2] Lerma's little application to the business of government was well enough known. So also was the corruption in high places. Don Pedro Franqueza, the adventurer who fell from power in 1607 as dramatically as he had risen to it, was, after all, a Catalan, and his career had been followed with interest. An ironic comment in Dr Pujades's diary for 1610 on the appointment of the youthful count of Lemos, Lerma's nephew, to the viceroyalty of Naples, shows that the Catalans had sized up pretty well the character of the new regime. 'Everyone is amazed that so young a man should be chosen for so important a post. It is true they say he is the wisest and the shrewdest man in Spain, but a powerful man is never foolish, nor a poor man wise. These are the consequences of the conjunction of the Lerma planet with the Spanish Leo.'[3]

The lowering of standards of government in Madrid naturally made itself felt in the government of the provinces. As the firm hand of Philip II was removed, there was an inevitable slackening of tension in their relationship with the Court, while viceregal administrations were

[1] See above, p. 52.

[2] E.g. Francesc Cosma Fivaller to Consellers of Barcelona, 14 July 1608 (AHB: CCO, 1608–11, fos. 40–41 v). Some of the letters written by Barcelona's agents at Court in these years are extremely scathing.

[3] Pujades, 2, fo. 227. Lemos in fact proved to be a very effective reforming viceroy (cf. Coniglio, *Il Viceregno di Napoli*, pp. 190–213).

left much more to themselves than they had been in the days of the old king. In some parts of the empire, Philip III's reign was an age of great proconsuls, like Osuna in Italy, because viceroys could now act with a freedom which had hitherto been denied them. But where there was no viceroy of proconsular abilities, as there was not in Catalonia during the first fifteen years of the reign, the new-found freedom of viceregal governments expressed itself in a sudden weakness. The government of Catalonia under Philip III's first viceroys fared very badly. It succeeded in antagonizing some of the most influential sections of Catalan society, while simultaneously revealing its inability to control the hostile forces it had managed to provoke. Much of this failure must be attributed to the character of the viceroys themselves, but behind it lay the deeper failure of the government in Madrid to provide its viceroys with the backing which alone could ensure, in a province like Catalonia, a continued respect for the power of the Crown.

Lerma's choice of viceroys during the first years of the reign was not inspired. It was believed in Madrid, not without justification, that Catalonia needed firm government, or, as Don Pedro Franqueza put it, 'for provinces as free as Catalonia, the proper medicine is severity'.[1] But if this accurately expressed the sentiments of Lerma and his colleagues, they did not behave as if they believed it. They replaced Philip II's last viceroy, the duke of Feria, a man of decided views and strong personality, with Joan Terés, the archbishop of Tarragona, whose viceroyalty from 1602 to 1603 was singularly unsuccessful. He was criticized by Franqueza for the weakness of his government.[2] None the less he managed to rouse the aristocracy to intense indignation by arresting a well-connected noble, Don Francesc Vilalba, for carrying a *pedrenyal* shorter than the statutory length. The Diputació, which had remained silent when a number of ordinary citizens were arrested for the same offence a few months earlier, was galvanized into action by this affront to the nobility, and claimed that the edict on *pedrenyals* was illegal—or that, if it was not, at least it did not apply to nobles.[3]

A viceroy who fell out with the aristocracy was likely to find himse l in serious trouble unless he could win the support of the towns, most of

[1] AGS: Cámara de Castilla, leg. 2796, Pieza 9 de Inquisición, fo. 351, Don Pedro Franqueza to Don Jaime Franqueza, 23 Dec. 1602.
[2] *Ibid.*
[3] ACA: CA, leg. 346, Archbishop of Tarragona to King, 5 Oct. and 9 Oct. 1602.

which had little love for the neighbouring gentry and would probably have been happy to see them deprived of their weapons. But the archbishop was not the man to gain their sympathy. His government was totally ineffectual in curbing the lawlessness that threatened the livelihood of the townspeople, and the fact that he was known to be a *nyerro*[1] suggests that he himself was involved in the terrible faction struggles that were tearing the land to pieces. The news of the termination of his viceroyalty was greeted with satisfaction: 'A letter has come from Court giving the viceroy leave to go and take a rest. God send us another who exercises more justice.'[2]

This pious hope was to be disappointed. The archbishop's successor was an engaging Neapolitan noble, the duke of Monteleón, a man with the best intentions but perhaps with too sophisticated a character to be really at home in Catalonia. He brought with him a cavalry company for operations against the bandits, and raised high hopes by personally going the rounds of Barcelona at night and arresting malefactors.[3] But, like every other viceroy, he found himself hampered by the lack of money in the treasury, and by the restrictions which the constitutions placed on the activities of royal officials.[4] It was true that both the Council of Aragon[5] and the city of Barcelona[6] spoke well of his government, but the frequent references to banditry in Dr Pujades's diary for these three years hardly suggest any very striking success. These were the years in which Roca Guinarda was most active, driving the king's ministers to fury and despair by his cheerfully provocative acts of defiance and his skill in evading capture. In January 1610, when Monteleón's viceroyalty was nearing its end, Dr Pujades wrote in his diary: 'The viceroy can do no more. The bandits laugh at him, and he has forfeited the respect of the *cavallers*, with whom he has failed to make friends.'[7]

A vigorous new viceroy was needed; one who could instil fear into the bandits, and win and keep the respect of the ruling class. On the recommendation of the Council of Aragon, the king appointed to the post a Castilian noble, Don Francisco Hurtado de Mendoza, marquis

[1] Pujades, I, fo. 165.
[2] *Ibid.* fo. 172, 19 June 1603.   [3] *Ibid.* fos. 181–181v, 31 July and 1 Aug. 1603.
[4] Reglà, *Els Virreis de Catalunya*, pp. 124–5.
[5] ACA: CA, leg. 267, no. 153, consulta, 27 Aug. 1609.
[6] Reglà, p. 124.   [7] Pujades, 2, fo. 206.

of Almazán.[1] Although Almazán had considerable experience of government, both in Milan and as a former viceroy of Valencia,[2] the appointment turned out to be extremely unfortunate. The marquis's departure for the Principality was delayed by illness for over a year, and the bishop of Tortosa was appointed interim viceroy—a post in which he distinguished himself only by issuing a large number of pardons to bandits. Almazán finally took up his duties at the beginning of September 1611, and very soon ran into trouble. It may be that his task was complicated by the magnanimous policies of his predecessor, as it was certainly complicated by the currency crisis which afflicted the Principality in these years.[3] In later years, he himself attributed his misfortunes to the mistakes of his predecessors: 'all the evils left in this province by my predecessors have fallen upon me'.[4] Whatever the truth of this, he did not make his task any easier by alienating the city government of Barcelona at an early stage in his career. Within six months of his appointment, the city was using all the influence it could command in Madrid to obtain his recall. In a letter to the king dated 12 March 1612, it complained that the Principality was swarming with bandits, and laid the blame on the viceroy for his negligence and for his willingness to let himself be governed by his wife and daughters.[5] It followed this up in the next few months with more complaints about Almazán himself, Almazán's wife, and the wretched state to which the province had been reduced, with ten different bandit gangs roaming at large. The viceroy was quite unfitted for government, being 'indolent by disposition, and, in addition, afflicted by an illness which his doctors pronounce incurable, and which causes him such continuous pain that he cannot attend to business'.[6]

Almazán indignantly rejected the charges, which he attributed to the self-interested motives of certain seditious persons in the city and Diputació, and justified himself by listing the punishments meted out by the Audiència during his first six months of office: hanged, drawn and quartered, 13; sentenced to the galleys, 25; tortured, 2; exiled, 37; whipped, 17—a grand total of 94, excluding many others sentenced to

[1] ACA: CA, leg. 267, no. 153, consulta, 8 Oct. 1609.
[2] Reglà, p. 126.   [3] See above, pp. 61–4.
[4] ACA: CA, leg. 355, Almazán to King, 25 Jan. 1614.
[5] Quoted in Carrera Pujal, *Historia de Cataluña*, vol. I, pp. 168–9.
[6] ACA: CA, leg. 485, petition from Barcelona, 30 Oct. 1612.

death by the *veguers* at the request of towns or barons.[1] In spite of this disclaimer, the king decided that the charges should be secretly investigated by Don José Pérez de Banyatos, who was at that moment conducting a *visita* of the royal officials in the Principality.[2] His report went a long way towards exonerating Almazán. According to Banyatos, the testimonies of both city and Diputació were unreliable, because each had come into conflict with the viceroy: the Diputats as the result of a quarrel between Almazán and Don Ramon d'Oms, the commander of the Catalan galleys, and the city because of a dispute over a point of precedence, involving the seating arrangements for Almazán's wife at a memorial service for the queen in Barcelona cathedral. All that could reasonably be said against the viceroy, in Banyatos's opinion, was that he had been somewhat remiss in despatching business because of illness which had confined him to bed.[3]

Banyatos's verdict may, or may not, have been more trustworthy than the original charges against Almazán, but in many ways it contrived to miss the real point. However well Almazán's character emerged from the investigation, certain facts were inescapable. He had succeeded in forfeiting the goodwill of the most influential people in Catalonia. He had antagonized the men who ran the city of Barcelona and the Diputació, and he had alienated the aristocracy as a class, thanks to a new pragmatic issued on 14 April 1612 forbidding the carrying of short *pedrenyals*.[4] Even more serious, he was a sick man. These were crippling disadvantages. Without some form of understanding between the viceroy and the Catalan authorities, there was little hope of bringing the bandits to heel; and a part-time viceroy was worse than useless.

Presumably reassured by Banyatos's report, Madrid left Almazán where he was. For three more years he ruled the country, ignored by city, Diputats and bandits alike. During these years, the Principality drifted into chaos, while Almazán protested to Madrid with such vigour against any slurs on his government that the Council of Aragon was forced to rebuke him for the 'indecent terms' in which he expressed himself in letters to His Majesty.[5] But even if Madrid was at last

[1] ACA: CA, leg. 396, Almazán to King, 7 April 1612.
[2] ACA: CA, leg. 269, no. 129, consulta, 20 Aug. 1612.
[3] ACA: CA, leg. 269, no. 129, Don Andreu Roig to King, 8 Oct. 1612.
[4] ACA: CA, leg. 362, Pragmatic; and see AHB: CCO, 1612–13, fo. 10, for the reaction of the nobles' confraternity of Sant Jordi in Girona.
[5] ACA: CA, leg. 356, Almazán to King, 9 Nov. 1613, and draft reply.

beginning to lose confidence in its viceroy, it was strangely slow in taking action. A successor to Almazán was chosen—the duke of Alburquerque, who announced himself ready to leave for Catalonia in April 1615.[1] But when Almazán finally died of his illness on 14 October 1615,[2] he was still viceroy of Catalonia, and Alburquerque had not yet started on his journey.

Alburquerque's delay no doubt has a personal explanation. Castilian grandees had a way of doing things in their own good time, and Alburquerque was the last man to allow himself to be hurried. But there was about Madrid's handling of the whole problem of banditry a lack of urgency, and almost an indifference, which seem all the more remarkable when it is considered how closely the vital interests of the Monarchy were involved. If Catalonia had been a remote and obscure corner of Spain, it might safely have been left to its own devices. But in fact it occupied a geographical position of paramount importance for the fortunes of the Monarchy. Not only did it represent Spain's first line of defence against a French attack, but it was also a vital staging-post on the route that linked Spain to its Italian possessions and thence to the heart of Europe. Along the road to Barcelona travelled the convoys of silver despatched by the king or his Italian bankers for shipment to Genoa. In 1603 a French traveller in Valencia passed one such convoy of thirty mules on its way to Barcelona, and noted with surprise that it had no military escort, 'so great is the respect they entertain for their king'.[3] The confidence shown here by the royal authorities was all the more surprising in view of a big silver robbery in Catalonia in 1587.[4] The dangers to the silver-route were fully confirmed when, on 8 January 1612, the notorious bandit Trucafort ambushed in the neighbourhood of Igualada a convoy from Zaragoza containing money belonging to 'the Genoese and other private persons', and made off with 16,000 *escudos*.[5] Although this incident made it perfectly clear that the road to Barcelona was no longer safe, the government in Madrid apparently took no action to prevent a recur-

[1] ACA: CA, leg. 269, no. 18, consulta, 24 April 1615.
[2] ACA: CA, leg. 270, no. 69, consulta, 29 Oct. 1615.
[3] 'Voyage de Barthélemy Joly en Espagne', ed. L. Barrau-Dihigo, *Revue Hispanique*, vol. xx (1909), p. 529.
[4] Reglà, *Felip II i Catalunya*, p. 117. See also Reglà, 'Los Envios de Metales Preciosos de España a Italia a través de la Corona de Aragón...', *Estudios de Historia Moderna*, vol. iv (1954), pp. 191–203.　　　　　　　　　　　　　[5] ACA: CA, leg. 396, Almazán to King, 14 Jan. 1612.

rence of the incident. Almost exactly a year later, in very much the same area, there occurred a similar but still more spectacular robbery, the story of which—as told by the Genoese commissioner accompanying the convoy[1]—throws a good deal of light on the mentality of bandits and populace, and on the problems of the royal authorities.

The convoy consisted of 108 cases of silver, part in bullion and part in silver *reales*, which were being sent to Italy, under royal protection and for purposes connected with the king's service, by one of his Genoese bankers, Niccolo Balbi. On 30 December 1613 the Genoese commissioner wrote to Balbi:

This is to bring you the worst news you have ever heard. Today, at one o'clock in the afternoon, the convoy was between the village of Hostalets and a place called Montmaneu (on the road from Lleida to Barcelona), guarded by more than eighty men from Cervera. Suddenly, more than a hundred bandits emerged from the mountains, each armed with four arquebuses and accompanied by horsemen. They looted the silver and the money, and only fifty-nine crates are left. The rest is missing; and of all the guard, not one man remained—they all fled, and the bandits forced open the boxes at their leisure. When I saw what was happening, I sent at once to Cervera, and more than two hundred men arrived, but not one of them would fight, in spite of my entreaties in the king's name. Many of them replied that they had children, and that His Majesty would not give them anything to eat if the bandits killed them. The bandits themselves carried off only ten or twelve crates, and all the rest were stolen by the local inhabitants whom we had called to our help. They were in league with the bandits, who said to them: 'Take as much money as you want, friends. Now's the time to make yourselves rich—this money belongs to the Genoese. And if you don't open those boxes, we'll break your heads open. If you can't carry off the silver bars, hide them—they'll come in useful in time.'...When I saw how these people were looting the money, I decided to go up to the bandits and speak to their captain, who is called Barbeta. So I went, and when I reached him, I threw myself down at his feet, begging him for God's sake not to allow them to carry off the bars. And he replied: 'It gives me more pleasure that these people should get rich on the wealth of the Genoese, than that I should carry off anything much for myself.'...You must know that all these people round here are great thieves—even the friars, and particularly two of the Order of Saint Bernard; and the women and children too, went and looted with the rest....

[1] AGS: Hacienda, leg. 528, two letters from Leandro Prebe to Niccolo Balbi, 30 Dec. 1613 and 1 Jan. 1614.

Barbeta, whose gang carried out this daring robbery, was an Italian, and he was finally caught in the Papal States in 1615, and sent back to Barcelona to be executed in the following year.[1] This very fact of his not being a native suggests that outsiders may have been tempted to try their luck by the prospects of easy money in a province lying athwart one of the main silver-routes of the king of Spain. If so, the success of the enterprise must have fully justified their hopes. The sum stolen was 180,000 ducats—sufficient to pay all the king's troops in Flanders for a month.[2] Since silver bars were not much use to villagers, some of the money was recovered, but the bulk of it disappeared for ever. The response of the authorities to this scandalous affair was tepid in the extreme. Balbi reported that the viceroy, Almazán, was ill, and displayed no great vigour in making investigations. Nor were the judges any more active, 'and it is believed that a large part of the stolen money is in Barcelona, in the hands of people who have good connections in the city and are treated with deference....'[3] The king agreed that a member of the Council of State should go to Barcelona, at Balbi's expense, to make inquiries, but there is no sign that Madrid took any further action.

If Madrid had hoped to see Catalonia destroy itself, the great robbery of December 1613 might have been expected to give it pause, and make it wonder whether the policy was worth the price. Yet in spite of the obvious implications of the robbery for Spain's vital interests, the government still did nothing.

The two most simple reasons that can be advanced to explain Madrid's passivity are also likely to be the most plausible. The first is the natural indolence of the duke of Lerma. One letter after another from Catalans in Madrid reported how impossible it was to persuade Lerma to attend to business or even to grant an interview. 'Here it is all a question of gaming, hunting and comedies, and no one will be bothered with anything.'[4] The second possible explanation of the government's inactivity is its shortage of money. The Crown had last gone bankrupt in 1607. Since then, the government had tottered from one fiscal crisis to another, living always from hand to mouth. The

[1] Reglà, *Felip II*, p. 119.
[2] AGS: Est., leg. 255, Juan Fernández de Heredia to King, 7 Jan. 1614.
[3] AGS: Hacienda, leg. 528, no. 14, consulta, 27 Jan. 1614.
[4] AHB: CCO, 1615–17, fo. 4, Fr Rafael Franc to Consellers, 10 Jan. 1615.

minimum expenses for 1614 were expected to be 6,280,000 ducats, and the maximum sum available would be 5,621,000 ducats.[1] The Council of Finance never knew where to turn to meet the expenses of the royal households or the cost of the fleet, and military operations in Catalonia would have entailed further heavy expenditure which the Crown's finances were simply not in a condition to bear. That such operations were in fact discussed and rejected on grounds of expense is made clear in a letter from Almazán to the king of October 1614, in which he mentions possible methods of crushing banditry, 'leaving aside the method of bringing cavalry and infantry from Castile, *which Your Majesty is not prepared to admit because of the expense in which it would involve the royal exchequer*'.[2]

The collapse of law and order in Catalonia is therefore intimately related to the failure of government at Madrid—a failure that was at once personal and financial. The king's ministers in Catalonia, their hands tied by the constitutions and by the emptiness of the treasury, had always in past crises been able to fall back on the government in Madrid for support. The authority of the Crown, the respect inspired by the power of Philip II, had at least acted as a restraint on the forces of disorder in the Principality during the later years of the sixteenth century. But now everything had changed. At a time when the government of Catalonia faced its severest challenge since the civil wars of the fifteenth century, the Crown itself was in no position to come to the help of its hard-pressed officials. This was not pure co-incidence. The rise of banditry in Catalonia was at least in some degree a natural response to the weakening of the king's grasp over the territories he ruled—a weakening that made itself apparent in the poor quality of his provincial ministers and in the complete passivity of the Court in face of constant provocation. In the final analysis, the break-down of government in the Catalonia of Philip III was only one more, neglected aspect of that general phenomenon so loosely described as 'the decline of Spain'.

[1] AGS: Hacienda, leg. 521, President of Consejo de Hacienda to King, 6 Dec. 1613.
[2] Reglà, *Els Virreis*, p. 126 (my italics).

CHAPTER V

THE RESTORATION OF GOVERNMENT
1616–21

By the spring of 1615 Catalonia's plight was terrible: worse, according to the Council of Aragon, than it had ever been before.[1] There seemed only one possible answer to the depredations of the bandit gangs: action by Madrid. The same was true, or believed to be true, of the acute shortage of small coins. At the end of January 1615 the *Consellers* of Barcelona drafted a letter to the duke of Lerma begging him to intercede with His Majesty:

...The dearth of coins is so serious that unless things are quickly put right by His Majesty, this city and the entire province will have reached the last extremity. It is spreading so fast that every day private and public commerce is dwindling, and the inhabitants of this city are unable to lay hands on ready cash to pay for their supplies of food. The shortage is so severe that we are afraid of some great revolution and disaster.[2]

The city of Barcelona, and indeed almost the entire Principality, had never been so anxious to see some striking assertion by the king of his regal authority as they were in the year 1615. Gone were the days when the Catalans were perpetually lamenting the interference of Madrid in their affairs. Now they were lamenting, even more bitterly, its non-interference. Father Franc, sent by Barcelona to negotiate on the currency question, was wringing his hands at Madrid over the attitude of the ministers: 'To get an interview with them one needs the patience of Job....This Court is a Cretan labyrinth....French and Italian affairs keep them so occupied that they will not discuss anything else....The duke refuses to do any business at Aranjuez....'[3] But the months passed, and still the duke did nothing. Coins were as scarce, and bandits as numerous, as ever. Finally, in September 1615, a week or two before the death of Almazán, the Diputació sent Carles de Calders on a

[1] ACA: CA, leg. 269, no. 18, consulta, 25 April 1615.

[2] AHB: Sótanos 1–12 (varios), draft letter of 24 Jan. 1615.

[3] AHB: CCO, 1615–17, fos. 7, 20, 54, 55. Letters from Fr Franc to Consellers of Barcelona, Jan. to May 1615.

special embassy to the Court, with secret instructions to represent to the king the afflictions of the province, and point out that the Principality was 'without hope of relief, unless it came from His Royal Majesty as King and Lord'.[1]

Castile never had a better chance than it had in 1615 to impose its will on Catalonia. The Principality was not only prepared to accept an intervention by Castilian troops; there was even reason to believe it would welcome it. This at least was the opinion of the bishop of Vic.

You must know [he wrote to Madrid] that the people of this Principality are heartily blaming the bishops for not getting together and requesting some remedy for these evils. They say that if the king sends troops and conquers them, they will all support him if he establishes justice in the manner of Castile, and removes the bad laws and customs which stand in its way.[2]

The fact that the bishop of Vic was a foreigner only recently arrived in the Principality, to some extent detracts from the value of his observation; his knowledge and understanding of the country may still have been superficial. But the events of the next year or two suggest that he was not greatly mistaken, and that the populace was willing to accept firm government at almost any price. Nor was there anything particularly surprising about this. The constitutions may have been sacrosanct in the eyes of some members of the ruling class, but the rest of the population can be forgiven if it felt less than enthusiastic about laws which gave unrestricted licence to nobles and gentry. If a choice had to be made between security and the constitutions, there was little doubt which the majority would choose.

A unique opportunity had therefore arisen for Madrid to castilianize Catalonia under the pretext of restoring order. Catalan historians, indeed, have implied that this had all along been the intention of the king's ministers. But it is hard to see what evidence there can be for this allegation. If the king's ministers means the Council of Aragon, then the charge is patently improbable. The regents of the Council of Aragon were none of them Castilians, and had no wish to see their homelands governed by the laws of Castile. Preoccupied with the problem of maintaining in the Crown of Aragon a government both acceptable and legitimate, they were careful to point out in their *con-*

[1] ACA: G, lib. 906–12, Lletres secretes 1605–74; instructions for Calders, 27 Sept. 1615.
[2] ACA: CA, leg. 358, Bishop of Vic to Vice-Chancellor, 1 May 1615.

8-2

sultas how important it was that the Aragonese, Catalans and Valencians should never be led to believe that, 'because the king of Aragon is king of Castile and other kingdoms, they might be deprived of one jot or tittle of what they would have had if he had been only king of Aragon'.[1] The king of all was essentially, for them, the king of each. If Catalonia was to be castilianized, the regents of the Council of Aragon were not the men to do it.

If, on the other hand, there was a conspiracy at a higher level, among Lerma and a few of his colleagues, to deprive the Crown of Aragon of its laws and liberties, they set about it very strangely. Ambassadors and representatives of the kingdoms of the Crown of Aragon were treated in the opening years of the new reign with a rare deference, and the Venetian ambassador reported in 1605 that 'Aragon, Valencia, Catalonia and Navarre put everything they have into preserving their many privileges', for which the times were clearly propitious.[2] It is difficult to believe that Lerma, himself a Valencian, had either the desire or the energy to set about altering the forms of government of the provinces of Spain. It was easier to let sleeping dogs lie. It must have been very irritating when some of them showed a distinct preference for getting up and barking.

By the summer of 1615 it was hard even for Lerma to go on ignoring the Catalan problem. But so far from seeing in the lawlessness of the Principality a perfect occasion for forcibly imposing on the Catalans the laws that governed Castile, he appeared to have no plans to meet the emergency, as he certainly had no money to implement them. It had been decided that Alburquerque should take with him to Catalonia two cavalry companies, to be paid for out of 12,000 ducats still owed by the Catalans from the subsidy voted in the Corts of 1599. These companies would patrol the plains, towns and roads, since it was believed that the bandits would not for long be able to hold out in the mountains because of shortage of supplies.[3] Some months after this decision had been taken, the ministers in Madrid were still bothered about how the Catalans might react to even this small contingent of foreign troops in their midst. The Catalan vice-chancellor of the Council of Aragon, Don Andreu Roig, assured the king that, while

[1] ACA: CA, leg. 267, no. 6, consulta, 26 March 1602.
[2] Barozzi e Berchet, *Relazioni*, 'Spagna', vol. I, p. 321.
[3] ACA: CA, leg. 269, no. 18, consulta, 25 April 1615.

this concern was justifiable in the light of what was generally known about the Catalan character,

in this instance there is no reason to fear their reaction, because the ordinary people, who suffer the most inconvenience from billeting troops, are so afflicted and anxious for redress, that not only will they show no resentment, but will be more than pleased, and give every possible assistance to the troops. We had experience of this in the time of the duke of Maqueda [viceroy from 1592 to 1596].

The real problem, according to Roig, was not the popular reaction but the question of pay. The gentry and 'powerful people' held the purse-strings, and it was they who encouraged the bandits, 'so as to maintain their own particular faction, and perhaps for other, worse, reasons'.[1]

While Madrid was debating the ethical, and financial, problems involved in sending two cavalry companies to Catalonia, the poor bishop of Vic was wringing his hands in despair.

Many young men are waiting to see how the new viceroy makes his entry [he wrote to Roig], and if he does not strike fear into their hearts on arrival, they will all become bandits, and their number will rapidly increase throughout the land. Among them are many heretics from France who go round disseminating their errors, and we are afraid that a new sect will arise, and rebellion follow in its wake. If you think this exaggerated, remember the beginnings of Mahomet and Tamburlane, of the Turks and many others....[2]

With his province on the brink of heresy and revolution, Almazán died on 14 October 1615. On hearing the news, the Council of Aragon insisted that his successor, Alburquerque, should leave for Catalonia at once,[3] but it was not until March 1616 that the new viceroy finally set foot on Catalan soil. Revolution or no, he would come at his own convenience. When he arrived, he took a roundabout route. Having taken the oath in Lleida on 15 March 1616, he went not to Barcelona but Tortosa, where he arrived on 17 March, and at once took the most vigorous measures to stamp out banditry and crime. The young men who were carefully watching the new viceroy before deciding on their future careers did not have to wait long before making up their minds. Alburquerque was no Almazán.

[1] ACA: CA, leg. 269, no. 18, Don Andreu Roig to King, 26 July 1615.
[2] ACA: CA, leg. 358, Bishop of Vic to Roig, 30 Sept. 1615.
[3] ACA: CA, leg. 270, no. 69, consulta, 29 Oct. 1615.

The new viceroy knew what he wanted, and he knew how to set about it. 'When I arrive at Barcelona', he wrote to the king on 8 April 1616, 'I shall put the entire Principality in the galleys.... And as regards the *fueros* and constitutions of this Principality Your Majesty must please not be surprised if I trample on some of them which stand in the way of the administration of justice.'[1] With these words, Alburquerque openly avowed what had long been obvious: that banditry could only be suppressed by means that were strictly 'unconstitutional'.[2]

Alburquerque's determination to disregard those constitutions which hampered his work of pacification, posed a problem which had always been implicit in the relationship between the Principality and the Court. The king had taken an oath to observe and uphold the constitutions. It was also his duty as king to see that his Catalan subjects were properly governed. What happened when, as in 1615, his obligation to uphold the constitutions conflicted with his obligation to govern? Was the Principality to be allowed to suffer ruin and desolation because of conscientious scruples about the letter of the law? Alburquerque at least had no hesitation as to where the king's duty lay. But his determination to disregard the constitutions for the sake of restoring justice and government, contained implications for the Catalans which he may not have appreciated. Their entire relationship with the king was legal and contractual. If their laws were even temporarily to be set aside on the plea of 'necessity', this radically changed the whole character of the relationship. It also set a dangerous precedent. 'Necessity' could be interpreted in many different ways, especially if the interpretation rested with the king. If he had once set aside the constitutions on the grounds of necessity, there was nothing to stop him from doing the same thing again. Although the Crown's rights were much more strictly limited in the Catalonia of Philip III and Philip IV than in the England of James I and Charles I, the question of the king's emergency powers, although not specifically formulated in Spain until the reign of Philip IV, was as crucial for the Catalans as it was to be for the English. In both countries the restrictions on royal authority which

[1] Soler y Terol, *Roca Guinarda*, pp. 422–3.

[2] Alburquerque was later to be accused of saying to an embassy from the Diputació, 'I shall observe such constitutions as I see fit, and not the others'. He vigorously denied ever having spoken these words (Soler y Terol, p. 437). Whether he really did or did not, is not of very great importance, since he certainly acted in the spirit of his alleged remark.

had been received from an earlier age, prevented the Crown in a very different age from doing certain things that it considered administratively essential. In one country as in the other, to allow the king special powers on the grounds of an alleged emergency would be to open the door to a whole succession of illegalities, and the end of it all might be arbitrary government.

This problem of 'necessity' versus 'legality', which had given Philip II such trouble in the Netherlands, was to be at the heart of all the struggles between Catalonia and the Court of Spain from 1615 to 1640. As soon as the Crown tried to increase its authority over the Principality, either—as in 1615—for the benefit of the Catalans themselves, or—as under Olivares—for that of Castile, the problem became inescapable. Catalan historiography might lead one to suppose that the king was always in the wrong. Technically this is no doubt correct, since almost any assertion of royal authority in Catalonia involved the violation of some law. But 'legality' can as easily degenerate into mere legal forms, as 'necessity' can degenerate into a convenient pretext for the imposition of absolutism. It was easy for historians who had studied the constitutions of Catalonia at the time of the Principality's medieval grandeur to forget that conditions change; that every law is open to abuse, and that a constitutional system designed successfully to protect the Catalans from the arbitrary rule of the king, might none the less deliver them up to the arbitrary rule of one dominant group among their own compatriots.

Catalonia's sorry state in 1615 suggests that something had gone radically wrong. The Principality's vaunted liberties, so far from being a guarantee of political freedom and social order, had become an invitation to licence. When a noble could commit a savage crime and escape justice on a plea of aristocratic immunity, it is difficult not to sympathize with Alburquerque's irreverent attitude to the constitutions. In this lies the interest, and the tragedy, of the seventeenth-century conflict between Castilian and Catalan. This conflict arose out of the divergence between the ideal Catalonia and the Catalan reality, between the imaginary and the actual relationship of the Catalans and their king, between the medieval laws of Catalonia and the stark modern needs of Castile. The king would allege necessity; the Catalans would cling to legality. Extremists on both sides would go beyond the bounds of common sense or reason, but in the middle stood a body of opinion genuinely puzzled by the problem of reconciling the stipulations of the law with the demands of government, and unable to find a way of escape from the dilemma. As the years passed, the very pressure of events would help to drive the moderates into the arms of the extremists; but the issue was not yet prejudiced when, in March 1616, the duke of Alburquerque set foot in the Principality and issued his declaration of war against the more obnoxious of Catalonia's laws.

Alburquerque's whole approach to the task of government promised a head-on conflict with the Diputació. The Diputats at any time would have been compelled by the terms of their office to protest vigorously against the violation of the laws, but at this moment they had a strong personal interest in hampering Alburquerque's work. 'The Neptune and guiding-star in this sea of the Diputació'[1] was none other than the irrepressible Don Alexandre d'Alentorn, who had the good fortune to be drawn as Diputat Militar for the triennial period 1614–17. The Alentorn family, for one reason or another, had for long been at odds with the royal administration,[2] and Don Alexandre, described in later life by Dr Pujades as 'a man who is always violent',[3] vigorously maintained the family tradition. His bandit activities were notorious. A *nyerro*, and friend of Roca Guinarda,[4] he later made common cause with a bandit known as the Sastre Domingo, and clashed violently with Don Alexos de Marimón, the Governador of Catalonia, who was probably a *cadell*.[5] If he did harbour a grudge against individual ministers, or against the royal administration in general, his position in the Diputació gave him the perfect platform from which to conduct his campaign. He obviously made the most of his opportunities. 'The wiles of Don Alexandre Lentorn are terrible,' reported Alburquerque, 'and he is determined to oppose everything connected with the royal service.'[6]

The complete silence of the documents about Alentorn's real intentions and ambitions is most disappointing. Was he simply waging a

---

[1] ACA: CA, leg. 358, Alburquerque to Vice-Chancellor, 27 Sept. 1616.
[2] See above, pp. 70–1, and 92, n. 3.
[3] Pujades, 3, fo. 20v, 15 April 1621. Don Alexandre died in the early 1620's.
[4] Soler y Terol, p. 258.
[5] ACA: CA, leg. 493, petition of Alentorn (1619).
[6] ACA: CA, leg. 357, Alburquerque to the Protonotario, Don Francisco Gassol, 17 Sept. 1616.

private vendetta against the royal officials, or was he the leader of some wider movement against a government taking its orders from Madrid? The vice-chancellor, in his note to the king of July 1615, had referred to a group of powerful Catalans keeping their hands tightly on the purse-strings of the Diputació, 'so as to maintain their own particular faction, *and perhaps for other, worse, reasons*'.[1] Could those 'worse reasons' possibly imply a conspiracy aiming at some sort of autonomy for the Catalans? If so, the inertia of Madrid becomes all the more puzzling. On the whole, it might be wiser to look upon Alentorn as the leader of a *Fronde* of discontented nobles, possibly with no very specific aims, but strongly appealing to the many members of the ruling class who had no wish to see any increase in the powers of the Crown. Among these must be numbered several royal officials, un-accustomed after the laxity of Almazán's government to receiving orders from the viceroy which they were expected to obey.

The truth is, as I have come to realize [wrote Alburquerque], that Diputados, Canciller, Regente and all the rest here, do not want to accept any orders from the Court, and are unwilling to recognize that there is a King, a Vice-Chancellor, Regents [of the Council of Aragon], a Protonotario, a chancery or anything else superior to them. And by God, there has to be more of this in my time than there has ever been before; but I am gradually disillusioning them whenever they come to protest.[2]

If Alburquerque was faced with the sullen resistance of an 'anti-Court' party, he could at least draw comfort from the knowledge that a large number of people were all too glad to see that something was at last being done about the general lawlessness.

The latest news we have here [wrote a citizen of Vic, then in Tarragona, to the councillors of his home town] is that the viceroy is acting with the utmost severity. He has pulled down several houses in Tortosa, and extracted from all the churches those who had taken asylum there—thanks to a special papal bull. May the Lord enable him to govern as well as we need. No privileges or exemptions of familiars of the Holy Office, or anybody else, are sufficient to make him hold his hand, and he has sent many inhabitants of Tortosa in chains to Barcelona.[3]

Alburquerque's methods were straightforward and ruthless. Having meted out summary punishment to the criminal inhabitants of Tortosa,

[1] See above, p. 117.   [2] Alburquerque to Gassol, 17 Sept. 1616.
[3] AMV: CR, 8, Bernat Costa to Consellers of Vic, 8 April 1616.

he went on by sea to Barcelona, and from there proclaimed a *sometent general*, or general hue and cry, throughout the Principality. At the same time, the Governador and the *jutges de cort* were sent to bandit-infested regions to take charge of operations.[1] By the seventeenth day of the *sometent*, large numbers of bandits had been brought to Barcelona, dead and alive, in spite of the fact that the two cavalry companies (which were anyhow undermanned and badly equipped) had not yet arrived in the Principality.[2] This success seems to have been achieved by the simple expedient of setting a bandit to catch a bandit. A drive was first begun against the *cadells*, in which the *nyerros* presumably co-operated with enthusiasm, only to discover when the work was done that they were the next victims on the list. These drives were followed up by the razing of castles and houses belonging to those who had befriended the bandits.[3] Practised on a large scale, this was something of a novelty to the Catalans, because it ran directly counter to their constitutions which forbade royal officials to touch a man's property. But the illegality of his proceedings did not worry Alburquerque. 'Experience has shown', he wrote later, 'that in Catalonia the execution of delinquents has ceased to act as a warning, while the destruction of the house of anyone who assists them has the most salutary effects; and the viceroy who cannot make use of this device commands no respect and cannot maintain his authority.'[4]

The ruthless trampling on privileges and immunities showed startlingly quick results. Frightened of what lay in store for them, several bandit nobles, like Don Bernardino de Marimón, the Governador's cousin, hastily withdrew across the frontier into France.[5] Within six months of assuming office, Alburquerque was able to inform the towns of the success of his campaign against the bandits. Peace once again reigned through the Principality,[6] and to ensure its continuation, he persuaded the towns to billet the cavalry which had at last arrived from Castile.[7] This does not seem to have caused him any difficulty. The

---

[1] Soler y Terol, pp. 423–6.   [2] *Ibid.*

[3] The Court chronicler, Gil González Dávila, states that Alburquerque razed three castles and 150 fortified houses. *Historia de la vida y hechos del Inclito Monarca...D. Felipe Tercero* (Madrid, 1771), p. 193.

[4] ACA: CA, leg. 357, Alburquerque to Don Francisco Gassol, 24 Feb. 1618.

[5] ACA: CA, leg. 378, Alburquerque to King, 3 Feb. 1628.

[6] AMV: CR, 8, Alburquerque to Consellers of Vic, 30 Aug. 1616.

[7] *Ibid.* 28 Nov. 1616.

towns had suffered severely from the decline of trade and business in the last few years, and the billeting of a few troops was a small price to pay for a return to normal conditions. Throughout his viceroyalty, Alburquerque could count on the support of the bourgeoisie. It was this support which enabled him to achieve success against the bandits within so short a time, and, in their gratitude to him, they never questioned his use of methods which flagrantly violated the constitutions.

The restoration of order was followed by a gradual recovery of the coinage,[1] and it was in a more hopeful atmosphere that a Jubilee, specially authorized by Pope Paul V, was celebrated in the Principality for two weeks in December 1617. Its purpose was to mark the end of the feuds between *nyerros* and *cadells*, and the removal from Catalonia of the scourge of banditry.[2] In both respects it was more than a little premature. But this was a moment of triumph, and there was widespread contentment. It was not, however, universal. There was muttering behind the scenes among those who had suffered from the viceroy's high-handed actions and those who were disturbed at the way in which the constitutions had been disregarded. Early in the new year, the Diputats lodged a protest at the Court about certain illegal actions of the viceroy, which included the destruction of houses, the depriving of Don Berenguer d'Oms, a distinguished Catalan noble, of his sword and shield, and the publication in its original Castilian of a pragmatic issued by the Council of State. Alburquerque had always expected protests from the Diputats about the destruction of houses, and pleaded necessity.[3] The plea was accepted by the king, although the viceroy was told to take care. But he was very sharply reprimanded by Madrid on the other two charges. The king's letter made it clear that if he was prepared to countenance the disregard of the constitutions at the height of the emergency, this was now no longer justified:

[1] There is some account of the monetary crisis in Carrera Pujal, *Historia...de Cataluña*, vol. II, pp. 36–96, but the actual means and the stages by which the currency recovered are extremely obscure, and the whole subject clearly needs much more study. Father Franc finally obtained from the Court in September 1617 the long-sought permission to devalue, but (p. 93) Barcelona did not in fact take advantage of this permission, and Catalan silver *reals* continued to be minted at 72 to the mark, instead of the 76 reluctantly authorized by Madrid. This suggests that the monetary crisis was only ephemeral, and the stability of Catalan prices from 1617–40 certainly indicates a more favourable financial position than that of Castile, where prices oscillated violently.

[2] N. Feliu de la Peña, *Anales de Cataluña* (Barcelona, 1709), vol. III, p. 235.

[3] ACA: CA, leg. 357, Alburquerque to Gassol, 24 Feb. 1618.

I have decided that, from now onwards, you should take care to see that the constitutions are observed. I charge you with this, and you are to pass on these orders to the royal officials. And from now on, you are to respect the privileges of the *militares*, allowing them to carry their customary swords and shields....[1]

So much for the belief that Alburquerque had been sent to Catalonia to subvert its laws and abolish its liberties.

In ordinary times, the publication of a pragmatic in Castilian instead of Catalan would have aroused the bitterest resentment and forfeited for the viceroy any popularity he enjoyed in the Principality. But in 1618 it hardly rippled the surface. The country seems to have felt deep gratitude for what Alburquerque had achieved, and a mutual warmth and sympathy had entered into the relations between Alburquerque and the Catalans such as can be found in the annals of no other viceroyalty of the time. The man who had arrived in Catalonia breathing fire and slaughter, and had condemned out of hand the entire royal administration, had nothing but praises to bestow when his term of office ended in March 1619.

Whatever I may deserve of Your Majesty [he wrote], give most of it to the Catalans, for they are very great vassals of Your Majesty, and they have placed me under an obligation to Your Majesty, with all humility, to favour them in every possible way—and especially all the judges of the Audiència, whose great services and qualities are most deserving of reward.[2]

The extraordinary warmth of this tribute to the Catalans is matched only by a corresponding tribute to the qualities of the viceroy in the official records of the city of Barcelona: he 'has conducted the government in the most excellent and saintly manner, to the great pleasure and contentment of this city and of all the Principality'[3]—and this of a viceroy who had infringed more constitutions than any other in the nation's history.

The glowing testimonials which speeded Alburquerque on his way should not be allowed to hide the fact that in some respects his achievement was very limited. He had restored order, but he had not wiped out banditry. Not long after his departure, the bandits were once again

---

[1] ACA: CA, leg. 493, King to Alburquerque, 10 March 1618.

[2] ACA: CA, leg. 362, Alburquerque to King, 16 March 1619.

[3] *Dietari del Antich Consell Barceloní...*, ed. F. Schwartz and F. Carreras y Candi (Barcelona, 1892–1922), vol. IX, p. 413.

stealing out of their hiding-places, and for many years to come, when the long winter nights drew in, bandits like Margarit del Pont and the famous Serrallonga would be a source of terror to the peasant in his cottage and the traveller on the roads. Nothing could have prevented this. The roots of banditry were deeply embedded in social and economic discontents, and no repressive measures could eliminate a lawlessness that sprang from overpopulation and rural unemployment. But one thing Alburquerque had achieved. Catalan banditry after his viceroyalty was very different in character from the banditry of the preceding years. The Principality had been brought to the verge of destruction in 1615 by lawlessness that was both popular and aristocratic. Alburquerque's greatest achievement was to frighten the nobles and gentry into withdrawing their support from the bandit gangs. This was a lasting achievement. A Junta of ministers in 1626 said that 'the bandits who roam at large today are the most inferior people, and enjoy no support from the *caballeros* of the province',[1] and the duke of Cardona reached a similar conclusion ten years later.[2]

While Alburquerque deserves much of the credit for this decline in the lawless habits of the aristocracy, it probably owes something also to the changing pattern of life of the Catalan nobility. The old grievances remained: the dearth of offices and honours, the absence of employment outside the Principality for younger sons. But all the while, those noble families which had taken up their residence in the towns were assuming more and more of the characteristics of the urban patriciate. However much the merchants in the towns originally distrusted the nobles, and however much the nobles despised the merchants, both sides began to find that their interests outweighed their differences. Nobles wanted to play a part in civic life commensurate with their social status; leading citizens, forming themselves into a tight little oligarchy, began to realize that they needed the personal and the financial support of the nobles in their midst. Most towns were short of money, and the nobles who lived in them refused to pay any dues as long as they had no part in the government. Girona opened the doors of its government to the resident nobility in 1601.[3] The next year Perpinyà followed suit, on the grounds that it saw no hope of escape

[1] ACA: CA, leg. 260, no. 2, Junta of ministers, 23 Feb. 1626.
[2] ACA: CA, leg. 390, Cardona to Protonotario, 15 March 1637.
[3] ACA: CA, leg. 347, paper on government of Girona, c. 1605.

from its financial troubles 'as long as this division persists between the town and the *militars*, who have no part in the government although they own almost all the property of any importance'.[1] By 1621, when the nobles resident in Barcelona were finally accepted for civic office, *militars* had obtained entry into the government of most towns in the Principality.[2] This gave them something to occupy their time and attention, while the ceremonial attendant upon the public appearances of municipal dignitaries helped to make up for the decline in the natural authority which they held to be theirs of right. Slowly, a feudal aristocracy was being transformed into an urban aristocracy, absorbed in the ceremonial functions and the petty intrigues which added a little spice to the comfortable routine of urban life.

If some of the urban nobles were not yet fully resigned to this new mode of life, Alburquerque's brusque measures acted as a salutary warning both to them and to their rural colleagues. It was very expensive to rebuild a house or a castle pulled down on the viceroy's orders, and it was perhaps better to forfeit the pleasure of entertaining bandits than to have no ancestral home in which to be able to do so. Nor can many nobles have wanted to join Don Bernardino de Marimón and his friends—or enemies—in France; a quiet life at home was to be preferred to a compulsory holiday abroad. Quietly, then, the aristocracy, except in the remoter mountain regions, ceased to consort with bandits and began to adjust itself to less violent pursuits. Now and again a group of young nobles would brawl in the streets of Lleida or Girona, and below the surface the feuds of *nyerros* and *cadells* still smouldered, but the aristocracy as a whole managed to turn its back on the past with surprising speed. The younger generation, more easily acclimatized, was to show itself one degree more sophisticated than its fathers. When, twenty years later, a group of discontented nobles again appeared on the centre of the stage, they would be found in the guise not of bandits but of national heroes.

The taming of the aristocracy represented the triumph of the towns. Alburquerque's victory was as much their victory as a victory for the royal administration, and without their loyalty to the viceroy it could

[1] ACA: CA, leg. 347, Feria to King, 15 March 1602.
[2] ACA: CA, leg. 364, Alcalá to King, 17 Oct. 1620. Tarragona is an exception to this, perhaps because the gentry living in Tarragona were few and unimportant. (I owe this information to Don Josep M.ª Recasens i Comes of Tarragona.)

not have been won. Leading citizens, the more responsible nobles, wealthy bourgeois with valuable rural estates, the prosperous peasant proprietors of eastern Catalonia—these were the people who stood to lose most from unstable conditions, and who saw in Alburquerque the belated answer to their prayers. It was he who represented their real interests, not a Diputació dominated by Alentorn and his friends.

There were considerable possibilities in this alliance forged by Alburquerque between these people and the Crown. If properly exploited by Madrid, it might have paved the way for a new, and happier, chapter in the relations between Catalonia and Castile; and at the very least it provided the Crown with a natural bulwark against the forces of the old order—with their *fueros*, their liberties and their privileges—which represented a permanent threat to the king's precarious hold over Catalonia. But instead of being skilfully exploited, such opportunities as existed were to be almost callously thrown away. Here were people who were prepared to pay almost any price so long as order and security were guaranteed. Yet, within little more than twenty years, those same people who, in Alburquerque's time, had applauded the successes won by the Crown at the expense of their country's traditional laws and liberties, were prepared to countenance—however unenthusiastically—a revolution in defence of those very laws. Much of the history of Catalonia between 1619 and 1640 is the history of how this happened: of the disenchantment of the Catalan bourgeoisie—a disenchantment that was already well under way within three years of Alburquerque's departure from the Principality.

If any single man could be held responsible for the disenchantment, it was Alburquerque's successor, Don Fernando Afán de Ribera y Enríquez, duke of Alcalá. An Andalusian aristocrat of great erudition,[1] Alcalá seems to have been entirely devoid of those sympathetic qualities which succeeded in endearing his predecessor to the Catalans. It soon became clear that his learning was greater than his tact. This was particularly unfortunate since his task was much more delicate than

[1] Diego Ortiz de Zúñiga (*Anales...de Sevilla*, Madrid, 1677, p. 665) describes him as an amateur painter, a patron of the arts, and a Latin scholar who devoted his spare time to the investigation of Castilian antiquities. He built up a fine library in his palace at Seville. See also José López de Toro and José Serrano Calderó, 'El libro de las sentencias del duque de Alcalá', *Archivo Hispalense*, no. 63 (1954), pp. 35–64.

Alburquerque's. Where Alburquerque had simply had to stamp out disorder, his successor had to heal the wounds of a bruised and battered country. This healing task needed great gifts of sympathy. The Catalans had been hurt in their self-esteem. They knew that, as a result of the long years of anarchy, their standing at Court was very low;[1] and many of them, while intensely relieved at Alburquerque's success, can hardly fail to have been disturbed by the unconstitutional methods which produced it. The kind of dilemma with which they had been faced can be appreciated from the comments of the lawyer, Dr Fontanella, on Alburquerque's government and his destruction of castles. 'It cannot be denied', he wrote, 'that these proceedings were contrary to the constitutions', but none the less they were held by some people to be justified by the cruelty of the criminals and the terrible state to which the Principality had been reduced. 'But we, who regard these proceedings as repugnant to our liberties and constitutions, cannot praise or approve them.'[2] Yet Fontanella knew as well as anyone what would have happened if Alburquerque had not acted as he did.

Alcalá was not the man to understand the uneasiness of those who felt that in some way they had betrayed their heritage by allowing Alburquerque to disregard their ancient constitutions. Ignoring the instructions given to his predecessor in 1618 that henceforth the constitutions should be respected, he continued the various practices employed by Alburquerque at the time when banditry was at its height. He antagonized the nobility by enforcing the pragmatic on *pedrenyals*, which had been allowed to lapse, and by forbidding the carrying of certain types of swords and daggers;[3] and he continued the destruction of castles, sometimes, as in the case of Antoni de Vilaplana's castle, on the strength of flimsy evidence.

From the standpoint of efficient government, there was justification for many of the viceroy's actions. He had very great successes against the remaining bandits, and he often earned hatred and resentment for measures that were in the Principality's best interests. This was particularly true of his clashes with the Diputació, the fiercest of which

[1] AHB: CCO, 1614, fo. 160, Fr Franc to Consellers, 29 Nov. 1614.
[2] *De Pactis Nuptialibus*, clausula VI, glosa II, pars 2, §16.
[3] ACA: CA, leg. 493, memorial against the government of Alcalá presented by the ambassador of the Diputació, 22 May 1620.

was provoked by a controversy over the small fleet of galleys which had been authorized in the Corts of 1599 for keeping the coast clear of pirates. Although Alcalá naturally put the worst possible construction on the behaviour of the Diputats, their attitude since the granting of this authorization goes a considerable way towards confirming his view that the Diputació was rotten to the core. The permission to build a minimum of four galleys had been greeted with immense enthusiasm by the Catalans, who saw in it the chance to revive their ancient prowess on the seas. The Corts voted what seemed ample provision for the construction and maintenance of the galleys. By increasing certain taxes paid to the Generalitat, 87,000 *lliures* a year would be raised annually for the purchase of the galleys and for their maintenance at the annual rate of 15,000 *lliures* a galley.[1] But, in the end, no more than two galleys were built, and their maintenance was a public scandal. The soldiers supposed to man them were never paid; the galley-slaves, fed only on biscuit, were dying of hunger. It was common knowledge that the dues intended for their upkeep were finding their way into the pockets of the Diputats and their friends, and that their collection was attended by the grossest frauds. In the three years' experience of one assessor of the Diputació, the French cloths that entered Barcelona for re-export to Valencia and other parts were never once registered at the customs house; and the extent of the fraud practised in connection with the tax levied on these cloths, known as the *bolla de Barcelona*, is suggested by the willingness of Don Francesc Reguer to pay the Diputats 10,000 *escuts* a year more than the highest official figure reached in recent years, for the privilege of administering it.[2] Thus ill-equipped and ill-administered, the galleys were not fit to put to sea, and Alcalá very properly refused to authorize their use for commercial purposes by the Barcelona merchants. The eventual fate of the vessels completely justified his attitude, but it won him no love among the Diputats, who insisted that jurisdiction over the galleys belonged to them.

Alcalá's troubles with the Diputació suggest something of the difficulties which faced anyone who had to govern Catalonia, and can hardly fail to inspire considerable sympathy even for viceroys as un-

[1] *Constitutions fetes...1599*, cap. 63.
[2] ACA: CA, leg. 364, Alcalá to King, 1 Aug. 1620.

sympathetic as this one. There was no ignoring the Diputació. Its role
was crucial in the life of seventeenth-century Catalonia, and its power,
its resources, and its functions were among the principal causes of the
distrust and dislike with which the government in Madrid viewed the
Principality. Although any institution whose main purpose was to
protect the Principality's ancient laws from any infringement by royal
officials could not be expected to endear itself to the Spanish Court, the
reasons for Madrid's hostility went deeper than this.

The Diputació is customarily treated in Catalan historiography as a
well-nigh perfect institution, the unchanging symbol of an unchanging
Catalonia. The excellence of its purpose may be readily admitted, but
this hardly precludes the necessity of studying how this purpose was
being fulfilled at a given moment. With the Diputació, as with any
institution, one needs to know who it really represented, and how it
really used its powers and resources.

The method by which the three Diputats and the three Oidors were
selected for office appears on the surface as a perfect example of the
strictest impartiality. Every third year, on 22 July, six names were
drawn at random by a small boy from a silver basin, and those fortunate
enough to be drawn formed the Diputació for the next three years.
With two clerics, two *militars* and two members of the *braç reial* com-
posing the Diputació, all three traditional classes in Catalan society
enjoyed equal representation, and the various divergent interests in the
Principality were considered to be properly balanced.

The way in which names were drawn from the silver basin is well
enough known, but it has not generally been appreciated how the
names found their way into the basin in the first place. In reality, the
ceremony of 22 July was only the last stage of a long and exciting
process. Although it was luck alone which determined the outcome
of the final lottery, a good deal more than luck was required to qualify
for the draw. The Principality's total population was something in the
neighbourhood of 400,000; those eligible for the triennial lottery numbered 524. The 524 places had been allotted on a geographical basis, as
agreed by successive Corts over the course of the sixteenth century.
Eligibility for participation in the draw was determined by the following distribution shown on pp. 131–2.[1]

[1] ACA: G, 78/4, *Llibre de Habilitacions.*

Ecclesiastics

For place of Diputat Eclesiàstic		For place of Oidor Eclesiàstic		Total
Bishops (all except Solsona)	8			8
Religious houses	11	Religious houses	12	23
Canons:		Canons:		
Tarragona	2	Tarragona	3	5
Barcelona	2	Barcelona	3	5
Lleida	1	Lleida	3	4
Girona	1	Girona	3	4
Tortosa	2	Tortosa	3	5
Urgell	1	Urgell	3	4
Vic	1	Vic	3	4
Elna	1	Elna	3	4
	30	Total	36	66

Militars

Vegueries of	For place of Diputat Militar	For place of Oidor Militar	Total
Barcelona	42	34	76
Lleida	12	4	16
Girona	17	15	32
Tortosa	2	—	2
Perpinyà	10	6	16
Tarragona	2	5	7
Cervera	12	23	35
Vic	6	7	13
Manresa	4	—	4
Puigcerdà	1	2	3
Vilafranca del Penedès	6	5	11
Montblanc	4	3	7
Balaguer	4	3	7
Tàrrega	7	2	9
Urgell	6	3	9
Camprodon	2	1	3
	137	113	250

Braç Reial

Town	For place of Diputat Reial	For place of Oidor Reial	Total
Barcelona	39	46	85
Lleida	6	11	17
Girona	10	20	30
Perpinyà	22	21	43
Tortosa	12	11	23
Vic	—	2	2
Puigcerdà	—	2	2
Cervera	—	2	2
Besalú	—	1	1
Torroella	—	1	1
Manresa	—	1	1
Balaguer	—	1	1
	89	119	208

Certain aspects of this distribution deserve attention. There were only sixty-six competitors for the two places available for clerics, who included not a single parish priest, as against 250 *militars* (about a third of the aristocracy) also competing for two places. Canons, except for the canons of Solsona cathedral which was not represented, had the best chance of any group in the Principality of becoming a Diputat or an Oidor: something which must materially have increased the desirability of acquiring a canonry. But the most curious anomalies were reserved for the towns. Some large, or growing, towns like Mataró, Vilafranca and Tarragona were entirely unrepresented, while others had what might be considered an excessive number of places. Barcelona in particular possessed unique advantages, although this was perhaps no more than its due. With five ecclesiastical places, seventy-six for *militars* and eighty-five for the *braç reial* allotted to it, it had excellent chances of being represented in the Diputació, and there were only two or three occasions between 1599 and 1640 when it was not.

With only 524 names eligible for the triennial draw, there was keen competition to join the band of the elect. This was achieved not by merit but by influence. An ordinary citizen of Girona, for instance, could not expect to be considered for one of the ten places reserved to his native town on the list of the Diputat Reial. 'As it is only just and reasonable that those who do the work and bear the municipal burdens should be preferred before other citizens in the distribution of honours and benefices', the vacancy could be filled only by a distinguished citizen—a *ciutadà honrat*.[1] Candidates, in fact, must come from the top drawer of the municipal oligarchy. Even here, though, the choice was not necessarily made on merit. Every year it fell to the current Diputats and Oidors to fill any vacancies in the list of the 524 names, caused either by death or by transference. To do this, they wrote, a month before making their choice, to the relevant towns and cathedral chapters, requesting a list of suitable names. Once they had the list, they could choose as they pleased. The final selection was the fruit of intensive bargaining, for all six men would have commitments to friends and relations. There were occasions on which disagreement over the filling of vacancies completely wrecked the unity of the Diputació, as in the period 1620–3 when, in spite of a signed agreement on the allocation of places, the Diputats fell out seriously among themselves. Ramon de Calders, the Oidor Militar, was accused by his colleagues of breaking the agreement. In 1622 he had managed to squeeze quite a number of his relations into vacancies: Don Ambrós Gallart i Calders for Diputat Militar for Lleida; Jeroni de Calders (brother), the same for Cervera; Lluís Joan de Calders for Diputat Militar for Barcelona, and Fra Josep de Calders (brother) for Oidor Eclesiàstic.[2] This might have seemed a good haul, but Calders was rash enough to demand for a friend a vacancy in the gift of one of his colleagues—and, in so doing, split the Diputació into two armed camps.[3]

The dissensions among Calders and his colleagues, though unusually violent, show something of the intensity that surrounded everything connected with places in the Diputació. 'All the affairs of this world boil down to questions of interest', remarked Matíes Murillo in a letter to his brother explaining how he had managed to obtain for him a

[1] *Capítols sobre redres del General...1542*, cap. 18.

[2] ACA: G, Dietari, 1620–3, part II, fo. 758, and Deliberaciones, 1620–23, part II, fos. 902–7.

[3] ACA: CA, leg. 272, no. 87, information on the excesses in the Diputació by Dr Miquel Carreras, 27 July 1623.

vacant place on the list for Oidor Eclesiàstic.[1] Bribes, influence, interest, were the order of the day, and people would go to extraordinary lengths for the sake of a vacancy. When the triennial draw itself came round, the excitement in the Principality was so intense that a sweepstake used to be held. The proceeds provided the winner with a handsome prize and enough remained for the upkeep of a small body of cavalry for chasing bandits.[2]

The competition for places in the Diputació was unfortunately prompted less by any desire to serve the fatherland than by a keen interest in the loaves and fishes. The Diputació had turned into an enormous racket run for the benefit of the ruling few. The preserve of a privileged minority, it had come to offer immense opportunities for the exercise of power and patronage. It was true that the power of the Diputats had to some extent been restricted by the obligation to follow the votes of the *Braços* and act only on the advice of the lawyers, but, as Alentorn had shown, a Diputat who was so inclined had ample scope for causing trouble. At the very least, Diputats and Oidors had enough nuisance value for it to be worth the Crown's while to bribe them into docility. Four members of the Diputació of 1602–5 were later rewarded for their services,[3] and it is to be suspected that this was a fairly common practice, although not of a kind that can be easily traced.

Neither the patronage in the bestowal of the Diputats, nor the general perquisites of office, were to be despised. Each Diputat and Oidor received an annual salary of 1314 *lliures* and 1085 *lliures* respectively[4]— more than a judge in the Audiència. On top of this, there were distributions on special days of the year, like the 25 *lliures* given to each before the Feast of Sant Jordi.[5] Then there were all the opportunities for profit connected with the filling of vacant places for the triennial draw, the appointment to posts, and the farming or collecting of taxes. These taxes were the *dret del general* on imports and exports (*entrades i eixides*), the *bolla* on textiles, and the new duties imposed by the Corts

[1] ACU: Cartes, 1615–19, M. Murillo to Archdeacon of Urgell, 28 May 1615. 'May the Lord send you success', wrote Murillo. He did. The Archdeacon was drawn as Diputat Eclesiàstic for the triennium 1626–9.
[2] AGS: GA, leg. 1330, Junta de Cortes, 11 Sept. 1626, consts. 5 and 6.
[3] ACA: CA, leg. 269, no. 76, consulta, 3 Aug. 1607.
[4] ACA: G, R. 1052, fos. 579–83.,
[5] ACA: G, Delibs., 1614–17, part II, fo. 385.

of 1599 for the upkeep of the galleys. Trustworthy figures are hard to find, but the following balance-sheet gives some indication of the sums passing through the hands of the Diputats during these years:[1]

	Income	Expenditure
1599–1602	599,486 *lliures*	828,776 *lliures*
1602–1605	563,977	627,363
1605–1608	468,435	471,509
1608–1611	501,288	674,169
1611–1614	490,998	544,793
1614–1617	518,718	514,322
1617–1620	512,485	481,124
1620–1623	504,405	529,779
1623–1626	477,161	458,540

In addition, the Diputats had floated two loans (*censals*) after the Corts of 1599: one of 300,000 *lliures* towards the subsidy voted to the king, and another of 80,000 for the galleys.

The figures in this balance-sheet make it clear that the Diputació could expect to receive an annual income of some 170,000 *lliures*—as compared with the 40,000 *lliures* entering the royal treasury in Catalonia. But they also show that expenditure frequently outran income. Exactly how this could be, was something of a mystery even to contemporaries. There were certain unavoidable expenses which came under the heading of ordinary expenses. These included interest on loans, which ran at the rate of about 50,000 *lliures* a year in the reign of Philip III,[2] and the payment of salaries. The salaries paid by the Diputació to royal officials accounted for some 10,000 *lliures* a year and the salaries to its own officials nearly 20,000.[3] This was a large sum, but the Diputació had become a large organization. It had sixty-five officials spread over the Principality, of whom twenty-one were known as *diputats locals*,[4] and some sixty officials either in, or directly connected with, the Diputació itself at Barcelona.[5]

[1] ACA: G, 147/2, *Balans de les Generalitats de Catalunya per les Corts del any 1632*, fos. 7v and 37v. It is to be presumed that the figures for income represent the net revenues of the Diputació after tax-collectors and Diputats had had their pickings. Elsewhere in Europe outside the Crown of Aragon the only body similar to the Diputació enjoying a comparable degree of control over taxation appears to have been the Small Committee of the Estates of Württemberg (cf. F. L. Carsten, *Princes and Parliaments in Germany*, Oxford, 1959, p. 35). For the *dret del general*, see Appendix III.　　　　[2] ACA: G, 147, Balance presented to Corts of 1626.
[3] *Ibid*.　　　　[4] *Balans* (1632), fo. 45.
[5] The officials are listed in ACA: G, Delibs., 1614–17, part II, fos. 385–387v.

If these ordinary expenses are assumed to be about 80,000 *lliures* a year—a figure confirmed by an ardent defender of the Diputació[1]—this should have left some 90,000 a year for extra expenses and for the building up of financial reserves from which to pay the subsidy voted in the next Corts. But in fact they were all swallowed up in extraordinary expenses, and no reserves remained. Enormous sums could be run up under the heading of 'extraordinary expenses'. No figures are available for the period after 1600, but a comparison of ordinary and extraordinary expenses for the period 1584–99 is revealing:[2]

	Ordinary	Extraordinary
1584–1587	115,248	126,925
1587–1590	174,975	197,457
1590–1593	187,681	152,977
1593–1596	174,768	38,694
1596–1599	158,710	400,153

Where did all this money go? Some of it was spent on building works on the palace of the Generalitat in Barcelona. There was heavy expenditure on festivities and celebrations, like the celebration of Corpus in 1610, when a large meal was laid out in the garden of the Diputació—136 plates of different kinds of birds, rabbit and meats of all sorts, fifty plates of preserves, and numerous other delicacies.[3] The embassies frequently sent by the Diputació to Madrid, either to attend some special occasion at Court or else to lodge a protest at the infringing of the constitutions, also represented a heavy outlay. In the triennium 1620–3, admittedly a period of unusual diplomatic activity, no less than 40,000 *lliures* were spent on embassies to the Court.[4]

There was a good deal of speculation as to how far this expenditure was really justified, and it was widely suspected that the Diputats and Oidors did extremely well out of their term of office. The Corts of 1585 and 1599 both attempted to curb these excesses by drawing up a long series of articles of reform: the Diputats were no longer allowed to create new posts or increase salaries on their own initiative;[5] ex-

[1] BC: Fullet Bonsoms 5204, *Resposta al paper del Duc de Alcalá* (1626).
[2] ACA: G, R. 1052, fos. 579–83.   [3] Pujades, 2, fo. 227v.
[4] ACA: G, R. 147. When Fr Franc was sent on a mission to Madrid by the city of Barcelona in 1614, he spent 30 *lliures* on the hire of two mules and a boy at Barcelona, 20 *lliures* on the journey, and 50ll. 8s. on forty-two days' living expenses in Madrid (AHB: CCO, 1614, fo. 135).
[5] *Capítols sobre lo redres del General...1585*, cap. 63.

penditure for ceremonial purposes was to be strictly limited,[1] and the Corts were so scandalized at 'the excesses of the Diputats in their shameless spending of the Generalitat's money'[2] that it was decided to hold a *visita* of the Diputació every three years.[3] In spite of the widespread indignation which the behaviour of the Diputats had aroused, it cannot be said that they changed their ways after 1599. The *visitas* soon degenerated into a farce. Costing 18,000 *lliures* a time, they seem only to have provided an opportunity for more people to cash in on the revenues of the Generalitat, whose affairs were as badly mismanaged as ever. In 1626, as in 1599, not only did the Diputació have no reserves, but it was owed some 570,000 *lliures* by creditors who had defaulted, and most of this money was not recoverable.[4]

The questionable financial proceedings of the Diputació, combined with its exclusiveness, made it unpopular in the Principality at large. Demanding a big reduction in the number of offices and a careful check on expenditure, the town council of Cervera committed itself to the comment—which it afterwards erased—that 'the house of the Generalitat in Barcelona is nothing but a house of damnation'.[5] It may be that the hostility of towns like Cervera sprang as much from the resentment of its citizens at their exclusion from this goldmine in Barcelona as from a desire to spare the public funds: 'the people of Catalonia ordinarily have little love for the Generalitat because they do not all enjoy offices in it'.[6] But, whatever the exact reasons, the general attitude is unmistakable. The Diputació had, over the course of the centuries, built up for itself so commanding a position that the nation would, in all probability, still rally instinctively to it at moments of real crisis. But in ordinary times the mass of the Catalans now tended to regard it less as the palladium of their liberties than as a happy hunting-ground for an unprincipled clique of racketeers, who used its political powers and its financial resources primarily to serve their own self-interested ends.

If this was the attitude of the Catalans themselves, the feelings of the

---

[1] *Capítols...1599*, cap. 2.
[2] ACV: Cartes, 1580–99, Canon Antoni Vila to Chapter of Vic, 12 July 1599.
[3] *Capítols...1599*, cap. 1.
[4] *Resposta al paper del Duc de Alcalá*.
[5] AHC: Varia, instructions for syndics to Corts of 1626.
[6] BC: MS 979, fos. 66–70, *Diversos Discursos*.

viceroys may easily be guessed. Here was an institution which, from their point of view, existed solely to cause trouble, and no doubt they did everything possible to discredit it in their letters to Madrid. What made matters particularly galling for them was the enormous wealth of the Diputació and the way in which the Diputats proceeded to squander it. While 170,000 *lliures* entered the coffers of the Generalitat every year, most of it to be thrown away on trivialities, they were expected to govern the Principality on an income of under 40,000. It was impossible to avoid the conclusion that if only they could somehow lay hands on the revenues of the Generalitat, the most difficult of their problems could be solved.

But unless the whole constitutional and administrative structure of the Principality were reformed—and this would be impossible without the most drastic action by the Crown—the coffers of the Diputació would remain as unapproachable as the ark of the covenant. And Alcalá needed money at once. The frontier defences had been hopelessly neglected;[1] the treasury was empty; by 1616 the king owed 38,825 *lliures* in arrears of *mercedes*;[2] and the alienation of Crown property and royal rights was still continuing.[3] Unable to lay hands on the revenues of the Diputació, Alcalá turned to the only obvious alternative source of money, the towns. And in the process he lost for the Crown the allies his predecessor had so recently won.

Dotted over the Principality, the towns were little worlds on their own, their horizons hardly extending beyond the walls behind which they sheltered. It was true that most citizens would have their plot of land outside the walls,[4] but there seems to have been considerable antagonism between town and country, 'peasants ordinarily' being 'envious of townspeople'.[5] Towns, indeed, were generally at loggerheads with all their neighbours—with the town over the hill and the gentry who interfered with the grazing rights of their inhabitants or encroached on municipal lands. 'The barons in these Comtats cause daily and continuous vexations to the citizens of Perpinyà, by not allowing them to pasture their animals on their own land or else-

---

[1] ACA: CA, leg. 363, Alcalá to King, 30 May 1620.
[2] ACA: CA, leg. 357, Count of Erill to King, 16 Jan. 1616.
[3] *Ibid.* Enclosures.   [4] See above, p. 28.
[5] Joan Baptista Sanz, 'Relació breu dels sucessos...en la ciutat de Vich', *La Veu del Montserrat*, vol. xxv (1902), p. 53 (see Appendix VI, section D).

where.... '[1] This was the very breath of urban life in seventeenth-century Catalonia.

The top social stratum of the larger towns, like Lleida, Girona, Vic, consisted of nobles, gentry and distinguished citizens (*ciutadans honrats*). Distinguished citizenship bestowed a status comparable to that of nobility. At Lleida, for instance, which in 1591 was granted a privilege to create distinguished citizens, the conditions for election had a distinctly aristocratic bias:[2] anyone aspiring to be a *ciutadà honrat* must be a native of the town, and the son and grandson of honourable persons; neither he nor his father could have been employed in any 'mechanical office', such as tailor, cobbler or carpenter; he must have sufficient income to live with dignity, and he must be elected on a secret ballot.

Just below this group, and often merging into it, were the merchants and the professional people—lawyers, doctors, notaries. These, together with the urbanized aristocracy and the distinguished citizens, made up that solid, prosperous, comfortable class which might be loosely described as the 'upper bourgeoisie'. It owned houses and land, and its money was safely invested at 5 per cent. In Catalonia, as in other parts of Spain, the development of an elaborate system of public and private loans, of *censals* and *censos*, offered widespread facilities for safe investment and had created a large *rentier* class. Widows, orphans, religious foundations, anyone with money to spare, would invest it in a loan floated by the Diputació, or the Catalan municipalities, or lend it '*a cens*' to a private individual. In return, the creditor paid an annual interest, or pension, which in early seventeenth-century Catalonia was customarily 1s. in the pound.[3] The estate of Esteve Gilabert Bruniquer, a famous Barcelona notary, includes a good deal of land at Granollers, all of it leased in return for an annual payment, several houses, similarly leased, and a number of *censals*: one of 800 *lliures* with an annuity of 40 *lliures*, paid on 1 November by Miquel Joan Taverner, gentleman of Barcelona; another of 500 *lliures*—annuity 25 *lliures*—paid in two parts, on 15 June and 15 December, by various inhabitants of Caldes de Montbui, and so on.[4] Bruniquer and his like represent the solid,

---

[1] AMP: B.B. 23, instructions of outgoing to incoming Cònsols (1609), no. 2.

[2] Rafael Gras y de Esteva, *La Pahería de Lérida. Notas sobre la antigua organización municipal de la ciudad, 1149–1707* (Lérida, 1911), pp. 61–2.

[3] AHB: LC, 1635–7, fos. 158–9, Consellers of Barcelona to Protonotario, 6 Sept. 1636.

[4] APB: A. J. Fita, lib. 9, d'inventaris, Bruniquer, 11 April 1641.

conservative element in Catalan society, interested in the maintenance of a stable currency, in the preservation of order and the avoidance of political excitements. These were the people who had wholeheartedly supported the duke of Alburquerque in his struggle against the forces of anarchy, and whom the duke of Alcalá was so soon to antagonize.

Beneath them in the towns were the mass of the citizens: the artisans and craftsmen, organized into their guilds, and the shopkeepers, apprentices and domestic servants. Although the guilds played a vital part in the ordinary life of the towns, municipal governments were generally dominated, in practice if not in theory, by the 'upper bourgeoisie'. Since the reforms introduced by Ferdinand the Catholic, it was not quite so easy for this group to turn itself into a closed, self-perpetuating oligarchy completely controlling municipal government, as it had been in the fifteenth century. Towns, like the Diputació, had adopted the system of *insaculació*, whereby the names of candidates for office were drawn by lot. This greatly reduced the chances of fraud, and destroyed the possibility of rigged elections. Similarly, there was a reasonably large and tolerably representative town council in most towns, which somewhat inhibited government by a clique operating behind closed doors.

In spite of these inconveniences, town governments were usually weighted heavily in favour of the higher social groups. At the top of the governmental hierarchy came three or four town councillors, who were responsible for the day-to-day administration of the town during their year of office. Their style varied according to the geographical area: around Lleida they were known as *Pahers*, round Barcelona as *Consellers*, round Perpinyà as *Cònsols*, and round Girona as *Jurats*. The method of their selection was similar to that employed in the Diputació. At Manresa, for instance, there were four Consellers. For the post of each Conseller there was a fixed list of names, vacancies being filled by vote of the rest, and a name once inscribed remaining there for life. At the time of the annual change of Consellers, these names were placed in four bags, and the person whose name was first drawn from each bag held the post for the coming year. The social suitability of the candidate, however, had already been predetermined by the presence of his name on the original inscribed list. At Manresa, unlike Lleida and other important towns, nobles and gentry at this time took no part in government, and in 1629 the four bags were composed thus:[1]

Bag 1 (First Conseller—Conseller-en-Cap)	Bag 2 (Second Conseller)
4 notaries	1 notary
1 apothecary	1 apothecary
2 doctors of law	2 doctors of medicine
1 bachelor of law	1 bachelor of law
6 merchants	2 shoemakers
	11 merchants
14	18

Bag 3 (Third Conseller)	Bag 4 (Fourth Conseller)
1 cloth-shearer	1 cotton dealer
1 cotton dealer	1 tanner
2 tanners	6 merchants
4 merchants	
8	8

The limited number of occupations considered suitable for the town's principal representatives is here very apparent. Out of forty-eight names, twenty-seven are those of merchants, thirteen are members of the professions, and only eight remain to represent all the other occupations in the town, although these were slightly better represented on the town council itself.

Although the Conseller-en-Cap and his colleagues were the nominal rulers of the town during their year of office, and represented it on all ceremonial occasions, they were by no means free agents in the business of government. It was their duty to put into effect decisions taken by the town council, which was summoned by the ringing of a bell whenever there were matters of moment to discuss. The town council was nominally a representative institution. For purposes of municipal representation, a town would be divided into different quarters, or else the citizens would be classed by groups, according to their social status. At Lleida, for example, the division was into major, medium and minor 'hands'. The first consisted of gentry and 'citizens', including doctors

---

[1] AHM, *Llibre de Ànimes*.

of law and medical doctors; the second of merchants, bachelors of law, surgeons, notaries and grocers; and the third of mechanics, tradesmen, labourers and peasants.[1] The town council—the *Consell General*—was formed of fifteen members of each of these groups, and five representatives of the guilds. In the Consell General, as among the town's councillors (or Pahers as they were called at Lleida), the interests of the 'upper bourgeoisie' predominated. The major and medium 'hands' were always in alliance, and so could consistently out-vote the artisans and tradesmen. Thus, although ordinary citizens did have some form of representation in municipal deliberations, control remained firmly in the hands of the dominant social group; and it was shaken only when the minority in the town council appealed to their comrades among the citizens at large, and a rioting mob forced an entry into the town hall.

In all towns there were several important posts connected with matters of general municipal administration. There were financial officials, custodians of the town hospital, officials for checking weights and measures, for seeing that municipal ordinances were obeyed and for supervising the market. The occupants of these various posts were again drawn by lot, but again from a restricted list of names, so that the lion's share of the more lucrative offices went to the dominant social group. The salaries attached to these posts were generally small, but in most of them there were opportunities for exercising influence and obtaining profit on the side, and they were not hard to fill. According to that sharp-eyed citizen of Vic, Joan Baptista Sanz, this was an age in which the public welfare was quickly forgotten, and everyone hastened to feather his own nest.[2]

While many individual citizens were wealthy, and were not likely to be overscrupulous in their attitude to the public funds, the towns they served generally had no money to spare. Their income was derived from a variety of municipal taxes, levied on almost everything bought and sold within the town, and probably supplemented in emergencies by a straight tax on property—1*d.* in the pound at Cervera.[3] A good example of the nature of these taxes and the way in which they were raised is provided by Lleida. With something like 6000 inhabitants, Lleida was one of the largest towns in Catalonia, as it was also one of

---

[1] Gras y de Esteva, *La Pahería de Lérida*..., p. 61.
[2] Sanz, *Sucessos*, p. 74.
[3] AHC: *Manifest nou de totes les cases y heretats*... (1622).

the wealthiest. A university town on the banks of the river Segre, a town of narrow, sloping streets, it was dominated by its great fortress-like cathedral set on the top of the hill. Lying on the main road from Zaragoza to Barcelona, and the first town of any importance on the western boundaries of the Principality, it was a natural trading centre, with 'the corn of Urgell and Tamarite de Litera, the wool on its way through from Aragon, the flocks that come down from the mountains to pasture on the grasslands, the silks and innumerable other objects for sale and purchase'.[1]

As befitted such a town, revenues and expenditure were both large.[2] Its revenue came from the following municipal dues:

(1) *pes i mercat*, a tax on all goods, at the rate of 2*d.* in the pound for both buyer and seller.
(2) The *menuderies*—on the sale of wood, salt, game and wildfowl.
(3) The *bladeria*—on all corn and grain sold in the town.
(4) Duty on all fresh fish (river and sea fish) sold in the town.
(5) Duty on salt fish and meat.
(6) Duty of about 120 *lliures* per annum paid by surrounding villages within Lleida's jurisdiction.
(7) Duty on sale and transit of wine (used to pay salaries of university professors).

These duties were not levied directly by municipal officials, but were farmed to the highest bidder at an auction held every second year. In 1600 the *pes i mercat* was farmed for 1040 *lliures*, the *menuderies* and *bladeria* for 200 *lliures* each, the duty on fresh fish for 305 and that on salt fish and meat for 150. Over a period of eleven years, these duties, excluding that on wine (farmed for 1610 *lliures* in 1600), averaged 2342 *lliures* a year.

This money was spent on the salaries of municipal officials, the conservation of the municipal fishponds, the repair of the town walls and the university buildings, and the entertainment of important guests passing through Lleida—no small item when it is considered how many dignitaries on their way to or from the Spanish Court would travel by the Barcelona route. Above all, the money went on the payment of interest on the *censals* raised by the city at various times—no less than 5765 *lliures* a year, 'a sum so excessive...that it absorbs all that the

[1] ACA: CA, leg. 360, petition from Lleida (1615?).
[2] ACA: CA, leg. 353, paper on revenues of Lleida, 10 March 1611.

city receives from the aforesaid dues'. In fact Lleida, like so many other Catalan towns, was in chronic financial difficulties.

Whether or not they were in difficulties was of no great concern to Alcalá. He needed money, and certain towns, he believed, had a legal obligation to provide it. He therefore determined to enforce such claims as the Crown possessed to a share in the revenues of certain municipalities—claims that were either disputed or had been allowed to lapse through the negligence of royal officials. Some towns were already, in accordance with the terms of their charters, paying a fifth part or *quint* of their revenues into the royal Treasury. Others were specifically exempted by their charters from any such fiscal obligation. But there was a third class of town which had either lost its original records, so that its status was not known, or else had a charter which neither specifically mentioned an obligation to pay the *quint* nor any exemption from it.[1] It was these towns against which Alcalá decided to take action.

There was nothing new about Alcalá's ideas. Uncertainty over the status of the third class of town had already induced royal ministers in the later sixteenth century to rummage in the archives for evidence of obligations to pay the *quint*. Their researches provoked considerable alarm in many a town, for who knew how many centuries' arrears of *quints* might not one day be suddenly demanded? It was therefore a matter for much rejoicing when Philip III in the Corts of 1599 renounced all claims to *quints* payable before that year, although he refused to waive his rights in perpetuity.

In the first years after the Corts of 1599, the Crown's claims to the disputed *quints* were not seriously pressed, although royal ministers were fully aware that they represented potentially the Crown's most valuable property in Catalonia. Cases did come before the Audiència, but were rarely brought to any conclusion; and many towns claimed exemption as 'streets' of larger towns like Barcelona which were held to be immune.[2] But the expenses of bandit-chasing made it impossible to ignore any potential source of revenue, and in 1612 royal officials again began searching the archives and visiting towns to examine their accounts. Their visits caused the most acute concern throughout the

[1] AGS: Hacienda, leg. 573, fo. 203, Vice-Chancellor to King, 30 May 1620.
[2] ACA: CA, leg. 347, Don Pere de Vilanova i Pernes to King, 16 Oct. 1606.

Principality, and did much to increase the unpopularity of the viceregal administration. Everywhere the officials met a hostile reception. The town of Cervera managed to eject them by a combination of force and guile, and the royal commissioner at Puigcerdà had to escape by night in disguise. The whole object of the municipalities, which were acting in concert, was to delay matters as long as possible, in the hope that, if they could manage to spin out their cases in the Audiència for ten years or so, the king would in the meantime have visited the Principality and renounced his claims as an act of grace.[1] But in January 1614, the case against Cervera, which was being used as a test case, was decided by the Audiència in the royal favour,[2] and the towns began to fear the worst. Slowly the Treasury's income from the *quints* began to rise,[3] partly perhaps because of the gradual return to normal conditions after the crushing of the bandits, but also because of the increased activity of the royal officials.

1611	5,577 *lliures*
1612	5,521
1613	4,359
1614	9,698
1615	10,611
1616	12,565
1617	19,332
1618	22,959

From these figures it is clear that royal officials had already shown considerable activity during the viceroyalty of Alburquerque, and that Alcalá was doing no more than continue the policies of his predecessor. But there was a world of difference between the attitudes of the two men, vividly illustrated by their letters to the king. Alburquerque:

As regards the *quintos*, only small sums are owed to Your Majesty, and these by a few towns so poor that they could only be collected by harsh methods which it would break my heart to employ. The only important outstanding sum is owed by the city of Vic, which owes Your Majesty 13,000 *lliures*; and although the city has suffered terrible floods, they may well agree to offer 8000 or 9000; and if your Majesty is willing to accept this, the Treasury should still have enough to meet its ordinary expenses.[4]

[1] ACA: CA, leg. 396, office of Mestre Racional to King, 2 June 1612.
[2] ACA: CA, leg. 355, Don Guerau de Guardiola to King, 18 Jan. 1614.
[3] Figures from ACA: CA, leg. 490 (paper of 1617), and leg. 364 (Don Guerau de Guardiola to Viceroy, July 1620).
[4] ACA: CA, leg. 479, Alburquerque to King, 25 Aug. 1618.

Alcalá:

On several occasions I have represented to Your Majesty that the entire royal estate in this Principality consists of the *quintos*....I therefore beg Your Majesty to have the proposed agreements with certain Catalan towns now before the Council of Aragon, most carefully scrutinized....[1]

The blunt expressions, often highly disrespectful to the king, and the complete lack of any of that compassion which, for all his bluffness, so distinguished Alburquerque, were typical of Alcalá.

The viceroy's obvious determination to extract his pound of flesh caused anguish and despair among the towns of Catalonia. Any gratitude they may have felt for the Crown's firmness in restoring order a year or two before, was now rapidly dissipated. In their moment of peril, they naturally looked to the Diputació for help, but the Diputació, which was not itself directly involved, showed not the slightest interest. 'There are no Diputats', wrote Cervera's agent at Barcelona, adding that the Diputat Militar 'does everything the viceroy asks of him to save his son, who is in prison, from exile...Look at poor Catalonia, the state it is in.'[2]

Driven back by the pusillanimity of the Diputació on to their own scanty resources, towns like Cervera and Manresa sent special ambassadors of their own to Madrid, to plead their case at Court. This was a desperate rearguard action, but help was at hand. The year 1620–1 was to be a turning-point in the history not only of the towns but of the entire Principality. In May 1620 Alcalá impetuously suggested that the time had come for the king to demand *quints* from no less a town than Barcelona itself.[3] Counting the arrears since 1599, this meant a sum of no less than 300,000 *lliures*—a figure beside which the *quints* of a town like Cervera paled into insignificance. The viceroy's proposal threatened to launch the Crown on a journey into uncharted, and dangerous, waters. There was no danger in challenging a small town like Manresa, too weak to hold out for ever against royal officials armed with documentary proof of an obligation to pay the *quints*. But

---

[1] ACA: CA, leg. 479, Alcalá to King, 12 Sept. 1620.

[2] AHC: CR, Carpeta B, no. 112, Jaume Puig to Pahers of Cervera, 8 Nov. 1620. The Diputat Militar was Nofre Jordà, who came from Fondarella, between Cervera and Lleida. The supreme concern of the Diputació at this moment was with the galleys, and it sent Dr Fontanella to Madrid in December to seek royal recognition of its jurisdiction over them.

[3] ACA: CA, leg. 363, Alcalà to King, 30 May 1620.

with Barcelona it was likely to be a different story. Barcelona's archives were full of privileges and royal charters; the city was well stocked with lawyers as good as any in the pay of the Crown; and it possessed great financial reserves and an important stake in the Diputació. In deciding to make a bid for the *quints* of Barcelona, Alcalá was pitting himself against the most powerful force in the land.

By the end of 1620, Alcalá had managed to array the entire Principality against him. The nobles had been antagonized by his repressive policies, the Diputació by his firmness over the Catalan galleys; he had alienated many of the smaller towns by his merciless extortion of the *quints*, and now, as rumours of his intentions spread, he alienated Barcelona too. The alliance forged between Alburquerque and the 'upper bourgeoisie' was crumbling. The citizens who composed the municipal oligarchies of Catalonia had been touched in their pockets, and touched also in their national self-esteem. The viceroy made no secret of his dislike of the Catalans. 'Only the torments of hell can be compared to governing Catalonia,' he was to write one day.[1] Already filled with a sense of guilty uneasiness at their surrender of constitutional propriety for the sake of personal security in the time of Alburquerque, the Catalans watched the activities of this antipathetic Castilian viceroy with growing concern. The latent nationalism of Catalonia, never far below the surface, was beginning to stir, and the bandits were crying, perhaps with an increased frequency, *Visca la terra* —Long live the land.[2]

The worst fears of the Principality, still only half voiced, were confirmed in March of 1621, when it awoke to discover that Alcalá had had the arms, not of Catalonia but of Castile and León, placed over the entrance to the *Dressanes*—the Barcelona dockyards: 'an abomination which, if our ancestors could see it, would make them turn in their graves'.[3] There could no longer be room for doubt. At the very moment when the king lay dying in Madrid, his ministers were plotting to deprive the Catalans of their laws and liberties. Over the Principality of Catalonia loomed the shadow of Castile.

[1] ACA: CA, leg. 272, no. 16, Alcalá to Vice-Chancellor, 24 July 1622.
[2] Soldevila, *Història*, vol. II, p. 263. Pujades (3, fo. 25 v.) reports a riot in the Barcelona gaol on 15 May 1621 among the gentlemen prisoners, who responded to an attempt to remove a prisoner named Pelgri, wanted in Aragon by the viceroy, with shouts of 'Long live the liberties of Catalonia'.   [3] Pujades, 3, fo. 14, 23 March 1621.

CHAPTER VI

THE SHADOW OF CASTILE

Philip III died at the age of forty-three on 31 March 1621. The Catalans had no great reason to lament his passing. Since his visit to the Principality in 1599 they had seen nothing of him, and he had given them no cause to hold his memory in love or respect. Mild and ineffectual to the last, he had entrusted the government of his dominions to favourites and ministers whom the Catalans had come to regard with supreme contempt. After neglecting Catalonia's pressing problems for a full fifteen years, he had belatedly sent two energetic viceroys, the first of whom ignored the constitutions on grounds of plausible necessity, but none the less ignored them, and the second of whom took a patent delight in disregarding them out of sheer hatred of the Catalans. What cause had Catalonia, racked and ravaged by the duke of Alcalá, to feel sorrow at the death of the king who appointed him? If the change of sovereigns meant a change of ministers, and, above all, of viceroys, then it could be nothing but a happy release.

The news of the king's death, officially communicated to the Principality on 9 April 1621, was accompanied by rumours of great changes at Court. Lerma's son and successor, the duke of Uceda, had fallen from power. In his place, the new king, the young Philip IV (III of Catalonia), had put the experienced Don Baltasar de Zúñiga, while choosing as his 'intimate favourite' Zúñiga's nephew, the count of Olivares.[1] Every letter from Madrid in the following weeks brought news of the institution of reforms long overdue, and of a great purge of ministers of the old regime. No wonder that Dr Pujades wrote with enthusiasm in his diary of 'a new dawn which has broken'.[2]

But although the change of regime held out promise of a brighter future, it also brought immediate difficulties in its train. The king's letter announcing the death of his father informed the Diputats that his urgent commitments prevented him from coming at once to the Principality. In the meantime, he had instructed the duke of Alcalá to

---

[1] Pujades, 3, fo. 17v. [2] *Ibid.* fo. 21v.

continue as viceroy.[1] Apart from being personally most unwelcome, this was also constitutionally embarrassing. After searching in vain for precedents, the lawyers of the Diputació uncompromisingly declared that 'in Catalonia it is the clearest, most certain and established fact that can be found...that, on the news of the death of the king, the viceroy's government is ended, and his jurisdiction is held to be extinguished'.[2] Ordinarily, a formal decree issued by the king, reappointing the viceroy for a further term of office, was all that was needed. But no royal decree was valid in Catalonia unless the sovereign who issued it had at some time been to the Principality and there sworn to uphold all its constitutions. Among his many other omissions Philip III had omitted to see that his son fulfilled this important task. As a result, the new king was not yet legally king in Catalonia, and there was grave doubt in the Principality as to whether any orders from him could be obeyed, and the prolongation of Alcalá's viceroyalty be accepted.

During the next few days, there was great discussion in Barcelona as to what should be done. A possible opportunity for ending the viceroyalty of Alcalá seemed too good to be missed, and a vigorous campaign against Alcalá's continuation in office was mounted by a group of influential Catalans headed by the abbot of Sant Cugat, Don Francesc de Erill, whose expectations of becoming Canceller had been disappointed by Alcalá.[3] On the other hand, no one was anxious to forfeit the favour of the new king at this early stage in the reign. When, therefore, the archbishop of Tarragona proposed to a packed meeting of the Braços (Estates) in Barcelona that the decree reappointing Alcalá should be accepted on the grounds of *necessity*, which overrides all laws,[4] a majority approved, and Alcalá, to his great relief, took the oath as viceroy of King Philip IV on 15 April 1621.

The viceroy's continuation in office had been accepted only on sufferance. It was generally assumed that the new king would visit the Principality in a matter of months, and the immediate prospect of a royal visit made it possible to tolerate even Alcalá's government a little

---

[1] ACA: G, 14, *Consistori de jurats de virreys no havent jurat SM*, fo. 3. [2] *Ibid.* fo. 13.
[3] ACA: CA, leg. 368, Alcalá to King, 10 April 1621. The post went to Dr Puigmarí, but Erill, the count of Erill's brother, finally obtained it, with tragic consequences for the Principality, in 1631 (RAH: Salazar K. 40, fos. 39–40, consulta of Council of Aragon, 9 Sept. 1631).
[4] *Consistori*, fos. 40 ff.

longer. But the months came and went, and still there was no news of a royal visit. The Principality was beginning to grow restless. Alcalá's government was as unpopular as ever, and the city of Barcelona was thoroughly alarmed by his determination to demand a fifth of all its revenues since 1599.

Barcelona was unaware that Alcalá's policy by no means commanded the full support of the ministers in Madrid. As so often happened in the reign of Philip III, the provincial agent of the government had moved faster than his superiors at Court. Alcalá had first hit upon the idea of demanding the *quints* from Barcelona when considering the poverty of the royal Treasury in the Principality, and the defenceless condition of Catalonia's frontiers. From here, he had moved on to a still more ambitious scheme. Anxious to save not only the government in Catalonia, but the entire Spanish Monarchy, from financial shipwreck, he proposed to Madrid in the last year of Philip III's reign that a fifth of the municipal revenues should be demanded from all the cities of Aragon, Valencia, and Portugal, as well as Catalonia.[1] As was to be expected, the king's financial ministers in the *Consejo de Hacienda* warmly welcomed this ambitious proposal;[2] and the Council of State, meeting a few days before the king's death, thought that a special Junta might be appointed to go into the matter. This was as far as things had gone. But Alcalá, impatient at the Court's delay, had pressed on with his plans without waiting for instructions. Nothing could have been better calculated to fill Barcelona with alarm, and the new regime, at a time of uncertainty over the new king's legal position in Catalonia, had everything to gain from keeping Barcelona contented. The king's advisers were clearly disturbed by the implications of Alcalá's precipitate action. After reading through his letters, Philip IV wrote the following minute: 'It seems that he has exceeded his orders, since he was merely asked to give an opinion. He should be told that in any case he is to act in such a way that the city can have no reasonable cause for complaint but appreciates the mildness and circumspection with which the matter is being handled.'[3]

Mildness and circumspection were quite alien to Alcalá's temperament. He had his own views on how the Principality should be treated,

[1] AGS: Est., leg. 2645, consulta, 27 March 1621.
[2] AGS: Consejo de Hacienda, leg. 573, consultas, 28 June and 11 Oct. 1620.
[3] AGS: Est., leg. 2645, decree by Philip IV, 3 Nov. 1621.

and was so accustomed to telling the king what to do that he was unused to complying with orders from Madrid. His immediate concern, however, was the question of a royal visit. His appointed three-year term of office was drawing to a close, and he had still received no intimation that the king was coming to the Principality. The experiences of April 1621 had made him certain that the Catalans would never agree to his own reappointment, or even the appointment of a successor, unless the king had first been to the Principality and taken the oath to observe its constitutions. He therefore suggested that the king should at once come to the Principality, hold a session of the Corts, and use the opportunity not to demand a subsidy but to revoke all those constitutions which impeded good government.[1]

When these suggestions came before the Council of Aragon, they were very badly received. Among the regents of the Council, each with the interests of his native province at heart, a viceroy like Alcalá had no friends. They were as anxious as everybody else that the king should soon pay a visit to his vassals of the Crown of Aragon, but they held Alcalá's anxiety about the effects of the king's continued absence to be unfounded: Alcalá knew nothing about the affairs of Catalonia, and had taken no trouble to understand the country he had been sent to govern, or he would never have suggested the revoking of constitutions without the full agreement of the Principality.[2] These comments, of a rare bitterness for so cautious a body as the Council of Aragon, testify to the extent of the hostility Alcalá had aroused. His violent letters to Madrid, and his clumsy handling of the Catalans, had made everyone want to be rid of him. By December 1621 the grievances of the Principality had reached such a pitch that the Diputats called a special meeting of representatives of the three estates to consider what should be done. Missions of protest to Madrid had met with no success. The one and only answer to all the Principality's troubles lay in a visit by the king. It was decided that letters should be written him begging for a visit and it was also agreed that the Diputats should come to Barcelona's help over the question of the *quints*.[3]

The Diputats' willingness to assist Barcelona over the *quints* contrasted strangely with their tepid reaction to the earlier complaints of

[1] ACA: CA, leg. 368, Alcalá to King, 1 Nov. 1621.
[2] ACA: CA, leg. 368, draft consulta, 12 Nov. 1621.
[3] *Consistori*, fos. 63–8, 10 Dec. 1621.

smaller towns from which *quints* had been demanded, but special circumstances gave the city of Barcelona a unique hold over the policy of the Diputació. The Diputats were by no means free agents in the shaping of policy. Not only did the prospect of a *visita* hang over them, with all its possibilities of heavy penalties for alleged neglect of duty, but their freedom was also limited by the terms on which they held office. The articles for the redress of the Generalitat drawn up in 1585 expressly stated that the Diputats were under no circumstances to interpret on their own initiative dubious constitutional points.[1] These points, after being submitted to lawyers, were to be put before a meeting of the Braços. This was a special gathering of members of the three Estates who happened to be in Barcelona at the time. In such a gathering the interests of Barcelona could not fail to predominate. There was usually insufficient time for those who lived further afield to ride into Barcelona to attend the meetings, so that the majority of those present inevitably consisted of inhabitants of Barcelona. Canons of Barcelona cathedral predominated in the *braç eclesiàstic*, and resident nobles and *cavallers* in the *braç militar*, while in the *braç reial* the chief councillor of Barcelona was expected to speak for the other towns, whose representatives, to their great annoyance, were forbidden attendance.[2]

Barcelona's preponderance in the meetings of the three estates meant that the city could exercise control over the Diputació whenever it felt inclined. As long as the city's interests were not at stake, the Diputats acted in their own interests or those of any particular group with which they were closely connected; but when Barcelona needed the extra support of the Diputació's prestige and authority it could mobilize those of its citizens eligible to attend meetings of the Braços, and in this way dictate to the Diputats the policy they should follow.

It was, then, an ominous sign when the Diputació promised to help Barcelona in its struggle to avoid payment of the *quints*. The city had marshalled its batallions, and the two most powerful bodies in Catalonia—city and Diputació—had begun to act in unison. When it was announced, in the spring of 1622, that Alcalá's term of office would be extended until September, city and Diputació both sent large embas-

---

[1] *Capítols sobre lo redres del General* (1585), cap. 34.
[2] AHB: Corts 1626, fo. 603, const. 43.

sies to Madrid, to plead with the king to delay his visit no longer. As the nine ambassadors of the Diputació made clear in their petition,[1] the king's failure to come to the Principality and take the oath raised vital constitutional issues, for 'between Your Majesty and your vassals there is a reciprocal obligation, whereby, as they must serve and obey Your Majesty as their king and lord, so Your Majesty equally should protect their laws and privileges'. In fact, the whole contractual nature of the relationship between the king and the Catalans was being jeopardized by the king's delay. Equally important was the *personal* relationship between king and vassals which in the last hundred years had become so tenuous. The Diputats' petition ended with an impassioned plea that the Catalans might enjoy the presence of their monarch—a plea that went to the heart of the problem of kingship in that intensely monarchical age:

How fitting it is that Your Majesty, as king, father and lord of all your states and kingdoms, should come personally to see all that you have in this Principality, and to console your most loyal vassals. We cannot but be jealous of the good fortune of others who enjoy the royal presence at first hand, and we beg the king's Majesty to come and acquaint himself in person with the affairs of this province so as to improve its government....In thirty-seven years, only twice have your vassals seen their king and lord, and it is this long absence which is responsible for the violation of their laws....Those who govern the Principality have infringed these laws, like the duke of Alcalá, who has not hesitated to break numerous constitutions, against the express orders of Your Majesty....

These eloquent phrases admirably expressed the feelings of the Principality. Everything had gone wrong, and it was natural to ascribe the misfortunes of recent years to the prolonged absence of the king, just as it was equally natural to assume that his presence would set everything right. Surely a king who had sworn to preserve the liberties of Catalonia would not remain passive when he saw for himself the injustice of demanding Barcelona's *quints* or the injustice done to the aristocracy in prohibiting *pedrenyals*. The king must come to Catalonia, take the oath, summon the Corts, and remedy the grievances of his afflicted vassals.

[1] BC: Fullet Bonsoms 15, *Discurso...hecho por F. Francisco de Copons y otros embajadores en la Corte de SM* (Barcelona, 1622).

Philip IV was no doubt genuinely anxious to visit the Principality. He told the Council of Aragon that he hoped to be free to undertake a visit in the early months of 1623, and explained that the delay had been caused by his urgent commitments in Madrid.[1] Although this was probably true, there was an additional reason for the postponement, which it would have been impolitic to make public. The Crown's finances were in such a state that the king could not pay for the journey.[2]

The spring of 1623 was still a long way ahead, and it seemed increasingly unlikely that Alcalá would remain in office until then. He himself was now agitating to be relieved of his post. His salary as viceroy was hopelessly in arrears, and he was having trouble in keeping his servants. If His Majesty would neither pay him nor relieve him of his office, all he asked was that his wife and children should be sent home while he was confined during His Majesty's pleasure in the castle of Salces or Perpinyà, as a punishment for having spent his entire estate in serving his king.[3] The discontent of Alcalá came as a fortunate windfall for the Council of Aragon. Here, surely, was the perfect chance to remove a viceroy it detested, and it suggested his replacement by Joan Sentís, the bishop of Barcelona and a native Catalan. On 6 August a letter was sent from the king to the Diputats informing them of the change of viceroys, and instructing them to attend the ceremonial swearing-in of the bishop of Barcelona as successor to Alcalá.[4] The latter packed his bags and prepared to leave the Principality he had governed for three and a half long years, 'ill-rewarded by the king and unloved by the land he had harried and destroyed'.[5]

In recommending the appointment of a new viceroy before the king had sworn his oath to maintain the liberties of Catalonia, the Council of Aragon had taken a very serious risk. Although the Catalans had reluctantly agreed, in the special circumstances following the death of Philip III, to let the customary practice be set aside, it was asking a good deal of them to agree a second time to an unconstitutional expedient. It soon appeared that the Council of Aragon had gravely underestimated the strength of feeling in the Principality about this implied threat to the sacrosanct constitutions: the sharpness of the Catalan re-

[1] ACA: CA, leg. 272, no. 16, consulta, 28 June 1622.
[2] BM: Add. MSS 13,997, fos. 30–1, *Parecer del Marqués de Aytona*, 28 Jan. 1624.
[3] ACA: CA, leg. 272, no. 16, Alcalá to Vice-Chancellor, 24 July 1622.
[4] *Consistori*, fos. 92–3.   [5] Pujades, 3, fo. 98.

action took the regents of the Council completely by surprise. Many Catalans believed at the time, and many more were later to maintain, that the ministers at Madrid deliberately set out to force the Catalans to accept a new viceroy before the king took the oath, as the first step in a carefully devised plan to deprive the Principality of its traditional laws and liberties.[1] But the bitter disputes of 1622–3 over the acceptance of a new viceroy were the result of muddle and miscalculation on the part of the ministers in Madrid, rather than of any sinister designs against Catalonia. The responsibility lay not with Olivares but with the Council of Aragon, which was so anxious to remove Alcalá from office that it rashly recommended his removal and substitution by a new viceroy without stopping to consider the probable reaction in the Principality. When the reaction came, it dared not retreat for fear of losing face,[2] and its behaviour consequently involved Olivares and the king's chief ministers in an embarrassing struggle they would willingly have avoided, but in which any apparent weakening seemed likely to compromise the authority of the king.

The struggle itself was both bitter and confused—so confused that Dr Pujades considered it impossible for anyone to write a comprehensible account.[3] It began on 10 September 1622, when Alcalá took ship at Tarragona, and lasted until 12 April 1623 when the bishop of Barcelona at last took his oath as viceroy before representatives of city and Diputació. In those intervening seven months, so much anger and bitterness were generated, both in Barcelona and Madrid, that the bishop of Elna, looking back in the summer of 1623 on the sudden storms that had shaken Catalonia, wrote that on more than one occasion he had thought the Principality to be lost.[4] His fears were not unduly exaggerated. Those months of 1622–3 were months of real crisis in the relationship between Castile and Catalonia, a commentary on the recent past and a tragic portent for the future.

When the bishop of Barcelona announced to the Diputats on 10 September that he would take his oath as viceroy in seven days' time,

[1] This was the line taken by all the pamphlets written in and after 1640 in justification of the Catalan revolt.
[2] AHB: CCO, 1620–2, fos. 156–7, Oms and Vinyes to Consellers, 15 Oct. 1622. The opinion of the city's two ambassadors is confirmed by the evidence of the consultas of the Councils of Aragon and State.
[3] Dietari, 3, fo. 138 v.
[4] ACA: CA, leg. 272, no. 16, Bishop of Elna to Vice-Chancellor, 10 Aug. 1623.

there was intense agitation in Barcelona. The bishop himself, an inoffensive character, was mercilessly lampooned as the son of a Frenchman who had earned his living by transporting fish from Tortosa to Zaragoza.[1] The Diputats, the Barcelona city council and the *braç militar* (the aristocratic Estate), all met to consider precedents from the reign of Charlemagne onwards. Even the artisans left their work and flocked to the *Casa de la Ciutat*—the Barcelona town hall—where they spent their time passionately arguing the rights and wrongs of the case.[2] The public demand was so great for copies of the petitions presented by the ambassadors of the Diputació to the king, that a reprinting had to be ordered, and it was in a city keyed up to the highest pitch of excitement that the lawyers of the Diputació unanimously advised the Diputats on 16 September not to attend the swearing-in ceremony.[3]

This decision was extremely grave. A refusal by representatives of city and Diputació to attend the inauguration of the new viceroy meant that they would not acknowledge him as the king's representative, and would regard all the actions of the viceregal government as invalid. Such defiance of the king's authority by the two most formidable bodies in Catalonia would be the equivalent of rebellion, and rebellion would presumably lead to the armed intervention of Castile. The implications of precipitate action were therefore so serious that even the Council of Aragon drew back when the bishop suggested that he should move to Tarragona with the entire Audiència and take the oath there instead of in Barcelona.[4] Unwilling to risk a complete break with the Catalans by authorizing the bishop to go ahead with the ceremony without the participation of city and Diputats, the Council dillied and dallied throughout October, and the inauguration of the new viceroy was deferred from one week to the next.

The legality of the Diputats' decision not to attend the ceremony is difficult to determine. As usually happened in Catalonia, precedents could be found to justify both sides. Archives would be ransacked for documents that were often barely relevant, and the lawyers would wrangle to their hearts' content. Dr Pujades, though a doughty defender of the Principality's liberties, privately believed that justice lay with the

[1] Pujades, 3, fo. 103.
[2] ACA: CA, leg. 367, Bishop of Barcelona to King, 15 Sept. 1622.
[3] *Consistori*, fos. 127–30.
[4] ACA: CA, leg. 367, Bishop of Barcelona to Juan Lorenzo de Villanueva, 14 Sept. 1622.

king,[1] though others could be as sincerely convinced of the opposite. Of more interest than the strictly legal issues were the conflicting interests at stake. The king's case was simple. It was impossible for him to come at once to the Principality, and it was ridiculous that viceregal government should cease simply because he had been unable to take the customary royal oath to observe the laws and protect the liberties of Catalonia. Even if there were not good legal precedents to be found on his side, *necessity* alone completely justified his action.

City and Diputació, however, could put forward equally cogent arguments. Their lawyers held that it was quite unconstitutional for the king to appoint a viceroy when he himself had not yet taken the traditional oath. If viceregal government ceased, the constitutions made provision for a perfectly adequate alternative form of government, known as government *vice-regia*, whereby the governor of Catalonia exercised authority until a viceroy could be legitimately appointed (though the prospect of being ruled by Don Alexos de Marimón, the then Governador, filled many people with dismay). This effectively disposed of the argument based on *necessity*, which maintained that unless the king could appoint a new viceroy, all government would come to an end. But behind these constitutional and administrative arguments were others which brought to the surface the whole problem of the future relationship of Castile and Catalonia.

Those who urged rejection of the bishop's appointment did so both on the grounds of its illegality, and on the grounds that its acceptance would 'close the door for them to enjoy the royal presence in the Principality'.[2] If once the appointment were allowed, might not the king appoint further viceroys in the future, and himself never come to Catalonia? If this happened, the perennial Catalan nightmare would begin to come true: the province would lose its privileges one by one, and gradually be subjected to the domination of Castile. Perhaps this was the real intention of the king's ministers, and the explanation of the constant postponements of a royal visit. A vital principle was involved, which affected not only the Catalans but the subjects of all the king's dominions united to the Crown of Castile by marriage and inheritance. In the arguments and counter-arguments that flew to and fro between

[1] Pujades, 3, fo. 146.
[2] ACA: CA, leg. 272, no. 16, consulta, 24 Oct. 1622.

Barcelona and Madrid in these agitated months of 1622–3, two rival theories of the nature and purpose of the Spanish empire stood face to face. Was it, after all, to be a Castilian empire, ruled by the laws of Castile, or was it to remain an empire of separate territories each maintaining its own individual identity and individual relationship to the king? On the accession of Philip III in 1598 the duke of Feria had offered this advice to the new king's favourite:

One of the most important considerations for His Majesty to keep in mind at this, the beginning of his happy reign, is that his peoples should regard him as very anxious to hold to his own promises or those made by his ancestors; and he should give such close attention to the affairs of each kingdom as to make it seem (following the example of Ferdinand the Catholic) that he has no other kingdom to govern.[1]

Would Philip III's son follow this advice? Would he keep the promises of his ancestors to observe the Catalan constitutions? Would the Spanish empire continue to be governed along traditional federalist lines or would federalism give way to a centralized, Castilian style of government?

The future character of the Spanish Monarchy was here at stake, as the ambassadors of the Diputació made clear in their second petition to the king—an attempt to lecture him on his duties and obligations as Prince of Catalonia.[2] The ambassadors warned him that he could not in good conscience justify his failure to take the oath by adopting the argument of 'certain persons' that 'the Monarchy should be ruled by uniform laws'. Such an argument was morally and historically unacceptable. It was just and proper that services to the Crown should be fittingly rewarded.

Therefore there *should* be differences in the laws and privileges of Your Majesty's kingdoms, when these privileges are rewards for services to the Crown....And it is right that, in return for the services rendered by the Catalans to their kings, their laws should be observed even when they differ from those of other kingdoms, for it is this very difference which gives Your Majesty's Monarchy its peculiar beauty.

Anyhow, there was no concealing the fact that the Spanish Monarchy was not united and uniform, 'for if all the kingdoms of Your Majesty

---

[1] ACA: CA, leg. 344, Duke of Feria to Marquis of Denia, 28 Dec. 1598.
[2] BC: Fullet Bonsoms 16, *Segundo discurso y memorial hecho por F. Francisco de Copons* (Barcelona, 1622).

regarded themselves as one body politic, there would be no prohibitions on the export of goods and provisions from one kingdom to another, and when they cross the frontiers they would not pay customs dues'.

The ambassadors' arguments put the case for federalism as well as it had ever been put. They reveal all too well the dilemma of an empire governed for over a hundred years by a constitutional formula which had been subjected to growing strain. If the empire was really federal, it was Philip IV's duty to visit his different kingdoms and have due regard to their individual laws. If he did not, then it became clear that the Castilians had determined to recreate the empire in their own image, and break faith with the past. The issue was so clear that there was really nothing to be added to the arguments put forward in 1622. When the Catalans finally revolted against Castile in 1640, they had nothing new to say: that is why the controversy of 1622 between Barcelona and Madrid, for all its apparent triviality, was of such vital consequence. It created a specific issue on which the Catalans, in speaking for themselves, spoke for all those who feared an attempt by the Castilians to alter the traditional constitutional structure of the Spanish empire to suit their own convenience.

It is doubtful whether the Catalans would have spoken so forcibly and reacted with such vehemence if it had not been for the experiences of recent years. The viceroyalty of Alcalá had filled them with foreboding. His provocative actions, his declared intention of destroying the constitutions, had made them sense danger from every quarter; and the king's failure to take the oath and his determination to impose a new viceroy on them by unconstitutional methods, were sufficient to confirm their fears. Never had a menacing Castile seemed so close as in the autumn and winter of 1622.

Yet whether the danger seemed real and serious to *all* Catalonia is by no means clear. One unsympathetic observer attributed the unrest to the actions of four unprincipled men, who stirred up sedition for their own private ends:

one, a discalced friar, a protector and concealer of thieves and the most ill-intentioned of them all; the second a most infamous character, a public thief, who lodges the first in his house; the third who keeps in his breast pocket the pardon given him for counterfeiting coins, and the fourth who has been condemned to death as a bandit. These, although *caballeros*, were responsible for all the riots and unrest.[1]

If this conspiratorial interpretation seems rather too far-fetched, there appears to be no justification for going to the opposite extreme and suggesting that the entire Principality rose like one man to defend its treasured liberties. There is no evidence of unrest in other towns than Barcelona, nor of any very vigorous support for the action of the Diputació. As the months passed, with no viceregal government and the Audiència at a standstill, the towns were growing restless, and began to show irritation at Barcelona's intransigence.[2] The opposition apparently came not from the Principality at large but from Barcelona and from the governing class—the aristocracy and the Barcelona oligarchy— through their mouthpieces, the *braç militar*, the Diputació and the city government.

This was the class that had most to lose from any violation of the traditional system by which Catalonia was governed. It was this class, with its social advantages and legal privileges, and its stake in the Diputació, which benefited most from the Principality's contractual constitution, and which would be most affected if Alcalá's ideas became the basis of Madrid's Catalan policy. The aristocracy wanted to ensure against any future violation of its privileges; Barcelona wanted to ensure against any attempt to exact the *quints*. Only the personal appearance of the king, and his promise on oath to respect the constitutions, would give them a real safeguard against a continuation of Alcalá's policies and methods of government; and the only hope of obtaining the personal appearance of the king now lay in refusing to accept the viceroy he had chosen.

The method by which this class conducted its struggle over the viceroy's appointment can only be understood in relation to Barcelona's system of government. The disputes of 1622–3 lift the veil for a moment on the workings of a city government which shrouded its proceedings in the formal, anonymous minutes of official registers. During these few months, through the letters of the viceroy-elect and the private

---

[1] Angel González Palencia, 'La Junta de Reformación, 1618–1625', *Archivo Histórico Español*, vol. v (Valladolid, 1932), document LXXXIII, 'Advirtimientos sobre las cosas de Cataluña', pp. 118–19. According to the author, any child in the street could point to the trouble-makers, so he omitted to mention their names, and it has not been possible to identify any of them with certainty.

[2] ACA: CA, leg. 367, Bishop of Barcelona to Vice-Chancellor, 30 Nov. 1622.

information of his friends and allies, it is possible to glimpse some of the powerful personalities who ruled the city, and to see the way in which they could manipulate the mechanism of city government to gain the maximum advantage for themselves and their friends.

Barcelona was a great city—great in size and wealth, and great for the power and privileges it had managed to obtain in a long and distinguished history. 'The treasure house of courtesy, the refuge of strangers, the hospital of the poor, the country of the valiant, the avenger of the injured, and the abode of firm and reciprocal friendships, unique in its position and its beauty', Cervantes had said of it.[1] Like Don Quixote and Sancho Panza, all travellers were impressed by the beauty both of its position and its buildings. Beside it rose the hill of Montjuic. In front lay the sea, a curving bay, with a 'harbour neither commodious nor safe'[2] but with 'a mold very strong and stately',[3] as befitted 'a maritime town, and one of the greatest in Spain, her chiefest arsenal for gallies and the scale by which she conveys her monies to Italy'.[4] Here in the large bay rode ships at anchor, galleys from Genoa, vessels from Alicante and Valencia, Canet and Marseilles, resplendent on the shimmering water, but always apprehensively watching for the east wind, which 'makes most dangerous seas and has sometimes driven ships home to the mold and stav'd them'.[5] But at least there was the consolation of good dockyards near at hand—the Dressanes on which Alcalá had dared to set the arms of Castile.

Toward the seaside within the walls is the public plaza for general resort, where the pleasant view invites the gallants and the donnas to spend the evenings in their coaches. Beside the plaza is the city's magazine for corn and over that is their armoury. Over against the magazine is a stately bourse for merchants, and adjoining this is the public house where sit the judges of maritime affairs, being a comely building and adorned both within and without. [This was the famous *Llotja*, the hub of Barcelona's life as a great trading port.] The city is in circuit about 3½ miles, having a very strong and stately stone wall, within the breastworks whereof coaches are driven quite round

---

[1] *Don Quijote*, part II, ch. LXXII. Translated J. M. Cohen (1950), p. 928.

[2] Bodleian: Rawlinson MS D. 120, *An Incursion into Catalonia* (1648), fo. 11.

[3] Bodleian: Rawlinson MS C. 799, Robert Bargrave, *A Relation of Sundry Voyages...* (1654), fo. 105v. The mole was under construction in the 1620's.

[4] *Epistolae Ho-Elianae. The Familiar Letters of James Howell*, ed. Joseph Jacobs (London, 1890), vol. I. Letter to Sir James Crofts, 24 Nov. 1620, p. 58.

[5] Bargrave, *Relation*, fos. 105v–108, for this and the description that follows. Bargrave has some interesting comments to make on Barcelona's commercial possibilities.

the city, and without it is a good dry trench, so that if they be masters of the port it seems impregnable....Its buildings are generally handsome, high and strong, yet nothing so stately without as they are rich within. Their rooms are very large, uniform, high roofed and nobly furnished. The streets are but narrow to screen out the sun....The town is full of convents....

A population of some 40,000 thronged these narrow streets—a population that was noisy and turbulent, a population of apprentices and craftsmen and artisans, with a sprinkling of sailors from the foreign and Catalan ships that put in at the port. It was a population easily excited, at once bustling and idle, happy to turn out to watch the sights —the latest ship putting into harbour, the arrival of some foreign dignitary—or to riot because corn was too dear, or simply because there was nothing better to do. It was restless and hungry and crowded and dirty, and now and again it would be ravaged by terrible epidemics. In 1589–90, perhaps a fifth of the population (over 11,000 people, according to contemporary records) had been carried off by the plague —plague that came in ships from Marseilles or the Levant, or overland from Castile or France.[1]

At the other end of the social scale, living in solid respectable houses, with their wide arched entrances opening into a spacious *patio*, from which a stone stairway led to the 'high roofed and nobly furnished rooms' on the principal floor, was the city aristocracy: nobles and gentry, merchants and lawyers. These were the people who took the evening air in their coaches; who bought from the bookshops the works of Lope de Vega and the latest comedies from Valladolid and Madrid, together with the more standard works—the colloquies of Vives, lives of the saints, works of devotion and popular romances;[2] who went to see the comedies in the city's theatre,[3] and who educated their sons at the college of Cordelles. They were the people who governed the city of Barcelona, and, through the Diputació, the Principality.

This Barcelona aristocracy numbered perhaps five hundred men. No figures are available for lawyers and doctors, who were waging an

[1] Robert S. Smith, 'Barcelona Bills of Mortality and Population, 1457–1590', *The Journal of Political Economy*, vol. XLIV (1936), p. 86.

[2] See the inventory of Narcís Pons, a bookseller of Barcelona (1608), in APB: A. J. Fita, lib. 1, d'inventaris.

[3] The agent of Vic, who went to call on Dr Fontanella, the lawyer, found that he was 'at the comedy' (AMV: CR, 12, Francesc Sala to Consellers of Vic, 24 May 1634).

interminable lawsuit to secure the same rights and privileges as the *ciutadans honrats*,[1] but they do exist for nobles, *cavallers* (or *donzells*), *ciutadans honrats* and merchants:[2]

Nobles	103
Cavallers	71
Ciutadans honrats	51
Merchants	154
	379

These men formed a small, closely knit group bound by ties of kinship and marriage. No less than three institutions were available through which they could express their opinions: Diputació, *braç militar* and city government. This meant that the same names constantly recur in the political life of the Principality—names like Bellafilla, Navel, Dalmau—sometimes in the actions of the *braç militar*, sometimes in those of the Barcelona city council. Josep de Bellafilla, for instance, who was perhaps the most influential man in Barcelona at this moment, and who played a leading part in the dispute over the viceroy's appointment, on this occasion conducted his campaign through the *braç militar* of which he had been elected *protector*. The *braç militar* existed simply to express the views of the aristocracy, and especially the Barcelona aristocracy, which was overwhelmingly represented in it. Its meetings were attended not only by the aristocracy proper, nobles and *cavallers*, but also by the *ciutadans honrats* of Barcelona, so that its own interests and those of the city government generally coincided. Wealthy and powerful, it could reinforce the actions of the city by mobilizing the resident aristocracy in the city's interests, by presenting its own petitions, and even by sending embassies to Madrid.

But it was the government of Barcelona which offered the best field for political manoeuvre, for the city of Barcelona, thanks to its wealth and its privileges, was almost an independent republic, a second Venice, linked to its Count, now king of Castile, by only the slenderest of ties. In wealth and importance it towered above the other Catalan towns. Tortosa collected 12,000 *lliures* a year in taxes, Girona and Perpinyà

[1] AHB: lib. 57, *Matrícula dels antichs ciutadans honrats de Barcelona*, fo. 108 v.

[2] From the lists compiled in 1639 by Joan Pi and others (ACA: G, caja 26) and by Francesc de Vilalba (caja 21). The figure for merchants, from the year 1625, is given by Carrera Pujal, *Historia...de Cataluña*, vol. I, p. 393.

6000—and Barcelona 80,000.[1] Its financial credit gave it a rock-like stability; the Taula, the deposit bank, contained some 400,000 *lliures* placed there by private persons and the Diputació.[2] Indulgent or impoverished monarchs had showered privileges upon Barcelona, leaving the Crown with scarcely a vestige of control. In the seventeenth century the king could still appoint to one or two city offices, and nominate the *veguer* of Barcelona; he still possessed a few financial rights, most of them disputed; and only he could confer new privileges upon the city. But this was all. Not even a royal garrison or castle survived to hint at the existence of a superior power.

The city spared no effort or expense in impressing its importance upon the world. Of all the cities of Spain, it was the only one to reserve a permanent box in the Plaza Mayor of Madrid at a minimum cost of eight ducats a bullfight.[3] It treated with the ministers in Madrid almost as if it were a foreign power, despatching ambassadors to conduct negotiations, and surrounding their entry and appearances with the most elaborate ostentation and ceremonial. When Josep de Bellafilla went to Valladolid in 1602 as the city's representative, he was accorded so magnificent a welcome that 'even the leading nobles of this Court say that the nuncio of His Holiness himself has never been given such a reception, nor the ambassador of the Emperor or other potentates, and the Castilians are all amazed and awestruck that an ambassador who is a vassal of the king should be received with so much honour'.[4] Barcelona's embassy of 1622 on the appointment of the viceroy was accompanied through the streets of Madrid by a cortege of no less than two hundred carriages, and was reported to be the most magnificent in living memory.[5] If this could be said of a Madrid which had lived through the reign of Philip III, it must have been a most remarkable sight.

Barcelona did not arrange all this finery simply through a passion for splendour. In an age when ostentation was visible proof of power and pre-eminence, it was a matter of policy to mount such costly ceremonial. When Olivares's servant, Simón, cried: 'Enter the City of

[1] AHN: Est., leg. 860, paper enclosed by the Count of Oñate, 28 Aug. 1632.
[2] ACA: CA, leg. 276, no. 9, Fontanet to President of Council of Aragon, 30 Dec. 1628.
[3] AHB: CCO, 1637, Joan Grau to Consellers, 1 Aug. 1637.
[4] AHB: CCO, 1600–3, fos. 62–63 v, Josep de Bellafilla to Consellers, 1 April 1602.
[5] AHB: CCO, 1622, fos. 86–9, Pau de Altariba to Consellers, 18 June 1622.

Barcelona', the ambassador who entered Olivares's study was the embodiment of his city, and the ceremonial that accompanied him, with all its suggestion of power and independence, strengthened his hand in the diplomatic negotiations he had come to conduct. No one could be left in any doubt that he represented a great city free and independent in all but name.

A share in the government of so influential a city was therefore extremely desirable. Those who possessed it enjoyed power, prestige, and offices—and especially power. Barcelona dominated Catalonia, determining its relations with the king and the policies that the Principality was to follow. Indeed, as Olivares was one day ruefully to admit, Barcelona *was* Catalonia.[1] This meant that the form of its government was a matter of considerable concern not only to the Principality at large, but also to the apprehensive ministers in Madrid.

Barcelona's municipal government, dating from the thirteenth century, had been reformed by Ferdinand the Catholic in 1498.[2] It was based on a representative council of 144 members, known as the *Consell de Cent*, or Council of a Hundred, half of which was replaced annually by the lottery system for the selection of officers which had been generally adopted in Catalonia. The members of the Consell de Cent can be broadly divided into four classes:

48 *ciutadans* (citizens)—32 *ciutadans honrats* and lawyers, and 16 *militars*, of whom two, after 1621, had to be nobles.[3]

32 *mercaders*—merchants registered and chosen by the *Llotja* of merchants, and confirmed by those already in the Consell de Cent. (Unregistered merchants, known as *negociants*, had no status and were not allowed entry into the government of city and Diputació.)[4]

32 *artistes*—notaries, barbers, apothecaries, grocers, etc.

32 *menestrals*—tailors, shoemakers and members of other smaller trades organized into guilds.

These men took part in the draw for city offices, and had to make the major policy decisions on questions of administration and on the city's relations with the king and his ministers. They would be summoned

---

[1] AHB: CCO, 1634, fos. 41–2, Jeroni de Navel to Consellers, 8 April 1634.
[2] See J. Vicens Vives, *Ferran II i la Ciutat de Barcelona* (3 vols., Barcelona, 1937), for details of Ferdinand's reforms and of the working of the city government.
[3] AHB: LC, 1620–2, fos. 54–6, rules for admission of nobles, 12 June 1621.
[4] *Discurso de Micer Francesc Soler...* (Barcelona, 1621), pp. 26–7.

by the tolling of the city bell—a sound which filled many a viceroy with alarm and which, at moments of tension, was itself sufficient to arouse an excited mob.

When the Consell de Cent was gathered, the issues were presented to it by the Consellers, and then debated and voted upon. The Consellers, who numbered five, were extracted by lot every St Andrew's Day, and were responsible for the daily government of the city and for the execution of the policies decided by the Consell de Cent. Of these five Consellers, the first (known as the *Conseller-en-Cap*), and the second and third, had their names drawn from the bags of citizens' names; the fourth Conseller was always a merchant, and the fifth either a *menestral* or an *artista*, alternating annually. The *artistes* and *menestrals* had for long been agitating for the creation of a sixth Conseller, so that each group should always have one town councillor, but nobles, *ciutadans honrats* and merchants resisted the demand.[1]

From the proportionate representation of different social classes both in the Consell de Cent and among the five town councillors, it is clear that the city aristocracy was again predominant, with eighty places in the Consell de Cent, four out of the five councillors, and the lion's share of the offices in the city government. Yet even with this preponderance, it could not always be sure of getting its own way. *Artistes* and *menestrals* might be in a minority in the Consell de Cent, but they represented the great majority in the streets outside. If the crowd was whipped up by agitators and rioted outside the town hall, the city oligarchy was well advised to fall in with the wishes of the mass of the populace. It was therefore natural enough for anyone aspiring to dominate the city to bid for the support of the *artistes* and *menestrals*. The control of Barcelona in the last resort lay not with the oligarchy, but with the thousands of humbler citizens, and an ambitious noble or citizen could successfully defy his colleagues by appealing over their heads to the crowd.

The oligarchy's ability to control the fortunes both of Barcelona and the Principality therefore at least partly depended on its ability to secure, either through persuasion or through agitation, the adherence, or at least the quiescence, of the citizens of Barcelona. This in turn was determined by its own solidarity. A small group of nobles in alliance

[1] ACA: CA, leg. 267, no. 4, consulta, 19 Jan. 1602.

with the crowd might successfully defy the rest of the Barcelona aristocracy. With a united front and the sympathy of the population, the oligarchy were invincible; with a united front but without popular sympathy they were vulnerable; without a united front and without popular sympathy their powers of resistance were very limited. This made it clear what tactics the Crown should adopt when it was involved in any dispute with the Principality. It must break the alliance of city and Diputació, win over by bribery, promises or threats as many influential members of the city oligarchy as possible, and either isolate or suborn the ringleaders of the opposition.

The Crown, apparently so weak in the Principality, possessed one unique advantage. By a judicious use of patronage, it could convert enemies into friends, and turn the most bitter opponents of the regime into willing partisans. The experience of these years was to show that very few Catalans could resist appeals to their self-interest. The desire for a title, or a pension, or a post in the administration was almost always too strong even for those who had fought the Crown most bitterly. Many, who were often perfectly sincere in their opposition, could be bought off by a well-timed bribe; others may have gone into opposition less for public than for private interest, in order to draw attention to themselves and force the Crown to give them satisfaction. Motives were so mixed as to be impossible to unravel, for it paid in city politics either to be very good or very bad—the very bad having a slightly better chance of ultimately securing a favour from the Crown. Josep de Bellafilla, who led the opposition to the appointment of the bishop of Barcelona, may genuinely have felt that a royal visit was essential for the survival of the Principality; but he may also have been influenced, to a greater or lesser extent, by personal grievance. He spent two years in prison under the marquis of Almazán for unspecified reasons,[1] and he had never been paid an annual pension granted him in 1599.[2] How far he was motivated by these personal considerations, no one can say, although his opposition was to come to an end when a personal approach was made to him on the question of his pension. There can be less doubt, though, about the motives of his most vehement opponent, and the most consistent defender of the interests of

---

[1] ACA: CA, leg. 487, Almazán to King, 20 Sept. 1614.
[2] ACA: CA, leg. 378, Josep de Bellafilla to Viceroy, 11 Nov. 1628.

the Crown throughout the controversy, Don Bernardino de Marimón. Marimón, an accomplice of the bandits, had taken the precaution of retiring to France at the outset of Alburquerque's viceroyalty, rather than await the outcome of the case pending against him in the Audiència.[1] But he was a poor noble with a family, and he was not anxious to spend the rest of his life in exile. He finally managed to return to the Principality on a safe-conduct, probably obtained with the assistance of his cousin, Don Alexos de Marimón, the governor of Catalonia, and set out at once to prove himself a model vassal of His Majesty. The dispute over the viceroyalty provided him with the perfect opportunity to show the extent of his transformation. From the first he braved the opposition in the *braç militar* and the Consell de Cent and spoke openly in the king's interest. His services were so considerable that, in spite of his background, they could not be overlooked. When the dispute was over, and the Council of Aragon was busily dividing the leading citizens of Barcelona into sheep and goats, Don Bernardino, heading the list of sheep, must naturally be given his due reward. His son was granted a pension of 200 ducats a year on the bishopric of Tortosa,[2] and he himself received the lucrative post of superintendent of the Barcelona dockyards.[3] The ex-bandit had made good, and the former penurious noble was on the way to becoming a prosperous royal official.

The confusion of motives, the mingling of public and private interest, defeat all attempts to understand the exact course of events in struggles like that of 1622–3 between the Principality and Madrid. The fiercest opponents of the Crown would change sides so unexpectedly and so suddenly that it would be natural to expect that they had been bribed; but proof of bribery is rare, and no more can be done than hint at the circumstances which might have induced a man to change his mind under pressure. Yet unless the existence of widespread lobbying and bribery is assumed, the story is incomprehensible, and the jigsaw can never be pieced together.

At the beginning of the controversy over the acceptance of the bishop of Barcelona as viceroy, the city oligarchy had been united in its determination to resist the bishop's appointment. The strength of the Principality's opposition derived, as the Diputats themselves pointed

[1] See above, p. 122.
[2] ACA: CA, leg. 371, Bishop of Barcelona to J. L. de Villanueva, 7 Aug. 1623.
[3] ACA: CA, leg. 370, consulta, 1623.

168

out, from 'the union and conformity which exists between these two houses [of city and Diputació] and the *braç militar* and all the rest, so that nobody holds a contrary opinion except the self-interested, and those who are always ill-disposed towards the fatherland'.[1] Yet within a very few weeks of the Diputats' refusal to attend the bishop's inauguration, this much-vaunted unity was beginning to crack. The ambassadors of the Diputació reported from Madrid that all the royal ministers were opposed to the Principality's claims, and that the doctrine of *necessity* was in itself sufficient to release the king temporarily from his obligations.[2] On receipt of this letter, the Diputats began to waver. Their lawyers, who had been so firm on the justice of the Principality's case a few months earlier, now admitted that certain learned persons held a contrary opinion, and announced that, although they personally still believed in the justice of their cause, it was not their duty to pronounce judgment.[3] Since they had always been happy to pronounce judgment in the past, this was a rather surprising retreat, in which the hand of the Fontanella family is to be detected. Here again, personal and professional considerations are impossible to disentangle, but the later reputation of Dr Fontanella as an intrepid defender of Catalonia's liberties makes it worth while to examine his activities at this particular moment.

Dr Fontanella, whose nephew happened to be the Diputat Eclesiàstic, enjoyed a great reputation in the Principality for his book on marriage contracts. As was natural, he had applied for a post in the Audiència, listing his many qualifications—his twenty years' service as a lawyer, his book, his general suitability.[4] His petition was unsuccessful, and his further petitions in the following years, although well supported by the members of the Audiència themselves, were equally ill-fated. On each occasion his appointment was opposed by Alcalá, who disapproved of the various commissions he had undertaken for the Diputació, and regarded him as a 'man of restless condition'.[5] Having failed to enter the royal administration, he continued to work for the Diputació, and signed the legal opinion rejecting the appointment of the bishop as

[1] *Consistori...*, fo. 193, Diputats to ambassadors, 8 Oct. 1622.
[2] *Ibid.* fos. 229–31, ambassadors to Diputats, 15 Oct. 1622.
[3] *Ibid.* fos. 255–9, paper by lawyers, 4 Nov. 1622.
[4] ACA: CA, leg. 359, petition by Dr Joan Pere Fontanella, 1617.
[5] ACA: CA, leg. 364, Alcalá to King, 28 Dec. 1620. He was rejected for three separate vacancies for the Audiència in 1621–2, at the instigation of Alcalá (ACA: CA, legajos 366 and 369).

unconstitutional. But within two months he and his nephew were wavering, and by the end of the year they had ranged themselves on the side of the Crown. Two of the more violent members of the Barcelona aristocracy, Monrodón and Espuny, were so angered by this that they treated 'the two Fontanellas, uncle and nephew, as traitors, and swore they would kill them, because Fontanella was one of the lawyers who drew up a memorandum against the King and now spoke in his favour'.[1]

There is no knowing why the Fontanellas changed their minds. It may well be that the Diputats and Dr Fontanella were by now convinced, on the basis of the letters sent by the ambassadors from Court, that there was no chance of success; in these circumstances, it would be better for them to accept a compromise solution than return empty-handed. If personal considerations entered into Dr Fontanella's *volte-face*, he had badly miscalculated. He continued to put forward his name for appointment to the Audiència during the following years, but each time, for one reason or another, his hopes were dashed, although he was acknowledged to be the best lawyer in Barcelona.[2]

The defection of the Fontanellas destroyed the united front which had been up to now so successfully maintained, and caused deep resentment in the city. The Diputats now favoured a compromise solution put forward by the duke of Sessa, but it was overwhelmingly rejected at a meeting of the Braços, convened by the blowing of trumpets at the unprecedented hour of nine o'clock on the night of 4 November. Only Don Bernardino de Marimón and two other nobles voted in favour of Sessa's compromise, which offered, in return for the Catalans' immediate acceptance of the bishop, that government *vice-regia* by the governor would begin at the end of a year if the king had not in the meantime come to the Principality. The vote was disappointing, but it could not be taken as indication that the Barcelona aristocracy were unanimously opposed to the compromise, since the more elderly nobles, weary of the violence that characterized the meetings of the *braç militar*, had ceased to put in an appearance.[3]

When the Consell de Cent heard on 8 November that the Diputats still thought of pursuing negotiations on the proposed compromise, it

[1] Pujades, 3, fo. 132.
[2] ACA: CA, leg. 380, Viceroy to King, 29 June 1630 (see below, p. 294).
[3] ACA: CA, leg. 367, Bishop of Barcelona to King, 5 Nov. 1622.

broke up in tumult. Arms were brought out, the city bell was rung, and the walls were plastered with lampoons against the Diputats. The unfortunate Diputats had to retract their recent actions and submit to the humiliation of writing to their ambassadors a letter (to be produced in the Consell de Cent before despatch) instructing them once again to insist on the king's granting government *vice-regia*.[1] Wherever power lay in the Principality, it clearly did not lie with the Diputats.

Somehow, the opposition of the nobility and the Consell de Cent must be broken, and it was on the nobility that the bishop of Barcelona now decided to concentrate his attention.[2] A letter from the king, dated 11 November, charged the nobles, as a matter of particular service to himself, to attend the bishop's inauguration whenever it should be announced.[3] The natural corollary of the word *service* was *reward*. Many nobles took the hint, and from this moment there was a definite weakening in the hitherto solid ranks of nobles and *militars*. Don Bernat and Don Francesc de Pinós, Don Miquel Clariana and Don Francesc Grimau, all of whom had fiercely opposed the bishop's appointment, now retired from active participation in the controversy.[4]

Only the Consell de Cent remained immovable, and indeed showed itself not less but more intransigent. Without government in the Principality, order was deteriorating and the bandits beginning to return. The bishop was growing desperate, and his desperation communicated itself to the Council of Aragon. The time had come, it suggested, for the king to order the bishop to take his oath, with or without the attendance of city and Diputats, inside Barcelona or outside it.[5] Only two members of the Council of Aragon questioned this recommendation, which the Council had rejected a few months earlier, and produced a minority *consulta* of their own. These two, the count of Chinchón and the Valencian regent Castellví, believed that the opposition to the appointment was still so strong and so general, that either the Barcelona mob would prevent the bishop from going to the cathedral, or, if he took the oath in private, no one would obey his orders. Either of these actions amounted to rebellion, which would

---

[1] ACA: CA, leg. 368, Bishop of Barcelona to King, 12 Nov. 1622.
[2] *Ibid.* 19 Nov. 1622.
[3] *Consistori*, fos. 285–6, royal letter, 11 Nov. 1622.
[4] ACA: CA, leg. 369, Bishop to King, 27 May 1623.
[5] ACA: CA, leg. 366, consulta, 24 (?) Dec. 1622.

oblige the king to undertake punitive action. But what was the probability of immediate success, they asked, in a city like Barcelona? There were no troops in Barcelona or elsewhere in the Principality capable of suppressing a popular tumult, and they reminded the king of the difficulty of suppressing revolts even in towns like Brussels and Naples which were commanded by royal artillery. If insurrection in Barcelona were not at once suppressed, there was danger of a repetition of the troubles that Philip II had faced in Aragon, and the rebels could always beat a retreat to France.

Reminders of the Aragonese troubles in the 1590's always alarmed the ministers in Madrid. The minority *consulta*, with its ominous hints of rebellion, set the issue squarely before the king. Was he to compromise, or run the risk of revolution—a revolution which, as Chinchón pointed out, was motivated by nothing more disloyal than a desire to see the king's person? The Council of State, which had up to now left the Catalan question to the Council of Aragon, could no longer refrain from intervention; and its intervention was to be the first real test for Olivares, who, since Zúñiga's death in October, had become sole favourite of the king. On 27 December 1622, therefore, the Consejo de Estado was summoned to discuss the two *consultas* of the Council of Aragon.[1] Its meeting was very important, for it was to be the first of many occasions when the correct treatment of the Catalans was debated by the ministers of Philip IV, and at this stage they spoke much more freely than in later years, when Olivares's domination was more firmly established.

Olivares had already been laying his plans, and had mooted the idea of a special mission to Catalonia by the young count of Osona, the son of the marquis of Aytona, and a popular figure among the Catalans. It was between this suggestion, and that put forward by the majority of the Council of Aragon, that the Consejo de Estado was asked to decide. The exchange of views provides a valuable insight into the attitudes of the leading ministers and the considerations predominant at this moment in the policies of Madrid. The duke of Infantado, who began the discussion, confined himself to a plea that rupture with the Catalans should be avoided, and warmly supported the proposed conciliatory mission of the count of Osona. But Osona's father, Aytona,

[1] AGS: Est., leg. 4126, consulta, 27 Dec. 1622.

who spoke next, took an entirely different line. In his view, his son's visit would not be much use, and Barcelona had long deserved a show of force, which the king, as a special favour, had long withheld. His only other suggestion was that an approach be made to Bellafilla, of whom he happened to be a friend; if the king offered Bellafilla payment of the pension so long owed to him, there was a good chance of his changing his mind, but this must be handled very diplomatically to avoid any suggestion that he and others were actuated by self-interest.

Negotiation and force now each had a partisan. Don Pedro de Toledo, who followed Infantado and Aytona, discoursed at length on diseases in the body politic, but finally cast his vote in favour of negotiation. A policy of force against the Catalans would cause a great deal of trouble at a time when their help was needed in assisting the king financially, and in defending the Indies, Italy and 'the Catholics of Germany'—'all of these matters of more importance and concern to the world than a domestic settlement with the Catalans'. The Council of Aragon's recommendation, while showing zeal for the king's authority, was very misleading about the prospects of a war in Catalonia 'when the king of France, ready armed, is so close, and is so well placed to encourage it'. This was not to be the last time when Catalonia's proximity to France emerged as one of the most effective arguments against the use of force by Madrid.

Don Agustín Mexía and Don Diego de Ibarra agreed with Don Pedro, while the marquis of Montesclaros, trying to make the best of both worlds, spoke in favour of moderate punishment. It only remained for Olivares to speak. Even at this early stage of his political career, his speech had all the characteristics which later became so notorious—excessive length and complication, a tendency to exaggeration, and to digressions on the art of politics. The content, as well as the manner, throws an interesting light on the workings of Olivares's mind. He was always attracted by the idea of a quick, forceful solution: 'with 4000 or 6000 men on those frontiers, or with naval forces in the vicinity of the province, everything would be so easily settled that a single *alguacil* could arrange matters according to Your Majesty's commands'. But, whenever he made this kind of statement, there were always second thoughts, as if to show that, while he could be tough when necessary, he was too good a politician to give way to such crude measures. 'The wisest course in such cases, though, is to use the most gentle measures, and this is the course followed by Your Majesty up to now, in refusing to agree to the Council of Aragon's demands for a policy of force.' On the other hand, he did not think that Don Pedro de Toledo's suggestions of conciliation had any hope of success, and there were certain inherent objections, for 'in my view the essence of statesmanship (*materia de estado*) is, and always will be, not to allow subjects to choose their own conditions, even in those cases where the right is on their side'. Questions of prestige and the maintenance of the king's authority always played an important part in Olivares's political decisions. If the Catalans were successful on this occasion, would they not be encouraged by their success to make more and more exorbitant demands? And might not the rest of the Crown of Aragon follow suit? (The possible reactions of Aragon and Valencia could never be over-looked in any discussion of Catalan affairs.) He had therefore come to a conclusion similar to that of Montesclaros: that it was advisable to use 'a little rigour, which is a more effective way with them than gentle-ness'. Rigour and gentleness—*rigor* and *blandura*: how many times were those words to echo through the Council chambers when the correct policy towards the Catalans was under discussion! There was nothing surprising about this. Because of the restricted power and limited police resources of seventeenth-century monarchies it was hard to know how to deal with recalcitrant subjects, and it always became necessary at a relatively early stage to choose between starting military operations, or making concessions which, although preventing rebellion, might seriously diminish the authority of the Crown.

Olivares's definition of 'a little rigour', however, turned out to be nothing more serious than a decision to send Osona to Barcelona with letters expressing His Majesty's determination to punish the excesses with the greatest severity. The Catalan authorities were at once to agree to attend the bishop's inauguration, and, in return for this, Olivares promised to throw himself at the king's feet and beseech him to grant whatever the Catalans might demand. Philip IV, as was always to happen, made the final decision along the lines suggested by Olivares, and the young count of Osona was despatched at the beginning of 1623 on his delicate, and peculiarly vague, mission to win over the intransi-gent citizens of Barcelona.

Osona's chances of success did not seem very hopeful. Bellafilla and his friends had spent Christmas-time attempting to force Diputats and nobles back into the fold of the patriots, and the only consolation that the bishop of Barcelona could report was the growing unpopularity of Barcelona among the majority of the Catalans: 'the complaints of the Principality against the city could hardly be exaggerated'.[1] But for all the opposition of the rest of the province, Barcelona held firm. Osona, who arrived in the city on 10 January 1623, was met by a deputation of the twelve most intractable members of the Consell de Cent, headed by Bellafilla, Lluís de Corbera and Jeroni de Navel. His negotiations with them continued for almost a fortnight, and it was only on 23 January 1623 that the fateful motion was put before the Consell de Cent: should it accept or reject Osona's proposal that the city's representatives attend the bishop's inauguration in return for Olivares's promise to intercede with the king?

The meeting of the Consell de Cent, which began at three o'clock on the afternoon of 23 January, and continued until four the next morning, was one of the most exciting to be held in that assembly, and on this occasion enough information leaked out for the proceedings to be roughly reconstructed. The meeting began with a report by Bellafilla and his eleven colleagues on their discussions with Osona, who was then himself admitted into the Consell to explain his mission. After this, Dr Vileta, the Conseller-en-Cap, put the proposition to the meeting in the usual manner, but ended, in an unprecedented manner, with the menacing words: 'And I warn you that you are not to obey, and I will not retreat even with a dagger at my throat.'[2] This uncompromising declaration was supported by the second Conseller, Francesc Cornet, who had already distinguished himself by his opposition to Alcalá two years earlier. He told the Council that an astrologer had forecast that he would die at the age of seventy, and as there were only two years to go, it hardly worried him what befell him in the short space of time that remained: so he also advised against acceptance of the Osona proposal. Miquel Fivaller, a *militar*, then formally proposed its rejection, and was supported by two other *militars*, Domingo Monrodón and Josep d'Espuny, who attempted, by threats and entreaties, to

[1] ACA: CA, leg. 272, no. 16, Bishop to King, 8 Jan. 1623.
[2] AHB: CCO, 1623–5, fos. 15–17, ambassadors to Consellers, 1 Feb. 1623.

secure unanimous support for Fivaller's motion. But they had over-looked the intrepid Don Bernardino de Marimón, anxious to shine in the service of his king. Marimón made an impassioned speech in favour of accepting Osona's proposal, only to find that Dr Vileta and the third Conseller, in an attempt to preserve the fiction of unanimity, refused to allow any reference to his speech in the official records. For an hour and a half the meeting was held up, as Marimón wrangled with the city clerk in an effort to get his opinions put on record, and the dispute was only brought to an end by the forcible ejection of Marimón from the Council chamber.[1] The voting was finally held after Marimón's removal, and, although he had managed to obtain forty sup-porters, Fivaller's motion was accepted. The Conseller-en-Cap was to be sent on a fresh embassy to Madrid to demand government *vice-regia* till the king could come. Osona's mission had ended in total failure.

Osona's failure showed the extent of the control exercised over the Consell de Cent by a few dominant personalities in the city, but it is hard to believe that the Consell would have resisted for so long if it were not genuinely convinced of the disadvantages of Osona's proposal. The nobles wanted a remedy for their grievances and the city wanted a renunciation by the Crown of its claim to the *quints*, and it was because of the general strength of feeling on these issues that the most outspoken opponents of the bishop's appointment, whether they acted for reasons of public or private interest, enjoyed such success. The city's ambassa-dors in Madrid, Oms and Vinyes, believed that Barcelona had lost a fine opportunity for an honourable settlement, and that, if the city had complied with the king's wishes, the ministers would have given it all it wanted.[2] But Osona's opponents, rightly or wrongly, believed that even partial surrender could be ruinous to their demands, and they had now committed themselves so deeply that no surrender, however prompt, could restore their personal standing with the ministers of the Crown.

The city's refusal to comply with the royal demands was very em-barrassing for the ministers in Madrid, and most of all for Olivares who had staked his authority on the success of Osona's mission. It was clear that he must give Osona a stronger hand to play, but he must do

---

[1] ACA: CA, leg. 272, no. 16, Bishop to King, 24 Jan. 1623.
[2] AHB: CCO, 1623–5, fos. 18–19, Oms and Vinyes to Consellers, 4 Feb. 1623.

it without giving the impression to the Council of State that he had in any way yielded to pressure from the city. Osona had managed to win Bellafilla by promising that his pension would be paid, and Bellafilla was now using his considerable influence in support of the cause he had formerly so assiduously opposed, but Osona must have something better to offer than a mere promise from Olivares of intercession with the king.

Some time during the course of February 1623 Osona was given the bargaining counters he needed, presumably in a private letter from Olivares which no longer exists. One day at the end of February, Osona signed and handed over to the Consellers a paper containing three promises: that the king would come to Barcelona and console his vassals; that the pragmatic forbidding the carrying of *pedrenyals* would be suspended; and that the royal ministers would make no attempt to collect the *quints* from Barcelona or from any other town where the royal rights were disputed, until the conclusion of the first Corts to be held.[1] The only condition attached was that the Consellers should keep these offers absolutely secret, in order to avoid prejudicing the king's authority with the Principality, or, more plausibly, Olivares's authority with his colleagues. The Consellers therefore had the difficult task of persuading the Consell de Cent to change its mind without being able to report why it was advantageous to do so. They did what was required of them, however, and on 3 March the Consell de Cent finally voted that the city authorities should attend the inauguration of the bishop.[2] Even now, further troubles threatened to wreck the settlement. Olivares, in his efforts to save face, had persuaded Dr Vileta to sign a paper saying that Barcelona had surrendered unconditionally, and the fury in the Consell de Cent when it learnt of the Conseller-en-Cap's action again delayed the ceremony.[3] It was perhaps fortunate for Olivares that a sudden discovery that Dr Vileta had appropriated thousands of ducats from the city funds conveniently diverted the Consell's attention from politics to finance. Finally, on 12 April 1623, seven months after his original appointment, the bishop of Barcelona took the oath as viceroy 'with much applause from the city'.[4] Olivares, on receiving

---

[1] AHB: CCO, 1620–2, fo. 77, undated paper signed by the count of Osona (incorrectly bound in volume for 1622).
[2] AHB: LC, 1620–3, fo. 185, Consellers to Grau, 3 March 1623.
[3] ACA: CA, leg. 272, no. 16, Bishop to King, 27 March 1623.
[4] ACA: CA, leg. 272, no. 16, J. L. de Villanueva to Olivares, with Olivares's reply, 15 April 1623.

the news in a note from the secretary of the Council of Aragon, heaved a sigh of relief and went to tell the king. 'This is very good news', he replied to the secretary, 'and I have told it to His Majesty who is delighted to see that we have escaped from so embarrassing a situation. . . .'

All that remained was for Olivares to induce the Councils at Madrid to concede to the Catalans what he had already conceded them privately. It seems from the *consultas* of the Consejo de Estado that it was ignorant of the concessions that Olivares had quietly made, but it was fully conscious of its obligation to reward the Principality for its 'unconditional' surrender.[1] Everything turned out as Olivares had wanted. The obvious reward was suspension of royal claims to Barcelona's *quints*, and to this the Consejo de Estado agreed, together with the restoration to the viceroy of the right to give the various small privileges known as *cosas de gracia* which had been withdrawn during the viceroyalty of Almazán.[2] The only remaining subject of discussion was the length of the bishop of Barcelona's tenure of office. Montesclaros wanted to rub salt into the wound by nominating a permanent viceroy to succeed the bishop, simply in order to show that the king had the right to appoint new viceroys as and when he wished. But, as the duke of Infantado pointed out, there would be two thousand contradictions if a third viceroy were nominated, and Montesclaros's imprudent suggestion was rejected. Consequently, the unfortunate bishop of Barcelona, who had never shown any enthusiasm for his post, was condemned to continue in office until such time as the king could at last come to the Principality. When that time would be, nobody knew.

The long, involved controversy had come to an end, but it would be hard to say with whom the victory lay, or indeed whether it was possible in the circumstances for either side to talk of victory. Madrid had been forced to make concessions which it would willingly have avoided. Barcelona had obtained a further postponement of the royal attempt to obtain one-fifth of its revenues, and the nobles had secured a suspension of the intolerable pragmatic about the carrying of weapons. But these issues, while important, had not been the fundamental issues at the beginning of the dispute. The crucial question had been whether or not the king's government of the Principality could continue if the

[1] AHN: Est., lib. 737, fo. 293, consulta, 21 June 1623.
[2] *Ibid.* fos. 311–13, consulta, 10 July 1623. For the *cosas de gracia* see above, p. 81.

king himself failed to visit it and take the traditional oath to observe its laws. On the answer to this question hinged the entire contractual relationship between the Catalans and their king; either the king, in governing the Principality, recognized certain legal restrictions on his freedom, or he did not. If he did not, then Catalonia would lose its traditional constitution, and come to be governed in the manner of Castile. The petitions of the Diputats, when the dispute began, make it clear that they had fully appreciated the constitutional implications of the appointment of a viceroy before the king had taken the oath. But during the dispute this issue had come to be overlaid with others, like those of the *pedrenyals* and the *quints*, and by making concessions on these, without conceding the main point, Olivares had managed to secure the appointment of the viceroy and had committed himself to no firm date for a royal visit. It was the Principality's failure to carry the main point which gives substance to Dr Pujades's comment on the outcome of the controversy. In his opinion, the city would have done better to have accepted the Sessa compromise, with its promise that government *vice-regia* would automatically begin if the king did not come within a year. This would have represented at least a partial victory on the central issue, instead of defeat on the central issue and victory on the side-issues. It would, as Dr Pujades said, 'in some way have set the seal of approval on the city's claim, which now is completely discounted'.[1]

Such success as Madrid enjoyed, however, was not a success for any deliberate policy aimed at destruction of the Catalan constitutions. The king's ministers had never looked on the dispute in these terms. For them, Philip IV was not simply the Prince of Catalonia and Count of Barcelona, but the ruler of a vast number of dominions, all of which had just as much right to his presence as the Catalans. In their eyes, Catalonia was behaving selfishly and even frivolously in demanding an immediate royal visit when there was still so much to be arranged in Madrid for the benefit not of one but of all his kingdoms. Why should the Catalans expect to be singled out for special favour when that favour meant neglecting the interests of his many other territories? They could not understand that the Catalans saw Philip IV's failure to visit the Principality in a very different light. To the Catalans, Philip IV was

[1] Pujades, 3, fo. 147v.

Prince of Catalonia, and that was all that counted. Because they thought of the king only as their king, they found it difficult to grasp why his visit should be delayed. Certain evil-intentioned ministers, they felt, must deliberately be preventing a royal visit, and the aim of these ministers was to subvert the laws of Catalonia.

The Catalan interpretation of Madrid's policy may seem far-fetched, and it did not correspond to the intentions of the king's ministers at that moment, but it was a perfectly comprehensible interpretation, given the original assumptions. Their experiences since the union of the Crowns, and especially in the last few years, had made the Catalans ready to see in any royal minister a conspirator against their sacred laws and liberties. They genuinely feared for the destruction of their traditional constitution, and there was much to lend colour to their belief that its ultimate destruction was the aim of the Castilian aristocracy. The Castilians, on their side, could not appreciate the intensity of feeling with which the Catalans looked on their laws and institutions, and there was some justification for *their* belief that those laws were simply a cloak to shield certain interested groups from the punishment they deserved.

The root cause of the difficulties between Castile and Catalonia was therefore a failure of comprehension on both sides. This failure of comprehension was the outcome of historical circumstances, of the way in which the Spanish empire had grown and developed. Catalonia's traditional form of government may have been admirably suited to the days before the union of the Crowns, but times had changed. In the words of one commentator who, although a Catalan, was unsympathetic to Catalonia's claims: 'the form of the empire and of the Monarchy has altered, and our province no longer possesses a king who rules in it alone, but one who rules over all four quarters of the earth...'.[1] This was the real explanation of Catalonia's troubles. The conflict over the viceroy revealed, perhaps more clearly than any previous dispute, the difficulty of reconciling the interests of one particular province with the wider interests of the Monarchy as a whole, and showed how hard it had become to maintain the fiction that the king of all was no more than the king of each.

The conflict of 1622–3 between the Catalans and the ministers in Madrid was not, then, the result of sinister machinations by one side or

---

[1] *Súplica de...Tortosa*, fo. 10.

the other. The leading players on both sides were to a large extent caught in the toils of a situation that was not of their own making. Catalonia had suffered incalculably from long-standing royal absentee-ism in an age when the presence of the king was still of vital importance to the proper working of government; and the fiercest opponents of the bishop of Barcelona's appointment, whether acting for public or personal ends, had all in some degree felt the consequences of their king's protracted absence. The Castilian ministers, on the other hand, were confronted with the almost superhuman task of governing and holding together an empire of innumerable provinces, each with differ-ent laws and privileges, each with its own particular problems, and each with its own traditional relationship to the king. How could an empire of this nature ever hope to survive in a warring world? This was the problem to which Olivares, entrusted by Philip IV with the task of governing this vast and variegated empire, had begun to turn his attention.

CHAPTER VII

OLIVARES AND THE FUTURE OF SPAIN

The crisis over the appointment of the Catalan viceroy was only one more symptom of the increasing derangement of the Spanish body politic. The ills of Catalonia were universal ills. Royal absenteeism, the lack of incentives and opportunities, the frustrations of the aristocracy, the inadequacy of a viceregal administration which suffered all the opprobrium of its connection with a distant and alien Court while obtaining no compensatory advantages from it, the increasing infiltration of the customs and habits and language of Castile—these were general complaints throughout the Spanish Monarchy. By the 1620's the whole institutional structure of the Monarchy was beginning to appear hopelessly inadequate to meet the needs and aspirations of the non-Castilian peoples who owed allegiance to the Spanish Habsburgs.

But grievances were not confined to the Aragonese, the Portuguese and the Catalans. The Castilians also had their discontents. For if the Monarchy was insufficiently federal to satisfy the ruling classes in the various kingdoms other than Castile, it was at the same time insufficiently centralized to satisfy many Castilians who felt that Castile's great empire was failing to yield the benefits it was capable of yielding. The desire of a section of the Castilian aristocracy to see Castilian forms of government imposed on all the Monarchy,[1] had not been fulfilled in the reign of Philip II. Provinces like Catalonia and Valencia still lived intact behind the shelter of their own laws. Those laws had hampered the workings of royal justice. Still worse, they had shielded these provinces from the heavy military and fiscal exactions imposed upon Philip II's Castile. And now, as a result of those exactions, Castile was threatened with ruin.

Castile's realization of impending diaster came suddenly and dramatically. As long as Philip II lived, the Castilians had been carried along, half proud, half reluctant, in the wake of a great imperial ideal. There had been great defeats but there had also been great victories, as if to

[1] See above, p. 17.

confirm that, while God's children had sinned grievously, yet at the end He had not forgotten them. And then, suddenly, everything changed. In 1598 the king died. In 1599 Castile and Andalusia were ravaged by a terrible plague. The years around 1600 were terrible years of famine and labour shortage and spiralling food prices.[1] And amid the ruin and the desolation of Castile, the carefree Court of the king of Spain celebrated its escape from the long winter of Philip II by launching out into a hectic round of festivities, more extravagant and more magnificent than any it had ever known.

The contrast was so sharp as to be overwhelming. It was like some Baroque painting: on one side, coffers overflowing with gold and jewels, set against a background of rich velvet hangings, and, on the other, a skeleton crumbling to dust. The skeleton was Castile, barren, impoverished, decayed. Shocked by the sudden realization, many thoughtful Castilians put pen to paper and set out to account for what had happened and to propose drastic remedies. It was this paradoxical character of Castile's situation which most forcibly struck Martín González de Cellorigo, one of the acutest of these economic writers, or *arbitristas*. Spain, with all the wealth of the Indies, was the richest of countries and yet it had the most poor; it was the greatest, and yet it stood in need, with 'the kingdom finished, the royal treasury exhausted, the subjects ruined and the republic consumed....It seems as if one had wished to reduce these kingdoms to a republic of bewitched men, living outside the natural order of things.'[2]

'A republic of bewitched men'—the land of Don Quixote; an enchanted land in which wealth turned into poverty, silver into ashes, windmills into giants. 'We have no money, gold or silver in Spain because we have it; we are not rich because we are rich.'[3] Then what was to be done? How was the enchantment to be exorcized and sanity restored? The *arbitristas* were surprisingly unanimous both in their analysis of Spain's ills and in their suggestions for a cure.[4] Trade and industry must be fostered; agriculture restored; the population

---

[1] There is great need for a proper study of Castile in the reign of Philip III, but see the stimulating article by Pierre Vilar, 'Le Temps du Quichotte', *Europe* (Paris, 1956).

[2] *Memorial de la política necesaria y útil restauración a la República de España*... (Valladolid, 1600). Quoted from J. Carrera Pujal, *Historia de la Economía Española* (Barcelona, 1943), vol. I, pp. 367–8.

[3] *Ibid.*

[4] There is still no really comprehensive study of the Spanish *arbitristas*, but R. Bona, *Essai sur le problème mercantiliste en Espagne* (Bordeaux, 1911), summarizes the ideas of many of them.

increased. The king must curb his expenditure and the weight of taxation on Castile be reduced.

It was at this point—the reduction of the burden of taxation on Castile—that Castile's constitutional relationship to the other parts of the Spanish Monarchy assumed importance. For, of all the paradoxes of the Spanish Monarchy, not the least seemed to be that Castile, the head of a great empire, instead of growing rich on the profits of empire was impoverishing itself in the defence of its own possessions. At the very beginning of Philip III's reign, an *arbitrista*, Álamos de Barrientos, pointed out in a long discourse presented to the new king, that 'in other states all the parts contribute to the maintenance and greatness of the head, as is only fair. . . . But in ours, it is the head which does the work and provides the other members with their sustenance.'[1] This theme—that Castile was being called upon to do too much in comparison with the other parts of the Monarchy—was to become one of the dominant themes in Spanish political life as the reign of Philip III proceeded, and it was to determine the character of much that happened in the reign of Philip IV.

When the Castilians complained of the intolerable burdens they were called upon to bear, they tended to forget that their imperial history had not been exclusively a saga of self-sacrifice. If they bore the burdens of empire, in the form of providing troops and money for the defence of their possessions, they had also come to achieve a near-monopoly of posts at Court and in the imperial administration. But these by no means contemptible profits of empire were easily overlooked; as easily as the fact that, if the wealth of the Indies had proved in the long run of singularly little advantage to Castile, it had only itself to blame.

But, setting aside these considerations, how far were the Castilians justified in claiming that they were bearing a disproportionate share of the burden (disproportionate on the assumption that the obligations of all were equal)? It is undeniable that the laws and the representative institutions of the other provinces of the Monarchy gave them a protection against the demands of the Crown which Castile had forfeited through the weakness of its Cortes. This made an obvious and immediate difference as regards the liability of the parts of the Monarchy other than Castile to provide troops for the Spanish armies. The king-

[1] Álamos de Barrientos, *L'Art de Gouverner*, ed. Guardia (Paris, 1867), p. 67.

doms of the Crown of Aragon, for instance, could not legally be compelled to raise troops for service beyond their own borders. As a result, they suffered none of that burden of recruiting which was denuding Castile of its able-bodied men. Their success in evading the specifically fiscal demands of the Crown is more difficult to estimate, for the relative incidence of all forms of taxation on Castile and the other provinces is at present impossible to measure. A rough comparison can, however, be made of the direct taxation levied by the Crown on laymen in Castile and in the States of the Crown of Aragon. In the first years of the reign of Philip III, Castile was paying three million ducats annually in the *millones* (a tax on basic foodstuffs), 400,000 ducats a year in the form of *servicios* voted by the Cortes, and 2,800,000 ducats a year in the *alcabala* (nominally a 10 per cent tax on sales, which the larger towns had long since compounded for an agreed yearly payment). The nominal annual yield of these taxes was thus 6,200,000 ducats.[1] The Crown of Aragon did not pay the *alcabala* or the *millones*, and its Cortes were very infrequently summoned to vote *servicios*. In all his twenty-three years as king, Philip III summoned the Cortes of Catalonia once, in 1599, and obtained a subsidy of 1,100,000 ducats; those of Valencia, which made him a grant of 400,000 ducats, once, in 1604; and those of Aragon not at all. Even allowing for the fact that the population of the Crown of Aragon was only one-sixth that of Castile, its fiscal contributions to the Crown obviously do not stand comparison with those of the Castilians. This does not necessarily mean that a Catalan artisan was paying far less in taxes than his Castilian counterpart: municipal dues and the indirect taxes levied by the Generalitat were both considerable, although their exact relation to his income is not known. But it does mean that the proportion of tax-money *which went to the Crown* was incomparably less in Catalonia than it was in Castile.

As the depopulation and impoverishment of a plague-stricken Castile made it increasingly difficult to collect the full quota of a tax like the *millones*, Castilians began to look enviously at the other, less heavily taxed provinces of the peninsula. Were not these lands flowing with milk and honey, when contrasted with the desolation of Castile? Why should they not contribute more to the royal treasury and relieve

[1] AGS: Hacienda, leg. 380, no. 5, *Relación de lo que valen las alcabalas*...(1598), and leg. 456, *Relación sumaria de la hacienda*...(1606).

Castile of some of its burden? Naturally, the Castilians tended to exaggerate the wealth and resources of the other provinces. In spite of the vitality of its agrarian life, it would be unrealistic to talk of seventeenth-century Catalonia as a prosperous country. But, significantly enough, it was beginning to appear prosperous in the eyes of a hungry Castile, and this in itself marked an important change in the life of the peninsula. Where sixteenth-century Castile had seemed well-populated in relation to a province like Catalonia, seventeenth-century observers would remark on the populousness of the peripheral regions, and contrast it with the emptiness of the centre.[1] This serves as a reminder that the Spanish peninsula did not live according to a single rhythm. Depopulation and acute monetary disorder in Castile did not by any means necessarily imply similar conditions in Catalonia or Portugal. These provinces led their own lives, and had up to now escaped total absorption into Castile's economic system. The 'decline of Spain' is therefore too loose a description of the economic trends of the seventeenth century, since it suggests a simultaneous and parallel decline in all parts of the peninsula. In practice, economic crisis overtook different parts of the peninsula at different times, and Castile's fate was not simultaneously shared by all Spain.

The early seventeenth century is predominantly the period of the decline of Castile, and it is this phenomenon which explains much of Spain's political history in the 1620's and 1630's. For the growing weakness of Castile naturally implied a changed relationship with the other parts of Spain. In the sixteenth century, Castile, its economy linked to that of a fabulous New World, had possessed a natural economic preponderance within the peninsula. By the early seventeenth century, this preponderance was no longer as overwhelming as it had seemed even fifty years before. With the absolute decrease in the national wealth, population and resources of the centre of the peninsula, there had been a relative increase in the economic status of the periphery. The time had not yet come when the centre of economic gravity in Spain would shift decisively from Castile to the peripheral provinces, but already the sixteenth-century pattern of a vigorous Castile and a relatively weak periphery was a thing of the past. In an effort to redress

[1] A Girard, 'La répartition de la population en Espagne dans les temps modernes', *Revue d'Histoire Economique et Sociale*, vol. XVII (1929), p. 358.

a balance that was tipping more and more against it, Castile would naturally seek to exploit the resources of provinces which had hitherto carried a less heavy fiscal and military burden than itself. Out of this would come the conflicts of the reign of Philip IV.

The emotional demand of certain Castilian aristocrats for the castilianization of the Spanish peninsula and empire was thus reinforced in the early seventeenth century by the still more powerful demands of fiscal and military necessity. If provinces like Catalonia could only be shorn of their traditional laws and liberties and be reduced to conformity with Castile, it would be easier to obtain from them the men and money required by the king. On three separate counts, therefore, the traditional laws and liberties of the States of the Crown of Aragon had become objectionable to a Castilian aristocrat like the duke of Alcalá. They were objectionable because they differed from the laws of Castile; because they made effective government impossible and gave every encouragement both to captious nobles and low-born bandits; and because, as long as they were allowed to survive, the Crown of Aragon would never contribute to the needs of the king on a scale comparable to that of Castile.

It was this last argument, based on economic necessity, which became of overriding importance in the last years of Philip III, and gave a new meaning and urgency to long-standing demands for the castilianization of Spain. As the *arbitristas* contemplated the miserable condition of Castile, and the ministers of the Crown contemplated the no less miserable condition of the royal finances, castilianization, or at least the introduction of fiscal parity between Castile and the other kingdoms, began to appear both logical and justifiable, if the Monarchy were to be saved from disaster.

It was from about 1615 that the case for action began to appear overwhelming. The estimated expenditure for that year was 8 million ducats, and, as the president of the Consejo de Hacienda (the Council of Finance) wrote to the king: 'The spending of eight million in a year is unheard of.'[1] In practice, this figure of 8 million ducats marked a disastrous failure on the part of the Crown to reduce its expenditure in time of nominal peace. It may be compared with the

[1] AGS: Hacienda, leg. 536, no. 1, President of Consejo de Hacienda (Don Fernando Carrillo) to King, 6 Jan. 1615.

estimated expenditure for the first ten months of the year 1608, when Spain was still fighting in the Netherlands. This came to 7,272,173 ducats, of which 2 million ducats were destined for the army in Flanders.[1] The Crown had already in 1607 been forced to repudiate its debts, and its difficulty in raising money and in persuading the bankers to make large new loans was finally to compel the signing of the Twelve Years' Truce with the Dutch in April 1609. In spite of the truce in Flanders, however, the anticipated need of 8 million ducats for 1615 showed that the Crown had dismally failed to keep its expenditure down. Any reduction in the cost of the Flanders army had been counterbalanced by unexpected military expenses in Germany and Milan, Chile, North Africa and the Far East.

By September 1615 it had become clear that the year's expenditure, so far from being the 'unheard-of' 8 million ducats, would in fact reach 9,332,000 ducats—a figure of which 'there is neither record nor tradition', wrote the poor president of the Council of Finance.[2] Nine months later, in the sternest note he had yet written to the king, he inveighed bitterly against the army commanders for their gross extravagance, and warned of impending disaster:

To expect the Crown of Castile to meet so many and such enormous payments is fantastic. Everyone knows how it has been drained of men and resources; and to ruin it, and try to squeeze out of it what is simply not there, in order to make ourselves important in Germany—this is a policy which in all conscience cannot be carried out.[3]

This was the voice of the Castile of the Comuneros, all but muted now, but still vainly protesting at being sacrificed to the grandiose policies of the House of Austria.

The 9 million ducats a year which the Crown was now spending simply could not be produced year after year from the traditional sources of revenue.[4] These traditional sources, with the income they produced at the beginning of Philip III's reign, were three in number:

---

[1] AGS: Hacienda, leg. 474, no. 405, *Relación*, 22 Dec. 1607.
[2] AGS: Hacienda, leg. 536, no. 95, Carrillo to King, 2 Sept. 1615.
[3] AGS: Hacienda, leg. 536, no. 162, Carrillo to King, 17 June 1616.
[4] These figures are taken from different relations from 1598–1607 in the documentation of the Consejo de Hacienda at Simancas.

Taxes paid by Castile—6 million ducats a year.

The three *gracias* (taxes collected in all the king's possessions by papal concession)—1½ million ducats a year.

Silver brought by the treasure fleet—about 2 million ducats a year.

Apart from what was collected in the three *gracias*, no money was entering the central royal treasury from the king's European possessions, since anything raised by a province like Milan in the way of taxes, was consumed on the spot and indeed often proved inadequate for the needs of the provincial government, which had to apply to Madrid for more.

Two of these three sources of revenue had fallen away heavily by the later years of Philip III. Of the taxes paid by Castile, the 3 million ducats raised in the *millones* each year at the start of the reign, had been reduced to 2½ million in 1607, and were to be reduced to 2 million a year from 1617;[1] and the money from the *alcabalas* had been reserved exclusively for the payment of interest on the Crown's debts, and so was not available to meet current expenses. Still more serious was the decrease in remittances from the Indies. The decade 1610–20, which marks a crucial change for the worse in the fortunes of Spanish trade with America,[2] saw also a sudden catastrophic decline in the quantities of American silver coming to the Crown. The president of the Council of Finance reported in December 1616 that 'in the last two years hardly a million ducats have come each year'[3]—instead of the 2 million ducats a year during the first years of the reign; and by 1620 the figure was to be as low as 800,000 ducats.[4]

The crisis in the royal finances coincided with a great increase in international tension and the outbreak of rebellion in Bohemia. When Lerma asked the Council of Finance in August 1618 for a special despatch of money to Germany and Italy, its president, now the count of Salazar, answered that 'the royal finances are not in a fit state to provide these sums at present.... The ordinary revenues and all the rest of the royal *hacienda* are pledged for a greater sum than their total value.' But the king only replied that 'these provisions are so vital that

[1] Vicente de Cangas Inclán, 'Carta o representación al Sr. Rey Don Felipe Quinto', A. Valladares, *Semanario Erudito* (Madrid, 1787), vol. III, p. 254.

[2] See the detailed study of American trade by H. and P. Chaunu, *Séville et l'Atlantique* (Paris, 1955–9), especially vol. VIII, 2, ii.

[3] AGS: Hacienda, leg. 542, no. 1, Carrillo to King, 23 Dec. 1616.

[4] AGS: Hacienda, leg. 573, no. 11, *Relación*, 20 Nov. 1620.

the Council of Finance must find them. Germany cannot possibly be abandoned.'[1]

What, then, was to be done? A scrutiny of the Council's fiscal documents shows that the Crown was paying out considerable sums for the defence of Spanish territory, and would have to spend still more if war came any closer. The usual annual expenditure on frontier defences and garrisons was something like 400,000 ducats, a figure which in 1611 had included the following individual payments:[2]

> Maintenance of troops in Catalonia—84,806 ducats
> Maintenance of troops in Aragon—82,144 ducats
> Maintenance of troops in Navarre—77,457 ducats
> Maintenance of troops in Portugal—222,156 ducats

Surely something could be done at least to relieve the Crown of this burden. This at least was the conclusion of the Council of Finance. In a strongly worded draft paper of 2 December 1618, the count of Salazar examined the Crown's few remaining sources of revenue and continued:

The kingdoms of Aragon, Valencia and Catalonia contribute nothing to Your Majesty's expenses beyond their own frontiers, and money even has to be sent to them from Castile to pay their garrisons. Would Your Majesty please consider the possibility of discussing with the Council of Aragon whether these kingdoms could themselves undertake the provision of the money required for paying the troops garrisoned in them....Everything is met out of the resources of Castile and out of what comes from the Indies, and literally nothing is contributed by Aragon, Valencia, Catalonia, Portugal and Navarre. As a result, Castile's revenues are pledged to the hilt, and it finds itself in such a state that one cannot see how it can possibly go on paying such vast sums.[3]

The count of Salazar's paper shows one group of ministers—the financial ministers—now pressing for a policy which would bring the other provinces of the peninsula into closer fiscal alignment with Castile. The Council of Finance was joined in its demands a few months later by a much more authoritative Council, the Council of Castile. On 1 February 1619 the Council of Castile presented the famous *con-*

---

[1] AGS: Hacienda, leg. 555, no. 212, consulta, 26 Aug. 1618.
[2] AGS: Hacienda, leg. 502, *Relación*, no. 5, 15 Oct. 1611.
[3] AGS: Hacienda, leg. 555, paper by the Count of Salazar, 2 Dec. 1618.

sulta in which it examined the causes of the depopulation and misery of Castile and proposed a number of remedies.[1] Among the proposed remedies (all of which had already been recommended by many *arbitristas*), it pointed out in its first clause, which dealt with the excessive taxation falling on Castile, that other provinces besides Castile were interested in the conservation of the Monarchy, 'and therefore it is just they should offer, and should even be requested to offer, some help, so that all the weight should not fall on so weak and exhausted a victim' as Castile.[2] The famous *arbitrista*, Fernández Navarrete, whose *Conservación de Monarquías* was written in the form of a commentary on the Council of Castile's *consulta*, glossed this particular clause in a way which vividly recalls the words of Álamos de Barrientos at the beginning of the reign of Philip III:

All monarchies have been accustomed to enrich the head of the empire with the spoils and tributes of provinces and nations won by arms or legitimately acquired by other means....Only Castile has pursued a different method of government, because, while it should, as the head, be the most privileged in the payment of taxes, it is in fact the most heavily taxed of all, and contributes the largest sum to the Monarchy's defence....It is only reasonable that the burdens should be distributed in proper proportion: that Castile should continue to provide for the royal household and for the defence of its own coasts and the route to the Indies; that Portugal should pay for its own garrisons and for the East Indies fleets, as it did before it was incorporated with Castile, and that Aragon and Italy should defend their coasts and maintain the necessary militia and ships for the purpose. It is quite unreasonable that the head should be weakened while the other members, which are very rich and populous, should simply stand by and look on while it has to bear all these heavy charges.[3]

By 1619, then, an influential body of ministers in Madrid had added their voices to those of the *arbitristas* who wanted a radical alteration of the present structure of taxation in the Spanish Monarchy. It was too much to hope, though, that anything of importance would be achieved by the present regime. Lerma had fallen from power in October 1618, but only to be succeeded by his own son, the duke of Uceda, who showed no greater inclination than his father to tackle thorny problems. Such pressure as came for a drastic change came from outside the Court:

[1] González Palencia, *La Junta de Reformación*, doc. no. 4.   [2] *Ibid.* p. 16.
[3] P. Fernández Navarrete, *Conservación de Monarquías* (Madrid, 1626), discurso XXIII.

from a viceroy like the duke of Alcalá, whose proposals for the exaction of the *quints* were inspired in the first place by the miserable state of Catalonia's defences.[1]

It was, above all, this problem of imperial defence which would sooner or later make attempts at fiscal re-organization inevitable. The 'conservation' of the Monarchy was the order of the day (few now talked about its expansion) and the obvious symptoms of economic collapse in Castile suggested that 'conservation' through the further exploitation of the traditional sources of revenue was no longer feasible. This became still clearer in 1621. In April of that year, the Twelve Years' Truce with the Netherlands expired, and was not renewed.[2] The resumption of war in the Netherlands after the twelve wasted years of peace meant the recruiting of new armies, for which Castile could not easily find the men. It meant a rapid enlargement of the fleet, which had been allowed to rot in the dockyards. Above all, it meant more money. During the last years of the truce, the annual expenditure on the troops in Flanders had stood at about $1\frac{1}{2}$ million ducats. On the resumption of the war, it rose at once to $3\frac{1}{2}$ million ducats, while the cost of the Atlantic fleet rose from 480,000 ducats to a million.[3] With the steep fall in the silver remittances from America, the problems involved in raising this money seemed insuperable, and the case for demanding that the various provinces pay for their own defences now appeared irresistible.

The greatest benefit from these frontier garrisons [the Council of Finance reaffirmed] accrues to the provinces themselves, and so they should reasonably be expected to maintain them, and Castile should not have to bear the entire burden, especially when the royal revenues are in such an impossible state, and the Castilians so exhausted and oppressed with tributes.[4]

[1] See above, p. 150.

[2] Since the war with the United Provinces dominated Spain's foreign policy during the first half of the reign of Philip IV and was responsible for many of its misfortunes, it is particularly unfortunate that there is no sign of the *consultas* in which the Council of State presumably made the grave decision not to renew the truce. It is possible that the crucial argument (and a very comprehensible one) for the resumption of the war was the way in which the Dutch had made use of the years of peace to force an entry into the overseas possessions of Spain and Portugal. (See the paper by Don Carlos Coloma, printed in Antonio Rodríguez Villa, *Ambrosio Spínola*, Madrid, 1904, pp. 382–92.) But it should also be remembered that, even if Spain had wished to prolong the truce, the triumph of the bellicose Orangist party in the United Provinces would have made prolongation unlikely.

[3] AGS: Hacienda, leg. 573, fo. 303, consulta, 10 Dec. 1621.

[4] AGS: Hacienda, leg. 582, consulta, 10 April 1622.

While this seemed obvious enough, the constitutional problems it posed were extremely delicate. Any attempt to raise the level of taxation in the various provinces of the Monarchy could in any event be expected to meet fierce resistance. But *regular* contributions either of men or of money would also require entirely new constitutional arrangements, and the abandonment of treasured privileges. A novel fiscal system presupposed a novel relationship between the kingdoms of the Monarchy and their king, and the sensitivity which a province like Catalonia had displayed in recent years at the slightest sign of a presumed affront to its traditional institutions did not augur well for major constitutional readjustments.

This was the problem which faced the ministers of the king of Spain at the moment when Philip III died at the end of March 1621 and the Netherlands truce expired. Within a few days of the new reign, it became clear that the new chief ministers, Don Baltasar de Zúñiga and the count of Olivares, were men of a very different stamp from Lerma and Uceda. If there was any man in Spain equipped to grapple with the enormous problems of the day, it was the count of Olivares. In spite of the poor showing he makes in most accounts of seventeenth-century Spain, his personal qualifications for the almost superhuman task that confronted him were by no means to be despised.[1] It is true that he was only thirty-four at the time when the affairs of the greatest monarchy in the world were entrusted to him, and that he was sadly lacking in any form of governmental experience. At least, however, he showed a burning determination to learn. It was not long before he was haggling personally with the Genoese bankers over the annual *asientos* (or contracts for financial provisions in the coming year), and as a result rapidly acquired a detailed knowledge of the royal finances. In this he differed sharply from Lerma, who never displayed any interest in financial affairs other than those of his own family. But in almost everything, Olivares was the complete antithesis of Lerma. Where Lerma was acquiescent and passive, Olivares was forceful and dynamic; where Lerma was bland and pliant, Olivares was harsh and ruthless; where Lerma was indolent and dilatory, Olivares would work himself to exhaustion; and where Lerma was notoriously corrupt, Olivares

---

[1] For the first serious revaluation of Olivares, see the remarkable 'psychological' biography by G. Marañón, *El Conde-Duque de Olivares* (3rd ed., Madrid, 1952), which, however, says almost nothing about his political activity.

displayed an almost puritanical integrity. The first measures of reform decreed at Madrid at the start of the new reign made it clear that the administration had at last been galvanized into life; there were signs of a new driving force such as had long been wanting. Another ten years of a regime like Lerma's, and the Monarchy was ruined. Now, with Olivares in power, there was hope.

Over the years, Olivares was to establish a complete and unchallenged supremacy at Court. This supremacy derived both from the unwavering confidence of the king and from Olivares's own fanatical devotion to work. Philip, while still heir to the throne, seems originally to have entertained a strong antipathy towards the domineering character who had been appointed a gentleman of his household.[1] But, while far more intelligent and quick-witted than his father, Philip suffered from a similar lack of self-confidence. Emotionally he required someone on whom to lean, and Olivares, with his driving energy and his fixity of purpose, fully met this need. He could put stiffening into the limp character of the king, fortify his resolution, and drive him back to his papers on the occasions when his fatal inertia seemed once again to be winning the upper hand.

In the first years of his power, Olivares (or the Conde Duque, as he was soon to be called)[2] would attend on the king three times a day. First thing in the morning he would come in, draw the curtains and open the window while the king lay in bed, and discuss with him the programme for the day; he would see him again after the midday meal, and then once more at night, before he retired to bed, to report on the day's work.[3] But as time went on he was able to relax this schedule, and he saw the king in private audience for only about a quarter of an hour a day. The lessening of time spent in audience with the king must have brought him welcome relief in the tightly packed programme of his own day's work.[4] He would be up by five to receive his confessor,

---

[1] Marañón, *Olivares*, pp. 35–40, and Conde de la Roca, 'Fragmentos Históricos de la Vida de D. Gaspar de Guzmán', published in Valladares, *Semanario Erudito* (Madrid, 1787), vol. II, pp. 154–6.

[2] On 5 Jan. 1625 he was created Duque de Sanlúcar la Mayor (see the Privilege in Conde de la Roca, *Fragmentos*, pp. 233–5). His title then became Conde de Olivares, Duque de Sanlúcar la Mayor. From this time, he was always known, in State papers as well as in conversation, as the Conde Duque.

[3] Marañón, p. 169; Martin Hume, *The Court of Philip IV* (London, n.d.), p. 50.

[4] For his usual timetable see Roca, *Fragmentos*, pp. 245–6, and Marañón, pp. 168–9.

and then, still in the early morning, would grant a series of private audiences. From nine o'clock until eleven he would see his secretaries and with them go through the *consultas* on which the king would be required to take a decision during the day. At eleven in the morning he would receive in audience all those persons, sometimes as many as a hundred, who had come from an audience with the king. When this was over he would take a quick meal and return to work at three; and, until eleven at night, or later, he would be seeing ministers, giving more audiences, attending—and invariably speaking at—meetings of the Councils and Juntas, writing draft papers and going through yet more papers with his secretaries. This routine was, more often than not, interrupted by unexpected intrusions on his timetable, and especially by the frequent Court *fiestas*, in which he would appear on horseback with the king, accompanying him in wild boar hunts and in other open-air sports.[1] But not a moment was wasted. He would continue to give audiences in the open air while the king was hunting. Much of his work, indeed, was done out of doors, for he would go for drives in his coach in the Prado or in the countryside round Madrid, followed in a second coach by two or three secretaries, whom he would summon to join him when he wished to dictate. And all the while, 'from his bed-chamber to his study, from his study to his coach, out strolling, in the odd corner, on the stairs, he...would hear and despatch an infinite number of people'.[2] No wonder that this hectic routine killed four of his secretaries, and that the Conde Duque himself, especially in his later years, seemed to stagger like a sleepwalker through the crowded hours of his endless working day.

The sheer physical energy of the man is obvious enough, but the dark, squat, heavily-built figure of Velázquez's portraits, with his puffed face and his hard eyes, had something more than brute strength and an infinite capacity for work. His intellectual powers were considerable. A great book-collector, he was also a voracious reader, and had acquired a vast store of erudition, together with a fund of political maxims from Seneca, Tacitus and Livy which did not always stand him in good stead.[3] After studying at Salamanca university he had

---

[1] He was a very good horseman but put on a great deal of weight in later life, and came to look rather ridiculous when competing in equestrian exercises.
[2] Roca, *Fragmentos*, p. 246. [3] Marañón, p. 162, quoting Melo, *Epanaphoras*.

spent long periods in Seville, whose leading writers and artists he came to know well; and he possessed more than an onlooker's interest in changing literary fashions, for he had himself tried his hand at writing poetry. He was, by all accounts, an eloquent, if long-winded, orator, exaggerated in his mannerisms but powerful and persuasive in argument. He wrote, as he talked, at great length and often obscurely, employing an excessive number of literary conceits. But almost all his papers are vigorous, and betray the stamp of a powerful mind.

Alongside his many qualities, however, there were certain grave defects which became increasingly obvious as the years passed, and as Olivares grew accustomed to the exercise of unrestrained power. Supremely confident of his own abilities, he was always impatient of criticism, and would bluster and rage at those who dared to express differing opinions. This meant that he tended to alienate the more intelligent, and was increasingly surrounded by flatterers and time-servers who would rather comply than run the risk of crossing swords with the Conde Duque. His temper could be frightening; he would fly into rages which terrified all those that saw him. Nor did he have the gift of making himself sympathetic to others. When he was trying hard to be persuasive and to win over his hearers by argument, there was an air of insincerity about him, which somehow suggested that he was acting a part. His delight in the subtle and the complicated tended to give the impression that he courted mystery for its own sake; there was a suspicion that some of his more complicated acts of policy and diplomatic manoeuvres were motivated less by the needs of the moment than by a desire to display the infinite resourcefulness of a fertile brain. Above all, he had a dangerous capacity for self-delusion, for becoming so entranced by the beauty of his own ideas that he became utterly incapable of judging them with a reasonable degree of objectivity, or of grasping the often very powerful objections that might be raised against them. 'He loves novelties,' wrote the Venetian ambassador Mocenigo, 'allowing his lively mind to pursue chimeras, and to hit upon impossible designs as easy of achievement. For this reason, he is desolated by misfortunes; the difficulties proposed to him at the beginning he brushes aside, and all his resolutions rush him towards the precipice.'[1] Hopton,

[1] *Relazioni*, ed. Barozzi and Berchet, Serie I, 'Spagna', vol. I, p. 650.

the English agent, confirmed this impression: 'the Conde is indeed a very provident servant, in which, and in his secretaryship, I conceive consist his greatest abilities, for in matters of state he tieth himself so obstinately to certain grounds he hath laid as he will hazard all rather than leave them'.[1] Having once decided upon some course of action no evidence that it might be impracticable or untimely could deter him. Against all obstacles he would press on, and when he failed, as he often did, his confidence would suddenly desert him, and he would be plunged into the deepest melancholy. Moods of euphoria would alternate with moods of despair, and a man who one day was arrogantly self-assured and ebullient would the next day be asking the king for immediate leave to retire.

While these temperamental defects might on more than one occasion jeopardize the success of Olivares's policies, the very fact that he had long-term policies for the government of the Monarchy was itself quite a novel feature in Spanish history. For too long, the Spanish empire had been allowed to drift. Philip II seems to have found it difficult to conceive of all his dominions as a whole, and to formulate policies which would treat them as a single unit.[2] As for Lerma, his policies did not rise above the level of expedients. As a result, the strains and stresses within the Monarchy had increased, the grievances of the provinces had begun to fester, and the decline of Castile had proceeded unchecked. The time had come, and indeed was long overdue, for a radical reappraisal of the whole structure and character of the Spanish Monarchy, and if it was a question of devising plans and drawing up blueprints, there was no more enthusiastic planner than Olivares.

---

[1] PRO: SP 94. 40, fo. 160, Hopton to Windebank, 26 July/5 Aug. 1638.

[2] There are signs, however, that the problems of imperial defence were gradually forcing him towards some realization of the unity and interdependence of his kingdoms. Cf. his reply to a *consulta* of 1589 (quoted by Koenigsberger, *The Government of Sicily*, p. 56): '...since God has entrusted me with so many [kingdoms], since all are in my charge, and since in the defence of one all are preserved, it is just that all should help me'. But, as Koenigsberger points out, the very fact that Philip saw himself as the only connecting link between the component States prevented him from conceiving the idea of an empire as 'a living organization with an inherent purpose, transcending the unity provided by the crown' (*ibid.* p. 57)—an idea which *was* grasped by one of his viceroys, the Italian Marc Antonio Colonna. For reasons suggested by Koenigsberger on p. 56, note 3, it may have been easier for a member of the 'subject' races, like the Italians, than for a member of the dominant race—the Castilians—to appreciate the idea of empire. It is natural to speculate whether Olivares's Andalusian origins gave him a certain detachment which enabled him to formulate the idea of empire in a way that escaped the pure Castilian.

Although none of Olivares's predecessors had taken any really effective steps to increase the unity of the king's dominions, the very absence
of unity, and its harmful consequences, had provoked a good deal of
thought, and indeed was a commonplace of the times. 'A great king
indeed,' wrote the Englishman Howell of the king of Spain, 'tho' the
French in a slighting way compare his monarchy to a beggar's cloak
made up of patches'; but 'if these patches were in one piece, what
would become of his cloak embroider'd with flower-de-luces?'[1] What
indeed? It was natural to believe that if only the king of Spain could
unify his territories, his power would be irresistible. This at least was
the opinion of the Italian political thinker Campanella, who, in his
Discourse Touching the Spanish Monarchy declared it to be 'an undoubted
truth that every great empire, if it be united within itself, is so much
the safer from the enemies' incursions'. And how was it to be 'united
within itself'? Campanella, never at a loss for ideas, suggested many
measures for promoting closer unity which were also to be put forward
by Olivares—the encouragement of intermarriage among the natives
of the different provinces, a general distribution of offices among all
the nationalities, and the abolition of their 'old customs...but not
upon a sudden'.[2]

Within Spain, too, there had been a certain amount of thought about
the structure of the Monarchy and the need for greater unity. It seems
that Olivares's own schemes owed much to the writings of Philip II's
famous secretary Antonio Pérez, and to those of Pérez's disciple, Álamos
de Barrientos, who was one of Olivares's advisers.[3] But the problem of
unity was most urgent for those professionally concerned with the
defence of the Spanish empire, and it is interesting to find Martín de
Aróztegui, one of Philip III's ministers and a consistent advocate of the
need to concentrate on building up Spain's naval strength, writing the
following words in a paper dated 17 August 1617: 'It is obviously

---

[1] *Epistolae Ho-Elianae*, vol. I, p. 204, Howell to Viscount Colchester, 1 Feb. 1623.

[2] T. Campanella, *A Discourse Touching the Spanish Monarchy* (Eng. trans. 1654), pp. 125–6.
A German edition, the first to be published, appeared in 1623. Although there are striking
similarities between Campanella's proposals and those of Olivares, I have been able to find no
evidence that Olivares knew of Campanella's work or was in any way influenced by it. The only
book by Campanella to be found in the catalogue of the Conde Duque's library is Campanella's
discourse to the princes of Italy, which again raises the question of union, though this time in
relation to defence against the Turk (RAH: D. 119, Bibliotheca Olivariense, fo. 278).

[3] G. Marañón, *Antonio Pérez*, vol. II, p. 738.

cheaper to increase and extend one's power if one's forces are united. This is shown by experience, for the king of France, with all his lands adjoining each other, has no need to maintain great fleets and armadas for their protection. And other kings with contiguous territories enjoy the same advantages.'[1]

There was, then, well before Olivares took over the government, a strong feeling that the maintenance of Spanish power depended on the king's ability to unite more effectively the resources of his scattered possessions. Two obvious difficulties stood in the way of this. The first was distance, which created insuperable problems so far as the empire as a whole was concerned, but was not so formidable when the question was only one of promoting greater unity within the Spanish peninsula itself. The other difficulty, which did exist in an acute form within the peninsula, was the diversity of laws among the king of Spain's dominions. So long as each kingdom retained its own laws and institutions, it was difficult to see how the various parts of the Monarchy could be brought together in a closer association and pool their military and fiscal resources in a common enterprise.

The replacement of diversity by unity must, therefore, mean the introduction of a uniform law. This at least was Olivares's conviction. According to the contemporary Italian historian Siri, Olivares had already decided, at the very beginning of his ministry, to subject all the kingdoms of the Monarchy to the same form of government, 'and was frequently accustomed to repeat these words: *Multa regna, sed una lex*'.[2] There could be no doubts as to the nature of this *una lex*. It must inevitably be the law of Castile, where the king's power was more effective than in any province which still retained all its traditional liberties. In fact the castilianization so long demanded in certain influential quarters, was now to be the official policy of the king of Spain.

This official policy found formal expression in a famous secret memorandum prepared for Philip IV by Olivares, dated 25 December

[1] AGS: Hacienda, leg. 554, paper by Aróztegui.

[2] Vittorio Siri, *Del Mercurio overo Historia de' correnti tempi* (2nd ed., Casale, 1648), vol. II, p. 43. Siri's remarks on Olivares's policies, as on other contemporary topics, must, however, be treated with caution. He was neither so detached, nor quite so well-informed, as he would like his readers to believe, and his comments should not be taken—as they sometimes are—as conclusive evidence as to Olivares's intentions. For his unreliability as a source for the historian, see Ludwig von Pastor, *Geschichte der Päpste*, vol. XIII (Freiburg, 1929), pp. 1022 ff.

1624.[1] This memorandum provided a detailed description of the nature of government in the Spanish Monarchy and of the various problems that faced it, and its theme was expressed in a key passage which has frequently been quoted by nineteenth and twentieth-century historians:

The most important thing in Your Majesty's Monarchy is for you to become king of Spain: by this I mean, Sir, that Your Majesty should not be content with being king of Portugal, of Aragon, of Valencia and count of Barcelona, but should secretly plan and work to reduce these kingdoms of which Spain is composed to the style and laws of Castile, with no difference whatsoever. And if Your Majesty achieves this, you will be the most powerful prince in the world.

How was the castilianization of these kingdoms to be achieved? The Conde Duque suggested three possible ways. The first 'and the most difficult to achieve, but the best, if it can be managed', was to favour the people of other kingdoms, 'introducing them into Castile, marrying them to Castilians', and, by admitting them into the offices and dignities of Castile, to prepare the way for a natural union. The second was for the king to start negotiations at a time when he had an army and a fleet unoccupied, so that he could negotiate from strength.

The third way, although not so justified, but the most effective, would be for Your Majesty—assuming you have these forces—to go in person as if to visit the kingdom where the business is to be done; and there to bring about some great popular tumult. Under this pretext, the troops could intervene. And in order to restore calm and prevent any further recurrence of the troubles, the laws could be reorganized (as if the country had been newly conquered) and brought into conformity with those of Castile.

The unscrupulous character of this proposal, combined with the fact that there are certain similarities between the 'third way' and the actual events surrounding the Catalan Revolution of 1640, has helped to damn Olivares in the eyes of posterity. 'This third method', wrote one Cata-

---

[1] BM: Eg. MS 2053, fos. 173–218. This memorandum has only once been printed in full, during the eighteenth century, by Valladares in his *Semanario Erudito*, vol. XI, pp. 162–224. It was ascribed by Valladares to Philip IV's (Catalan) tutor, Don Galcerán Albanell, and perhaps for this reason passed unnoticed. The nature of the memorandum first became generally known as a result of the reproduction of the key passages by Cánovas del Castillo in his *Estudios del Reinado de Felipe IV* (Madrid, 1888), vol. I, pp. 56–63. Cánovas got it from a manuscript in the Biblioteca Nacional of Madrid, and seems to have been unaware that it had been printed in Valladares. Marañón, in the appendix to his biography of Olivares, prints from Valladares several important passages, but again not the entire memorandum.

lan historian, 'was the one adopted by Philip IV in pursuance of the perfidious and Machiavellian advice of his favourite, that astute and omnipotent minister, to annihilate Catalonia.'[1] The accusation is, however, by no means a new one. Just after Olivares's fall from power, the Italian Siri wrote that it was common knowledge among those best informed about what went on in the 'royal cabinet of Spain, that the principal document presented by the Conde Duque to Philip IV at the beginning of his reign suggested that the Catalans should be given some occasion to revolt, so as to have a reasonable excuse for depriving them of their privileges'.[2] It has to be remembered that this passage was written after the outbreak of the Catalan revolution, and that if the contents of Olivares's memorandum had in fact leaked out, it was natural to connect the rather mysterious events of 1640 with the intentions Olivares was believed to have expressed in the document written fifteen years before. While the presumption of a direct cause and effect relationship between Olivares's words and the Catalan Revolution is perfectly natural, it remains a presumption. No clear proof has ever been adduced. In watching the unfoldment of events in Catalonia, the charge that Olivares deliberately instigated revolution as a pretext to castilianize Catalonia can and must be borne in mind. But it is not proven, and should not be considered as any more than one possible hypothesis to explain the strange pattern of events.

The emphasis given to the 'third method' has not only prejudged the issue of the Catalan Revolution. It has also obscured the other things that Olivares had to say in his memorandum. Olivares does not simply make a plea for bald castilianization, as might be assumed from most references to the document. The 'first method' advocated for reducing the various kingdoms to conformity with the laws of Castile, consists of the mingling of the various nationalities by intermarriage and the conferring of offices on non-Castilians. Elsewhere in his memorandum, Olivares has more to say on this theme, and he says it with considerable vigour.

What reason is there that these [non-Castilian] vassals should be excluded from honour or privilege in these kingdoms [of Castile] ? Why should not they equally enjoy the honours, offices and confidence given to those born in

---

[1] Ferran de Sagarra, *Les Lliçons de la Història. Catalunya en 1640* (Barcelona, 1932), p. 18.
[2] Siri, *Mercurio*, vol. II, pp. 43–4.

the heart of Castile and Andalusia?....Is it surprising that, with these Castilian vassals being admitted to all the honourable positions round Your Majesty, and enjoying the royal presence, there should be jealousy, and discontent and distrust? There is the greatest justification for discontent in those other kingdoms and provinces, which have not only put up with government for so many years without the presence of the king, but are also regarded as unfitted for honours and unequal to the other vassals....

If Olivares is considered a typical advocate of Castilian domination in the Spanish Monarchy—as the heir to the Castilian extremists of the sixteenth century—these words ring very strangely. For they express, apparently with deep feeling, all the complaints and discontents of the Aragonese, the Catalans and the Portuguese during the preceding decades. Here is a ruler of Spain who not only appreciates that the provinces of the Monarchy have just cause for complaint at the way in which they have been treated, but actually goes so far as to suggest remedies. Of the two fundamental grievances, the first—royal absentee-ism—could be counteracted by the king's travelling from one province to another instead of residing permanently in Madrid; while the second —exclusion from offices—could be remedied by ending the Castilian monopoly.

An expressed wish to abolish the Castilian monopoly of posts and offices in the Monarchy runs directly counter to the traditional picture of Olivares as the arch-exponent of a Castilian empire. It may, of course, be objected that the Conde Duque's intentions were insincere, and that, if he ever did intend to admit Aragonese into Castilian posts, then this was only to facilitate the introduction of Castilians into offices in Aragon. Yet this is a secret memorandum, intended only for the eyes of the king, and there seems no reason for Olivares to dwell on the grievances of the Aragonese or the Catalans if he did not mean what he said. And if he did mean what he said, then there was all the more reason to keep the memorandum secret, for while knowledge of his plans for castilianization would cause an outcry in the Crown of Aragon and Portugal, a knowledge of his plans to open offices to all nationalities could be expected to provoke no less an outcry in Castile.

It may be that this fear of Castile's reaction was the reason why in the following years, he failed to open the posts in the Monarchy to everyone, irrespective of their province of origin. He did indeed appoint an

Aragonese, Miguel Santos de San Pedro, to be president of the Council of Castile—itself a striking break with tradition—but otherwise his policy made little headway. There were too many vested interests for him to change a long-standing practice overnight, and it is also possible that his consciousness of the enormous burdens being shouldered by Castile made him hesitate to remove, in its monopoly of imperial offices, one of the few compensations that Castile still possessed.

In spite of this failure, Olivares's words have the stamp of sincerity, and suggest that he was aiming at something nobler, and more ambitious, than a crude castilianization of all the king's dominions. That he did intend to castilianize, in the sense of introducing the laws of Castile into the other provinces, he himself makes clear. Such a policy is not attractive to liberal or nationalist minds in a later age, but it is hard to see that a seventeenth-century monarch, anxious, like all his contemporaries, to extend his authority and secure greater control over the resources of his kingdoms, had any alternative to some such scheme. Medieval privileges and exemptions had come to be looked upon as irritating obstacles to effective government, and some form of absolutism seemed the only answer to the vast fiscal, military and administrative problems of seventeenth-century monarchies struggling for survival in a world at war. In advocating uniform laws, uniform taxes, the abolition of customs barriers, Olivares was doing no more than contemporary statesmen all over Europe. The striking feature of Olivares's plans is not his advocacy of the castilianization of laws, which was normal enough in the circumstances of the age, but his suggestions for the *de*-castilianization of office. At this point he seems to be groping towards some wider concept of Spanish nationality, in which 'Castilian' and 'Aragonese' would both be subsumed. The plan, like so many of the Conde Duque's plans, came to nothing, but it did enshrine an ideal which might conceivably, if tactfully pursued, have set the Spanish Monarchy on a new and happier course.

Olivares's policies become easier to understand if he is seen as the champion not of Castile but of Spain: of an organic, unified state in which the peoples of every part of the peninsula should have an equal stake. Although the State was to have a Castilian form of government, this did not mean, in the Conde Duque's eyes, that the Castilians would be conceded a superior status. In this he differed sharply from the old school of Castilian aristocrats, who naturally tended to regard Catalans or Portuguese as second-class citizens. On more than one occasion Olivares went out of his way to scotch any such idea. In 1632, for example, the loyalty of the Catalans was questioned by a number of ministers, and Olivares turned on them very sharply in a meeting of the Council of State.

In making an exception of the Catalans because of their nationality [he said] and in not trusting in their loyalty as much as in that of the Castilians, the Council is doing them a grave injustice. Your Majesty can certainly place in those vassals the same confidence as he places in those born in Madrid, and the baseless difference with which people have tried to treat the nations of Spain has been most prejudicial to the service of Your Majesty and to the conservation of the Monarchy, and it will be its total ruin to permit it. In saying 'Spaniards' it must be understood that there is no difference between one nation and another of those included within the limits of Spain, and the same is to be understood of the Portuguese as of the Catalans.[1]

This might imply the obligation of Catalans and Portuguese to pay the same taxes and be governed by the same laws as the Castilians, but it also implied that they deserved to receive the same confidence and enjoy the same privileges. Castilians and Catalans alike were no longer to be thought of simply as Castilians or Catalans: they were *Spaniards*, equally valued and equally trusted partners in the renovated Monarchy of the king of Spain.

Olivares himself, however, was the first to recognize that a united Monarchy of this nature could not be created in a day. The work of 'familiarizing'[2] the natives of the different kingdoms with each other was bound to be slow, and in the meantime the empire had to be defended and Castile relieved of some of its many burdens. It was for this reason that he devised a second project, rather less ambitious in scope, known as the Union of Arms. The theme of this project was again the idea of union, with community of interest leading naturally to community of defence. 'The only remedy for all the ills that can occur is that, as loyal vassals, we all unite...considering it certain that

[1] AGS: Est. leg. 2651, consulta, 6 Jan. 1632.

[2] This is the word used by Olivares's favourite and confidant, the Protonotario of the Crown of Aragon, who strongly objected to an attempt to prevent the Aragonese from receiving ecclesiastical pensions from bishoprics outside Aragon. The king's whole object, he said, was to 'familiarize the natives of the different kingdoms with each other so that they forget the isolation in which they have hitherto lived' (AHN: Cons., lib. 1884, fos. 173–4, August (?) 1626).

all the enemies of His Majesty will give up the struggle when they see that each of his kingdoms can count on the support of all the others, and that they form one single body.' Was it not true that an attack on the king and kingdom of Aragon was also an attack on the king and kingdom of Castile? Then it was clear that each kingdom should come to the assistance of the other.

This mutual assistance was to be achieved by the creation of a common reserve of 140,000 men, supplied and maintained by each province in the following proportions:

Catalonia	16,000 paid men
Aragon	10,000
Valencia	6,000
Castile and the Indies	44,000
Portugal	16,000
Naples	16,000
Sicily	6,000
Milan	8,000
Flanders	12,000
Mediterranean and Atlantic islands	6,000

The king, drawing on this reserve, would come with the seventh part of it—20,000 infantry and 4000 cavalry—to the help of any province which was attacked. Catalonia, for example, would send to the help of Flanders one-seventh of its contribution, or 2286 men, and if at the same time there were war in Italy, another 2286 men would be sent there. The reserve troops were not to be maintained permanently under arms, but would continue in their normal occupations, be exercised on fiesta days, and be called upon only in time of emergency. If Catalonia itself were invaded, it would not be compelled to send any men abroad, but instead would have, in addition to its own 16,000 men, the 20,000 infantry and 4000 cavalry from the other kingdoms which the king had promised.[1]

This plan had certain obvious advantages. By accustoming the different provinces to the idea of military co-operation, it would pave the

[1] BM: Add. MS 13,997, fos. 11–16, *Conveniencias de la unión de los reynos desta monarquía, representadas a los de la Corona de Aragón*; and BM: Eg. MS 347, fos. 119–26, *Papel que escribió el Conde Duque deseando entablar la unión de los reynos desta monarquía.* . . .The first of these is a printed tract intended for distribution to the Cortes of the Crown of Aragon, and may also be found bound into the register of the Catalan Corts of 1626, in ACA: G, Cortes, R. 1057, fo. 181.

way towards that complete union of the provinces of the Monarchy which was the Conde Duque's ultimate aim.

Today, the common people look on the various nationals as if they were little better than enemies, and this happens in all the kingdoms. If Castile can be seen as a feudatory of Aragon, and Aragon of Castile, Portugal of both and both of Portugal, and the same for all the kingdoms of Spain, those of Italy and Flanders being brought into a close relationship, then the blindness and separation of hearts which has existed hitherto must necessarily be ended by the close natural bond of a union of arms. For when the Portuguese see the Castilians and the Castilians the Portuguese, they will know that each sees the friend and feudatory of the other, who will help him with his blood and his men in time of need.

This closer union would bring immediate relief to Castile, while going a long way towards solving that problem of imperial defence which first brought home the need for more adequate co-operation among the provinces of the Monarchy.

Olivares received much praise at the council-table for his ingenious plan for the Union of Arms: 'the only remedy for this Monarchy', said Don Pedro de Toledo; 'the only way to preserve and restore the Monarchy', echoed the Confessor.[1] But however admirable the scheme might appear when considered in Madrid, it was not likely to be greeted with such enthusiasm in the provinces. Not all the skilful arguments of the Conde Duque could conceal the disagreeable fact that, if the plan were successful, kingdoms and provinces hitherto relatively immune would now be contributing regularly with money and troops. They would in all probability regard such regular contributions as objectionable in themselves, and as an infringement of their *fueros*. Although Olivares claimed that he was not requesting 'a thing against the *fueros*', not everyone was likely to agree with him. Very strict rules governed the recruiting and use of troops in the kingdoms of the Crown of Aragon. In Aragon and Valencia, vassals could not be obliged to go beyond their own frontiers for military purposes, though they had fairly extensive obligations if their kingdom was attacked.[2] In Catalonia, military service was regulated by an archaic usage known as *Princeps Namque*.[3] If the Principality were invaded, the Catalans might

---

[1] AGS: Est. (Flandes), leg. 2040, consulta, 6 Oct. 1626. The king's confessor was the Dominican Fray Antonio de Sotomayor.   [2] ACA: CA, leg. 233, no. 28, consulta, 20 Feb. 1634.

[3] AHN: Est., leg. 860, no. 4, *Cabos que de orden de SM se consultan en el Consejo de Aragón*, 10 Feb. 1629.

be called to arms by the proclamation of *Princeps Namque*, although custom suggested that the proclamation was only valid if the king were present in person. In the event of offensive and not defensive war, it appeared difficult to make the Catalans serve beyond their own frontiers at the king's expense, and impossible at their own expense, unless they were feudatories of the Crown.

In mobilizing the resources of the various Spanish provinces, Olivares was certain to find his efforts hampered by innumerable archaic feudal privileges and medieval immunities of this kind. It was easy enough to say that they bore no relation to the changed circumstances of the seventeenth century: easy enough to point out that their survival hindered the successful prosecution of war against a more effectively organized enemy. But, however desirable their abolition, they could not simply be spirited away by a magic wand waved in Madrid. Too many people had an interest in their survival and continuation for them to be abolished with ease.

Perhaps only an immediate and generous offer to treat non-Castilians on the same basis as Castilians in the distribution of offices and the organization of commerce, stood any chance of inducing Aragonese and Catalans and Portuguese to abandon some of their privileges and unite in a common cause. Even then its successful outcome was far from assured. But it hardly lay within the ability of Olivares to make an offer of this nature: Castile would scarcely have tolerated any attempt to make it relax its grasp on offices or commercial privileges. All that Olivares could do was to approach the various provinces with the utmost delicacy, and attempt to show that any sacrifices they were willing to make would be amply rewarded. This itself would be difficult enough, for Castile's urgent need of relief made it hard to proceed with delicacy and caution, while the only reward obviously available was the dubious one of closer collaboration in the fighting of a distant war with the Dutch.

Yet Olivares seems to have entertained an almost childlike confidence in the ultimate success of his plans. Now and again he admitted that he expected them to run into difficulties, but he never displayed any fear lest the difficulties prove insuperable. His project of a closer union seemed to him so eminently reasonable that he could not see how it could fail to appeal to anyone who considered it dispassionately. That dispassionate consideration of so potentially explosive a project was the last thing to be expected never crossed his mind. He clung to the belief that a rational appeal to the Catalans, Aragonese and Valencians to contribute men and money for the help of their hard-pressed king could not fail of success, and he even appears to have believed that it might succeed without his having to summon their Cortes.

It might have been thought that one or two unfortunate experiences with the Catalans in the years following their acceptance of the bishop of Barcelona as viceroy would have done something to temper his optimism. Recent attempts to collect from the Catalans a feudal aid known as the *coronatge*, automatically payable on the accession of a new king, had been held up both by riots[1] and by complaints from the Diputats that the aid could not legally be demanded until the king had honoured the country with his presence.[2] Although the objections were overruled by Madrid, the collection of the money proceeded very slowly, and it was several years before it was completed, and the sum of 29,565 *lliures* entered the royal treasury.[3] Long before this money had been successfully gathered in, the ministers were busy devising other methods of obtaining money quickly from the Crown of Aragon. An appeal was launched in Castile in 1625 for a voluntary gift to the king, known as a *donativo*, and the Court saw no reason why it should not be extended to the Aragonese, Catalans, and Valencians, who between them might offer at least 1½ million ducats.[4] This plan, however, was stillborn. The bishop of Barcelona saw that it was unwise even to mention a voluntary gift at this stage,[5] and, in spite of much discussion, nothing was done.

So great was the desire in Catalonia for a royal visit and the convocation of the Corts that it would seem that any attempt to obtain money from the Principality before such a visit had no possibility of success. The bishop of Barcelona, who knew the province intimately, certainly believed this, and the Catalan attitude to the collection of the *coronatge* justified his fears. Olivares's persistence in the idea that he might secure

[1] ACA: CA, leg. 372, Bishop of Barcelona to King, 27 Jan. 1624.
[2] ACA: CA, leg. 273, no. 3, Bishop of Barcelona to King, 11 Jan. 1624.
[3] ACA: CA, leg. 378, relation by José Carvajal, 10 Oct. 1629. This sum is the equivalent of 270,975 *reales*. The Aragonese *coronaje* brought in 87,235 *reales*, the Valencian 130,000, the Sardinian 201,412 and the Majorcan 63,529½.
[4] AHN: Cons., lib. 1882, fo. 136, consulta of Council of Aragon, 31 Jan. 1625.
[5] ACA: CA, leg. 273, no. 30, consulta, 6 July 1625.

the co-operation of the Catalans without committing the king to an expensive and troublesome journey to their country appears to have sprung from that lack of personal knowledge or understanding of the Catalans which bedevilled all his dealings with them. Throughout his career, Olivares, like any other principal minister, was forced to depend when formulating his Catalan policies, on the information provided him by the Council of Aragon, by secret agents and by any supposedly well-informed persons who obtained his confidence. The Council of Aragon was not necessarily reliable, and had shown itself badly mis-informed at the time of dispute over the new viceroy. Agents and informers could be equally misleading, either through genuine mis-apprehension or through a determination to further their own interests. In later years, Olivares was to rely, with unfortunate results, on the advice of Jerónimo de Villanueva, the Protonotario of the Crown of Aragon.[1] At this stage, however, he had yet to discover the skill and ingenuity of the Protonotario, and had apparently placed his confidence in a member of the Valencian Audiència, Dr Silverio Bernat.

Dr Bernat's qualifications for the post of adviser were a little dubious. He had been charged in a *visita* of the Valencian Audiència with 'making use of his office for immoral purposes' and the charge was at present pending against him.[2] For either this or other reasons he was engaged in a bitter vendetta with the Council of Aragon, and it was this that made him useful for Olivares's purposes, though it did not necessarily make his testimony reliable. An informed but unofficial view of the Crown of Aragon had obvious attractions for the Conde Duque, if only as a check on the Council of Aragon's activities. Dr Bernat had therefore been asked in January 1625 to prepare a paper on possible ways of obtaining revenues from the Crown of Aragon 'in order to relieve the urgent necessities of the Monarchy of the king our Lord'.[3] Much of his reply consisted of a violent attack on the Council of Aragon, which would later play its part in hastening the Council's reconstruction.[4] Turning to possible methods of raising money, Dr

[1] See below, pp. 256–9.
[2] AHN: Cons., lib. 1884, fos. 248–9, consulta, 20 Jan. 1627; and lib. 1885, fos. 85–6, consulta, 3 July 1627.
[3] AGS: Hacienda, leg. 618, *Discurso sobre el donativo que se ha de pedir en los reynos de la Corona de Aragón* (10 Feb. 1625), by Dr Bernat.
[4] See below, pp. 254–6.

Bernat declared himself strongly opposed to a convocation of the Cortes. Not only would the expenses of a royal visit to the Crown of Aragon be very considerable, but any subsidy voted by the Cortes of the three kingdoms would take a very long time to collect. It had taken twenty years for the Catalans to pay the subsidy voted in 1599, and the collection of the Valencian subsidy of 1604 was not yet complete. A further objection to the holding of the Cortes was the attitude of the aristocracy. In Aragon and Valencia, the nobles had suffered severely from the expulsion of the Moriscos, and would vote a subsidy only if they received very liberal *mercedes* from the king. In Catalonia the nobles and gentry had 'usurped' 400,000 ducats worth of annual revenues formerly in the possession of the Crown.[1] As always happened with the Catalan Corts the nobles would refuse to consider voting a subsidy unless the king promised to defer consideration of a resumption of alienated Crown property until the next Corts were held. In this way, the recovery of Crown lands was indefinitely postponed, and the Crown in Catalonia was annually losing 400,000 ducats to the nobility. Dr Bernat dismissed the idea of voluntary gifts or *donativos* as an alternative to a subsidy voted by the Cortes; nor did he hold out much hope of obtaining loans from cities and towns, although much might be obtained from the Church. In his view, the most satisfactory method for securing assistance from the Crown of Aragon was to request armed men for specific military purposes, paid by the provinces for a fixed period of time.

Dr Bernat's proposal for obtaining armed infantrymen may possibly have inspired Olivares's scheme for the Union of Arms. More probably it helped to reinforce or define ideas which the Conde Duque was already turning over in his mind. In spite of the numerous letters from the Diputats of Catalonia and Aragon begging for a royal visit, and the equally numerous letters from the viceroys maintaining that such a visit was essential, Olivares decided to take Dr Bernat's advice and make an attempt to secure the Crown of Aragon's acceptance of the Union of Arms without summoning the Cortes. In the autumn of 1625 he sent

---

[1] It is impossible to judge the accuracy of this statement. Many nobles had certainly at one time or another obtained Crown land and jurisdiction, either by direct usurpation or as the result of a grant from the king. Whether these grants were temporary or permanent could only be determined by examination of the original privilege in every instance—a task that had already become impossible by the seventeenth century.

three senior regents of the Council of Aragon to Catalonia, Valencia and Aragon in order to persuade their compatriots to accept the scheme for the Union of Arms.[1] Salvador Fontanet, the Catalan regent, received instructions to 'procure that the inhabitants serve His Majesty with a sufficient number of paid men to help the other kingdoms and provinces of the Monarchy in time of war, promising in return that they will come to the help of the Principality when necessary'.[2] If, as seems probable, he was given more specific instructions, they have not come to light.

Fontanet arrived to find a discontented province. The dispute over the viceroyalty and the failure of the king to come to Catalonia had left a mark which even the discreet government of the bishop of Barcelona had not succeeded in effacing. In addition, national pride had been badly hurt by the loss of the two Catalan galleys to the Algiers Moors in July 1623. The loss had occurred in the most scandalous circumstances and fully confirmed the wisdom of Alcalá's refusal, during the time of his viceroyalty, to let them sail without his permission. Instead of doing their proper work of defending the Catalan coast against the pirates, they had been used as merchantmen and laden with goods belonging to the private company of Canoves and Morgades, for sale in Sicily. Being not only laden but overladen, they had been unable to escape when Moorish vessels appeared over the horizon, and had fallen intact into Moorish hands. Since both ships and goods were insured, the direct loss did not fall on the Diputació, although much of the insurance had been in the hands of its officials who had hoped to reap a handsome profit from the expedition. 'God allowed it to happen because they are all thieves there', remarked Dr Pujades, but this was little consolation for the 'most infamous loss that the Catalan nation ever suffered'.[3]

The loss of the precious galleys, which had originally been hailed as the vanguard of a restored Catalan navy, reflected little credit either on the Catalan commanders or on the Diputació, and did much to increase the Principality's acute national sensitivity. Indeed, these years seem in many respects to have been a time of heightened nationalism in Catalonia, which revealed itself in various ways. There were, for example, fierce anti-Genoese riots in Barcelona in 1623, and there was much

[1] RAH: G-43 Dormer, *Anales de la Corona de Aragón en el reinado de Felipe el Grande*, lib. II, cap. I.
[2] ACA: CA, leg. 274, no. 56, Fontanet to King, 17 April 1627.
[3] Pujades, 3, fo. 164 v.

public discussion as to whether foreign merchants should continue to do business without any form of restriction.[1] It is clear that the tide was flowing strongly against the free-trade sentiments of the Corts of 1599. The protectionist movement, a European phenomenon, was presumably inspired in Catalonia by the commercial troubles of recent years: troubles that increased between 1624 and 1626 with the sudden worsening of political relations between France and Spain.

With the defeat of the Bohemian rebels and the successes of Spínola in Flanders, the fortunes of the House of Austria were in the ascendant; but the advent of Richelieu to power in 1624 heralded the beginnings of a more active French foreign policy, designed to withstand the mounting Habsburg pressure. The weakest point in the Habsburg system was the Valtelline, an essential link between the Spanish and Austrian Habsburgs, and a vitally important passage for Spanish troops on their way from Milan to Flanders. In January 1625 the French occupied the Valtelline and made an alliance with Venice and Savoy against Spain's ally, Genoa. At this moment of considerable tension a serious incident was provoked by the duke of Guise, who was governor of Provence. More than $3\frac{1}{2}$ million *escudos* had reached Barcelona for shipment to Genoa, and Guise, with the connivance of Paris, laid plans to intercept the silver convoy on its way to Italy, and so disrupt the supply system of the Spanish forces in Milan and Flanders. The alarm at Barcelona, already considerable, was increased when, in March, a French galley seized three Genoese barques off Marseilles, with 160,000 ducats on board. The Genoese promised to give Olivares half this sum if he could recover the money for them, and on 2 April the Conde Duque ordered the seizure of French property in Spanish ports to the value of the stolen silver. France retaliated on 29 April by prohibiting all trade with Spain; Madrid riposted by ordering the sequestration of all French property on Spanish soil. Although on this occasion open war was averted, tension between the two countries remained acute for the rest of the year, and it was only in March 1626, at the Treaty of Monzón, that agreement was reached on both the Valtelline question and on a mutual restoration of the confiscated property.[2]

[1] See Carrera Pujal, *Historia...de Cataluña*, vol. I, pp. 375 ff., for examples of protectionist pamphlets.

[2] For the whole incident, see Albert Girard, 'La saisie des biens des français en Espagne en 1625', *Revue d'Histoire Economique et Sociale*, vol. XIX (1931), pp. 297–315.

Although the boycott of trade during these months was never complete, it none the less hit Catalonia hard, and Dr Pujades commented gloomily on the resulting high prices and the scarcity of goods.[1] In the summer and autumn of 1625, therefore, Catalonia was in an uneasy frame of mind. Trade was bad; war seemed close; and the Principality was busily preparing against a possible French invasion.[2] In the charged atmosphere, rumours spread quickly and were magnified in the spreading. Vague reports of Olivares's intentions had reached the Catalans during the summer, and appeared to receive confirmation when Don Jerónimo Pimentel was appointed captain-general of Catalonia in July.[3] Pimentel had simply been appointed because the dual office of viceroy and captain-general could not be satisfactorily combined in the person of a viceroy who was a bishop, and the menacing international situation made the presence of a military commander in Catalonia very necessary. But it was believed in Barcelona that Pimentel's appointment portended the use of force against the Catalans by Madrid, and the city began fortifying its harbour, ostensibly against a possible English attack.[4]

This atmosphere of suspicion can hardly be said to have enhanced the prospects of success of Fontanet's delicate mission. As his colleague from the Council had already been active in Aragon, the Catalans had a pretty shrewd idea of the reasons for his visit, by the time he actually reached Barcelona on 8 December. In the words of Dr Pujades,

the Catalans had taken the measure of this regent Fontanet very well...and when various gentlemen went to see him, they said that it was common knowledge in the city that His Excellency had come to ask for the contribution requested by His Majesty, etc., etc., and that there was talk of there being in Castile and Aragon one crown, one law, one coinage; and that no intelligent man would expect this of him, who was such a good Catalan, and so sensible and discreet.[5]

The rumour that Olivares intended to establish 'one king, one law, one coinage' (*un rey, una ley, una moneda*) appears to have spread throughout Spain. It was not a bad summary of his supposedly secret plans for the future of the Monarchy, although the accuracy of the reference to

[1] Pujades, 3, fo. 274v, 30 June 1625.
[2] ACA: CA, leg. 273, no. 26, consulta, 21 June 1625.
[3] ACA: CA, leg. 273, no. 28, consulta, 21 July 1625.
[4] Pujades, 3, fo. 296v. The fiasco of the Prince of Wales's visit to Madrid in 1623 had been followed by Anglo-Spanish hostilities, and Lord Wimbledon's expedition was now being fitted out for its disastrous attack on Cadiz in October 1625.   [5] Pujades, 3, fos. 299–299v.

'one coinage' is not certain. According to the contemporary Italian historian Assarino, Fontanet brought with him secret instructions to try to introduce the Castilian *vellón* coinage into Catalonia.[1] There is no documentary proof of this, and the sources for Assarino's history were Catalan, so that his statement is not necessarily trustworthy. The establishment of a uniform coinage would undoubtedly have been one means of uniting the provinces of the peninsula, and the Crown's expenses would have been appreciably lightened if it had been able to pay in *vellón* currency for goods and services in other parts of the peninsula than Castile alone. But if this was indeed the Conde Duque's intention (and his plans for the gradual withdrawal of the debased Castilian *vellón* make it rather unlikely)[2] there could hardly have been a worse advertisement for the new-style Monarchy of his dreams, for the other provinces would do anything to save their currencies from suffering the fate which had befallen the coinage of Castile.

The Catalans' skilful treatment of Fontanet had the desired effect. In company with the other regents, he reported to Madrid that there was no hope of acceptance of the Union of Arms without the holding of Cortes. This was bad news, but the plan for the Union was now so dear to the heart of Olivares that, if the summoning of the Cortes were indispensable for its success, then summoned they must be, regardless of the inconvenience to the king and his ministers. When the reports of the regents arrived, the king asked the Council of State whether he should visit the Crown of Aragon. The Council unanimously approved the journey, and the king replied: 'God willing, I shall leave on 7 January.'[3]

So at last, five years after his accession, the date for Philip IV's long-awaited visit to his kingdoms of the Crown of Aragon was fixed. A royal letter of 17 December 1625 summoned the Cortes for January 1626, those of Aragon in Barbastro, those of Valencia in Monzón, and those of Catalonia in Lleida.[4] Whether he succeeded or failed in his mission, his journey would mark a new epoch for Spain. Castile needed the help of the Crown of Aragon as it had never needed it before. The years of neglect were over, the years of exploitation about to begin.

[1] Luca Assarino, *Le Rivolutioni di Catalogna* (Bologna, 1648), p. 22.
[2] For these plans, see Fernando Urgorri Casado, 'Ideas sobre el gobierno económico de España en el siglo XVII', *Revista de la Biblioteca, Archivo y Museo (Ayuntamiento de Madrid)*, vol. XIX (1950), pp. 123–230.   [3] AHN: Est., leg. 860, no. 4, consulta, 21 Dec. 1625.
[4] ACA: Canc., Procesos de Cortes, 51, fo. 1.

CHAPTER VIII

THE CORTS OF 1626

The King and Olivares arrived at Zaragoza on 13 January 1626 on the first stage of their visit to the Crown of Aragon. The Aragonese Cortes were opened a week later, and those of Valencia on 31 January.[1] From the start, the Cortes of both kingdoms ran into trouble. It soon became clear that the project for the Union of Arms aroused no enthusiasm among Valencians or Aragonese, who were much more concerned to obtain remedies for their grievances than to vote a novel kind of subsidy to the Crown. The days at Barbastro and Monzón passed in angry controversy, as the Cortes wrangled interminably while Olivares attempted to hasten their proceedings by a combination of bullying and bribery. This hardly augured well for the success of the Corts in Catalonia, and, needless to say, the Catalans were watching the Valencian and Aragonese Cortes with the closest interest. The syndic of the cathedral chapter of Vic wrote back from Barcelona what was to prove a startlingly accurate prophecy: 'The king has requested the Aragonese for men and money, and it is understood that he will do the same here ...and as he has a fiery temperament they doubt whether he will conclude the Cortes but expect him to lose his temper over some point or other and go back to Madrid. Woe to the land whose king is a child.'[2]

Every extra day spent by the king in Zaragoza meant a further postponement of the opening of the Catalan Corts. The syndics of the Catalan towns, congregated at Lleida, were kicking their heels in impatience, and passing the days in acrimonious disputes with the syndics of the city of Barcelona, over the proper location for the Corts. It was customary for the Corts of Catalonia to be held in Barcelona, but the bishop-viceroy had suggested to the king that they be held elsewhere, 'in a rather inconvenient place', in order to reduce the influence of Barcelona over the proceedings and perhaps dissuade various un-

---

[1] Dormer, *Anales*, lib. II, cap. IV. Dormer's manuscript, which Martin Hume seems to have been the only historian to use, is informative on the Cortes of Aragon and Valencia, but has little to say about those of Catalonia.
[2] ACV: Cartes, 1620–29, Dr Don Enric d'Alemany to chapter of Vic, 29 Jan. 1626.

desirable elements from attending.[1] The king had accordingly chosen
Lleida, to the delight of the citizens of that town, and to the fury of
Barcelona, which at once proceeded to bombard the Court with letters
of protest. After two of Barcelona's five syndics, Jeroni de Navel and
Joan Francesc Rossell, returned from an unsuccessful mission' to Barbastro to persuade the Conde Duque to change his mind, they devoted
themselves to insisting on the nullity of the convocation at Lleida before
the king had taken his oath at Barcelona.[2] These activities endeared
them neither to the syndics of Lleida, nor to those of the other towns,
who had no wish to undertake another expensive journey, this time
from Lleida to Barcelona. Confronted with the unanimous opposition
of all the other towns represented in the Corts, Rossell decided to resort
to a little blackmail, and remind them of their obligations to Barcelona,
such as the provision of corn at time of dearth, 'so that I may surreptitiously oblige them to follow me'.[3] Such measures were not in the
end to prove necessary, for the obvious disadvantages of holding the
Corts at Lleida could hardly fail to impress the Conde Duque. Not only
was the accommodation at Lleida totally inadequate for a royal suite
some two thousand strong,[4] but it was hardly good policy to offend so
influential a city as Barcelona even before the Corts had begun. On
15 March, therefore, the duke of Cardona entered the Consell de Cent
to report that, by the special intercession of the Conde Duque, the king
had agreed to the transference of the Corts from Lleida to Barcelona.[5]
Barcelona displayed an almost hysterical enthusiasm on the receipt of
this welcome news. A special service was held in the cathedral to offer
thanks to God, the Virgin Mary and St Eulalia (the city's patron saint),
and the municipal artillery was ceremonially fired.

The king, however, could not set foot in Catalonia before he had
disposed of the Aragonese and the Valencians. It was clear that the
Aragonese Cortes would take much more time than the king was
prepared to spend in Barbastro, and finally, on 15 March, Olivares
managed to persuade them, after great difficulties, to agree to continue
under the presidency of the count of Monterrey in the absence of the

[1] BM: Add. MS 13,997, fo. 48, Bishop of Barcelona to Count of Chinchón, 4 May 1624.
[2] ACA: Canc., Procesos de Cortes 51, fo. 22, 26 Jan. 1626.
[3] AHB: CCO, 1626, fo. 18, Rossell to Consellers, 30 Jan. 1626.
[4] AHB: CCO, 1626, fo. 68, Bishop of Barcelona to Consellers, 21 March 1626.
[5] AHB: Delibs., 1626, fo. 60.

king. This enabled the king to leave for Monzón and concentrate on the rapid conclusion of the Valencian Cortes. He arrived to find the Valencians showing themselves unexpectedly prickly. In a desperate attempt to end the Cortes quickly, Olivares gave them the date of 21 March as a deadline, and they found themselves in constant and frenzied session from seven to twelve in the morning and then again from two in the afternoon until midnight. Even working under intimidation and to a rigid timetable, the Valencians made it plain that they would not consent to the Union of Arms in the form that had been proposed to them. Like the Aragonese, they considered it a 'hard condition that the troops should run the risk of having to leave the kingdom whenever they were ordered',[1] and Olivares decided to modify his plan and make the military service voluntary, while still insisting on the money to pay the men. The Valencians were finally harried and brow-beaten into agreeing to a subsidy in this form. Under great pressure they voted 1,080,000 ducats, which the king accepted as sufficient to maintain 1000 infantrymen for fifteen years, at the rate of 72,000 ducats a year. Immediately the subsidy was voted, the king held the traditional cere-mony concluding the Cortes, and left Monzón the same day, 21 March. The day after, he crossed the frontier into Catalonia and was met by the bishop of Barcelona, whose viceroyalty automatically expired at the same moment. Now at last, after twenty-seven years, their prince and count was among his faithful Catalan vassals, and the light and warmth of the royal presence, for so long denied them, was again their own.

The king was enthusiastically acclaimed on his arrival in the Princi-pality, but his progress towards Barcelona was marred by one or two unfortunate accidents. On the road between Cervera and Igualada stood the count of Santa Coloma's castle of Aguiló, which had been decorated with a large number of blue and yellow flags in honour of the king; but a sudden gust of wind ruined the display, and to Santa Coloma's chagrin, the king scarcely noticed it.[2] The count of Santa Coloma, extremely ambitious and always anxious to please and im-press, was not the man to shrug off his misfortune with a laugh. Even more unfortunate was an argument that arose at the outskirts of Barce-lona, between Olivares and the admiral of Castile, the duke of Medina

---

[1] ACA: CA, leg. 233, no. 28, consulta, 20 Feb. 1634.
[2] BUB: MS 115, Sevillà's history, fo. 63.

de Rioseco, over the carriage in which the admiral should ride.[1] Since the admiral, although entirely Castilian, had originally come from the old Catalan family of Cabrera, the Catalans naturally took his side, and the episode served only to detract further from the already diminished popularity of the Conde Duque. Nor did the first sight of Olivares on his entry into Barcelona do anything to restore it: 'along came a fine coach and inside it there was only one person, a very fat man with a thick beard', reported a sixteen-year-old boy who was watching the entry of the royal party into Barcelona on 26 March.[2] More pleasure was given by the appearance of the king, dressed in 'rose, with a hat adorned with feathers and diamonds'[3] as he entered the city on horseback and was greeted by the Diputats, the Consellers of Barcelona, the judges of the Audiència and the more distinguished citizens. The next day Philip IV took his long-deferred oath to observe the liberties, privileges and constitutions of Catalonia, and on 28 March, in the monastery of Sant Francesc, the session of the Corts began.

The Catalan Corts consisted of three Estates, or *braços*, ecclesiastical, *militar* and *reial*, deliberating separately. The ecclesiastical estate, presided over by the archbishop of Tarragona, was composed of the bishops, abbots and priors together with syndics from the cathedral chapters; the *braç militar* of all the nobles and *cavallers* who chose to attend (some 500 on this occasion);[4] and the *braç reial* of forty-one syndics representing the thirty-one towns allowed a place in the Corts, Perpinyà having three syndics, Lleida, Girona, Tortosa and Balaguer two, and Barcelona five, headed by the Conseller-en-Cap, who was president of the Estate.[5]

The purpose of the Catalan Corts, as the Catalans never tired of explaining, was very different from that of the Cortes of Castile. In Castile, laws were made by royal pragmatics, and the task of the Cortes was not to pass laws but to grant taxes. In Catalonia, on the other hand, no laws could be made outside the Corts, the first object of which was to 'establish or amend our laws.... The second object is to remove

---

[1] BM: Eg. MS 347, fos. 126–8, *Relación de lo que pasó al Almirante de Castilla.*

[2] BUB: MS 224, *Dietari de Miquel Parets*, vol. I, fo. verso. I have preferred the original Catalan version, with its spontaneity and vividness, to the Castilian version printed by Pujol y Camps in the *MHE*, vols. xx–xxv.

[3] Dormer, lib. II, cap. xv.

[4] The names of those present can be found in ACA: Canc., Procesos de Cortes, 51.

[5] ACA: CA, leg. 260, no. 49, list of syndics, 1626.

the grievances of the natives of this Principality. The third, to give His Majesty some service, and the king to give to all of us general and individual *mercedes.*'[1] It will be seen from this that the Catalan Corts, unlike those of Castile, worked more to the advantage of the Principality than to that of the prince. The granting of a subsidy or service— an act known, significantly enough, as an act of *grace*—took very much a third place to matters of *justice*—the redress of grievances and the amendment of laws. For decisions on matters of justice, a majority vote in each Estate sufficed; but when it came to granting a subsidy, there had to be *unanimity* throughout the Corts. The granting of supplies was therefore entirely dependent on the preceding redress of grievances.

In a parliamentary system of this nature, proceedings were bound to be slow. Every grievance brought before the Corts had to be properly investigated. The Corts would nominate certain persons to receive and classify the complaints of all those who claimed to have been wronged either by a royal minister or by any other person. Their grievances, or *greuges*, were then submitted to eighteen judges of *greuges*, nine appointed by the king and nine by the Corts, to decide whether they were justified, and, if so, what compensation should be given.

While the grievances were being investigated, another committee of eighteen persons, of whom six were appointed by the king, was at work on the amendments to the laws and constitutions. A preliminary draft of some new or amended constitution would be given them either by an individual or by the lawyers attached to each Estate. It was their task to examine the draft of the proposed new law, give it proper shape, and return it to the Estates for consideration. The Estates would often disagree among themselves over the wording, and three representatives of each would then be elected to smooth out the disagreements. Once this had been done, the proposed new law was submitted to the royal ministers who had to decide if it could be accepted in its present form. If it could not, the king's representatives had to settle down with those of the Corts to find a formula satisfactory to both sides.[2]

[1] BN: MS 2358, *Respuesta a un papel del Duque de Alcalá en razón de las Cortes de Cataluña año 1626*, fo. 305.
[2] For all procedural matters, see Luys de Peguera, *Pràctica, Forma y Estil de Celebrar Corts Generals.*

Much the most important work of the Corts was therefore done outside the sessions of the Estates themselves, by the committees appointed to examine grievances and consider laws. This was essential, for no royal ministers could attend meetings of the Estates, so that the only opportunity for ministers and Corts to discuss and work together was in the meetings of the committees. In spite of the importance of the committees, however, the Corts themselves were paramount. The committees depended on them for instructions, and reported back to them on all matters that had been considered; and the Corts retained long-distance but effective control over all their proceedings.

Debates in the Corts of Catalonia bore no relation to those in the seventeenth-century English parliament. Indeed, debates as such can scarcely be said to have existed. As was perhaps logical in an institution primarily concerned with defending the rights of the subject, the Catalans had devised a unique form of procedure which gave the individual member of the Corts unlimited power over the proceedings of the body as a whole. This was known as the act of dissent, or *dissentiment*. Any member of any Estate could rise from his seat to say that he wished to place a *dissentiment* to all matters of grace, or of justice, or of both, until such time as a particular point which he raised had been investigated. Other members of his Estate might signify their adherence to his act of dissent, and, if the Estate accepted it, it would then be reported to the other two Estates. As soon as this happened, all proceedings throughout the Corts, or all those that concerned matters of grace or justice, according to the wording of the *dissentiment*, came to a standstill. Nothing could be considered except the point raised in the *dissentiment*, until a decision was reached and the *dissentiment* removed.[1]

This remarkable device was a political weapon of the first importance. By its skilful use, an individual or a group could force the committees to consider or press on with one particular problem, or could bring pressure on the king to yield on some point by keeping the Corts inactive for day after day until he was willing to surrender. The Catalan Corts did not therefore have debates ending in motions and resolutions, but proceeded by fits and starts from the placing of one *dissentiment* and its withdrawal, to the placing of the next. Work might halt for

[1] Michel Sarrovira, *Cerimonial de Corts* (Barcelona, 1701), pp. 24-5 (first published 1585).

days or even weeks while the grievance raised in the *dissentiment* was investigated, or while the dissenter and his opponents refused to yield an inch.

This unusual method of conducting business by means of bringing it to a halt, gave the Corts a real protection against any attempt by the Crown to impose its desires upon unwilling Estates. But its use clearly demanded a very high degree of political maturity. It offered each member of the Corts so excellent an opportunity to divert the course of proceedings he disliked, that the temptation to use it for private ends was extremely strong. A *dissentiment* could easily degenerate into a form of blackmail, with one unscrupulous clique threatening to keep the entire Corts inactive for days on end. The real victim of the un-principled use of the *dissentiment* was, of course, the king. If he was anxious for the rapid granting of a subsidy, as he usually was, *dissentiments* could be used to extort from him one concession after another. It became almost impossible to control the Corts when they were in an intransigent mood without making large concessions and resorting to bribery on a vast scale. This was how Philip III had managed to secure a subsidy from the 1599 Corts, and his son would need to use the same methods if the 1626 Corts were to prove equally fruitful to the Crown.

Philip IV's difficulties, in any event, were likely to be much greater than those that had faced Philip III. He was intending to request a new kind of service of unprecedented size, and he would be requesting it from a Principality where no Corts had been held for twenty-seven years. Philip III had had difficulty enough in obtaining a service after a lapse of only fourteen years. Worse still, those twenty-seven years had been years of widespread discontent, marked by the anarchy of 1615, the harsh measures of Alburquerque and Alcalá for the restoration of order, and the acute uneasiness aroused by the disputes of 1622-3 over the appointment of the bishop of Barcelona as viceroy. There would be private and public grievances in plenty to dispose of before the Corts would begin to discuss a service to the Crown, and many demands for institutional and administrative reform.

Of all the Estates, the ecclesiastical was likely to be the most docile. The syndics of the cathedral chapters were always vocal, but they were outnumbered by the bishops and abbots whose hopes of preferment inclined them to good behaviour. The *braç militar* was likely to give much more trouble. More than one noble nurtured a grievance because his castle had been pulled down on the orders of Alburquerque and Alcalá, and the aristocracy as a whole resented the infringement of its privileges by these viceroys. It was likely to demand that its privileges be treated with more respect by the royal authorities; that it be allowed to carry *pedrenyals* and other weapons; and that the jurisdictions of such rival bodies as Church and Inquisition be reduced.

The best prepared of the three Estates was the *braç reial*, since each town gave its syndics detailed instructions of the demands they were to put forward in the Corts. These instructions vary comparatively little from town to town, and, when analysed as a group, they make it possible to reconstruct the desires of a section of the community which was perhaps more representative of the Principality as a whole than either clergy or aristocracy. It was, of course, true that a body which contained neither peasants nor artisans could scarcely represent very accurately the demands of the Catalan nation, since most of the nation was politically mute and could make its feelings known only by acts of mob violence. But the instructions of the syndics, even if they primarily reflected the demands of the municipal oligarchies, certainly expressed at some points the desires of the humbler urban classes and of the wealthier class of peasants, many of whom now lived in the towns. There was little hope of getting any closer to 'public opinion', in a nation where perhaps 40 per cent lived in towns or small villages, and the rest were small landholding peasants or illiterate agricultural labourers.

The first class of demands which the syndics were instructed to make [1] covered all the problems of municipal life and government which seemed so petty in themselves and meant so much to the inhabitants: new rules for the selection of members of the town council, the confirmation of old privileges, the extension of municipal jurisdiction. Apart from these specific demands, there were demands of more general interest on which most of the towns seem to have been united. The syndics were instructed to press for a renunciation by the king of all claims to the *quints*. This was perhaps their greatest anxiety, for very

[1] The instructions for syndics to the Corts are generally to be found in the municipal registers or boxes of municipal correspondence for the relevant year kept in local archives. I have not felt it necessary to specify the source of each reference where many examples can be found.

often the exaction or renunciation of the *quint* made all the difference between solvency and bankruptcy. Immediately after this in order of importance came the demands for the reform of the Diputació: 'that the immoderate and unlimited expenditure in the house of the Diputació be moderated'.[1] 'Item', said a paper drawn up in Cervera, 'because, in the filling of offices of Diputats and Oidors in the said Generalitat, little attention is paid to the good character and qualifications of those chosen, and the choice is governed solely by kinship, friendship and bribes', the entire method of filling the posts should be altered; and Cervera even went so far as to recommend that the selection of *militars* for the Diputació be entrusted to the viceroy.[2] The towns also wanted a diminution in the private jurisdictions and immunities both of the barons and the Inquisition, and a reduction of the excessive power and privileges of Barcelona: 'that the city of Barcelona be not allowed to determine anything affecting the public welfare of the Principality without the syndics of the towns being first summoned and heard'.[3] Finally, there were demands for the regulation of trade, which revealed the protectionist tendencies of the Catalan bourgeoisie at this time. Vic wanted a prohibition on the export of unworked wool,[4] and Lleida restrictions on the import of French cloths and on the export of money.[5] In many of these demands there is a hint that the towns would have liked to see not less but more government. The Crown was the natural ally of the smaller towns in a world dominated by Barcelona and the aristocracy, and more positive action by the royal ministers—so long as it did not entail any new demands on municipal finances—was likely to be welcomed. But the towns were certain to show themselves adamant in resisting all financial demands that they considered excessive or unwarranted.

It would obviously not be easy to reconcile these various municipal demands with those of the other two Estates, and still less easy to secure a satisfactory balance between the interests of the Principality and those of the king. There was much to be said for a modified version of Alcalá's suggestion that when Corts were held, the king should not demand a subsidy but devote his attention entirely to alterations of the

---

[1] AMV: Acuerdos, 1622–30, instructions of 16 Jan. 1626, no. 37.
[2] AHC: Carpeta I, no. 28, paper headed 'General de Cathalunya'.
[3] AMV: Instructions of Vic, *ibid.* no. 7.   [4] *Ibid.* no. 9.
[5] APL: R. 744, Llibre de Corts (1632), nos. 28 and 29.

laws.[1] So many reforms were needed in the government of Catalonia that the Corts could have been kept fully occupied by the full-time discussion of a reforming programme. But a session of this nature was out of the question. The king urgently needed money, and he could not be expected to let slip the rare opportunity of a visit to Catalonia for doing something to restore his ramshackle finances.

Olivares therefore displayed considerable optimism when he hoped that the Catalans would accept his Union of Arms. It would be difficult enough even to obtain agreement on reforms desired by the Catalans. Could Olivares ever consent, for example, to a renunciation of the Crown's alleged right to the *quints*, with the consequent loss to the royal Treasury? And if he could not, was there any hope of bringing the Corts to a satisfactory conclusion and of inducing it to vote even an ordinary form of service to the king? Olivares held one strong card, but only one. The Catalans were likely to be as anxious as he for the Corts to be concluded, because the new laws and constitutions which they wanted would not otherwise come into effect. A decisive rupture with the king would be not only politically disastrous for the Principality, but would mean that trade remained unprotected, the Inquisition unrestrained, the appointment of foreigners to Catalan benefices unchecked, and that Barcelona and the other towns would still be liable for the payment of the *quints*. Both sides would have to make concessions, but it still remained an open question whether, even with the best will in the world, the gulf between King and Principality could ever be properly bridged, after twenty-seven years of royal absence and the viceroyalty of Alcalá.

Whatever happened, Olivares and his colleagues would have to handle the Corts with the utmost tact, and the omens were not auspicious. The Conde Duque had not succeeded in making himself popular since his entry into the Principality; the marquis of Aytona, whose influence among the Catalans might have counted for much during the Corts, had died on 24 January,[2] and the Treaty of Monzón, ratified in Barcelona in March, had done something to reduce the alleged urgency of the Union of Arms by ending the war with France. Aware that it would be necessary to smooth the path as far as possible, Olivares had hoped to exclude one or two of the more undesirable syndics like Navel

[1] See above, p. 151.   Dormer, lib. ii, cap. vii.

and Rossell, but had found that this could not be done.[1] A more profitable method of obtaining acquiescence was to hold out hopes of liberal rewards for the well-behaved, and there is no reason to believe that anything that might be done in this way was left untried. But it still remained difficult to know how to guide and control five hundred nobles and *cavallers* in the *braç militar*, and it was therefore decided to take the president of the *braç*, the duke of Cardona, into the royal confidence, in the hope that his influence and his large personal following would keep the rest of the Estate in line.

These preliminary precautions having been taken, the Corts opened on 28 March with the traditional speech from the throne, known as the proposition before the Corts. The proposition explained how the king was prevented from coming earlier to hold the Corts because of his preoccupations with the military commitments of the Spanish Monarchy—a statement that enabled him to enlarge on the successes that had followed: the defence of the Valtelline, the defeat of the English before Cadiz, a successful naval battle with the Dutch. But the demands of defence were heavy and the Crown's resources limited. 'I therefore hope that as faithful vassals you will set out to do everything possible, since it will all redound to your own benefit.'[2] This speech, it was noticed with satisfaction in the Corts, 'differed from that made to the Aragonese and Valencians, as nothing is said about soldiers, and it simply represents the king's troubles and difficulties, and the large sums that have been spent on the defence of the faith, with a request for as much help as possible'.[3] Olivares was wisely holding back his project till a more suitable moment.

After the delivery of the speech and a formal reply by the bishop of Urgell, the Corts were prorogued until Monday, 30 March, when they began on the slow and tedious business of examining the credentials of those attending. This was always a source of interminable disputes over problems of precedence and seating arrangements, and as early as 2 April the king found it necessary to urge on the Corts the need for speed, as his health made it necessary for him to leave Barcelona before the coming of the hot weather.[4] But Olivares was determined to show

[1] ACA: CA, leg. 260, no. 4, consulta, 25 Feb. 1626.
[2] ACA: Canc., Procesos, 51, fo. 98.
[3] AMV: CR 10, Dr Pere Vicens Sayz to Consellers of Vic, 1 April 1626.
[4] Procesos, 51, fo. 112.

himself conciliatory, and the king acceded to a request by Cardona that, in spite of the urgent need for discussion of a service to the Crown, all matters affecting the government and welfare of the Principality should first be discussed.[1] In the eyes of the Catalans this was no more than the proper order for proceedings in the Corts, but it showed restraint on the part of Olivares, for whom the sole purpose of the Corts was the granting of a subsidy with all possible speed. At the same time, in order to show that the king was anxious to assist in the recovery of trade, he despatched his confessor, Salazar, to the house of the Conseller-en-Cap of Barcelona on 4 April to tell him of the king's wish to make Barcelona 'the centre of trade for Italy, Alexandria, Alexandretta and other ports of the Levant'. A Junta of royal ministers and Catalan merchants was to discuss the problem of creating a trading company, and report back with advice.[2] Schemes for trading companies stood high among Olivares's plans to strengthen and reform the Monarchy and an approach to the Catalans through their commercial interests might do much to link them more closely to the interests of Madrid.

It was only on 6 April, a week after the opening of the Corts, that business really began. A *dissentiment* was placed, and at once raised, by Don Joan de Peguera in order to draw attention to the problems of lawlessness and banditry in the Principality.[3] The Crown had nothing to fear from Peguera, but a further *dissentiment* in the *braç militar* on the same day showed that others than the friends of Cardona were also at work. Miquel Fivaller, who had played a leading part in the disputes over the bishop of Barcelona's appointment, dissented to everything until measures had been discussed for ensuring the better observance of the laws and constitutions of the Principality.[4] This raised a matter of extreme importance, which was to prove one of the main sources of conflict with the king. It was obvious that, if the constitutions were to mean anything, they must be properly observed by the royal ministers. Ferdinand the Catholic in 1481 had agreed to a constitution known as *De Observança*, which began 'laws and constitutions would be of little value if they were not observed by us and our officials'.[5] This constitution, which stipulated the measures to be taken in the event of

[1] ACA: G, R. 1057, fo. 65.
[2] AHB: Delibs., 1626, fo. 79; and see below, p. 274.
[3] ACA: G, R. 1057, fo. 66.   [4] AHB: Corts, 1626, fo. 129.
[5] *Constitutions y altres drets de Cathalunya*, vol. I, pp. 47–50.

infringements of the constitutions, had become the cornerstone of Catalan liberties, but it possessed certain defects in the eyes of many of the nobles. Constitutions had frequently been ignored or deliberately infringed by viceroys like Alburquerque and Alcalá, and each time this had happened, the Diputació had become involved in great expense and endless debates over the correct interpretation of the laws. To obviate this, Fivaller wanted amendments to the original version of the constitution *De Observança*.

The need for some form of amendment seems to have been generally agreed, but Fivaller was acting as the spokesman of a particular faction in the *braç militar*. This faction was advised by a well-known Barcelona lawyer, Dr Vinyes, who was to play an outstanding part in the life of the Principality during the coming years. Vinyes, the son of a parish priest of Ripoll,[1] had first achieved notoriety at the time of the dispute over the viceroy, and had been sent as one of Barcelona's ambassadors to Madrid. Ambitious and impetuous by temperament, or *coleriquísimo* as he was one day to be described,[2] he was at this time the friend and adviser of a bevy of nobles, and it was he who drafted for them a proposed new constitution on the observance of the laws.[3] When the new draft constitution was submitted to the Corts on 11 April, it clearly betrayed its origins. It might well be unacceptable to the king, but it was not even acceptable to the other Estates. On the assumption that 'the principal purpose of laws is to administer justice with equity, and in order to avoid providing the powerful with an opportunity to oppress the weak', Barcelona took objection to it in its present form, since the new procedure would leave the decision on the defence of the constitutions to meetings of the Braços, which were easily packed.[4] No one was willing to put yet more power into the hands of the aristocracy.

The threatened disagreements over the proposed new constitution were likely to hold up proceedings indefinitely. Already on 7 April the syndic of Girona had protested that the numerous *dissentiments* prevented him and his colleagues, who were coming morning and evening to the Corts, from getting any business done.[5] If these delays were

---

[1] ACA: CA, leg. 224, no. 13, Fontanet to Cardenal Infante, 30 Jan. 1633.
[2] ACA: G, caja 32, Santa Coloma's marginal reply to letter from Protonotario, 14 May 1640.
[3] ACA: CA, leg. 274, no. 61, consulta, 28 July 1627.
[4] AHB: Delibs., 1626, Dietari del xxiv, 20 April 1626.   [5] ACA: G, R. 1057, fo. 80.

irksome to the syndics themselves, they were infinitely more annoying to ministers in a hurry. A message was brought from the king on 12 April complaining of the slowness of the proceedings, and asking the Corts to finish their business within a week so that they might begin discussion on the king's business. 'To finish within a week when we shall need all April!' exclaimed one angry syndic.[1] Olivares, however, was not content to rely on mere requests to the Corts. Measures must be taken to induce those who had placed *dissentiments* to raise them. Presumably at the tactful suggestion of some royal official, Fivaller on 13 April presented a petition asking for a title of nobility,[2] and the following day he at last raised his *dissentiment*.[3] It was probably at the same moment that approaches were also made to Dr Vinyes. He was summoned to the room of the marquis of Eliche, one of the nobles who served as a liaison officer between the king and the Corts, and the marquis, acting under superior orders—presumably those of his father-in-law the Conde Duque—hinted that he might be given a vacant place in the Audiència if he behaved in a manner consistent with the royal service.[4] A dazzling prize hung before the eyes of Dr Vinyes, and he found it irresistible. He now set about undoing all the work he had so laboriously done, winning over even the most 'contrary spirits'.[5] He was to win his prize eventually, although it was to elude him for another four years, but the repentance and regeneration of one man were insufficient to alter the course of a session which was going less and less to the liking of the king.

On the day Fivaller raised his *dissentiment*, a long paper from the king was read to the Braços.[6] This paper was a good deal sharper than anything they had yet heard. While the king expressed his desire to confer new favours upon them daily, he found that, in spite of all his requests for speed, the Corts were constantly being held up by new and unnecessary *dissentiments*. 'It has seemed advisable to warn you again by word of mouth, and, so that there shall be no mistake, in writing also, that whoever introduces delays is conspiring against my life because he is undoubtedly prejudicing my health.' This remarkable statement

---

[1] AHC: CR, Carpeta B, no. 160, Joan Fuster to Pahers of Cervera, 13 April 1626.
[2] ACA: CA, leg. 499, petition of Fivaller.   [3] ACA: G, R. 1057, fo. 110.
[4] ACA: CA, leg. 274, no. 83, Duke of Medina de las Torres to Count of Chinchón, 29 Nov. 1626.
[5] *Ibid.*   [6] ACA: G, R. 1057, fos. 114-15.

was followed by the revelation that he intended to leave for Madrid at
the start of the coming week, and the note ended with an exhortation
which again showed the gulf between the natives of an individual
province and ministers who were compelled to watch over the Monarchy as a whole. 'Look how, for your petty interests, my great
undertakings have been shaken.'

Behind the wording of this message there does seem to have lain a
genuine concern about the effects of the Barcelona heat on the king.
On the day the message was delivered, Olivares wrote a private letter
to the duke of Alcalá: 'We are working as fast as we can in the Cortes
of this Principality, so as not to endanger the king's health.'[1] The royal
hypochondria, however, was most unfortunately timed. The very procedural methods of the Catalan Corts made it impossible to conclude
a session quickly. The Catalans needed time to discuss their problems
and still more time to reach agreement. In trying to make them work
'as fast as we can', Olivares was running the risk of throwing out of
gear the entire procedural machinery of an institution which he was
either unable or unwilling to understand. 'I hope,' continued his letter
to Alcalá, 'that although the matter is very big and new, and for this
reason very difficult, we shall achieve something of value.' He had left
himself only a week to do so.

The king's message created considerable alarm. The ecclesiastical
Estate, always the most subservient, resolved to send an embassy to the
king to inform him that, of the eight constitutions brought before it,
it had already approved five; it had also submitted the constitution on
Observança to the lawyers, and was now discussing with all possible
speed the constitution on the reduction of the powers of the Inquisition.[2]
The *braç militar* also assured the king that it was working as fast as
possible, but it was already becoming clear that the demand for speed
was subjecting the cumbersome procedural machinery to a heavy
strain. Nobles were not remaining in their places and were being
counted twice when votes were taken;[3] and the lawyers were failing
to appear on time.[4] When the Protonotario entered on Thursday, 16
April, to say that all the private business of the Corts must be finished
by Saturday, they were in a state bordering on chaos, with various

[1] RAH: 11-13-3, fos. 14-16, Olivares to Alcalá, 14 April 1626.
[2] ACA: G, R. 1057, fo. 116.   [3] *Ibid.* fo. 122.
[4] AHB: Corts, 1626, fo. 183.

persons placing and raising *dissentiments* at a bewildering speed. It was too much to hope that Cardona, for all his influence, could control so large a body as the *braç militar*, which had just been swept off in a new direction by its desire to get a glimpse of the balance-sheet of the Diputació, only to be checked by a *dissentiment* placed by Josep d'Espuny over an alleged threat to aristocratic privileges, to which 'almost all those present, who are numerous, have signified their adherence'.[1]

When Saturday, 18 April arrived, it was clear that the Corts could not possibly bring their business to an immediate close. But Olivares could wait no longer to bring the king's business before them. Just after a *dissentiment* had been placed in the *braç militar* protesting at the undue speed at which the Corts were being compelled to work, the regents of the Council of Aragon and other important ministers entered the room and took their seats. Then the Protonotario, seated and bareheaded, started to read a long paper from the king. This was to be the decisive moment. Olivares had waited till now to introduce to the Corts his great plan for the Union of Arms; and, before the printed paper outlining the plan was distributed to the members, he had decided that its circulation should be preceded by a dramatic appeal from the king.

The speech read by the Protonotario on the afternoon of 18 April is one of the most moving ever made in the name of Philip IV, and the most eloquent expression of Olivares's hopes for the reorganization of the Spanish Monarchy.

My Catalans [it began],[2] your count comes to your doors, besieged by his enemies, in order to request money not to be spent on vain display, but on obtaining satisfaction against them.... You may choose your own means, for my intention is not to alter the laws and prerogatives which the counts and kings, my ancestors, gave you, but to give you as many new ones as you reasonably request.... My enemies have formed against me and all my kingdoms an offensive and defensive league for fifteen years. For the same period I ask that my kingdoms and territories unite their arms, so that the terror inspired by their power may frighten God's enemies and mine, and dissuade them from their unjust and perfidious intentions.... My children, one and a thousand times I say and repeat that I have no wish to remove your *fueros* and immunities, but only to give you many new ones.... To serve with

---

[1] ACA: G, R. 1057, fo. 148. The *dissentiment* is given in AHB: Corts, 1626, fo. 180.
[2] ACA: G, R. 1057, fo. 181. This speech was reproduced by N. Feliu de la Peña in his *Anales de Cataluña*, vol. III (Barcelona, 1709), pp. 243-4.

paid men, as is proposed to you, is not to infringe your constitutions nor to do anything contrary to custom, but to revive the glory of your nation, and the name that for so long has been forgotten, but was once feared throughout Europe. And by this means I wish your countrymen to obtain the leading places in my kingdoms—places to which their valour and heroism will surely take them.

This speech may perhaps be read as no more than a clever attempt to lure the Catalans into voting a particularly large service. But it can also be seen as an imaginative effort to fire the enthusiasm of the Catalans and induce them to abandon their cramping provincialism for the sake of participation in the great work of creating a new and more glorious Spain. A knowledge of the actual condition of Spain at this moment, and of how little Olivares had to offer the Catalans except a greater share in the sacrifices, may legitimately provoke scepticism both about his ability to keep his promises, and their intrinsic value. But the offer of promoting a trading company for the restoration of Catalan commerce was doubtless intended as an earnest of things to come—of Olivares's genuine hopes for a restoration of Spain's fortunes by a closer co-operation between the peoples of the peninsula.

All the king's references to the more glorious future that awaited a Catalonia working in unison with the rest of Spain, appeared to make not the slightest impression. The Corts's attention was riveted by the accompanying demand for 16,000 men, 'which caused a commotion'.[1] In the ecclesiastical Estate, Dr Don Enric d'Alemany, canon of Vic, supported by Pau Claris, canon of Urgell, and the syndics of other cathedral chapters, dissented to any consideration of the royal proposal until all matters of justice had first been settled.[2] He was only acting according to the instructions that his chapter had given him before the Corts began:

to resist fervently any claims by His Majesty which will involve the ecclesiastics of this Principality in new contributions for soldiers or anything else because we are already paying excessive sums in *quartas* and *excusados*; also to resist any attempts to allow foreigners to enjoy Catalan ecclesiastical revenues.... Warned by the weakness of the Aragonese we have a better opportunity to protect ourselves in advance.[3]

[1] AHC: CR, Carpeta B, no. 179, Joan Fuster to Pahers of Cervera, 18 April 1626.
[2] ACA: G, R. 1057, fo. 197.
[3] ACV: Cartes, 1620–29, Vic chapter to Alemany, 14 Feb. 1626.

Reactions were similar in the other Estates. In the *braç reial*, which the syndics of Barcelona had hitherto managed to keep under close control in their great anxiety for the Corts to proceed smoothly to a satisfactory conclusion, the syndic of Vilafranca del Penedès placed a *dissentiment* to all matters of grace and justice until such time as the proposed constitution on the *quints* was approved.[1] But it was the *braç militar* that produced the epitaph on the Union of Arms in the form of a *dissentiment* by a *cavaller* of very recent creation, Narcís Ramon March:

> Considering that in this Principality of Catalonia the inhabitants are free and cannot be obliged to go and serve His Majesty except of their own free choice, and considering also that the magnitude of the service demanded of us makes its execution impossible, I dissent expressly to all matters of grace, and in particular to the service of soldiers demanded by His Majesty.[2]

In spite of these setbacks, Olivares still hoped for success. The Corts were summoned on the afternoon of Monday, 20 April, to meet the king, who told them that he hoped to leave on Saturday, 'and offered to confer more *mercedes* on this occasion than all those conferred by his predecessors....It is nothing but flattery and praise for the Principality of Catalonia, to make us give a generous service.'[3] Certainly, the Corts were anxious to please the king; anxious also for the king to accept their proposed new constitutions; but working a twelve-hour day,[4] they were tired and overwrought, and they were conscious of nothing but the many grievances that remained to be set right, and of the appalling size of the service that was asked of them.

In this tense atmosphere, rumours spread fast, and the Corts were easily stampeded by alarms. A strange incident occurred on 21 April.[5] Cardona, presumably to incite the Corts to a greater display of loyalty, announced in the *braç militar* that the French ambassador, who had been negotiating the peace of Monzón at the Court, had expressed his regrets to Philip IV at the unwillingness of the Catalans to give the service he had asked of them, and had offered the help of Louis XIII's army in bringing them to their senses. Whether or not the French ambassador ever said anything of this nature, the effect of Cardona's announcement

---

[1] AHB: Corts, 1626, fo. 216.   [2] *Ibid.* fo. 227.
[3] AHC: CR, Carpeta B, no. 165, Fuster to Pahers, 20 April 1626.
[4] BN: MS 2358, *Respuesta a un papel*, fo. 306.   [5] *Ibid.*

was electric. 'We rose up in fury at this insult to our loyalty', and immediate measures had to be taken to protect the person of the unwise, or unfortunate, envoy of His Most Christian Majesty. It was some time after this incident, so revealing of the mood of the Corts, before they could be induced to settle down again and return to the more humdrum business of daily routine, and almost at once Cardona made another tactical mistake. For the duration of the Corts he had been allowed by the king to grant *mercedes* on his own account, if they were likely to further the royal interest. On 23 April, exercising this right, he conferred the title of *cavaller* on his personal legal adviser, Dr Josep Ramon, thus enabling him to take a seat in the *braç militar*.[1] This privilege, conferred when the king had as yet conferred none of his own, greatly upset all those nobles in the *braç militar* who entertained hopes of *mercedes*, and stimulated the beginnings of secret but organized resistance to Cardona's leadership.[2]

Although Cardona enjoyed a very large personal following, he could not afford to alienate a single noble or *cavaller*. It was true that many would follow him to the end, like Don Andreu de Marles, who declared in a petition to the king that he was 'actively serving Your Majesty in these Cortes, following the advice of the duke of Cardona in everything, as being most compatible with the service of God and Your Majesty'.[3] But not every noble could be expected to see the path of duty so clearly stretching before him. Many were discontented and saw little hope of obtaining satisfaction. Others, while anxious to gratify the king, were not so anxious to gratify the duke of Cardona. The duke had many enemies, not least the count of Santa Coloma, always eager for public applause; the two men were at daggers drawn since a quarrel between their wives at the bedside of a mutual friend whom they had come to congratulate on the safe delivery of a son.[4] So much depended on personal relationships that private feuds of this nature could suddenly flare up with renewed animosity when fanned by the winds of political discontent.

Since the dissensions in the Braços held up all discussion of the service, the king was compelled to postpone his threatened departure from one

[1] ACA: CA, leg. 260, no. 51, mercedes. King to J. L. de Villanueva, 23 April 1626.
[2] Assarino, *Rivolutioni*, p. 28.   [3] ACA: CA, leg. 500, petition, 29 April 1626.
[4] Sevillà's history, fo. 59. The duchess of Cardona took the seat nearest the bed, to the fury of the countess, who considered herself by birth the equal of the duchess.

day to the next. He might have given up in despair and gone home at once if he had been fully informed of the attitude of the municipalities. The town council of Cervera, for instance, had instructed its syndics that they were 'on no account to consent to His Majesty's request for soldiers'; and that, on condition that the Corts were satisfactorily concluded and His Majesty renounced his claims to the *quint*, they might then consent to a subsidy of 1,100,000 *lliures*.[1] Since it was now being rumoured that he would ask for 3,300,000 *lliures* in lieu of soldiers,[2] and since he was extremely unlikely to abandon his claims to the *quints*, the chances of agreement were slight. But Olivares, though now realizing that he would have to abandon his plea for soldiers, appears to have been unaware of the general consternation at the rumoured size of the sum to be asked. Determined to push the business through as quickly as possible, he decided to apply more pressure. The Braços were again summoned before the king on 25 April, this time to be told that he must leave on 3 May, and it now appeared as if he really meant to carry out his threat. 'We all returned confused and bewildered, asking each other how we could cut things short....Everywhere was confusion and distress.'[3] How, they asked themselves, could the constitutions possibly be completed, the grievances be remedied and the service be decided upon, all in the space of eight days? Eight days in which to set right the wrongs of twenty-seven years! 'Time, which is so prodigally wasted, had become our first enemy.' In a desperate attempt to show that something had been achieved, the eight draft constitutions nearest to completion were hastily prepared for submission to the king.[4]

In spite of the real effort being made to hasten the discussions, *dissentiments* were still being placed, to the anger of the ministers, who were losing patience. When, on 27 April the syndic of Pals dissented to everything until the constitution on the *quints* was approved, and refused to withdraw his *dissentiment*, Cardona and the Protonotario unwisely entered the *braç reial* and ordered him on pain of death to withdraw it forthwith.[5] This was not the way to handle intransigent syndics. There was immediate uproar in the *braç*, and the two men beat

[1] AHC: Llibre de xxiv, 1605–34, fo. 17, 23 April 1626.
[2] AHC: CR, Carpeta B, no. 175, Fuster to Pahers, 25 April 1626.
[3] *Respuesta a un papel*, fo. 307.   [4] AHB: Corts, 1626, fo. 355.
[5] AHC: CR, Carpeta B, no. 178, Fuster to Pahers, 27 April 1626.

a hasty retreat. In the records of the *braç reial* for the next day appeared
the sinister note: 'this morning, because of the dissents placed yesterday
in the present *braç* and the *braç militar*, nothing at all was done'.[1]

Olivares may well have wondered how to deal with these impossible
Catalans. Threats were having no effect; nor were the bribes that were
now being profusely offered.[2] The ministers had gone so far as to
draw up a list of *mercedes* to be offered at the conclusion of the Corts,
and it is to be presumed that those who were to receive favours had
been advised of the prize that lay in store for them. Thirty-eight titles
of nobility were to be given; seventeen privileges of *cavallers*; eleven
places in the military orders, and eighteen honorary citizenships of
Barcelona.[3] The list was not, it was true, to be compared to the enormous list of honours granted in 1599, but no one could be expected to
compete with the boundless generosity of Philip III. Not everyone
could be pleased, but it was now beginning to seem questionable
whether *anyone* could be pleased. The syndic of Cervera had reported
in his letter of 27 April that not one of the towns had received what it
had requested, and any request that threatened to diminish the royal
patrimony in Catalonia was answered with the words: *no ha lugar*—
the petition is rejected.

The rejection of petitions from the towns requesting an extension of
their jurisdiction shows the dilemma that faced Olivares. The royal
patrimony in Catalonia was already so small that he dared not diminish
it further. Concessions in this direction were therefore impossible. The
same difficulty arose over the eight constitutions that had been submitted for the king's approval. The royal authority in the Principality
was already so weak that the king dared not make further large administrative concessions for fear of losing all control over Catalonia. As a
result, six of the constitutions were returned so altered by the ministers
that they bore little relation to the original drafts.[4] When an embassy
was sent to the king begging him to approve the constitutions in their
original form, it met with an uncompromising refusal.

I am amazed that you have come to complain to me about the decisions
on the constitutions, in which I have conceded more—especially on the

---

[1] AHB: Corts, 1626, fo. 370.   [2] Fuster's letter of 27 April.
[3] ACA: CA, leg. 260, no. 50, *Apuntamientos...en favor de los que se siguen*, 28 April 1626.
[4] ACA: G, R. 1058, fo. 300, 28 April 1626.

constitution *De Observança*—than all my predecessors.... And take note that I have been here five weeks, and my service has not yet been discussed. I have to leave on Monday... and I warn you that I have seen into your hearts and know the manner of your proceeding....[1]

The realization that only four days remained to them had a marked effect on the Corts. Caught between the 'brevity of the time and the magnitude of the matter to be discussed', a final heroic effort was made, and no less than seventy *dissentiments* were raised during the course of the day.[2] But the gap was so wide between the minimum demands of the Principality and the maximum administrative and fiscal concessions the king was prepared to make, that the chances of agreement were slender. King and Catalans were talking different languages. In the eyes of the king, any more administrative and fiscal concessions would leave the Crown so fatally weakened in the Principality as to transform it into an independent republic. To the Catalans, or at least to those sections of the community represented in the Corts, concessions were necessary and desirable, though there was so much rivalry between towns and aristocracy that it was questionable whether they could even reach preliminary agreement among themselves on what was to be asked of the king.

The gulf dividing king and Corts over administrative and fiscal reform suggests that the Corts of 1626 were in any event condemned to failure. On three outstanding points—the *quints*, Observança, the powers of the Inquisition—there was complete deadlock. It is just possible that Olivares could have broken this deadlock by surrender on one question—the *quints*. It was the aristocracy, not the *braç reial*, which was really insistent on the other two constitutions. Renunciation of royal claims to the *quints*, at least until the next Corts, could well have swung the *braç reial* into line behind Olivares.[3] Barcelona was so anxious to escape payment of its *quints* that it would have used all its powerful influence to bring the Corts to a quick conclusion. The *braç militar* would then have found itself isolated, and the very fact that it possessed no real coherence or unity would sooner or later have allowed its resistance to be broken down. Individual nobles under pressure

---

[1] AHB: Corts, 1626, fo. 392.   [2] *Respuesta a un papel...*, fo. 307.
[3] 'All the syndics are agreed that if the King wants a service, he must remit the *quints* for the entire Principality at least until the conclusion of the next Corts.' Dr Sayz to Consellers of Vic, 1 May 1626 (AMV: CR, 10).

simultaneously from both the king and the rest of the Corts would not hold out indefinitely. Once again, therefore, an alliance between the Crown, Barcelona and the municipal oligarchies appears, as it appeared in the days of Alburquerque, to have been the only solution to the king's difficulties. But the price that the king must pay was high— perhaps too high for it to be worth paying. It meant at least temporary renunciation of the *quints*; and it meant the asking of a subsidy no larger than that which the towns themselves considered reasonable.

Olivares, obsessed by the poverty of the Crown, could not, and dared not, comply. He showed no sign of giving way on the *quints*, and on the subsidy he was adamant. He was prepared to abandon his request for paid infantrymen, as he had abandoned it in Valencia, but he would not yield on the figure he regarded as necessary to pay for the Principality's defence. On 26 and 27 April the syndics of the towns were individually informed that:

Considering the difficulties raised by the province over the levying of paid men, His Majesty's final resolution on the fifteen-year service...is that he shall be given 250,000 ducats a year for these fifteen years. The money is to be spent solely in this province, for the defence of its frontiers and the upkeep of galleys, not galleons. It is to be entirely collected by natives of the province, and is not to pass through the hands of royal officials; and if the funds of the Generalitat are inadequate, new expedients are to be found.[1]

The sum of 250,000 ducats a year horrified the Corts. A citizen of Vic, Pau Beuló, wrote home urgently from Barcelona warning his town council on no account to agree to the

horrific sum of 3,700,000 ducats demanded by His Majesty, which, at 11 *reals* to a Castilian ducat, works out at 4,125,000 Barcelona *lliures*, which as I understand and as can well be believed, would mean the total ruin and destruction of this kingdom....They say that to raise this money, a tax of one thirtieth would be levied on all grains, vines, oils and other fruits for a period of fifteen years, so that all Catalonia would be desolated....So be brave and constant, for if we allow ourselves to be oppressed in this way, not only we but all our descendants in perpetuity will be slaves and captives. We want to please our king, as is only right and proper, but in such a way that we all stay alive, not being—as we are not—a conquered but a free people, as we have made clear in all the offers we have made, and as can be found in the volumes of all the constitutions....[2]

[1] ADP: Série B, liasse 385, note in Castilian, dated 26 April 1626.
[2] AMV: CR, 10, Pau Beuló to Consellers of Vic, 27 April 1626.

The intensity of feeling expressed in this letter, allied to the fact that a town like Cervera had been thinking in terms of a service of 1,100,000 *lliures*,[1] suggests a sharp divergence between the king's advisers and the Catalans over the fiscal resources of the Principality. Was 4 million *lliures* spread over fifteen years an exorbitant figure for the Principality to pay? The Catalans thought that it was, the ministers thought it was not. Strangely enough, both sides seem to have been basing their calculations on a far larger figure for population than was really correct. Olivares consistently spoke and acted on the assumption that the population of the Principality was at least one million; and the Catalans themselves apparently accepted this figure. The Catalan merchant Jaume Damians, in a paper of 1630 on Catalan commercial problems, wrote of

the great number of inhabitants, of whom today there are so many that, without doubt, the population exceeds one million persons. This can be estimated from the fact that in the Principality and Comtats there are today 250,000 hearths, as I have been informed of a certainty by various intelligent and trustworthy persons, who made an investigation at the time of the Corts; and computing that there are more than four persons in each household, the total number exceeds one million.[2]

Since the census of 1553 had given the Catalans a total of 71,690 hearths, a figure in 1626 of 250,000 hearths would have meant that the population had more than trebled in seventy years. Yet no one seems to have queried a figure which suggested so rapid and large an increase. Moreover, a population increase of this magnitude would surely have been reflected in a significant rise in the dues paid to the Generalitat, such as had not occurred; it would also have been reflected in a much higher figure than the 62,000 *lliures* collected annually in the Catalan *cruzada*[3] —a tax which most Catalans would have paid, and which, at 2 *reals* a person, would suggest a total minimum population of 340,000. If the real figure for the population was somewhere between 360,000 and 400,000, as seems probable,[4] there was a wild inaccuracy in the commonly accepted figure of one million which was to have tragic political consequences, for Olivares was attempting to exploit a country whose population and resources had been greatly exaggerated.

The Principality was at present paying in taxes to the Generalitat

[1] See above, p. 234. [2] BC: Fullet Bonsoms 5404, *Parer de Jaume Damians*.
[3] ACA: CA, leg. 383, note on income from *cruzada*, 18 Dec. 1632.
[4] See above, p. 26.

about 160,000 *lliures* annually. The king was now asking it for about 260,000 *lliures* a year, and in addition the Catalans would still have to pay sufficient dues to meet the ordinary expenses of the Diputació. Even if the Diputats were to make large economies, it is doubtful whether they could have cut their annual expenditure below 100,000 *lliures*, so that the Principality would have had to raise at least 360,000 rather than 160,000 *lliures* a year if the king's demands were accepted. This was a very big increase, especially at a time when the dues of the Generalitat were declining, and the figures for import and export dues in the period 1623–6 had shown a marked drop.[1] On the other hand, the Diputació, if it had been functioning properly, would have had a considerable reserve of money from which a significant proportion of the subsidy to the king could have been met. It was the general custom for the services granted by the Catalan Corts to be drawn largely from the revenues and reserves of the Diputació, with the remainder being found from new taxes specially levied for the occasion. But in 1626 the Diputació had no reserves, and this was the real source of the trouble.

The story of what had happened to the Diputació's funds is revealed in a letter from Dr Sayz, the syndic of Vic and a fellow-citizen of Pau Beuló, who had written in such vehement tones about the exorbitant demands of the king. Sayz was one of the syndics who had been elected to inquire into the finances of the Generalitat, and his discoveries seem genuinely to have shocked him. They also throw an interesting light on the motives behind Beuló's letter.

I and the others have been trying to find out, for the relief of our consciences, exactly where the water has been leaking, because although the Generalitat receives an income of 164,000 *lliures* and pays only 54,000 *lliures* in interest on *censals*, there is no money in the Diputació for a service to the King.... We have discovered that the larger part of it has been mis-spent, because anyone legally occupying an office in it takes on three colleagues to assist him, all of them drawing extra salaries. This has made us decide to get rid of twenty or thirty surplus officials in the Diputació, of whom one is Mr Pau Beuló who, with others, assists in one of these offices....From the balance-sheet which I enclose, you will see that more than 50,000 *lliures* a year have gone in unnecessary expenses, so that in the past twenty years 1 million could have been set aside towards the service requested by the king....[2]

[1] See the figures given in Appendix III.
[2] AMV: CR, 10, Sayz to Consellers of Vic, 1 May 1626.

Sayz's letter puts Beuló's ringing appeal to his fellow citizens in a rather different light. If the Corts were concluded and the proposed reforms of the Diputació approved, he would be out of a job. But the patriotic fervour of Beuló's letter need not be entirely discounted as a mere hypocritical effusion. Public and private interest were always hopelessly confused in seventeenth-century Catalonia, and the grossest egoism combined quite happily with a patriotic idealism that was perfectly sincere. What was undeniable was the fiscal exhaustion of the Diputació, and at this moment the reasons for its exhaustion were irrelevant. If the Diputació could contribute nothing, the money would have to be raised in the Principality through new devices which would not be received with favour. Most of the towns were so heavily indebted as to be scarcely able to make ends meet. The clergy had no intention of paying more dues, 'in view of the intolerable burden they are bearing'.[1] Such fierce opposition both in cathedral chapters and town councils to a royal request for a service of over 4 million *lliures* suggests that Olivares had no chance of success.

The Conde Duque, however, seems to have been oblivious to the violent reactions his proposal had aroused. He even had some reason to feel encouraged, for on 1 May the Braços had actually gone so far as to nominate representatives to discuss the service. For the first time in four weeks it seemed that the goal was in sight. But it was important that the Corts should vote on the service quickly, without having time to examine the matter too closely and embark on detailed discussions which would last for ever. When, therefore, the Corts sent a new embassy to the king on the afternoon of Saturday, 2 May, only two days before the date arranged for his departure, and asked him to accept the original draft of the six constitutions and spend a few days more in Barcelona, it received an icy reply: 'I have not granted this audience to listen to you, but for you to listen to me. Only God can make me change my mind, or else the definitive concession of the service.'[2] This unpleasant rebuff did not have the expected result. 'These words have created such a stir that the Corts are in chaos, and it is feared that the Principality is threatened with some terrible disaster if the king goes, as it is considered certain he will go, before Tuesday.'[3]

[1] ACV: 1620–9, draft reply of Vic chapter to Alemany, 5 May 1626.
[2] AHB: Corts, 1626, fo. 417.
[3] ACV: 1620–9, Alemany to chapter of Vic, 3 May 1626.

The Catalans were not accustomed to this kind of treatment. Rather pathetically the syndic of Cervera wrote home: 'These Corts are very different from those held by other kings, because when they wanted something they would ask for it, whereas now there are nothing but threats.'[1] Olivares was not handling the Catalans well; but would a more diplomatic approach have met with any greater success, given the size of the service he was demanding, and the small number of concessions he felt able to make? The grievances of individual dissenting *militars* alone were, it was alleged, capable of involving the Crown in an expenditure of 6 million *lliures*.[2] How far could Olivares possibly give way? Even if he had let the Corts work at their own pace, instead of hustling and harrying them, there was no guarantee that he would have fared any better. Relations between Cardona and Santa Coloma had grown so bad, that every day the Corts continued added to the fear of a clash between their supporters in the *braç militar*.[3]

Olivares did, however, decide that one big concession must be made. On Sunday, 3 May, the Protonotario came to the *braç reial* with a promise that the king would cancel the arrears of *quints* of all towns which voted the service he had asked, and would make no further claims on them until the next Corts.[4] This promise may have had some effect, for the towns appear to have been thinking now in terms of a subsidy of 2 million *lliures*, although the Corts had come no closer to agreement on the ways in which the money was to be raised. A paper composed by the commission appointed to discuss the service was read to each of the Estates, outlining possible new taxes: '6*d*. on every pair of shoes, a *real* on playing cards, 4*s*. on the carrying of *pedrenyals*, 10*s*. a year payable by every unmarried French immigrant....'[5] But the paper was badly received in the *braç reial*, and all discussion was prevented by the placing of *dissentiments*. In the *braç militar*, where tempers were frayed and feelings running high, it met a similar fate, and was again greeted by numerous *dissentiments*, including one placed by the irrepressible Josep d'Espuny. There followed a violent altercation between him and Cardona, whose patience was nearing exhaustion.[6]

---

[1] AHC: CR, Carpeta B, no 186, Fuster to Pahers, 3 May 1626.
[2] *Ibid*. no. 187, Dr Montornès to Pahers, 3 May 1626.
[3] Sevillà's history, fo. 67v.
[4] AHB: Corts, 1626, fo. 420.   [5] AMV: CR, 10, Sayz to Consellers, 3 May 1626.
[6] BN: MS 6745, *Cortes en Barcelona año 1626*, fo. 29.

Once again, Cardona had shown that he did not have the equability of temperament nor the capacity for dissimulation needed for presiding successfully over the *braç militar*.

In spite of the misfortunes of that Sunday morning, the ministers had decided to force a vote on the subsidy during the course of the afternoon. While the king was enjoying a naval pageant in the harbour, the president of each Estate formally proposed a grant of 3,300,000 ducats for the king, taking care to point out that if it were not voted, nothing could stop the king from leaving the next day. In the *braç eclesiàstic* objections were overruled against taking a vote while *dissentiments* remained in force. The voting began, and one by one the bishops and abbots cast their vote in favour of 3,300,000 ducats. It came to the turn of the syndics of the cathedral chapters. With one exception they had protested that the proceedings were null and void, and now, when their turn came, they rose up and left the chamber.[1] In the *braç reial* the syndics would not even allow the proposition to be read, and all marched out. But the greatest drama was reserved for the *braç militar*.

Having carefully primed 'many *caballeros*, relations, friends and servants of his house',[2] Cardona rose to propose the vote. The response was far from encouraging. Seeing the way the wind was blowing, the count of Santa Coloma now placed himself squarely on the side of the dissidents, and a few barbed words were enough to make Cardona reach for his sword. While the two nobles stood facing each other with drawn swords, other nobles and gentlemen also drew theirs, and were followed by their servants who had heard the uproar from outside.[3] For a few moments a clash seemed certain, but the royal guards intervened and calm was momentarily restored. Almost immediately, however, two former supporters of Cardona rose to object, and found strong support from all quarters. Cardona, seeing that everything was collapsing around him, stood up with the words: 'Those who want to serve the king follow me.' 'Many *caballeros* put themselves at the door, begging him to calm the *braç*, and assuring him that all were anxious to serve the king, but he would not stop, and although the door was blocked and he could only make his way through it with difficulty, he left the room, and I and others followed him.'[4] The number who

[1] ACV: Cartes, 1620–9, Alemany to chapter of Vic, 4 May 1626.
[2] *Respuesta a un papel...*, fo. 308.
[3] BN: MS 6745, fo. 29.　　　　　　　　　　　[4] *Respuesta*, fo. 308.

242

followed Cardona seems to have totalled 142 out of about 400 persons present. They included many distinguished names—the counts of Vall-fogona, Montagut and Erill, Don Berenguer d'Oms, Don Lluís Des-catllar—but that of the count of Santa Coloma was not among them.

With the dissolution of the Braços in turmoil on the evening of 3 May, Olivares decided that the king should remain in Barcelona no longer. At six o'clock the following morning, he left the city.[1] As a parting shot a message was read by the Protonotario to the Braços the same morning, in which the king told them that he had already gone, and that when they had drawn up a list of grievances they could forward it to him for consideration.[2] Nothing more.

The news of the king's abrupt departure led to an immediate re-action. The Consell de Cent of Barcelona was immediately summoned, and the Consellers asked it what they should do, in view of the fact that the city was extremely anxious to receive certain privileges, especially exemption from the *quints*. It decided that the city should offer the king an immediate loan of 50,000 *lliures* to meet the expenses of his journey, and that the Conseller-en-Cap, taking the money with him, should lead an embassy which would depart at once and beseech him to return to conclude the Corts.[3] Barcelona, which had striven so hard for a satisfactory conclusion to the Corts in its hope of obtaining exemption from payment of the *quints*, would do everything in its power to prevent a break with the king as long as the hope remained.

The Corts had gone into urgent discussion when they heard that the king had left. At eleven in the morning, the *braç eclesiàstic* informed the others of its decision to vote 3,300,000 ducats for fifteen years, in spite of the objection of all the syndics from the cathedral chapters. The *braç militar*, crumpled by the news of the king's departure, began to take a vote on the service, in spite of the fact that more than two hundred *dissentiments* still remained in force. Cardona and 165 others voted for the full 3,300,000. Votes were also cast for smaller sums:

3,000,000 =	3 votes	1,100,000 =	24 votes
2,000,000 =	27 votes	1,000,000 =	1 vote
1,700,000 =	34 votes	100,000 =	1 vote
1,500,000 =	86 votes		

[1] AHC: CR, Carpeta B, no. 189, Fuster to Pahers, 4 May 1626.
[2] ACA: Canc., Procesos, 51, fo. 173.   [3] AHB: Delibs., 1626, fos. 115–16.

This meant that a total of 342 members of the *braç* had voted specific sums, their vote to take effect *sublatis dissentimentis*.[1]

In casting their votes, the majorities in both the ecclesiastical and aristocratic Estates had infringed the constitutional procedure whereby no vote could be taken on a service to the Crown until grievances were redressed and all *dissentiments* raised. When Dr Alemany reported the day's events to his cathedral chapter, they expressed the liveliest indignation:

Those gentlemen of the ecclesiastical and aristocratic Estates have behaved in a very extravagant fashion over the service, with so many *dissentiments* still in force, when one considers that a single *dissentiment* is enough to prevent any vote being taken. It looks as though their very anxiety to bend the nation to their own sinister designs has confused and undermined them. May God help them to see their wickedness in preferring their own interests to those of the land; and may He be pleased so to settle matters that His Majesty is contented with what can reasonably be borne, and the Principality gets the constitutions it needs for its well-being.[2]

The reaction of the canons of Vic to the vote of the *braç militar* underlines once again the distrust in which the Catalan aristocracy was held. Already the Estates had clashed over the aristocracy's efforts to extend its powers, and now, in this latest vote, it again seemed to be putting sectional interests before those of the nation. The 'nation', needless to say, was represented by the cathedral chapters and the towns —and particularly by the cathedral chapters. The clergy were more heavily and regularly taxed than anybody else, and their resentment turned them into the most doughty defenders of an oppressed Catalonia. There was nothing insincere about this. Private discontents added fuel to the flames, but the aggrieved never had any doubts in their own minds that when they spoke for themselves they spoke for all their fellow-countrymen.

Although the canons remained intransigent, a majority of the towns represented in the Corts had now come to accept in principle the figure of 2 million *lliures*,[3] as long as it was voted in a constitutional manner. Barcelona was doing its utmost to get the *dissentiments* raised in the *braç reial*, but its efforts were not very successful, and as long as they

[1] AHB: Dietari del xxIV, fo. 277.
[2] ACV: Cartes, 1620–29, chapter of Vic to Alemany, 6 May 1626.
[3] AHC: CR, Carpeta B, no. 190, Fuster to Pahers of Cervera, 5 May 1626.

remained, no vote could be constitutional. While a minority resisted Barcelona's threats and blandishments it does not seem as though there was any conspiracy to sabotage the Corts. Everyone wanted to see them brought to a satisfactory conclusion and the king go away contented with his Catalan vassals. But many people simply could not see their way to granting the service that he asked. The syndic of the small town of Camprodon spoke for them when he placed a *dissentiment* on 5 May: 'Today the Principality of Catalonia is very poor and exhausted, and overburdened with dues, and it is impossible to find the sum demanded by His Majesty—a sum which is very excessive in view of the poverty of the towns, and could only bring ruin and destruction upon them.'[1]

If at this moment the king had shown himself ready to return and accept a service of two million *lliures*, the Corts might eventually have been brought to agree. On the other hand, innumerable problems remained over the drafting of the new constitutions, and it is hard to see how these could have been resolved without a whole succession of conflicts. Olivares certainly saw no reason to change his mind, in spite of the obvious desire of the city of Barcelona for some form of settlement. Its eagerness was brought home by the hectic journey of the Conseller-en-Cap to catch up with the king. When he finally overtook him, he presented him with the 50,000 *lliures* and the city's petitions. The king briefly replied: 'I thank the city for what you have said to me on its behalf. I shall remember this all my life and will deal swiftly with your petitions.'[2] But he did not turn back; nor did he keep his promise.

The embassy returned to Barcelona disconsolate. 'The people were so indignant at the failure to give His Majesty satisfaction that they received the Conseller angrily, because they thought he could have gone faster.... We were all downcast and confused because the light of our prince had gone from us.'[3] Worst of all, there was no indication that the light would ever shine again. Day after day the Corts were prorogued, until at last, at the end of May, the syndics went home. It was all too obvious that the king was not coming back. He had stopped only to pray at the Pilar of Zaragoza for a few hours before continuing his journey to Madrid.

[1] AHB: Corts, 1626, fo. 436. [2] AHB: Delibs., 1626, fo. 121.
[3] *Respuesta*, fo. 308.

It must have been some comfort to the king and his advisers that the Aragonese eventually offered either two thousand paid volunteers for fifteen years, or alternatively the 144,000 *escudos* a year needed to pay this number of men. But the king's visit to his Levantine kingdoms in search of money was to be crowned by a nice irony. On 3 May he had borrowed from Bartolomé Spínola the sum of 17,847 *escudos* to meet the expenses of his journey. The money was to be paid back in Italy in August. Such was the state of the royal finances in the summer of 1626, however, that it was far from clear how the debt could be cancelled on time. After grave consultation it was eventually decided that the only possible course was to draw on the Castilian *donativo* of 1625, which had been carefully set aside for other purposes. Laconically, the king agreed.[1]

The indebtedness to Spínola might seem a suitably tragi-comic ending to the king's foray into the Crown of Aragon, but one man at least professed himself highly satisfied with the outcome of the visit. Olivares was not to be baulked of his plans for the closer association of the kingdoms of the Spanish peninsula. On 25 July he published in Castile a decree proclaiming the official inauguration of the Union of Arms. It explained that the king had undertaken his arduous journey to the Crown of Aragon for the purpose of bringing some relief to Castile; and as an earnest of the benefits which would flow from a project already far advanced, he generously offered to pay one-third of the Castilian contribution out of the Crown's private revenues, 'hoping in the future to do even more and to relieve it of still larger quantities'.[2] How it was hoped to fulfil this promise on an empty treasury was not explained.

Ignoring the uncomfortable fact that none of the kingdoms had voted for troops for service beyond its own frontiers, and that the Catalans had not even voted a sum of money, Olivares commended to the Infanta Isabella the introduction of the Union of Arms in Flanders, with the words: 'in the kingdoms of Aragon, Valencia, Sardinia and Majorca it has been settled; in Catalonia, everything is well disposed'.[3] This was, to say the least, a rather misleading interpretation of what had happened and the Infanta was too shrewd to be convinced.

[1] AGS: Hacienda leg. 621, consulta, 28 June 1626.
[2] AGS: Est., leg. 4126.
[3] AGS: Est. (Flandes), leg. 2040, consulta, 6 Oct. 1626.

Olivares, however, was not at this moment disposed to take even the Catalan reaction too tragically. The king could always return to the Principality and resume the Corts at the point at which they had been broken off. It would take time for Olivares and the world to realize that, from the moment of the king's silent departure from Barcelona in the early morning of 4 May, nothing could ever be quite the same again.

CHAPTER IX

THE TURN OF THE SCREW, 1626–32

Although the failure of the Catalan Corts of 1626 seemed at the time no more than a temporary setback to Olivares's schemes, it marked in reality a decisive stage on the downward path to open conflict. Until 1626, the problem of Catalonia had been no more than a part of the more general problem of the Crown of Aragon as a whole: the problem of how the Crown's resources could be harnessed to the advantage of Castile. As a result of the king's visit in 1626, Aragon and Valencia had made some contribution to the royal treasury. Catalonia, on the other hand, had contributed nothing. In failing to contribute, it had differentiated itself from Aragon and Valencia; the problem of the Crown of Aragon had turned itself into an embryonic Catalan problem.

However optimistic Olivares may have been about a prompt solution to the problem, the very fact of the failure of the Corts would inevitably affect Castile's view of the Catalans, and the Catalans' view of Castile. The Catalans had never been popular in Madrid, and the wave of brigandage under Philip III, followed by the troubles over the appointment of the new viceroy, had done nothing to enhance their reputation. Now, with the failure of the Corts, another mark was chalked up against them. It is not surprising if the king's ministers began to talk about the Catalans with increased asperity, in the years after 1626. Harsh words and biting remarks became more frequent. When, for example, the Council of State was discussing a new constitution proposed by the Catalans which would enable their nobility to engage in trade without prejudicing its status, Don Pedro de Toledo objected to any measure that would 'enrich the Catalans, since, the better off they are, the less obedient they will be'.[1] On this occasion he was in a minority, but such remarks were increasingly to be heard in Madrid.

The Catalans were naturally sensitive to the growing coolness with which the king's ministers treated them. The clash over the viceroy, the royal demands in the Corts, the open break between the Principality

---

[1] AGS: Est. (Inglaterra), leg. 2849, consulta, 21 Oct. 1626.

and its Prince, had undermined their confidence and provoked growing anxiety about Castile's intentions. Olivares's talk of union had made it clear that the king's ministers intended to force them into a closer relationship with Castile. The Catalans, not unnaturally, entertained considerable doubts about the nature of this new relationship, and an opportunity arose for them to express the doubts publicly when a memorandum written by the duke of Alcalá somehow fell into their hands. In this memorandum, Alcalá advised the king against returning to Catalonia for the conclusion of the Corts. The failure of 1626 had confirmed his gloomiest expectations, and there seemed no purpose in exposing His Majesty to the insolence of the Catalans yet again. Instead, pressure should be brought to bear on the Principality, which was capable of serving the king with not three but seven million ducats. Let Barcelona and the other towns pay their arrears of *quints*; let the alienated royal patrimony be recovered, and the finances of the Diputació be investigated. This was the way to bring the Catalans to heel.[1]

Alcalá's memorandum inspired at least two written answers which have survived. One confined itself to disputing the figure of seven million ducats as a sum within the capacity of the province;[2] the other, more ambitiously, examined the whole project for the union of the Monarchy.[3] While the author admitted the theoretical excellence of a scheme for common defence, he pointed out the obvious difficulties.

Kingdoms which feel strong enough to defend themselves consider that they risk a great deal in committing themselves to the assistance of others. For this reason, Catalonia hesitates to promise assistance to Flanders, because it does not expect any need of such help from Flanders as Flanders requires from it. Aragon, similarly, is afraid to tie itself to Milan, which is always under attack.

If these were the objections to a union for defence, the objections to a more complete constitutional union were still more formidable. 'The duke wants to make us all one, and to have us all judged by the same judges. This can only be achieved in one of two ways. Either Castile enjoys the privileges and liberties of Catalonia...or Catalonia pays the same taxes and is judged by the same laws as Castile.'

Union meant castilianization: this was the real objection to the

---

[1] BC: Fullet Bonsoms 5203. [2] BC: Fullet Bonsoms 5204.
[3] BN: MS 2358, fos. 304–31, *Respuesta a un papel del Duque de Alcalá.*

schemes of Olivares and Alcalá. The abuses to which the constitutions had led, the archaic exemptions behind which irresponsible aristocrats took shelter, may well suggest that castilianization would have been less of a disaster for the Principality than the author of the reply to Alcalá feared. But it would be wrong to judge the Catalan constitutions solely by the behaviour of the seventeenth-century aristocracy. Those constitutions had been devised to guarantee to the subject certain fundamental rights. However distorted or abused, they did enshrine certain ideals which, the Catalans believed, were not to be found in the laws of Castile. A minor incident in 1629, concerning none other than Alcalá himself, vividly reveals the divergence between Castilian and Catalan viewpoints, and suggests the real dangers to individual liberty implicit in seventeenth-century schemes to replace the laws of Catalonia by those of Castile. A clash occurred at the Catalan port of Cadaqués between the local population and the soldiers from the Maltese galleys in which the duke of Alcalá was sailing to Italy. The *batlle* of the town, a vassal of the duke of Cardona, wounded the general of the galleys. Alcalá demanded his immediate execution. Cardona told him that he was informed by his council that it was against the laws of the land to execute summary justice, and the man must be properly tried. Alcalá replied that all the constitutions of Catalonia had to be thrown on the bonfire. Fortunately at this moment the wind changed, the galleys put out to sea, and the *batlle* was despatched to Barcelona for his case to be tried in the customary manner.[1]

If Alcalá's behaviour typified the Castilian attitude, the Catalans had real reason to fear castilianization. Olivares might offer the Catalans greater opportunities and wider horizons, but would he also guarantee protection of individual liberties? If not, were the gains worth the sacrifice, especially when the gains were no more than hypothetical and the sacrifice, judicial as well as fiscal, immediate and obvious? Catalan doubts were naturally deep-rooted, and Alcalá and his like did nothing to lessen them. It is not, then, surprising that the years after 1626 saw a growing uneasiness among the Catalans, and that the antipathy reflected in Castilian comments upon them was wholeheartedly reciprocated.

Aroused by recent events to a fuller awareness of Castile's inten-

[1] Pujades, 4, fos. 106 ff.

tions, they watched anxiously for every sign of confirmation of their fears. In the political and constitutional sphere there would soon be confirmation enough, but the first sign of danger came from a different quarter. In the Catalonia of Philip IV as in the England of Charles I, an ill-timed attempt at ecclesiastical reform added new issues to the causes of conflict and helped to extend an already wide area of mistrust.

In the Corts of 1599, an attempt had been made to prevent the appointment of foreigners to Catalan benefices.[1] This attempt was renewed in the Corts of 1626. The constitutions said nothing about the appointment of non-Catalans to bishoprics in Catalonia, and a new constitution was drafted which would reserve all ecclesiastical benefices and revenues in the Principality exclusively to Catalans.[2] This was a matter which closely affected both the aristocracy and the clergy. The aristocracy wanted benefices and bishoprics for the provision of its younger sons. It also wanted pensions granted by the king on ecclesiastical revenues, and by 1630 no less than forty-one such pensions were being drawn by non-Catalans.[3] The clergy resented the appointment of Castilian bishops, who naturally preached in Castilian and had little personal knowledge of the country in which they now resided. Of the bishops appointed in Catalonia between 1600 and 1626 about a dozen—rather under half the total number—were strangers to the Principality.[4] Although subservient bishops had their political uses, and Castilian bishops in Catalonia might be expected to be particularly subservient, there is no evidence that these appointments were deliberately made for political reasons. Non-Catalans might be appointed to bishoprics in the Principality because there was a dearth of candidates with sufficient spiritual or cultural qualifications among the Catalan clergy; or, more probably, because the king found himself under obligation to so many people that a vacant Catalan bishopric was a most convenient means of reward.

Whatever the motive behind their appointment, Castilian bishops were not popular in their Catalan dioceses. Cathedral chapters were rarely on friendly terms with their bishops, and when the bishop was a Castilian the motives for antagonism were much increased. Resent-

[1] ACA: G, 1051, fo. 464v.   [2] ACA: G, 1058, fo. 224.
[3] ACA: CA, leg. 277, no. 14, consulta, 8 March 1630.
[4] See Pius Bonifacius Gams, *Series Episcoporum* (2nd ed., Leipzig, 1931), for names of bishops. There is unfortunately no indication of their province of origin.

ment was therefore always smouldering in Catalonia over matters ecclesiastical. During the viceroyalty of the bishop of Solsona from 1627 to 1629, however, the Castilian-Catalan feud over religious appointments spread alarmingly to all types of ecclesiastical institution in the Principality. The bishop of Solsona himself was unwise enough to appoint a Castilian to a vacant canonry in his church, and there were angry protests.[1] But it was in the abbeys that the most serious trouble occurred. There were fourteen abbeys in Catalonia, most of them Benedictine. The standard of learning and morality among the monks was not high.

In matters of learning, what professorial chairs do they hold in Catalonia? What sermons do they preach? In what controversies do they distinguish themselves? What books and treatises have they written? None. On the contrary, it is almost a matter for pride among them that they possess no books and do not talk of the sciences; and if any of them should want to read, they abuse him; and it is a miracle if ever an abbot preaches a sermon.... When the duke of Feria was viceroy of Catalonia, he gave one of these abbeys to a Dominican, and, as usual, the Benedictines began to draw up petitions and send embassies, and went to complain to the viceroy. But he said to them: 'Gentlemen, don't you know why I didn't give you this abbey? You don't? Then I'll tell you straight. All I can find among you is ignorance, vice and pride. The proper way to complain is to come not with petitions but with deserving candidates.' And they went away, not knowing how to reply....[2]

This was the testimony of an observer bitterly opposed to the Benedictines, but there is no reason to believe that his views were unduly harsh. Evidence abounds of scandals in Catalan religious institutions, though not all the incidents are as dramatic as the affair at the abbey of Banyoles in 1622, when the abbot was blown up by barrels of gunpowder placed in the cellar of his house by three unruly monks.[3] There was perhaps room for reform, but, when reform at last came, neither its timing nor its manner was opportune. In 1627 the bishop of Solsona, as viceroy, began a campaign, presumably under orders from Madrid, to introduce stricter observation of the rule of St Benedict. This was not likely to be a simple task in a province which had stub-

[1] ACA: G, Delibs., 1626–9, vol. I, fos. 148–50.
[2] AAE: Corresp. Espagne, sup. no. 3, fos. 350–3, paper by Gaspar Sala (after 1640). The reference is presumably to the third duke of Feria (viceroy 1629–30) rather than to his father.
[3] ACA: CA, leg. 272, no. 6, Alcalá to King, 30 April 1622.

bornly resisted all attempts to execute the Tridentine reforms; and it was unwise to begin with so powerful an abbey as Ripoll, where violent altercations had already occurred between the reformed and the un-reformed Benedictines. The publication of the papal brief in 1628 was a signal for the renewal of these quarrels. The issue was complicated by the decision that, while the present monks should be allowed to leave Ripoll for any other monastery of their choice, and would continue to draw their income for life, their place would be taken by discalced Benedictines from Castile. At once the religious issue was overlaid by national considerations; and, to make matters worse, the baronies and jurisdiction of Ripoll were to go to the king, and part of its revenues be diverted to the support of the recently founded convent of San Plácido in Madrid. The proposed changes therefore at once became a matter of passionate concern. Here were the rapacious Castilians once again poaching on Catalan preserves: more Castilian monks in Catalan monasteries,[1] and Catalan ecclesiastical revenues diverted to Madrid for the sake of a new convent to which the king had taken a fancy. 'What a reason for the king to agree to the exile of our poor Catalans, and for the curs of Castile to come and drink the blood of our fathers and eat the bread of our sons!'[2]

The anti-Castilian bitterness of Dr Pujades's comment on the at-tempted reforms at Ripoll—a bitterness without parallel in the earlier part of his diaries—suggests how fast the antipathy of Catalonia to Castile was growing. This antipathy was reflected in a number of inci-dents: in a clash in October 1629 between Castilian soldiers from the Spanish galleys and peasants crying *Visca la terra*—long live the land!;[3] in the near destruction of a party of Castilian cavalry and infantrymen on their way through the Principality.[4] In the abbeys and monasteries singled out for reform, tempers ran high, and Castilian and Catalan monks pursued a fierce vendetta. The Catalans, made aware in a hundred ways of the suffocating proximity of Castile, watched with sharp eyes all that went on in Madrid. Dr Pujades's references to the king's ministers become more frequent and more scathing—in April 1629, of the uncertain relations between Spain and France: 'No one understands this method of governing Spain';[5] in July of the same year:

---

[1] There had been Castilian monks in the monastery of Montserrat since 1585.
[2] Pujades, 4, fo. 7.
[3] *MHE*, vol. xx, pp. 40–5, Parets's diary.
[4] Pujades, 4, fo. 134.
[5] *Ibid.* fo. 94v.

'Alas, Count of Olivares: Please God you may not be a Count Julian for the second loss of Spain, foretold in the prophecies of San Isidro. First, marriage treaties with England, now peace with Rohan—what more can one expect?'[1] Such remarks are made the more ominous by warm references to the king of France, 'so young and warlike and catholic'.[2]

The mounting criticism of Philip IV's ministers, bitter and sardonic, was by no means uninformed. The Catalans had seen Olivares and his colleagues when they came to the Principality in 1626, and what they had seen they had not liked. Their unfavourable impressions were confirmed in the years after 1626 by Catalans who had met the ministers on visits to the capital, and by the pasquinades produced at Court, many of which found their way into the pages of Dr Pujades's diary. It would not be easy for the Conde Duque to restore his reputation in the Principality, and it was particularly unfortunate for him that his right-hand man in Catalan affairs had acquired a most unsavoury reputation almost at the beginning of his ministerial career. This man was Jerónimo de Villanueva, the Protonotario of the Crown of Aragon.

The rapid rise of Villanueva, which was to have fateful consequences for both Castile and Catalonia, is to be explained by Olivares's need for new men and new instruments of government. The councils which governed the Spanish empire under the House of Austria were powerful bodies with enormous vested interests in the provinces they governed. If Olivares were ever to gain real control of the government of the Spanish empire, and reshape the Monarchy in his own way, he must first break the power of the councils. The Council of Aragon was an obvious and early candidate for remodelling along lines more favourable to the designs of the Conde Duque. Its advice to the king over the appointment of the bishop of Barcelona as viceroy suggested that it was blessed with neither insight nor wisdom; its permanent feud with Alcalá suggested that its relationship with leading Catalans was closer than might be considered desirable for the impartial government of the Principality. The all-important post in the council was that of vice-chancellor. If that post could be wrested from the hands of natives of the Crown of Aragon, Olivares would have taken the first and most

---

[1] Pujades, 4, fo. 104. Count Julian was the governor of Ceuta whose treachery was instrumental in bringing the Arabs to Spain in 711.   [2] *Ibid.* fo. 11v.

important step towards bringing the council more closely under his own control.

The office of vice-chancellor conveniently fell vacant through the death of its incumbent, the Catalan Roig, in 1622. Olivares flouted tradition by appointing to succeed him first Don Pedro de Guzmán, and then, on his sudden death in 1623, Garcí Pérez de Araziel. Both of these were Castilians. Their appointment caused a storm in the kingdoms of the Crown of Aragon, which alleged that, in choosing Castilians, the king had infringed the *fueros*.[1] But Pérez de Araziel was also to die, even before he had a chance to take the oath of office, and the post was left unfilled. It was fairly soon after this that Dr Bernat wrote his paper for Olivares on ways of obtaining money from the Crown of Aragon; a paper which maintained that there was no hope of success as long as the councillors were presided over by a native vice-chancellor and continued to favour all their friends and relations in the provinces.[2] Dr Bernat's motives were dubious, but his advice was opportune. It was possibly with Dr Bernat's paper in mind that Olivares wrote of the Council of Aragon in his great memorandum on the government of Spain:

This council is the one which most needs great subjects, and which today is most short of them. It is common opinion that they tyrannize over their kingdoms, that each regent is left to look after his own province, and that they share among themselves the distribution of offices. If great men are needed in all the presidencies they are more needed here than in all the others put together, to prevent such things from happening. It is almost impossible to find suitable subjects if the vice-chanceller has to be a native. Similarly, the president of the Council of Castile should be a native of the Crown of Aragon....So it is important to discover by judicial means whether the post of vice-chancellor can be taken from the hands of natives.[3]

The question of the status of the vice-chancellor was therefore submitted to legal experts. It seems probable that their decision was unfavourable, for in December 1627 the Council of Aragon was asked whether there was anything to prevent the council from having a president, like the other councils, irrespective of any constitutions about the nationality of the vice-chancellor.[4] The council fought the proposal,

[1] AHN: Cons., lib. 1882, fo. 172, consulta, 28 Feb. 1625.
[2] See above, p. 209.
[3] BM: Eg. MS 347, fo. 275.   [4] AHN: Cons., lib. 1885, fo. 188.

but lost the battle. On 1 February 1628 the king ordered the appointment of a president of the Council of Aragon, enjoying the same preeminence as that formerly accorded to the vice-chancellor, whose post now quietly lapsed.[1] Olivares had won his way, and the council was skilfully remodelled to suit his own designs. Its former treasurer-general, the count of Chinchón, had been despatched at the end of 1626 to govern Peru. Chinchón's successor, the marquis of Montesclaros, one of Olivares's closest friends, became the first president; Olivares's son-in-law, the duke of Medina de las Torres, succeeded him as treasurer-general. Some of the regents, including the Catalan Fontanet, the most influential of them all, had been kept out of the way in the Crown of Aragon for two or three years, and when they returned to Madrid they found their power gone. As would happen with each of the councils, Olivares had brought the Council of Aragon under direct surveillance by placing his own chosen instruments in the key positions.

Of these chosen instruments, the most important proved to be not Montesclaros or Medina de las Torres, but a figure whose duties were normally confined to the chancery section of the Council—the Protonotario. Since 1620 the post had been held by Jerónimo de Villanueva. The Villanuevas, like the Pérez before them, were members of an Aragonese dynasty which had successfully established itself in the bureaucracy at Madrid; one Villanueva after another served as secretary either to the king or to his councils. Jerónimo was the son of Agustín de Villanueva, who had worked in the royal service in Madrid since 1571 and became secretary to Philip III. Profiting from his father's position, Jerónimo served in the secretariats of Aragon and Majorca and in the office of the Protonotario, before himself becoming Protonotario in 1620.[2] For the first few years he appears to have been restricted to the traditional functions of his office. These included, however, the despatch of business in the Cortes of the Crown of Aragon, and here he seems to have made his mark, for already by June of 1626 the letters of Barcelona's agent in Madrid suggest that the Protonotario was a figure to be reckoned with when the Catalans wanted anything from their king.[3]

[1] AHN: Cons., lib. 1885, fo. 219.
[2] AGS: GA, leg. 916, draft petition by Jerónimo de Villanueva, 1625.
[3] AHB: CCO, 1626, fos. 138–9, Sebastià Cormellas to Consellers, 6 June 1626.

Villanueva had obviously managed to attract the attention of Olivares, and had hitched his wagon to Olivares's star. Through policy or conviction he became a passionate devotee of the Conde Duque's designs. Loyal and industrious, he could be relied upon to do what was asked of him, and he gradually made himself indispensable to the favourite. From 1626 his progress was unchecked. He attended and spoke at the meetings of the Council of Aragon.[1] He became secretary of the Consejo de Estado and a member of the Council of War. He was appointed to all the important Juntas which Olivares created to circumvent the work of the councils. It was he who came to write the royal replies in the margins of the *consultas* of the Council of Aragon when the king did not write them personally. Enjoying direct access to the king and the Conde Duque, and complete control over the papers of the Council of Aragon; with a brother who was *Justicia* of Aragon, with a nephew as secretary of the Council of Aragon for Catalan affairs, and another for Aragonese affairs, he dominated the government of the Levantine provinces. Every occurrence in the Crown of Aragon was subjected to his scrutiny: all appointments, judicial, administrative, ecclesiastical, passed through his hands.

All the scraps of evidence that come to light have a way of adding to the mystery that surrounds the character and career of this forgotten minister. He is known to history, in so far as he is known at all, in connection with the scandals surrounding the convent of San Plácido in Madrid, which was originally founded by his brother-in-law's sister.[2] It was in this connection that his name first made its impact in Catalonia, to judge from a breathless and indignant entry in the diary of Dr Pujades.

By the post from Madrid [he wrote on 17 June 1628] horrible news and a providential discovery. The king's secretary, one Villanueva, an Aragonese, founder or principal benefactor of the convent of reformed Benedictine nuns at Madrid, commonly known as San Plácido, has been accused of

---

[1] It is not clear, however, how far this was a new departure. A paper of 1588 (Riba y García, *El Consejo Supremo de Aragón*, doc. 60) suggests that the Protonotario was advancing his position at the expense of the secretaries, who insisted that he ought to be present in the chancery during the hours when the council was in session.

[2] For the scandals of San Plácido, see Marañón, *El Conde-Duque de Olivares*, pp. 198–201, and his detailed studies of the subject there mentioned. Lea, *History of the Inquisition*, vol. II, pp. 133–58, tells the story of Villanueva's case, and produces some curious details about his religious and astrological interests.

being a member of the sect of the *alumbrados* [the *Illuminati*]. Twenty-seven nuns from the convent have been arrested, and it is said they have a familiar spirit. When the news came, it was found in Barcelona that the three friars who had introduced the reforms into the monastery of Ripoll had fled, and one has been captured by the Inquisition....[1]

This is all the evidence so far available of a hitherto unsuspected link between Villanueva, the affair of San Plácido, and the monastic reforms in Catalonia. The story is so curious, and may have such important political implications, that the lack of further information is particularly tantalizing.

Whatever the role of Villanueva in the scandal of San Plácido, it was only in the 1640's, after the fall of Olivares, that the Inquisition was able to begin investigations against him. Until then, he reigned supreme in Madrid, although his contemporaries regarded him as an atheist and a sorcerer.[2] This contemporary reputation makes it exceptionally difficult to fathom the character of a man who successfully won and retained the complete confidence of Olivares; a man who came to be the most unpopular figure in Spain after the Conde Duque himself, as bitterly hated in Madrid as he was in Barcelona. The conversations reported in detail by many Catalans who visited him in Madrid suggest an unattractive character, hard, ruthless, quick to anger; a man of crude, blunt manners and impetuous language, 'who always blurts out what he has in his mind'.[3] To the Catalan regent Magarola, who worked with him daily in the 1630's, he was 'a terrible man, which he would not be if he were not so powerful'.[4] Perhaps this was the truth about Villanueva: that power had made his position impregnable and his character intolerable. As Olivares became weighed down with the burden of business, the confidant began to step into a leading role. 'Who is the favourite?' asked the Catalan Dr Martí, 'And who keeps the archive of his thoughts?'[5] All the secrets of the Conde Duque, his hopes, his ambitions, were locked in the bosom of the Protonotario. It was he who provided the Conde Duque with the information he required for the formulation of his policies. In providing the information, he came also to proffer ideas, and from proffering ideas it was

---

[1] Pujades, 4, fo. 28 v. [2] Marañón, *Olivares*, p. 205.
[3] APL: R. 854, Don Francesc Virgili to Pahers of Lleida, 7 Aug. 1638.
[4] ACA: G, caja 9, Dr Magarola to Santa Coloma, 30 Oct. 1638.
[5] Martí, *Noticia...de Cataluña*, p. 109.

only a short step to framing policies on his own initiative. It is impossible to disentangle where the Protonotario begins and Olivares finishes. He may well be more to blame than Olivares for the tragic blunders of Madrid's Catalan policy in the reign of Philip IV. But what were his real motives, whether he was any more than the zealous servant concerned only to stand high in his master's favour—to this there is no clue.

Villanueva's presence had a blighting influence on the Council of Aragon, which found itself reduced to the minor role of executing policies devised in higher circles. Between 1626 and 1632, however, no single consistent policy towards Catalonia was pursued by Madrid. In spite of Alcalá's warning, Olivares clearly intended that the king should return to the Principality as soon as possible to resume the session of the Corts.[1] His return was prevented by illness in 1627, and, although confidently expected in 1628 and 1629, had, for one reason or another, to be repeatedly postponed. The uncertainty over a royal visit made the formulation of a long-term policy impossible. This was essentially an interim period in the Principality, as was suggested by the appointment in succession of the bishops of Urgell and Solsona as viceroys. Bishops were not chosen as viceroys when there was serious work to be done.

The lack of any comprehensive plan for the treatment of Catalonia did not, however, mean that the Catalans would be left in peace. Even if they had not worked out the details of their policy the general attitude of the king's ministers was clear enough. This attitude was, as always, determined by the fiscal difficulties of the Crown and the economic troubles of Castile.

Five years after the accession of Philip IV, the royal finances, burdened with the debts incurred by Philip III, were once again on the verge of disaster. Olivares's hopes of reducing the Crown's debts by tax reforms and the establishment of a banking system, had foundered on the resistance of interested parties and of the Castilian Cortes.[2] The

[1] A Junta was at work in Madrid in the autumn of 1626 on the draft constitutions that had been put forward in the abortive session of the Corts (AGS: GA, leg. 1330, Junta de Cortes, 11 Sept. 1626).

[2] See Antonio Domínguez Ortiz, *Política y Hacienda de Felipe IV* (Madrid, 1960), Part I, ch. 2. This book represents the first serious attempt to study as a whole the royal finances in the reign of Philip IV on the basis of the numerous documents of the Consejo de Hacienda at Simancas.

solution to the problem of putting the Crown's finances on a stable footing, and of providing the government with adequate financial reserves on which it could draw in time of war, thus remained as far off as ever. Instead, the ministers had their usual recourse to expedients, like the voluntary *donativo* of 1625, and, all the time, expenses grew, while the Italian bankers became increasingly reluctant to offer loans.

The co-operation of the bankers was essential to the working of the system by which the Spanish Habsburgs traditionally financed their wars. This system, known as the *asiento* system,[1] was the outcome of elaborate negotiations between the ministers of the Council of Finance and the bankers (usually Germans or Italians) at the Spanish Court. Towards the end of each year, the Council would prepare a statement of the expected expenditure of the Crown, both inside and outside Spain, during the forthcoming year, and would then attempt to arrange with the leading bankers *asientos* or contracts for the provision of the money at the necessary place and time. The *asentistas*, or bankers, would agree to provide certain specified sums in Italy or Flanders or in Madrid at specified dates in the year, on the security of the silver in the next treasure-fleet and of taxes still to be collected, or even still to be conceded by the Cortes. The nominal rate of interest was 8 per cent, which was augmented by a so-called 'gratuity' (*adehala*) of 4 per cent,[2] and there were always numerous honours, titles and other perquisites which, it was hoped, would induce the bankers to continue their services to so notorious a security risk as the king of Spain.

During the reign of Philip II the Fuggers had yielded first place as royal bankers to the great Genoese banking families, and at the start of Philip IV's reign it was still the Genoese—Strata, Imbrea, Centurión—who provided the bulk of the Crown's financial supplies. But their uneasiness was growing, and some of them were beginning to show signs of wishing to retire from business. It took until February of 1624 to induce them to contract for the provisions for that year;[3] the provisions for 1625 were arranged only with the very greatest difficulty and at enormous expense to the Crown, and, at the beginning of 1626, the Conde Duque himself had to spend a whole night arguing with the

---

[1] There are brief but clear descriptions of the system in Domínguez Ortiz, Part II, ch. I, and in the introduction to Henri Lapeyre, *Simon Ruiz et les Asientos de Philippe II* (Paris, 1953).

[2] Domínguez Ortiz, pp. 98–9.   [3] *Ibid.* p. 29.

bankers over provisions which finally totalled, with costs, 7,300,000 ducats.[1]

The uneasiness of the Genoese was fully justified. Not only was it difficult to see how the Crown could hope to meet its obligations, but there had appeared on the stage in August 1626 a consortium of Portuguese businessmen who offered the Crown a loan of 400,000 *escudos* in Flanders. The implications of this were obvious. The Council of Finance now had a second group of bankers to which it could turn for help, and which it could play off against the Genoese in order to bring down the rates of interest.[2] Olivares made the most of his opportunity. No *asiento* had been arranged for 1627, and on 31 January of that year the Conde Duque suspended all payments to the bankers. Twenty years after Lerma had defaulted on his payments, the Monarchy had again declared itself bankrupt.[3]

This convenient postponement of pressing obligations enabled the king, at a meeting of the Council of Castile, to present a glowing picture of the restored fortunes of the Monarchy: a new-found solvency, household reforms, victories on land and sea. But he admitted the heaviness of the burden still borne by Castile, and declared he would rather see the day when Castile's taxes could be reduced than the day of the capture of Constantinople.[4]

Certainly he had good reason to feel uneasy about the condition of Castile—a condition for which the financial policies of his own ministers bore a heavy responsibility. The years 1627 and 1628 were years of great hardship. There was a startling rise of prices in *vellón* currency.[5] This was partly the result of bad harvests and of the scarcity of foreign goods, which arose from the partial closing of the frontiers between 1624 and 1628,[6] but it may also be ascribed to the government's monetary policies. In five years it had manufactured 19,728,000 ducats worth of *vellón* coins, which, after costs had been met, left the Crown

[1] *Ibid.* p. 31.
[2] AGS: Hacienda, leg. 621, fo. 92, consulta, 17 Aug. 1626.
[3] AGS: Hacienda, leg. 632. Much information on this bankruptcy, which has never been studied in detail, can be found in this legajo. The so-called 'bankruptcy' was in fact, as usual, the conversion of short-term into long-term debts.
[4] BM: Eg. MS 338, fos. 136–51.
[5] Important documents on the inflation of these years are printed in González Palencia, *La Junta de Reformación*.
[6] Domínguez Ortiz, p. 276, note 16.

with some 13 million ducats[1]—the equivalent of over one and a half years' expenditure. Minting was at last suspended by a royal decree on 8 May 1626 as the premium on silver in terms of *vellón*, which had stood at some 4 per cent in 1620, rocketed to 50 per cent.[2] But the damage was done. Castile was henceforth the victim of a monetary instability which was to afflict it throughout the reign of Philip IV.

After a futile attempt at price-fixing, the Crown ordered on 7 August 1628 'the most drastic and significant deflationary measure since the days of Ferdinand and Isabella',[3] with the reduction of the tale of *vellón* by 50 per cent. The deflation, which inevitably caused grave hardship in Castile, brought immediate relief to the royal treasury, no longer burdened with the heavy premium it had been compelled to pay the *asentistas* for silver. It might now have been possible to consider seriously the preparation of a reform programme designed to place the Crown's finances on more solid foundations, especially as the 1627 treasure fleet had brought valuable silver supplies for the king.[4] But unfortunately the Conde Duque had already compromised the chance of reform by embarking on a costly new venture, which would come to be regarded by many of his contemporaries as his cardinal error in the field of foreign policy.

Since the Treaty of Monzón of 1626 the international situation had continued to favour the Habsburgs. The duke of Feria dominated Italy; the Imperial generals had defeated the Danes and were triumphant in Germany; and Richelieu was heavily preoccupied with the Huguenots. But in December 1627 the duke of Mantua died. The candidate with the best claim to succeed him was a Frenchman, the duke of Nevers. The duchy occupied a position of great strategic significance, and its possession by a client of France might well endanger Spain's hold over North Italy and Milan. The governor of Milan, Don Gonzalo de Córdoba, was acutely aware of this, and was convinced that it was vital for Spain to secure control of the duchy. The Conde Duque, equivocating over an action which offered glittering prospects but which would place the king of Spain in an invidious position in the eyes of Europe, gave him tacit encouragement by sending supplies; and

---

[1] Domínguez Ortiz, p. 256.

[2] See Table 7 (p. 96) of Earl J. Hamilton, *American Treasure and the Price Revolution in Spain* (Cambridge, Mass., 1934).

[3] Hamilton, p. 83.   [4] Domínguez Ortiz, p. 39.

in March 1628, on orders from Madrid, his troops entered Montferrat. The French could not afford to stand by and see their candidate deprived of his rights, and, almost before he realized its implications, Olivares found himself involved in war in Italy.[1]

The Mantuan War of 1628–31 proved in every respect to be disastrous for Spain. It brought the French across the Alps and gave them, in 1630, the fortress of Pinerolo; and, in doing so, it brought a full-scale Franco-Spanish war appreciably closer. It revealed the unexpected weakness of Spanish arms, which failed to secure a favourable peace. It branded Spain as an aggressor in the eyes of the world, and it committed the Monarchy to heavy new expenses at a time when some degree of financial reorganization might otherwise have been possible.

Spain's expenses in Italy and in Germany, where Wallenstein was besieging Stralsund—a potential naval base from which Spain might one day strangle Holland's Baltic trade[2]—placed heavy strains on a depleted royal treasury. In August 1628 the Council of Finance found itself two million ducats short on the year's provisions,[3] and future prospects were still further darkened when one month later the Nueva España treasure-fleet was captured by Piet Heyn. The increasingly gloomy financial situation inevitably meant more pressure on the king's subjects, and not least on the Catalans.

One of the most effective means of applying this pressure would be to start turning the screw on the two wealthiest and most powerful institutions in the Principality—the Diputació and the city council of Barcelona. The ministers in Madrid had for some time been considering methods of weakening the Diputació and exploiting its presumed resources, and in the years immediately following the failure of the Corts they momentarily believed that they had hit on an ingenious scheme which would give them what they wanted. This scheme was nothing less than a plan to detach the Comtats—the counties—of Rosselló and Cerdanya from the Principality and to establish them as an independent province.

The original initiative for the dismemberment of the Principality

---

[1] See Manuel Fernández Alvarez, *Don Gonzalo Fernández de Córdoba y la Guerra de Sucesión de Mantua y del Monferrato* (Madrid, 1955).

[2] G. Pagès, *La Guerre de Trente Ans* (Paris, 1949), p. 107, and Michael Roberts, *Gustavus Adolphus*, vol. II (London, 1958), pp. 316–17.

[3] Domínguez Ortiz, p. 41.

apparently came from the counties themselves. In the reign of Philip III the town of Perpinyà sent the king a petition claiming that its survival was endangered so long as Rosselló and Cerdanya remained united to Catalonia. It maintained that the union had brought no benefit to the counties, since the Principality had not sent help when the French invaded them in 1597; and Barcelona had simply made use of the union to exploit them.[1] It was certainly true that the condition of the counties was far from happy. In 1617 one of the king's ministers in Rosselló produced an alarming report on its economic distress. Perpinyà itself, formerly a town of 6600 houses, now had less than 2000; there had not been a good harvest since the end of the sixteenth century; the town's fortifications had collapsed, and many of the citizens had emigrated to other parts of Catalonia where they felt themselves more secure.[2] It was presumably these conditions which inspired a prophetic utterance from the canons of Elna: 'what today is Spain may tomorrow be France'.[3]

There is no evidence to show how widespread was the resentment in the counties as a whole against Catalan hegemony. There were good enough reasons for general discontent, but Perpinyà, alone of the towns in the counties, voiced it. Relations between Perpinyà and Barcelona, as rival capitals, had always been strained, and it is difficult to avoid the suspicion that the ruling group in Perpinyà had certain ulterior motives in first proposing the separation from Catalonia. It was jealous of the wealth of Barcelona, which contrasted so strongly with the poverty of Perpinyà, and it is not likely to have ignored the advantages that would have come from the counties possessing a Diputació of their own. Whatever their exact motives, the idea of separation had obviously found favour among certain influential citizens of Perpinyà, and they took the opportunity provided by the Corts of 1626 to press their claim once more for an end to the union.[4]

Their request must have come as a pleasing windfall for Madrid. If the counties could be divorced from the Principality, the Catalan Diputació would be deprived of their dues, which could then be applied to the upkeep of the frontier castles. Olivares therefore had no objections

[1] *Súplica de... Tortosa*, fo. 13.
[2] ACA: CA, leg. 347, Don Gabriel de Llupià to King, 1 June 1617.
[3] ADP: Série G, liasse 63, canons of Elna to Canon Llobet, 7 April 1626.
[4] ACA: CA, leg. 274, no. 1, petition by Dr Boldó.

to offer when, in 1627, Dr Boldó of Perpinyà was sent to Madrid with a long memorandum explaining the advantages to be gained from turning the counties into an independent province.[1] But unfortunately for Madrid's hopes, Fontanet, the Catalan regent on the Council of Aragon, produced a very damping report on the feasability of separating the counties from Catalonia.[2] He explained that the contributions of the counties to the revenues of the Diputació had averaged only 12,000 *lliures* during the past four years, and even if these dues were to be increased by taxing the small quantities of iron they produced, their total revenue would still be insufficient to meet the extra administrative expenses of an independent province and simultaneously to pay for its defence. There were nine fortresses in the counties and 70,000 ducats a year were said to be needed for their upkeep. The counties, so far as Fontanet was concerned, did not form a viable economic, administrative or strategic unit.

Although Fontanet's report might have seemed conclusive, Madrid was reluctant to drop the idea of a separation. When the duke of Feria (the son of Philip II's last viceroy) was appointed viceroy in succession to the bishop of Solsona in 1629, he was instructed to investigate the matter further, and simultaneously to examine the whole question of the maladministration of the funds of the Diputació.[3] He arrived to find Barcelona and Perpinyà engaged in a private war. In February 1629 a riot broke out in Perpinyà on the occasion of the despatch of French cattle through Rosselló for delivery in Barcelona, under the auspices of one of the city's meat-suppliers, Joan Francesc Brossa.[4] Perpinyà claimed that dues were payable to it on all French produce sent through Rosselló. A similar dispute had occurred in 1627,[5] but this time tempers ran higher and both sides sought an opportunity for reprisals. The citizens of Perpinyà brought out the flag to march against Barcelona; Barcelona offered the viceroy 10,000 men if he would march against Perpinyà[6]—a reaction understandable enough since it

[1] ACA: G, Delibs., 1626–9, vol. I, fo. 77, Don Joan Grau to Diputats, 27 Feb. 1627.

[2] ACA: CA, leg. 274, no. 1, paper by Fontanet.

[3] ACA: CA, leg. 235, no. 19, consulta of President of the Council of Aragon, the Protonotario and the Duke of Feria, 5 May 1629.

[4] Pujades, 4, fo. 77. See also p. 66, n. 1 for Brossa.

[5] ACA: CA, leg. 276, no. 5, relation of events at Perpinyà, June 1627–Feb. 1629.

[6] ACA: CA, leg. 378, Viceroy to J. L. de Villanueva, 31 March 1629.

found itself subjected to an economic blockade, unable to obtain either meat or corn from the counties.[1]

Even a viceroy predisposed in favour of Perpinyà's pleas for a constitutional separation found himself unable to condone its behaviour over the transit dues. But although Perpinyà had lost this particular round, the struggle left a legacy of bitterness on both sides which came by no means amiss to the king's ministers. It enabled Feria to keep alive Catalonia's fear that the king would agree to the separation of the counties in response to the wishes of the inhabitants. This gave him a useful instrument for applying pressure on the Principality; and indeed he still seems to have believed that the creation of a separate province out of the counties offered real advantages to the king. It would make Barcelona's trade with France more difficult, and push up the price of wool, most of which came from the counties, so that Catalonia's cloth trade with Italy would suffer. This would surely reduce the Principality to a more compliant frame of mind.[2]

The hopes of Feria and the projects of Madrid in the end came to nothing. His viceroyalty ended abruptly in 1630 when he was sent to succeed Spínola in Milan, and the scheme for the separation of the counties was quietly shelved. The difficulties were too numerous, the advantages too few, for it to have had any chance of success. Weak, undefended, with a population that was increasingly French and an economy ever more closely tied to that of France, the counties could never have stood upright on their own. In the 1620's and 1630's, they had already become a kind of no-man's land between Spain and France. Thirty years later, the dissidents of Perpinyà would achieve their aim, although hardly in the manner they had planned. In 1659 the counties would be permanently sundered from Catalonia—but only to be permanently joined to France.

The abortive scheme for the divorce of the counties from Catalonia was only one of the weapons that Madrid had been sharpening for its battle with the Principality. At the same time as it was considering ways and means of weakening the Diputació, it was also concerned to extract what it could from the city of Barcelona. Here there was rather more hope of speedy success. The city was anxious to retain the king's

---

[1] ACA: CA, leg. 379, Viceroy to T. Fermat, 12 March 1629.
[2] ACA: CA, leg. 276, no. 71, Feria to King, 28 May 1630.

sympathy because it wished for a favourable decision on the petitions it had presented him on his departure from the Principality in May 1626. These petitions were concerned largely with certain concessions which would affect the administration of the city and the collection of municipal dues, but they included a request that the Crown should renounce all its claims to Barcelona's *quints*. The abandonment of these claims meant more than anything else to Barcelona at this moment, and therefore, so long as it believed there was the slightest chance of success, it would do everything in its power to work for cordial relations with Madrid.

The ministers in Madrid, however, were in no mind to make concessions. The Council of Aragon decided that any decision on Barcelona's petitions should be indefinitely delayed, so that the city should be on its best behaviour when the Corts were resumed.[1] It was perhaps unwise of the council to make no gesture which might inspire Barcelona with hopes of eventual success. As the months passed, and the king acceded to not one of the city's petitions, Barcelona's attitude hardened. It had no intention of offering the king money so long as the king had no intention of accepting its requests.

Only a resumption of the Corts could end the deadlock, once both sides had taken up their positions. But a resumption of the Corts created special fiscal problems of its own, for the king could not afford to make the journey to the Principality unless he received financial assistance, and Barcelona would give no such assistance unless it were sure that the king would come. In the autumn of 1628, however, the prospects of a royal visit seemed brighter, and the viceroy was instructed to approach the city for a loan, to enable the king to come. Careful preparations were made; the five Consellers of Barcelona were bribed,[2] and the Consell de Cent agreed on 9 October 1628 to lend the king 100,000 ducats for his travelling expenses. But rumours of plague meant a fresh postponement of the king's visit. Meanwhile, the king's expenses in Italy were mounting. He therefore asked Barcelona to send the 100,000 ducats to Genoa and Milan, where money was urgently needed, and added that he hoped to come to the Principality in April.[3] The city was determined not to fall into a trap. It replied that it would

[1] ACA: CA, leg. 273, no. 4, consulta, 16 Aug. 1626. A list of the city's petitions is enclosed.
[2] ACA: CA, leg. 501 and leg. 379, consulta, 21 Oct. 1628.
[3] ACA: CA, leg. 276, no. 9, King to Barcelona, 8 Jan. 1629.

only anticipate the loan and forward the money to Italy if the king gave ample security for it; and the security demanded was nothing less than the entire royal patrimony in Catalonia. The viceroy and the Council of Aragon agreed in finding this condition intolerable: better to refuse the offer of a loan from the city than accept it at this price.[1] This was the end of the negotiations. Barcelona's money would not be sent to Italy, much to the private satisfaction of Dr Pujades. If the loan were reserved for a royal visit, a large part of it would be used to meet Court expenses in Barcelona, to the advantage of individual citizens and the municipality alike, whereas it would be folly to send it to Italy, 'when all Spain is drained of silver'.[2]

Barcelona's attitude smacks more of the hard bargaining traditions of a mercantile city than of the instinctive loyalty of faithful vassals, but the king can scarcely be said to have shown the generosity that might provoke an outburst of loyal enthusiasm. The ministers in Madrid, however, could find no excuses for Barcelona's shameless conduct. It was time to devise measures which would 'reduce the arrogance of those people'.[3] If Feria considered the time opportune he should revive the lawsuit over Barcelona's *quints* and press other claims by the Crown to certain of the city's dues, which had long been in abeyance. Similar instructions were given to Feria's successor. On 7 November 1630 the duke of Cardona, Catalonia's sole duke, was named viceroy of Catalonia, perhaps in the belief that he might meet with more success than a Castilian viceroy in his relations with the Catalans. Before he left for Catalonia, Cardona was briefed at the Escorial by Olivares himself,[4] and was given a sheaf of instructions prepared for him under the signature of the Protonotario, over and above the usual standing orders for Catalan viceroys.[5]

Cardona's instructions had less to do with Catalonia than with the state of the Monarchy in general, for Madrid was at this moment mainly concerned with the reverses which the king's armies were suffering in Italy. Cardona was to examine the possibility of obtaining the help of Catalan troops, and, above all, he must obtain money from the Princi-

[1] ACA: CA, leg. 276, no. 9, Viceroy to King, 27 Jan. 1629.
[2] Pujades, 4, fo. 71 v.
[3] ACA: CA, leg. 276, no. 9, consulta, 6 Feb. 1629.
[4] ACA: CA, leg. 382, Cardona to King, 28 Nov. 1631.
[5] ACA: Varias de Cancillería, R. 332, instructions for Cardona, 9 Oct. 1630.

pality, since it had not yet given the king a single service, in spite of the example set by the rest of the Crown of Aragon. But he was assured that it was not His Majesty's intention to oppress the Catalans, although they were the least heavily taxed of all his subjects, and even a loan would be welcome.

Cardona's viceroyalty began well. To the surprise of Madrid he managed to obtain from Barcelona not a loan but an outright gift. On 14 February 1631 the Consell de Cent voted 12,000 *lliures* to the king to help him in his present necessities.[1] It was true that this sum was small compared with that which Olivares had in mind, and the Catalans had refused point-blank to provide troops for Italy. But this was the first time in the ten years of Philip IV's reign that Barcelona had actually given the king money, although it had lent him 50,000 ducats when he left the Principality in 1626, and another 12,000 on 11 June 1630 to help pay for the journey to Barcelona of the king's sister, on her way to be married in Austria. The gift was particularly welcome because the other towns of Catalonia felt themselves obliged to follow Barcelona's lead. Tortosa and Tarragona each offered 40,000 *reales* (4000 *lliures*), Girona 30,000, Vic 20,000 and Perpinyà 12,000 until the king had been given by the autumn of 1632 a total of 316,000 *reales*, or 31,600 *lliures*.[2]

These contributions to the Italian campaign no doubt reflected the Catalans' desire to preserve the goodwill of their sovereign, and it would be reasonable to assume that Cardona's intervention had played its part in stirring Barcelona to action. His honeymoon with the city, however, proved to be brief. The impulsiveness which he had shown in his handling of the Corts made it difficult for him to maintain the poise and patience always necessary for the preservation of smooth relations between the representative of the Crown and the city of Barcelona. The city was notoriously touchy about its privileges, and it was not long before it clashed sharply with Cardona over questions of jurisdiction. Plague threatened Catalonia in 1629 and 1630.[3] Food prices were high and profiteers flourished. It was discovered in 1631 that the bakers of Barcelona, making the most of their opportunities, had been replacing flour with earth and robbing the city of 18,750

[1] ACA: CA, leg. 503, Cardona to King, 15 Feb. 1631.
[2] ACA: CA, leg. 503, list of contributions, 28 Oct. 1632.   [3] See below, p. 273.

pounds of bread a day.[1] Cardona, not trusting the city to make a full
investigation, sent royal officials to the municipal warehouses to take
samples of the corn. The clash between city and viceroy over the bread
scandal spread to embrace the whole question of plague precautions.
Should royal or municipal officials enforce quarantine regulations and
issue orders for ships from plague-stricken areas not to enter the harbour?[2] Cardona wrote privately to the secretary of the Council of
Aragon: 'My desire has been to take nothing from them, but only to
fulfil my obligations.'[3] But his handling of the plague precautions,
which had always been a bone of contention between Crown and city,
only served to exasperate the Consell de Cent. As the viceroy floun-
dered in deep waters, as suggestions were followed by orders and
orders by arrests, the city abandoned all hope of direct negotiation
with the viceroy and despatched Josep de Bellafilla to Madrid to lay
its case directly before the king.[4]

Bellafilla arrived in a Madrid which showed not the slightest interest
in Barcelona's disputes with the viceroy. The councils were meeting
day and night over a question of far greater moment: the deteriorating
situation in Germany since Gustavus Adolphus's landing in July 1630.
Bellafilla quickly appreciated that the Swedish successes made almost
inevitable a determined new attempt to touch the Catalans for money.
'As a man who has seen three Corts and is curious to see many more',[5]
he was at first hopeful, but the feverish activity in the Court filled him
with increasing gloom. 'This journey is more the result of the necessities of war than of any desire to hold the Corts', he reported on
24 January 1632.[6] He still hoped that the city could make use of the
king's necessities to obtain a good bargain, but three weeks later he
was doubtful even of this. All that Madrid wanted was a good sum in
ready cash. A verse from the Psalms seemed particularly apposite:
Et super dolorem vulnerum meorum addiderunt. 'The only thing to do is to
be alert and attempt to save yourselves, giving what you can but no
more.'[7]

[1] ACA: CA, leg. 381, Dr Berart to M. Bayetolá, 19 July 1631.
[2] ACA: CA, leg. 226, correspondence between Cardona and City on the plague, 1631.
[3] ACA: CA, leg. 382, Cardona to J. L. de Villanueva, 1 Nov. 1631.
[4] AHB: LC, 1630-2, fos. 97-8, City to King, 30 Oct. 1631.
[5] AHB: CCO, 1632-3, fo. 8, Bellafilla to Consellers, 10 Jan. 1632.
[6] *Ibid.* fos. 18-20, the same, 24 Jan. 1632.   [7] *Ibid.* fos. 37-8, the same, 14 Feb. 1632.

Bellafilla had correctly gauged the attitude of the ministers and the extent of their alarm. During the first ten years of the reign, Spain and its allies had won some notable victories. The victories, however, had brought peace no nearer, and now the Monarchy, humiliated by the outcome of the Mantuan War and shaken by the progress of Gustavus Adolphus in Germany, saw itself once again on the point of war with France.[1] The Conde Duque therefore needed every penny he could get. In February 1632 he appealed to the Castilians for a so-called 'voluntary' gift to save Flanders and Italy.[2] The same month a new, and entirely unexpected, blow fell. The treasure fleet of Nueva España was reported lost at sea. In a state of deep depression the Conde Duque addressed a melancholy meeting of the Consejo de Estado:[3] 'Everything depended on this nerve of the royal estate which was on its way to Your Majesty and was larger than ever.... Today we are short of two millions in silver, which would have been sufficient, with the outcome of measures at present being taken, to meet this year's requirements.' The ways of Providence were indeed inscrutable when the money which had been intended to castigate the enemies of the Faith was removed beneath their very eyes.[4]

It was left to the other members of the council, while agreeing with the Conde Duque's apocalyptic utterances, to point out that, with the divine will as yet unknown, it was necessary to follow the course dictated by prudence and reason. The count of Oñate acted as their spokesman. He totted up the Crown's principal obligations. The needs

[1] A. Leman, *Urbain VIII et la Rivalité de la France et de la Maison d'Autriche de 1631 à 1635* (Lille, 1920), p. 101. The concessions wrested by Richelieu from the duke of Lorraine at the Treaty of Vic of 6 January 1632—concessions which potentially endangered the security of Spain's military route up the Rhine—provided a further motive for a Franco-Spanish conflict which might have broken out at this moment but for Spain's shortage of money and the reluctance of the Emperor to follow Madrid's lead.

[2] RAH: 11–219, Papeles varios, fos. 334–5, instructions for collection of *donativo* given by the President of the Council of Castile. Everyone in Castile was to be asked, and every city, town and village visited. Nobles were to give 1500 ducats and *caballeros* 150. The collectors were to explain that the loss of Flanders would mean the loss of Italy, and the loss of Italy be followed by that of the Indies and everything that had been conquered by earlier generations.

[3] AGS: Est., leg. 2651, consulta, 19 March 1632.

[4] The news eventually turned out to be incorrect. It was brought by an *aviso* despatched on 28 December 1631 from Havana, where the galleons had been vainly awaiting the Nueva España fleet, with which they were to join forces for the return journey to Seville. This fleet, after losing its *capitana* and *almiranta* in a storm off the coast of Campeche, had put back to Vera Cruz. The return journey of the silver fleet was thus delayed, but it finally reached Cadiz in April 1632 (H. and P. Chaunu, *Séville et l'Atlantique*, vol. v, p. 221).

of Flanders and Italy must at all costs be met; the Emperor must receive his subsidy, Wallenstein 50,000 florins a month, the duke of Orleans 4000 *escudos* a month (to be increased to 20,000 if he should invade France); an army must be raised in Alsace, and another army of 2000 infantrymen in the Crown of Aragon to defend the frontiers with the help of troops from Milan. The king, without going as far as Barcelona, should assemble the Catalan Corts at Tortosa and prorogue them to Barcelona afterwards, to allow their conclusion by one of his brothers.

So there could no longer be any doubt that the king, after six years' absence, would return to continue the Corts. If Bellafilla was not optimistic, neither was Olivares. He confessed that he would not have recommended a royal visit to Catalonia but for the loss of the fleet. He had heard of the lack of enthusiasm in the Principality, but 'considering the straitened circumstances of the royal finances, there is less disaster involved in risking a clash than in losing the two million ducats which can be got from the Catalans'.[1] But he was determined that a clash should, if possible, be avoided, and so he rejected Oñate's suggestion that the Corts be held at Tortosa. As a gesture to Barcelona, he also granted it the jurisdiction in times of plague which Bellafilla had been sent to Madrid to request.[2]

The prospects of success enhanced by these measures, the king and his two brothers, accompanied by Olivares, set out on their journey to Catalonia. They entered Barcelona on 3 May 1632. Two days later, the Protonotario signed a paper enabling him to borrow from the city 110,000 *lliures* for the expenses of the royal journey. He offered as security the revenues of the entire royal patrimony in Catalonia.[3] Madrid as well as Barcelona might well exclaim: *Et super dolorem vulnerum meorum addiderunt.*

[1] M. Danvila y Collado, *El Poder Civil en España*, vol. VI, docs. 950–5, no. 1, Olivares in the Consejo de Estado, 23 March 1632.

[2] ACA: CA, leg. 282, no. 41, consulta, 30 March 1632.

[3] ACA: CA, leg. 285, no. 6, Vinyes to Protonotario, 14 Feb. 1640.

CHAPTER X

THE STRUGGLE WITH THE CITY, 1632-5

Olivares had chosen a bad moment to renew his appeal to the Principality, for around 1632 its economic fortunes took a grave turn for the worse. Harvests had been poor in 1628 and 1629, years of severe drought. Prospects for 1630 looked brighter, but, in both France and Spain, the crops were suddenly struck by disease in mid-April and were ruined within a week.[1] In Barcelona corn sold at famine prices, ranging from 60s. to 110s. a quarter between the autumn of 1630 and July 1632,[2] and the dearth of these years was said to be worse than any in living memory.[3]

Over a dearth-stricken land hovered the threat of plague: a plague that was already raging in Italy and in the South of France.[4] Guards had been posted along the frontier to prevent the entry of French merchants, but, in spite of all precautions, the plague spread into Catalan territory in December 1629.[5] The vigorous measures taken to combat it were only partially successful, for in September 1630 the epidemic hit Perpinyà, where it claimed over four thousand victims.[6] Fortunately it receded during the winter without ravaging the Principality itself, but it would seem none the less that the plague of 1629–31 heralded the opening of a new and catastrophic period for the population of Catalonia—a period of high mortality and of demographic stagnation.[7]

The epidemic also disrupted the Principality's trade. All through 1630 trade with France and Italy was prohibited by viceregal proclamation.[8] Coming on top of the boycott of French trade in 1625, this latest prohibition represented another grave setback to Catalan commerce, which was reflected in the decrease in the import and export

[1] AHC: *Llibre vert de les notes*, fos. 149–51.
[2] See table of corn prices at College of Sant Guillèm (Appendix II).
[3] AHC: Lletres missives 1631–6, fo. 2v. Pahers of Cervera to Dr Mora, 23 March 1631.
[4] This was the Milanese plague so vividly described in Manzoni's *I Promessi Sposi*. In the cathedral of Le Puy (Haute Loire) there is a picture showing a procession held on 22 April 1630 to give thanks for the town's deliverance.
[5] Nadal and Giralt, 'Ensayo metodológico para el estudio de la población catalana', p. 251.
[6] Nadal and Giralt, *La Population Catalane*, p. 42, n. 1.
[7] *Ibid.* pp. 21 and 42.　　　　[8] Nadal and Giralt, 'Ensayo metodológico', p. 251.

dues levied by the Diputació.[1] The sources of wealth on which Olivares hoped to draw were already beginning to run dry.

An important outcome of the decline in trade was the almost total eclipse of the Barcelona Llotja. For some years now the Llotja, formerly the centre of Barcelona's commercial life, had betrayed scarcely even the shadow of its medieval greatness. Although in 1625 it numbered 154 registered members, as against 146 in 1552,[2] they seem as merchants to have been neither enterprising nor influential. 'There are no merchants left of estate, quality and credit, as there were in former times,' reported the viceroy in 1628, 'because all the commerce of the Llotja is at an end.'[3] Competition from the foreign merchants established in Barcelona had no doubt made inroads on the traditional preserves of the Llotja, but the institution itself seems to have been betrayed from within. A wealthy merchant would be strongly tempted by the privileges and prestige of the *ciutadà honrat* to sacrifice his commercial activities for a place in the highest circles of the municipal oligarchy. Those merchants who remained in the Llotja formed a closely knit group apparently more concerned to profit from the financial resources of their corporation, and obtain collectively the status of *militars*, than to expand their trade. They had shown only the most tepid interest when Olivares had put forward his plans for the creation of a Levant Company based on Barcelona.[4] Although two of their number had finally been sent to Madrid in 1629 for discussions on the establishment of the Company, they spent much time and money in the capital to no effect.[5] This was partly because the usual kind of problem arose as to whether the ultimate control of the Company should lie with Madrid or Barcelona,[6] but it is unlikely that the Llotja possessed either the resources or the enterprise to launch out on new commercial ventures. Such little credit as it possessed had been badly shaken in 1628 when two *cavallers*, Dimas Polit and Gabriel Miret, went bankrupt,[7] and their bankruptcy was followed by that of five merchants in the Llotja. The

[1] See Appendix III. A melancholy note to this effect was inserted in the balance-sheet of the Diputació drawn up for presentation to the Corts of 1632 (ACA: G, 147/2, fo. 49).
[2] Carrera Pujal, *Historia...de Cataluña*, vol. I, p. 393.
[3] ACA: CA, leg. 275, no. 42, Bishop of Solsona to King, 30 Sept. 1628.
[4] See above, p. 226.
[5] ACA: CA, leg. 382, petition from Barcelona Llotja, 10 Oct. 1630.
[6] BM: Eg. MS 340, fos. 151–65, consulta of Council of Aragon (Nov. 1630).
[7] Pujades, 4, fo. 15.

trade depression of 1629 and 1630, following hard on the bankruptcies, effectively ended any possibility of the Llotja's playing a useful part in the Conde Duque's plans for the restoration of Spanish trade.

Even if the antagonism of 1626 had left no bitter memories in the Principality, the commercial depression and general distress of the following years must in any event have reduced the chances of obtaining a substantial subsidy from the Catalans. Olivares was determined, however, that the mistakes of 1626 should, so far as possible, be avoided. The most obvious blunder in those Corts had been the attempt to carry through the Crown's programme at excessive speed. This time, the Catalans would be given as long as they liked for their deliberations. As the king could scarcely be expected to remain in the Principality for an indefinite period, his place would be taken by his brother, the Cardenal Infante Don Fernando, who would simultaneously act as president of the Corts and viceroy of Catalonia. This substitution of Don Fernando for the king was not welcome to the Catalans. They believed that his powers and his ability to confer privileges and *mercedes* would be severely restricted,[1] and it was only after a sharp tussle with the towns that Olivares finally persuaded the Corts to accept Don Fernando as their president.

Immediately the Cardenal Infante had been vested with office at a formal ceremony of the Corts on 18 May 1632, the king and Olivares hurried home to Madrid. They had taken care to see that Don Fernando would not be left a lone Daniel in the den of lions. Although a young man of considerable energy and character, he had as yet no political or administrative experience, and Olivares left him with a heavy bodyguard of ministers, of whom the most outstanding was the count of Oñate. 'A very wise man,' wrote the English ambassador in Madrid, 'but I hold him fitter to govern a people more flexible than these, who are not to be dealt with with a high hand.'[2]

Although the Cardenal Infante had the count of Oñate to guide him, the Protonotario had drawn up a set of instructions for his eyes alone.[3] 'This province', the instructions said, 'is of all provinces in the

---

[1] Matías de Novoa, *Reinado de Felipe IV, Codoin*, vol. LXIX, p. 153.

[2] BM: Eg. MS 1820, Hopton's MS notebook, fo. 199.

[3] AGS: Est., leg. 2651. These are draft instructions, many in Villanueva's own hand. A. Van der Essen found a copy in the Brussels archives and published a short summary in his *Le Cardinal-Infant* (Brussels, 1944), vol. I, pp. 62–4.

Monarchy the one least burdened with taxes, and the one with the most obligation to assist me because it has given me no service since I came to the throne, and is the most extensive, abundant and populous.' The king expected from it a subsidy of three million ducats. Naturally, there would be difficulties to be met and overcome before the subsidy was voted: the Protonotario pointed particularly to the draft constitutions on Observança, the Inquisition and the *quints* which had been drafted in the Corts of 1626. But by securing agents among the members of the committees appointed to draft new constitutions, it would be possible to discover the proposals under consideration and to arrange for the drafts to be voted down when they came before the Corts.

The Cardenal Infante was unfortunately to have no occasion for putting the Protonotario's advice to the test. A strange series of events destroyed all hope of a successful conclusion to the Corts from the very day of their opening. The trouble arose from a long-standing claim by the city of Barcelona that its Consellers were entitled to a privilege enjoyed only by Spanish grandees—the privilege of remaining covered in the royal presence. The attempt to exercise this supposed right had given rise to some unfortunate incidents during the visit of the king's sister to Barcelona in 1630. Anxious lest a repetition of the incidents should damage the prospects of the Corts, the king wrote to the Cardenal Infante from Montserrat suggesting that he should have the city's claim examined.[1] Since the precedents for the claim were buried in the Barcelona archives and were not accessible to royal officials, the task would not be easy.[2]

Before there was time to examine the matter properly, an occasion arose when Barcelona might be expected to assert its right. The Corts were to open on 27 May, and the preceding day the Cardenal Infante was to take his oath as viceroy in Barcelona cathedral. The Consellers of Barcelona would be present at the ceremony, and would presumably wear their hats, as they claimed to have worn them when they accompanied the king to the High Altar in 1626.[3] The duke of Cardona was quite sure they had not worn hats on that occasion, and proof to the contrary was surprisingly scanty. The Cardenal Infante's advisers had no desire to upset the city just when the Corts were beginning, and

[1] ACA: CA, leg. 260, no. 1, King to Cardenal Infante, 20 May 1632.
[2] ACA: CA, leg. 277, no. 56, Junta, 24 May 1632.
[3] ACA: CA, leg. 278, Oñate to King, 26 May 1632.

Oñate devised an ingenious temporary solution. The only person with an undoubted right to remain covered throughout the ceremony was the duke of Cardona, as a Spanish grandee. Would it not be possible for Oñate to induce Cardona, as a special service to His Majesty, to forgo his right for this particular occasion? The Consellers, seeing that Cardona remained uncovered, would follow suit, and the tricky problem would be evaded.

Oñate's plan worked all too well. Cardona, as a loyal vassal, made the great sacrifice of agreeing to remain uncovered throughout the ceremony in the cathedral. The Consellers put on their hats at the moment of entering. The Cardenal Infante pretended not to notice, while the secretary of the Council of Aragon whispered to them to uncover as the duke of Cardona was also uncovered. In a fateful moment they complied, and the ceremony proceeded to its conclusion without further incident.[1]

The news of the Consellers' pusillanimous behaviour spread quickly through the city. Painfully aware of the public indignation caused by his action, the Conseller-en-Cap, Dr Bernat Sala, spent a sleepless night wondering how he could avert the wrath of his fellow-citizens.[2] There was to be no escape. The Consell de Cent duly met the following day, and decided that precedents should first be considered before any action was taken.[3] The short delay gave time for a meeting to be arranged between four royal ministers and the representatives of the city, at which the ministers reached the conclusion that precedents varied for different occasions. In formal ceremonies where the Consellers sat before the king they had always worn hats; in private visits they had never worn hats; and in entering and leaving churches in the royal presence, there appeared to be some precedents but these were doubtful.[4] Hoping to pacify the city, the Cardenal Infante offered to intercede with the king for the extension of the privilege to the second and third types of occasion, but the Consell de Cent would have none of this. Furious at the loss of a right which it had long claimed to possess, it voted on 7 June to send an ambassador to Madrid to lodge a protest, while boycotting all public functions normally attended by the Con-

---

[1] ACA: CA, leg. 278, Cardenal Infante to King, 26 May 1632.
[2] ACA: CA, leg. 260, no. 54, Sala to J. L. de Villanueva, 27 May 1632.
[3] AHB: Delibs., 1632, fo. 258.
[4] ACA: CA, leg. 278, relation of events, 29 May–9 June 1632.

sellers, and placing a *dissentiment* in the Corts to all acts of grace and justice.¹ That which the ministers greatly feared had come upon them.

Barcelona's decision to bring the Corts to a standstill because of a disagreement over the right of its Consellers to wear hats in the royal presence looks at first glance unworthy and irresponsible. But the city's indignation was deep and genuine, and not entirely without justification. In the seventeenth century, questions of ceremonial and precedence were supremely important, since they were the visible evidence of the degree and status of each individual and corporation in the great hierarchical society of mankind. This, of all privileges, was dear to Barcelona, since it was enjoyed by no other city in the entire Spanish Monarchy; the city's ambassador, Francesc Bru, told Olivares that it was 'the apple of the city's eye'.² The fact that the actions of Madrid over the last ten or fifteen years were generally interpreted as revealing a determination to destroy the privileges and liberties of the Catalans one by one, certainly added to the sharpness and speed of Barcelona's reaction. It was as important to defend this supposed privilege as it was to defend the privilege of exemption from payment of the *quints*, for the existence of each privilege added to the power and prestige of Barcelona, and the currency of prestige was worth as much as the ducats demanded of Barcelona by the king.

The ministers in Madrid naturally saw Barcelona's claim in a very different light. How, they asked, could Barcelona possibly enjoy a *right* to be covered in the royal presence when even the grandees only enjoyed it as a special act of grace, granted afresh on each occasion by the monarch? Olivares recalled in his interview with Bru how on one occasion the duke of Alburquerque put on his hat in the king's presence without awaiting the royal command, and was immediately told to uncover. For the king to concede that Barcelona's Consellers could *of right* remain covered was unthinkable, for it would place the city in a unique position, higher than that of a grandee. 'Do the Consell de Cent not realize', Olivares asked Bru, 'that this affair keeps the whole world in suspense and that all the kingdoms of the Monarchy have their eyes fixed on what is happening?'

From the very beginning of the dispute, then, the parties concerned

¹ AHB: Delibs., 1632, fos. 267–8.
² AHB: CCO, 1632–3, fos. 141–2, Bru to Consellers, 12 Aug. 1632.

found themselves trapped by considerations of status and prestige which left them almost no room for manoeuvre. Negotiations proceeded constantly both in Barcelona and in Madrid, but neither Olivares nor the Consell de Cent felt themselves able to yield any ground. Meanwhile, all formal deliberations of the Corts had come to a halt, although work was being done behind the scenes on various draft constitutions. Such news as emerged about these constitutions did not allow much hope of a satisfactory conclusion to the Corts, even if the city should one day raise its *dissentiment*. Constitutions were being prepared, as the Protonotario expected, on those very points where the relations between the Crown and the Catalans were most delicate: on the *quints*, the Inquisition, the appointment of foreigners to Catalan benefices, and, above all, on the observation of the constitutions. This last constitution on Observança promised endless difficulties. Not only had it small chance of proving acceptable to the Court, but it also threatened to create interminable wrangling between the Estates themselves. The *braç militar* wanted the creation of a new tribunal, known as the Sala de Sant Jordi, to pronounce on all alleged infringements of the constitutions by the royal authorities.[1] Since it would ignore any illegal proceedings by barons and their officials, it was interpreted as another attempt by the aristocracy to obtain hegemony over Catalonia, and was fiercely opposed by the ecclesiastics and the towns.[2]

A further strain was put on tempers already frayed over the constitution on Observança, when Barcelona blocked all attempts to get it to raise its *dissentiment* and refused an independent judicial inquiry into its controversy with the Crown. The syndics of the towns resented kicking their heels in Barcelona day after day when nothing was done; they were angry at the city's obstructionist tactics and at the domineering behaviour of Barcelona's syndics; and on 22 June they rebelled, and sent a message to the Cardenal Infante imploring his protection against oppression by the city of Barcelona.[3] But the city was not to be moved.

Barcelona's intransigence was partly the result of its belief that, if it could only hold out, the king would eventually concede all that it wished. As the weeks passed, however, other issues began to push the original point of dispute into the background. Relations between the

[1] ACA: CA, leg. 278, no. 29, draft constitution, 1632.
[2] AMG: corresp., 1630–9. Dr Camps and Joan Clapes to Jurats of Girona, 28 May 1632.
[3] ACA: CA, leg. 383, relation of events, 17–25 June 1632.

city authorities and the Cardenal Infante were made worse by a quarrel over the city's fortifications. This was a matter about which Madrid had long been uneasy. At the time of the king's visit in 1626, the city authorities had been constructing a bulwark on the wall above the dockyard. Their idea was to top the bulwark with artillery, which incidentally would command the site of the royal artillery in the dockyard below. When the Council of State reported on this, the king expressed deep indignation,[1] natural enough in an age when a town like La Rochelle could defiantly resist the forces of a powerful sovereign. On this occasion a royal veto effectively brought work in Barcelona harbour to a halt; but the city was waiting for its chance to resume operations, and seized the pretext provided by a letter from the king ordering the Principality to strengthen its defences against a possible French attack. Work on the parapet in the harbour was resumed, and the city authorities studiously refrained from informing the Cardenal Infante of the fact. He naturally protested, only to be told that the city was carrying out orders from the king and would continue to do so.[2]

On this occasion, Barcelona won the day. When challenged, it produced its trump card in the form of an ancient royal charter allowing it to repair walls and build fortresses. The Council of Aragon and the Protonotario reluctantly decided that, in the circumstances, it would be wiser to let the work continue.[3] This new success for Barcelona deepened the gloom of the Cardenal Infante's advisers. As far back as the beginning of June, the count of Oñate, on learning of the constitutions being drafted in the Corts, warned the king that the Corts were aiming to turn the Principality 'virtually into a free republic, under Your Majesty's protection'.[4] The events of June and early July only strengthened this impression. A Junta composed of Oñate, the marquis of Montenegro and the Cardenal Infante's confessor advised Madrid that, even if Barcelona could be induced to raise its *dissentiment*, there was no hope of bringing the Corts to an amicable conclusion, because the Catalans were determined to secure for themselves a virtual republic, and settle their affairs for once and all, 'so that no

[1] AGS: Est., leg. 2646, consulta, 3 Sept. 1627.
[2] ACA: CA, leg. 277, no 81, correspondence forwarded to Madrid by Cardenal Infante, 10 July 1632.
[3] ACA: CA, leg. 277, no. 81, consulta, 23 July 1632.
[4] ACA: CA, leg. 278, no. 23, Oñate to King, 2 June 1632.

more Cortes will be necessary'. The king's best course would therefore be to dissolve the Corts without delay, and then to attempt to exact the *quints* from all those towns not yet paying them, and to recover all the alienated rights and properties of the Crown.[1]

As often happens on such occasions, the ministers on the spot were more pessimistic than those further away from the scene of action. The Protonotario, in particular, was surprisingly hopeful: he thought it would be possible to secure a prolongation of the Corts beyond the original six months agreed by the towns, and he also believed that the dispute over Barcelona's claims could be settled to the advantage of the Crown by a judicial action in which a majority of the judges could be bribed.[2] It seems odd that the Protonotario should have thought both that Barcelona would place no further obstacles in the way of the Corts once its claim had been duly considered, and that the Corts could finally be concluded to the satisfaction of all parties. The reason for his confidence may perhaps be explained by the nature of the source on which he relied for information. His closest confidant in the Principality at this moment was none other than Dr Vinyes.[3]

It had taken Dr Vinyes four years to obtain fulfilment of the promise made to him during the Corts of 1626 that he should be given a post in the royal administration. The duke of Feria had written to Madrid on 25 June 1630 about the importance of honouring the king's word, and the Council of Aragon finally agreed to recommend Vinyes for a post in the Audiència.[4] In the long run the appointment was to prove very advantageous to the Crown. Not only was Vinyes an energetic man and an outstanding lawyer: he was also in close touch with city and Diputació, both of which he had faithfully served for many years. His contacts with influential circles in the city made him very useful to the Cardenal Infante and to the Protonotario, but it is by no means certain that he had yet managed to shed all his old loyalties in the short time since he had become a royal minister. As late as January 1633 the regent Fontanet reported that Vinyes was not to be trusted where the claims of the city were concerned,[5] and it is perfectly possible that Vinyes was playing a double game during the summer of 1632. If he could persuade

---

[1] AHN: Est., leg. 860, no. 20, report of Junta, 16 July 1632.
[2] AHN: Est., leg. 860, no. 28, paper by Protonotario, 18 Aug. 1632.
[3] See above, pp. 227–8.   [4] ACA: CA, leg. 280, no. 9, undated consulta.
[5] ACA: CA, leg. 224, no. 13, Fontanet to Cardenal Infante, 30 Jan. 1633.

Madrid that there was still much to be hoped of the city and the Corts, he might delay, and perhaps prevent, the rupture that Oñate considered inevitable.

The optimism of the Protonotario and the Council of Aragon was to some extent shared by the Conde Duque when he came to summarize the views put forward by the councils at Madrid.[1] He pointed out that all the ministers in Barcelona favoured a dissolution of the Corts, while all those in Madrid wanted their continuation, although opinions differed as to whether Barcelona's claim should be conceded or the case be handed over to judges. It was generally agreed that the Cardenal Infante's advisers had allowed things to go too far, and had taken insufficient care to humour a people so passionately addicted to its privileges. The Conde Duque was not attracted by Oñate's proposal that the Corts be dissolved, since this involved a rupture with the Catalans, and the state of the Monarchy would not allow a prompt, forceful settlement of the affairs of Catalonia. Instead, the ministers in Barcelona should continue negotiations by every possible means; they should display the utmost 'tolerance and gentleness, and be prepared to consider any measure that would conclude the Cortes to the general satisfaction, *even if it brings little benefit to the royal treasury*'.[2] These few words of the Conde Duque reveal how far the events of the past few months had compelled him to modify his original plans. It was no longer a question of securing three million ducats from the Catalans at any price, but simply of ending their Corts without seriously diminishing the prestige of the Crown.

And if the Corts could not be brought to a satisfactory end, what then? The unpleasant question must at least be faced. Olivares thought that, in such an eventuality, the king would have to return to the Principality to close the Corts in person, but only after certain precautions had been taken. The duke of Feria, in Italy, should be warned to have 1000 Spanish and 1000 German troops ready for embarkation by mid-September. With this preparation, and a convocation of the Cortes of Aragon and Valencia, all would be well. The Conde Duque in fact envisaged, as a last resort, a forcible conclusion of the Corts, such as the Court had been expecting since July, when rumours began to circulate that men would be sent from Naples and Castile for use against

---

[1] AHN: Est., leg. 860, no. 23, paper by Olivares, 25 Aug. 1632.   [2] My italics.

the Catalans.[1] 'There want not some', reported the British agent in Madrid, picking up the rumour in September, 'that (out of a custom to lay hold on the worst things) publish that the people of Cataluña begin to suspect that under a colour of service against the French, these forces are to be employed to reduce them to reason.'[2]

But the Conde Duque had made it clear that the attempt to reduce the Catalans to reason must first be made by negotiation rather than threats. In accordance with his instructions, six representatives of the Corts were summoned into the Cardenal Infante's presence on 7 September to hear a paper couched in the most conciliatory language and explaining the justice of the king's case.[3] This was followed by a special letter from Olivares to Barcelona, which the Cardenal Infante handed over to the city on 21 September. It contained vague promises and an impassioned appeal: 'The royal service is for the good of the province. If you assist it by an exemplary display of behaviour in the Cortes, His Majesty will feel justified in bestowing more favour upon you than has ever been dreamt of by any city or kingdom of his Monarchy.'[4]

The Conde Duque's letter failed to move the hearts of its recipients. Three or four members of the Consell de Cent—Beltran Desvalls, Dr Ribas, Dr Martí[5]—dared to speak in favour of the Conde Duque's plea, only to find themselves abused and shouted down.[6] They made one final bid to obtain a proper discussion, and secured thirty supporters, but the majority voted that the city's *dissentiment* in the Corts should not be raised. The battle was now lost, but the Cardenal Infante determined to try yet once again, and asked the bishop of Barcelona to address the Consell de Cent. For an hour and a quarter he harangued

---

[1] AHB: CCO, 1632–3, fo. 122, Bru to Consellers, 23 July 1632. According to M. de Pény, writing from Madrid, a contingent of 5000 Neapolitans actually embarked for Catalonia in July. Of the 5000 'not half survive, because some were lost at sea, and the others were attacked by the Catalan peasants, who saw that they had come to ravage their country. This war between the villagers and the foreign soldiers is still going on' (M. de Pény to M. Hotman, 6 Sept. 1632. AAE: corresp. Esp., vol. 16, fo. 368).

[2] BM: Eg. MS 1820, fo. 209, Hopton to Coke, 23 Sept. 1632.

[3] ACA: CA, leg. 261, no. 22, paper read by J. L. de Villanueva, 7 Sept. 1632.

[4] BC: Fullet Bonsoms 5211, Olivares to Consellers, 9 Sept. 1632.

[5] Desvalls had been Conseller-en-Cap in 1627; Dr Ribas had written several papers for the Cardenal Infante about the disputes with the city, to be found, badly burnt, in BM: Add. MS 25,686; Dr Martí was angling for a place in the viceregal administration (see his petition in ACA: CA, leg. 501) which he eventually obtained.

[6] AHN: Est., leg. 860, no. 30, relation, 11–25 Sept. 1632.

it, on the morning of 25 September. He dwelt on the dangers that would come from a failure to conclude the Corts, and on the military activities of Louis XIII who was reported in the neighbourhood of Narbonne. But episcopal eloquence proved no more effective than ministerial epistles: the Consell de Cent remained unconvinced.

The city council is said to have been encouraged in its resistance by nine actively seditious members, including Dr Estevanell, whom Cardona had arrested the year before over the bread scandals, two merchants, Fornes and Cormellas, and an apothecary and a barber.[1] The exact motives of this heterogeneous group of dissidents are impossible to determine, but there is reason to believe that not all the opponents of the Court in the city council were moved solely, or even primarily, by the question of the Consellers' right to wear hats. A considerable amount of unsavoury wrangling had been going on behind the scenes in the Corts during June and July over the question of filling vacant offices in the Diputació.[2] The scandals in the administration of the Diputació, which provoked more constant bitterness and dissension in Catalonia than any other issue, might have been ended, or at least diminished, if the reforms mooted in the 1626 Corts had ever been put into effect.[3] But the reform projects failed with the failure of the Corts, and the Diputats and their friends continued their nefarious activities unchecked. If the city were now to raise its *dissentiment* and the Corts to continue, the question of the reform of the Diputació would certainly be aired again. There were several influential persons in Barcelona who would rather have seen the Corts fail a second time than run the risk of the Diputació being reformed, and the Cardenal Infante's advisers were convinced that these persons were deliberately encouraging the Consell de Cent in its resistance, so that Barcelona's veto should never be raised.[4] Others, who were not royal officials, shared these suspicions. 'The Corts are dying', wrote the syndic of Lleida,[5] 'and no one is doing anything to stop it. In fact, many interested persons would like to see them expire so as to avoid a reform of the Generalitat.'

[1] ACA: CA, leg. 282, no. 27, rough note (from J. L. de Villanueva?), probably 24 Sept. 1632.
[2] See the relation of events 17–25 June 1632 (ACA: CA, leg. 383), and the register of the 1632 Corts (ACA: G, R. 1058), where the activities of Francesc Despujol show something of the inter-relation of the politics of city and Diputació.
[3] See above, pp. 239–40.
[4] ACA: CA, leg. 282, no. 27, Villanueva's (?) note.
[5] APL: R. 744, Llibre de Corts (1632), Alexandre Calaff to Pahers of Lleida, 23 Oct. 1632.

If certain persons were deliberately planning to wreck the Corts, their plan succeeded perfectly. Barcelona's stubbornness was equalled by that of Madrid; deadlock was complete. Since Olivares was not prepared to make the one concession which would have induced Barcelona to raise its *dissentiment*, there was nothing for it but to consider ways and means whereby the Corts could be wound up without too much loss of face. Even this confronted the ministers with serious dilemmas. Should the Corts be prorogued, or should they be formally ended? There were arguments in favour of each of these two courses, and they were thrashed out in endless debates among the ministers in Barcelona and Madrid.[1] During the discussions on the Catalan problem from August to October 1632 the ministers consulted by Olivares showed several different shades of opinion. The count of Castrillo was cautious and conciliatory;[2] on the other hand, José González, one of the 'new' men whom Olivares had gathered around him, revealed himself a militant advocate of castilianization. The Catalans, he maintained, could not be allowed to keep their present constitutional system, but should be reduced to uniformity with the rest of Spain, 'being vassals by conquest, who properly have no more prerogatives than any other similar vassals'. Their liberties and privileges should gradually be pared away, and the process could begin at once with the billeting of troops in the Principality as a means of punishment.[3]

Olivares eventually decided that the Corts should be indefinitely prorogued. This had the advantage of deferring a final decision on the affairs of Catalonia to a moment when the international situation was more auspicious. It had been agreed at Madrid that immediate help must be sent to the rebellious duke of Orleans, to divert the French from foreign adventures.[3] Since this entailed a reinforcement of the Spanish frontier, a neat solution to the vexed problem of the Corts presented itself: the Cardenal Infante should prorogue the Corts and move to Girona, on the pretext of inspecting the frontier fortifications. An order to this effect was sent to him on 24 October, with the rider that he should avoid 'any further action which would complete the loss of those vassals'.[5]

[1] Several documents surviving from these debates are printed in Danvila, *El Poder Civil*, vol. VI, docs. 956–72.   [2] Danvila, docs. 956–72, no. 3.   [3] *Ibid.* no. 4.
[4] AHN: Est., leg. 860, no. 29, King to Cardenal Infante, 27 Sept. 1632.
[5] ACA: CA, leg. 282, no. 37, King to Cardenal Infante, 24 Oct. 1632.

The farce of the 1632 Corts had drawn to its dismal close. For the second time in the space of six years, the Catalans had failed to grant the subsidy requested by their king, and the constitutional machinery for the making of laws and the righting of wrongs had been paralysed. Superficially, the Catalans might be regarded as the victors in the contest with the Court, since they had evaded the payment of taxes; but in the context of the struggle, to talk of 'victory' for one side or the other would be meaningless. The relationship between Catalonia and its king was contractual. The traditional constitution of the Principality depended for its working on the preservation of a harmonious relationship between two equally balanced parts, and in so far as the scales were tipped in favour of one side or the other, the delicate machinery of the balanced constitution was damaged. The damage caused by the failure of the 1626 Corts was great; the further failure of the 1632 Corts may have made it irreparable.

Olivares was for the moment too busy to attend to the consequences. Catalonia was only one among the many provinces in the great empire he governed, and others besides the Catalans were capable of causing trouble. On this occasion it was the inhabitants of Vizcaya, angered by a new salt tax. Riots and risings in Vizcaya kept the Conde Duque fully occupied during the autumn and winter of 1632, and effectively diverted his attention from Catalonia. But paradoxically the risings in Vizcaya ensured that the Catalan question would not for long be neglected, for the resistance of both provinces to Madrid had many similarities and possessed common constitutional origins. The English ambassador believed that the Vizcayans' resistance was inspired by that of the Catalans, 'for the voice of privilege spreads far'.[1] As long as Olivares governed Spain he would never be allowed to forget that similar problems faced him in a dozen different provinces; that each of those provinces would strenuously resist any attempt to abolish its traditional laws and privileges; and that, as long as those laws and privileges survived, the king might be king of Castile and Aragon and *Señor* of Vizcaya, but he would not be king of Spain.

But how to make Philip IV king of Spain: that problem seemed no nearer solution in 1632 than it was when Olivares wrote his great memorandum on the government of the Monarchy eight years before.

[1] BM: Eg. MS 1820, fo. 216, Hopton to Coke, 19 Nov. 1632.

Now that the second failure of the Catalan Corts, together with the risings in Vizcaya, had confirmed the extreme difficulty of obtaining the co-operation of the provinces, Olivares's mind turned once again to the possibility of using force. The two Catalan regents on the Council of Aragon, Fontanet and Magarola, were asked for their views on the relative merits of a gentle or harsh policy towards the Principality. Fontanet died in February 1633. Magarola, however, wrote a detailed report.[1] He agreed that the Catalans were obstreperous and intractable, having persuaded themselves that 'this province, because of its geographical position, will always have to be humoured by Your Majesty'. On the other hand, he was certain that, if the French should invade Catalonia, the Catalans would throw themselves heart and soul into the struggle against their traditional enemy. As to the proper method of handling them, he would hardly recommend a 'rigorous' policy. He assumed that, if force were used, the province would eventually be compelled to surrender; the surplus revenues of the towns and the Diputació would be appropriated, and regular taxation introduced. But this would require an army of occupation, and the expense of maintaining such an army would certainly exceed the new revenue which its presence in the Principality was intended to bring the Crown.

Magarola could hardly be expected to show any enthusiasm for projects aimed at the conquest of his native province, but his argument about the ultimate futility of conquest was not easy to answer. It is doubtful whether Spain, with all its international commitments, could at that moment have put and kept in Catalonia an army capable of enforcing permanent submission; and it is even more doubtful whether the Principality possessed sufficient resources, either in men or money, to make it worth singling out for such special treatment. This second consideration was not likely to be entertained by the Conde Duque. For him, Catalonia was a province with a million inhabitants and abundant wealth. But the problems involved in establishing an army of occupation in Catalonia were too obvious to be ignored, and they effectively deterred him, in the circumstances of 1633, from pursuing a line of policy directed towards conquest. For the time being, the Catalan question must wait. So no troops were called in; the Cardenal Infante left for Italy in April 1633, on his way to take up the government

[1] ACA: CA, leg. 230, no. 55, *Respuesta del Regente Magarola...*, 27 Feb. 1633.

of Flanders, where more dazzling prospects awaited him; and the long-suffering, conscientious duke of Cardona was once again appointed viceroy of Catalonia.

After the conflicts of the preceding years, 1633 was singularly free of incident. The Catalans were left unmolested, and all the news was from Silesia and Alsace where the successes of Wallenstein and Feria restored the balance upset by the two years of spectacular Swedish victories under Gustavus Adolphus. War with France, which had looked so inevitable, had still not come, and Olivares began the year 1634 in an optimistic frame of mind.[1]

This year was to be marked in Catalonia by a renewal of discord, springing again from the fiscal demands of the Crown. Of all the classes in Catalan society, the clergy were the most exposed to these demands. Unlike the rest of their compatriots, they were already subjected to regular taxation by the Crown, and their benefices were, they considered, wretchedly poor, especially when they compared them with the fat benefices of Castile. A mere 250 *lliures* a year for a canonry, 120 for a rectory and 80 at the most for an ordinary benefice—the stipends were utterly inadequate, and all of them required 'increase, not diminution'.[2] Yet further diminution they were now called upon to face. In 1632 the king had obtained from Rome a papal brief for the imposition of a *décima* or tenth on the revenues of the Church in Spain, in order to raise a subsidy for the aid of the Emperor. Those canons who happened to be in Barcelona at the time hurriedly arranged an emergency meeting[3] and managed to enlist the support of the Diputació. By means of legal quibbles the Diputats successfully prevented the collection of the money during much of 1633,[4] but the day of reckoning could not be indefinitely postponed. When the collection began, however, the collectors met bitter resistance in the diocese of Vic, which was then *sede vacante*. The canons of Vic seem to have been more anxious about the precedents involved than about the quantity actually

[1] RAH: 11–13–3, fo. 30, Olivares to Alcalá, 4 Jan. 1634.
[2] ACT: Cartera 68, fo. 59, Tarragona chapter to Diputats, 21 March 1632. The canons of Tarragona were particularly poverty-stricken at this moment because they had been engaged in a long and expensive struggle since 1628 with the Castilian archbishop, Don Juan de Guzmán (Josep Blanc, *Arxiepiscopologi de la sancta església metropolitana i primada de Tarragona*, ed. Joaquim Icart, Tarragona, 1951, vol. II, pp. 178 ff.). For the sake of peace, the king had Guzmán transferred to Zaragoza in 1633.
[3] ACT: Cartera 39, Don Diego Girón de Rebolledo to Tarragona chapter, 14 March 1632.
[4] ACA: CA, leg. 386, Bishop of Girona to Protonotario, 23 July 1633.

demanded of them on this occasion: 'it is true that the tax is moderate but the question arises as to whether it is to be demanded in perpetuity.'[1] They were encouraged in their resistance by the chapters of Girona and Urgell, and no money was forthcoming. As so often happened in Catalonia with disputes of this nature, argument led to violence. Two *agutzils* sent to Vic by the viceroy in April were manhandled; an angry Cardona decided to retaliate by despatching twelve cavalry companies to be billeted in Vic and its neighbourhood, and was only dissuaded by urgent appeals from two or three distinguished members of the Vic aristocracy.[2] Instead of troops he finally sent Drs Grau and Mir of the Audiència, who ordered the sequestration of ecclesiastical property in Vic. The clergy riposted by closing the churches, and handbills were distributed through the city branding the judges as traitors.

The resistance of the canons was well organized. It was led by the archdeacon of Vic, Dr Melcior Palau, with the assistance of the sacristan, Dr Enric d'Alemany, together with two canons of Barcelona and two of Urgell, Pau Claris and Jaume Ferran.[3] They seem to have had at their command certain agitators from outside who were surreptitiously introduced into Vic.[4] The situation looked grave, especially as a company of 250 ill-disciplined foreign troops happened at that moment to be passing through the Vic region on their way to Rosselló, and clashed with the villagers all along the route. Over a thousand inhabitants of the Vic region turned out to attack this company: 'the whole countryside was prepared and united, with none of the old dissensions of *nyerros* and *cadells*; all were friends on this occasion.'[5] The company failed to survive the onslaught, and the parish priests of Vic were subsequently kept very busy with confessions.

The combination of religious agitation in the city of Vic and popular unrest in the countryside made it appear for one moment in June 1634 as if Cardona was confronted with an organized rebellion. But the sequestration order and the arrest of three clergymen served to damp the spirits of the more ardent, and Alemany negotiated a settlement in Barcelona on 22 July, whereby the pope would be informed of their

[1] ACV: Cartes, 1630–9, Dr Diego Palau to Canons of Vic, 1 March 1634.
[2] AMV: CR, 12, Don Miquel Clariana to Consellers of Vic, 15 May 1634.
[3] ACA: CA, leg. 280, no. 4, Bishop of Girona to J. L. de Villanueva, 24 June 1634.
[4] AMV: CR, 12, Pau Mallol to Consellers of Vic, 18 June 1634.
[5] Sanz, *Relació breu dels sucessos...de Vich*, pp. 25–6. Sanz gives a vivid account of all the events at Vic in this year.

complaints, the prisoners would be released, and payment of the *décima* would be deferred until mid-November.[1] The tension slackened, calm was restored. It was, however, no accident that the man eventually appointed to the bishopric of Vic was Gaspar Gil, a close friend of the Protonotario and formerly the confessor of his nieces, who were nuns in the convent of San Plácido.[2] It was important for Madrid that the Crown should have a thoroughly reliable agent in so troubled a diocese.

The troubles at Vic in the spring and summer of 1634 show how close to the surface was the latent antagonism between the Spanish Court and the Catalan clergy. The canons lived in a state of turbulence, the parish priests in poverty. Few had any prospect of preferment. For the ambitious, there were only two paths to positions of distinction: conformity, which entailed subservience, or rebellion. Of the leaders of the 1634 troubles, Palau would one day conform, while Claris would rebel.[3] Meanwhile, they and their colleagues nursed their grievances, and added one more bitter memory to their accumulated store of resentment.

However rebellious the clergy, Madrid could usually count on getting the better of a leaderless and downtrodden Church. A much tougher problem was to crack the resistance of the proud and ancient city of Barcelona. It was Barcelona which had wrecked the Corts of 1632. It was Barcelona which had persistently parried all attempts by Madrid to obtain money from the Catalans. Sooner or later a conflict between Madrid and Barcelona was inevitable.

The issue on which the Court would make its challenge was easily guessed. It had never allowed the king's claim to one-fifth of Barcelona's revenues to be forgotten, although the Crown had not pressed its demand for the *quints* since the viceroyalty of Alcalá. It was true that Olivares had promised not to demand the *quints* again until the conclusion of the Corts, and they had not yet been concluded. It was also true that the legal basis of the king's claim was shaky. Barcelona could show an imposing list of privileges, including one from Don Alfons in 1286 confirming the city's imposts and renouncing all royal claims over them for himself and his successors.[4] But if the city's impositions were

---

[1] ACA: CA, leg. 280, no. 4, Bishop of Girona to J. L. de Villanueva, 22 July 1634.
[2] BUB: MS 115, Sevillà's history, fo. 116.   [3] See below, pp. 436–7.
[4] AHB: LC, 1632–5, fos. 66–70, memorandum for Navel, 18 Feb. 1634. The reference is to Alfonso III of Aragon (1258–91).

worth 80,000 *lliures* annually, and a fifth of this sum could be claimed for the Crown every year since 1599, the royal treasury would benefit to the extent of 560,000 *lliures*[1]—considerably less than the sum demanded of the Corts, but by no means a contemptible figure. The prize was worth a struggle.

There was much to be said for launching the struggle while Cardona was viceroy. As a member of a family Catalan by origin, he might succeed where an outsider could fail. The appropriate orders were therefore sent from Madrid, and on 30 January 1634 the Consellers of Barcelona were told to present the city accounts at the office of the Mestre Racional.[2] As was to be expected, representations to the viceroy were useless. The city decided to appeal directly to the king in order to avoid a battle which could lead to fiscal, and even political, disaster. Already, by a decision of the Consell de Cent of 31 January, Jeroni de Navel, a *ciutadà honrat*, had been chosen to go to Madrid as the city's spokesman in a controversy with the cathedral chapter over the sale of meat. He was now given the additional, and far more important, task of speaking for the city in the matter of the *quints*, and of pressing for at least a suspension of the viceroy's order.[3]

Navel took the precaution of making his will before he left for Madrid.[4] Since he was to prove the most formidable figure in Barcelona politics in the years before the Catalan revolution, it is unfortunate that the will is more than usually reticent. But various sources make it possible to discover a little of his background. He came of an old-established Barcelona family. For unspecified reasons, his grandfather had been deprived by royal officials of a hereditary office in the Barcelona dockyards, worth more than 500 *escuts* a year. The Crown had offered compensation in the form of a pension of 200 *lliures* annually, but in eighteen years this had been paid only two and a half times, although it had persistently been claimed by the family.[5] The claims were made by Jeroni's father, Julià de Navel, who had been Conseller-en-Cap of Barcelona during the reign of Philip III, and directed the city's operations against the bandits.[6]

[1] ACA: CA, leg. 385, paper sent by Cardona to King, 15 Nov. 1634.
[2] AHB: LC, 1632–5, fos. 58–61, embassy of Consellers to Viceroy, 15 Feb. 1634.
[3] AHB: LC, 1632–5, fos. 63–5, instructions for Navel, 18 Feb. 1634.
[4] APB: A. J. Fita, lib. 7, de testaments, fos. 11 v–13 v.
[5] ACA: CA, leg. 490, petition of Julià de Navel, 1617.
[6] Soler y Terol, *Roca Guinarda*, p. 50.

Julià de Navel's last term of office as Conseller-en-Cap of Barcelona was from 1625 to 1626. His son Jeroni followed in his father's footsteps, and himself became Conseller-en-Cap for the first time in 1629–30.[1] He seems first to have attracted the unfavourable attention of the viceroy early in 1632 when he intervened in a dispute between city and viceroyalty over the administration of certain corn dues, and, with a group of friends, raided the Customs House and threw several chests into the street while the city bell incessantly tolled.[2] In spite of this incident, the Cardenal Infante was able to bribe him during the struggle with the city in the summer of 1632, although there is nothing to show what services he performed.[3] Navel, however, was an elusive character, too slippery for anyone to hold for long. He was a born demagogue, and came to exercise an almost hypnotic control over the Consell de Cent, where he took care always to choose a seat near the more humble citizens. The flattery was very successful: they regarded him as an oracle and believed what he said 'as if he were St Paul'.[4] 'This man', Cardona was to report to Madrid, 'is dangerous, and I doubt if his intentions are any less seditious than those of the rebels in The Hague, but as his power is not so great, he is more restricted in his activities.'[5] But whether Navel entertained long-term political aims or was simply an opportunist who delighted in power, there is no means of judging.

Chosen now as Barcelona's representative for a mission of the highest importance, he took the high road to Madrid. He reached the Court on 25 February 1634, and wrote from it a number of letters describing his interviews with the ministers in the most vivid detail. After the usual courtesy calls, his first important visit was to the Protonotario, 'the man who has the biggest hand in everything, and without whose permission nothing is done'.[6] Villanueva told Navel that he had examined all the relevant documents, and it was quite clear that the city was in the wrong—a conclusion that Navel at once rejected. If only, the Protonotario continued, the city had given *something* to help His Majesty in his moment of difficulty, then perhaps the question

---

[1] *Rùbriques de Bruniquer* (Barcelona, 1912–16), vol. I, pp. 52–3, List of Consellers.
[2] ACA: CA, leg. 385, Cardona to King, 4 Oct. 1634.
[3] ACA: CA, leg. 277, no. 70, Cardenal Infante to J. L. de Villanueva, 24 Aug. 1632.
[4] ACA: CA, leg. 385, relation of events in Consell de Cent.
[5] ACA: CA, leg. 385, Cardona to J. L. de Villanueva, 4 Oct. 1634.
[6] AHB: CCO, 1634, fos. 11–13, Navel to City, 4 March 1634.

would never have been raised. Navel reminded him of the loan of 50,000 *escuts* in 1626, and the Protonotario, acknowledging this with gratitude, promised to obtain for Navel an audience of the king.

This was the usual kind of skirmish that occurred in interviews between representatives of Barcelona and the king's ministers in Madrid. Navel had few illusions. The duke of Sessa, who disliked Olivares and made a point of expressing his own affection for the Catalans, had warned him that the ministers were 'so greedy for money that, at the slightest prospect of it, they would never stop until they had it all'. Navel therefore realized that all he could do was to delay the execution of Cardona's orders for as long as possible, and in the present climate of crisis at Madrid even this would test his skill and diplomacy to the limit. The optimism with which the new year opened had been summarily dispelled by the discovery of Wallenstein's treachery, and at the end of February Olivares had summoned ministers from various councils to consider a *consulta* of the Council of State representing that the Spanish Monarchy was in danger of final ruin.[1] The interview with the Conde Duque would not be easy.

'Enter the city of Barcelona', cried the Conde Duque's servant, and Navel entered for his first interview with Olivares. It was short, and not very cordial. The *quints*, maintained Olivares, belonged to the king, who was now forced by his necessities to claim them. He had forborne to do so up to now, because the city had done him certain services, but since it showed no desire to continue them, action must be taken. Navel protested that the city was in such financial straits that it could do no more. Olivares would not accept this argument: 'Aragon has given and Valencia has given, while from Catalonia we have got almost nothing. And why? Because the city of Barcelona is so powerful; and since it refuses to give anything, the other towns follow suit....In these circumstances, His Majesty must avail himself of what belongs to him.'[2]

But how was Olivares's threat to be carried out? In Barcelona the twenty-days' time limit for the city to present its accounts was running out, and nothing had happened. Uncertain what to do next, Cardona decided that a ten-days' extension should be given. If by 5 April the

[1] ACA: CA, leg. 233, no. 28, consulta, 20 Feb. 1634.
[2] AHB: CCO, 1634, fos. 23–4, Navel to City, 18 March 1634.

city's books had not been handed over, the *advocat fiscal patrimonial* was to arrange for a visit to the city's archives.[1] This was mere temporizing, since Cardona must have been perfectly aware that the city would never voluntarily allow a royal official to burrow among its documents. A further note of piquancy was added by the fact that Cardona's *advocat fiscal patrimonial* was none other than Dr Vinyes, whose vigour and acumen singled him out for rapid promotion in the viceregal administration; and Dr Vinyes's personal position was not entirely without its embarrassments, since in 1621 he had written a forceful paper maintaining Barcelona's exemption from the *quints*, which the city now forwarded to Navel with glee.[2]

Vinyes had now put his past behind him, even though on occasions like this it had an unpleasant way of catching up with him again. The king had no servant in the Principality more energetic than Dr Vinyes. But the city was well defended. Dr Vinyes met his match in the other great Catalan lawyer of this period, Dr Fontanella, now Barcelona's principal legal adviser. The similarities and contrasts between the careers of Vinyes and Fontanella added a note of personal rivalry and bitterness to a constitutional struggle which was to have far-reaching implications for the future of Catalonia. Like Vinyes, Fontanella had been one of the more fiery defenders of Catalan 'liberties' during the viceroyalty of Alcalá.[3] Like Vinyes, he none the less attempted on innumerable occasions to obtain a place in the Audiència, but, unlike Vinyes, failed. His last application for a post was made as late as 1630; after that, he ruined any surviving chance he may have possessed by writing in defence of Barcelona's claims in 1632. The Canceller remarked of him on this occasion: 'it is only reasonable that those who aspire to the Crown's service should take more care about the way they behave'.[4] With these words, the door to office was slammed in Fontanella's face.

The failure to obtain a post in the highest tribunal in the Principality must have been particularly galling for a man with Fontanella's great legal reputation. Salt was rubbed into the wound by the success of his former, and less distinguished, colleague, Dr Vinyes. Now, for the first time, the two men stood face to face on an important issue. They

[1] ACA: CA, leg. 384, Cardona to King, 1 April 1634.
[2] AHB: LC, 1632–5, fos. 97–100, City to Navel, 15 April 1634.
[3] See above, pp. 169–70.   [4] ACA: CA, leg. 224, no. 8, consulta, 14 Oct. 1633.

found themselves occupying positions exactly the reverse of what might have been prophesied for them a few years earlier. Vinyes, by origin an outsider, by temperament a rebel, found himself transformed by rapid stages into the foremost champion of the established order, while Fontanella, of respectable family and established reputation, was gradually compelled to become a revolutionary.

It was Fontanella who, in the struggle over the *quints*, came to devise a doctrine of revolutionary implications for the Principality. He maintained that it was useless for city and Diputació to seek judicial remedy for grievances in the Audiència, since the clearer the rights of the province, the more certain was the Audiència to pronounce in favour of the king.[1] Up to 1634 at least, the doctrine of a biased Audiència was not borne out by its judicial decisions. Viceroys tended to complain of its ineffectiveness and unreliability in suits affecting the interests of the Crown. 'Up to now', wrote Dr Ribas in 1632, 'no fiscal case has been won, or, if it has, it has been only by the imposition of strict limitations on the Crown's rights.'[2] The judges in the Audiència were too personally involved in the affairs of the Principality, and too restricted by the constitutions, to behave as the agents of despotism. It was possible that all this might change as Vinyes came to take the Crown's fiscal interests in hand, and the pressure from Madrid grew stronger. But if Fontanella's doctrine of an Audiència subservient to the Crown was not strictly true at the time of its formulation, its usefulness was undeniable. He had forged what was to prove the deadliest weapon in the legal arsenal of city and Diputació.

Acting on the advice of Fontanella, the city decided not to present its accounts in the office of the Mestre Racional. It put all its trust in the diplomacy of Navel, who was still battling with the ministers in Madrid. Olivares insisted again that Catalonia was the one province which had failed to come to the king's help, and said that he held Barcelona responsible, since Barcelona *was* Catalonia. He had, however, no desire to ruin the city, and would be willing to consider any way out of the impasse that Navel might propose.[3] The Protonotario, whom Navel visited on Easter day, showed himself much less amiable than the Conde Duque. What, he asked, did Navel think of the recent

---

[1] ACA: CA, leg. 393, Vinyes to ?, 7 July 1640.
[2] BM: Add. MS 25,868, fos. 90–3, paper by Dr Ribas, 1632.
[3] AHB: CCO, 1634, fos. 41–2, Navel to City, 8 April 1634.

arrest of the duke of Aerschot? If Aerschot could be arrested, so could a Conseller of Barcelona. Navel hastened to protest the city's loyalty; the Protonotario altered tack, exchanging threats for praise, and the interview ended inconclusively.

The Protonotario, for all the mixture of honey and gall in his conversation, cannot have been unaware that the Crown's position was difficult. The ministers in Madrid had apparently failed to take the obvious precaution of deciding on the measures to be adopted if, as they might have guessed, Barcelona refused to produce its books.[1] When the Council of State finally came to discuss the question, it was obviously baffled: the duke of Villahermosa expressed the sense of the meeting when he said that the behaviour of the Catalans justified 'violent measures', but the times were unpropitious for them.[2] This was the perpetual dilemma of the ministers whenever they discussed Catalonia. In all their plans for the future of the Principality they constantly felt themselves inhibited by the proximity of France. This drove them back on compromise measures, which made the worst of both worlds. On this occasion, for example, the king decided that royal officials should take the books from the city archives, but should act with the utmost 'gentleness' and circumspection.

It was left to the unfortunate Cardona to obey this impossible order. In the circumstances, it was not surprising that his plans miscarried. The seizure of the books was planned for 2 o'clock on the afternoon of Friday, 16 June. The city, as always, got wind of what was intended, and had a large number of armed men posted in the area of the town hall.[3] A riot was imminent and was only prevented by the prompt action of the Conseller-en-Cap, Don Guerau de Peguera, who had the bell-rope of the city bell pulled up to the bell-tower, and a guard placed on it.[4] Realizing that, with the city in its present state, it would be folly to go ahead with his plan, Cardona cancelled his orders, but sought retribution by arresting four members of the Consell de Cent who had played a prominent part in the day's disturbances: Dr Pere

---

[1] AHB: CCO, 1634, fo. 61, Navel to Consellers, 22 April 1634.
[2] AGS: Est., leg. 2654, consulta, 23 May 1634.
[3] ACA: CA, leg. 343, Cardona to King, 24 June 1634.
[4] AGS: Est., leg. 2655, Vinyes to King, 7 Jan. 1635. Documentation of the struggle between Cardona and the city is scanty. The story is told briefly by L. Assarino, *Le Rivolutioni di Catalogna*, pp. 44–5.

Joan Rossell, son of Dr Joan Francesc Rossell, the most eminent physician in Catalonia, and a leader of the city in the troubles of 1622; Jaume Pi, a merchant, and Rossell's brother-in-law; Rafael Matali, another merchant, and Pau Boquet, who had assisted Navel in the Customs House affair of 1632.

The unexpected and unpremeditated arrest of the four citizens only complicated an already involved situation. Cardona was universally reviled as an 'enemy of the fatherland',[1] and, in forfeiting the last remnants of goodwill in the city, had gained nothing but four prisoners in return. The impotence of a viceroy, without troops and without a castle in a hostile city, was painfully apparent, and underlined the weakness of the king's authority in Catalonia. The next move, as Cardona himself pointed out, lay once again with the ministers in Madrid; when they gave the orders, he would obey.[2]

Cardona would have to wait a long time, for the ministers were in a quandary. It is probable that they were again discussing the possibility of using force, for rumours were again circulating in Madrid that troops were to be sent to Catalonia.[3] A decision of such magnitude would, however, need much discussion, and in the meantime it was decided that Cardona was best away from Barcelona. War with France again seemed imminent, and the viceroy was ordered to Perpinyà, from where he could keep an eye on the frontier. On his way to Perpinyà he successfully negotiated with the towns of Girona and Figueres for three hundred paid soldiers,[4] but when he published at Perpinyà on 15 August a proclamation of *Princeps Namque* for the convocation of troops,[5] scarcely a soul in the Principality stirred. The whole province was watching Barcelona, and at Barcelona, Jeroni de Navel, who had returned from Madrid at the end of July, was again in command. As long as the four citizens remained imprisoned, and the threat of a forcible exaction of the *quints* hung over the city, Navel would see to it that the city ignored all the king's requests for troops.

During the autumn of 1634 Navel persistently obstructed in the Consell de Cent any measure which might be considered to further the

---

[1] ACA: CA, leg. 343, Vinyes to J. L. de Villanueva, 24 June 1634.
[2] ACA: CA, leg. 384, Cardona to J. L. de Villanueva, 29 July 1634.
[3] BM: Eg. MS 1820, fos. 375–6, Hopton to Coke, 13 Aug. 1634.
[4] ACA: CA, leg. 279, no. 4, Don Pedro Coloma to King, 16 Dec. 1634.
[5] See above, pp. 206–7.

royal service. He introduced interminable delays when the king asked Barcelona for soldiers; he held up attempts by the Diputats to mediate between Cardona and the city over the *quints*;[1] he dissuaded the city from giving the duchess of Mantua a ceremonial reception when she arrived at Barcelona on her way from Italy to Madrid, on the pretext that the king had not personally notified the city of her visit.[2] As if all this were not of itself sufficient to drive Cardona to exasperation, Navel achieved his final triumph on St Andrew's Day when (by one of those coincidences in Catalan public life of the time, almost too good to be true) he was drawn by lot as Conseller-en-Cap of Barcelona for the coming year.

For all the apparent strength of his position, however, Navel had to play his cards with extreme care. The continuation of the struggle over the *quints* was of no advantage to Barcelona. Already it was losing heavily from the termination of all business in the Audiència, which had ceased to function since Cardona's arrival in Perpinyà on 10 August.[3] There was no knowing what further offensive measures the king might not take to bring the city to heel. Nor was Navel's own personal status entirely secure, as he must have been fully aware. A writ of *regalia* had long been hanging over him for his part in the Customs House affair of 1632, and if it should be enforced against him he would be ineligible for city office. In addition, certain irregularities in his private life left him unpleasantly exposed. At this very moment, correspondence was being exchanged between Cardona and Madrid over the fact that Navel had in the past maintained a scandalous relationship with a nun in a Barcelona convent.[4] This in itself might offer sufficient pretext for his arrest.

All these circumstances suggested the advantages of preventing a final break between the king and Barcelona, so long as the city could do so without paying the *quints* in full. Navel therefore let fall a few well-placed remarks in a conversation with the *veguer* of Barcelona, Don Francesc de Ayguaviva, a friend and dependant of the duke of Cardona.[5] He would, he said, like to reach an agreement with the

[1] ACA: CA, leg. 385, Cardona to J. L. de Villanueva, 1 Nov. 1634.
[2] ACA: CA, leg. 385, relation of events in Consell de Cent, Oct. 1634.
[3] ACA: CA, leg. 385, Vinyes to Cardona, 17 Oct. 1634.
[4] ACA: CA, leg. 385, undated note to Cardona, and Cardona's reply to king, 22 Nov. 1634.
[5] He had been governor of Cardona's estates (cf. AHB: CCO, 1626–9, fo. 14, town of Igualada to Barcelona, 4 Aug. 1627).

Crown, and thought he could prevail on the Consell de Cent to offer the king 50,000 or 60,000 *escuts* if he would renounce the lawsuit over the *quints*.[1] These remarks duly reached the quarters for which they were intended, and negotiations began, under cover of night, between the Canceller of Catalonia, Don Francesc de Erill, and the second Conseller of Barcelona, Joachim Valls, a close friend of Navel. It was quite clear from the conversations that the city would accept nothing less from the king than a renunciation in perpetuity of all claims to the *quints*. In return for such a renunciation, Erill believed that the city would give the king 100,000 *lliures*; he also believed, from his knowledge of Navel, that a bribe would help to smooth the path.

None of the ministers in Catalonia, however, had the authority to negotiate a settlement, and no orders had come from Madrid. The delay was serious: Cardona found himself a solitary, neglected, figure, unemployed in Perpinyà; the judges of the Audiència, unable to continue work in the viceroy's absence, sat unemployed in Barcelona; and the suspension of all the judicial tribunals was causing distress throughout the Principality.[2] With the blessing of Cardona, Dr Vinyes had gone to Madrid in November to point out to the ministers the serious consequences of delaying either a decision or a settlement. He suggested, as one means of simultaneously bringing pressure to bear on Barcelona while solving the problem of the judicial tribunals, that the Audiència should be removed from Barcelona for the time being, and ordered to join Cardona at Perpinyà.[3]

During the winter of 1634 and the early spring of 1635 Vinyes was to have unlimited first-hand experience of the paralysis which affected all discussion of business in Madrid. His proposal was supported by the Council of Aragon, but then had to be debated by the Council of State. The discussion was held at a meeting on 26 December 1634, the Conde Duque himself being absent.[4] The only member of the Council to approve the suggestion that the Audiència be removed from Barcelona was the Inquisitor-General,[5] and even he was unhappy about pressing

[1] ACA: CA, leg. 385, Chancellor to Cardona, 9 Dec. 1634.
[2] ACA: CA, leg. 385, Cardona to King, 28 Dec. 1634.
[3] AGS: Est., leg. 2655, paper by Vinyes, 7 Jan. 1635.
[4] AGS: Est., leg. 2655, consulta, 26 Dec. 1634.
[5] Fray Antonio de Sotomayor, archbishop of Damascus and confessor of the king. He was already 77 at the time of his appointment in 1632, and resigned his office under pressure after the fall of Olivares in 1643. He died in 1648 (Lea, *Inquisition*, vol. I, p. 309).

the affair of the *quints* too strongly at a time when war with France threatened. The other members, Cardinal Zapata,[1] the marquis of Mirabel and the duke of Villahermosa, all found themselves in general agreement with the outspoken count of Castrillo, who, as in the discussions of 1632, was not afraid to come to the defence of the Catalans. If they should be proved right about the *quints*, the king should drop his claims; moreover, Catalonia was in the state 'we well know', and it was for His Majesty to 'extinguish any spark capable of producing a conflagration which it would then be difficult to put out'. The Audiència, therefore, should not be moved; Navel should not be arrested, and efforts should be made to settle amicably the question of the *quints*.

Another two months were allowed to pass before this mild and conciliatory *consulta* was itself debated. During those two months, preparations for war against France continued. The English ambassador was of the opinion that, 'if they can by any means excuse it they will never break with France', but thought that the king might make use of the military preparations 'to settle the disorders of Cataluña, if not by fair means, by foul'.[2] Colour was given to this belief by the activities of two *tercios*, which had been billeted in the Principality for some months, officially as part of the defence preparations. As always, the soldiers frequently clashed with the population, and, as always, there were those who believed that the troops had been billeted in the Principality for purposes of political coercion. Such accusations were levelled so regularly against all European monarchs in the seventeenth century that it is difficult to know how seriously to take them: soldiers always had to be quartered somewhere, and their presence was never likely to be welcome to the local population. But it is true that Cardona had planned the billeting of soldiers in and around Vic at the time of the religious disturbances in 1634 in order to put pressure on the local population, and the *tercios* may well have been billeted in the Principality with the same end in view. Whatever the reasons for their presence, they incited rather than cowed the population, and the Diputats sent the indefatigable Bellafilla to Madrid to complain both about the arrests of 16 June and about the behaviour of the troops.[3]

Olivares was clearly dissatisfied with the *consulta* of the Council of

---

[1] Sotomayor's predecessor as Inquisitor-General (1627–32).
[2] BM: Eg. MS 1820, fo. 428, Hopton to Windebank, 11 Jan. 1635.
[3] ACA: CA, leg. 279, no. 29, petition to be presented by Bellafilla.

State. On 26 February 1635 he summoned a large Junta of members both of the Council of State and the Council of Aragon to discuss once again the question of the transfer of the Audiència and the arrest of Navel.[1] It was not perhaps without significance that, on this occasion, Olivares himself was present, while the count of Castrillo was not. Since the whole question had been under discussion for the best part of four months, there was nothing startlingly fresh about the views expressed. Of the members of the Council of Aragon, the president of the Council, the duke of Alburquerque, with his intimate knowledge of the Principality, considered that the transfer of the Audiència would be impolitic. He was supported in this by two regents, while the three others joined with the Protonotario in recommending a transfer. The members of the Council of State repeated what they had already said, the Inquisitor-General again advocating relatively strong measures, while the marquis of Leganés and the count of la Puebla, who had not been present at the earlier meeting, supported Mirabel and Villahermosa in their milder views.

When all these ministers had spoken, it remained for the Conde Duque himself to speak. So far, seven ministers against five had advocated a conciliatory policy. If discussions in councils and juntas had been decided by the vote of the majority, Olivares's intervention could have made no difference one way or the other, but, as the favourite, his voice inevitably carried the preponderant weight with the king. He came down in favour of those who advocated a strong policy. The divorce of viceroy and Audiència was in his view unnatural; Cardona could not possibly move far from the French frontier, and the best solution would be to establish both him and the Audiència at Girona. He agreed that the removal of the Audiència might induce Barcelona to recognize the error of its ways, and drew a parallel, not perhaps entirely happy, with his handling of the revolt in Vizcaya. Not only a single city but a whole province had been at fault in Vizcaya, but the final outcome had been singularly satisfactory. His Majesty had first 'broken their pride and strength by removing their trade', and had then asked what he could do to meet their demands. The province was now contented and quiet. Olivares omitted to add that the salt tax, which had originally provoked the rebellion, had not been enforced.

[1] AGS: Est., leg. 2655, Junta, 26 Feb. 1635.

The Conde Duque had spoken and there was no more to be said. The king endorsed Olivares's views on the back of the *consulta*, and, at the end of March, Cardona received two orders: one, to let it be known that Navel was the subject of a writ of *regalia* and therefore ineligible for his office, and the other to move his establishment to Girona and summon the Audiència there to join him.[1] The second order was eventually carried out, though with considerable reluctance on the part of the judges. The first order, about Navel, baffled Cardona, who did not know how to set about it.[2] Cardona, however, was to be saved from embarrassment, and Navel from arrest, by a new development. The marquis of Villafranca, of the proud house of Toledo, had been sent to Barcelona to organize the transport of troops to Italy. This mission, as Olivares probably intended, would give him the opportunity to negotiate with the city over the *quints*. While still in Madrid Villafranca had already put out feelers,[3] and he began personal negotiations with the Consellers on his arrival in Barcelona.

During the delicate negotiations, Cardona decided that it would be wise to suspend any action against Navel.[4] Navel and his fellow-Consellers had been told by Villafranca that the city should ease the way for a settlement over the *quints* by serving the king generously. When they pressed him to elaborate on this, they discovered that he was thinking of a grant of 2000 soldiers and 60,000 ducats. The revelation seems to have appalled them, for they wrote to Joan Francesc Codina, their special ambassador in Madrid, that the city did not have a penny.[5] Ordinarily, the demand would probably have been rejected out of hand, but this was a serious moment, both for the city and for Navel. Codina, from Madrid, wrote to Barcelona that the marquis of Villafranca's attempts at a settlement offered the city the best chance of release from its afflictions, to which the transfer of the Audiència to Girona had now to be added, but he ended with a warning: 'As I see it, each is trying to look after his own interests without regard for the common welfare and for the peace of the Principality.'[6]

---

[1] ACA: CA, leg. 279, no. 15, orders of 21 and 31 March 1635.
[2] ACA: CA, leg. 279, no. 15, Cardona to King, 11 April 1635.
[3] AHB: CCO, 1635, fos. 16–17, Don Joan Grau to City, 10 March 1635.
[4] ACA: CA, leg. 279, no. 15, Cardona to J. L. de Villanueva, 24 May 1635.
[5] AHB: LC, 1635, fos. 7–8, City to Codina, 30 May 1635.
[6] AHB: CCO, 1635, fo. 46, Codina to City, 26 May 1635.

There is no knowing to whom this cryptic reference was intended to refer, but events in Barcelona were taking a strange turn. Navel, either to save himself or because he believed a settlement was now indispensable for the safety of the city, decided that a bargain must be struck. Doubting his ability to carry a vote through the Consell de Cent single-handed, he turned to a friend, Francesc Dalmau, for assistance. Dalmau, a very influential figure in Barcelona, was anxious for his son Agustí to obtain the next vacancy in the office of Mestre Racional in the viceregal administration.[1] Agreement was quietly reached, and on 27 May Dalmau, presumably aware that he risked losing his reputation with the city if ever the truth emerged, proposed that Barcelona should serve the king with 1500 men and 35,000 ducats. He managed to talk the Consell de Cent into voting 30,000 *lliures*, but no troops. Villafranca rejected this offer as trivial, and on the following day Navel and Dalmau went back again and induced the city council to raise the figure to 40,000 *lliures*, a sum which Villafranca was graciously prepared to accept.

The news of Barcelona's gift was received in Madrid with jubilation.[2] It was the first outright gift of any significance made by Barcelona to Philip IV, although it had lent him over 150,000 ducats since his accession. Since 40,000 *lliures* represented half Barcelona's income for one year, the gift did entail a real sacrifice for the city, although against this must be set the fact that the Principality had paid almost nothing in taxes to the king, while Aragon alone was contributing 144,000 ducats a year. Perhaps for this reason, Madrid's pleasure at the news was not expressed in any tangible gesture of gratitude. Although the city waited anxiously, not one of the requests it had made to the king in 1626 was granted in acknowledgement of its service. Rather desperately, it pinned its hopes on intercession by Villafranca. Codina, who knew the ways of Madrid, thought that all Villafranca's powers of intercession would be necessary, and promised to approach Olivares and the Protonotario personally. This was a critical moment. 'Since it looks as though the fruit is beginning to ripen, pick it in time, for things are going in such a way that we must not miss our opportunity.'[3]

---

[1] ACA: CA, leg. 280, no. 25, consulta, 18 June 1635.
[2] AHB: CCO, 1635, fo. 57, Grau to City, 10 June 1635.
[3] AHB: CCO, 1635, fo. 66. Codina to Consellers, 30 June 1635.

The fruit, unfortunately, was not as ripe for the picking as the city's ambassador believed. Madrid was not to be cheated of its prospects of 500,000 ducats by the gift of a mere 40,000 *lliures* and for that very reason the struggle over the *quints* could not be abandoned. As the dispute stood at the end of May 1635, neither Barcelona nor Madrid could be said to have emerged with much advantage. Madrid, it was true, had gained 40,000 *lliures* through the complicity, either prudent or self-interested, of two of Barcelona's leading citizens, and it had to some extent weakened Barcelona by removing the administrative and judicial capital of Catalonia to Girona. On the other hand, it had failed to obtain either the co-operation or the surrender of a city whose resistance had proved to be one of the principal obstacles to Olivares's plans for the establishment of fiscal uniformity in Spain. The battle between Madrid and Barcelona must inevitably continue. Its nature, however, was to be profoundly changed by great new developments of international moment. One week before Barcelona voted its gift of 40,000 ducats, a more stirring event of rather less debatable significance had occurred in another important city of the Spanish Monarchy. On 19 May 1635 a French herald arrived at the gates of Brussels to announce an event long feared and long foreseen. France was at war with Spain.[1]

[1] The Cardenal Infante declined to receive the herald, who had to post up his challenge and depart without an audience (Manuel Fraga Iribarne, *Don Diego de Saavedra y Fajardo y la diplomacia de su época*, Madrid, 1956, pp. 152–3, n. 272).

CHAPTER XI

WAR WITH FRANCE

By May 1635 a Franco-Spanish war had come to seem a necessary evil. Neither Richelieu nor Olivares entertained many illusions about the internal condition of their respective countries; both longed for a durable peace which would allow them to set their houses in order; but both had been driven to the reluctant conclusion that the only possible prelude to such a peace was war.

The arguments that prompted this conclusion stemmed from the conviction of each of the two statesmen that the policies of the other gravely endangered the vital interests of his country. So far as Spain was concerned, those interests were primarily determined by the strategic problems involved in bringing help to the Emperor and in continuing the war against the rebellious United Provinces. One of the principal axioms of Spanish policy, under Olivares as under his predecessors, was that the route from Milan to Flanders must at all costs be kept open.[1] It was to secure a route safe from French attack that Spanish troops under the duke of Feria had occupied the Valtelline in 1620. It was to obtain control of the passages of the Rhine that Spain had seized on the opportunity afforded by the revolt of Bohemia and by the misdemeanours of the Elector Palatine to station its troops in the Lower Palatinate. It was in the hope of annexing the strongpoint of Casale, which would consolidate Spain's command of the route from Barcelona to Vienna, that Olivares embarked on his unfortunate Mantuan War.[2] The successes of the Swedes, and the French occupation of the duchy of Lorraine in 1633, had both endangered the 'Spanish road'. To counter the threat a Spanish army of Alsace was established under the duke of Feria in 1633[3] and the next year the danger temporarily receded when the Cardenal Infante beat the Swedes at Nördlingen on his march from Italy to Flanders.

---

[1] See A. van der Essen, *Le Cardinal-Infant*, vol. I, ch. 3.
[2] See above, p. 262, and Michael Roberts, *Gustavus Adolphus*, vol. II, p. 430.
[3] Van der Essen, vol. I, p. 105. The duke of Feria, the former viceroy of Catalonia and one of the few surviving Spanish commanders of any ability, died in January 1634.

Spain's victory at Nördlingen made France's entry into the war inevitable. The road that was a lifeline to Spain seemed to Richelieu to threaten France with death by strangulation. Now that the noose was closing again, and the Swedes were no longer strong enough to come to France's rescue, it could count only upon itself. Yet Richelieu had grave doubts as to his country's capacity to stand the strain of war.[1] Like Olivares, he shrank from open conflict, and it was significant that the actual outbreak of war in May 1635 was both preceded and almost immediately followed by negotiations for peace.[2] Both men, while preparing themselves for battle, spent much of their time anxiously looking over their shoulders at the disarray in the rear, and neither found much cause for comfort. France, painfully adjusting itself to heavier taxation and to changed economic circumstances as prices ceased to rise and harvests failed, had been shaken by a whole series of riots and revolts.[3] But at least Richelieu had largely succeeded in keeping his country free from the central European conflagration of the 1620's and early 1630's. Spain, on the other hand, had been consistently at war since 1621. Spanish troops had been fighting in Flanders, in Italy, in Central Europe and in the New World. Spanish money had financed innumerable military operations. Reserves of men and money were therefore already running low by May 1635, at the very moment when vast new supplies of both would be necessary.

It was true that the Castilians, unlike the French, had borne their sufferings with remarkable stoicism. Castile, however, was running dry as a reservoir of manpower. The recruiting of troops was a pitiful affair.

I have observed these levies [wrote the English ambassador within a fortnight of the outbreak of war], and I find the horses so weak as the most of them will never be able to go to the rendezvous, and those very hardly gotten. The infantry so unwilling to serve as they are carried like galley-slaves, which serves not the turn, and so far short in number of what is purposed as they come not to one of three....[4]

---

[1] G. Pagès, *La Guerre de Trente Ans* (Paris, 1949), p. 182.

[2] See A. Leman, *Richelieu et Olivares* (Lille, 1938).

[3] See B. F. Porshnev, *Die Volksaufstände in Frankreich vor der Fronde* (Leipzig, 1954), and R. Mousnier, 'Recherches sur les soulèvements populaires en France avant la Fronde', *Revue d'Histoire Moderne et Contemporaine*, vol. v (1958), pp. 81–113.

[4] BM. Eg. MS 1820, fo. 474, Hopton to Windebank, 31 May 1635.

The sight of the ragged columns that trudged the roads beneath the Castilian sun brought home the urgent need for recruits from the other provinces. Men were needed not only for the defence of Spain itself, but for service abroad. It was essential to have proper information about the numbers of men in the country capable of bearing arms, and during the spring and summer of 1635, viceroys were kept busy trying to extract from the towns details of the number of adult male inhabitants and of the contents of the municipal arsenals. The duke of Cardona, in Catalonia, had managed by September to obtain answers from 211 towns and villages. Since the towns themselves were expected to provide the necessary information, the list finally forwarded to Madrid was inevitably incomplete and incorrect. The 211 places could boast between them 26,981 men fit for war, and 23,157 weapons, but the names of a number of important towns were missing, and the figures provided by others looked very untrustworthy.[1] In Spain, as all over early seventeenth century Europe, the increasing awareness of the need for statistical information was as yet unaccompanied by administrative methods which would ensure its accuracy.

If Castile's declining reserves of manpower must be supplemented from the resources of the Crown of Aragon, the same had long been true of its diminishing financial reserves. The tax system in Castile, badly organized, badly administered, unevenly distributed, was increasingly self-defeating: the more taxes imposed on Castile the less appeared to be their yield. Olivares guessed that seven millions out of every ten disappeared in the process of collection.[2] At the beginning of May 1635, even before the coming of war with France, the Council of Finance found itself committed for the current year to an expenditure of no less than 11 million ducats, compared with 8 million ducats a decade earlier. It considered and turned down one suggestion after another for new methods of raising this money. A further increase in the *millones* was rejected because, as a tax on articles of consumption, it primarily affected the poor, who simply could not pay. Past experience suggested the folly of restarting the minting of a *vellón* coinage. 'A general property tax—an expedient never tried in these kingdoms, nor in others except perhaps in some republics—would not be well

[1] AGS: GA, leg. 1366, *Lista de los hombres aptos para la guerra*...13 Sept. 1635.
[2] BM: Add. MS 25,689, *Consulta del Conde Duque a SM*, fo. 232.

20-2

received. . . .' The creation of more offices would be useless, since there were insufficient applicants for the present offices on sale. The confiscation of money coming from the Indies for private persons would have serious consequences for Sevillan trade. . . . The Council of Finance, as so often, was at a loss.[1]

While the outbreak of hostilities with France inevitably meant more demands for men and money from the various provinces of the Monarchy, and a heavier Castilian pressure on each and all of those provinces, it meant something further to Catalonia. The Principality was France's immediate neighbour. Already in an area of considerable strategic importance, as a transit centre for men and money despatched from Spain to Italy, it now became in addition a potential battlefront. The new military significance of Catalonia as Spain's outer bastion against a French attack immediately lifted the problem of Castilian-Catalan relations on to a different level of importance. Indeed, from May 1635 a third stage may be said to have opened in the relationship of the two countries. Until 1626 the problem of Catalonia had been the problem of the entire Crown of Aragon: how Madrid could tap the resources of provinces which were not contributing to the needs of the Monarchy in proportion to their presumed ability. From 1626 to 1635 it had constituted a separate problem, which had remained embarrassingly unsolved. The great contest that had raged around the independent behaviour and financial power of the city of Barcelona had proved indecisive. Olivares felt frustrated, the Catalans felt trapped, and the mutual mistrust that arose from each new source of friction—from the Crown's failure to obtain loans, from the disaster of the Corts of 1632, from the dispute over the *quints*—only made it more difficult to preserve a sense of proportion. With each failure, Olivares was confirmed in his conviction that the Catalans were evading their responsibilities at a moment when the future of the Faith and of the Monarchy was at stake; and each time, the universal preoccupations of the Monarchy had made it impossible to reach any satisfactory decision on the specific problem of Catalonia.

Now, in 1635, came a new danger, long foreshadowed. Was it not possible that, instead of the Crown's general preoccupations interfering with the solution of the Catalan problem, the specific problem of

[1] AGS: Hacienda, leg. 730, no. 168, consulta, 2 May 1635.

Catalonia might itself begin to impinge upon matters of more universal concern? In fact, might not the Catalan problem, until now only a marginal question, be transformed by mismanagement or mischance into the central problem of the Monarchy? The chances of this may still have seemed remote in the spring of 1635, but the changed international situation at least gave these questions some meaning. The key to Spain's security lay in the response of the Catalans to a French invasion. Those who knew the Catalans argued that, with war on their doorstep, they would abandon their uncooperative behaviour of the preceding years. But supposing they did not? If the menace of a French attack had done something to increase the possibility of closer cooperation between Barcelona and Madrid, it had also immeasurably increased the dangers if the two capitals remained estranged. If anything were to go wrong, a national problem could very easily assume an international complexion. The French could hardly be expected to stand idle on the frontier in the event of a Castilian-Catalan conflict. There was little comfort for Olivares in the knowledge that the province which represented the first line of defence against France was entering the war politically disaffected, its many problems of relationship with Castile all unsolved.

The disadvantages of embarking on a war saddled with a liability of this kind very soon became apparent. On 14 June 1635 Olivares prepared a master-plan of campaign, which, in his own words, would either 'win and finish the war with supreme brevity, or else utterly finish with the Monarchy'[1] The plan involved turning Catalonia into the *plaza de armas*—the parade-ground—of Spain. The king should go in person to the Principality, and there head an army of 40,000 men, of whom 10,000 would be raised in the Crown of Aragon. Depending upon the requirements of the Emperor, it could then be decided where this army could most usefully undertake a diversion. If the state of Italian affairs so demanded, the king could move with his entire army and the Catalan militia to Italy; Louis XIII, occupied in Flanders, would then lose his Italian allies. If Louis should decide to come to the help of Italy, the Flanders-based cavalry of the Cardenal Infante would strike towards Paris. Alternatively, if all were going well in Italy, the army in Catalonia could advance into southern France, and the French,

---

[1] AGS: Est., leg. 2656, *El Conde Duque sobre lo que se debe disponer para executar la jornada de VM*, 14 June 1635.

caught by a triple-pronged attack from Flanders, the Empire and the Pyrenees, would surely sue for peace.

The formulation of this grandiose plan for rapid victory left the Conde Duque prostrate, but heroically aware of the vast gamble on which he was embarking. At the end of the document he scrawled in his own hand:

My head cannot bear the light of a candle or of the window.... To my mind this will lose everything irremediably or be the salvation of the ship. Here go religion, king, kingdom, nation, everything, and, if our strength is insufficient, let us die in the attempt. Better to die, and more just, than to fall under the dominion of others, and most of all of heretics, as I consider the French to be. Either all is lost, or else Castile will be head of the world, as it is already head of Your Majesty's Monarchy.

The Conde Duque was probably correct in his assumption that Spain's best hope of survival lay in a rapid end to the war. Even sudden defeat would be preferable to creeping exhaustion. But any military scheme conceived on so vast a scale demanded gifts of organization such as neither the Conde Duque himself, nor any other Spanish leader, had yet displayed. It was always difficult for the Conde Duque to grasp that an army of 40,000 on paper was not necessarily an army of 40,000 on the battlefield. But even assuming that such an army could be gathered at short notice, a further difficulty must be taken into account. The choice of Catalonia as a military base introduced certain complications which could not for long be ignored.

One obvious complication, which worried the duke of Cardona more than it worried Olivares, was the difficulty of provisioning a large army in Catalonia. The harvest of 1635 was poor, producing in the counties of Rosselló and Cerdanya only a quarter of its normal yield. Cardona reported that an army could not be maintained in Catalonia on the local supplies of barley and corn,[1] but his warning was ignored by Madrid, and on 26 August 1635 the city of Barcelona was informed of the king's intention to return. The grand design was getting under way.

The news of the king's forthcoming return gave satisfaction in Barcelona, which was now on very bad terms with the king's representative, the duke of Cardona. The absence of viceroy and Audiència

[1] ACA: CA, leg. 279, Cardona to King, 11 Aug. 1635.

angered the city, which rejected a request from the king, forwarded by Cardona, that it should raise 2000 men to resist the French. It had given the king 40,000 *lliures* and could do no more.[1] Barcelona clearly expected some *merced* or reward for its service, but none had been given, in spite of repeated requests to the marquis of Villafranca by the city authorities during the summer months. It was only in early September that the city received a token of the royal grace in the release of the four men imprisoned fifteen months earlier for their part in the riot over the *quints*.[2]

The act of royal clemency was not, however, followed, as might have been expected, by the arrival of the king. September and October passed, and still the king did not come. Delay was nothing new at Madrid, but on this occasion it was increased by unexpected opposition at the Council table to Olivares's grand design. The project was easy enough to criticize, especially the part of it relating to Catalonia, since a royal visit to the Principality would naturally revive the much-discussed question of whether the Catalan Corts should continue in a state of suspended animation. The return of the king was well enough in its way, but the return of the king with an army at his back raised difficult questions of governmental policy towards the Catalans. Did the dispatch of an army to Catalonia imply that force was to be used against the Principality? The count of Castrillo, who had shown himself an advocate of leniency to the Catalans in the discussions on the *quints*, assumed that it did, and opposed the scheme accordingly. While he admitted that the plan had its conveniences for the prosecution of the war in Italy, he considered that there was no need for the king to leave Madrid. It was, he held, in no way expedient to use armed force against the Catalans, least of all at a time when the king was present in the Principality. The Inquisitor-General agreed with Castrillo that a royal expedition was unnecessary. 'Barcelona', he said, 'is a trivial thing to justify the moving of so vast a machine. Any minister of Your Majesty could crush Barcelona to the ground.'[3]

The opposition of Castrillo, the Inquisitor-General and others to the king's projected journey drew a written reply from Olivares.[4] It was

---

[1] AHB: LC, 1635–6, fo. 34, City to King, 21 July 1635.
[2] ACA: CA, leg. 280, no. 25, consulta, 3 Aug. 1635.
[3] AHN: Est., leg. 860, no. 39, *Votos*, 7 Nov. 1635.
[4] AHN: Est., leg. 860, no. 39, paper by Olivares, 14 Nov. 1635.

rumoured that he was forcing the king to go on this journey. Such reports were absurd. The journey was essential if Milan and Catalonia were to be saved. Almost ten years had passed during which the king had been unable to conclude the Catalan Corts, 'and those vassals have played no part in assisting the Crown, have shown themselves useless for service, and have been tolerated in their attitude in a manner little befitting the dignity and power of His Majesty. And indeed I can see no occasion for correcting things, if the present opportunity is missed.' Castrillo's assumption was right: Olivares's grand design for the defeat of France included a grand design for the settling of the Catalan question.

When the matter of the king's journey was brought before the Council of State on 17 November, the Council proved to be evenly divided, with the Catalan problem as one of the outstanding points of disagreement. The duke of Alburquerque, the count of Castrillo and the Inquisitor-General all opposed the plan, while the duke of Villahermosa, the count of la Puebla and the marquis of Mirabel spoke in its favour. The count of la Puebla thought that it represented an excellent opportunity for settling the affairs of Catalonia,

not because I think that things will reach such an extreme as to make the use of force necessary, but because, with Your Majesty in such difficulties, they will be obliged to do what they have hitherto refused to do. And Your Majesty by appearing in arms, will be better placed to exercise the royal prerogative of clemency, guaranteeing their laws and constitutions, and only demanding of them equality with the other kingdoms in their contributions to the king's service. For it would be very unfortunate and unjust if the Catalans, while sharing with the other kingdoms the benefits accruing to the Monarchy, should be unwilling in time of need to contribute towards its defence.[1]

The division at the meeting of 17 November was unsatisfactory to the Conde Duque, and the unfortunate Council found itself having to debate the same subject once again only two days later. It was not surprising that opinions remained unchanged, but it was significant that in this discussion the emphasis had shifted from the military possibilities of the king's journey to a consideration of its consequences for Catalonia. The *consultas* produced on the subject are interesting because of the unexpectedly strong opposition to Olivares which they reveal—an opposition that crystallized on the Catalan question. Open defiance of Olivares in the Councils became increasingly infrequent during the

[1] AGS: Est., leg. 2655, consulta, 19 Nov. 1635.

later years of his government, and Alburquerque and Castrillo spoke now with a directness which is not to be found at the Council table in the crucial years 1639 and 1640. But it is impossible to tell how far the Catalan question was responsible for this opposition, and how far it merely served as an excuse. One of the many unsolved problems surrounding the Catalan revolution of 1640 concerns the extent to which the Catalans received encouragement from nobles like the duke of Sessa, who were determined to bring about the downfall of Olivares. There was certainly a group at Court which disapproved of Olivares's Catalan policy and secretly or openly sympathized with the Catalans in their misfortunes.[1] Some of this sympathy may well have sprung from a genuine conviction that Olivares's centralizing policy towards the Spanish empire was mistaken and misguided, but it is hard to resist the impression that the Catalans' opposition to Olivares gave considerable satisfaction to the many dissident elements at Court. The Conde Duque's attempts to extract money from Castilian nobles had antagonized the entire aristocracy, while his arrogant demeanour had alienated one after another of the great houses of Castile. When the count of Castrillo spoke in defence of the Catalans he may therefore have been fighting the battles of the aggrieved house of Haro, rather than taking a stand for the rights of the provinces.

Whatever the exact motives of those who opposed the king's expedition, Olivares knew perfectly well that the treatment of the Catalan problem, on which his critics had seized, made his scheme particularly vulnerable. He was always extemely sensitive to criticism, and his manœuvres when under attack displayed even more duplicity than usual. His general attitude at the Council table was often carefully calculated to leave those who heard him profoundly uncertain as to his real intentions. According to the English ambassador, 'it is usually his manner of proceeding to deliver his opinion in public contrary to that he thinks and means shall take effect, because on either side he finds his justification, in the good success of the action by the success itself, in the bad by his voice'.[2] On this occasion, rumour at Madrid held that the king was determined to go on the expedition, but the Conde Duque was secretly opposed to such a plan and intended to

[1] See Matías de Novoa's defence of provincial liberties, and his acid comments on Olivares's Catalan policy, in *Codoin*, vols. LXXVII, p. 332, and LXXX, p. 225.
[2] BM: Eg. MS 1820, fo. 266, Hopton to Lord Treasurer, 9 May 1633.

thwart it while apparently complying with his master's wishes.[1] There can be no doubt of Philip IV's desire to lead his armies to war in person. A little over a year later he was writing to his brother, the Cardenal Infante, of 'the supreme desire that I have to be a soldier'.[2] But the king's presence with his army seemed such an integral part of the grand design on which Olivares had set his heart, that it is hard to believe that he was working all the while to prevent the king's journey. He did however contrive in the November discussions to give the impression that he had lost his enthusiasm for the expedition, possibly in order to provoke enthusiasm among those who had been opposing it. If this was the purpose of his tactics, they were unsuccessful. Opposition remained as strong as ever.

It was on the Catalan question that the Conde Duque must silence his critics. The king's long reply on 19 November to the *consulta* of the Council of State took Alburquerque and his colleagues to task for assuming that it was his intention to use violence against the Catalans, 'or to conquer them....This is something that has never entered my mind.' It was the count of la Puebla's remarks which most accurately reflected the king's intentions.[3] Yet even if the king appeared in Catalonia with an army and used it only to overawe the Catalans, as the count of la Puebla suggested, the problem of what should be done with the Catalan Corts still remained. A large Junta, which included Dr Vinyes, was summoned for 6 December to discuss this point. All the Junta except Alburquerque agreed with Vinyes that the king must conclude the Corts, so that the various abuses in the government of the Principality might be reformed. Administration had collapsed in Catalonia, the Junta reported, because the royal patrimony in Catalonia was worth no more than 5000 ducats and there was no money for government. Alienated royal revenues could only be recovered if the king came in person, with troops to confer an additional authority on him. Once the war was over, it would be difficult to find such a good excuse for the presence of troops, which could exercise 'a restraining influence on those who try to prevent the passage of reforms in the Corts for reasons of self-interest'.[4]

---

[1] M. Hume, *The Court of Philip IV*, pp. 297–8, quoting Hopton.
[2] BM: Add. MS 14,007, fo. 65, Philip IV to Cardenal Infante, 12 April 1637.
[3] AGS: Est., leg. 2655, royal decree, 19 Nov. 1635.
[4] AGS: Est., leg. 2655, Junta, 6 Dec. 1635.

A hand-picked group of ministers had at last reached a clear-cut decision in favour of the king's journey, leaving Alburquerque, the sole representative of the dissidents to be summoned to the Junta, in a minority of one. This was the signal for which Olivares had been waiting. 'Now', he wrote to the Cardenal Infante, with whom he maintained a close correspondence,

it is all a question of the royal expedition.... To me, the Cortes appear absolutely necessary, although I feel so ill that I doubt whether I shall survive another day. But I must say what I think—that it is a scandal that those Cortes should still remain unfinished after ten years. Would to God a way might be found of avoiding this.[1]

The Conde Duque had good reason to feel embarrassment over the exact purpose of the expedition to Catalonia. The Catalan constitutions made it illegal to hold the Corts when there was an army in the Principality. If the king announced his intention of holding a Corts and arrived with an army, he would be acting unconstitutionally. If, on the other hand, he arrived without an army, he could neither further his designs against the French, nor enjoy that extra authority in his negotiations with the Catalans, which the presence of an army would confer upon him.[2]

This paradox, so perplexing to the Conde Duque, was no more than a new version of the problem he was always meeting in his policy towards Catalonia: the problem of whether to employ gentleness or harshness, *blandura* or *rigor*, in his dealings with the Principality. Temperamentally he seems to have longed for a swift and simple solution which would settle the question for once and all, but all the time he was uneasily aware of the impracticability of such a 'solution'. 'The purpose of the expedition', he wrote, in an endeavour to conjure away the dilemma, 'is not to crush the Principality, but only to overawe it a little, since the attitude of those vassals has not up to now compelled the resort to more drastic measures.' Anything else would make of Catalonia the 'ruin that has been made of Castile'.[3]

The unfortunate Philip IV was therefore to be cast in a somewhat ambiguous role, descending upon Catalonia with an olive branch in one hand and a sheathed sword in the other. This vision of royal

[1] RAH: 11-10-5, leg. 6, Olivares to Cardenal Infante, 10 Dec. 1635.
[2] AHN: Est., leg. 860, no. 39, paper by Olivares, 12 Dec. 1635.   [3] *Ibid.*

power allied to royal mercy long haunted the Conde Duque. It seemed to offer such an attractive compromise between excessive *blandura* on the one hand, and the many inconveniences of conquest on the other. The vision was not, however, to be realized. Marching orders were given for 21 January 1636 and then suddenly cancelled. No direct evidence has appeared to account for the cancellation, but it can perhaps be attributed to the unexpected resistance of the Castilian Cortes to the Crown's new fiscal demands,[1] and to the surprising strength of the opposition which the project had aroused. The decision to abandon the expedition seems to have been taken with reluctance, for the king, in a message to the Council of State on 30 March 1636, expressed the hope that they would not soon be regretting his final agreement with those who opposed the journey.[2]

The abandonment of the king's expedition meant that the Cardenal Infante's advance on Paris, which reached Corbie in August 1636, was deprived of the advantages which would have come from a simultaneous thrust by Spanish forces into the south of France. It also meant that the Catalan problem was again to be shelved. This was all the more unfortunate because of the unhappy state of the Principality since the removal of the viceregal administration to Girona. The departure of the government had entailed a heavy financial loss for the city of Barcelona, although, on the advice of its agent in Madrid, it was careful to refrain from making a formal protest.[3] It seemed wiser to wait and see whether the king might not be compelled to order the return of the administration to Barcelona of his own accord, for it was the viceregal administration itself which suffered most. The duke of Cardona resented his exile; he found himself 'totally useless, the way in which I have been left here, a viceroy in no more than name'.[4] The members of the Audiència shared his annoyance. All the documentary records had been left in Barcelona, accommodation in Girona was quite inadequate, and it had been necessary to prorogue a large number of cases indefinitely.[5] Although there may have been an element of special pleading in the unhappy picture of the Audiència's troubles painted by its own

[1] A. Rodríguez Villa, *La Corte y Monarquía de España en los años de 1636 y 37* (Madrid, 1886), p. 13.
[2] AGS: Est., leg. 2658, royal reply to consulta of 30 March 1636.
[3] AHB: CCO, 1635, fos. 179–81, Grau to Consellers, 17 Nov. 1635.
[4] ACA: CA, leg. 386, Cardona to King, 27 Dec. 1635.
[5] ACA: CA, leg. 279, no. 53, Audiènca to King, 9 Nov. 1635.

members, its request to return to Barcelona was fully supported by an outsider, Matías de Bayetolá. An Aragonese regent of the Council of Aragon, he had been commissioned in June 1635 to conduct the first full-scale *visita* or inquiry into the viceregal administration to be held since the reign of Philip III.[1] The time might not have seemed very opportune for an inquiry into the activities of the harassed royal officials in the Principality, but at least Bayetolá could see for himself the unfortunate effects of Olivares's Catalan policy upon the organs of the viceregal administration.

Not only was the government of Catalonia weakened and demoralized, but relations between the viceroy and the Catalans had become so bad that Barcelona sent a special ambassador to Madrid in March 1636 to request that Cardona should not be reappointed to the post when his three years of office came to an end.[2] It was becoming doubtful how far a province so disgruntled with its rulers could be relied upon in the event of foreign invasion. Bayetolá's first-hand experience of Catalonia made him pessimistic. 'The attitude of this people is terrible', he reported.[3] The Catalans would not offer money as a voluntary gift to the king to meet the emergency, since nobody was willing to give a penny unless he could make a profit out of it.[4] Nor would they offer themselves as soldiers. The only recruits were pardoned criminals; the rest had no mind to serve outside the Principality.[5]

With the growing manpower problem in Castile, the persistent refusal of the Catalans to take service under the king's colours was beginning to be of some consequence for the military fortunes of the Monarchy. Almost immediately after the abandonment of the projected royal visit, the situation in Italy deteriorated, and Olivares sent an urgent request to Cardona to cross at once by sea to Genoa, taking a contingent of Catalans with him. Cardona was compelled to reply not only that this was quite impossible, but that the Catalans even refused to enlist men for the defence of their own frontier. Only a few days before, some of the infantry so laboriously recruited by Bayetolá had moved off in the direction of France, taking their weapons with them,

[1] ACA: CA, leg. 280, no. 10, instructions for Bayetolá, 20 June 1635.
[2] AHB: LC, 1635–6, fo. 115, Consellers to Olivares, 22 March 1636.
[3] ACA: CA, leg. 235, no. 19, Bayetolá to J. L. de Villanueva, 3 Nov. 1635.
[4] *Ibid.* 12 April 1636.
[5] ACA: CA, leg. 386, Bayetolá to King, 29 Dec. 1635.

on hearing an entirely false rumour that they were to be ordered to embark.[1]

Further disappointments followed. At one moment, it was thought that an extra 8000 men at Milan might turn the tide, but the 8000 could only come from Catalonia. The king offered to suspend the lawsuit on the *quints* until the next Corts, if Barcelona would raise 3000 or 4000 men for six months,[2] but his offer was rejected.

If Barcelona were to behave as it should [burst out Olivares on hearing of the rejection] the whole province would follow suit... but it attempts to bargain over questions not only of grace but even of justice, to the detriment of the public welfare and of royal authority. And it is impossible not to add that, unless these vassals recover from their present blindness, it will be necessary to take some terrible steps which Your Majesty, in his mercy, has always been anxious to avoid....[3]

Barcelona continued to negotiate with just enough show of sincerity to make such measures unjustifiable, but the two sides were too far apart for success. Barcelona was interested in obtaining immunity from all further attempts to collect its *quints*, by offering payment of a lump sum. The ministers, on the other hand, were particularly anxious to break the city's spirit of independence,[4] and refused even to consider composition for the *quints* unless Barcelona first offered a paid force of infantrymen. The city council had no intention of levying citizens for foreign service against their will, and its unwillingness fully accorded with popular feeling. There was an ugly riot in Barcelona on 12 June when a gentleman of Barcelona called Joan Agustí Forés attempted to recruit a company of twenty-five men in return for a promise that the king would appoint him *veguer* of the city. He sought his recruits among the *segadors* who came to Barcelona at this season of the year to hire themselves out for harvesting. Since it happened to be a wet day, the *segadors* were unemployed. As they stood idly around, a rumour spread among them that some of their number had been forcibly detained by Forés to make up his company of recruits. The *segadors* set off for Forés's house, which they sacked with gusto, and the unfortunate owner was only saved by the prompt action of the city

[1] ACA: CA, leg. 232, no. 26, Cardona to King, 3 April 1636.
[2] AGS: Est., leg. 2658, consulta, 30 March 1636.
[3] AGS: Est., leg. 2658, consulta, 10 April 1636.
[4] AGS: Est., leg. 2657, consulta, 15 May 1636.

authorities in incarcerating him in the municipal prison. 'This province survives by a miracle,' commented Bayetolá, 'since there is no viceroy and nobody to administer justice.'[1]

Popular hostility and the threat of unrest provided an unfavourable background for the negotiations which the marquis of Villafranca, as the king's special representative, was conducting with the city for the supply of troops. For one moment he seemed near to success, but was foiled at the last minute by a reversal of votes in the Consell de Cent.[2] As a result of his failure, the unfortunate Valencians, who had offered 5000 men and several *donativos* during the last few years, were again called upon to fill the galleys that had just arrived from Italy.[3] It was not the first occasion on which Catalan stubbornness had cast an extra burden upon the Principality's neighbours.

The Conde Duque was losing patience. It was not only that the Catalans refused to give any troops of their own, but they were even encouraging desertions among the men who marched through the Principality for embarkation at Barcelona. 'If there were anyone', he said at a Junta in August, 'who would dare reduce that province without the presence of Your Majesty (a task which, with Your Majesty's presence, one hopes to God will be easy), he would deserve the greatest imaginable honours and rewards from Your Majesty. And really, it raises serious questions of principle to allow this business to drag on.'[4]

Although Olivares's remarks were made in the secrecy of the council chamber, the Catalans could be in no doubt about his general attitude. It was both unpleasant and unwise to remain perpetually in disfavour with the king and his minister. Moreover, the continued absence of the Audiència represented a considerable financial loss to the city. It seemed, then, that the time had come to make a conciliatory gesture. The moment was favourable. The duke of Cardona, after refusing the viceroyalty of Sicily,[5] had his viceroyalty of Catalonia prolonged for another three-year period, beginning in August 1636. He had no wish to remain exiled in north Catalonia, especially now that the appointment of Don Felipe de Silva to organize the defences made

[1] ACA: CA, leg. 387, Bayetolá to J. L. de Villanueva and to King, 14 June 1636.
[2] ACA: CA, leg. 386, Villafranca to King, 14 July 1636.
[3] ACA: CA, leg. 280, no. 47, consulta, 30 July 1636.
[4] AGS: Est., leg. 2657, consulta, 9 Aug. 1636.
[5] Rodríguez Villa, *La Corte y Monarquía*, p. 24.

his presence on the frontier unnecessary. Similarly, the city of Barcelona was anxious to have a viceroy in residence once more. Shortly after Cardona was sworn in for his next term of office at Perpinyà, a request arrived from Barcelona that he should take the oath there too. At the same time the city let it be known that it wished to settle its differences with the Crown, and Cardona decided that the time had come to resume negotiations.[1]

The Council of Aragon was willing to allow Cardona to negotiate, although without committing either himself or the king. The Protonotario made it clear, however, that Cardona would not be authorized to bargain away future revenues from the *quints*, although a settlement might be reached on the arrears. His reasons were less financial than political: 'these annual dues are the best curb on the city, and the only way to make it move in the direction desired by Your Majesty'.[2] Unaware that the Court intended at the most only a limited settlement, the city prepared to negotiate, and appointed sixteen commissioners to treat with Cardona, who had returned to Barcelona on 15 September. Negotiations went slowly, since the Court was in no hurry, and was at this moment more anxious for signs of submission from the city than for a full and immediate fiscal settlement. Cardona was instructed to obtain some token of submission before he reached any agreement on compounding for arrears of the *quints*, and it was suggested this token might take the form of six months' payment for a body of five hundred dragoons to be recruited in the Principality by the reformed bandit, Don Pere de Santa Cília.[3] The Consell de Cent took kindly to this suggestion, hoping that, as a minimum reward, the king would restore the Audiència to Barcelona,[4] and finally voted on 24 January 1637 to serve the king with 40,500 *escuts*.[5] The ministers at Madrid, while not impressed with the size of this unconditional gift, welcomed it as the first sign of thaw in the long winter of harsh relations with the Principality, and the Audiència was duly allowed to return.

This gift of money in January 1637 brought the sum total obtained from Barcelona since the outbreak of war with France to 80,500

---

[1] ACA: CA, leg. 279, no. 7, Cardona to King, 5 Sept. 1636.
[2] ACA: CA, leg. 279, no. 7, consulta, 12 Sept. 1636.
[3] ACA: CA, leg. 232, King to Cardona, 31 Dec. 1636.
[4] ACA: G, caja 2, M. Pérez to M. Tafalla, 24 Jan. 1637.
[5] ACA: CA, leg. 279, no. 6, Cardona to King, 25 Jan. 1637.

lliures, or the equivalent of one year of Barcelona's income. This was a considerable sum, but it came too late to repair Castilian-Catalan relations. The king's advisers were by now unable to see good in anything Catalan, and received any financial service from Barcelona as no more than the Crown's belated due. The Catalans, for their part, resented the indifference with which the king received their services, and watched with alarm the growth of anti-Catalan feeling among the ministers. Madrid's policy made them increasingly sure that their independence was threatened: that Olivares was determined to pick a quarrel with them however well they behaved. The Castilian assault on the Principality seemed all the time to be mounting, and adequate defence against the assault was becoming imperative.

While Barcelona was perfectly capable of conducting its own defence, the wider defence of the Principality's interests fell, in default of any vigour in the Diputació, to the Catalan clergy. They had already displayed their powers of resistance in the Vic troubles of 1634,[1] and, in spite of a temporary setback, they had no intention of abandoning their struggle against excessive taxation. While Barcelona was sparring with Madrid during 1636, the Provincial Council of the ecclesiastical province of Tarragona was in turbulent session. It had been summoned in February to vote the continuation of the *subsidio* and *excusado* for another five years. In spite of frantic manœuvres by the bishops and abbots, the canons, as always, were proving troublesome.[2] In a gathering over fifty strong, the bishops found themselves outnumbered, and when the Council was adjourned in July it had agreed to continue payment of the taxes only under certain stringent conditions.[3] The Council insisted that the king should not ask the pope for any new grace to impose taxes on the clergy during the next five years; it also agreed that all preaching in the Principality should be in Catalan.[4]

This linguistic provision by the Council of Tarragona inaugurated a vigorous pamphlet debate on a question of fundamental importance. Ever since the union of the Crowns, the Castilian language had been gaining ground among the upper classes in Catalonia, and Catalan was being permeated by Castilian expressions. The works of Castilian authors

[1] See above, p. 289.
[2] ACA: CA, leg. 280, no. 38, Prior of Sta Anna to Cardona, 12 Feb. 1636.
[3] ACA: CA, leg. 280, no. 38, Don Lluís Monsuar to Cardona, 19 June 1636.
[4] ACA: CA, leg. 387, Bishop of Barcelona to King, 4 April 1637.

were published in Castilian by Barcelona publishers, and enthusiastically read by the Barcelona public. In some Catalan churches, sermons were being delivered in Castilian, although it was not clear how far, if at all, Castilian was understood by the lower classes in Catalan society.[1] Although the Catalan language retained its vitality, the Principality had produced no native writers of real distinction during the sixteenth century, and some Catalans, like the embittered Alejandro de Ros,[2] had begun to regard their native language with contempt.

In attempting in 1636 to prevent the further dissemination of Castilian from the pulpits, the Catalan clergy had made an important move towards safeguarding Catalonia's existence as an independent national entity. Some Catalans had long recognized the danger to their national survival in the spread of the Castilian language: as early as 1557 Cristòfol Despuig had warned his compatriots that Castilian might gradually oust Catalan until finally the Principality would 'appear to have been conquered by the Castilians'.[3] The Castilians, for their part, had early seen the possibilities of political domination implicit in linguistic monopoly. 'Language is the perfect instrument of empire', remarked the bishop of Ávila to Isabella the Catholic, when Nebrija's Spanish grammar was presented to her in 1492.[4] The struggle that was now opening between the Castilian and Catalan languages, after a century of slow but unchecked Castilian infiltration, was therefore only one more aspect of the wider struggle between centralization and regionalism, between uniformity and diversity, that was being fought in the Spanish peninsula. 'La Castellana es lengua del Imperio'[5]— Castilian is the language of the Empire—and as long as Valencian or Catalan, or Portuguese, was talked in preference to Castilian, the unity of Spain for which Olivares was working could never be achieved.

As far as Olivares was concerned, the clergy's refusal to allow preaching in Castilian must have seemed only one more manifestation of an obstinate spirit of independence which strained the relationship between the Principality and its natural prince, and threatened to jeopardize the fortunes of the entire Spanish Monarchy. Why could the

---

[1] BC: Fullet Bonsoms 9967, Dr Diego Cisteller, *Memorial en defensa de la lengua catalana* (Tarragona, 1636).

[2] *Cataluña Desengañada*, p. 241.   [3] *Col·loquis de Tortosa*, p. 21.

[4] Quoted in Lewis Hanke, *Aristotle and the American Indians* (London, 1959), p. 8.

[5] BC: Fullet Bonsoms 9966, *Memorial en defensa de la lengua castellana* (n.d.).

Catalans not behave like the king's loyal vassals in his other provinces? Why did they insist on remaining so aloof from the heroic enterprise on which the Monarchy was engaged? Unable to recognize or appreciate in the behaviour of the Catalans a desperate anxiety about the future and an instinctive defensive reaction in the face of an overbearing Castile, Olivares attributed their intransigence to a wilful spirit of sedition. Somehow or other the spirit must be curbed and broken, if ever the Principality was to play its rightful part in the great international conflict.

In his plan for the Union of Arms, the Conde Duque had suggested that military co-operation between the provinces represented the most hopeful first step towards their eventual integration. He never abandoned this idea. An essential feature of his dealings with the various provinces of the peninsula was his persistent attempt to secure troops for service beyond their own frontiers. This would at once dispose of those mediaeval traditions which imposed careful restrictions on the use of the provincial militias, and would help to dispel the deeply engrained assumption that a province's obligations to its monarch ended at its own frontier. In 1635 and 1636 he had met with some success in this policy: Valencia in particular had performed considerable services, including the provision of 5000 volunteers for Italy.[1] But Catalonia, in all the sixteen years since the accession of Philip IV, had provided no more than a few hundred amnestied criminals for service in the royal armies.

It was essential, then, both for immediate military necessities and for the purpose of pressing Catalonia into the common Spanish mould, that the Principality should provide an adequate body of troops as soon as possible. Since Catalonia lay along the enemy frontier, a pretext was easily found: troops were required for the Principality's own defence against the French. On 6 May 1637, at a meeting of the *Junta de Ejecución*—a recently created body which soon established itself as the principal policy-making organ at Madrid—it was decided that Cardona should lure the Catalans into offering five or six thousand men by telling them that the existing garrison was needed for service in Italy and native troops would now be expected to man their own frontiers.[2] Cardona was doubtful about this manœuvre.

---

[1] ACA: CA, leg. 280, no. 47, consultas of 30 July and 26 Aug. 1636.
[2] AGS: GA, leg. 1182, Junta de Ejecución, 6 May 1637.

As regards using the Catalans for their own defence [he replied to Olivares], we shall try to do so by the most subtle methods. But I beg Your Excellency to permit me to tell you that these people are temperamentally so lacking in docility, even when their own welfare is at stake, that even when aware of this they remain suspicious, and will take no action until necessity compels.[1]

Olivares, accustomed by long experience to this particular Catalan characteristic, had already decided to give necessity a helping hand. The plan of campaign against France for 1637 was to take the form of a diversion against Languedoc, which would relieve the pressure on Italy, Flanders and the Empire. This diversion was to be carried out from Catalonia by an army 15,000 strong, of which 6,000 troops were to be Catalans.[2] The existence of military operations on the Catalan frontier would provide complete justification for the summoning of Catalans to the standards. This was done on 13 June 1637 in the traditional manner and according to the proper forms, by calling all able-bodied men to arms for the defence of the Principality in conformity with the usage of *Princeps Namque*.[3]

In deciding to play a traditional game, Olivares had unfortunately failed to take the precaution of abiding by the traditional rules. According to expert Catalan opinion, the proclamation of *Princeps Namque* was only valid if the king were present in the Principality at the time. Philip IV had not been present, and the Catalans were quick to take advantage of the legal loophole this gave them. The marquis of Villafranca acidly reported that the 6000 men were being transformed into 6000 lawsuits 'which will last for years, while the province looks on and laughs'.[4] While the Catalans argued that the proclamation was invalid, the Council of Aragon decided that it was justified by precedent, and a special Junta at Madrid agreed that, in the event of a test case coming before the Catalan Audiència, Cardona should take care to win over any intransigent judges by the use of bribes and threats.[5]

With the shadow of war and constitutional conflict hanging over the Principality, August was a gloomy month. 'May God set things right! Those who have gone will not have a very good time, and I

---

[1] AGS: GA, leg. 1182, Cardona to Olivares, 12 May 1637.
[2] AGS: GA, leg. 1182, instructions for Cardona, 26 May 1637.
[3] BC: Fullet Bonsoms 5394, proclamation dated Madrid, 4 June 1637.
[4] AGS: GA, leg. 1182, Villafranca to Olivares, 17 June 1637.
[5] ACA: CA, leg. 349, consulta, 3 Aug. 1637.

fear that those of us who remain will not fare very much better.'[1] But those who had gone were very few indeed. When the army crossed the frontier on 29 August 1637 and laid siege to the French fortress of Leucata, there was not a Catalan to be seen, although Girona was raising one company, and another was on its way from Empordà.[2] While the Catalans had no love for the French, they liked to do things in their own time, and the machinery for raising troops in the various towns of the Principality always moved with ponderous slowness on these occasions. Barcelona itself, disgruntled at the king's failure to recognize its recent service by the granting of some signal *merced*, refused for a long time even to consider the enlisting of troops, but finally responded to Cardona's persistent appeals by agreeing on 7 September to raise a company of five hundred men, with three months' pay. The Council of Aragon was very pleased: 'Really, although it is hard to make them act as they should whenever they think that something is being asked of them which conflicts with their constitutions, they have never failed on the actual occasion; and this city has itself rendered some outstanding services since Your Majesty's succession.'[3]

The contribution from Barcelona which called forth this unexpected tribute proved to be of little more than symbolic value. It took several weeks to assemble even three hundred of the five hundred men, and when the company was eventually formed, its behaviour on the march was no better than that of the foreign troops about whom the Catalans so constantly complained. According to one of the Barcelona company commanders, 'they are dissolute men, quite shameless about stealing hens and sheep....It is all wrong that these soldiers, who are natives of the province, should conduct themselves so badly.'[4]

While Barcelona's troops were still on their inglorious march, the French relieving force unexpectedly broke the lines of the besieging armies at Leucata on 27 September and inflicted a sharp defeat upon them. The news caused consternation in Madrid. The king ordered

[1] ACA: G, caja 2, Dr F. Millet to Don Cristóbal Icart, 7 Aug. 1637.
[2] AHB: CCO, 1637–8, fo. 19, Cardona to Barcelona, 3 Sept. 1637.
[3] ACA: CA, leg. 282, no. 58, consulta, 14 Sept. 1637. Cardinal Borja had become president of the Council of Aragon in succession to the duke of Alburquerque in July 1637. According to one contemporary, 'il était sans valeur, il n'avait aucune aptitude pour les affaires politiques; l'on voyait, par son exemple, que l'Espagne était entièrement dépourvue d'hommes et que ce vaste empire allait à la ruine'. Quoted in A. Leman, *Urbain VIII et la Rivalité de la France et de la Maison d'Autriche*, p. 119.   [4] AHB: CCO, 1637–8, fo. 45, Miquel Rodo to City, 3(?) Oct. 1637.

a full investigation of this 'disgraceful, disastrous and unauthorized action...if only because history will condemn the engagement, and with reason'.[1] Olivares recognized that the blame lay with the army commander, Juan Cerbellón, who displayed a notable lack of judgment;[2] but there were many in Madrid ready to point an accusing finger at the Catalans.[3] If the Catalans deserved blame, however, it was less for their part in the day's disaster than for their almost entire absence from it. Although most of the towns in the Principality had by now offered troops, the only ones actually to have reached Leucata by the day of the battle were those from Girona, Empúries, Olot, Santa Pau and Peralada.[4]

Campaigning weather was now past, and revenge for the defeat at Leucata must be postponed till the following year. The Catalans were as anxious as Madrid for this revenge. The defeat had come as an unpleasant surprise, and the royal officials in the Principality found the towns and cathedral chapters unusually willing to promise troops for three months' service in the coming spring. The aristocracy, however, still proved recalcitrant. Only two barons had offered men: the others not only refused, but attempted to persuade the Diputats that they should declare illegal a general convocation of the militia.[5] The barons had no intention of spending money when it could be avoided; nor did they wish to lose their vassals to the army. Their vassals themselves showed a similar lack of enthusiasm, Cardona's own vassals seeking legal aid against his orders that they should enlist, and protesting that they were under no obligation to endure this kind of servitude. Every one of them would rather have paid for exemption than gone to the war.[6]

Since the campaign had proved a disaster, and the Catalans had given so little effective help to the royal armies, the Leucata affair was a sad disappointment to the Conde Duque. By enlisting companies, however belatedly, the Catalans had certainly shown some signs of grace; but they had equally shown that they had no mind to infringe their own constitutions by crossing the borders of the Principality. The issue of Catalan co-operation therefore remained open, with a conclusive test

[1] AGS: GA, leg. 1182, King on consulta of 6 Nov. 1637.
[2] BM: Add. MS 14007, fo. 87, Olivares to Cardenal Infante, 28 Oct. 1637.
[3] AHB: CCO, 1637–8, fo. 57, Joan Grau to Consellers, 17 Oct. 1637.
[4] AGS: GA, leg. 1182, Cardona to King, 7 Oct. 1637.
[5] ACA: CA, leg. 282, no. 64, Cardona to King, 26 Nov. 1637.
[6] AGS: GA, leg. 1182, Cardona to King, 22 Oct. 1637.

yet to come. For the present, the troops must be billeted in Catalonia for the winter, and preparations made against the next campaign. It was to be hoped that the coming year would be more successful than the present, 'when our fortunes could hardly be in a worse state'.[1] It was also to be hoped that the new year would see the real entry of the Catalans into the Union of Arms. But if this occurred, it would not be under the leadership of Cardona. Always sensitive to any slurs on his reputation, and quick to sulk when he felt his efforts belittled, Cardona was not prepared to remain at his post while he was being regarded as a scapegoat for the Spanish defeat. He therefore submitted his resignation as viceroy of Catalonia after four hard years of service which had earned him no love and few thanks. This was not, however, to be the end of his public career. In spite of his disgrace, he still had one more brief appearance to make on the stage. But that was two years ahead. In the meantime he disappeared from the public eye, and Catalonia stood in need of a viceroy.

[1] BM: Add. MS 14,007, fo. 87, Olivares to Cardenal Infante, 28 Oct. 1637.

CHAPTER XII

THE DIPUTACIÓ RESURGENT

If Olivares's Catalan policy was to succeed, it was necessary to find for the viceroyalty of Catalonia a man who could combine authority among the Catalans with a proper degree of subordination to Madrid. The duke of Cardona, with his vast Catalan estates and his natural sense of dignity, had always enjoyed the respect of the Catalans, even when they regarded him with dislike. On the other hand, he had never been a consistently pliable instrument of the Court. Always very conscious of his own importance—'being who I am'[1]—he had never been afraid to strike out on an independent line, and was ready to threaten resignation whenever he felt that he was not being properly treated.[2] There was much to be said for finding a more compliant character as his successor, but he must, like Cardona, be at least nominally a native of the Principality if he were to have any chance of carrying out successfully the unpopular policies devised by Madrid.

The choice of the Court fell on a Catalan noble of secondary rank, Don Dalmau de Queralt, the count of Santa Coloma. The truculent behaviour of Santa Coloma in the Corts of 1626 would hardly seem to have singled him out as a future loyal servant of the king, but Olivares and the Protonotario had chosen their man with care. They knew that he was extremely ambitious for promotion to the rank of marquis, which would raise the family of Queralt above its rivals, the Rocabertí. They knew also that he was a man of intelligence and cunning, and the noble with the largest clientele in Catalonia. They hoped now to capitalize on the great influence enjoyed by Santa Coloma in the Principality—an influence which had in the past caused considerable concern to Madrid. As recently as 1637 the Council of Aragon reported that he was restless and aggrieved because he considered himself out of favour, and that this made him a potential danger in the Corts.[3] The Council suggested that his energies should be harnessed to some useful

---

[1] ACA: CA, leg. 503, Cardona to Protonotario, 6 March 1632.
[2] Cf. his letter of resignation to the King, 26 Sept. 1635, ACA: CA, leg. 279, no. 64.
[3] ACA: CA, leg. 281, no. 21, consulta, 11 Feb. 1637.

employment, like the command of the still non-existent Catalan galleys, but the king replied that the most important thing was to get him out of the Principality. He was accordingly offered the post of ambassador to Venice, which he declined.[1] His refusal, which he may have lived to regret, left the problem of his future as perplexing as ever, until it was characteristically solved by Cardona, who on his own initiative made Santa Coloma his representative as captain-general of Catalonia while he was away at the front.[2]

Santa Coloma had therefore already enjoyed some taste of office when he received the king's letter of 6 February 1638 offering him the viceroyalty. He consulted with his friend Don Josep Margarit, who advised him not to accept, on the grounds that he would forfeit his popularity among the Catalans in general and the aristocracy in particular.[3] Santa Coloma ignored this wise advice, and on 13 February accepted the appointment.[4] Don Alexos de Marimón, the wily old Governor of Catalonia, whose sins of omission and commission had exasperated Cardona, was quick to congratulate his new master: 'Better late than never to admit that there are natives capable of governing Catalonia, without having recourse to bishops or other outsiders....'[5]

Marimón's letter of congratulation suggests that, by virtue of being a native Catalan, Santa Coloma could count on an initial fund of good-will in the Principality as he entered on his term of office. But this very advantage automatically became a disadvantage in his dealings with Madrid, which could not be expected to place such immediate confidence in a native viceroy as it would in a Castilian grandee. Since Santa Coloma was determined to obtain the trust and esteem of Olivares, it was clear that he would have to walk very delicately along the tight-rope between Barcelona and Madrid. The precarious character of the balancing act was emphasized by the very first letter that the new viceroy received from the Conde Duque. After the conventional congratulations on his new appointment, the letter continued: 'the maintenance of the troops which are in the Principality or are on their way to it, is

---

[1] ACA: CA, leg. 281, no. 21, Cardona to King, 9 May 1637.
[2] ACA: CA, leg. 281, no. 21, Cardona to King, 3 Aug. 1637.
[3] BUB: MS 115, Sevillà's history, fo. 130.
[4] ACA: CA, leg. 389, Santa Coloma to King, 13 Feb. 1638.
[5] ACA: G, caja 3, Marimón to Santa Coloma, 17 Feb. 1638.

a matter of supreme importance....[1] The Conde Duque could not afford to lose the army which had been fighting on the Catalan frontier, for it contained seasoned men, and there were few enough of these for all the tasks demanded of the Spanish armies. Only a month later he was writing again to Santa Coloma:

I wish I could express to Your Excellency the great concern which the conservation of these troops gives me. I have constantly to write to Your Excellency on this point, since if it is overlooked, everything that has been spent and will in future be spent, and all the work that has been done, will have been lost...For God's sake stop these desertions, which are the ruin of everything....[2]

Olivares's natural concern for the survival of the army was unfortunately not easily reconciled with the interests of the country on which it was billeted. For several years, troops had marched across Catalonia on their way to the ports, while others had been quartered in the Principality. These troops often behaved badly: in December 1637 the Diputats submitted a detailed complaint about the tribulations which the province had been suffering at the hands of the military—how the Neapolitan *tercio* quartered for eight months in Vilafranca del Penedès had seized its own billets and extorted money from the citizens, while in a small town in Rosselló the four cavalry companies there had billeted eighteen men to a house.[3] Such complaints, and such behaviour, were normal in Europe at a time when semi-mercenary armies were indifferently disciplined and irregularly paid, and although governments were well aware of the misery and resentment caused by the presence of troops among the local population, there was little they could do about it. The Leucata army billeted in Catalonia over the winter of 1637 consisted of over 10,000 men of differing nationalities, and while the ministers at Madrid were agreed on the importance of avoiding conflicts between these men and the local inhabitants,[4] it was not easy to translate this determination into practical measures. Santa Coloma's predecessors, the dukes of Feria and Cardona, had both tried and failed. Santa Coloma himself issued a printed order emphasizing the need for preserving peace between the soldiers and civilians. Troops

[1] ACA: G, caja 3, Olivares to Santa Coloma, 2 Feb. 1638.
[2] ACA: G, caja 4, Olivares to Santa Coloma, 6 March 1638.
[3] ACA: CA, leg. 280, no. 13, Memorial from Diputats, 4 Dec. 1637.
[4] ACA: CA, leg. 281, no. 24, consulta, 17 Oct. 1637.

were to take nothing from householders except the very limited necessities to which they were entitled under the Catalan constitutions. The first offence would be punished by strokes of the lash, the second by relegation to the galleys.[1] But as the captains cheated their men of half their pay of one *real* a day,[2] the troops took to robbery to keep themselves alive, and the offences continued.

While Santa Coloma was expected to keep the peace between the troops and the Catalans, and so run the risk of discontenting both, he was also expected to ensure that the Principality was properly fortified. This again threatened to embroil him with his compatriots. Some 370,000 *escuts* were required to build and strengthen the fortifications, and the Council of Aragon considered that, as the royal revenues in the Principality were insufficient, the money should come from the Catalans themselves as it was to be used for their own defence.[3] A sum of money had been set aside by the Corts of 1585 for purposes of defence, but Cardona, after a long tussle, had prized out of the Diputats most of the remainder of this sum.[4] In the past, when more money was needed, the kings of Aragon had assembled the Corts. Since this was now out of the question, the Audiència could only suggest that the viceroy should negotiate with individual towns, offering them new privileges in return for cash.[5] It was obvious that some such measures must be adopted if the fortifications were ever to be completed, and the town with which it was natural to begin was Barcelona.

Convinced that a reconciliation between Barcelona and the Court was essential if the Principality were ever to participate fully in the war, Santa Coloma felt that a gesture from Madrid offered the best hope of breaking the deadlock. Barcelona should be given one of the *mercedes* which it had for so long been led to expect, and then negotiations could begin again on the *quints* and on other outstanding points of dispute.[6] The Council of Aragon gave qualified approval to this plan, but the king's reply to its *consulta* only emphasized that rigidity of ministerial policy towards Catalonia which Santa Coloma was so anxious to soften: 'It is for them to meet these expenses, and their

[1] ACA: G, caja 4, proclamation, 3 March 1638.
[2] ACA: G, caja 5, Dr Francesc Joan Magarola to Santa Coloma, 2 April 1638.
[3] ACA: CA, leg. 228, no. 3, consulta, 1 Feb. 1638.
[4] AGS: GA, leg. 1182, Cardona to King, 30 Oct. 1637.
[5] ACA: CA, leg. 390, report from Audiència, 27 March 1638.
[6] ACA: CA, leg. 390, consulta, 6 April 1638.

general obduracy is forcing me to take special steps to prevent the delays in fortification from proving prejudicial.'

The king's concern at the delay was to be explained by the probability that the Catalan frontier would again be a theatre of operations in the coming campaign season. Olivares hoped to revenge Leucata and to attract the enemy to Catalonia.[1] When he had originally proposed this, he came into conflict with the count of Oñate, whose years at the Court in Vienna had not made him forget his unpleasant experiences with the Catalans in 1632. Oñate's opinion, unusual at a period when sycophancy had reduced the majority of the king's advisers to ciphers, was that a further campaign on the Catalan frontier would be very unwise. It was essential, he maintained, that provinces to be used as a base for military operations should be well affected to the government. Catalonia was not. It was unwilling to be a theatre of operations both because it had no desire to see the king any more powerful within its borders, and because war would interfere with its trade. Anyhow, prices in Catalonia were exceptionally high and everything pointed to the wisdom of selecting another province, from which the French could be attacked more cheaply and to better effect.[2]

Oñate's arguments were brushed aside by the Conde Duque, but it so happened that neither Olivares's hopes nor Oñate's fears were to be realized in 1638. Possibly still unaware of the political benefits that might be gained from putting military pressure on Catalonia, Richelieu chose the other end of the Pyrenees for his new campaign, and forestalled a Spanish invasion from Catalonia by sending the French armies across the border of Guipúzcoa. Fuenterrabía, to which the French laid siege, was a long way from Catalonia, but the siege was nevertheless to have important consequences for the Principality.

The attention of Olivares and his colleagues was riveted on the French invasion. Unable to think of anything but the dangerous situation in Guipúzcoa, they had little time to devote to the problems of Catalonia. This was particularly unfortunate because Santa Coloma's policy of restoring good relations between the Principality and the Court depended on the co-operation of Madrid. As far as Catalonia was concerned, the moment was unusually favourable for breaking the

---

[1] RAH: 11–10–5, leg. 6, fo. 71, Olivares to Cardenal Infante, 27 May 1638.
[2] AGS: Est., leg. 2660, Junta del Aposento del Conde Duque, 12 March 1638.

deadlock. The city of Barcelona had no wish to remain perpetually out of favour with the king. It was anxious to profit from the financial embarrassments of the Crown and settle the affair of the *quints,* and it was anxious to receive those *mercedes* for which it had repeatedly asked since 1626. Santa Coloma therefore found it in exactly the right conciliatory frame of mind for negotiating a settlement. Friendly conversations between him and the city authorities resulted in an offer by Barcelona to compound for the *quints* by making an outright gift to the king of all the services, including loans, it had granted since 1626, together with an additional 10,000 *lliures.*[1] These services were listed by Barcelona as follows:[2]

July 1626	Loan	50,000 *lliures*
June 1630	Loan for the queen of Hungary's visit	12,000
July 1631	Gift for the Italian war	12,000
May 1632	Loan at start of Corts	110,000
	Interest paid by city on this sum (to 1638)	33,000
July 1635	Gift	40,000
Jan. 1637	Gift	40,500
Oct. 1637	Expenses of 500 men for army	11,000
		308,500

Over a period of twelve years, 308,000 *lliures* for a city with an annual income of something like 70,000 *lliures* and with heavy municipal expenditure, was a considerable sum, although it was only half the value of the arrears of *quints* to which the Crown held itself entitled since 1599.

Santa Coloma thought Barcelona's offer a good one, and wrote specially to Olivares to tell him that negotiations on the *quints* had made unprecedented progress. At the same time he urged him to encourage the city to offer troops by allowing the Consellers' traditional claim to wear hats in the royal presence.[3] But if Santa Coloma had succeeded in obtaining an offer from Barcelona, he could make no impression on

[1] ACA: CA, leg. 228, no. 3, Santa Coloma to King, 3 July 1638. In addition the city claimed that in the years between 1547 and 1626 the Crown incurred debts to Barcelona amounting to 631,764 *lliures.*
[2] ACA: CA, leg. 282, no. 58, *Memorial de los servicios que representa la ciudad de Barcelona,* June 1638.
[3] ACA: G, caja 8, Santa Coloma to Olivares, 5 July 1638.

Madrid. The ministers proved quite unresponsive. They said this was no time to offer services that had already been rendered in the past; nor was 10,000 *lliures* in any way adequate for the present. Instead, the viceroy should tell the city that concessions on the *quints* or on the Consellers' claim to wear hats meant such a sacrifice on the part of His Majesty as to demand an outstanding service from the city in the form of troops and of money for the fortifications. Indeed, the Catalans should now be thinking about making a military diversion to relieve the pressure caused by the French invasion of Guipúzcoa.[1] 'What the Catalans ought to be doing on this occasion,' wrote the king on the back of a *consulta* a few days later, 'and what everyone else is doing, when the troops intended for the invasion of Languedoc are having to be sent to Italy and Fuenterrabía, is to cross the frontier and make the diversion that is expected of them.'[2]

Madrid's intransigent attitude, which hopelessly weakened Santa Coloma's hand, was quite unrealistic. Santa Coloma knew perfectly well that it was futile to expect the Catalans to undertake a diversion. They had no trained soldiers, and in any event a diversion across the frontier would be considered an infringement of the constitutions since the Principality itself was not under attack. All Santa Coloma could hope to do was to induce the Catalans to have an army of 10,000 or 12,000 men signed on to meet an invasion.[3] Even here he met with little success. Every town wanted a good price for its services. Lleida was willing to offer 3000 *lliures* for fortifications, and a hundred men paid for three months in the event of invasion, but only on condition that the men should not be ordered beyond the frontiers, and that a dispute with the town of Monzón should first be settled.[4] Tortosa offered 6,000 *escuts* and the same number of men, but only if it were first given all the jurisdiction in its neighbourhood at present belonging to the Crown.[5] As for Barcelona, resentful at its inability to obtain any sign of favour from the king, it took Santa Coloma three months to induce the city to fulfil its earlier promise of five hundred paid men for three months, of which one month still remained.[6]

[1] ACA: CA, leg. 228, no. 3, consulta, 10 July 1638.
[2] ACA: CA, leg. 228, no. 63, King on consulta of 19 July 1638.
[3] ACA: G, caja 8, Santa Coloma to Olivares, 18 July 1638.
[4] ACA: CA, leg. 282, no. 61, consulta, 7 Oct. 1638.
[5] ACA: CA, leg. 282, no. 61, consulta, 8 Oct. 1638.
[6] AHB: LC, 1637–9, fo. 109, Consellers to Santa Coloma, 20 Sept. 1638.

Naturally the Catalan municipalities saw in the embarrassments of the Crown a golden opportunity for securing privileges long desired. But to Madrid, carried away in the summer of 1638 by heroic conceptions of a great national struggle at Fuenterrabía, this could only look like shabby trafficking for something that should never be bought or sold. The Catalan attitude appeared so despicable because Fuenterrabía had become for Olivares the symbol of national unity, of the achievement of the Union of Arms on which he had set his heart. From all over Spain, troops were flocking to the town's defence. Here surely was proof of the Conde Duque's claim that there was indeed 'no difference between one nation and another of those included within the limits of Spain'.[1] This indeed was a true Union of Arms.

But the Union was not quite complete, for the Catalans were missing. When the Aragonese and Valencians, for all their privileges, were coming to the help of the army at Fuenterrabía, it seemed a 'hard thing', wrote Magarola, the Catalan regent of the Council of Aragon, that the Catalans should even refuse to raise men for the defence of their own province.[2] And when the struggle at Fuenterrabía was crowned with a Spanish victory, Magarola could not forbear to express his grief that his countrymen alone had failed their king.[3]

The Principality itself showed no sign of having qualms of conscience over its inglorious role. In its own eyes, it had more grounds for complaint than the king. It had rendered great services to its ruler, and what acknowledgement had it ever received? 'All the slowness of this people', confided Santa Coloma to the secretary of the Council of Aragon, 'stems from their complaint that, after giving so many services, they have received not a single *merced*.'[4] There was much truth in this, but it was not the full explanation. The Catalans did nothing at the moment of crisis partly because they were angry at their treatment by the Court, partly because they were temperamentally inclined to do things at their own time, in their own way, without taking orders from others, but also because they were profoundly uninterested in what happened beyond their own borders. This is a reflection on the mentality of a bourgeoisie whose interests were confined to the events that

[1] See above, p. 204.
[2] ACA: G, caja 8, Magarola to Santa Coloma, 24 July 1638.
[3] ACA: G, caja 9, Magarola to Santa Coloma, 11 Sept. 1638.
[4] ACA: G, caja 9, Santa Coloma to Pedro de Villanueva, 24 Sept. 1638.

occurred within the walls of its home town; but it also testifies to a historical process, which had created a mental gulf between the Principality and a world-wide empire with no meaning and no reality for the inhabitants of Catalonia.

This failure of understanding tragically shaped the course of Castilian-Catalan relations. Catalonia could only feel incomprehension at Castile's desperate pleas for help, while the rulers of Castile could only feel anger and bitterness at Catalonia's refusal to come to the aid of its king. The two sides were talking a different language. The failure of comprehension, the mutual inability of each side to enter imaginatively into the problems of the other, is displayed in a typical interview held at Madrid in the summer of 1638.[1] Don Francesc Virgili had been sent by Lleida, his native town, to discuss with the ministers at Madrid a dispute between the town and its cathedral chapter. His conversations included a discussion with the Protonotario, Villanueva, who brought it round to the question of Lleida's contribution to the Principality's defences. Virgili said that the town was very short of money, but offered 2000 *escuts* on condition that his business in Madrid was promptly despatched. The Protonotario replied:

This is not a proper service. If I were in the Council I should not accept a memorandum of this nature. Although His Majesty requests this money as an act of grace, it is really a question of justice, and very soon he will be ordering all the towns to pay. You know very well how little His Majesty possesses in Catalonia—there is not even enough to pay the viceroy—and who is to pay for the defences except his vassals? Things should not be offered to His Majesty conditionally, as if it were a question of buying and selling what is judicially his.

Virgili pointed out that in 1632 Lleida contributed 2000 *escuts* without asking for a *merced*; another 1000 in 1633, and last year it raised an infantry company.

The Protonotario. It is a fine thing to call self-defence against French invasions a 'service'...look how you people defend your constitutions and how the Aragonese defend their laws, and refuse to go to war beyond the frontier....No, Sir, payment for fortifications is a matter not of grace but of justice. Here is the Diputació spending its money on fans and posies, and expecting the King to pay for the

[1] APL: R. 854, Don Francesc Virgili to Pahers of Lleida, 7 Aug. 1638.

fortifications and to defend the country. The Valencians and Aragonese have served, and are serving at this very moment, and are
sending troops to Fuenterrabía, and the Catalans refuse.

Virgili. We have enough on our hands, Sir, with the defence of the
coast and of Perpinyà.

Protonotario. I won't interfere in any of that. You do well to defend
your laws, but the Valencians and Aragonese have served, and the
Catalans have not.

Virgili. Because their Corts never finished.

Protonotario. They will never finish, because they don't want them to.

Virgili. But, as always, they will offer more than all the rest put
together.

Protonotario. Don't go on fooling yourselves. This has got to stop. . . .

The Protonotario, who, according to Virgili, had a reputation for
saying exactly what he was thinking, spoke for his master as well as for
himself. Neither could forgive the Catalans for their behaviour. And
worse was to follow. The very months of the Fuenterrabía campaign
saw in Catalonia the beginnings of a new struggle, which would confirm Madrid's worst impressions, and prepare the way for the decisive
break between Catalonia and the Spanish Court.

When the count of Oñate had argued against a summer campaign
along the Catalan frontier, one of his principal points had been that the
Catalans would object to the inevitable interference with their trade.
The coming of war with France had already had serious consequences
for Catalan maritime trade. Between the outbreak of the war in May
1635 and September 1638 forty-five Catalan and Genoese ships, containing Catalan cloth and other goods, had fallen into the hands of the
French. Their total value was estimated at 114,800 *escuts*.[1] Apart from
these direct losses caused by the hazards of war, the Principality's
normal commercial life had been disrupted by legal prohibitions
on trade with France. On instructions from Madrid, Santa Coloma
had published on 15 March 1638 an edict similar to an earlier one
published by the duke of Cardona on 9 August 1635. This edict prohibited all trade with France, imposed heavy financial penalties for any

[1] ACA: G, caja 9, Jaume Damians to Santa Coloma, 16 Sept. 1638.

infringement, and threatened confiscation of all illegally imported goods, whether manufactured in France or passing through French territory.[1]

In spite of the edict, a total cessation of Catalan-French trade was out of the question. The Principality was dependent on France for too many of its supplies of essential goods, and the viceroy had constantly to give special licences for the import of goods which could not be obtained elsewhere. When, for example, Barcelona's meat supplies ran short in the autumn of 1638, Santa Coloma was compelled to authorize the import of ten thousand sheep from France.[2] In addition to such authorized imports, illegally imported goods abounded. The viceroy's orders were inevitably ignored and disobeyed. There was not a shop in the Principality which did not sell French goods, publicly brought into the Principality with the connivance of undersalaried royal officials.[3]

In matters of contraband, as in everything else, the frontier region was a law unto itself. All along the border between Rosselló and France lay the estates of great landowners like Don Joan de Llupià, who claimed that only the French gave them a good price for their wool.[4] To these men, Madrid's prohibition of trade with the enemy threatened ruin. Some of them were fortunate enough to obtain special trading licences from the viceroy, but these licences only served as an additional source of conflict among the feuding border families. Some were favoured by the viceroy, some were not. It was pleasant to settle old scores by reporting to royal officials the unauthorized possession of French goods, although the manœuvre sometimes misfired, as when an army captain, Fernando Gallo, an old enemy of Francesc Pasqual i de Cadell, seized some prohibited goods from him, only to discover that Pasqual had been given a special licence by the viceroy.[5]

Everyone took a part in this obscure frontier war: the troops, the clergy, the local aristocracy. Perpinyà itself was the centre of an organized network of smugglers, and large quantities of forbidden goods were found there by a zealous official in the houses of a priest,

[1] ACA: CA, leg. 392, report by Dr Vinyes, 7 Aug. 1638.
[2] ACA: Canc., R. 5526, fo. 292v, Santa Coloma to Governor of Vall d'Aran, 30 Oct. 1638.
[3] ACA: CA, leg. 396, Governador to King, 8 May 1638.
[4] ACA: G, caja 27, Don Joan de Llupià to Santa Coloma, 8 Jan. 1640.
[5] ACA: G, caja 28, F. Gubert to Santa Coloma, 7 Feb. 1640. Gallo was married to a Llupià.

Francesc Reart, and of the cavalry commander, Don Josep d'Oms.[1] Even the king's secret agent in Catalonia, Captain Joan de Torres, took advantage of his official duty of reconnoitring the frontiers to import bales of tobacco into the Principality.[2]

Smuggling was not, however, confined solely to the French frontier. The long coastline offered innumerable opportunities for smuggling under the very eyes of royal officials. These officials were hampered in their task by the fact that all customs dues on imported goods were paid to the Diputació, which kept its own officials in the ports to examine and register the cargoes. Since a significant proportion of the Diputació's revenues came from these import dues, the Diputats had never looked kindly on royal proclamations prohibiting trade with France. Customs dues—the *dret de entrades i eixides*—had already fallen heavily during the past decade, as the combined result of plague and war in the Mediterranean area. The figures in the Diputació's books show a striking contrast between the income from this tax for the year July 1626 to June 1627, and July 1636 to June 1637:[3]

	1626–7	1636–7
All check-posts other than		
Barcelona	18,602 *lliures*	9,340 *lliures*
Barcelona	21,078 *lliures*	14,955 *lliures*

Effective prohibition of trade with France would reduce these already low figures still further. While the customs dues appear to have been farmed for a fixed sum for a three or four-year period from 1637, the Diputats could not be expected to watch the decline of trade with equanimity; and there was reason to suspect that at least one of the current Diputats possessed a personal interest in the sale of French cloths, which can have done nothing to reconcile him to the royal proclamation.[4]

The business of evading the terms of the proclamation was easily managed. French ships would put in at the port of Mataró, which,

---

[1] See the letters of Dr Balet to Santa Coloma, 15 Dec. 1638 (ACA: G, caja 10) and 21 March 1639 (ACA: G, caja 12).

[2] ACA: G, caja 8, Dr Subirà to Santa Coloma, 28 July 1638.

[3] ACA: G, 85, nos. 27 and 29. See also Appendix III.

[4] ACA: G, 909, Lletres secretes (1605–74), Diputats to Dr Puig, 25 Dec. 1638. The suspicion may have been correct, but it has not been possible to identify the Diputat concerned. The contraband controversy, although mentioned by contemporaries, has been ignored by later historians, and many mysteries remain.

almost alone of the check-posts, showed an actual increase of customs dues between 1626 and 1636, and their cargoes would immediately be seized by officials of the Diputació on the pretext that the dues of the Generalitat had not been paid. This effectively prevented their confiscation by royal officials from the captaincy general. The goods were then stored in the Diputació's warehouses, from which they were sent to be sold, presumably at considerable profit to the Diputats and their officials, in the shops of Barcelona and other towns.[1]

Since the government at Madrid was very naturally concerned at the extent of contraband trade with France, it ordered Santa Coloma to protest vigorously to the Diputació. During the summer of 1638 his protest elicited only vague words and general promises. Increasingly annoyed by the evasions of the Diputats, the viceroy decided to act. It was ridiculous that French goods should enter Spain with the aid and approval of that very body which in theory represented the Catalan nation in its struggle with France. Legally, the only interest of the Diputats in the affair lay in the dues which all imported goods paid to the Generalitat; once these dues were paid, the Diputats could properly claim no further interest in the fate of the goods themselves.[2]

On 19 July 1638, therefore, Santa Coloma informed the Diputats that the contraband goods stored in their warehouses would be confiscated, but that the dues for which they were liable would be paid to the Generalitat in the normal manner.[3] This appeared to safeguard the interest of the Diputació, while striking hard at illegal trade with France. The Diputats, however, rejected Santa Coloma's request that they should help in the collection of the contraband goods, and sent officials to prevent a forcible entry of the viceroy's agents into the warehouse at Mataró. But the royal *agutzil* Monrodón broke into the warehouse and had the goods transferred to royal warehouses, having first offered the Diputats payment of their dues. On 30 July similar measures were taken at the important frontier post of Salces.[4]

Technically, the royal officials had put themselves in the wrong by breaking into the warehouses of the Diputació, but the behaviour of the

---

[1] ACA: CA, leg. 392, report by Dr Vinyes, 7 Aug. 1638.
[2] Dr Vinyes's report, *ibid.*
[3] ACA: Varias de Cancillería, R. 387, fo. 35, Santa Coloma to Don Guerau de Guardiola, 19 July 1638.
[4] ACA: G, Dietari, 1638–41, part I, fo. 9.

Diputats provided a reasonable excuse for their action, and responsible opinion in Barcelona seems to have considered it justified.[1] The Diputats on their side, however, considered that their rights of jurisdiction had been grossly violated, and took immediate steps to pronounce the action of the royal officials unconstitutional.

The controversy that broke out in July 1638 between viceroy and Diputació was the first serious dispute in which the Diputació had been involved since the quarrels over the appointment of the new viceroy in 1622 and 1623. In the intervening years the Diputats, either through indolence or self-interest, had given the Crown little trouble. The occasional protest, the sending of an embassy—nothing that would seriously disturb Madrid. It was Barcelona, not the Diputació, which had led the Principality's opposition to the policies of the Court, while the clergy conducted a separate action on their own. But Barcelona and the clergy had primarily been concerned with the safeguarding of their own welfare: Barcelona struggling to avoid payment of the *quints*, the clergy protesting at the level of taxation and the granting of pensions and benefices to foreigners. The Diputació, which might have co-ordinated and organized resistance to Madrid's policies, had remained quiescent.

Now, for the first time in almost twenty years, the Diputació had been stirred to action—but only by something that directly affected its own interests. For this very reason the effectiveness of its protests might be diminished. While many people had an interest in the continuation of the French trade, it would not be easy to justify the precipitate behaviour of the Diputació, and there were probably many who felt that, if Madrid were to be resisted, it would be desirable to find other and better motives for opposition. Nor was this the moment which all the ruling class of Barcelona would have chosen for a renewal of the struggle. The progress of negotiations on the *quints* had led to real hopes of a settlement, and it would be folly to throw them away by incurring the king's displeasure on a new issue of doubtful validity.

These considerations might in due course have tempered the first hot-headed reactions of the Diputats, had they remained in office. But by an unfortunate accident their three-year term of office drew to a close in the opening stages of the controversy, and the luck of the

[1] Sevillà's history, fo. 145.

341

draw on 22 July 1638 produced a new Diputació whose composition was to have profound consequences for the future of the Principality and its relations with Madrid.[1]

Oddly enough, both of the ecclesiastics in the new Diputació, Pau Claris, the Diputat Eclesiàstic, and Jaume Ferran, the Oidor Eclesiàstic, were canons of the cathedral chapter of Urgell. This in itself was unfortunate, since the history of the diocese of Urgell was one of unusual turbulence in which the cathedral chapter was particularly implicated. Set close to the Pyrenees and to the French frontier, the small town of the Seu d'Urgell, with its little Romanesque cathedral, was the centre of a vast but impoverished diocese that covered the barren lands of west Catalonia. The town itself was full of priests, 27 per cent of its houses belonging to ecclesiastics, according to the census of 1553.[2] As so often happened in Catalan cathedral towns in the seventeenth century, relations between the municipality and the cathedral chapter were bad. As far back as 1615 the town council of the Seu d'Urgell had sent an agent to Madrid to protest about the behaviour of the canons and their habit of consorting with criminals and bandits.[3] The canons, indeed, dominated Urgell, exercising their control through the powerful aristocratic family of Boquet, owners of the nearby barony of Calvinyà. It was not unknown for Baron Boquet, who looked after the estates and jurisdiction of the cathedral chapter,[4] to parade through the Seu d'Urgell with a body of armed followers.[5] When the new bishop of Urgell, Pau Duran, arrived in his diocese, he found it and its neighbourhood terrorized by the large Boquet clan, and by the Boquets' relatives, the traditional bandit family of the Cadells of Arsèguel, who were masters of the road between the Seu d'Urgell and Cerdanya.[6]

For many years the canons had had things very much their own way, but the appointment of Pau Duran as bishop of Urgell in 1634 seriously threatened their dominance for the first time, and introduced a fresh element of discord into an already troubled diocese. Duran's pre-

---

[1] The new Diputats were Dr Pau Claris (*eclesiàstic*); Francesc de Tamarit (*militar*) and Josep Quintana (*reial*). The new Oidors, Dr Jaume Ferran (*eclesiàstic*); Rafael Antic (*militar*); Rafael Cerdà (*reial*). [2] Pere Gil, *Geografia*, p. 122.

[3] ACU: Cartes, 1615–19, secret instructions for syndic of Urgell, 30 March 1615.

[4] For the income from these estates, see Appendix II.

[5] AMU: Llibre de Consells, 1617–57, fo. 317.

[6] ACA: G, caja 6, Bishop of Urgell to Santa Coloma, 6 May 1638.

decessors had preferred to be non-resident, rather than run the risks of living in a town ruled by their turbulent canons.[1] Pau Duran was made of sterner stuff. A native Catalan, the son of poor parents from the town of Esparraguera, he had studied at Salamanca, held a chair at Huesca, and then became vicar-general of the bishop of Majorca.[2] A tough, violent and very ambitious man, he was remorselessly making his way up the Catalan ecclesiastical hierarchy. His appointment to Urgell gave ample scope to his energies. He would curb the canons, restore peace to the diocese, and show His Majesty that he had here a bishop worthy of the fullest confidence. He took up residence in the city, had various delinquents arrested for carrying arms in the streets, and got Cardona to billet a troop of 150 cavalrymen on the town.[3] These measures restored at least a temporary peace to the Seu, but they did not endear him to the canons, who were unused to the presence of an energetic bishop in their midst. As one conflict followed another, relations between the bishop and the cathedral chapter became exceptionally bitter and violent.

The chapter's resistance to the bishop was directed and organized by one of the most energetic of its canons, Pau Claris. Born at Barcelona in 1586, the son of a well-connected lawyer, Claris had been presented in 1612 to the chapter of Urgell in whose affairs he had played an increasingly important part.[4] He acted as a syndic of the Urgell chapter in the Corts of 1626,[5] and had also been appointed to represent it at provincial councils and on business in Barcelona, where, indeed, he seems to have spent much of his time. Together with his colleague Jaume Ferran, the new Oidor Eclesiàstic of 1638, he played a leading part in the religious disorders at Vic in 1634.[6] By now his experience must have made him a skilful agitator, and from 1636 he was busily organizing the opposition to Pau Duran,[7] for whom he seems to have

[1] AMU: Lletres del Bisbe als Consellers, 1512–1630, Bishop of Urgell to Cònsols, 9 Aug. 1635.
[2] ACA: CA, leg. 359, petition of Dr Pau Duran.
[3] ACA: G, caja 6, Bishop of Urgell to Santa Coloma, 6 May 1638.
[4] There is an adulatory biography, *Pau Claris* by A. Rovira i Virgili (Barcelona, 1922), but it is uninformative on Claris's early career.
[5] Most of Claris's letters to his chapter at this and later periods appear to have been deliberately removed from the cathedral archive at the Seu d'Urgell. One or two, however, seem to have escaped the notice of the person who removed them—enough to make one hope that, if the missing letters survive, they will one day be recovered.
[6] ACA: CA, leg. 280, no. 4, Bishop of Girona to J. L. de Villanueva, 24 June 1634.
[7] ACA: CA, leg. 280, no. 38, Cardona to Bishop of Urgell, 23 June 1636.

cherished a personal hatred of peculiar bitterness.[1] The rancour which Pau Claris and Pau Duran entertained for each other can partly be explained in terms of a conflict between two ambitious and forceful personalities, both proud, energetic, and quick to anger.[2] But there was a deeper division between them than this. Duran, having once obtained a foothold on the ladder of promotion, had thrown in his fortunes with the Court. He was essentially a royalist bishop, who was to show himself as capable of expounding and defending the policy of Madrid as the Protonotario himself.[3] Claris, on the other hand, like most of the other canons in Catalonia, would never receive promotion; his energies were cramped and restricted by the limitations of ecclesiastical life in a province where the plums went to foreigners or to time-servers; he knew nothing of the world beyond Catalonia, which indeed was all his world. He hated his bishop, he hated the Castilians, and reserved all the passionate love and loyalty of which he was capable for his cathedral chapter and his native province. Because he loved these things, he must preserve and protect them from the attacks of the enemy and from the subtly eroding influence of time. This was the theme of his life: to conserve and defend, with all the vehemence that accompanied an acute but narrow vision. Nothing reveals Claris's passionately conservative character better than a letter he wrote to his cathedral chapter about the iniquities of the bishop.

You know the bishop's character well—indeed, it is notorious not only in this province but in many other places too. And the worst of it is that you have got the bishop for life (according to informed opinion he will die bishop of Urgell). So arm yourselves with the courage that your forebears always showed, to resist him in his anger, and see to it that in your time your holy church does not lose an atom of its prerogatives and privileges. If the said gentleman sees any sign of weakness in you—something I cannot believe possible—the church will certainly fall into a state for which future canons will hold you responsible.... And once again I beg you—do not let us lose in our time what our forebears so bravely won.[4]

[1] His will, dated 2 December 1637, contains a nice touch of irony: 'Item, if I have any obligation to do so, and not otherwise, I leave what is customary to the Rev. Bishop of Urgell.' APB: A. J. Fita, leg. 30, lib. 6, de testaments, fo. 166 v.

[2] Duplessis-Besançon describes Claris as 'd'une humeur véhémente, et qui avait plus d'esprit, d'éloquence naturelle, et de fierté que de science acquise par étude', and speaks of 'cette aversion qu'il avait commune avec tous les catalans contre les castillans'. AAE: Corresp. Espagne, Supplément no. 3, fo. 189 v.

[3] See his letter to Santa Coloma of 25 Jan. 1639 (ACA: G, caja 11).

[4] ACU: Cartes, 1630–40, Claris to Canons of Urgell, 20 Dec. 1639.

In these closing words lies the guiding principle of Claris's life: that intense feeling of obligation to the past and to the future which seems to have come as second nature to the Catalans of the seventeenth century. To defend the legacy of the ages, so that not one iota was lost— this, with all its strength and its weaknesses was the supreme ideal of the Catalans: the ideal of a nation which can be accused of excessive veneration for its own past and a dangerous inability to lift its gaze towards the wider horizons of the future, but an ideal so intensely held as to command sympathy and perhaps a little admiration.

The very fact that Claris's career exemplified so perfectly the national characteristics would seem to have made him the ideal representative of his people at this dangerous moment in its fortunes. For this reason, it has been suspected that the extraction of Diputats was rigged in 1638 to ensure the selection of characters worthy of the occasion.[1] The possibilities of this are, however, slight. Apart from the sheer mechanical difficulty of rigging a lottery system when all those present are anxious to see their own names drawn, Claris was in no sense a national figure in 1638. It is also probable that he was not without enemies in the Diputació itself, as the result of a rather unsavoury affair when he was one of the investigating judges in a *visita* of the Diputació in 1627. In that incident, he had shown a gift for attacking his opponents which was only excelled by an ambition for office which made him retract his accusation within the hour.[2] For some years he had been on the roster of names from which the Oidor Eclesiàstic was drawn, as the third representative of the Urgell chapter, but had never been drawn for office; he had then in 1632 been promoted by a lucky draw to the roster for Diputats, where in 1638 he had a chance of one in twenty-three of being selected.[3] On this occasion he was fortunate. Office had come his way at last.

From the summer of 1638, therefore, the Diputació had as its president a man of energy and resourcefulness who had on more than one occasion shown his willingness to take an active part in organizing resistance to unpopular men and measures; a man passionately convinced of

[1] E.g. by Rovira i Virgili, *op. cit.* p. 18.

[2] It was known that he was a *visitador* of the Diputació in 1627 but no one seems to have searched in the Diputació's records for evidence of what happened in the *visita*. The story is too long and too trivial to recount, but can be found in ACA: G, Delibs., 1626–9, vol. II, fos. 157 and 326–30.

[3] ACA: G, 78/4, Llibre de habilitacions, 17 July 1638.

the justice of the causes he was defending; a man with a personal animosity towards his bishop, who happened to be the most vehement supporter of the Court among all the bishops of Catalonia; a man who was linked by his family connections to some of the most influential personages in Barcelona, and by his religious vocation to one of the regions of Catalonia with the closest commercial and cultural affiliations with France. All this could hardly be reassuring to Santa Coloma at a moment when Diputació and Crown had suddenly come into conflict. But even this did not exhaust Claris's potentialities for causing trouble. According to at least two contemporary sources,[1] Claris and Santa Coloma were already personal enemies of long standing as the result of Claris's intervention in a long legal struggle for possession of the barony of Pons in the diocese of Urgell, which was finally won by Santa Coloma in 1627.

As if the presence of Claris at the Diputació were not of itself a sufficient threat to the authority of Santa Coloma, he also had to face another difficult character in Francesc de Tamarit, the Diputat Militar. Tamarit came of an aristocratic Barcelona family. His father had been arrested by the Crown on 8 February 1593 and exiled from the neighbourhood of Barcelona for five years. During this period his estate suffered losses for which his son had for years been trying to obtain compensation.[2] Tamarit, like Claris, also seems to have been on bad personal terms with the new viceroy as the result of a close friendship with one of Santa Coloma's enemies.[3] Like Claris, too, he was a stickler for the laws and privileges of his country. After the outbreak of revolution in 1640 a political opponent wrote of him: 'This patriot was a man of great experience and modesty, possessing a love of his fatherland and *fueros* rather than a spirit of sedition.'[4] The Diputats Eclesiàstic and Militar between them made a formidable pair.

Santa Coloma is reported to have been so concerned about the rise of these two men to public office that he decided to make a bid for their friendship by a delicate form of bribery: Claris was to be given an important post at Lleida University, and the vacant canonry at Urgell would be offered to a close relation of Tamarit.[5] For some reason the

---

[1] Assarino, *Rivolutioni*, pp. 32–3, and Dr Sevillà, fo. 141.
[2] AHB: Corts, 1632, fos. 83–4, petition by Tamarit, 30 May 1632.
[3] Sevillà, fo. 142.   [4] *Súplica de Tortosa*, fo. 52.
[5] Sevillà, fos. 142–5.

gesture was never made, but it is doubtful whether it would have had the desired effect, for the new Diputats took such vigorous action in the contraband controversy during their very first week of office as to create an almost unbridgeable chasm between the viceroy and themselves.

Their predecessors had ended their careers in the grand manner by citing the constitution Observança against Monrodón and his colleagues for breaking into the property of the Generalitat. Monrodón naturally rejected the charge that he had infringed the constitutions. This was the moment at which the new Diputats arrived on the scene.

In evaluating their behaviour during the next few days, it is necessary to take into account a tragic occurrence, the news of which was at this very moment spreading horror throughout the Principality. Since the retreat from Leucata, troops had been continuously billeted on the little town of Palafrugell, to the north of Palamós. Being underpaid and short of food, they had treated the inhabitants atrociously. On 20 July, St Margaret's Day, when the town was on holiday, the towns-people, joined by outsiders, clashed with the troops, and two captains and five soldiers were killed. The troops' vengeance was swift and ter-rible. Ten cavalry companies descended upon the town and set out deliberately to sack and to pillage.[1] The inhabitants fled from their homes, leaving them to the mercy of the soldiers. Mindful of Olivares's warnings about the urgent need to preserve the army, Santa Coloma's first reaction was to rebuke Dr Puig of the Audiència for recounting at length the excesses of the troops while saying nothing of those com-mitted by the townspeople.[2] He hastily changed his tune, though, when Puig replied that there were no townspeople left to investigate, and ordered the troops to be billeted elsewhere.[3]

The new Diputats therefore assumed office under the shadow of the sack of Palafrugell. This was only the most recent of a series of incidents concerning the behaviour of the troops which had formed the subject of many protests by the Diputació during the past few years. It is pos-sible that the sack of Palafrugell convinced the new Diputats that mere protests were no longer adequate and that the time had come for a trial of strength with Madrid. The dispute over smuggling provided them

[1] See the terrible description by Dr Claresvalls, printed as Appendix III of Jose Sanabré, *La Acción de Francia en Cataluña* (Barcelona, 1956).

[2] ACA: G, caja 8, Santa Coloma on letter from Dr Puig, 28 July 1638.

[3] ACA: G, caja 8, Puig to Santa Coloma, 31 July 1638, and the viceroy's marginal note.

with a useful pretext, of which they at once took advantage. If their predecessors had acted with undue precipitation, this was not the moment to beat a retreat. On 2 August they boldly declared that Monrodón's case should be heard not in the Audiència but in the Diputació.[1] Outraged by this attempt to usurp its jurisdiction, the Audiència replied on the following day by formally announcing that no constitution had been infringed, and summoning Dr Fontanella and the other lawyers of the Diputació to appear before it.[2] The Diputats riposted by claiming that they were fully entitled to take action against the goods and persons of royal officials, and ordered Monrodón to pay a fine of 2000 *lliures* within ten days.[3] The Audiència, stung by this open defiance of its authority, promptly outlawed Dr Fontanella and seven other lawyers, who took refuge first in the Diputació itself and then in a monastery.

In their first six days of office, the new Diputats had displayed a vigour and determination such as had not been seen in the Generalitat for many years. Their action was likely to be welcomed in many parts of the Principality, and not least in Claris's own town of Urgell, which, in company with Mataró, had defied the general trend in the Principality by showing a significant increase in the yield of its customs dues during the past few years. The frontier regions could hardly fail to applaud such vigorous resistance to a royal proclamation which threatened to destroy their livelihood.

By acting in a manner agreeable to the frontier regions, the new Diputats had taken a step of considerable significance for the future alignment of forces within the Principality. In the previous decades, the Diputació had almost always allowed itself to be guided by the Barcelona aristocracy, acting through meetings of the Braços. The rest of the Principality had little or no control over the direction of policy. But Claris himself knew the border country intimately: he had influential friends and relations there, and must have appeared as a true representative of the interests of north Catalonia and the counties when he defied the Crown on the question of French trade. An effective alliance between the Diputació and the clergy and aristocracy of the border country was something new in seventeenth-century Catalan political

---

[1] ACA: G, Dietari, 1638–41, part I, fo. 8.
[2] ACA: CA, leg. 281, no. 77, report by Dr Vinyes for 1–6 Aug. 1638.   [3] *Ibid.*

life, and it was being forged just at the moment when the whole region was itself in a state of transition. For many years its inhabitants had been left to their own devices. Now, for the first time since the reign of Philip II, the influence of the Crown was beginning to make itself felt in the towns and villages of the Pyrenean foothills. The king's troops were everywhere to be seen; the king's officials were probing into commercial transactions which had previously been a private affair between the frontier-dwellers and the French over the border. As an automatic response to this new pressure from Spain, they were beginning to gravitate towards France, both in self-protection from interference by Madrid, and as a necessary means of meeting their economic needs. Simultaneously they found themselves championed by the Diputació, which for so long had neglected their interests. As a result, it may not be entirely fanciful to discern for the first time in 1638 a new and unexpected combination still unsuspected even by the participants themselves: the combination, to materialize two years later with such devastating effect, of the Diputació, the frontier regions, and France.

While the Diputats' stand may have been welcomed in the north, it seems to have been greeted with less enthusiasm by the city of Barcelona. All Barcelona's correspondence at this period shows it desperately anxious to recover the royal favour and obtain at least one of the *mercedes* for which it had asked at the time of the Corts of 1626.[1] The granting of a *merced* would be a sign that the king had at last recognized Barcelona's services and looked once again with favour upon the city. It would be folly for Barcelona to jeopardize its chances of receiving a *merced* or of reaching a settlement on the *quints* by hurrying to the assistance of a Diputació which had so unhesitatingly challenged the authority of the Audiència and the king.

Barcelona might indeed hope to gain capital out of the contraband controversy, if it played its hand with skill. Successful mediation between the king and the Diputats would surely entitle the city to some sign of royal favour. Instead of coming to the help of the Diputats, therefore, the city struggled to find a compromise. A suggestion that both sides should suspend judicial proceedings failed because Santa Coloma was unwilling to allow the outlawed assessors of the Diputació

---

[1] E.g. AHB: CCO, 1637–8, fos. 191–2, Joan Grau to Consellers, 9 Oct. 1638, and the Consellers' reply of 16 Oct. (LC, 1637–9, fo. 111).

to return to their homes.[1] He refrained, however, from proceeding against the lawyers in the hope that the city would put forward a more satisfactory proposal. Finally, in November, Barcelona suggested that the Diputats retract all their actions and waive their claims, although allowing them, if they wished, to raise the issue when the next Corts were held. In return, the viceroy should suspend the action of *regalia* which was hanging over Dr Fontanella and his colleagues.[2]

This compromise, which in effect represented a damaging blow to the claims of the Diputats, nearly found acceptance at a meeting of the Braços. But opposition was whipped up by Don Joan de Peguera (a cousin of Claris), assisted by Don Miquel de Rocabertí and Jeroni de Navel. At the decisive moment Lluís Llull y de Boxadors, the *protector* of the *braç militar*, changed sides and the proposal was defeated.[3] Since Boxadors had one son serving in Milan, another in the dragoons, and a third as Inquisitor at Murcia, the ministers at Court were naturally scandalized by his behaviour. He and his friends appeared to be motivated solely by self-interest. 'It is a great misfortune for our nation', commented the Catalan regent Magarola, 'that four or five people have so much power that they can direct the course of a controversy in which the king's point of view is so fully justified, and stir up things as much as they can simply to further their own personal interests.'[4]

Whatever his personal interest in the contraband controversy may have been, Boxadors's change of heart saved the Diputats from accepting an unfavourable compromise. They followed up this success by sending Canon Puig on an embassy to Madrid to present their case to the ministers. But, as they probably realized, their personal position was precarious. At the end of November, Santa Coloma had everything prepared for their arrest,[5] and judicial proceedings were only delayed because the Council of Aragon felt that Puig should first be heard.[6] Their best hope of escape from the dangers that threatened them lay in obtaining the public support of Barcelona. If only the city would formally approve their refusal to allow royal officials to enter their

[1] ACA: CA, leg. 392, report of events, 13–26 Aug. 1638.
[2] ACA: CA, leg. 281, no. 77, City's proposals to Diputats, Nov. 1638.
[3] ACA: CA, leg. 281, no. 77, Santa Coloma to King, 22 Nov. 1638.
[4] ACA: G, caja 10, Magarola to Santa Coloma, 20 Nov. 1638.
[5] ACA: CA, leg. 392, Santa Coloma to King, 30 Nov. 1638.
[6] ACA: CA, leg. 281, no. 77, consulta, 9 Dec. 1638.

warehouses, the sight of combined resistance by city and Diputació might be sufficient to deter Madrid from taking drastic action.

It is difficult not to believe that at this moment the Court lost an excellent opportunity for seizing the initiative in the Principality. The hesitations of Barcelona at least hinted at the possibility of driving a wedge between the two most powerful institutions in Catalan life. Even one *merced* or token of favour bestowed upon the city might have been sufficient to keep it neutral in the contraband controversy, and so leave the Diputats in a position where they would either have to withdraw their claims or run the risk of judicial proceedings. Realizing the possibilities, Santa Coloma sent one letter after another to the Conde Duque and the Council of Aragon, asking for a gesture to be made. 'I must represent to Your Excellency, setting aside any bias I may have as a Catalan', he wrote to the Conde Duque, 'that some *merced* would encourage them to continue their services. . .for they are a people whose rulers look more to the reward than to their obligations.'[1] It was no use. The Conde Duque and the Protonotario were incapable of forgetting the behaviour of the Principality during the siege of Fuenterrabía and could not bring themselves to bestow favours upon such undeserving subjects; and so Santa Coloma was compelled to stand by, with his hands tied, and watch the opportunity to divide city and Diputació slip away.

It could now be only a question of time before a disgruntled and disappointed Barcelona came round to the open support of the Diputats. Chance played its part. In the annual change of city officers on St Andrew's Day, the name of Francesc Claris, the brother of Pau Claris, was drawn for the post of second Conseller. This was a happy stroke of fortune, but it would not in itself have proved sufficient to win the city's full support for the Diputats, if the course of events had not been pushing Barcelona in that direction.

As the contraband controversy dragged on from month to month, it was natural that more and more people should find themselves involved. As always in conflicts of jurisdiction between two rival bodies, feelings ran high and each side looked for opportunities to score off the other. The Diputació considered that the Audiència had encroached upon its jurisdiction; the Audiència held that the Diputats had chal-

---

[1] ACA: G, caja 9, Santa Coloma to Olivares, 23 Sept. 1638.

lenged its authority. One of the victims of the constant skirmishes between the two bodies was a certain Dr Josep Vinyals, a lawyer and minor royal official who had upheld the Crown's rights in the Consell de Cent and elsewhere.[1] Unfortunately he owed a small sum to the Diputació, and the Diputats seem to have used his indebtedness as a pretext for his arrest and incarceration in the prisons of the Generalitat. The viceregal government retaliated by arresting three officials of the Diputació, on the orders of Santa Coloma. It also attempted, unsuccessfully, to arrest Francesc Joan de Vergós, a Barcelona *militar* who held an important post in the Diputació and was implicated in Vinyals's arrest. The Diputats wrote an indignant description of the scene to Canon Puig in Madrid:

Twice this very evening royal officials searched the house with pistols in their hands...From all of which you can judge the state of mind of the judges of the Audiència, when they are capable of acting with such precipitation...If the King's ministers behave in this way we can never feel safe, and not a privilege or constitution will remain secure.[2]

In attempting to lay hands on Vergós, the royal officials had made a lasting enemy of a man who enjoyed considerable influence in the affairs of the city. This was not the best moment to antagonize Barcelona's governing class, especially as Madrid was preparing new and unpleasant measures which were publicized within a very few days of the attempted arrest of Vergós. Two pragmatics were issued on 2 January 1639, both of a highly controversial nature.[3] The first ordered all Frenchmen living in Catalonia to purchase a special residence permit, under pain of five years in the galleys. The second decreed a general levy for 1639 and 1640 of 50,000 *lliures* a year to contribute towards the expenses of repairing the Principality's fortifications. This levy, which was decided upon in Madrid after the failure to obtain voluntary contributions from the Catalans towards their own defences, entailed a payment by Barcelona of 4455*ll.* 5*s.* 6*d.*, assessed at 15*s.* 5¾*d.* a hearth on the city's alleged total of 5756 hearths.[4]

Barcelona at once appealed to the lawyers for a ruling on the legality

[1] ACA: CA, leg. 508, petition of Dr Vinyals, 25 May 1642.
[2] ACA: G, 909, Lletres secretes (1605–74), Diputats to Dr Puig, 25 Dec. 1638.
[3] The texts of the pragmatics are bound between fos. 39 and 40 of AHB: Delibs., 1639.
[4] AHB: Delibs., 1639, fo. 55. Ten houses in every hundred had already been deducted, as belonging to the poor.

of the pragmatics. The lawyers, including Dr Fontanella, still in hiding in his monastery, held that both of them infringed the constitutions.[1] They claimed that the king was not entitled to make statutes outside sessions of the Corts and could publish no edicts except in the event of war within the borders of the Principality. In addition, both pragmatics contravened the constitution called *Nous vectigals* which forbade the levying of money in Catalonia without the approval of the Corts, and the pragmatic on French residents ran contrary to a custom of Barcelona allowing strangers who resided in the city for a year and a day to enjoy all the privileges of full citizens.

In the city's indignation over the pragmatics, the Diputats saw their opportunity to gain Barcelona's support in the contraband dispute. They promptly organized a large embassy to go and protest to the viceroy, and were careful to keep the city council fully informed, in view of the 'close correspondence' which had always existed between city and Diputació.[2] In spite of this 'close correspondence', Barcelona had not yet seen fit to declare its public support for the Diputació's actions over the contraband, and time was running short. Early in February 1639 Canon Puig was ordered by the king to leave Madrid.[3] This could only mean that judicial proceedings against the Diputats were imminent. On hearing the news, the Diputats took the only course still open to them. They sent a message to the Consell de Cent to report that the Diputació was now prepared to accept one of the two compromises proposed by the city on 18 November, which it had previously rejected.[4]

This move can be interpreted either as a surrender by the Diputats, or as an attempt to play for time. If they could only hold out for a few more weeks, it was possible that royal pressure on Barcelona would drive it into the arms of the Diputació. This, indeed, was exactly what happened. Apparently oblivious of Barcelona's resentment at the publication of the pragmatics, the king chose this moment to appeal to the city for a loan of 70,000 ducats. On 2 March the city declined on the grounds that it had no money.[5] The following day the viceroy ordered

---

[1] AHB: Delibs., 1639, fo. 39v, decision of lawyers, 11 Jan. 1639.
[2] AHB: Delibs., 1639, fo. 50, 22 Jan. 1639.
[3] ACA: CA, leg. 390, draft reply on letter of Diputats to King, 5 Feb. 1639.
[4] AHB: Delibs., 1639, fo. 75, 15 Feb. 1639.
[5] AHB: LC, 1637–9, fo. 128, City to King, 2 March 1639.

that the collectors of one of the municipal taxes, known as the *dret de la neu*, should pay the next instalment on 4 June not, as was usual, to the city but to the royal Treasury in Barcelona.[1]

Threatened with the appropriation of one of its taxes, the city decided that Jeroni de Navel should be sent on a special mission to Madrid. He left on 10 March with instructions to try to persuade the ministers to withdraw the pragmatic on the levy for fortifications and the order confiscating the municipal impost; to express the city's regret at its inability to raise the loan for which the King had asked; and finally to remind the Protonotario that last year's offer still stood, of a gift of all past services and an additional 10,000 *lliures* in return for suspension of the lawsuit on the *quints*.[2]

There was no reference in these instructions to Canon Puig's mission on behalf of the Diputats about the contraband, but a restoration of complete unity between city and Diputació was close. Navel's first report from Madrid was not encouraging. In his first interview with the Protonotario, who 'is omnipotent', he had pointed out that the king's only reply to the city's offer of a settlement on the *quints* had been the publication of the obnoxious pragmatic on the levy for fortifications. Villanueva answered that he had repeatedly told the king that the city deserved *mercedes*—a claim which his remarks in council meetings do not bear out—but that a mere 10,000 *escudos* was not much of an offer for the *quints*.[3]

But already before it received this report the city had decided that it could no longer remain aloof from the contraband dispute. Its neutrality had gained it nothing. On 24 March, therefore, an additional letter of instructions was despatched to Navel, ordering him to give Canon Puig all possible help because the viceroy's behaviour over the contraband was contrary to the laws of Catalonia and prejudicial to its welfare.[4]

With Barcelona's belated decision to come out in support of the Diputats, complete unity of action between the two most influential bodies in the life of the Principality was restored. But it was a unity with a new emphasis. Instead of the customary picture of a weak Diputació

[1] AHB: Delibs., 1639, fo. 107. This was a tax on the ice brought down from the Pyrenees and sold in Barcelona for purposes of refrigeration.
[2] AHB: LC, 1637-9, fos. 134-9, Navel's instructions, 2 March 1639.
[3] AHB: CCO, 1639-40, fo. 4, Navel to Consellers, 26 March 1639.
[4] AHB: LC, 1637-9, fos. 147-8, Consellers to Navel, 24 March 1639.

tagging along in the city's rear, a resurgent Diputació had now assumed direction of the Principality's relations with Madrid and had persuaded a somewhat hesitant city to follow its lead. The city's hesitation is understandable: the question of contraband, with its taint of private interests and treasonable practices, was hardly the ideal issue on which to challenge the Court. But the obstinacy of Olivares and the Protonotario, their refusal to make any conciliatory gesture to Barcelona, had gradually forced it out of its neutrality into openly supporting the extreme position adopted by the Diputació. Once again the complete inflexibility of the ministers in Madrid and their apparent blindness to the effects that their actions produced in Catalonia, had led to results directly opposed to their own best interests. It had always been an axiom of the government at Madrid in its dealings with the Principality that city and Diputació should be kept apart. The Protonotario had disregarded this axiom, with the inevitable consequences. In an interview with Navel he said that the Claris brothers, one in the Diputació, the other in the city council, were working hand in glove, and that the city's policy was being directed from the Diputació.[1] If this was correct, there could hardly have been a more damaging admission of the failure of his Catalan policy.

The new co-operation of city and Diputació set the seal on a series of events which in one year had transformed the political life of the Principality. During that year, Catalonia had been given a new, and not unintelligent, viceroy who had come into sudden and violent conflict with a new set of Diputats headed by the dynamic Pau Claris. Surviving their first crisis less through their own skill than through the mistakes of their enemies, the Diputats had recovered their traditional role as protectors of the laws and liberties of Catalonia. Claris had successfully challenged Madrid on an issue of vital concern to the frontier regions, and had at the same time managed to obtain a dominating influence over the policies of Barcelona. With his new-found assurance of wide support from the Principality, he now awaited the attack which was being prepared in Madrid against the laws and liberties of his beloved fatherland.

[1] AHB: CCO, 1639–40, fos. 17–20, Navel to Consellers, 30 April 1639.

CHAPTER XIII

'THE DEVIL TAKE THE CONSTITUTIONS!'

The ministers in Madrid were by now convinced that strict observance of every detail of the Catalan constitutions was incompatible with the security of the Spanish Monarchy. That this ran counter to the king's solemn oath and to his contractual obligation towards the Principality does not seem to have unduly distressed either the Conde Duque or the Protonotario. By their behaviour over the question of contraband, and by their refusal to raise troops and money voluntarily for their own defence, as well as by their manner of proceeding in the Corts of 1626 and 1632, the Catalans had, they considered, shown themselves unworthy of the laws and liberties granted by grateful kings to their ancestors. Moreover, Olivares had always maintained that self-defence was the supreme law, and this doctrine now came into its own. 'No law can stand in the way of natural defence', insisted a special Junta on fortifications when it produced its report on methods of raising money for the Principality's defences.[1]

In so far as a mutual failure of trust had already undermined the entire contractual system on which Catalonia's relations with its prince were grounded, Olivares's doctrine of a supreme law was no more than a formal justification for a policy that circumstances seemed to render inevitable. Since traditional forms of government were apparently inadequate to meet the needs of the age, new ways and means must be sought. There was indeed ample evidence to support the argument that the Catalan constitutions had become dangerous anomalies in the altered conditions of the seventeenth century, and that the Catalans themselves had offended against the spirit, if not the letter, of the contract. Yet it is difficult to avoid the suspicion that the government in Madrid *wanted* the Catalans to fail in their obligations, simply to justify its own conviction that the constitutions were merely the archaic quibbles of narrow-minded lawyers and deserved no place in the new, united, Spain of the Conde Duque's dreams.

[1] ACA: CA, leg. 390, Junta para la fortificación de Cataluña, 18 Jan. 1639. The Junta consisted of the Protonotario and the regent Magarola.

That anti-Catalan feeling was now very strong among the king's ministers cannot be doubted. 'This is a bad time for those of us who serve the king, and will always be so as long as the ruling ministers are so unfavourable to our nation', wrote the Catalan regent of the Council of Aragon, Dr Magarola, in April 1639.[1] Jeroni de Navel, who had a unique opportunity for watching the ministers at work during much of 1639, saw in Villanueva the Principality's most formidable enemy. 'Everything done in the Crown of Aragon', he wrote, 'runs through the hands of the Protonotario, to such an extent that the Conde Duque keeps only a general oversight. Neither of these two men is well disposed to the province, but much less so the Protonotario.'[2]

Although the Protonotario may well have entertained some personal antipathy towards the Catalans, the general situation of the Monarchy was by now so gloomy that this alone could have been quite sufficient to account for his attitude. The high hopes of the first years of the war with France had not been fulfilled. The French victory at Leucata in September 1637, itself of no great military significance, was the prelude to a slow but decisive change in the fortunes of the war. In October 1637 the Dutch recaptured Breda, which had fallen to Spínola in 1625. In spite of the failure at Fuenterrabía, the year 1638 was otherwise favourable to France and culminated in the capture of Breisach by Bernard of Weimar on 17 December. The fall of Breisach, the news of which did not reach Madrid until the evening of 17 January 1639,[3] proved to be an irremediable disaster for Spain. It meant that the road from Milan to Flanders was cut, and that the Spanish armies in the Netherlands were now totally isolated unless reinforcements could be brought to them through an English Channel patrolled by the Dutch.[4]

These reverses had occurred in spite of all the heroic efforts made by Spain to raise money for its armies—efforts energetically promoted by Villanueva, who had turned himself into the Conde Duque's factotum. Since the outbreak of the war with France, the Monarchy's scale of expenditure had been enormous. For the financial year that ran from

[1] ACA: G, caja 13, Magarola to Santa Coloma, 23 April 1639. Magarola only dared write so openly to Santa Coloma because he believed that the viceroy was destroying his letters as soon as he had read them.

[2] AHB: loose folder of *Cartas Comunes Originales del siglo XVII*. Navel to Francesc Pons, 7 April 1639.

[3] Fraga Iribarne, *Don Diego de Saavedra*, p. 289, note 529.

[4] See Pagès, *Guerre de Trente Ans*, pp. 211–12.

October 1636 to October 1637, for instance, the Council of Finance had attempted to arrange the following provisions:[1]

For Flanders	4,384,000 *escudos*
For Germany	1,500,000
For Milan	2,500,000
To be provided in Spain	2,000,000
For the fleet	500,000
For the royal household (in the event of an expedition by the King)	64,000
For ambassadors	150,000
	11,098,000

In addition to this, a further 2,050,000 *escudos* were needed for the royal households, the ordinary expenses of the fleet, and the frontier garrisons.

These figures were in practice quite unrealistic, all the more so in that they did not include interest for the *asentistas* or the cost of reducing *vellón* to silver. Even with new taxes like the tax on paper (*papel sellado*) and with 1,350,000 *escudos* brought by the silver fleet, the Crown could count on being able to raise only about half the sum required.[2] It was now making a practice of forcibly converting into *vellón* or government bonds (*juros*) the silver that came in the fleet for individual merchants,[3] but any relief that this brought was only temporary, and the long-term results were disastrous in that the whole system of Spanish trade with America—on the prosperity of which the Crown's credit ultimately depended—was fatally undermined.

As a result of the Crown's inability to raise anything like the figure of 13 million ducats needed for 1637, Olivares had been compelled to cut down on his expenditure and was quite unable to build up the great army of which he dreamed.[4] The provisions for 1639 were more modest —some 7 million ducats[5]—but the ministers had the greatest difficulty in inducing the bankers to undertake even this.

As Navel watched the frantic coming and going of ministers and their desperate search for new sources of revenue, he was quick to appreciate the way in which the situation could be exploited to Barce-

---

[1] Domínguez Ortiz, *Política y Hacienda de Felipe IV*, pp. 54–5.

[2] *Ibid.* p. 55. *Papel sellado* was introduced in 1636. It was specially stamped paper bearing a duty, to be used henceforth for all official and legal documents.

[3] *Ibid.* p. 290.   [4] *Ibid.* p. 57.   [5] *Ibid.*

lona's advantage. 'There has never been a better opportunity than the present', he wrote home,[1] 'because they do not possess a single *real*, and need our help for the wars with France. So if anything is to be done, let it be done quickly, because the emergency will be over when the treasure fleet arrives, and then they will remember nothing.' The Protonotario, for his part, was perfectly aware that Barcelona was attempting to take advantage of the Crown's financial troubles, and had no intention of playing the city's game. He was convinced that the Principality was rich enough to offer substantial help, and only refused to do so because of the self-interest and disloyalty of the Diputats. What had they ever done to help the king? he suddenly burst out in one stormy interview with Navel.[2] They had never rendered him any service; they had done nothing whatsoever at the time of the Leucata campaign, and they spent all their money on festivities and banquets; above all, they had sabotaged the Corts in order to save the Diputació from being reformed.

It was little use Navel insisting that the Diputació simply did not have the money to spare: that it was spending more than 50,000 *lliures* a year in interest on *censals*, and 16,000 on the salaries of royal officials as well as large sums on the dockyards, the hospitals and the prisons.[3] The Protonotario was certain that money was to be found in Catalonia, if only the king could lay hands on it. Why not, for example, a two months' loan of 70,000 ducats from the Catalan towns, at an interest rate of 8 per cent and full security?[4] Navel replied that Barcelona could not afford it. Then what about the Llotja of Barcelona merchants? Impossible, replied Navel. Trade had suffered badly from the war, and anyhow it could get 10 per cent on its loans. And if the king raised his offer from 8 to 10 per cent, what then? Again, no chance: past delays in payment had ruined the king's credit and Barcelona would not lend a *real*. Then what was to be done? asked the Protonotario. Give the city a *merced*, answered Navel....And so the conversations went round and round, always coming back to the king's desire for money and Barcelona's desire for a *merced*.

Navel himself felt that the correct policy was for Barcelona to agree

[1] Navel to Francesc Pons, 7 April 1639.
[2] AHB: CCO, 1639–40, fo. 8, Navel to Consellers, 9 April 1639.
[3] AHB: CCO, 1639–40, fo. 17, Navel to Consellers, 30 April 1639.
[4] AHB: CCO, 1639–40, fo. 12, Navel to Consellers, 16 April 1639.

to a financial service, but to make it conditional on the obtaining of the *mercedes* for which the city was so anxious.[1] He obviously considered the city to be in real danger, and thought it vital that the Consell de Cent should take some action before the arrival of the treasure fleet, which was expected in May.[2] The machinery of city government, however, moved slowly, and for an anxious Navel awaiting his instructions in Madrid, the deliberations of that august body seemed intolerably protracted.

Meanwhile, the Crown's shortage of money was making itself felt in the Principality. Work had come to a halt on the frontier defences because no cash remained. Even the necessary repairs to Perpinyà castle had been abandoned because the workmen refused to continue after remaining unpaid for forty-six days; no supplies could be sent to the fortress of Salces because the transport could not be afforded; the bakers of Elna had stopped baking bread for the troops until their bills were paid, and, worst of all, the army itself was in imminent danger of disintegration because the troops had not received their pay.[3]

The outlook was particularly serious because it was almost certain that the summer campaign of 1639 would be fought along the Catalan frontier. The French invasion of Guipúzcoa in 1638 had been unsuccessful, and it was natural that Richelieu should wish to probe the defences of Catalonia once again, especially as the general discontent of the Principality cannot have been unknown to him. But, ironically, Olivares as well as Richelieu had pinned his hopes on a campaign on the Catalan border. In laying his plans for the campaigning season, early in March 1639, he had picked upon Catalonia as the best part of Spain from which to wage war against France.[4] His reasons were both military and political. Catalonia was 'a rich province, abundant in men and supplies, and the most unburdened of all these kingdoms. It would be a very different matter to make war from Cantabria, which is poor and can offer very few men and supplies.' As the Principality had a coastline, galleys could be used, and troops be brought from Naples and Sicily. Catalonia, too, was farther from Castile than was the Cantabrian frontier, 'and these provinces of Castile are the most exhausted. Also,

---

[1] Navel to Consellers, 30 April 1639.
[2] AHB: CCO, 1639–40, fo. 21, Navel to Consellers, 7 May 1639.
[3] ACA: G, caja 13, Santa Coloma to King, 16 April 1639.
[4] AGS: Est., leg. 2663, paper in Olivares's hand, dated 12 March 1639.

we shall fulfil the hope we entertain of the Catalans, that when once provoked or attacked by the French, they will turn out gallantly to resist them....' While it was true that Catalan troops would be raw, this was a small price to pay for the help that Catalonia could give 'finding itself directly involved, as up to now it seems not to have been involved, with the common welfare of the Monarchy and of these kingdoms'.

In these fateful words lies the Conde Duque's recognition of his failures over so many years, to make Catalonia 'involve' itself in the fortunes of the Monarchy; and in his plan lies the determination to ensure that, this time, failure should be replaced by success. The Union of Arms, rejected by the Catalan Corts, would be imposed on the Principality by the logic of events.

Now that the Conde Duque had deliberately chosen Catalonia as the theatre of operations, it was not very comforting to discover that military preparations in the Principality were in a state of total disarray. Money for the defences *must* be found. The king wrote to the viceroy of Valencia ordering the sale of royal estates in Alicante,[1] but it was from Catalonia, not Valencia, that the main contribution was expected, and it is doubtful how far Catalonia was in a position to help. Such money as was to be found in the Principality belonged not to institutions but to private persons: to burgesses, to some of the *militars*, and to the wealthier peasants. Most of the Catalan municipalities were in debt, and all were husbanding their resources against the day of invasion.

It was therefore not surprising that the collection of the compulsory levy for fortifications was slow and inadequate, and accompanied by numerous incidents. Santa Coloma, faced on one side with the resistance of the Principality, and on the other with very specific instructions from Madrid, was perplexed and distraught. He had been ordered to have 6000 Catalans ready for the defence of the frontier, remembering that 'the supreme law is that of common defence and protection, and your power is in no way limited in such instances'.[2] This was all very well in theory, but as the towns positively refused to provide men before an invasion actually occurred, there was very little Santa Coloma could do. He had therefore confined himself to trying to build up

---

[1] ACA: CA, leg. 390, Junta for fortifications, 9 April 1639.
[2] ACA: CA, leg. 286, no. 6, Santa Coloma to King, 1 May 1639, summarizing his instructions.

stocks of supplies, dividing the Principality into twelve areas, each under the control of a judge of the Audiència. It was asking too much to expect him to raise troops and money, too. The marquis of Aytona wrote to commiserate with him upon 'the diversity of duties thrust upon you. They fail to realize you cannot work miracles without the where-withal. And I imagine not the least of your troubles is this business of fortifications, which is utterly impossible. I do not know where 100,000 *escudos* is to be found, when you think of the poverty of the land.'[1] Santa Coloma, once so ambitious for office, was beginning to discover, as his friend Magarola had already discovered from his experiences in the Council of Aragon, that this was not 'a time in which one can serve His Majesty with pleasure'.[2]

Fortunately for Santa Coloma, Languedoc was in little better state than Catalonia and the French were no better prepared for the cam-paign than the Spanish. Indeed, the operations that began in June 1639 and continued until January 1640 were a model of inefficiency on both sides. The commanders of both the French and Spanish armies were either incompetent, or sharply divided by personal enmities which extended to their planning of military operations; their armies, while containing good, if undisciplined, troops, suffered considerably more from poor leadership, poor provisioning and bad weather, than from their relatively infrequent clashes with each other.

The beginnings of the campaign are briefly but movingly described in the diary of a Catalan peasant from the region of Vic.

The year 1639 began with great news of war. We had news that the *gavatx*—the French—were massing and gathering a great army. And then on the eve of Quinquagesima, which was 11 June, they entered our Catalonia and did great damage to the crops. Then they laid siege to the castle of Salces. Then our men went out to meet them. Soldiers were sent according to the size of the village. From our place eleven went, and they left the day after St John, on 25 June.[3]

The French army under Schomberg and Condé was to capture the fortress of Salces on 19 July, and the following six months were to be spent in attempts by the Spanish armies to recover Salces, which was

---

[1] ACA: G, caja 13, Aytona to Santa Coloma, 9 April 1639.
[2] ACA: G, caja 13, Magarola to Santa Coloma, 23 April 1639.
[3] Diary of Joan Guardia of Corcó.

finally surrendered by the French commander Espenan on 6 January 1640.[1] But behind these bare details lay the story of a tragedy which was to engulf the Spanish Monarchy, beginning with the sufferings of those six months, and mounting to climax in which viceroy, Principality and the power of Spain itself, were successively swept away.

The six months' drama of the Salces campaign was enacted on a stage with four constantly alternating scenes. There was Madrid, where the Conde Duque and the Protonotario read their correspondence from the Principality with growing indignation, and poured forth in reply an unending stream of orders and reprimands. There was the Rosselló frontier and Perpinyà, where the harassed Santa Coloma did his best to follow his instructions and keep together an army without any money. There was Barcelona, where Santa Coloma's deputy, the Canceller of Catalonia, Francesc de Erill, abused and harried his compatriots in a way that suggested he was more interested in acquiring a bishopric for himself than in adding to the reputation of his country. Finally, there was the Principality itself, the towns and villages which found themselves subjected to constant pressure from the judges of the Audiència for more men, more supplies, more money.

The sufferings of the Catalans did not cause the Conde Duque any loss of sleep. 'Better that they should complain than that we should all weep', he wrote complacently to Santa Coloma, in an extraordinary letter, part bluster, part threats, part amateur strategy.[2] The Principality was to raise 8000 men, together with a further 6000 at His Majesty's expense until the arrival of reinforcements from Italy. There would be no shortage of money, the Conde Duque promised, and more than enough when the treasure fleet arrived.

The treasure fleet did not in fact arrive until late July, and in spite of Olivares's promises, Santa Coloma never had enough money to keep the army paid. But his immediate task was to raise enough native troops to meet the first French onslaught. As a start, he had, or expected, 2000 paid men offered by the municipalities during the past twelve months. He also had some 260 fief-holders of the Crown, whose

[1] See C. Vassal-Reig, *La Guerre en Roussillon sous Louis XIII* (Paris, 1934), for the military details of the campaign. The author's references to his sources are erratic, and it is not clear how far he has used Spanish documents. His valuable picture of French operations is not matched by a similarly well-informed account of events in Catalonia, or of the activities of the Spanish commanders.

[2] ACA: G, caja 15, Olivares to Santa Coloma, 18 June 1639.

legal obligation to serve with horse and arms for the duration of the campaign had been finally established after years of wrangling in the vice-regal tribunals.[1] These included several important members of the Catalan aristocracy, like Don Miquel de Rocabertí and Don Josep Margarit.[2] To swell the size of the native army, a *sometent general* was proclaimed, imposing heavy penalties on all those who failed to go to the front, and the ministers of the Audiència were dispatched to the various towns to negotiate for more troops.[3]

Santa Coloma's task was eased by the prompt response of Barcelona, which immediately voted to raise a company of 500 men and then increased the number to 700.[4] In gratitude for this, he revoked the order confiscating the *dret de la neu*—the city tax he had threatened to appropriate earlier in the year—and wrote to the king in praise of Barcelona.[5] Navel's hopes that the city would receive a *merced* rose once again.[6] He was unaware that the Protonotario, in a session of the Junta Grande for Catalan affairs, had admitted that Barcelona was serving 'well', but advised that it should not be given a *merced* because any more concessions by the king would destroy the last remnants of royal control over the city.[7]

Unhappily for the future harmony of the Principality, the viceroy's letter had contrasted the enthusiasm of Barcelona with the apathy of the Diputats. Santa Coloma was acting on the information sent him by his private agent in the city, Jeroni Torres, who told him that the Diputats were behaving 'worse than ever'.[8] By passing on the information to Madrid, the viceroy did great harm both to the Principality and to himself. Madrid immediately sent a sharp rebuke to the Diputació for raising no more than a thousand men.[9] This rebuke came as a shock to the Diputats, who had been particularly proud of their efforts.

We have no doubt [they wrote to Grau, their permanent agent in Madrid] that calumnies are being spread about us; in fact, we are certain of it, in view

[1] ACA: CA, leg. 286, no. 2, Dr Vinyes to King, 20 June 1639.
[2] ACA: CA, leg. 391, T. Fontanet to Santa Coloma, 6 March 1639.
[3] ACA: CA, leg. 286, no. 2, Santa Coloma to King, 24 June 1639.
[4] AHB: CCO, 1639–40, fos. 76–7, Santa Coloma to City, 21 June 1639.
[5] ACA: CA, leg. 391, Santa Coloma to King, 24 June 1639.
[6] AHB: CCO, 1639–40, fos. 106–7, Navel to Consellers, 16 July 1639.
[7] AGS: GA, leg. 1257, Junta Grande, 13 July 1639.
[8] ACA: G, caja 16, Torres to Santa Coloma, 22 June 1639.
[9] ACA: G, Dietari, 1638–41, part II, fo. 226, King to Diputats, 1 July 1639.

of the hatred with which we are regarded by the ministers here who invent them, and we are well aware of the favourable reception they have in Madrid. So it comes as no surprise to learn that our actions are viewed in an unfavourable light. But, God willing, the well-intentioned will one day be disabused, and our rivals confounded.[1]

While the Diputats were finding enemies in every quarter, the viceroy changed his mind about them. 'From what I understand about their efforts to increase the size of the levy...Your Majesty will find them so willing that further pressure to induce them to make a supreme effort will not be needed. Their fault was at the beginning, when they were no more than lukewarm.'[2] Unfortunately, this recantation came too late. The Diputats were by now convinced that in Santa Coloma they had an implacable enemy who would seize every available opportunity to belittle their efforts, and they noted in confirmation the speed with which he had forwarded the royal reprimand of 1 July, and his delay in forwarding an earlier letter bringing the joyful news that the king would suspend all judicial action in the contraband controversy.[3] The misunderstanding of these early weeks of the Salces campaign widened the rift between viceroy and Diputats until it became a permanent feud, of incalculable consequence for the future of the Principality.

By 11 July 7500 Catalans had arrived at the frontier and more were arriving daily.[4] But 5000 of these were to be reserved for the defence of the frontier, so that only 2500 remained to join the army of 8000 Castilians, Italians and Flemings which was to relieve the besieged fortress of Salces. A force of this size had no hope against a French besieging army of 16,000 men, and Salces surrendered to the French on 19 July.

The fall of Salces played an important part in hastening the deterioration of relations between the Principality and the Court. On returning from his mission to Madrid, Canon Puig had warned the Diputats that in the Court, 'they are pleased that the French have entered, and do not care two pins for Salces'.[5] But they affected to care mightily as soon as it fell into the hands of the French. The regent Magarola, in one of a

[1] ACA: G, LT, 1638–9, fos. 335–6, Diputats to Grau, 9 July 1639.
[2] ACA: G, caja 18, Santa Coloma to King, 17 July 1639.
[3] ACA: G, LT, 1638–9, fos. 345–6, Diputats to Grau, 16 July 1639.
[4] AGS: GA, leg. 1257, Santa Coloma to King, 11 July 1639.
[5] ACA: G, caja 17, Erill to Santa Coloma, 15 July 1639.

series of letters to Santa Coloma which repeatedly spoke of the Protonotario's hatred of the Catalans, had warned him that in victory all the
credit would go to the Castilians, and in defeat all the blame to the
Catalans. His prophecy proved accurate. Those Catalans unfortunate
enough to be in Madrid at the time of the fall of Salces dared not go into
the streets,

afraid that the boys will throw stones at us when they see we are Catalans;
and everyone speaks of us in such a humiliating way that it is terrible to
listen to them. One can only hope that things go better during the rest of the
campaign, so that at least we recover some of our lost reputation, though
there is no hope of recovering it all. And God forgive those who are most to
blame, who I know are not the Catalans. But we take the blame, and they the
glory if anything goes well.[1]

The fall of Salces had indeed become the signal for general recrimina-
tions. Madrid, as Magarola had warned, blamed the Catalans. Barcelona and the Diputació, anxious to absolve themselves, wrote to Madrid
blaming Santa Coloma for not attacking the enemy. The fact that
Santa Coloma's agent in Madrid ascribed the Diputats' letter to their
desire for revenge suggests how serious the feud between viceroy and
Diputats had become.[2] Santa Coloma himself was much too concerned
about his own reputation at Court to ignore the attacks upon it. He
wrote numerous letters to his friends at Court defending himself against
the charges made against him,[3] and pointing out, quite correctly, that
he had been dissuaded from attacking the enemy by none other than
the commander of the troops of the Diputació.[4] The trouble was that
the Catalans 'want to get the war over in a day, and do not consider
the risk involved in moving without proper precautions'.[5]

'Proper precautions' included adequate financial resources, and Santa
Coloma seems to have been starved of money during June and July.
Magarola, watching the Protonotario at close range, believed that this
was deliberate.

I think they will do nothing of any use about money.... They expect the
miracle to be achieved with the province's money, and enjoy telling each

[1] ACA: G, caja 18, Fructuoso Piqué to M. Pérez, 30 July 1639.
[2] ACA: G, caja 19, Bernabé Camacho de Carvajal to Santa Coloma, 12 Aug. 1639.
[3] E.g. to the Marquis of Aytona, 24 Aug. 1639 (ACA: G, caja 20).
[4] ACA: G, caja 20, *Parecer de Don Josep de Sorribes*, 17 Aug. 1639.
[5] ACA: G, caja 20, Santa Coloma to Olivares, 1 Aug. 1639

other that the Catalans are a people who know how to defend themselves. In short, I don't know what to say except that they are our enemies, and their treatment of the Catalans is a scandal.[1]

It is not clear whether or not Magarola's remarks about Madrid's malign intentions were entirely justified. By the Conde Duque's reckoning, Santa Coloma should have had an actual surplus of no less than 36,000 *escudos* for supplies. He had started June with 177,000 *escudos*; he had an army of 1500 cavalry and 5000 infantry, rising to 8000 in July, and at a monthly rate of pay of 10 *escudos* for a cavalryman and 7 for an infantryman, he should not have spent more than 140,750 *escudos* all told.[2] These calculations may have appeared convincing in Madrid. To Santa Coloma, confronted with the high cost of provisions in Catalonia, they naturally appeared unrealistic. 'The expense is much greater than Your Excellency imagines', he wrote to Olivares, pointing out that the devastation of Rosselló made it necessary to bring all the army's supplies from afar.[3]

The ministers in Madrid were not impressed by the viceroy's arguments about the cost of obtaining provisions. If corn were needed for the army, it should be requisitioned without any attempt at paying on the spot, since the requirements of defence excused all delays in payment. But when Santa Coloma passed on this order to the judges of the Audiència, whom the shortage of officials in the viceregal administration had converted into executive ministers in charge of recruiting and provisioning, they refused to obey. All the leading members of the Audiència, Miquel Joan Magarola, Dr Puig, Dr Vinyes, agreed that the order ran counter to the constitutions of the Principality.[4] In spite of their scruples, however, the army's requirements made it almost essential for the ministers of the Audiència to indulge in high-handed behaviour if they were to find their quota of supplies. This led to innumerable incidents. At Granollers, for example, the aged Dr Berart almost lost his life at the hands of a crowd over five hundred strong shouting *Via fora fam*.[5] In the town of Lloret in the diocese of Girona

---

[1] ACA: G, caja 18, Magarola to Santa Coloma, 16 July 1639.
[2] ACA: G, caja 20, King to Santa Coloma, 6 Aug. 1639.
[3] ACA: G, caja 20, Santa Coloma to Olivares, 1 Aug. 1639.
[4] ACA: CA, leg. 287, no. 126, Santa Coloma to King, 8 Aug. 1639.
[5] Literally 'down with hunger!' ACA: G, caja 19, Dr Berart to the Canceller, Erill, 25 Aug. 1639.

there was an outcry when Dr Ramon demanded a number of sheep, barrels of wine and quantities of corn against the transit of some infantry companies, and demanded them 'not as a free gift but as an obligation, threatening to seize them at their expense...'. On hearing this, the cathedral chapter of Girona wrote to the Diputats that if these excesses continued

the province will be utterly destroyed...and most of all this diocese, where the peasants cannot work their fields because most of their animals have been taken to the camp, while the remainder are being used for the transport of baggage and provisions. And on top of all this, it breaks one's heart to hear of the frauds and bribery practised by the officials entrusted with rounding up the animals.[1]

From all accounts, the insatiable demands of an increasingly large army were fast completing that alienation of the Comtats which had already begun with the publication of the royal decrees on trade with France. Troops and inhabitants were involved in constant clashes. Many of the troops, like the duke of Modena's Italians, were utterly uncontrollable,[2] but the villages did their best to make the troops feel unwelcome,[3] whether or not they maintained a reasonable discipline. One of the better company commanders, Don Diego de Brizuela, wrote ominously to the viceroy, 'Holland is not more rebellious than Cerdanya; only the preachers are missing, to make them lose their faith along with their obedience'.[4]

The unrest in the frontier regions, and the general desire for a rapid victory which would free the Principality from the burdensome presence of the army, help to explain why the fall of Salces had such devastating psychological consequences in Catalonia. Prepared neither by organization nor by temperament for a concentrated effort spread over a long period, the Catalans could have found some consolation for hostilities on their soil only in a swift campaign and glorious victory. The fall of Salces, and the prolonged siege that would be required for its recovery, meant that victory would be long deferred, and the delay might well place a heavier strain on the fragile Castilian-Catalan partnership than it was able to bear. It was significant that the Castilian

[1] ACG: Registrum litterarum, 1627–41, Chapter of Girona to Diputats, 20 Aug. 1639.
[2] ACA: G, caja 18, Marquis of Toralto to Santa Coloma, 10 July 1639.
[3] ACA: G, caja 18, Rafael Manegat to Santa Coloma, 8 July 1639.
[4] ACA: G, caja 17, Brizuela to Santa Coloma, 7 July 1639.

and Catalan troops were already quarrelling in the barracks: on 1 August they became involved in a fight which went on for over two hours and led to the death of seven or eight men.[1] This kind of incident only served to increase the bitterness not only in the camp itself, but in Madrid and Barcelona, too. From this moment, such enthusiasm as had buoyed up the Catalans during the first few weeks of the campaign rapidly melted away. It was now, with a long campaign in prospect, and little chance of anything but abuse from Madrid in recognition of their efforts, that the Catalans began to lose interest in the proceedings, to come to the front only as they were driven by the royal officials, and desert as soon as the occasion offered. Richelieu had few military successes more pregnant with political consequences than the capture of Salces by his armies, and their ability to hold it for six months against the besieging Spanish forces. The emergence of a powerful Diputació had been the first landmark along the road to a Castilian-Catalan conflict. The fall of Salces on 19 July 1639 was the second.

The immediate consequence of the fall of Salces was a change of commanders. The Protonotario, to whom the Juntas and Councils in Madrid turned more and more as the 'expert' on Catalan affairs, told them that Santa Coloma's letters showed him full of good intentions but singularly ineffective in their realization, and recommended the immediate despatch to the Principality of the marquis of los Balbases, son of the great Spínola, to take command of all but the Catalan troops.[2] The rumour of his appointment as Captain-General of the army for the relief of Rosselló and Cerdanya came as unwelcome news to the Principality. 'They say he comes with great powers, and that he is a terribly cruel man. This cannot be a good thing for us Catalans—it is bad enough his being Genoese.'[3]

Balbases took with him very specific instructions, prepared for him by a Junta which included Olivares and the Protonotario.[4] It was explained to him that the Catalans, although very loyal, had 'an excessive regard for the observance of their laws' and were afraid to allow a single modification of them, lest it should open the way to others. They could, for example, have prevented the French invasion by having

---

[1] AMV: CR, 13, Francesc Sala to Consellers of Vic, 2 Aug. 1639.
[2] AGS: GA, leg. 1262, Junta Grande, 1 Aug. 1639.
[3] AMV: CR, 13, Francesc Sala to Consellers of Vic, 31 Aug. 1639.
[4] ACA: CA, leg. 286, no. 28, instructions for los Balbases, 18 Aug. 1639.

6000 men on the frontier before it was launched, 'but I perfectly realize that this is not a suitable time for attempting to change an attitude as apprehensive on this point as that of the Catalans.' For the present, all that could be done was to appeal to their patriotism by making much of the heroic example of their forefathers. Since the campaign was now likely to be long, the three Catalan *tercios*, or 6000 men, should remain on the frontier, and should be indefinitely maintained by the Catalan municipalities. This would avoid the loss of men from industry and agriculture, and would, incidentally, accomplish the first stage of Olivares's schemes for making the Catalans contribute a standing force to the defence of the Monarchy.

Balbases was told that Dr Escartín, Fiscal of the Audiencia of Aragon, who was to investigate the behaviour of the troops, was also to make secret inquiries as to how many Catalans were actually present in the army. The question of numbers was now assuming considerable importance. The first serious hints that things were far from well with the Catalan regiments appear in the second week of August. 'Disease is beginning to spread, and the hospitals are full', reported the captain of the company sent by the town of Vic. 'All the *cavallers* are getting bored because they see that nothing is happening and that we are all sitting here with our hands folded doing nothing.'[1] Such was the behaviour of the nobles that Santa Coloma commented very sharply on it in a letter to Madrid of 24 August. Many of the aristocracy had not come to the front; others had simply left without leave, like Don Ramon de Guimerà, Don Ferran Fivaller and Narcís Ramon March, against all of whom he was instituting judicial proceedings.[2] Santa Coloma's remarks drew from the king a letter addressed to the Catalan nobility, in which he expressed his surprise at their half-heartedness in 'arriving late or departing prematurely, as some of you have done'.[3] The humiliating letter from their monarch did nothing to enhance the popularity of Santa Coloma among the Catalan nobles. The viceroy could begin to count the aristocracy, as well as the Diputats, among his enemies.

But it was not only the nobles who were leaving the army. The rank and file also were deserting fast. Again it was the viceroy who sent the

[1] AMV: CR, 13, Francesc Sala to Consellers of Vic, 11 Aug. 1639.
[2] ACA: G, caja 20, Santa Coloma to King, 24 Aug. 1639.
[3] ADP: Série B, 390, no. 11, King to Catalan nobles, 31 Aug. 1639.

I THE FORTRESS OF SALCES

news to Madrid. Stung by the malicious stories being circulated against him by the Diputats, Santa Coloma retaliated by expressly rejecting the claims of the Diputació to have rendered great services to the Crown.[1] So far from having begun its preparations well before the French invasion, it was far less ready than Barcelona and the towns. Although the enemy had crossed into Catalan territory on 10 June, not a single soldier levied by the Diputació had reached Figueres even as late as the 30th. All the blame for this lay with the Diputats themselves, the most ill-disposed persons in all Catalonia. As for their claim that there were 12,000 Catalans at the front, the Principality may well have been paying 12,000 men, but only 9000 were effective, and these had been raised with no thanks to the Diputació.

It was unfortunate for the Principality that the dispute between viceroy and Diputats should have helped to bring to light the undoubted fact that many of the Catalan troops had deserted. Although the Principality was indeed paying 12,000 men, a muster at Perpinyà on 13 August revealed no more than 6654.[2] The rest, according to a Barcelona company commander, had simply gone absent.[3] Boredom, illness, insufficient pay and constant bickering with the Castilians had all helped to reduce the numbers of the Catalans, and there was even a suspicion that desertions were being deliberately encouraged. The duke of Cardona, for example, discovered and arrested a familiar of the Inquisition called Pere Mijars, who had gone the rounds of the barracks of Cardona's company telling the men that they had fulfilled their obligations and were free to go home.[4]

In spite of their defections, Balbases's first reports on the Catalan troops when he finally reached the Principality were relatively encouraging. Although raw troops, their potential was good, and time and work would remedy their inexperience.[5] But there was to be no time. On 19 September there was a sharp clash between the besiegers and the besieged, in which, according to Dr Vinyes, the French themselves said that the Catalan troops had 'fought like lions'.[6] Then, at a muster

[1] ACA: CA, leg. 391, Santa Coloma to King, 4 Sept. 1639.
[2] ACA: CA, leg. 285, no. 1, report by the *escribano de mandamiento*.
[3] AHB: CCO, 1639–40, fo. 121, Don Antoni d'Oms to Consellers, 3 Aug. 1639.
[4] ACA: G, caja 21, Cardona to Santa Coloma, 6 Sept. 1639.
[5] AGS: GA, leg. 1262, Balbases to Olivares, 15 Sept. 1639.
[6] ACA: G, Dietari, 1638–41, part II, fo. 273, Vinyes to Diputats, 31 Oct. 1639.

held three days later, the startling discovery was made that only 3100 Catalans still remained in the camp. More in sorrow than in anger, Balbases wrote to the Conde Duque that, at the present rate of desertion, there would shortly be none left. 'And even worse, Sir, we don't know what to do with those who remain, because they will not obey, or work, or stay in quarters where the enemy artillery can reach them.... The country either cannot or will not help. I don't know how to tell Your Excellency this, but many of them are fleeing....'[1]

The news that some 8000 out of a supposed total of 12,000 were missing from the camp caused dismay throughout the Principality. The Diputats' first reaction was to write to their company commander saying they had rather the men had died fighting than infamously deserted the flags.[2] But indignation soon gave way to incredulity. The Canceller Erill reported:

The Diputats pretend that the flight of our men is imaginary...and they are supported in this by their agents in the camp, who claim that the figure of 3100 is wrong, and that there are really more than 5000 Catalans, and many sick and wounded. And they say the number of desertions is insignificant, and that Your Excellency's secretariat has given many leave-passes to the men.[3]

In so far as the truth about the desertions can be discovered, it appears to lie between the two extremes; the Catalans attempted to minimize them, while Balbases failed to explain them. There can be no doubt that they were deserting: Santa Coloma wrote on the margin of Erill's letter to him that 'more Catalans are fleeing every day, and, as you can imagine, their reputation is ruined...', but he pointed out that the real cause of the desertions was the lack of any hospital facilities for the Catalans. As sickness was raging in the camp, there was nothing to be done with the seriously ill except to give them leave to return home. Dr Vinyes alone had issued 1200 leave-passes to men certified sick by the doctors.[4] Although Santa Coloma was sure that no frauds were committed in the issue of these passes, he was certainly misinformed. Some men who had returned from the front with passes were in perfectly good health.[5] But a large number, probably the majority, of the

[1] AGS: GA, leg. 1262, Balbases to Olivares, 23 Sept. 1639.
[2] ACA: G, LT, 1639–40, fos. 65–6, Diputats to Sorribes, 24 Sept. 1639.
[3] ACA: G, caja 22, Erill to Santa Coloma, 1 Oct. 1639.   [4] Vinyes to Diputats, 31 Oct.
[5] E.g. there was a very robust sergeant from Maduxer's company who was found in Barcelona with a pass signed by his captain (ACA: G, LT, 1639–40, fos. 152–3, Diputats to Tamarit, 26 Nov. 1639).

absentees were genuinely sick or wounded. The roads going south from Perpinyà were crowded with diseased and dying Catalan soldiers who could find no one to confess them, and the casualty list, particularly of nobles, was growing fast.[1]

The desertion of the Catalan troops is put in clearer perspective by a fact to which Madrid gave no publicity. Non-Catalan troops were also deserting, and their number, which was about 12,000 at the end of August, was down to less than 9000 by the beginning of October.[2] If over a quarter of the non-Catalan soldiers had deserted, as compared with between a half and two-thirds of the Catalans, the difference may largely be explained by the Catalans' resentment at the manner in which they were treated, and by the lack of adequate medical help.

But Madrid was not interested in explanations. The fact that a large number of Catalans had deserted, merely confirmed the general opinion of the Catalan character, and strengthened the hand of those who advocated the use of harsher measures against the Principality. These were now considered to be fully justified by the urgency of the military and fiscal situation. Some time during 1639 a special Junta had been convened to consider the 'great tribulations' of the king's many subjects. But

none [it was pointed out] can compare with those of Castile. When our storm-tossed Monarchy is involved in a war forced upon it by implacable enemies, it is right and proper that all should suffer and that the burden should be equally shared, rather than that some should be exempt from all obligations while others are reduced to extreme distress.

Bearing this in mind, the Junta was to pronounce on ways in which the king could legitimately increase the military contributions of certain regions.[3] Although Catalonia was not mentioned on this occasion, it was clear that the plan for the Union of Arms was everywhere to be vigorously pressed. Inasmuch as the Catalan desertions offended against the spirit and the letter of this plan, they provided a convenient excuse for radical action. A meeting of the Council of Aragon attended by the Protonotario and Cardinal Borja suggested 'how useful it would be for Your Majesty to take advantage of events arising out of

---

[1] ACA: G, caja 22, Don Joan to Don Bernardino de Marimón, 3 Oct. 1639.

[2] AGS: GA, leg. 1261, Balbases to Olivares, 2 Oct. 1639.

[3] BM: Eg. MS 2082, fos. 149–50, *Decreto de SM sobre que contribuyan para la guerra con Francia las provincias separadas de lo de Castilla con 10,000 hombres.*

the behaviour of the Catalans, for arranging with the utmost care for such future action in Catalonia as may be thought desirable'.[1]

Those ministers who, like the Protonotario, demanded a harsher policy against the Catalans had no need to look far for their justification. It was not simply a question of desertions. The general attitude of the Catalans to the war had become intolerable. Balbases reported that they refused to send supplies for the army, or reinforcements to replace the missing and the dead. He found himself in a quandary.

If only we were in a province which gave help like all the rest, there would be some hope....But in this country, I do not know what to say to Your Excellency, who already knows too much about it. Why, in Perpinyà itself a soldier even has to pay for the sacraments if he wants to die. Although there are many honourable people and good *caballeros* in this Principality, I am afraid there are also some who will be pleased if the troops are so weakened as to lack the strength to billet themselves.[2]

Balbases was not exaggerating. The scant humanity with which the inhabitants of the frontier regions treated the troops supposedly sent for their protection, was leading to wide-scale desertion. Even the usually impassive Philip IV was sufficiently moved by the news from Catalonia to turn to someone beside him with the words: 'What do you think of the Catalans?'[3] It was clear that something must be done before the army in Catalonia melted away. On 3 October the Protonotario drafted for the king a letter to be sent to Santa Coloma. 'My intention', it began, 'has always been to conform to the demands of the constitutions, and if this had been compatible with the defence of the province...it would have been my wish to observe them scrupulously.' But the refusal of the Catalans to bring supplies to the front unless they received immediate payment, had made it impossible for him to continue in this way. He had therefore been obliged to take the 'final resolution' in order to prevent the province from destroying itself. By this 'final resolution', the royal ministers in Catalonia were to be absolved from their oath to observe the constitutions when any point arose connected with the maintenance of the army. They were in future to go through the province collecting forage without giving

---

[1] ACA: CA, leg. 283, no. 8, consulta, 28 Sept. 1639.
[2] AGS: GA, leg. 1261, Balbases to Olivares, 6 Oct. 1639.
[3] AHB: CCO, 1639–40, fo. 165, Navel to Consellers, 1 Oct. 1639.

immediate cash payment, and they were to see that the troops had every comfort.[1]

The Conde Duque had no doubts about his decision. To him it seemed incredible that at a time when the king had sent an army to the defence of Catalonia, and corn was being sent to the Principality from all over Spain, the Catalans

should make a fuss about transporting it the three leagues from the sea to the barracks. They should be doing this—forgive the expression—on the shoulders of the town councillors, if no other way can be found. By now I am nearly at my wits end, but I say, and I shall still be saying on my deathbed, that if the constitutions do not allow this, then *the devil take the constitutions* and whoever observes them, myself included. For no man can observe them who has not been abandoned by God, and who is not an enemy of His Divine Majesty, of his king, and of his fatherland.[2]

'The devil take the constitutions!' Time after time they had stood in the way of the Conde Duque's policies, and now the pent-up exasperation of eighteen years could no longer be contained. But while it was no doubt satisfying to pour wrath on the Catalans, Olivares showed little awareness of the true implications of his decision. For Madrid, it seemed necessary and legitimate to disregard the more obnoxious Catalan constitutions. For the Catalans, on the other hand, even a limited infringement allowed of no justification. The king had sworn to observe all their laws, and the arbitrary revocation of even one of them implied the breaking of the sacrosanct contract on which their existence as a nation was founded.

While the ultimate effects of any decision to disregard certain of the Principality's traditional laws must be to do incalculable harm to the relationship between the Catalans and their prince, those most immediately affected were the king's ministers in Catalonia, especially the judges of the Audiència. They had been brought up to regard the constitutions as inviolate; on taking office, they had sworn never to infringe them. Now they found themselves presented with a tragic personal dilemma. If they obeyed the new order and disregarded the constitutions, they both did violence to their own convictions and made themselves liable to penalization by the Diputació for breaking their oaths.

[1] ACA: CA, leg. 390, King to Santa Coloma, 3 Oct. 1639.
[2] ACA: G, caja 22, Olivares to Santa Coloma, 7 Oct. 1639 (my italics).

If, on the other hand, they disregarded the order, they failed in their duty to their king, and rendered themselves liable to the charge of treason.

Even before they were confronted by this conflict of loyalties, they were working under an intolerable strain. Since they were the only reliable officials of the Crown in the Principality, it had been found necessary to suspend the sessions of the Audiència and send them through the province to recruit troops and gather supplies. They all had separate areas to stump. Accompanied only by a notary or a commissioner, they would ride from village to village attempting to persuade the sullen inhabitants to send more men to Rosselló. Their salaries unpaid, without money and without military protection, the unfortunate judges moved about the country in peril of their lives.[1] Under such conditions it is only surprising that more of them did not imitate Dr Martí, who exempted villages from providing men or supplies in return for not inconsiderable bribes;[2] or the aged and infirm Dr Gori, who virtually abandoned the struggle, preferring the lash of the Canceller's tongue to the fury of the mob.[3]

In spite of their difficulties, the ministers had done their best during these trying months to observe the constitutions even while they attempted to satisfy the demands of the Canceller and the viceroy. Now they were expressly ordered to ignore those same constitutions they had sworn to observe. Madrid could scarcely have hit upon a more effective method of destroying the last vestiges of royal authority in the Principality. In spite of Dr Fontanella's allegations that the Audiència had ceased to be an impartial tribunal, its record in the years before 1639 does not suggest that it had become a mere instrument for castilianization. Indeed, the judges were nowhere regarded with more distrust than in Madrid itself. The regent Bayetolá reported in his *visita* of 1635–6 that 'they are terrible people, whom the Conde Duque knows better than I did before I came here, because I remember him saying that the worst of the lot were the ministers'.[4] The Conde Duque was right. The personal background and inclinations of the judges effectively prevented them from behaving in judicial matters as mere lackeys of

[1] This description is based on a letter from Erill to Santa Coloma, dated 23 July 1639 (ACA: G, caja 17).

[2] ACA: G, caja 19, Erill to Santa Coloma, 26 Aug. 1639.   [3] *Ibid.*

[4] ACA: CA, leg. 325, no. 19, Bayetolá to J. L. de Villanueva, 15 July 1636.

the Court, although the pressure upon them to carry out the dictates of Madrid had been growing constantly stronger. But, by and large, it had always been possible for them to take shelter behind the constitutions when faced with embarrassing decisions.

None the less, the very ambiguity of their position had also tended to undermine Catalan confidence in their impartiality. Since the Audiència was an advisory council to the viceroy as well as a judicial tribunal, it was invariably associated in the popular mind with the actions of a hated viceregal administration; and this association was made all the closer on occasions when the inadequacy of its local officials compelled the administration to send out the judges to their assistance. This had happened at the peak of the bandit movement in 1614, when Almazán had prorogued the Audiència for two months, in order to send the judges into the localities,[1] and Santa Coloma had been reduced to similar emergency measures in 1639 when he turned them into recruiting officers and quartermasters.

The employment of the judges to minister to the needs of the army in the summer and autumn of 1639 made them for the first time personally known, and personally hated, throughout the Principality.[2] The king's order of 3 October commanding them to ignore the constitutions, sealed their fate. From this moment they came to be regarded, fairly or unfairly, as traitors to the fatherland, as the minions of Castile. If ever the Principality were to rise in revolt, the judges of the Audiència were marked down as the first victims of the insurrection.

The unfortunate judges themselves were in no doubt as to the unpleasant situation in which they found themselves. The new orders from Madrid held Dr Vinyes 'in great suspense, since I see so many dangers and inconveniences in the execution of them'.[3] Yet the heavy losses incurred by the army besieging Salces left the viceroy with no choice but to press the Principality for more men and more supplies so that the siege should not have to be raised; the lack of enthusiasm in the Princi-

---

[1] See above, p. 87.

[2] Erill wrote to Santa Coloma in a tone of rather pained surprise on 6 Oct. 1639 that 'we are looked upon as infamous, and bad Catalans, and as enemies of the fatherland' (ACA: G, caja 22). A contemporary writer, Tormé i Liori, confirms the unfortunate consequences of the despatch of the judges of the Audiència through the Principality. He says that the people became increasingly disrespectful of royal justice when they saw them employed on duties so far removed from their proper occupations (BC: MS 762, *Miscelaneos históricos y políticos...*, p. 47).

[3] ACA: G, caja 23, Vinyes to Santa Coloma, 11 Oct. 1639.

pality meant that the pressure could only be successfully applied if the constitutions, particularly those which touched upon the commandeering of provisions, were disregarded; and the only ministers capable of applying the pressure were the judges. Their exertions alone enabled the army to survive.

Inevitably the cost to the Principality was terrible. In one of his more generous moments, the Canceller, usually so ready to condemn, wrote to Santa Coloma: 'we cannot deny that the province is spending more than it can afford'.[1] The heaviest financial burden fell on the towns, whose resources had been severely strained by the maintenance since June of companies of up to 100 men, at a monthly cost of 10 *lliures* for a *militar* and 7 for a musketeer.[2] For all of them this entailed the attempt to raise municipal loans, often without much success: the town of Cervera raised a loan of 2000 *lliures* in November, and another of 2000 in December;[3] Lleida attempted to raise 1000 on a *censal* in August, but could find no takers.[4] The heaviness of the burden was increased by the fact that it was unequally distributed. The *batlle* of Talarn, for example, reported at the end of October that many *militars* and citizens in his area had not gone to the camp, and had refused to contribute to the expenses of the infantry company maintained by the town.[5] Sanz, surveying events from Vic, wrote in his diary that 'at this time many showed their faults publicly by not going to the camp; some because they were afraid of illnesses and the possibility of plague, others because they were cowards or idlers; and so in the end almost everyone round here avoided it'.[6]

The Canceller, writing to the viceroy from Barcelona, let slip no opportunity of passing adverse comments on the behaviour of the Diputats and the city authorities. Santa Coloma, in turn, had no scruples about forwarding them to Madrid. He was so terrified at the prospect of ruining his reputation that he attempted to obey all his instructions to the letter, and hastened to apportion the blame in such a way that no ill-success could cause any reflection on his own shortcomings. Dr Vinyes made one or two attempts to stiffen his resolution,

[1] ACA: G, caja 22, Erill to Santa Coloma, 6 Oct. 1639.
[2] ACA: G, Dietari, 1638–41, part II, fo. 212.
[3] AHC: Llibre de Consells de Vintyquatrena, 1635–43, fos. 120v and 128.
[4] APL: R. 440, fo. 215.
[5] ACA: G, caja 23, Pau Prior to Santa Coloma, 29 Oct. 1639.
[6] Sanz, *Relació Breu*, p. 38.

reminding him that it was always possible to make counter-suggestions when inexpedient orders were issued,[1] but his efforts met with no success. Santa Coloma was bent on escaping censure, whatever the cost to others. 'The Diputats and city of Barcelona are setting such a bad example,' he wrote to Olivares, 'that they are slowing everything down, and all the blame must fall on them because it is all their fault.'[2] But what else could the Diputats have done? They claimed that their income was now only 140,000 *lliures*[3]—a figure that was probably correct. It had been about 180,000 a decade earlier, and since then not only had trade declined, but the tax of 24,000 *lliures* a year for the upkeep of the galleys, religiously collected for fifteen years after the galleys themselves had been lost, had eventually, and very conveniently, been suspended in 1638. Their ordinary annual expenditure was in the region of 100,000 *lliures*; the costs involved in the contraband controversy and the embassy of Canon Puig to Madrid had been heavy, and they had spent 51,324 *lliures* on the payment of their *tercio* at Salces, up to the beginning of October.[4] At this rate of expenditure, they could not go on much longer: 'we do not own a silver-mine, and we are not able to borrow'.[5]

It was probably Barcelona, more than the Diputació, which was dragging its heels in October. The refusal of the ministers in Madrid to give it any *merced* for its very considerable services during the summer had produced the consequences that might have been foretold. Angry and disillusioned, it appeared to have lost all interest in the war, which might just as well have been taking place in the Antipodes, as Erill acidly remarked.[6] The Consellers showed themselves in no hurry to discuss the contents of the viceroy's plaintive letters, nor to summon the Consell de Cent for deliberations, and they carried their obstruction to such lengths that when the city was asked for the loan of a spare shed to store provender for the cavalry, the Consellers responded by having it dismantled so that it should not be taken.[7]

In Madrid, the Conde Duque fumed at the 'extravagance of the pro-

[1] ACA: caja 23, Vinyes to Santa Coloma, 29 Oct. 1639.
[2] AGS: GA, leg. 1261, Santa Coloma to Olivares, 13 Oct. 1639.
[3] ACA: G, caja 22, Diputats to Santa Coloma, 22 Oct. 1639.
[4] ACA: G, caja 22, Diputats to Santa Coloma, 5 Oct. 1639.
[5] ACA: G, LT, 1639–40, fo. 104, Diputats to Grau, 22 Oct. 1639.
[6] ACA: G, caja 22, Erill to Santa Coloma, 4 Oct. 1639.
[7] ACA: G, caja 22, Erill to Santa Coloma, 9 Oct. 1639.

vince, which in the past and now defies description, when it is a matter of ejecting the enemy from their homes'.[1] As the Conde Duque's orders grew harsher, the fears of the Catalans increased. On 28 October, the Diputats received a letter from Madrid, forwarded by Santa Coloma, telling them that as the province was being lost by their scandalous behaviour, the dues of the Generalitat would be collected by royal officials for the duration of the war. They immediately formed a committee of eighteen, which included some of the names most prominent in the annals of resistance to Madrid: Don Joan de Peguera, Francesc Joan de Vergós, Pau Boquet, Josep Fontanella. This committee was to consider what might be done 'for the sake of the constitutions and in defence of the Generalitat'.[2] Two days later they convened the Braços. In a meeting of no less than one hundred there was an exactly equal division on the policy to be adopted: half said that the Diputats should again write to the king telling him that they could do no more, while the other half thought that the Diputat Militar should go to Salces, as Santa Coloma had long been urging. The Diputats finally decided that Tamarit should set out for Salces, taking with him a company specially raised for the occasion. The costs would be borne by a loan from the city on the security of the Diputació's silver, 'for we are reduced to the last extremity'.[3]

Tamarit, mounted on a white horse, at the head of a long procession, left Barcelona on 8 November, to the accompaniment of drums and trumpets.[4] On the 13th he arrived at the camp. The Diputats had now genuinely done all they could, but they could not resist following up their exertions by writing to the king a letter that contained a vicious personal attack on Santa Coloma. They accused him of lack of foresight in his preparations for the siege; of setting a bad example in not sending his eighteen-year-old son, Don Lluís de Queralt, to the war; and of using his opportunities as captain-general to pay off his family debts, as could be proved by a bill of exchange for 2000 *escuts* delivered to the Barcelona bank on 23 August.[5]

The Diputats were not alone in their hatred of Santa Coloma. By his

[1] RAH: 11–10–5, leg. 6, fo. 113, Olivares to Cardenal Infante, 23 Oct. 1639.
[2] ACA: G, Dietari, 1638–41, part II, fo. 261.
[3] ACA: G, LT, 1639–40, fo. 116, Diputats to Enric d'Alemany, 31 Oct. 1639.
[4] ACA: G, 114, *Dietari i Itinerari del Molt Ill. Sr. Francesc de Tamarit.*
[5] ACA: G, 909, Lletres Secretes, Diputats to King, 2 Nov. 1639.

latest measures he had succeeded in alienating the entire governing class of the Principality. He had decided that the only way to obtain the Principality's full co-operation was to compel the aristocracy to fulfil its military obligations. On 27 October proclamations throughout the Principality ordered all *militars* to go to the front, whether or not they held municipal office,[1] and Erill instituted judicial proceedings against twenty members of the Barcelona aristocracy who had stayed at home.[2] Threatened with arrest, or with compulsory departure to the front, nobles and wealthy burgesses prudently retired to the churches until the crisis had passed.

Santa Coloma was in despair. The siege appeared to be endless; sickness was spreading through the camp, and the Catalan contingent was scarcely a shadow of what it once had been. Olivares bombarded the viceroy with letters containing urgent postscripts written in his own hand complaining of the behaviour of the Catalans, and urging Santa Coloma to press on with the recruiting of more men to fill the empty ranks.[3] The viceroy was determined to obtain a further five hundred men from Barcelona, but in Barcelona, and indeed all over the Principality, people were refusing to go to the front, even though some municipalities were offering a bonus of 20 or 25 *lliures* to anyone who signed on.[4] In the Consell de Cent, Cristòfol Sangenís, a merchant, was bold enough to propose that all artisans who went to Salces should have the opportunity of matriculating as merchants if they closed their shops within a year and a day, but his fellow merchants reacted so violently that the proposal had to be withdrawn.[5] To encourage the city, Erill had two merchants and a *militar* arrested, but this only made it the more defiant. The inhabitants would do anything rather than go to the war, and the Consellers were terrified of provoking an insurrection. 'It all springs from fear of the populace', commented Erill on the failure of the Consell de Cent to authorize the raising of another company.[6]

Although the arrests continued, nothing could move the city; not even a letter from Santa Coloma reporting that, of the 11,237 men being paid for by the Principality, 9091 were missing, while the city company

[1] ACA: G, caja 22, Erill to Santa Coloma, 27 Oct. 1639.
[2] ACA: G, caja 24, Erill to Santa Coloma, 5 Nov. 1639.
[3] E.g. Olivares to Santa Coloma, 19 Nov. 1639 (ACA: G, caja 24).
[4] ACA: G, caja 22, Erill to Santa Coloma, 25 Oct. 1639.
[5] ACA: G, caja 24, Erill to Santa Coloma, 5 Nov. 1639.
[6] ACA: G, caja 24, Erill to Santa Coloma, 15 Nov. 1639.

had fallen to a mere 136 men.[1] The annual change of Consellers at the end of November brought no comfort to Erill: the chief Conseller, Lluís Joan de Calders, was 'as old and worn as Your Excellency knows', while the fourth, a merchant called Xirau, was 'the creature of J. de Navel'.[2] By the middle of December the number of Catalans in the army had fallen to 800, and it was known that a French force was gathering to attempt the relief of Salces.[3] In spite of this the Consell de Cent, swayed by the speeches of Francesc Joan de Vergós,[4] still refused to send a Conseller to Salces, or to bring out the banner of the city's patron, Santa Eulàlia: this, it claimed, was reserved only for occasions on which Barcelona itself was in danger.

The city's persistent refusal to raise the banner of Santa Eulàlia struck the ministers in Madrid as particularly outrageous. As if the failure to recover Salces would not in itself represent the gravest danger that had ever threatened Barcelona! For the moment it was necessary to dissimulate, but the city's behaviour showed that something must eventually be done.[5] All that the Council of Aragon could do for the time being was to send Santa Coloma two letters to be passed on to the city at his own discretion: the first annulling all those privileges of Barcelona which prevented the prompt levying of troops, the second ordering that all those who went to Salces should be given preferential treatment in appointment to city offices.[6]

Erill decided on the presentation of the second letter, and handed it to the Consellers on 23 December. The following day, Santa Coloma issued a startling proclamation which announced that all who had spent thirty days at Salces would automatically be declared to have passed all their professional examinations; that all *militars* who were not nobles and went to Salces would receive a privilege of nobility; that *ciutadans honrats* of Barcelona and the other towns who did the same would become *militars*, and all ordinary citizens *ciutadans honrats*.[7] The contents of the proclamation had already been foreshadowed in proposals made by Erill at the beginning of the month, which had been

[1] AHB: Delibs., 1639, fo. 372, Santa Coloma to City, 23 Nov. 1639.
[2] ACA: G, caja 25, Erill to Santa Coloma, 1 Dec. 1639.
[3] AHB: Delibs., 1640, fo. 37, Santa Coloma to Consellers, 19 Dec. 1639.
[4] ACA: CA, leg. 286, no. 40, Santa Coloma to King, 15 March 1640.
[5] ACA: CA, leg. 283, no. 60, consulta, 30 Nov. 1639.
[6] Drafts of both these letters, dated 14 Dec. 1639, are to be found in ACA: G, caja 25.
[7] ACA: G, Dietari, 1638–41, part II, fos. 279–80.

rejected by the Consell de Cent on the grounds that they would subvert the whole order of municipal government.[1] Now Erill's suggestions had been embodied in a royal proclamation. The city oligarchy rightly saw in this proclamation a formidable threat to their control of municipal life. All their power, all their lucrative offices would be wrested from them by the mob. They promptly rejected the proclamation as an infringement of the municipal charter granted the city by Ferdinand the Catholic.

It remained to be seen whether the Barcelona oligarchy's concern for the retention of its privileges was shared by the populace at large. On 26 December news reached Barcelona that Espenan had agreed to surrender Salces on 6 January if no relief force had by then arrived. In spite of a letter from Santa Coloma begging the citizens of Barcelona to come 'at once! at once!',[2] the Consell de Cent voted on 27 December against sending a Conseller or any more troops to Salces.[3] This was too much for the Barcelona populace. The days that remained until the promised capitulation were few, the risk relatively slight; and each man doubtless cherished dreams of ranking as a *ciutadà honrat*. That same evening the people rioted, and forced the Consellers to summon another meeting of the Consell de Cent for the following day.[4] At that meeting, a terrified city council reversed its earlier decision, and agreed that Calders should leave at once for Salces, at the head of a company drawn from the city guilds.[5] Once again, the populace had proved itself the master.

The departure for Salces of the Conseller-en-Cap of Barcelona brought out the entire Principality.[6] Companies from all the towns of Catalonia streamed along the roads that led to the besieged fortress, but the man who had done so much to bring this about was in no condition to appreciate his handiwork. After the tumultuous events of the past few days in Barcelona, the Canceller Erill had suddenly fallen ill—of passion and anger through his failure to obtain a bishopric, reported an unkind observer[7]—and he died on 6 January 1640. On the same day, the fortress of Salces surrendered.

[1] AHB: Delibs., 1640, fo. 12, 6 Dec. 1639.   [2] *Ibid.* fo. 43 v.
[3] *Ibid.* fo. 48.
[4] ACA: CA, leg. 284, no. 3, Erill to King, 29 Dec. 1639.
[5] AHB: Delibs., 1640, fo. 51.
[6] AGS: GA, leg. 1358, Santa Coloma to King, 6 Jan. 1640.
[7] BUB: MS 224, Dietari de Parets, fo. 48.

The long siege was over, and the Rosselló campaign had ended in victory, of a kind, for Spain. The price paid in human suffering had been out of all proportion to the extent of the victory. The price paid in terms of the strain on Castilian–Catalan relations had yet to be calculated. Six months of threatening and harrying by royal ministers on instructions from Madrid would not be lightly forgotten. Nor could Madrid itself forget that the threatening and the harrying had been necessary. Catalonia considered that its services had not been appreciated; Madrid considered that there were none to appreciate. This was partly because it had no intention of lavishing gratitude upon the Catalans, but also because the letters of Erill and Santa Coloma since the end of July had contained little but condemnation of their compatriots.

Perpetually waiting for troops that never arrived, Santa Coloma was understandably impatient, but he failed to take into account the political implications of the letters of condemnation he wrote to Madrid. At the very end, he did try to make amends, and wrote when Salces surrendered that 'the Catalans have stood up for themselves on this occasion'.[1] But the belated tribute carried little weight after five months of denigration. He could well have placed more emphasis in his correspondence with the Court on the sufferings and sacrifices of the Principality. Now it was too late.

The sufferings of the Principality are undeniable, but there is no way of measuring the fiscal strain imposed by the six months' campaign. The Diputació and the towns had emptied their coffers and drawn heavily on credit but it is possible that the strain on the Principality's resources was not as great as the volume of complaints might suggest. Rather surprisingly, Joan Guardia, the peasant-farmer of Corcó, after referring in his diary to the heavy casualties among the Catalan troops, 'all paid with our money', added these words: 'but in spite of all this, at that time we had enough money'.[2] It was the cost in lives, and the uselessness of the sacrifice, that was really terrible. A diarist at Girona wrote: 'it is considered certain that 10,000 men died of disease at the siege of Salces, and most of them were Catalans. Not 500 died fighting.'[3] Guardia put the Catalan casualties at 7000; another writer at 4000.[4] This

---

[1] AGS: GA, leg. 1336, Santa Coloma to King, 12 Jan. 1640.
[2] Guardia's diary, 1639.
[3] BN: MS 3619, Dietari de Sucesos de la Ciudad de Gerona (by Jeroni de Real), fo. 18.
[4] *Súplica de Tortosa*, fo. 46.

lowest figure would mean a casualty rate of ten in every hundred Catalans if some 40,000 men went to Salces all told. But the percentage of nobles who died at Salces was something like 25 per cent. About 400 Catalan nobles and *cavallers* went to the siege at some time or other.[1] About half of these—or about one-quarter of the entire Catalan aristocracy—lost their lives.[2]

That all this misery was to such little purpose was the result of the nature of siege warfare, in which the real enemy was not the besieged garrison but time and disease. It was asking much of the Catalans to remain at their posts through a long siege conducted under foul conditions and in bad weather, with no more than two Perpinyà churches to receive their sick. Yet the Principality itself cannot be exonerated from all blame for the course of events in the autumn of 1639. There were those who believed that the sick who remained at the camp were paying for the cowardice of the others, many of whom, besides being healthy, were also rich.[3] A number of *militars*, especially in the region of Vic, and many of the wealthy burgesses, were quick to make themselves scarce when a minister arrived in the district to search for recruits and money. Such behaviour ensured that the conscientious, and those least able to resist, found themselves at the camp, and that many of the more humble citizens bore a heavy expenditure while their wealthier colleagues refused to contribute.

For the time being, however, the horrors of the siege were forgotten in the joy of victory. The Catalans were immensely pleased with themselves, and expected many *mercedes* from a grateful monarch. The Conde Duque himself was elated, and wrote ecstatically to Santa Coloma: 'a thousand thanks and a thousand congratulations.... Many thanks to God and very many to Your Excellency who has worked miracles.... No general has done as much as you....' But were the Catalans after all to receive the rewards to which they felt themselves entitled? The Conde Duque's next sentence suggested that they were not.

Your Excellency is to study at once the subject on which I am writing to you —namely, the way to set things right in that province. And also, with the same secrecy, and in your own hand, you are to inform me personally how

---

[1] See the lists in ADP: Série B, 390, no. 19, and ACA: G, caja 21.

[2] Jeroni de Real says 184: Don Ramon de Rocabertí, in his *Presagios fatales del mando francés en Cataluña* (Zaragoza, 1646), p. 88, gives the figure as 225.

[3] ACA: G, caja 22, Erill to Santa Coloma, 31 Oct. 1639.

we can induce it to serve His Majesty with 5,000 native troops at the beginning of the spring, paid for the duration of the campaign, and also 2,000 pioneers, because this is indispensable....[1]

Even the first-fruits of victory were sour. Peace had come to the Principality, but with it no rest from its afflictions.

[1] This letter, dated 12 January 1640, comes from the appendix to the political pamphlet by Gaspar Sala, *Secrets Públichs* (Barcelona, 1641). The appendix, which was attached to some, but not all, copies of the pamphlet, and was reproduced in Siri's *Mercurio*, vol. II, pp. 56–129, consists of letters found in Santa Coloma's correspondence after his death. The 33 boxes of the viceroy's correspondence in the Archivo de la Corona de Aragón do not contain these letters, although copies of some of them are to be found elsewhere. There seems, however, no reason to dispute their authenticity, in spite of the political purpose which motivated their publication. Many phrases come straight from *consultas* still surviving at Simancas, and, in any event, Olivares's letters were in general so outrageous from the Catalan standpoint as to make invention and alteration unnecessary.

CHAPTER XIV

AN ARMY TO BE BILLETED

The general tone of Olivares's letter of congratulation to Santa Coloma showed that the Catalans had little hope of finding either sympathy or gratitude in Madrid for their sacrifices of the previous autumn. A considerable number of *mercedes* were indeed bestowed upon deserving individuals on the recommendation of Santa Coloma,[1] but the expected letter of royal thanks to Barcelona and the Diputació did not arrive. There seemed to be not a single person at Court willing to put in a favourable word for the Catalans when conversing with the king.[2]

To the Catalans the lack of gratitude might seem incomprehensible; to Olivares and his colleagues it was no more than the Principality deserved. What reason was there to be grateful for the behaviour of a province which had done nothing but obstruct and delay? The time for simulated gratitude was past. A province which had played no part over the past eighteen years in the bearing of the common burden, and which had not even responded with firmness and vigour to an attack on its own territory, could scarcely expect to obtain generous recognition from its king. At least it was clear that the Catalans must not be allowed to persist indefinitely in their obstinate ways. Since the French remained in possession of the fortresses of Ópol and Taltavull, military operations along the Catalan frontier would again be necessary with the return of spring, and Madrid dared not risk a repetition of the events of the preceding year. 'In order to be ready for all eventualities this year', resolved the Junta de Ejecución on 14 January 1640, 'it was felt that one of the most important things to be done is to settle matters in Catalonia, in such a manner that no obstructions are placed in the way of Your Majesty's service'....[3]

---

[1] Some of these are to be found in ACA: CA, leg. 391.

[2] ACA: G, caja 27, Joan Grau to Diputats, 28 Jan. 1640.

[3] AGS: GA, leg. 1326, Junta de Ejecución, 14 Jan. 1640. The Junta de Ejecución had become by 1640 the most important council of ministers in Madrid. Its composition seems to have varied slightly according to the nature of the subjects under discussion, but its hard core of members consisted of the following ministers, all of whom attended regularly: the Conde Duque de Olivares; the duke of Villahermosa; the marquis of Castrofuerte; José González; the Protonotario; Don Nicolás Cid; Pedro de Arce.

25-2

How was this settlement of 'matters in Catalonia' to be achieved? Santa Coloma was to be summoned to Madrid to offer his suggestions and the ill-fated Corts of Catalonia were once again to be convened. The place of meeting was to be the town of Montblanc, deliberately chosen for its inaccessibility, and the date was fixed for 15 April.[1] Olivares was determined that these Corts should not be a repetition of those of 1626 and 1632. His unhappy past experiences had apparently converted him to the duke of Alcalá's views that the Corts should be firmly treated as a mere vehicle for the passage of reforms required by the Crown.[2] 'Nothing is to be discussed in them except the reform of government—we will have none of that usual business of prayers and petitions', he wrote to Santa Coloma.[3]

When Olivares talked of the 'reform of government', it is clear that he was thinking of a programme which would compel the Catalans to make a larger contribution to the Monarchy's fiscal and military needs.

It is undeniable [he wrote in another letter to Santa Coloma] that the Catalans in their present condition are not useful to the Monarchy, and are not serving in person or with their possessions. Moreover, there is no province subject to the king, and not even a province outside the Spanish Monarchy, which conducts its affairs in this way, in a manner offensive to everybody and one that sets a very bad example to other vassals....Now, Sir, I want you to tell me the best and cheapest method of getting a good body of Catalan troops—some two or three *tercios* of 2000 men each. This is a measure that has been adopted in Castile, Italy and Flanders, and is to be introduced into Portugal this year, where we are asking for 8000 men....[4]

Olivares was clearly still hoping to achieve the Union of Arms. Rejected by the Corts of 1626, it must be accepted by the Corts of 1640, and the laws and privileges that stood in its way must be formally repealed. But the Corts of Montblanc were never to meet. The ever vigilant Dr Vinyes reminded Madrid of the document signed by the Protonotario in 1632 which promised that all the Crown's revenues in Catalonia would be forfeit to the city of Barcelona if its loan of 110,000 *lliures* were not repaid before the Corts expired.[5] Since the summoning of

---

[1] ACA: G, Dietari, 1638–41, part II, fo. 295.
[2] See above, p. 151.
[3] ACA: G, caja 28, Olivares to Santa Coloma, 3 Feb. 1640.
[4] Olivares to Santa Coloma, 14 Jan. 1640, in appendix to *Secrets Públichs*.
[5] See above, p. 272.

a new Corts at Montblanc automatically terminated the prorogued Barcelona Corts of 1632, the city could quite legitimately insist on the agreement being honoured. In the Principality's present state, it was perfectly capable of such an action. The consequent surrender by the Crown of all its patrimony in Catalonia was not a prospect to be viewed with equanimity.

This little problem of the security for the loan would presumably not have defied the collective ingenuity of the ministers in Madrid, if events in the Principality had not themselves been taking a course unfavourable to the Conde Duque's plans for a session of the Corts. During January and February of 1640 everything in Catalonia became subordinate to the overriding problem of the survival of the army which had been fighting on the frontier.

Since further military operations would be necessary on the frontier in 1640, it was obvious that the army must be conserved as a fighting unit, and be properly housed and fed during the winter months before the advent of the next campaigning season. There was obvious convenience in quartering this army in Catalonia. It would be close at hand for the next campaign; its maintenance would impose upon the Catalans a burden which Olivares considered it was their duty to bear; and its presence in the Principality would facilitate the passing of unpopular measures through the Corts. In 1635 Olivares had been unable to decide how to reconcile the holding of the Corts with the introduction of an army to fight the French;[1] but on this occasion the army would already be installed in the Principality for its own defence, so that the Conde Duque would have all the advantages of its presence without the onus of looking for a plausible reason for its introduction.[2]

The quartering of an army in a province which had already borne the brunt of a long campaign seems to have aroused a few scruples even in Madrid. In the winter of 1639 a Junta of thirty theologians was apparently summoned by the king to consider the moral question of

---

[1] See above, p.315.

[2] Sanabre (*Acción de Francia*, p. 90), has a story from Duplessis Besançon that M. de Saint-Aunés, the former governor of Leucata, who had defected to the Spaniards, himself suggested to the Spanish generals, and indeed to Olivares, that the *tercios* should be ordered to remain in Catalonia. He was thus all the time secretly acting in Richelieu's interests, and skilfully trapped the Conde Duque into taking the action most likely to exacerbate Castilian-Catalan relations. There might conceivably be some truth in the story, but in view of the dubious character and career of Saint-Aunés, it is to be hoped that it will be treated with the utmost caution, and regarded as no more than an intriguing possibility, unless or until further evidence is forthcoming.

whether the Principality could justifiably be called upon to house and feed the troops.[1] Delicate consciences were duly reassured by its verdict, and orders were sent out that the army should winter in Catalonia.

There were two serious objections to quartering an army in Catalonia and insisting on its maintenance at the expense of the inhabitants. The first was legal, the second practical. On the legal side, the constitutions were very clear about the extent of the Principality's obligations to an army quartered on its soil. A householder was expected to give a soldier a bed, a table, a light, and service, and provide him with salt, water and vinegar. Nothing else could be demanded of him, in accordance with the constitution of *Nous vectigals* which expressly forbade the viceroy or any other minister of the Crown to place any imposition on towns or private persons which was not authorized by the Corts.[2] Since the constitutions were so specific, doubts had naturally arisen in the viceroy's mind as soon as he received the order that troops were to be fed at the householder's expense. He summoned the Audiència early in January, and the judges agreed that the order was entirely illegal and could not be executed.[3]

The Council of Aragon, reduced to impotence when the Protonotario was absent, felt that, in view of the Audiència's objections, Santa Coloma should be left to billet the army as best he could.[4] The superior ministers had other ideas. Santa Coloma was informed that the Audiència's behaviour was ridiculous. The constitution of *Nous vectigals* was irrelevant because the province's contribution was not going to the king but to the army stationed there for its own defence; and, after all, the supreme law was that of self-defence.[5]

Olivares himself could find no rhyme or reason in legal objections to the maintenance of the troops by the Principality. Determined to keep an army in Catalonia, and obsessed with the need to make the Catalans play a larger part in Spain's struggle with France, he ignored any argument which stood in the way of his plans.

As regards billeting [he wrote to Santa Coloma], I must repeat how vital it is to arrange it properly, because it is against all reason that a province or a king-

[1] Assarino, *Rivolutioni*, p. 63.
[2] The text of this constitution, passed in the Corts of 1553, is to be found in *Constitutions y altres drets de Cathalunya*, vol. I, p. 304.
[3] ACA: CA, leg. 287, no. 21, consulta, 20 Jan. 1640.　　　　　　　　[4] *Ibid.*
[5] ACA: CA, leg. 287, no. 21, draft reply from King to Santa Coloma.

dom should be defended by an army and not be prepared to quarter it. Similarly, it is unreasonable that a king who has no fixed income from a province, should be expected to meet this expense, while the province itself supports neither the king nor the army. And, by your leave, I cannot easily allow myself to be persuaded that a province which has contributed and is contributing nothing, should have less substance than those that are heavily taxed....[1]

It is natural to wonder whether Catalonia did indeed possess sufficient 'substance' to support an army of some 9000 men. Unfortunately, the necessary information simply does not exist on the resources of a peasant household in relation to the demands made upon it by billeted soldiers. Neither the complaints of the householders themselves, nor the testimony of eye-witnesses, however impartial, provide a really satisfactory substitute for exact quantitative information. All that can be said is that both Santa Coloma and Balbases were agreed that Rosselló was not in a fit condition to support an army. The ravages of the Salces campaign, the lack of labourers to sow the fields, and the spread of epidemics which, according to Santa Coloma, had killed 4500 civilians in Perpinyà alone, had reduced Rosselló to a state in which the billeting of troops would prove fatal.[2] To relieve the ravaged frontier regions, it was therefore agreed in Madrid that most of the army should be withdrawn from Rosselló and quartered in eastern Catalonia between the Rosselló border and Barcelona, and in the Camp de Tarragona.[3]

In spite of the army's withdrawal to parts of the country more capable of sustaining it, the marquis of los Balbases foresaw many practical difficulties before his troops were satisfactorily billeted. He disliked the vagueness of instructions which stipulated that the royal ministers should simply attempt to arrange for the billeting as best they could. 'With no fixed agreements or rules', he wrote to Madrid, 'the disorderly will destroy the province, while the more meek and compliant will die of hunger, or desert.' To prevent this, he felt it would be best to 'arrange something moderate with the agreement of the province, and compel the soldiers not to go beyond this point. If this could be done it would be better both for the province and for Your Majesty's troops.

[1] ACA: G, caja 28, Olivares to Santa Coloma, 7 Feb. 1640.
[2] ACA: G, caja 28, Santa Coloma to Olivares, 1 Feb. 1640. There is a vivid and terrible contemporary description of life in the garrison town of Perpinyà in Paul Masnou, *Mémoires de Pierre Pasqual* (Perpignan, 1905).
[3] AGS: GA, leg. 1336, Junta Grande, 20 Jan. 1640.

Winter is far gone, the soldiers are very tired, and little time remains for them to rest.' He therefore proposed a moderate arrangement whereby the householders would give the troops a reasonable quantity of food. The ministers in Madrid agreed to this, but felt that the expense of feeding the troops should be generally shared among the towns, instead of falling on the individual householders.[1]

As Balbases himself admitted, the weakness of his plan was the difficulty of persuading the Catalans to accept it, although he pointed out that once the troops destined for Italy had left the Principality, the remainder would be few. Of these few, the infantry were on the whole well disciplined, although the cavalry were not. Unfortunately, details of the cavalry are not available, but the size and composition of the infantry regiments billeted in Catalonia can be discovered. They were drawn from two armies, the Ejército de la Vanguardia and the Ejército de Cantabria. These armies were composed as follows:[2]

Vanguardia	Companies	Officers	Other ranks	Total	Monthly pay (in *reales*)
Conde Duque's regiment (commanded by the *maestre de campo* Juan de Arce)	20	178	762	940	66,338
		122		122	18,450
		(attached officers)			
Aragonese tercio of Don Justo de Torres Mendoza	14	126	369	495	32,100
Tercio of the count of Molina	12	82	514	596	20,620
Cantabria					
Regiment of His Majesty's guard (commanded by the marquis of Mortara)	20	165	1,127	1,292	81,220
Regiment of the count of Aguilar	12	115	470	585	37,870

[1] AGS: GA, leg. 1336, Junta Grande, 20 Jan. 1640.
[2] AGS: GA, leg. 1364, *Relación de la gente que se halla effectiva*, 16 April 1640; and AGS: GA, leg. 1334, report sent by Luis Fernández de Vega, 23 April 1640.

Cantabria (cont.)	Com- panies	Offi- cers	Other ranks	Total	Monthly pay (in *reales*)
Tercio of Don Diego Caballero	10	99	307	406	20,920
Tercio of Irish under Tyrconnel	9	106	487	593	44,790
Tercio of Walloons under Baron de Molinguen	19	175	856	1,031	65,005
Tercio of Neapolitans under Don Leonardo Moles	16	171	885	1,056	70,700
Tercio of Neapolitans under Don Jerónimo de Tutavila	12	125	534	659	40,330
Tercio of Modena troops	20	137	266	403	29,030
	164	1,601	6,577	8,178	527,373

At a time when veteran troops were becoming scarce, the survival of this army was a matter of the deepest concern to the Conde Duque. Almost every letter he wrote to Santa Coloma contained some such phrase as: 'I beg you on my knees, and from the bottom of my heart, to billet that army well.'[1] Santa Coloma was uncomfortably aware that this was more easily said than done. He tried to explain to the Conde Duque that the country was not as rich as it appeared, and that it would not be easy for it both to billet the troops and find sufficient money for this year's contribution towards the cost of fortifications. But he would obey.[2] This was the tragedy of Santa Coloma. Avid for new honours for the house of Queralt, and moved by a fatal desire to please, he could not bring himself to contradict his superiors or to warn them forcefully of the dangers that attended their policies. Unlike his predecessor, the duke of Cardona, he never once threatened to resign. Instead, all he did, as a contemporary remarked, was to 'write, consult, doubt and obey'.[3] In letter after letter which he wrote to Madrid in

[1] ACA: G, caja 28, Olivares to Santa Coloma, 3 Feb. 1640.
[2] ACA: G, caja 28, Santa Coloma to Olivares, 1 Feb. 1640.
[3] F. Martí, *Noticia Universal de Cataluña*, p. 170.

January, February and March of 1640 was to be found some such phrase as: 'In spite of all this, I shall continue to execute Your Majesty's orders until I am otherwise instructed.'[1] Even with the world collapsing about him, Santa Coloma would have been capable of no more than a faint bleat of pained surprise. He doubted—and obeyed.

The effect of Madrid's orders about the billeting of the troops did not take long to make itself felt. By 26 January the syndic of the town of Pals in the bishopric of Girona was complaining to the Diputats about the behaviour of a Neapolitan cavalry company quartered in the town.[2] Within a fortnight, troops and local population were clashing all over eastern Catalonia.

The people refuse in many areas to give the troops food [wrote the acting Governador, Don Ramon de Calders, to Santa Coloma on 9 February]. The soldiers have not a single *real*. The entire province has arms in its hands, and many of the soldiers are taking the opportunity to desert because they are in such danger.... There is not a town which has not sent a representative to Barcelona, and the Diputats are liberally distributing papers to stop people from feeding the troops.... The cavalry is utterly disintegrating....[3]

Catalan nationalist historians have tended to lay all the blame for the incidents on the behaviour of the troops. This is to oversimplify both the incidents themselves and the motives of the participants. The Catalans in the past had shown no excessive respect for troops passing through their Principality,[4] and they often proved themselves more than a match for the soldiers. During the spring of 1640, marauding bands of Catalans would come down from the mountains at night and attack the soldiers in their billets.[5] Reports of the clashes between soldiers and civilians make it impossible to determine with certainty who struck the first blow, and the question is really immaterial. Tempers were running high, and each side gave as good as it got. It would be wrong, however, to minimize the element of desperation in the behaviour of the troops. Often they found themselves without money and without food, as when the peasantry refused to give anything to the cavalry company commanded by Don Manuel de Ariarán, with the result that by the beginning of February 130 cavalrymen had already deserted,

[1] ACA: CA, leg. 286, no. 109, Santa Coloma to King, 2 Feb. 1640.
[2] ACA: G, LT, 1639–40, fo. 201, Diputats to Santa Coloma, 26 Jan. 1640.
[3] ACA: G, caja 28, Calders to Santa Coloma, 9 Feb. 1640.
[4] See above, p. 289.
[5] ACA: CA, leg. 286, no. 40, Santa Coloma to King, 15 March 1640.

taking their horses and arms with them.[1] It was hardly surprising that soldiers were roaming through the countryside starving and almost naked; nor that others, in desperation, took by force what they could not obtain by consent. 'As long as food is not assured to the soldiers', wrote Dr Jacinto Valonga, who was sent to the Principality by Madrid to investigate the clashes between the troops and the population, 'it is impossible to keep them under control, because a hungry man must eat off the land if His Majesty does not come to his help.'[2]

While sheer hunger provoked many of the troops' most atrocious actions it was not the sole cause. Many of the troops were foreign mercenaries, naturally given to plundering the land in which they found themselves. Dr Valonga's careful inquiries add up to a damning indictment, especially of the foreign regiments; and the worst were the officers.[3] Baron Molinguen's Walloon regiment, for instance, consisting of 1300 men, was stationed from 6 to 11 February at Blanes, a coastal town with rather more than 1000 inhabitants. On the first two days, the town had to provide the *maestre de campo* with '1 sheep, half a cask of wine, 2 capons, 4 chickens, 6 lb. of bacon, 2 lb. of sugar, 1 lb. of sweets, 30 loaves at half a *real*; wood, oil, candles, and 30 measures of barley a day'. On the following four days it was forced to give him 100 *reals* daily, and his captains 28 *reals*—a total of 632 *reals* a day. During the days they were quartered there, the troops robbed and maltreated the population, and the *maestre de campo* did nothing to check them. On the final day, the *batlle* of the town arrested a soldier who had struck an inhabitant. The troops retaliated by shooting, and many soldiers lost their lives in the resulting clash.

Some regiments behaved better than this, some worse. The natural indiscipline of these troops is obvious enough, but it would be desirable to know how far, if at all, there was any element of deliberate brutality in their behaviour. The reactions both of Balbases and of the ministers in Madrid to the excesses of the troops make it difficult to accept the thesis that the excesses were deliberately encouraged by Madrid in order to provoke the Catalans into revolution.[4] But malice aforethought

[1] ACA: G, caja 28, Ariarán to Santa Coloma, 4 Feb. 1640.
[2] ACA: CA, leg. 394, Valonga to Protonotario, 17 March 1640.
[3] ACA: CA, leg. 393, *Relación del proceso que en este año de 1640 ha hecho el Dr Jacinto Valonga en la visita de los quarteles....*
[4] For this thesis, see the introduction, p. ix.

need not be attributed exclusively to Madrid. Some of the troops had already had unpleasant experiences when quartered in Catalonia in the past; others had quarrelled with the Catalan companies during the siege of Salces; and many of them had a rough notion of the Principality's generally uncooperative attitude. It is significant that, according to the account of one judge of the Audiència, the troops went around saying openly that they had come to Catalonia to get rid of the *non vol fer*—the refusal to do anything.[1] Added to this was the violent antipathy that the Neapolitan regiments had conceived for the Catalans. During the last weeks of the siege of Salces, Santa Coloma had become involved in a bitter quarrel with the commander of the Italian regiments, the marquis of Torrecuso, and eventually had both the marquis and his son placed under arrest.[2] The feud between the two men communicated itself to their respective compatriots, and at least two contemporaries suggest that the Italian troops attempted to avenge the insult to their commander by deliberately maltreating the population on which they were billeted.[3]

Of all the incidents between the troops and the native population during the first month of the billetings, none was more fateful than the murder of Don Antoni de Fluvià on 1 February. This inoffensive gentleman, devoted to painting and the practice of religion,[4] was killed by soldiers in the chapel of his castle at Palautordera.[5] According to Don Ramon de Calders, the Principality took Fluvià's tragedy as its own.[6] In Barcelona, the Diputats immediately summoned the Braços, which agreed on the necessity for a full investigation of the tragedy. At the same time they wrote to their agent in Madrid, Joan Grau, telling him of the 'heart-rending state this province is in. Things are going from bad to worse, and the only hope is that His Majesty, in his mercy, may discover some remedy. Here in the Principality all the ministers are deaf to our complaints, and we are afraid of a general

---

[1] Bodleian, MS Add. A. 137, fos. 74–157, *Relación del Levantamiento de Cataluña por Don Ramón Rubí de Marimón*, fo. 76. See Appendix VI, Sources, section D.

[2] This quarrel caused a great stir, and much distress to Santa Coloma. A large bundle of correspondence about it may be found in AGS: GA, leg. 1326.

[3] *Súplica de Tortosa*, fo. 47; and one of the Jesuit newsletters, *Cartas de algunos PP. de la Compañía de Jesús*, MHE, vol. XV, p. 392. 10 Jan. 1640.

[4] Rubí, *Levantamiento*, fo. 76.

[5] There is a detailed account of this tragic incident, from a strongly Catalan point of view, by F. de Sagarra in *Miscellània Prat de la Riba* (Barcelona, 1923), vol. I, pp. 307–40.

[6] ACA: G, caja 28, Calders to Santa Coloma, 9 Feb. 1640.

conflagration....'¹ It was clear that Santa Coloma would have to return quickly to Barcelona. He had spent the three weeks since the fall of Salces in Perpinyà recuperating from the rigours of the campaign, putting off the evil hour when he would have to obey the summons to visit Madrid. On receiving the news of Fluvià's death, he wrote a letter of sympathy to the Diputats and promised an inquiry into the affair. He also promised to send four judges round the Principality to help pacify the country.² But nothing less than his own presence in Barcelona seemed adequate to deal with the great volume of complaints coming in from all over Catalonia from civilians and soldiers alike.

As Santa Coloma made his way southwards, Balbases wrote from Girona giving him warning and advice. He was sure that the Diputats would co-operate if Santa Coloma told them that the king's decision was firm: that the troops had to be properly looked after, and that there must be no disorders. If they refused,

it looks as though we shall be compelled to take measures which will stop this army from disintegrating—especially the cavalry, because the salvation of the Monarchy depends upon its survival. I can think of no other means than that you and I should give orders that the soldiers should be content to live moderately and should not claim anything except subsistence until His Majesty is pleased to send new instructions. In some areas I have already managed this, and it shall be done in the rest. And any soldier or officer who disobeys these orders must be severely punished.³

For all Balbases's reputation, there was about him a kind of bluff common sense which prevented him from being the mere compliant agent of civilian ministers issuing orders from afar. His highest duty was to the army he commanded, but he was under no illusions about the behaviour of his troops and about the difficulty of disciplining them in their present circumstances. It was essential for the Diputats to agree to the distribution of printed orders stipulating exactly the obligations of householders to the troops, because without such fixed arrangements no army could be controlled.⁴ Santa Coloma, on the other hand, had no practical experience of handling troops, and considered his sole duty

¹ ACA: G, LT, 1639–40, fo. 208, Diputats to Grau, 4 Feb. 1640.
² ACA: Documentación Incompleta, caja 11, Santa Coloma to Diputats, 5 Feb. 1640.
³ ACA: G, caja 28, Balbases to Santa Coloma, 10 Feb. 1640.
⁴ *Ibid.* 13 Feb. 1640.

to be the carrying out of all the instructions he received from Madrid. His reactions to the behaviour of the population therefore generally tended to be harsher and less understanding than those of Balbases. To Balbases, soldiers and civilians alike were the largely innocent victims of ministerial inefficiency. To Santa Coloma, they were both responsible parties because they stubbornly refused to obey orders.

Santa Coloma's attitude had already forfeited all sympathy for him in the Principality. His reception on entering Barcelona by coach on 12 February was very different from that accorded to Tamarit and the Conseller-en-Cap of Barcelona on their triumphal return from Salces. The register of the Diputació contained the following laconic entry for the day of his return: 'It is to be noted that neither their Excellencies nor the city went out to receive him, but only a few *cavallers* and the marquis of Villafranca, who was in the city at the time. This note was inserted by order.'[1]

The Diputats were at least gracious enough to call on Santa Coloma the following day, but could obtain no satisfaction from him. He refused to admit that the billeting contravened the constitution of *Nous vectigals* and was consequently illegal. The viceroy, in turn, could obtain no assurance of co-operation from the Diputats in attempting to get the troops settled in their quarters without excessive friction. Failing to secure their help, he called Balbases to Barcelona to see if anything could be done, but it was clear to both that everything depended on the orders from Madrid, and Madrid was in no mood to yield. The Junta de Ejecución simply repeated that it was the duty of the Diputats to co-operate in the billeting, and laid it down that the troops should be billeted in such a way that they outnumbered the inhabitants, 'so as to avoid the usual incidents caused by the local population'. It also criticized the viceroy for not sending the judges of the Audiència round the Principality, as instructed.[2] Indeed, the ministers seem to have been losing their confidence in Santa Coloma: rumours were circulating in Madrid that he would be transferred to a post in Flanders.[3]

By February of 1640 the unfortunate viceroy would have been far happier in Brussels than in Barcelona. Feeling was running very high in the city over his failure to restrain the troops. Its strength is suggested

[1] ACA: G, Dietari, 1638–41, part II, fo. 297.
[2] AGS: GA, leg. 1336, Junta de Ejecución, 23 Feb. 1640.
[3] ACA: G, caja 28, Count of Molina to Santa Coloma, 11 Feb. 1640.

by an incident in the Consell de Cent on 19 February. The viceroy himself scrawled the details on the back of a letter he had just received: 'Joan de Vergós, *cavaller*, proposed that the city officials should leave off their ceremonial robes and order the guilds to cancel all dances. Lleonard Serra, merchant, that the Consellers should go into mourning. He was not supported.'[1] Francesc Joan de Vergós, who had already been in trouble with the viceregal administration[2] and had opposed the sending of a Conseller to Salces,[3] spoke for many people, including his close acquaintances, the Diputats. Their anxiety over the course that events were taking was now acute. 'Catalonia is in more imminent danger of destruction than it has ever been', they wrote to their agent in Madrid. In addition to the violence of the troops, 'many villages are so exasperated as to be on the point of explosion, and every day brings the death of more Catalans and more soldiers'.[4] Uncertain what their next step should be after the failure of their talk with Santa Coloma, they summoned the Braços. Fifty-nine members were present, and they agreed on an immediate embassy of nine to the viceroy to complain of the behaviour of the troops.[5] The same day, 21 February, Santa Coloma also received a deputation from the Consell de Cent, bearing a similar complaint. His assurances that the offenders would be punished failed to satisfy the deputations. It was clear that some striking gesture must be made to bring home to the viceroy the gravity of the situation. On 23 February the Braços decided that three solemn deputations should be sent to Santa Coloma on three successive days, pointing out to him that the constitution of *Nous vectigals* expressly forbade the viceroy or any other minister to demand any unauthorized imposition, and making clear that, unless he revoked his orders on billeting within three days, the Audiència would be called upon to pronounce them illegal.[6] The first deputation went on 23 February; the second on the 24th; the third on the 25th. It was the last warning Santa Coloma was to receive.

The unhappy viceroy, now a lonely and sorry figure, poured out his troubles in a long letter to Madrid, which revealed all the conflicts and uncertainties within him: his anxiety at the state of the Principality, his

---

[1] ACA: G, caja 28, Santa Coloma, on back of letter from Juan de Sala, 16 Feb. 1640.
[2] See above, p. 352.　　　　　　　　　　　　　　[3] See above, p. 382.
[4] ACA: G, LT, 1639–40, fos. 220–1, Diputats to Grau, 18 Feb. 1640.
[5] ACA: G, Dietari, 1638–41, part II, fo. 307.　　　　[6] *Ibid.* fo. 316.

anger at the behaviour of Barcelona and the Diputats.[1] The ministers had continued, he wrote, to press the villagers to supply the troops with food, but 'such is the poverty of the Principality that, although the householders may be able to hold out for a few more days, they cannot go on, because they do not have the resources...and the army, particularly the cavalry, will fall to pieces'. Unfortunately, the impact of these remarks was rather blunted later in the letter by strictures on the behaviour of the town of Granollers, which had refused to take any troops. Apparently Santa Coloma had asked that both the Conde Duque's regiment, and the Walloons should be quartered in it by way of punishment, but Balbases had refused to agree on the grounds that it would be unwise. This remark is significant because it helps to confirm that no secret agreement had been made between Madrid and the army commanders to crush the towns. The demands for strong-armed action came from Santa Coloma; the caution from Balbases.

Santa Coloma also recounted the scandalous behaviour of Vergós and Serra in the Consell de Cent, and enclosed a copy of the memorandum on the illegality of the billetings presented to him by the embassies from the Diputació. Since he would not revoke his orders, 'they will have recourse to the Audiència, which, as far as I can judge, will pronounce in favour of the Diputats. I felt I should inform Your Majesty of this, so that the appropriate action may be taken.' It was clearly the behaviour of the Diputats which most annoyed him. 'From the moment I arrived here, the persons of the Diputats have given proof of their seditious spirit not only by refusing to co-operate, but even by deliberately stirring up the people and trying to destroy the army.' The old feud between viceroy and Diputats was approaching its tragic climax.

When Santa Coloma's letter reached Madrid, Olivares could scarcely contain himself.

I have never heard of anything so ridiculous as the behaviour of the Diputació and the Consell de Cent on this occasion. And forgive my language, which is the most restrained I can manage, but no king in the world has a province like Catalonia....It has a king and lord, but it renders him no services, even when its own safety is at stake. This king and lord can do nothing that he wants in it, nor even things that need to be done. If the enemy invades it,

[1] ACA:CA, leg. 286, no. 101, Santa Coloma to King, dated 22 Feb. but written on 23 Feb. 1640.

the king has to defend it without any help from the inhabitants, who refuse to expose themselves to danger. He has to bring in an army from outside; he has to maintain it; he has to recover the fortresses that have been lost. And then, when the enemy has not yet been driven out...the province refuses to billet it....We always have to look and see if a constitution says this or that. We have to discover what the customary usage is, even when it is a question of the supreme law, of the actual preservation and defence of the province.... Sir, we all admire your wisdom, but we all without exception consider that a viceroy of that province, and especially a native of it, like yourself, should have made an example of these people....How is it possible that, of thirty-six ministers who have seen the despatches this morning, there is not one who is not clamouring, clamouring against Catalonia?...Sir, the king our lord is king of Castile, which has billeted troops; he is king of Navarre, which has billeted and is today billeting them. He is king of Aragon, which is doing the same, and Valencia, too. He is king of Portugal, which, although one of those kingdoms with many *fueros*, has never objected to billeting. And Milan, Naples, Flanders, the Indies, the Franche-Comté, than which there is probably no state or province with more liberties and immunities. Not one of these objects to billeting, not only when it is helping in its own defence but even when His Majesty chooses to station troops in it. Should all these kingdoms and provinces follow the example of Catalonia?....Really, Sir, the Catalans ought to see more of the world than Catalonia...[1]

Behind the withering sarcasm of this great tirade lay the gravamen of the Conde Duque's persistent charge against the Principality: why should it, and it alone, be different? If this complaint had now become an obsession with him, and if his language at times bordered on the hysterical, this was hardly surprising in view of the terrible crisis which was at this very moment threatening to engulf the Spanish Monarchy. The inadequacy of the silver consignment brought by the 1639 treasure fleet meant that it had been possible to arrange provisions to the value of only 6,351,000 *escudos* for the year 1640.[2] The premium on silver in terms of *vellón*, slowly and inexorably mounting once more after the deflationary decree of 1628, had shot up in the last two years to nearly 40 per cent.[3] Still worse, the financial crisis and the Crown's seizure of private incomes had virtually paralysed Seville, and its American trade was coming to a standstill.[4]

[1] *Secrets Públichs*: Olivares to Santa Coloma, 29 Feb. 1640.
[2] Domínguez Ortiz, *Política y Hacienda*, p. 59.
[3] Hamilton, *American Treasure*, table 7, p. 96.
[4] Chaunu, *Séville et l'Atlantique*, vol. v, pp. 344–5.

The military situation was correspondingly grave. Except in Italy, where the marquis of Leganés had seized Turin during the 1639 campaign, Spanish and Imperial arms were everywhere under pressure. Moreover, the attempt to establish communications by sea with the Spanish armies isolated in Flanders had ended in disaster with the victory of Tromp over the fleet of Don Antonio de Oquendo at the battle of the Downs on 21 October 1639.

Short of money, short of ships, short of men, the Conde Duque was straining every nerve in the opening months of 1640 to mobilize his country more effectively for war. Great new efforts were made to recruit troops in Castile, and a Junta presided over by the Conde Duque was hard at work in January attempting to make the Spanish nobility and gentry—most of whom had long since lost all interest in military pursuits—turn out in person for the war against France.[1] But while he rushed from Junta to Junta, exhorting, commanding, rebuking, he now knew that, if the final disaster were to be averted, he must make peace. 'God wants us to make peace', he wrote in a memorandum for the king, 'for He is depriving us visibly and absolutely of all the means of war'.[2] But on what terms *could* Olivares make peace? In one form or another he had been negotiating with both France and the United Provinces for years, and the discussions had led to nothing. Over the years he had gradually reduced his terms. In February 1638 he had insisted that the Dutch should restore Brazil, Breda and one of the Rhine passages; that Spain should keep one fortress in Piedmont or Monferrat; and that the duke of Lorraine should have specially favourable treatment in the negotiations.[3] Now, in February 1640, it looked as though, as a last resort, he would be prepared to leave the duke of Lorraine to his not undeserved fate, and would insist only on the retention of Spanish conquests in Italy, at least during the period of truce, and the restoration of Brazil by the Dutch.[4]

[1] A. Domínguez Ortiz, 'La movilización de la nobleza castellana en 1640', *Anuario de Historia del Derecho Español*, vol. xxv (1955), p. 808.
[2] Cánovas del Castillo, *Estudios del Reinado de Felipe IV*, vol. I, Appendix, 2nd series, doc. xii, p. 414 (*Informe* of March 1640). He was particularly concerned at the lack of Spanish commanders.
[3] *Ibid.* doc. vii.
[4] *Ibid.* doc. xii, p. 425. A combined Spanish-Portuguese expedition led by Don Fadrique de Toledo had recaptured in April 1625 the town of Bahia in Brazil taken by the Dutch the previous year. But in 1630 the Dutch sent a new expedition which successfully installed itself in the captaincy of Pernambuco in north-east Brazil, and the Spaniards and Portuguese had failed to dislodge them (see C. R. Boxer, *The Dutch in Brazil 1624-1654*, Oxford, 1957).

Desperate as the Conde Duque was for peace, and anxiously awaiting some favourable sign from Paris, he was determined that, as long as the war continued, it should be fought with every weapon at Spain's command. The entire Monarchy must be swung behind him in a supreme effort to stave off disaster—and perhaps even to reverse the tide of war, for Richelieu also had troubles enough of his own. At such a moment it was out of the question that the Catalans, alone of the king's subjects, should be allowed to evade their obligations by taking refuge behind 'vague and airy points, such as all privileges must be on occasions like the present'.[1] Of course they must billet the troops.

But what if they should still refuse? The choice before Olivares was appallingly difficult. Either he must leave the Catalans to their own devices, deprive himself of the help they could give him, leave their frontier dangerously exposed to French attack, and run the risk that other parts of the Monarchy might choose to follow the Catalan example; or he must compel them to accept obligations equal to those of the other kingdoms, at the risk of driving them into armed resistance. It seems probable that at this moment he did not believe in the possibility of an insurrection. The Catalans, while tiresomely addicted to their privileges, were fundamentally loyal and, in the last resort, would never revolt against their natural lord.... And so he chose compulsion. Detailed orders were to be sent to the Principality on the exact method of billeting troops; the viceroy was to arrest one or more of the Diputats and institute judicial proceedings; he was to discover who had circulated seditious papers in the Consell de Cent, and arrest all those who had voted for the city to go into public mourning; and since Barcelona was the source of all the trouble, the troops should be billeted there also, although its privileges granted it exemption. The Audiència was to be solemnly warned against declaring in favour of the Diputats on the question of legality, and any disobedient judge was to appear before the Council of Aragon within twenty days.[2]

As if these draconian measures were not in themselves quite enough to keep the viceroy fully occupied, the Junta de Ejecución made another drastic decision a few days later. It had been agreed that troops should be levied in the Crown of Aragon, and the Junta decided that 6000

[1] ACA: G, caja 28, Olivares to Santa Coloma, 29 Feb. 1640.
[2] ACA: CA, leg. 285, no. 7, consulta, 27 Feb. 1640.

Catalans should be conscripted for service in Italy. It would be necessary for a minister to be sent from Madrid to organize the raising of these troops. Was not the Protonotario exactly the right man for this? The king, in replying to the *consulta*, recognized that the Protonotario was very busy, but hoped he would agree, 'since it is a question of nothing less than bringing that province back to the strait and narrow path'.[1]

A personal visit by the Protonotario to the Principality might perhaps have opened his eyes to the true state of affairs in a province on which he had for so many years posed as the sole expert; but unfortunately he never went. In his absence, the viceroy and his ministers had to interpret and execute the orders from Madrid as best they could. In happy ignorance of the new instructions which were on their way to him, Santa Coloma was still struggling to get the troops properly billeted. It seems that the resistance of the towns and villages was at last being overcome.

We have continued all the necessary measures to persuade the villages to give the soldiers food [he wrote to Madrid on 5 March].[2] As a result some of them are doing so, although the commanders are not really satisfied because the country simply does not have the resources to look after them as well as Flanders or Italy.... Other villages refuse to conform, thanks to the encouragement they receive from the Diputats and the lawyers acting for the towns in Barcelona—all of them very free with bad advice.... And it has been necessary to use compulsion against these villages, *which is something I wanted from the beginning, but which was not done because the marquis of los Balbases had not made up his mind to do it.*[3] But now, seeing that things were going badly, he has agreed. The *tercios* of Don Leonardo Moles and Don Francisco de Castilla have therefore been sent to Sant Feliu and Llagostera, which had not done as they were told...and the same with Sitges and Vilanova....To help with the billeting of the cavalry in the plain of Urgell I have sent Dr Francesc Joan Magarola, assessor of the Batllia General, and in the plain of Tarragona, Dr Jaume Martí, assessor of the Capitanía General. All this is so colossal a business that day and night there is time for nothing but smoothing out the troubles between troops and inhabitants....And it is essential that Your Majesty should make a decision with all speed....

Shortly after he had written and despatched this letter, the decisions taken in Madrid at the end of February reached Santa Coloma. The

---

[1] AGS: GA, leg. 1327, Junta de Ejecución, 4 March 1640.
[2] AGS: GA, leg. 1364, Santa Coloma to King, 5 March 1640.
[3] My italics.

orders about the arrest of a Diputat and the billeting of troops in Barcelona were for the moment set on one side, pending consultations with Balbases, who at that moment was out of Barcelona. On 8 March, however, he summoned the Diputats to his house, and presented them with the new orders about the proper method of billeting. These orders, which he had printed and circulated through the Principality, laid down that billeting should be carried out in what was known as the 'Lombardy' style:[1]

(1) All soldiers to be given service, i.e. bed, wood, light, oil, vinegar, salt, bowls, dishes, and cooking-pots.

(2) Every soldier to be given by the country his ordinary pay of 1 *real* daily, his basic ration of bread being provided by the king.

(3) Soldiers also to be allowed to accept from householders such food as can reasonably be supplied and as they can extract without payment. Meals to be taken with householders. All offences to be punished.

(4) A captain to be entitled to five persons' rations; an ensign to four; a sergeant to three; a squadron-leader to two; a *maestre de campo* to sixteen.

(5) For all cavalry soldiers, 1 *quartà* of oats or barley daily for their horses, and sufficient straw.

Even before they were told that Lombardy style billetings were to be introduced, the Diputats had come to the conclusion that the situation was so grave as to warrant taking the 'final and most effective steps to obtain redress': the sending of a special ambassador to Madrid to prostrate himself at His Majesty's feet. The man chosen for this delicate mission was a Capuchin, Fra Bernardino de Manlleu, 'in spite of the impediment in his speech, for Moses suffered in the same way, and yet

---

[1] ACA: G, Dietari, 1638–41, part II, fo. 334. This may be compared with the form of billeting for garrison troops in sixteenth-century Andalusia:

(1) Bed and lodging to be free of charge.

(2) Every soldier to be provided with 1 *fanega* (1·6 bushels) of wheat a month, or the equivalent quantity of bread, together with such other foodstuffs as were locally available, and fuel and oil. A cavalryman to have 4 additional *fanegas* of barley a month for his horse.

These commodities were to be charged at rates fixed by local councils. Householders would keep a tally of the commodities supplied to their guests, and a claim would be sent to the company paymaster, who deducted the money from the soldier's pay (K. Garrad, *The Causes of the Second Rebellion of the Alpujarras, 1568–1571*, unpublished Cambridge Ph.D. dissertation, 1955, pp. 335–6). I am very grateful to Dr Garrad for allowing me to quote from his dissertation.

The 'Lombardy' style was the one employed by the Spanish armies in Milan, with which Balbases had previously held a command. The greater demands which it imposed on the householder were considered to be justified by the fertility of the country. (See Francisco Manuel de Melo, *Historia de los Movimientos, Separación y Guerra de Cataluña*, ed. Madrid, 1912, p. 19.)

was chosen by God to redeem the children of Israel'.[1] While they were still negotiating for the authorization of Manlleu's Superior for his journey to Madrid, the Diputats now received, in the new billeting orders, a further and still more cogent argument for a direct appeal to the king. Whatever their personal inclinations the Diputats were not free agents, as they themselves recognized. The very nature of their office as Diputats bound them to pursue the course of action laid down in the constitutions. The new orders from Madrid, they pointed out to their agent, Grau,

> directly conflict with the constitutions of Catalonia, which are so clear on the subject of billeting that no alternative interpretation is possible. The defence of these constitutions is specifically entrusted to us, and by virtue of this we must act in accordance with the obligations entailed in our office, under penalty of condemnation for perjury, and of sentence of excommunication.... And even if they did not conflict with the constitutions and privileges, it would be almost impossible to have them obeyed, because the peasantry is utterly ruined, and the towns are without money and without resources.[2]

The dilemma of the Diputats was very real. If the ministers at Madrid were driven by the desperate circumstances of the Monarchy into formulating a supreme law which gave them almost absolute powers, the Diputats were no less driven, by the historical nature of their function, to adhere to the sole laws which were valid in the Principality. Even if those laws were wholly or partially obsolete—something they would never have conceived as possible—they were none the less binding until such time as they were repealed in the traditional manner. The Diputats were therefore to some extent the creatures of historical necessity, just as Olivares and the Protonotario were the creatures of immediate circumstance. There are few contests of wider import and greater significance than that between the demand for change and the insistence on the sanctity of tradition. All over Europe in the middle of the seventeenth century, this contest was being fought out in terms of power versus law. The struggle between Madrid and the Catalans was therefore part of a general pattern. The significance of the issue under debate is not in doubt; only the question of whether

[1] ACA: G, 909, Lletres secretes, 1605–74, Diputats to Provincial Father of the Capuchins, 6 March 1640.
[2] ACA: G, LT, 1639–40, fos. 234–5, Diputats to Grau, 10 March 1640.

the participants on either side were of a stature equal to that demanded by the occasion.

The tension of those days, and the burden of responsibility that weighed upon him, seem to have affected the health of Pau Claris. The register of the Diputació recorded that he was not able to attend meetings on 11 March because of indisposition.[1] There is a slight possibility that the illness was either feigned or exaggerated in order to ensure his safety, for Santa Coloma had arrested Vergós and Serra the day before, and there was an obvious danger that he might lay hands on the Diputats. But a canon of Urgell who arrived in Barcelona later in the week reported that he found 'Canon Claris in a state of continual fever. He has been bled twice, and on Saturday a third time, and he still remains in danger...'.[2]

While Claris was away from his post, Balbases returned to Barcelona and the viceroy called both him and the marquis of Villafranca into consultation on the recent orders from Madrid about the arrest of one or more Diputats. To judge from his reply, Santa Coloma was not happy about ordering the arrest.[3] He claimed that the imprisonment of Vergós and Serra had already had the most salutary results, and all over the Principality the disorders over the billeting were gradually dying down. In these circumstances, Villafranca, Balbases and he were all agreed that it would be wise both to defer the arrest of a Diputat and to give up for the present the idea of billeting troops in Barcelona.

Unfortunately for Santa Coloma, the distance between Madrid and Barcelona meant that his letters and those from Madrid never kept in step. While circumstances were changing from day to day in the Principality, Madrid was at least three days behind the news, and still legislating as if the situation was exactly the same as when the viceroy had written his last set of despatches. At this moment, all that the ministers in Madrid knew for certain was the information contained in Santa Coloma's letter of 5 March, with its news of incessant clashes between troops and civilians, and of the hesitations of Balbases in billeting a large contingent of soldiers on recalcitrant towns. They also had a first-hand account by the Baron de Molinguen, who had just arrived in Madrid as a special emissary from Balbases to report that the

[1] ACA: G, Dietari, 1638–41, part II, fo. 339.
[2] ACU: Cartes, Canon Sullà to Canons of Urgell, 20 March 1640.
[3] ACA: CA, leg. 286, no. 40, Santa Coloma to King, 15 March 1640.

army was rapidly disintegrating. Naturally unaware of the very real improvement in public order in the Principality after about the first week in March,[1] they took the gloomiest view of the situation. The most important fact, for them, was that the army was being destroyed. Beside this, nothing else mattered. Such a situation demanded urgent measures. A sharp letter was despatched to Balbases on 14 March: 'There can be no doubt that if the remedy is not applied, it will be through lack of proper action or of a real desire to apply it, and this is not to be expected of a person with such obligations as yourself.'[2] On the same day, the Council of Aragon, with the Protonotario present, decided that Tamarit should immediately be arrested and conveyed by sea to Perpinyà; that an ecclesiastical judge should start collecting information against Claris, and that the dues of the Diputació should be seized.[3]

This order reached Santa Coloma at two o'clock on the afternoon of 18 March. Although by the time it arrived, the situation might not have appeared to warrant such drastic action, the order was so precise that Santa Coloma felt bound to obey. At seven o'clock the same evening, Tamarit was put under arrest.[4] Although a galley was all ready for his removal, the viceroy suddenly faltered; it was unprecedented for prisoners to be taken away from the town in which the Audiència was sitting, and Santa Coloma felt that he would have to ask for the assistance of the Consellers because the city authorities controlled the town gates. Tamarit therefore remained in prison at Barcelona— the first Diputat to be arrested since March 1602.

At the news of Tamarit's arrest, the Braços were summoned by trumpet, and the city bell rang at six o'clock the next morning to call together the Consell de Cent. As a result of their deliberations, the Consellers called on Santa Coloma at four o'clock on the afternoon of the 19th to ask for the release of Tamarit, and were followed by a nine-man deputation from the Braços with the same request. When the viceroy explained that the arrest had taken place on the orders of the king, and that he could not intervene, both city and Braços decided

---

[1] An indication of the improvement is to be found in the letter of Juan de Solar to Pedro de Villanueva, 17 March 1640 (ACA: CA, leg. 393).

[2] ACA: G, caja 29, King to Balbases, 14 March 1640.

[3] ACA: CA, leg. 286, no. 108, consulta, 14 March 1640.

[4] ACA: CA, leg. 286, Santa Coloma to King, 19 March 1640.

to send respectively a three-man and nine-man delegation to Madrid to plead directly for the freeing of Tamarit, Vergós and Serra. The delegation from the Diputació, headed by Don Francesc de Oluja, a canon of Lleida, included that veteran among travellers along the high road from Barcelona to Madrid, Jeroni de Navel.

In spite of the decision by the city and Diputació to send special missions to Madrid, Santa Coloma seems to have been satisfied with the course that events were taking. He had obeyed his orders, except for the removal of Tamarit to Perpinyà, and there had been no violent popular reaction. He had also succeeded in persuading the Audiència to go some way towards condoning the billetings. The wretched judges, under pressure from the viceroy, had hit upon a flimsy formula whereby the constitution of *Nous vectigals* was said to refer only to excessive contributions by householders, and it was therefore incumbent upon them to provide the soldiers with sufficient food.[1] The difficulty about this formula was that it did not allow proceedings to be instituted against delinquents by use of the *regalia*, which was the form of prosecution most feared in Catalonia.[2] But Santa Coloma, while expressing satisfaction that the Audiència had felt itself able to go so far, had ideas of his own, which he sent to Madrid for consideration. Any personal contributions would surely help to redeem his reputation, and satisfy the Conde Duque that he had no more loyal or efficient servant in all the Monarchy. Only on one point of importance did Santa Coloma feel himself unable to comply immediately with his orders: the levy of 6000 Catalans for Italy. There was, he pointed out, no chance of persuading 6000 men to come forward voluntarily. Compulsory recruiting would inevitably lead to revolt and this would require the presence in Catalonia of a larger army than the one now billeted there. This was not the moment, he hinted with as much delicacy as possible, to recruit Catalans for service abroad.[3]

The Protonotario had other ideas. The news of Tamarit's arrest, which reached Madrid on the evening of 23 March, caused jubilation among the ministers,[4] and obviously increased their confidence that

---

[1] ACA: CA, leg. 286, no. 43, decision of Audiència, sent by Santa Coloma, 19 March 1640.

[2] *Secrets Públichs*: Santa Coloma to Olivares, 19 March 1640. I have not been able to discover in what way it differed from other forms of prosecution.

[3] ACA: G, caja 32, Santa Coloma to King, 19 March 1640.

[4] ACA: G, caja 29, Bernabé Camacho to Santa Coloma, 31 March 1640.

they could now carry through their Catalan policy without fear of contradiction. When the Junta de Ejecución met on 26 March to consider Santa Coloma's letter, and asked the Protonotario to express his views, it was therefore not surprising that he completely ignored the practical difficulties suggested by Santa Coloma. The use of Catalan troops abroad was admittedly forbidden by the constitutions, but His Majesty was aware of this when he ordered the levy of 6000 men and had made his decision because they were needed for the defence of the Monarchy and of the Faith. The men could be taken from among those who failed to go to Salces. They would not, of course, come forward of their own free will, and compulsion would have to be used, 'although His Majesty had no intention of applying force to all the province at the same time. His only idea was that the ministers should have the backing of the cavalry when they went recruiting, in order to enhance their authority.' The Junta fully agreed with this. Catalonia's sacrifices were not equal to those of other provinces; its population greatly exceeded one million, and there were so many nobles in the Principality that if they made themselves responsible for raising 2000 men, and if the ecclesiastics and the towns raised another 2000 each, the troops could be recruited with ease.[1]

The conclusions of the Junta suggest that the ministers' determination to exploit Catalonia's allegedly large resources of money and manpower had become an obsession. They appear to have had no understanding of the administrative problems involved in conscripting troops in Catalonia, and no conception of the general state of feeling in a Principality which had been subjected to two months of violence by ill-disciplined troops, and had just seen one of its titular heads cast into prison. It was true that Tamarit's arrest had passed off without any untoward incident. But it was a serious mistake to equate the comparative calm in Barcelona with a resigned acquiescence in the policies of the viceregal administration. The immediate reaction to the arrest of the Diputat Militar was certainly one of fear: Claris (now recovered from his fever) and his four colleagues remained permanently in the palace of the Diputació for fear of arrest.[2] But the grave turn of events in Barcelona, followed by the news that the king was demanding a

[1] AGS: GA, leg. 1327, Junta de Ejecución, 26 March 1640.
[2] ACU: Cartes, Canon Sullà to Canons of Urgell, 22 March 1640.

levy of troops, had brought the possibility of a popular insurrection appreciably closer. This was hinted at by a canon of Urgell who was in the city at that moment.[1] Much more important, it was also hinted at in a letter to the Protonotario himself by Dr Jacinto Valonga, who was still busily investigating the clashes between the soldiers and the population. He warned the Protonotario that from his own personal observation, it would be extremely unwise at this moment to take any further measures which would antagonize the Catalans.

This province is very different from others [he wrote]. It contains a villainous populace, which can easily be excited to violence, and the more it is pressed, the harder it resists. For this reason, actions which would be sufficient to make the inhabitants of any other province submit to orders of any kind from above, only succeed in exasperating the inhabitants of this province, and in making them insist more stubbornly on the proper observance of their laws.[2]

Dr Valonga's warning on the state of Catalonia was the most forceful comment on the dangers involved in Madrid's Catalan policy to have reached the ministers from a person of authority with first-hand experience of the Principality. None of Santa Coloma's many letters to the Court had contained comments of this nature. This was the measure of the viceroy's failure—that it was left to a visiting royal official to tell Madrid the unpleasant fact it had for so long managed to ignore; the fact that, whatever the minister's plans for making the Principality conform with the other provinces of the Monarchy, the Catalans had other ideas of their own, and were not by temperament a people to be bludgeoned into unquestioning compliance with their sovereign's wishes.

The forcefulness, and possibly the novelty, of Dr Valonga's remarks impressed the Protonotario sufficiently to make him underline them, and put a marginal note to the effect that they would be communicated to the king. But they do not seem to have had any very marked effect on ministerial policy. The letter ordering Santa Coloma to proceed with the levy of 6000 men was duly despatched on 31 March.[3] On the following day, the Protonotario attended a meeting of the Council of

---

[1] *Ibid.*
[2] ACA: CA, leg. 394, Dr Valonga to Protonotario, 24 March 1640.
[3] AGS: GA, leg. 1327, King to Santa Coloma, 31 March 1640.

Aragon which was compelled to redraft in his presence a *consulta* which it had originally composed in his absence a week before, and which had been rejected by the king (or, more probably, by Olivares and the Protonotario) as being too indecisive and too mild.[1] Santa Coloma was rebuked for not transferring Tamarit immediately to Perpinyà, but at least it was left for him to decide whether the risk was now too great for this to be done. Tamarit was only to be sent for trial if the case against him could certainly be won. Finally, it was time to put some stiffening into the judges of the Audiència and compel them to fulfil their obligations more effectively.

The unfortunate Audiència had for long been under suspicion in Madrid. The allegedly pusillanimous behaviour of individual ministers had caused much adverse comment, as when the king remarked on a *consulta* that one of them deserved to be garrotted or flung into the sea with a millstone round his neck;[2] and the collective behaviour of the Audiència, with its refusal to pronounce unhesitatingly on the legality of the billetings, had convinced the Protonotario of its unreliability. Well aware of the distrust with which they were viewed in Madrid, all sixteen judges joined in signing a letter of protest to Santa Coloma, representing the great services they had rendered in nine continuous months of hard work all over the Principality, first in recruiting men for Salces and then in arranging quarters for the troops.[3]

By the end of March, there can be no doubt that the Audiència was thoroughly demoralized. Continual pressure to act in a manner that offended their own deepest convictions and ran counter to the constitutions they were sworn to observe was placing an intolerable strain on a group of men who, for almost a year, had found themselves employed in unfamiliar occupations which earned for them nothing more than the hatred of their compatriots. They had done their best to billet the troops satisfactorily, while calming an excited populace, and all they received for their efforts was abuse from Madrid. To some extent they could claim to have been successful. The printed instructions laying down the exact obligations of householders had at least ended the earlier period of uncertainty, and had reduced the Principality

[1] The rejected *consulta* of 23 March, with the royal reply written by the Protonotario, and the rewritten *consulta* of 1 April, in ACA: CA, leg. 286, no. 43.
[2] AGS: GA, leg. 1336, King on *consulta* of Junta de Ejecución, 13 March 1640.
[3] ACA: CA, leg. 286, no. 41, Audiència to Santa Coloma, 24 (?) March 1640.

to a state of uneasy calm. 'The orders which have been issued have had a good effect, thanks be to God,' reported Dr Valonga at the end of March, 'although the appetite of the commanders is insatiable.'[1] But, as he pointed out, the continued success of the orders depended on the capacity to enforce them, and in this lay the greatest danger to Madrid.

The Audiència knew these orders to be illegal; it had only succeeded in salving its conscience by inventing a formula which, although allowing the execution of the orders, did not authorize punishment of the disobedient by the Principality's only effective method of judicial prosecution.[2] This, as Santa Coloma realized, was an insuperable obstacle to any satisfactory and permanent solution to the problem of billeting. It was for this reason that he had taken Dr Vinyes and Dr Miquel Joan Magarola into his confidence, and that the three men had between them worked out an alternative procedure. They suggested that the king should issue a pragmatic to cover the period of the emergency, ordering the Lombardy style of billeting, as already arranged, and laying down for the expenditure a general contribution in the form of a hearth-tax. A draft pragmatic to this effect was prepared by Magarola and Vinyes and forwarded to Madrid for approval.[3]

The technical advantage of a pragmatic lay in the fact that the Audiència would be compelled to obey. The Diputats could challenge its legality and press for a decision by the Audiència, but there was no time limit in which this decision had to be reached, and it could consequently be indefinitely postponed. Santa Coloma thought that by this device he had hit upon a perfect method of keeping the country calm while allowing the Audiència to escape from its dilemma over the enforcement of unconstitutional regulations. But the Protonotario never accepted anything without adding a few emendations of his own. It was with consternation that Santa Coloma and Vinyes discovered, on receiving the pragmatic authorized by Madrid, that their original draft had been radically changed. The pragmatic, as modified by the Protonotario, laid it down that the entire burden of supporting the troops, including the provision of the daily ration of bread,[4] which had

---

[1] AGS: GA, leg. 1355, Dr Valonga to F. Ruiz de Contreras, 31 March 1640.
[2] See above, p. 409.   [3] *Secrets Públichs*: Santa Coloma to Olivares, 19 March 1640.
[4] *Pan de munición*. The monetary equivalent of this was calculated by Balbases as ½ *real* a day for every man (ACA: CA, leg. 286, no. 40, Santa Coloma to King, 15 March 1640).

hitherto been at the king's expense, should now be shouldered by the Principality.

The entire Audiència rose up in revolt against this new and impossible demand. In a vigorous protest it pointed out that the original orders, by stipulating the payment by householders of 1 *real* a day without any further obligations to feed the soldiers, had made it possible to carry out the billeting successfully. Not once in the past nine hundred years had a pragmatic been issued placing on the population the *entire* expense of maintaining an army, and past viceroys had always taken action, at the instance of the Diputats, when soldiers tried to compel householders to feed them. Moreover, the Principality was poor. Over half of it was too mountainous to be cultivated, and the rest was not very productive. The inhabitants were already spending 84,000 *escuts* a month on the upkeep of the troops—more than 1 million *escuts* a year—and the 100,000 ducats for fortifications had been collected only with the greatest difficulty. All these considerations made it essential to delay the publication of the pragmatic.[1] Dr Vinyes supported this protest in a strong personal letter to the Protonotario:

This province can in no way bear so heavy a burden.... The first order from His Majesty, which was moderate, has enabled us to quieten the villages and the soldiers, and the publication of this pragmatic, with the enormous burden it entails, will risk the ruin of all that we have so far achieved under the direction of the count of Santa Coloma.... No province has rendered greater services than those which this province has rendered and is at present rendering....[2]

Santa Coloma himself rallied to the defence of his ministers: even in Milan the basic food ration was provided at His Majesty's expense, and the Principality was quite incapable of supplying it.[3] Having committed himself so far to disobedience to royal orders, the viceroy was probably glad to escape the need for expressions of personal opinion on a second paper by the Audiència which he forwarded to Madrid the same day. This paper, even stronger in content than the first, spoke for itself. It was the outcome of the Audiència's findings on the order sent to the viceroy for appropriating the revenues of the Diputació.[4]

[1] ACA: CA, leg. 394, paper by Audiència, 16 April 1640.
[2] ACA: CA, leg. 394, Dr Vinyes to Protonotario, 16 April 1640.
[3] ACA: CA, leg. 394, Santa Coloma to King, 16 April 1640.
[4] See above, p. 408. The Audiència's paper is in ACA: CA, leg. 394.

It began with an impressive list of constitutions which proved that the Crown could not touch the revenues of the Generalitat, and reminded the king that he had sworn to observe these constitutions when he came to the Principality in 1626. If he laid hands on these revenues, the Diputats had the right to suspend the payment of all taxes in the Principality. If the Crown then chose to take action against anyone refusing to pay taxes, the case would come before the Audiència, and the Audiència would be obliged to act in conformity with the oath taken by each of its members to observe the laws of the province and the contracts made between king and Estates in the Corts of Catalonia.

The warning could hardly have been clearer. Taken in conjunction with the paper on the Protonotario's pragmatic, it showed that the Audiència had reached a point where it felt it could no longer yield another inch. Since the dispute on the *quints*, the Audiència's difficulty in serving two masters had become increasingly obvious. The events of the last year, the siege of Salces, the billeting of the army, had brought it to breaking-point. Forced to choose between blind obedience to the king, and adherence to the traditional laws and privileges of Catalonia, it had finally made its choice: the judges were Catalans first, vassals of the king second. But both for themselves, and for the Principality, the decision had come too late.

When Santa Coloma's despatches and the protests of the Audiència reached Madrid, the Junta de Ejecución, now joined by Balbases, who had arrived at Madrid from Barcelona at the end of March, decided that it was called upon to weigh in the scales two opposing arguments. On the one hand, it had to consider the loss of face involved in preparing a pragmatic which was then withdrawn. On the other, it had to consider the risk of disorders that its publication might entail. It is some indication of the character of those who directed Spain's policies at this moment, that the first of these dangers—the loss of royal authority through failure to publish—appeared graver than the second. Santa Coloma was to go ahead with the publication of the pragmatic, since the extra financial burden was not likely to be great, and the campaigning season was so close that time itself would provide a way of escape.[1]

The decision appears to be that of a body which had lost all contact

---

[1] ACA: CA, leg. 394, Junta de Ejecución, 22 April 1640.

with reality. Yet, argued from the standpoint of Olivares and the Protonotario, it appeared perfectly consistent. For them, there were two decisive questions: the survival of the army, and the extension of royal authority over the Principality. 'Anything which prevents the soldiers from being comfortably settled in their quarters is felt most acutely here', Balbases wrote from Madrid to Santa Coloma.[1] 'And as the Crown is so short of money, they refuse any expenditure which elsewhere is not borne by the army, in spite of the fact that they must be aware of the province's incapacity to meet it.'[2]

The lack of money was certainly one vital consideration, but there was also the question of royal control over Catalonia. During the past year, Madrid had gradually made headway in forcing the Principality to assume the obligations it had for so long evaded. The Catalans had been compelled to raise troops for their own defence; they had been obliged to billet the army, and provide money both for the maintenance of the troops and for the repair of fortifications. Slowly, but not unsuccessfully, Catalonia was being drawn into the Union of Arms. This was what Olivares had always intended. When the marquis of Villafranca wrote from Barcelona at the end of March to urge that the army should be let loose on the Principality, his suggestion was politely set aside.[3] There was no need for such crude measures. A Diputat had been arrested; the Principality was already cowed. Everything was going according to plan. By the time Santa Coloma had raised his 6000 men for foreign service, and had obtained a general contribution for upkeep of the billeted army, Olivares's Catalan policy would be on the verge of success. Catalonia would at last have become part of Spain.

Madrid might have cause for optimism. The Principality was indeed outwardly calm. But no one in Catalonia could forget that one Diputat and two members of the Consell de Cent were in gaol. Nor could anyone in the Principality be unaware that the peace between soldiers and civilians was only precariously maintained, although the viceroy tried his best to ignore the unpleasant realities that stared him in the face. On 24 April he wrote to Madrid that the billeting was being quietly settled, and that the only serious trouble was with the troops

---

[1] ACA: G, caja 30, Balbases to Santa Coloma, 14 April 1640.
[2] *Ibid.* 28 April 1640.
[3] AGS: GA, leg. 1327, Junta de Ejecución, 7 April 1640.

under the command of Juan de Arce, who found themselves in difficulties because of the pusillanimous behaviour of the member of the
Audiència entrusted with their billeting.[1] On the 24th also, he had to
report that the judge who had been investigating the behaviour of the
Diputat Eclesiàstic, could find nothing against him, and there was no
case for proceedings by an apostolic brief.[2] On the same day, Claris's
indisposition officially ended,[3] and he returned to the head of affairs at
the Diputació. These two events—the troubles of Juan de Arce, and the
return of Claris—heralded between them a fresh storm in the Principality, far heavier than any yet experienced by Santa Coloma and an
unsuspecting Court.

[1] ACA: CA, leg. 286, no. 42, Santa Coloma to King, 24 April 1640.
[2] ACA: CA, leg. 394, Santa Coloma to King, 24 April 1640.
[3] ACA: G, Dietari, 1638–41, part III, fo. 363.

CHAPTER XV

ANARCHY

During January and February of 1640, Balbases had arranged the billeting of the troops in such a way that the foreign *tercios*—the Italians and the Walloons—were quartered in north-east Catalonia while the native Spanish *tercios* were in the south and west of the Principality, towards the borders of Aragon and Valencia. So many troops were deserting with the connivance of the inhabitants, however, that it was decided to make the two halves of the army change places.[1] As part of this operation, Juan de Arce's *tercio* of Spaniards now found itself marching through the western regions of the province of Girona; harsh, inhospitable land, 'mountainous and wooded, and so high up as to be perfect for sheltering lawless men'.[2] Here were the old haunts of the bandit gangs, places of refuge for criminals and outcasts, and now for those who had left their homes in terror at the approach of the troops.

In a region such as this, trouble was to be expected. Juan de Arce's *tercio* had arrived at the little town of Sant Feliu de Pallarols. The town council could not make up its mind whether or not the troops should be allowed to enter, and for eight days the *tercio* waited outside the town walls while the council deliberated.[3] During much of this time the soldiers were without food, and dared not go far from each other because the countryside was in an uproar. The local population had posted sentinels in the hills to give warning of the arrival of more troops, and Dr Meca of the Audiència found it impossible to reason with the 'barbarous' inhabitants of the valley, who were all ready to take to the mountains at the first hint of a general movement by the *tercio*.

Santa Coloma put the blame for Arce's difficulties on Dr Meca, who, in his opinion, should have arrested the town councillors of Sant Feliu for their disloyal behaviour.[4] The name of Dr Meca, who was an in-

---

[1] Rubí, *Levantamiento*, fo. 78.
[2] Diputats to Grau, 4 May 1640. To be found in *MHE*, vol xx, doc. 113, where Pujol y Camps has printed a useful, but by no means exhaustive, series of documents on the events in this region during April and May.
[3] ACA: CA, leg. 286, no. 42, Dr Meca to Santa Coloma, 22 April 1640.
[4] ACA: CA, leg. 286, no. 42, Santa Coloma to King, 24 April 1640.

experienced young man appointed straight to his post in the Audiència from the College of Oviedo at Salamanca,[1] was duly noted by the Protonotario, who arranged that he should be called to Madrid to answer before the king for his conduct.[2] But neither Dr Meca nor any other minister could have induced the inhabitants of this region to take soldiers into their houses other than by force, and the commanders had not given their men orders to use it.

While Juan de Arce's troops waited patiently outside the walls of Sant Feliu, those under the command of Don Felipe de Guevara were doing the same outside the walls of Santa Coloma de Farners, further to the south. The town had refused to billet the soldiers in any form whatever, and two deserted houses provided their only shelter for the night.[3] Since the *tercio* of Don Leonardo Moles in turn would shortly have to pass through Santa Coloma de Farners, the viceroy determined that the inhabitants should not be allowed to escape their obligations a second time, and sent the *agutzil* Monrodón to arrange the billeting in advance. Monrodón was a notorious figure throughout the Principality. A violent and arrogant fellow, liable to drunken rages,[4] he had personally carried out almost all the unpopular orders of the viceregal administration, including the arrest of Tamarit. The citizens of Santa Coloma de Farners therefore knew exactly what to expect when Monrodón appeared in their town on 27 April. They also knew what lay in store for them once Moles's troops arrived. There were plenty of people ready to give them warning and encouragement, including a noble, Don Ramon de Farnés, who owned a house in the town, and who sent to the inhabitants two muskets, three arquebuses and two carbines, accompanied by a letter containing the following rousing words: 'If by any chance the soldiers are so shameless as to want to sack the place, there is nothing for it but to fight bravely and defend yourselves like men.'[5]

Santa Coloma de Farners had long enjoyed a reputation for lawlessness. The jurisdiction of it belonged to the viscount of Joc,'a gentleman

---

[1] ACA: CA, leg. 508, petition by Dr Meca, 14 Feb. 1642.
[2] AGS: GA, leg. 1328, Junta de Ejecución, 3 May 1640.
[3] AGS: GA, leg. 1328, Santa Coloma to King, 4 May 1640.
[4] ACA: CA, leg. 356, Almazán to King, 20 Sept. 1614.
[5] AGS: GA, leg. 1328, letter from Don Ramon de Farnés of 28 April found in a deserted house after the town had been sacked.

so good as to allow it to fall under the control of a clergyman called Dr Francesc Montagut—an evil intentioned man, and disloyal to Your Majesty'.[1] It was presumably under Montagut's direction that the inhabitants prepared themselves against the arrival of the troops by removing from their houses anything on which the soldiers could possibly lay hands. According to one account, Monrodón attempted to prevent this, lost his temper with a householder who refused to obey, drew his pistol and fired.[2] According to another, he had ordered that no one should carry pistols in the town, and, seeing his orders disobeyed by four men at the town gate, attempted to arrest them.[3] Whatever the exact cause of the original dispute, the people rioted, and Monrodón retreated with his servants to the inn, which was surrounded by a furious crowd and set on fire. Monrodón and all but one of his servants were burnt to death.

By the following day, 1 May, the news of Monrodón's death had reached Leonardo Moles, whose troops were quartered in the villages of Les Mallorquines and Riudarenes, only a short distance from the scene of the crime. Almost at the same moment, Moles's own men discovered themselves in danger. The town of Santa Coloma had sent out appeals for help, and large bands of armed men had come down from the hills in response. Estimates of their numbers varied, 'because they had to return to their homes for meals, but at their maximum they reached 4000 and their minimum was 800'.[4] These men seem to have been irate peasants, villagers from all the neighbouring region, and members of that floating rural population which always collected quickly in Catalonia when trouble was brewing. Well armed and well led, these groups of rebels moved down towards Les Mallorquines to snipe at Moles's troops.[5] Seeing himself at a disadvantage, Moles decided to retreat to the coast, but, before leaving, his men set fire to the village and the church of Riudarenes, in which the villagers had stored their possessions. They then retired to Blanes, on the coast, which they reached safely on 4 May.

The rebels, who had been following in pursuit, got as far as Tordera

[1] Santa Coloma to King, 4 May 1640.
[2] ACU: loose paper dated 27 May 1640, and sent by Don Llorenç de Barutell to Canons of Urgell, purporting to be an eyewitness account.
[3] Rubí, *Levantamiento*, fo. 78 v.
[4] *Ibid.* fo. 79 v.   [5] ACA: G, caja 32, Dr Puig to Santa Coloma, 4 May 1640.

and then realized that Moles was now safe.[1] Some of them returned home; others made for Amer, to the north of Santa Coloma de Farners, where they laid siege to part of the *tercio* of Spanish troops commanded by Juan de Arce. For four days, from 4 to 7 May, Arce's position appeared hopeless. The besieging force, over 3000 men strong, far outnumbered his own troops, and was described as 'well armed and desperate'.[2] But on 7 May a relief force composed of Don Felipe de Guevara's troops and those companies of Arce's own *tercio* which had been quartered at Sant Feliu, managed to break through the encircling ring and join up with Arce's beleaguered men. The peasant forces withdrew, and Arce himself, an elderly man worn out by the exertions of the past few days, reached the safety of Girona on 11 May.[3]

The relief of Arce at Amer came at the end of a week of violence which had transformed the face of the Principality. Until the beginning of May, the troops had been moving among a sullen and resentful population, but had encountered resistance only from a few desperate householders and from the odd marauding band. But during this first week of May the ineffectual individual protests had been replaced by a collective protest of frightening proportions. The whole countryside in the western areas of the provinces of Girona and La Selva had caught fire, and the few small groups of protesting peasants had turned into an army of three or four thousand men, apparently well organized and well armed.

The speed with which the insurgents organized themselves into something like an army might have seemed remarkable in any other country but Catalonia. But the Principality had a long tradition of collective action. In the civil wars of the fifteenth century, the peasants had formed very effective 'syndicates'. During the sixteenth and early seventeenth centuries the feuds of *nyerros* and *cadells* and the activities of bandit gangs had certainly helped to keep in being a network which stretched across the country, bringing information or assistance very quickly to those who needed it. When the soldiers from the galleys clashed with the inhabitants of Cadaqués in 1628, the duke of Alcalá was amazed at the speed with which the inhabitants obtained reinforcements from outside, and was able to discover for himself 'how the

[1] AGS: GA, leg. 1328, Santa Coloma to King, 6 May 1640.
[2] AMG: Corresp. dels Jurats, 1639–53, Jurats of Girona to Santa Coloma, 6 May 1640.
[3] ACA: G, caja 31, Don Ramon Calders to Santa Coloma, 11 May 1640.

Catalans respond to a call for help'.[1] It took little time for news of trouble to spread from one village to the next, especially as it was common practice in Catalonia for villages to ring their church bells whenever help was needed. The bells were ringing in all the valleys from Sant Feliu to Tordera during that first week of May. The country-side stood armed and ready.

All this land, by which I mean the peasantry, is so disaffected [wrote Don Ramon Calders to the viceroy from Girona], that I doubt if there are any who do not feel the same way as those of Santa Coloma. And the common people in this town are by no means well-disposed. It is true that the town council-lors and the superior classes are showing themselves to be devoted to His Majesty's service, but few of the clergy and the members of the religious orders are similarly inclined, and most of them follow the voice of the people.[2]

There were certainly agitators at work, and Santa Coloma sent orders to the judges of the Audiència to discover the names of 'towns and individuals who have given support, favour and assistance to the con-federates, helping them either in person or by sending provisions and arms; and those who have had the church bells rung, and have approved of the confederation and its crimes, either in conversation or other-wise'.[3] But the judges discovered little. Dr Puig reported from Girona that he had arrested a certain Francesc Cuch from Anglés, a familiar of the Inquisition, whom he believed to be implicated in the disturbances;[4] but it is only very rarely that even as little specific information as this is available, and the destruction of all the records of the Audiència makes it impossible to find out about the background and origins of the one or two rebel leaders whose names can be discovered.

Santa Coloma reacted to the news of Monrodón's death and the massing of the peasants by insisting on immediate punishment and retaliation. He ordered the destruction of a number of houses in Santa Coloma de Farners, and wrote to Madrid asking for permission to raze the entire town.[5] He also suggested that up to 3000 infantry and 500 cavalry should join forces to attack the insurgents.[6] The Council of

---

[1] Pujades, 4, fo. 107.
[2] AGS: GA, leg. 1328, Calders to Santa Coloma, 8 May 1640.
[3] ACA: Canc. R. 5527, fo. 26v, Santa Coloma to judges of Audiència, 12 May 1640.
[4] ACA: G, caja 32, Dr Rafael Puig to Santa Coloma, 13 May 1640.
[5] AGS: GA, leg. 1328, Santa Coloma to King, 4 May 1640.
[6] AGS: GA, leg. 1328, Santa Coloma to King, 5 May 1640.

Aragon, while deeply shocked by the murder of Monrodón, felt that it would be advisable to destroy no more than three or four houses in Santa Coloma de Farners, and to confiscate the possessions of the inhabitants.[1] The king, after a meeting of the Junta de Ejecución, wrote on the Council of Aragon's *consulta*, that troops were to back up the judicial punishment of the guilty, using force to stifle the rising, but *'without starting a new war'*.

There is little reason to doubt that he meant what he said. The Junta de Ejecución had agreed in its meeting of 9 May that 'it would be better for the present not to make a demonstration against the entire province, but to keep this for a more opportune time'.[2] The important thing was to stop the movement from spreading, not to 'make a war where there isn't one'.[3] It was also necessary to make an exemplary punishment of the troops responsible for burning the church at Riudarenes, and to have the church rebuilt exactly as it was. Spain's international situation was such that the insurrection in Catalonia must be localized and put down while the rest of the Principality was kept quiet.

As further bad news reached Madrid from Catalonia, with reports of the siege of Arce's troops at Amer, the alarm of the ministers increased. Time was getting on; it was essential to increase the size of the army in Lombardy, and disturbances in Catalonia could be extremely inconvenient.[4] The Council of Aragon even wondered whether it would not be advisable to defer punitive action against Santa Coloma de Farners, but the king replied that he saw no reason to change his orders. He did, however, insist again that the guilty soldiers must be severely punished: they had 'in the space of a short time caused incomparably greater destruction than any other undisciplined troops over a long period'.[5]

No one in Madrid seems to have seen any incompatibility in ordering that troops guilty of excesses should be punished, while simultaneously ordering those same troops to castigate summarily a rebellious population. Santa Coloma himself was all for prompt punitive action by the

---

[1] AGS: GA, leg. 1328, Council of Aragon, 8 May 1640 (my italics).
[2] AGS: GA, leg. 1328, Junta de Ejecución, 9 May 1640.
[3] AGS: GA, leg. 1328, further consulta of Junta de Ejecución, 9 May 1640.
[4] AGS: GA, leg. 1328, consultas of Junta de Ejecución, 11 and 12 May 1640.
[5] ACA: CA, leg. 285, consulta, 13 May 1640.

tercios. They should return to Santa Coloma de Farners, destroy the houses, as ordered, and then take up quarters in all the more rebellious villages of the Girona region. The risks attendant on this do not seem to have occurred to him, but were all too obvious to Dr Jacinto Valonga, whose continued inquiries into the behaviour of the troops had led him to Girona, where he had met the acting governor, Don Ramon Calders, and Drs Puig and Anglasell of the Audiència. The havoc wreaked by the *tercios* on their punitive expeditions, he wrote to Santa Coloma, had provoked such anger that 'although for the time things seem to be quiet, the calm is deceptive; and they have stirred up such bitter hatred that people will do everything to escape harm and seek revenge for the treatment they have received'.[1]

Santa Coloma, however, was determined to have summary justice done, and he was supported in this by the army commanders. Their only doubt was over the danger which dispersing the troops would involve. They therefore decided

not to separate...and to march all together on Sunday morning back to Santa Coloma de Farners, where we shall act in accordance with Your Excellency's orders and the instructions of the governor....As regards the reputation of His Majesty's forces, it seems desirable that all these men should billet for one night in Santa Coloma, even if they have to take with them their food for that night. It would not be possible for them to stay any longer—they have already put up with enough these last few days. We must add that our orders were to destroy the houses of the *batlle* and town councillors but the governor tells us there are no such houses. Will Your Excellency therefore please inform us why we are to go there, unless it be to demolish all the houses since all are guilty.[2]

Santa Coloma thoroughly approved these plans:

I fully support your decision to set out on Sunday, as it is highly important that you should go to Santa Coloma de Farners and carry out the measures I have ordered....It is a very good idea to billet the troops together, as you suggest...and I have sent orders to the governor that this should be done in the worst-behaved villages in the plain. The villages in the mountains, although more rebellious, are not suitable for billeting because the troops will not be sufficiently comfortable...Since there are no houses belonging

[1] AGS: GA, leg. 1328, Dr Valonga to Santa Coloma, 13 May 1640.
[2] ACA: Documentación incompleta, caja 11, Don Leonardo Moles, the Conde de Tyrconnel and Juan de Arce to Santa Coloma, 11 May 1640. Printed in *MHE*, vol. xx, doc. 133.

to the *batlle* and the town councillors, I have ordered the governor and Don Josep d'Oms to destroy twenty houses belonging to the most guilty inhabitants, while awaiting the reply to the inquiry I sent to His Majesty as to whether the whole town should be destroyed (which I am sure he will order)....

In a postscript he added: 'It is very important that you go to Santa Coloma and billet all the *tercios* there and do as I have instructed you, otherwise His Majesty will be ill-served.'[1]

This exchange of letters leaves no doubt as to the respective parts played by the viceroy and the army commanders in the fateful punishment of Santa Coloma de Farners. Santa Coloma was acting on his own initiative, although complete approval for his action was in fact on its way from Madrid. Armed with the viceroy's instructions, the *tercios* set out for Santa Coloma de Farners, and reached it between four and five o'clock on the afternoon of 14 May. They found the town deserted, but large quantities of wine and a certain amount of food had been left in the houses. Don Ramon Calders and the *maestres de campo* made an effort to restrain the men, but nothing could prevent them from sacking and setting fire to one house after another.[2] By the time they had finished their work, only two houses were left standing, both of them belonging to Don Ramon de Farnés, and immediately the troops departed the next afternoon, the inhabitants returned and burnt these also, shouting that Don Ramon was a traitor.[3]

After completing their punitive action with considerably more thoroughness than their orders warranted, the troops turned back towards Girona, quite gratuitously destroying on their way what remained of the village of Riudarenes. The news of the sack of Santa Coloma and Riudarenes caused panic in Girona, which feared that its turn was coming next, and when the *tercios* arrived outside the city walls, they found the gates barred against them. Realizing that the soldiers would either die of starvation or get involved in a separate struggle with armed bands which were flocking towards Girona from every quarter, Don Ramon Calders gave the order for retreat on the night of 17 May.

The only hope was to get the *tercios* to the coast, at Blanes, but the

---

[1] *Ibid.* Draft reply of Santa Coloma.
[2] AGS: GA, leg. 1328, Calders to Santa Coloma, 15 May 1640.
[3] AGS: GA, leg. 1328, Calders to Santa Coloma, 18 May 1640.

route ran across country that was now in open revolt. The sack of Santa Coloma de Farners, instead of pacifying the countryside, had served only to inflame it, just as Dr Valonga had foretold. From as far away as Reus in south Catalonia, came reports of the change that had come over the country with the news of the sack. 'We had got these places all settled and content with the billetings', wrote a royal official, Dr Martí, 'and now they are so transformed that I am in despair, with most of them pretty well determined not to feed the troops, and threatening to kill them.'[1] If this was the impact on a distant town, the effect on villages in the vicinity of Santa Coloma de Farners is easily imagined. Dr Anglasell reported from Girona that a localized movement had now turned into a general rising, with insurgents moving in to attack the *tercios* from Vallès, Vic, Camprodon, Ripoll, Besalú and Empúries.[2]

While the principal cause of this general movement in the countryside was the sack of Santa Coloma de Farners, it was encouraged by two further circumstances of considerable importance. Since April, there had been no rain, and by the middle of May it looked as though the harvest would be ruined unless the drought ended soon.[3] The prospect that the harvest would be lost did much to add to the desperation of a peasantry which already saw itself threatened with destruction by the troops. In this highly charged atmosphere, rumours of strange and miraculous events spread with extraordinary speed. When the troops burnt the church of Riudarenes, tears were seen to fall from the eyes of the Virgin in a picture in the church.[4] The news was carried to Girona by two Capuchins, who brought with them the reliquary they had saved from the flames. The bishop of Girona, fray Gregorio Parcero, appears at this moment to have been in Barcelona, where the Provincial Council of the archbishopric of Tarragona had been summoned for 4 May to vote on the renewal of the ecclesiastical taxes.[5] The council's attention was focused on the behaviour of the troops, to the exclusion of all else—and particularly of the unwelcome subject of taxes.[6] Par-

[1] ACA: G, caja 32, Dr Martí to Santa Coloma, 20 May 1640.
[2] ACA: CA, leg. 287, no. 123, Dr Anglasell to Santa Coloma, 20 May 1640.
[3] AGS: GA, leg. 1368, Santa Coloma to King, 11 May 1640.
[4] ACU: report sent by Barutell, 27 May 1640.
[5] J. M. Madurell Marimón, 'El Concilio Tarraconense de 1640', *Analecta Sacra Tarraconensia*, vol. xxi (1948), p. 126.
[6] ACA: CA, leg. 384, Bishop of Barcelona to King, 25 May 1640.

cero, who was not a Catalan, could hardly be expected to ignore the obvious strength of feeling about the troops, especially as Riudarenes was in his own diocese. After collecting all the available information about the burning of Riudarenes, and the destruction of the sacraments, he placed a sentence of excommunication on the entire *tercio* of Don Leonardo Moles, as being responsible for the sacrilege. 'This, Sir, has happened in Spain, where our Faith is preserved in the purest form,' he wrote to Santa Coloma on 14 May, 'and the crime has been perpetrated by soldiers fighting beneath the Catholic banners of His Majesty.'[1]

The bishop of Girona's action, while inspired by the deepest spiritual sincerity, was not distinguished for its worldly wisdom. It was only one step from excommunication by the bishop to a proclamation by the rebels that they were fighting for God and their churches.[2] Inevitably, the episcopal censure was regarded by the insurgents as a complete vindication of their activities. It gave their rising the character of a Holy War—an idea already suggested by the miraculous tears of the Virgin and encouraged by the clergy and members of the religious orders, who told them that divine retribution was now being meted out to soldiers whom temporal justice had failed to punish.[3]

Fortified by the sanction of the Church, the rebel bands which had gathered at Girona started in pursuit of the retreating troops. These had begun their march towards Blanes on the morning of 18 May. All along the route they were harried by the rebels.[4] By an extraordinary feat, the *maestres de campo* somehow managed to prevent their half-starved men from retaliating, to the subsequent regret of both the viceroy and Madrid.[5] Pursued by cries of 'Help against the enemies of the Holy Catholic Faith and the Church!'[6] they reached the coast at Blanes, weary and famished, on 19 May. Their march was completed, but revolution had begun.

Unaware that the sack of Santa Coloma de Farners and the bishop of Girona's pronouncement had between them unleashed a general insurrection in the provinces of Girona and La Selva, the Junta de

[1] *MHE*, vol. xx, doc. 72.
[2] ACA: G, caja 31, Villafranca to Santa Coloma, 14 May 1640.
[3] ACA: G, caja 31, Dr Guerau to Santa Coloma, late May 1640.
[4] ACA: G, caja 31, Calders to Don Tomàs Fontanet, 18 May 1640.
[5] AGS: GA, leg. 1328, Santa Coloma to King, 19 May 1640.
[6] ACA: CA, leg. 285, no. 29, Jurats of Blanes to Santa Coloma, 19 May 1640.

Ejecución assumed that its orders would by now have had the desired results. 'Nothing', it agreed, 'is so important as to continue billeting in that province. If this is not done...we shall have committed ourselves to a proposition that we have always tried to avoid: that in the event of war it is not obliged to billet troops.' The point would by now have been driven home to the Principality by the punitive action of the *tercios*. There was no need for the destruction of more houses. The Catalans would have learnt their lesson.[1]

While Madrid was still insisting on points of principle, it was beginning to dawn on Santa Coloma that it was high time that principle should be sacrificed. The spread of rebellion and the retreat of the troops to Blanes had at last begun to open his eyes to what was happening. 'This province feels so deeply about the billeting', he wrote to the king on 19 May, 'that the people are in a state of turmoil and take up arms wherever the soldiers go....Everything is in such a dangerous state that I do not know how to describe it to Your Majesty. There is not a man who can be counted on in the entire province....'[2] This was not the voice that had so imperiously ordered the destruction of Santa Coloma de Farners only a week before.

The situation was by now extremely dangerous. The revolt had spread southwards to Vallès, where on 20 May the insurgents attacked the duke of Modena's *tercio* and the cavalry of Chirinos and forced them back towards Barcelona.[3] The city itself still seemed to be quiet, but Santa Coloma was extremely uneasy. A few days earlier, Madrid had sent him instructions to 'seize Barcelona in case of danger',[4] but he had been obliged to reply that he was not clear how this was to be done, as there was no castle in the city and he had no troops.[5] The viceroy was therefore at the mercy of the city, and the city itself was ceasing to be its own master. By the evening of 21 May, Barcelona was full of reports that the *tercios* at Blanes were marching on the city. The bishop of Barcelona, seeing that the people were stirring, closed the cathedral so that the bells should not be rung, and hastily sent a message to the Consellers that the reports were false.[6] But his precautions were useless.

[1] AGS: GA, leg. 1328, Junta de Ejecución, 18 May 1640.
[2] ACA: CA, leg. 285, no. 18, Santa Coloma to King, 19 May 1640.
[3] Sanabre, *Acción de Francia*, p. 63.
[4] AGS: GA, leg. 1328, Junta de Ejecución, 11 May 1640.
[5] AGS: GA, leg. 1328, Santa Coloma to King, 20 May 1640.
[6] ACA: CA, leg. 285, no. 26, Bishop of Barcelona to King, 22 May 1640.

The peasant forces from Vallès, armed with muskets, arquebuses and pistols, were moving towards the relief of the supposedly threatened city, where handbills were being passed around announcing that they intended to finish with the viceroy and with all traitors.[1] On the morning of the 22nd they were inside the walls of Barcelona.

It has always been a mystery who opened the gates to the insurgents that morning. But a plausible account, containing a more detailed description than most, is provided by Dr Rubí of the Audiència.[2]

There has been much discussion on the decision of the rebels to enter Barcelona [he wrote]. The most probable explanation is that the Diputats, afraid of summary punishment being meted out to Tamarit, had previously sent out messengers to the rebel forces well before daybreak. Finding them at Sant Andreu, resting after the exertions of the previous day, they persuaded them to enter and release the Diputat from prison, promising them that the city would not put any obstacles in their way or do them any harm....

The rebels then nominated nine men to organize the entry. They held up all the vehicles bringing supplies to Barcelona, and put a group of two hundred men behind them, followed at a distance by the remainder of the insurgent army.

Shielded by the carts and the pack-mules, they got very close to the New Gate, when the gate-keepers discovered them and tried to close the gate. But a body of twelve who had gone ahead to act as a guard prevented them from doing this by skill and entreaty, and the entire band entered. As they did so, they shouted out that they had only come to free the Diputat, and would harm no one.

According to another account, they entered with cries of 'Out of the way, if you value your life!', and marched along behind an image of Christ, shouting 'Long live the King! Death to traitors! Down with bad government!'[3]

Once inside the city, the rebels made straight for the prison, where they arrived in remarkably good order. Quietly and efficiently they set to work to pull down the prison gates.[4] Within a short time, the

[1] AGS: GA, leg. 1328, Santa Coloma to King, 22 May 1640.
[2] Rubí, *Levantamiento*, fos. 91–91 v.
[3] AMG: Corresp. 1640–9, Don Ramon Xammar to Jurats of Girona, 23 May 1640. The bishop of Barcelona, on the other hand, says they had no flag or other insignia. He also says that they had no leader.
[4] Tormé i Liori, *Miscellaneos*, p. 109.

entire prison was emptied, and Tamarit, Vergós and Serra were freed—
as also were several thieves, bandits and ordinary criminals, together
with the soldier who had killed Don Antoni de Fluvià at Palautordera
three months before.[1] The time was now about 11.30, and the Consellers had sent an urgent message to the bishop of Barcelona to come
to their help. He arrived with the bishop of Vic, and the two bishops
together approached the rebels who were milling around the streets,
and asked them to leave the city. The request was well received. Some
of the rebels kissed the bishop of Barcelona's hand, and there were
cries of 'Long live Holy Mother Church and the King our Lord!'[2] The
two bishops made the most of their opportunity, and carefully shep-
herded the insurgents, estimated at from two to three thousand, back
through the New Gate, and outside the city walls. The immediate
danger to Barcelona had passed. Not a single drop of blood had been
shed, and the Diputat Militar was free.

May 22nd was a day of triumph for the insurgents. They had discovered
their strength. Full of confidence, they prepared for a general assault
on the *tercios* now sheltering at Blanes. They set up their camp at Sant
Celoni and sent out appeals for help, written from Tordera, near Blanes,
by someone calling himself the *mestre de camp cathalà*.[3] Realizing that
the position of the troops in Blanes would be desperate, the army commanders and Santa Coloma decided that the only hope was to get their
men to Rosselló. Since the cavalry could not be taken off by sea,
this meant an overland march all the way from Blanes up to Roses.
Juan de Arce broke out of Blanes on 27 May, and slowly made his
way northwards, under constant attack from the peasants, who had
occupied all the narrow passes on the road to Sant Feliu de Guíxols.[4]
By 30 May he had arrived at Montiró, where his men set fire to the
church. Finally, with most of his cavalry destroyed, Arce reached
safety at the strongly fortified garrison town and port of Roses on
31 May.[5]

While the *tercios* were making their dangerous journey to Roses, the

---

[1] *Súplica de Tortosa*, fo. 70.
[2] ACA: CA, leg. 285, no. 26, Bishop of Barcelona to King, 22 May 1640.
[3] ACA: G, caja 32, *Copia del paper que escriu lo cap dels amotinats*, 24 May 1640.
[4] AGS: GA, leg. 1328, Marquis of Villafranca to King, 29 May 1640. A useful diary of the
events of these days is provided by Pujol y Camps in his *Melo y la Revolución de Cataluña en 1640*
(Madrid, 1886), pp. 83–90.
[5] AGS: GA, leg. 1328, Juan de Arce to Santa Coloma, 1 June 1640.

rebellion was spreading through all the Principality north of Barcelona, and was already beginning to display signs of the savagery and vindictiveness which characterized its later stages. On 26 May four or five hundred insurgents appeared at Mataró, shouting 'Traitors of Mataró— you are the guilty ones. It was you who first gave shelter to the soldiers'.[1] The same day, much more serious incidents took place at Vic. The Consellers of Vic had refused to pass on the letters they had received from the rebel commander appealing for recruits to join his peasant army.[2] Handbills began to circulate in the city, naming thirteen or fourteen citizens, all of whom happened to be rich, as traitors to the fatherland. On the 26th there were disturbances among the university students in the town,[3] and suddenly, on the firing of two shots as an agreed signal, a band of about thirty armed men broke in through one of the gates, shouting 'Long live the land and the King! Death to traitors and bad Christians!' They made straight for the house of Miquel Joan Granollachs, one of the best-appointed private houses in the Principality, where Dr Bernat Pons of the Audiència was lodging. The house was set on fire, but Pons escaped by jumping into the garden and finding refuge with a priest. The insurgents moved on from Granollachs's house to the house of the chief Conseller of Vic, Antoni Illa, to which they also set fire. Illa rushed to the window to pour water on the flames, and was shot and killed. Attempts were then made to set fire to the houses of two wealthy citizens, but without success. The next day the insurgents walked openly around the town, but some effort seems to have been made by the more responsible citizens to raise a guard: 'they saw that the common people were the cause of all the trouble, and especially those who want to live without working, spending everything in taverns and gaming-houses without having a penny in the world'. The rebels finally left the town, nominally to fight the soldiers, but it was not very long before they were back.

The pattern of events in Vic was closely followed in many other towns and villages of northern Catalonia. At Girona, for instance, armed bands arrived at the city on 26 May, apparently believing that Arce's troops would pass through it on their march northwards. On

[1] ACA: CA, leg. 287, no. 37, report written by Don Acacio Ripoll.
[2] Sanz, *Relació*, pp. 39 ff., gives a vivid description of the incidents, which I have followed here.
[3] A university, of no great repute, had been founded in Vic in 1599 (Gustave Reynier, *La Vie Universitaire dans l'Ancienne Espagne* (Paris, 1902), p. 102).

entering they started sacking convents in which a few soldiers were taking refuge, and set off in search of the acting governor, Calders, and Drs Meca and Corts of the Audiència, who were known to be in the city. Calders and his colleagues happily found refuge in the cathedral and succeeded in escaping from Girona at midnight on the 30th, making their way on foot to Blanes, from where they managed to obtain a sea passage to Roses.[1]

The events in Vic, Girona and elsewhere make it clear that the first stage in the spread of revolution was the arrival of a group of armed outsiders at the gates, generally coinciding with disturbances inside the town. The gates would be opened to the outsiders by some prearranged agreement, and they would make for houses in which they expected to find royal ministers or prominent figures who were regarded as 'traitors'. Having sacked or burnt these houses, they would then turn their attention—with the connivance and encouragement of the more underprivileged and lawless townspeople—to the houses of the rich. During the early days little attempt was made by people in positions of authority to check them. In some places the town councillors were personally ineffective. In Girona, the chief Jurat absented himself after rebels had burnt down two of his houses; the second died, allegedly of shock or anguish, three days after being called a traitor by women in the streets; the third was in the last stages of a fatal illness, and only the fourth remained to offer Calders any kind of assistance.[2] In other towns the municipal councillors were so paralysed with fear as to be incapable of taking independent action.

News has reached this city [wrote the Consellers of Manresa pathetically], which has filled us with alarm and confusion. They say—and on two occasions we have actually seen for ourselves—that there is a great uproar, and a ringing of bells from town to town, and much crying for help against the soldiers who are going around laying waste the land. . . . And we know that the tumult has reached the city of Vic and the town of Moià, and that if the town councillors refuse to do what they are told, the rioters kill them and set fire to their houses on the pretext that they are traitors. So it looks as though we shall suffer one of two misfortunes: we shall either provoke the anger of the king our Lord (by following the general current) or else the anger of the country. We should like to do the right thing, and escape, if we can, from this labyrinth. . . .[3]

[1] ACA: CA, leg. 287, no. 41, Don Ramon Calders to Santa Coloma, 2 June 1640.
[2] *Ibid.*
[3] AHM: leg. 1089, Consellers of Manresa to Ma. Victoria Font, 31 May 1640.

The poor town councillors, rudely jolted out of the even tenor of their comfortable lives, were not the men to face with determination a violent popular movement. The rebellion swept to and fro across north Catalonia, unresisted, irresistible. Santa Coloma, his nerve shattered by the events of 22 May, saw his world collapsing about him. The bells were ringing, the province was in arms, the judges of the Audiència were being hounded to death. 'It is impossible to do anything or to administer justice. Everything has come to a stop.'[1]

Santa Coloma's letter reporting the release of Tamarit reached Madrid on 27 May. The Council of Aragon went into immediate session. This was the moment for which its two most vigorous members, Cardinal Borja and the Protonotario, had been waiting. Under their direction, the Council recommended the king to do what it had so often advised—to 'bridle that province'. Here was the perfect occasion for the use of force against the Catalans.[2] A similar plea was shortly to be sent by the marquis of Villafranca, now at Palamós with the galleys under his command: 'If they are not promptly punished, it could cause a troublesome war in Spain.'[3] The pressure for ruthless measures against the Catalans, such as had been demanded in 1622, 1632, 1636, was reaching its climax.

Everything now depended on the Conde Duque. His entire Catalan policy over the best part of twenty years had been directed towards making the Principality play the active role which he had designed for it in Spain's wars. For some time it had seemed as if he had found the perfect middle way between *suavidad* and *rigor*—between an excessive compliance with the wishes of the Catalans and a policy of naked force. By tempting the French to invade the Principality, by driving the inhabitants to participate in the Salces campaign, and then by billeting the army in Catalonia to be maintained at the Catalans' expense, he could almost be said to have achieved his object: the integration of Catalonia into a united Spain. And now, suddenly, there came news of insurrection and the release of Tamarit. His policy lay in ruins.

A few days before, when the first hints of disorders in the Principality were reaching Madrid, the Junta de Ejecución had agreed on the importance of restraining disturbances there, 'especially at this time,

[1] AGS: GA, leg. 1328, Santa Coloma to King, 26 May 1640.
[2] AGS: GA, leg. 1328, Council of Aragon, 27 May 1640.
[3] AGS: GA, leg. 1328, Villafranca to King, 29 May 1640.

because of the serious consequences that could arise from any insurrection'.[1] Now that insurrection had actually begun, was Madrid to change its policy and execute summary punishment upon the entire Principality, as the Council of Aragon demanded? This was the question with which the Conde Duque was faced. There was much to be said for action of the type demanded by the Council of Aragon. It might permanently 'settle' the affairs of the Principality in a manner satisfactory to Madrid, and put an end to the long series of manœuvres by which the Catalans had sought to escape their obligations. But Olivares was responsible for the welfare of the entire Spanish Monarchy, in a way that the Protonotario and the Council of Aragon were not. It was for him to balance the demands for forceful measures in Catalonia against the wider interests of the Spanish Crown. If the supreme task of Spain was the defeat of France, as Olivares had always insisted, would the achievement of this task be hindered or facilitated by the forcible pacification of the Principality?

At a combined meeting on 27 May of the Consejo de Estado and Junta de Ejecución, with thirteen ministers present, Olivares announced his decision. It amounted to a complete rejection of the demands of the Council of Aragon. The Barcelona authorities should be thanked for their good behaviour on 22 May; all Spanish grandees who had estates in the Principality should go there at once to calm their vassals; city and Diputats should be asked for advice on how to pacify the province.

In my view, Your Majesty should accept any measure suggested by these people for some form of accommodation; and although I consider that discussions should be held to arrange for the best possible settlement, my view is that a settlement which they consider satisfactory to Your Majesty may well be a good deal better than the best settlement that could be expected from the present state of affairs. For matters have got so entangled, and things have dragged on for so long, that we cannot hope that a single blow or a single decree can reduce that province to a proper frame of mind.[2]

In this belated recognition that the Catalan problem had become too complex to allow of a rapid, clear-cut solution, Olivares had contradicted one of the fundamental assumptions of Madrid's Catalan policy. Whenever they had become embroiled with the Catalans during the

[1] AGS: GA, leg. 1328, Junta de Ejecución, 21 May 1640.
[2] AGS: GA, leg. 1328, Junta Grande, 27 May 1640.

past decade, the ministers in Madrid had always tended to draw comfort from the thought that, if the worst came to the worst, they could solve their difficulties by the use of force. But now, when the royal mercy had been tested to its limits and the state of affairs in Catalonia might surely be regarded as serious enough to justify the most drastic measures, Olivares found that the weapon he had been holding in reserve had fallen to pieces in his hands. The complexity of the Catalan problem, the gravity of the military position in Germany and Italy, and the strain already being placed on Spain's armies, precluded him from applying the panacea he had cherished for so long.

It was all very well for the Conde Duque to recommend, and the king to approve, a 'lenient policy',[1] but neither Olivares nor any other minister in Madrid seems to have grasped the full implications of such a decision. Measures which seemed lenient to Madrid might well appear very far from lenient to the Catalans. There was, for example, the problem of the *tercios* which had retired to Rosselló. Were these troops to be allowed to remain where they were, in a country they had driven to the verge of revolution? In his speech on 27 May, Olivares had said nothing about withdrawing them. On the contrary, their numbers were to be increased. 'I shall not insist on the importance of enlarging that army, because it is so obvious. I shall only say that we must press on fast with our preparations for Naples and Germany....'

From the strictly military point of view, Olivares's remarks were fully justified. It would be foolhardy to denude the Catalan frontier of troops when the French were reported to be massing for a new invasion. Without reinforcements the *tercios* at Roses could not possibly hope to prevent their entry.[2] Yet the chances of restoring order in Catalonia as long as the *tercios* remained on Catalan soil, appeared to those on the spot to be non-existent.

The peasants are so roused [wrote the Diputats to their delegation in Madrid on 26 May] that as long as the billeting continues they will not hesitate to face any danger to save themselves from the injuries, insults, sacrilege and devastation of their homes perpetrated by the soldiers. The sole remedy is to withdraw the soldiers and issue a general pardon.[3]

---

[1] King on consulta of 27 May: 'el medio de la blandura, que appruebo...'.
[2] AGA: GA, leg. 1368, Don Alvaro de Quiñones to Santa Coloma, 4 June 1640.
[3] AGA: G, LT, 1639–40, fos. 303–4, Diputats to their envoys, 26 May 1640.

Santa Coloma was of the same opinion, and had actually gone so far as to order on his own initiative that the troops which had gathered in Rosselló should be evacuated by sea to Vinaroz in Valencia.[1]

The marquis of Villafranca had refused to obey the viceroy's order for a general evacuation without first consulting Madrid. He rightly suspected that the order would not be confirmed. The Junta de Ejecución, meeting on 3 June, rejected it out of hand, and stood by the decisions it had reached two days before.[2] In that earlier meeting, there had been general agreement that the Rosselló army must be increased. Olivares, although confessing himself afraid of another Sicilian Vespers, had even advocated that the reinforcements, instead of going by sea, should march the entire way from Alfaques up to Rosselló. Balbases, who had a rather better idea than the Conde Duque of what this really entailed, managed to dissuade him, pointing out the importance of doing nothing which could give rise to new disorders in the Principality.[3]

There is no doubt that the ministers were very much divided in their own minds. Olivares himself, although he had taken the lead in advocating a general pacification by lenient measures, none the less hoped that the troops in Rosselló might find an opportunity for a sharp crack at the insurgent forces.[4] The Protonotario and Cardinal Borja had accepted the lenient policy, but only with a very bad grace. The rebels, they pointed out, had got all they wanted: they had exempted themselves from the obligation of billeting, freed the Diputat and reduced Santa Coloma to impotence. But this was the natural outcome of leniency.[5]

The confusion of thought that prevailed in Madrid at the beginning of June, and the complete inability of the ministers to visualize what was really happening in Catalonia, are vividly brought home by the account of a curious conversation held in Madrid on 3 June. It took place between Don Fernando Ruiz de Contreras, the secretary of the Council of War, and Don Melcior Palau, the archdeacon of Vic. Palau, who had taken the lead in the ecclesiastical disorders at Vic in 1634,[6] was now a reformed character. The appointment to the vice-

---

[1] ACA: CA, leg. 287, no. 33, Santa Coloma to King, 27 May 1640.
[2] AGS: GA, leg. 1328, Junta de Ejecución, 3 June 1640.
[3] *Ibid.* 1 June 1640.   [4] *Ibid.* 3 June 1640.
[5] AGS: GA, leg. 1328, Council of Aragon, 3 June 1640.
[6] See above, p. 289.

royalty of Santa Coloma, who was a personal friend, had dramatically changed his prospects. 'Expectations of promotion alter a man's whole nature', remarked Sanz of Vic, observing the transformation in Palau's character.[1] As an intimate friend, Santa Coloma had chosen Palau as his personal envoy to Madrid to give the ministers first-hand information on the state of Catalonia.[2] Palau reached Madrid on the afternoon of 3 June, and was taken by Ruiz de Contreras in his coach to the Buen Retiro. He found himself subjected to a barrage of questions. Why, asked Contreras, did Santa Coloma not send royal officials to investigate the disturbances? Palau did his best to describe the state that Catalonia was in, and how it made any such inquiry impossible. Then what was to be done? asked Contreras. Palau told him that Santa Coloma had suggested two possible measures: either punishment, which must be vigorously administered, or unconditional pardon. This second suggestion shocked Contreras—the king would have no authority left in Catalonia if the rebels escaped unpunished. Palau admitted that punishment might eventually be possible, but at present it was hardly feasible, as the rebels would simply retire to the mountains and make contact with France. Were the nobles strong enough to quieten the populace? asked Contreras. They were not. Then perhaps Barcelona and other large towns should be responsible for administering punishment. And Cardona, with his large number of vassals, surely he was powerful enough to punish them? 'That man is in no way acceptable to the Principality', answered Palau. What about Santa Coloma? The billeting had made him universally unpopular. Or the bishop of Barcelona? Was he influential enough to induce the Catalans to punish their own rebels? Palau explained what the bishop of Barcelona was like, and how 'he had no friends because he was solely concerned with feathering his own nest'. After criticising the behaviour of the bishop of Girona, whose sentence of excommunication he held responsible for all that had happened, Contreras then asked if the Audiència was helping Santa Coloma as it should, adding in an unpleasant tone of voice, 'and Vinyes?'[3] Palau replied that Dr Vinyes had not left Santa Coloma's side for a moment, and no minister was in greater danger.

[1] Sanz, *Relació*, p. 46.
[2] AGS: GA, leg. 1328, Santa Coloma to King, 27 May 1640.
[3] There had been a good deal of suspicion in Madrid about Dr Vinyes's reliability. See the urgent note sent by the Protonotario to Santa Coloma on 14 May (ACA: G, caja 32).

Contreras went on to inquire about the viceroy's personal safety, and expressed himself glad to hear that in future Santa Coloma's servants were to be armed.[1]

The kind of questions asked by Contreras show how far the ministers were from understanding the nature of recent events in the Principality. As ministers of the Crown, in close contact with the king, they instinctively thought first in terms of royal authority, which to them was something very real. They saw in the rising of the Catalan peasantry a challenge to this authority, which justified punitive action either now or later because *lèse-majesté* was a heinous affair.[2] They conceded that the soldiers had behaved extremely badly, but they considered that the pretexts for insurrection had now been removed. With the burden of billeting now lightened and the army paid at the king's expense, the two fundamental causes of the disturbances had ceased to exist.[3] Consequently, the Principality ought now to be returning to normal, and it was the duty of all loyal vassals to assist in the restoration of order and the punishment of the seditious.

Such an outlook might be regarded as betraying a somewhat naïve idea both of the nature of revolutionary movements and of the degree to which the Crown possessed effective authority even in ordinary times. It ignored the fact that revolutions gather a momentum of their own, and that they are accompanied by strains and tensions within a society which can fatally disturb its normal equilibrium. It assumed that royal government was based on infinitely more solid foundations than a mere handful of hard-worked, underpaid officials issuing orders which were more or less obeyed, sitting in judicial tribunals which were more or less effective, according to the degree to which their actions happened to coincide with the desires and the interests of the province's natural governing class. In a word, it forgot that Barcelona was some four hundred miles away, and that it was not Madrid.

It was true that Palau's personal impressions of the state of Catalonia had at least a temporary impact. After Olivares had seen him in private audience, the Junta de Ejecución agreed that the rebels should be in-

---

[1] ACA: CA, leg. 391, Palau to Santa Coloma, 4 June 1640.
[2] The burning of Monrodón was regarded by Madrid as *lèse-majesté*, and the ministers expressed great indignation at the failure of the Audiència to pronounce it as such (AGS: GA, leg. 1328, Council of Aragon, 24 May).
[3] AGS: GA, leg. 1328, Council of Aragon, 3 June 1640.

duced to ask for a pardon, which it would be advisable for the king to give.[1] But as further news came from Catalonia, with reports that the insurrection, so far from dying down, was actually spreading, the perplexity of the ministers increased and their earlier resolution began to be shaken. The Council of Aragon reacted to Santa Coloma's letter of 2 June reporting that the rebels were forcing the towns to provide them with men, by bluntly declaring that lenient measures had failed, and that a new policy was required. But what was the new policy to be? Punitive action? Impossible, because the army could not be moved from the frontier, and it would be fatal to become involved in civil war when a French invasion threatened. An attempt to 'preserve respect for justice'? There was little future in this, since neither the Diputats nor the towns could control the rebels. The only remaining line of policy was to do everything possible to calm them down, even at the expense of a considerable loss to royal prestige. The Council pronounced no decisive opinion but contented itself with suggesting that Santa Coloma should at once be recalled, as his authority was gone.[2]

The Junta de Ejecución still had faint hopes that its earlier decisions might bear fruit. 'On the assumption that the method considered most effective for settling the present disturbances is to display gentleness and leniency', it would be advisable to await the views of the Diputats and of the Barcelona authorities, especially as there was always a danger that the Catalans in their present mood might be willing to allow the French to enter. As an afterthought the Junta added that, although on previous occasions efforts had been made to divert the enemy from other areas by attacking them from Catalonia, a repetition of this in the present circumstances would be unwise, and the commanders in Italy should be instructed to launch a diversion.[3] It was also agreed that Olivares should have another talk with the delegation of the Diputació, which he had seen for the first time on 3 June, after keeping it waiting for many weeks outside Madrid. As might have been expected, the delegation had a paper prepared which stated that only a general pardon and the withdrawal of the troops could hope to restore normal conditions in the Principality.[4]

[1] AGS: GA, leg. 1328, Junta de Ejecución, 4 June 1640.
[2] AGS: GA, leg. 1328, Council of Aragon, 8 June 1640.
[3] ACA: CA, leg. 287, no. 57, Junta de Ejecución, 9 June 1640.
[4] ACA: CA, leg. 285, no. 8, paper presented by the envoys of the Diputació.

The withdrawal of the troops appeared to the Junta a ridiculous and impossible condition, but it was necessary to give the impression of taking it seriously in order to keep the delegation from the Diputació hopeful of eventual agreement. At the same time, the Junta was considering one or two more quite contradictory ideas submitted to it by the Council of Aragon. Should the king, for instance, renounce his claims to the *quints* in order to retain the loyalty of the towns? The Junta agreed that the *quints* were not very profitable since Barcelona did not pay them, but considered them the best 'curb' that the king possessed on the behaviour of the Principality, and rejected the idea of a wholesale renunciation. On the other hand, it agreed that those towns which had behaved particularly well, like Blanes and Mataró, should obtain at least a temporary remission of their *quints*. Some tangible expression of gratitude should also be bestowed upon deserving individuals like Don Ramon Calders. Another idea suggested by the Council of Aragon was that, following the precedent offered by the handling of the Vizcaya revolt of 1632, Catalonia should be submitted to an economic boycott. The Junta considered this seriously. Catalonia had three types of trade.[1] There was trade with France across the borders of Rosselló and Cerdanya, the bulk of this consisting of meat, of which Catalonia was very short. The second type of trade was the cloth trade, largely with Sicily. The volume of this trade was believed to have declined by more than half,[2] with the development of cloth manufacture outside Spain, but it would always be possible to destroy the rest of the trade by imposing import restrictions in Sicily if this should be found necessary. Catalonia's third source of commercial profit was Italian trade with the Spanish peninsula. This was not large because the heavy dues to which the goods were subjected on their journey from Barcelona to Castile had induced the majority of the merchants to divert them from Barcelona to Cartagena. Some goods did still come through Barcelona, however, and it would not be hard to prevent this trade. Taken as a whole, these various restrictions on Catalan trade would not have any very striking immediate consequences, but were worth holding in reserve as a possible weapon for the future.[3]

The number of conflicting policies which the Junta de Ejecución was

[1] The Junta ignored or overlooked Catalonia's trade with other parts of the Iberian peninsula.
[2] The Junta fails to say since when.
[3] AGS: GA, leg. 1328, Junta de Ejecución, 9 June 1640.

able to contemplate in the course of a single day suggests something of the confusion and the uncertainty with which the ministers viewed the Catalan problem. It was so difficult to decide whether the Catalans should be treated as hardened sinners, or wandering sheep, or simply as naughty children. This uncertainty is itself the best refutation of the belief that Madrid deliberately instigated revolution in Catalonia in order to have a suitable pretext for depriving the Principality of its liberties. The whole course of their discussions during the first fortnight of June suggests that the Catalan revolution had taken the ministers completely by surprise.

It is typical of Olivares that, at this moment of general confusion, he should have returned to a vigorous advocacy of the guiding principles he had formulated at the start of his political career. In the same way as his conduct at the time of the Salces campaign of 1639 showed that he had never abandoned his scheme for a Union of Arms, so his reaction to the news of the insurrection of 1640, with its implications of Spain's political dissolution, showed that he had not abandoned his plans for a wider union of the peoples of the peninsula. On 11 June, at the height of the discussions over the correct policy to be adopted towards the Catalans, he made an impassioned speech on the theme of unity to the Junta de Ejecución:

The Conde Duque has explained to this Junta...that he cannot forbear to repeat what he has already said on other occasions and has even written in a published book[1]—that one of the things he considers most important in this Monarchy is to establish that in this Court no deserving vassal of His Majesty who is a native of the kingdoms subject to his rule and included in this Monarchy should be treated as a foreigner, as regards appointment to dignities and offices. For if all equally enjoy all offices and positions, this will help to create such unity and mutual understanding between the various kingdoms as to produce very fruitful consequences....And if this arrangement is equal and reciprocal, all without exception will be eligible for office in the councils of different provinces....As a start, he proposes that an Aragonese should at once be appointed an *alcalde de corte*, so that without delay they can know the honour that Your Majesty is conferring upon them.

The Junta declared itself in full agreement. It was highly desirable that the vassals of the different kingdoms should equally enjoy the honours and rewards offered in them by Your Majesty; and that by this means the other

---

[1] I do not know to what this refers.

provinces will lose the disconsolate feeling created by the present ineligibility of their inhabitants for offices in Castile, specially in the councils and chancellories.... This could be a very efficacious means for securing a closer unity and interrelationship among the various crowns, since they will not only look for rewards in their own province but also for those which Your Majesty can confer upon them in Castile....

It was accordingly agreed that all future nominations for secular and ecclesiastical appointments should be drawn from all the provinces.[1]

At last the government in Madrid had agreed to something which the different realms of the Spanish Monarchy had been demanding for over a hundred years. The Junta's decision represented a radical change in Castile's attitude to the other territories owing allegiance to its king. But it had come only under pressure—under the threat of the dissolution of Spain's empire—and it had come too late. When the fruit was ripe it had been enjoyed exclusively by the Castilians, while the rest had watched with envious eyes. Now that it had turned rotten, it was to be shared among them all.

If a decision to throw open offices in Castile to non-Castilians had been made even twenty years before, it might perhaps have done something to dissipate that general air of frustration in Catalonia which came from the lack of outlets for nobles, clerics and lawyers. But even then it would almost certainly have been regarded as no more than an artful device for enabling Castilians to work their way into offices in Catalonia. By 1640 there was no chance of the measure being considered as anything except self-interested. Even if it had been publicized, it would have come too late to have any impact on the course of events in the Principality, and it was not publicized, perhaps because the Junta feared the reaction in Castile.

While the traditional policies governing the organization of the Spanish empire were quietly jettisoned on 11 June 1640, unhonoured and unsung, the ministers also managed to make up their minds on something of more immediate relevance to the needs of the Principality. Santa Coloma must go. His recent letters had made it clear that he had lost his nerve, and enjoyed neither influence nor authority among the Catalans. José González, one of Olivares's most trusted advisers, opened

[1] AGS: GA, leg. 1328, Junta de Ejecución, 11 June 1640.

another meeting of the Junta de Ejecución on 11 June by recommending the replacement of Santa Coloma by Cardona in the viceroyalty of Catalonia as the most effective means of pacifying the Principality. He should have full powers to act without prior consultation with Madrid, and should be free to offer a general pardon. Don Pedro de Arce, brother of Juan de Arce, the commander of the *tercios* in Catalonia, disagreed. He was not in favour of appointing Cardona, and preferred a Castilian viceroy. Don Nicolás Cid did not feel that Santa Coloma could be disposed of so summarily. The Protonotario agreed with González, but felt that a general pardon should only be offered if there were no alternative. Balbases, who had consistently advocated the importance of not antagonizing the Catalans, also approved the appointment of Cardona, and supported the idea of a general pardon. Finally, Olivares also agreed with González. Cardona should be made captain-general, with the task of pacifying the province, for which he must be given a free hand.[1]

This was the first decision after a fortnight's discussion which really entailed any immediate and substantial change in the affairs of the Principality. Although a lenient and conciliatory policy had been officially laid down on 27 May, all the decisions taken since then in pursuance of this policy could be reduced to a request to the Diputats and Barcelona for advice, and an order to grandees owning estates in the Principality, to visit them forthwith. Two weeks of hesitation had now been brought to an end with general agreement that the Catalans should be given a general pardon, and that Santa Coloma should be replaced. At last a positive, practical decision had been taken. There was only one drawback. Unknown to the Junta, Santa Coloma had been dead for four days.

Since the release of Tamarit on 22 May, Santa Coloma had lived in a haunted, fearful world of his own. The events of that day had brought home to him his appalling isolation. There was only a handful of people on whose loyalty he could rely;[2] he was not allowed a guard of more than fifty halberdiers,[3] and there was no royal castle in Barcelona to which he could retire for safety, if a revengeful mob should turn its wrath upon him. His fears for his personal safety were therefore by no

---

[1] AGS: GA, leg. 1328, Junta de Ejecución, 11 June 1640.
[2] Santa Coloma lists their names in letters to Madrid of 22 and 24 May (AGS: GA, leg. 1328).
[3] Assarino, p. 86.

means unjustified, nor the repeated complaints in his letters to the Court that there were no galleys ready in Barcelona harbour to take him off in the event of an emergency.[1]

That an emergency would arise, he had no doubt. The rebels were shouting for death to all traitors, and the name of Santa Coloma must surely stand at the head of the list. It is, indeed, perfectly possible that plans had been laid for his assassination: one of Olivares's spies, in a paper written three years later, claimed that he informed the Conde Duque of the 'communications that were passing between the Catalans at Court and those in the Principality, and how, having planned here the death of the count of Santa Coloma, they carried it out there within twenty days'.[2] This may or may not have been true, but the revolutionary situation in Catalonia carried obvious risks to the viceroy, and Santa Coloma himself seems to have had strong premonitions of his impending death. There were several stories in circulation within a very short time of his death, which may have been fabrications, but possibly had some foundation in fact. It was said, for example, that when he was young a fortune-teller of Barcelona had told him that at the age of forty-four he would occupy one of the most honoured posts in his country—and then refused to continue with the prophecy....[3] It was also said that he had been sent a paper telling him to settle his affairs, as the writer had been warned by a divine revelation that he had but a little time to live.[4] There was much talk of his having received special warnings of a miraculous nature, which he apparently attempted to shrug off as frauds designed to intimidate and demoralize him.[5]

As June approached, Santa Coloma's fears increased. The country was in a state of tumult, as the rebels passed from town to town, killing, burning, intimidating. It was some cause for comfort that the Principality's prayers for rain had at last been answered at the end of May,[6] but if the long drought had ended just in time to save the crops from destruction, the rains had come too late to save the country from revolution. The sights and sounds of the last few months had caused profound agitation through the Catalan countryside. The ceaseless

[1] ACA: CA, leg. 287, no. 40, Santa Coloma to King, 2 June 1640.
[2] *Codoin*, vol. LXXXI, *Copia de la Relación...que hizo...Don Marcelino de Faria*, pp. 566–7.
[3] Tormé i Liori, p. 112. [4] *Ibid.* p. 113.
[5] AGS: GA, leg. 1361, Don Felip to Don Josep Sorribes, 24 June 1640.
[6] ACA: CA, leg. 391, Dr Guilló to Santa Coloma, 31 May 1640.

clamour of church bells, the terrible rumours of the coming of the troops, of the burning of churches and the sacking of villages, the long processions through the streets of a penitent people praying for rain, the inflammatory sermons from the pulpits rousing the congregations to fight for the preservation of their liberties,[1] the strange stories that passed from village to village of figures of the Virgin or the Christ which had turned pale and shed tears—all these had roused the rural population to a state bordering on hysteria.

The coming of June brought fresh cause for alarm. This was the traditional season for the arrival in Barcelona of the *segadors*—the casual labourers who arrived from all over the countryside to hire themselves out for the harvesting. Even in ordinary times, town councillors would breathe a sigh of relief when these rough, lawless people were once more safely outside the city walls. On this occasion, with Catalonia in its present excited state, their coming could only arouse acute anxiety. The Consellers of Barcelona would themselves apparently have liked to forbid the *segadors* entry, but were afraid of the reaction of the Consell de Cent and asked Santa Coloma that the request should come from him.[2] He duly made the request, and it was duly rejected.[3] The rejection may well have been the result of fear, rather than of any sinister intentions. The Barcelona populace was in a very ugly mood. The galleys of the marquis of Villafranca had reached the port on 5 June, but the Inspector-General of the army, Don Juan de Benavides, had been unable to come ashore because of the threatening crowds on the quayside.[4] Santa Coloma himself would have liked to have gone aboard the galleys and was urged to do so by the judges of the Audiència, but he remembered the reproaches heaped upon him when he thought of embarking on 22 May, and reluctantly changed his mind. He had missed his last chance: Villafranca decided to go on with the galleys to Cartagena, and failed to leave any ships at the viceroy's disposal.[5]

Santa Coloma now knew that no means of retreat remained open to him. The day of Corpus Christi, 7 June, on which the *segadors* were due

---

[1] AGS: GA, leg. 1328, Santa Coloma to King, 19 May 1640.
[2] Rubí, *Levantamiento*, fo. 93.
[3] ACA: CA, leg. 287, no. 40, Santa Coloma to King, 2 June 1640.
[4] ACA: CA, leg. 393, Santa Coloma to King, 6 June 1640.
[5] Rubí, fo. 94.

to enter Barcelona, was very close. 'My life will be in great danger tomorrow', he is reported to have written to Olivares on 6 June. 'I will run the course with a brave heart. May God help me, so that I may send to Your Excellency an account of all that happens.'[1] The same day, to his credit, on hearing the news of the burning of the church at Montiró he wrote a letter of deep reproach to Juan de Arce about the conduct of his troops.[2]

It was too late now to do anything but wait, and hope. But the grounds for hope were few enough, and in the event all the worst fears and predictions for Corpus day were tragically fulfilled.[3] A group of four or five hundred men dressed as *segadors* entered Barcelona early on the morning of Thursday, 7 June. Mingled among the genuine *segadors* were insurgents who had been fighting the troops in the countryside north of Barcelona. Between eight and nine o'clock three or four of them passed by the house that had belonged to the *agutzil* Monrodón, and became involved in an altercation with a youth who is believed to have been one of Monrodón's servants. He drew his dagger and struck one of the *segadors*, fatally wounding him. Within a matter of minutes, it seemed as if all the *segadors* in Barcelona had arrived at the spot, but the culprit had disappeared, and the angry *segadors* set off for the Rambla and thence to the viceroy's palace. On reaching the palace they began stacking wood against the doors to set the building on fire. Fortunately for Santa Coloma, the Minorites, whose convent was immediately opposite, came out with an image of Christ which they placed on the piles of wood, and then brought out the Sacrament. Their

---

[1] Rubí, fo. 94.   [2] ACA: G, caja 32, Santa Coloma to Juan de Arce, 6 June 1640.
[3] There is a study of the events of Corpus by A. Rovira i Virgili, *El Corpus de Sang* (Barcelona, 1932). Many eyewitness accounts have survived, and more are coming to light. The description which follows is simply an attempt at a brief reconstruction, based on the following sources: Letters from the bishop of Barcelona, the bishop of Urgell, Don Ramon Calders, Don Joan Francesc de Melgar, printed in the appendix of Ferran de Sagarra, *Les Lliçons de la Història. Catalunya en 1640* (Barcelona, 1931); Rubí, *Levantamiento*, fos. 96v ff.; letter from Padre Esteban Fenoll printed by M. Batllori, S.I., 'Un nuevo testimonio del Corpus de Sang', *Analecta Sacra Tarraconensio*, vol. XXII (1949), p. 31; Don Llorenç de Barutell to Chapter of Urgell, 7 June 1640 (ACU: Cartes, 1630–40); Don Francesc to Don Josep de Sorribes, 8 June 1640 (AGS: GA, leg. 1361); Dr Vinyes to Pedro de Villanueva, 11 June 1640 (ACA: CA, leg. 287, no. 131); Relación del Suceso de Barcelona...hecha por Don Josep d'Oms, etc. (AGS: GA, leg. 1368); the official account in the Dietari of the Diputació, 1638–41, part III, fos. 381–6; Barcelona's letter to the King of 8 June (AHB: LC, 1639–40, fos. 127–9). The name of *Corpus de Sang*—Corpus of Blood— by which 7 June 1640 is commonly known, was not used by contemporaries, and was popularized by a nineteenth-century historical novel by Manuel Angelón, who gave it this title (Rovira i Virgili, *Corpus de Sang*, p. 5).

action diverted the attention of the *segadors* sufficiently to allow time for the arrival of the Consellers, the Diputats and the bishops of Barcelona, Vic and Urgell.

These dignitaries gradually managed to calm the rioters and started shepherding them towards the gate of St Anthony; but 'certain diabolical spirits' urged them not to leave before they had at least achieved something, and a group of those at the front broke away from the main stream, and made for the house of Dr Berart of the Audiència, which was in the Rambla.[1] Dr Berart escaped to the convent of the Discalced Carmelites, but the rioters broke into his house, threw his books, papers and furniture out of the windows, and made two enormous bonfires of them. They then moved on to do the same to the houses of Dr Puig, of the Audiència, and Don Guerau de Guardiola, who, as *lloctinent del mestre racional*, had been responsible for the collection of the *quints* and for other financial exactions in the Principality.

Meanwhile, the Consellers returned to the viceregal palace and offered Santa Coloma a guard of three companies, which he gratefully accepted. Shortly after arriving back at the town hall to decide what they should do next, they heard that Guardiola's house was being sacked and went to the scene of the riot. The time was now about two o'clock. They gradually managed to move the rioters back towards St Anthony's gate, but their route happened to pass the house in which the marquis of Villafranca had been living, and some of Villafranca's servants, thinking the house was about to be attacked, started firing from the windows, killing one of the *segadors*. The other *segadors* rallied round, stormed the house and set it on fire; seeing some of the servants and guard fleeing, they pursued them into the convent of Los Angeles, where they killed five or six of them, and followed this up by entering one convent after another in search of fugitives. The hiding place of the unfortunate Dr Berart was discovered and he was brutally murdered.

During this uproar, Santa Coloma sent to ask if he was safe in his palace and either decided, or was persuaded, to make his way down to the dockyards, in order to embark. A Genoese galley had arrived off Barcelona that morning, and signals were made to it to put in to the wharf. The Diputats having, as they thought, escorted the viceroy to safety, left him and returned to patrol the city. Santa Coloma was

[1] Rubí. fo. 96 v.

apparently just about to go on board ship when his cousin, Don Cristòfol Icart, told him that on no account should he leave before the return of the Consellers, and that he should go aboard only at the last moment, since his departure would mean the total loss of Barcelona.[1] The viceroy therefore delayed. While he was waiting at the dockyards, the Consellers were still doing their best to quieten the tumult round the marquis of Villafranca's house, and in the mêlée the third Conseller either tripped or was knocked down. A rumour at once spread round the city that one of the Consellers had been killed by the servants of the marquis of Villafranca. A furious mob moved down towards the harbour in search of Villafranca's servants, shouting 'Death to the traitors who have killed the Conseller!' As the rioters approached the dockyards and began to force their way in, the three bishops and the large number of nobles who had been with the viceroy scattered, leaving with him only a small group, which struggled towards a broken-down rampart that had a way out towards the hill of Montjuic. Having safely arrived at this spot, Santa Coloma sent Don Josep d'Oms to reconnoitre. He returned to report that no one was around and that it would be easy to embark from there. At this point, there seems to have been some disagreement and delay, and, while the party was arguing, Don Bernardino de Marimón arrived with the news that the rebels had broken right into the dockyards and that all was lost. Santa Coloma ordered that signals be made to the galley, but a surgeon called Novis climbed the tower in the dockyards and forced the artilleryman, at the point of a dagger, to shoot at it, effectively keeping the galley at a distance.[2] Seeing that there was no hope of embarkation within range of the artillery, the party left the shelter of the rampart and set off along the shore in the direction of Montjuic. Shots were being fired at it from the dockyards, and the little group, picking its way over a rocky shore, began to straggle. The viceroy's son, and a number of others, managed to reach a skiff and escape, but Santa Coloma, a fat man, floundering over the rocks in the heat of the afternoon sun, was left far behind, with only a servant or two to assist him. Overcome by heat and fatigue, he was forced to sit down and rest. But the rebels were coming closer, and he struggled up to carry on for a few yards

---

[1] *Relación...que hizo...Don Josep d'Oms.*
[2] Rubí, fo. 99 v. Rubí calls the surgeon Munes.

more. Stones and shots were now raining down on the little group, which was driven to take shelter among the rocks. As he picked his way over the boulders, Santa Coloma slipped and fell, apparently breaking his wrist in the fall.[1] He fainted with the pain, and almost at the same moment a few of the rebels caught up with the fugitives. One of the *segadors* asked Santa Coloma's servant who he was. The servant, an Andalusian, replied in the best Catalan he could muster that he did not know.[2] Another rioter, a sailor aged about twenty, came up at that moment, saw Santa Coloma on the ground, recognized him and plunged a dagger into his stomach. A companion gave him three or four more blows, and then the group moved off, leaving the viceroy of Catalonia dead on the beach.

Back in Barcelona the rioters were behaving more or less as they pleased. A group of them, having discovered a mechanical monkey on a clock they had taken from the marquis of Villafranca's house, bore it off in triumph to the Inquisition, claiming that they had seized the marquis's familiar. The judges of the Audiència had gone into hiding, but their houses were systematically looted during the next two days, by mobs which the city authorities did little or nothing to restrain. Unfortunately, information does not exist which would allow an examination of the composition of these mobs. There is no doubt that many of the townspeople either joined the *segadors* or tacitly supported them. One witness, whose testimony is not necessarily reliable, said that a quarter of the population, all the dregs of the city, were actively engaged in the disorders; another quarter, composed of the nobles and gentry, the merchants, the tradesmen and skilled artisans, attempted to stop them; and the other half of the city was neutral but untrustworthy.[3] Several eye-witnesses report that the *segadors* enjoyed the active co-operation of many of the populace, and it seems that the women in particular showed great ferocity.[4] But it was probably less the active assistance of part of the populace than the acquiescence of almost all of

---

[1] *Ibid.* fo. 101 v.

[2] Declaration of Santiago Domínguez de la Mora on the death of Santa Coloma, reproduced in the appendix to Sagarra, *Les Lliçons de la Història.*

[3] AGS: GA, leg. 1361, Don Felip to Don Josep Sorribes, 24 June 1640. The report may be untrustworthy because Don Felip Sorribes was one of the leaders of the Catalan revolution; his brother, Don Josep, had been planted in Madrid as a spy, and it may well have been intended that his letters should reach the eyes of the Protonotario, as they eventually did.

[4] Rubí, fo. 99.

it which allowed the *segadors* to act with such freedom. The city companies, provided by the guilds, never went near the scene of action, except to guard the Taula—the City Bank.[1] The townsmen are reported to have called the rioters 'brothers', and when the Consellers ordered the guilds' companies to go out, they refused with the words: 'we won't fight our brothers'.[2]

It is possible to discover the names of only two of the *segadors* who played a leading role in the events of Corpus. One of them was Sebastià Estralau, the leader of the rebels from Empordà; the other, who seems to have been responsible for much of the organization, was a certain Rafael Goday, leader of the rebels of Prat, who had escaped from prison on the day of Tamarit's release, while under sentence of death for certain unspecified crimes. It was he who organized the burning of the houses of Drs Puig, Massó and Mir, all of whom had been his judges. After committing these acts of incendiarism he is said to have gone through the city accompanied by a band of friends, and even to have entered the town hall, where he was fêted and congratulated by the Consellers and the city officials.[3]

There is no evidence as to how far, if at all, the Consellers and Diputats were in collusion with the rebels. If they entertained Goday, their action may have been prompted by fear more than by any real sympathy with his aims. The bishop of Urgell, who can hardly be called a sympathetic eyewitness, reported that the Consellers had 'done everything possible, and exposed their persons to danger. And if the results of their efforts were not commensurate with their zeal, this was not through any fault of theirs.'[4] The truth of the matter was that the *segadors* had the city at their mercy. The Barcelona oligarchy was powerless as long as most of the populace looked upon the activities of the rioters with more or less friendly eyes. But after the first shock was over, the oligarchy seems slowly to have recovered its courage; on 9 June all the nobility went into session in the town hall from eight in the morning to five in the evening to discuss what should be done, and agreed to form two companies one hundred strong to patrol the

---

[1] ACA: CA, leg. 287, no. 31. Vinyes to Pedro de Villanueva, 11 June 1640.

[2] Rubí, fo. 97.

[3] Vinyes to Villanueva, *ibid*. The reading of Estralau is uncertain. The name might possibly be Estraban or Estralan.

[4] ACA: CA, leg. 287, no. 58, Bishop of Urgell to King, 7 June 1640.

city day and night.[1] The important thing was to get the *segadors* out of Barcelona. The longer they stayed there, the greater became the danger that they would turn on the aristocracy and the rich, who usually came to be classed as 'traitors' when other more obvious 'traitors' had been exterminated. On 11 June the third Conseller went on horseback through the city accompanied by most of the nobility, and the same day the Conseller-en-Cap managed to lead the *segadors* out of Barcelona on the pretext that Girona was in danger of attack by the *tercios* and must be defended.

Once outside the city walls, the rebels amused themselves by sacking the country residences of the ministers of the viceregal administration. For the moment at least, Barcelona's ordeal was over. Five days of anarchy and rioting had come to an end, leaving behind a trail of destruction wherever a judge of the Audiència had had a house. All the king's ministers in the Principality—the main targets of the rebels— had taken refuge in churches and convents. A dozen to twenty people had lost their lives, including the viceroy. Yet on 11 June 1640 the predominant emotion in Barcelona was one of relief, and almost of hope. The Consellers' success in getting the rebels out of Barcelona had been followed by such a striking and immediate improvement in public order that, in the words of the syndic of Manresa, 'it seems that we are in paradise in contrast to the state we were formerly in....It is now considered certain that the soldiers of the king are no longer in Catalonia. There is not much fear that they will come back for the time being, and it is hoped that they will also leave Rosselló, where they are at present.'[2] The revolution seemed to have ended in triumph almost before it had begun.

[1] AGS: GA, leg. 1361, Don Felip to Don Josep Sorribes, 10 June 1640.
[2] AHM: leg. 1089, Syndic of Manresa to Consellers of Manresa, 11 June 1640.

CHAPTER XVI

REVOLUTION

The news of the murder of Santa Coloma stunned the Court. The king himself wrote:

This is something the like of which has never been seen in any province or kingdom of the world. Thus do I express the depth of my feeling and my indebtedness. The count of Santa Coloma died with the greatest possible merit, since he died expressly for me, and I will reward his sons in such a manner that all my debts will be paid. Send immediately for these boys to be fetched, and the daughter of the marquis of Aytona who is to marry the elder of them. Do this with all speed because my justice must not be deferred on a point of such pressing obligation. The general preparations that have been agreed upon must be carried out at once....Everyone must surpass himself in obeying orders, for if Our Lord does not come to our aid with a rapid settlement, or else with general peace, Spain will be in a worse state that it has been in for many centuries....[1]

The envoys of Barcelona and the Diputats found the Conde Duque almost out of his mind when they called upon him shortly after the news had reached Madrid. To Barcelona's representative, Pau Boquet, he cried three times 'Go away!' and refused to accept the copy of a letter from Barcelona addressed to the king.[2] To Manlleu and the other envoys of the Diputats he said that, on hearing the news, he felt as if he had been shot by an arquebus; and that 'he was in such a state that he was not in his right mind, and did not know if he was eating or sleeping'. He lamented the failure of his efforts to pacify the province by offering a general pardon, and confessed himself at a loss for a remedy.[3] And he wrote to the Cardenal Infante: 'the troubles of Catalonia have reached an extreme, and I confess to Your Highness that, like family troubles, they are driving me out of my senses. The loss of this *caballero* is great, very great, for I assure Your Highness that the count of Santa Coloma was a subject capable of undertaking the most responsible

---

[1] ACA: CA, leg. 287, no. 89, royal reply to consulta of Consejo de Estado, 12 June 1640.
[2] AHB: Delibs., 1640 (bound between fos. 218–19), Pau Boquet to Consellers, 12 June 1640.
[3] *Ibid.* Manlleu to Diputats, 12 June 1640.

duties in any part of the Monarchy.'[1] Such was the Conde Duque's epitaph on the man whom, one week before, he had decided to remove from his post.

Others took a less tragic view of the events of Corpus. When the representatives of the Diputació left the Conde Duque's room, they were met by four nobles, two of whom were grandees—almost certainly the duke of Híjar and the duke of Sessa. Both Híjar and Sessa hated Olivares. Both of them had relations, and estates, in Catalonia and both of them had on various occasions in the past presented themselves as ostentatious supporters of the Catalans in their quarrels with the Court. Sessa had gained such applause for his behaviour in the Corts of 1626 that, after the release of Tamarit, the ministers had thought seriously of taking advantage of his popularity to help pacify the Catalans.[2] Híjar, restless and ambitious, had been appointed general of the cavalry in Catalonia in the spring of 1640, but had declined the post because it involved taking orders from Santa Coloma—and Santa Coloma had imprisoned Don Jeroni de Pinós, a close relation of the duchess of Híjar, for surrendering Canet to the French in August 1639.[3] Both dukes had lavishly bestowed advice and encouragement on the official envoys of the Principality during May and early June, at a time when other nobles had felt it advisable to keep clear of the representatives of a seditious province.[4] On seeing the envoys as they came away from their meeting with Olivares, they again insisted that they were 'very devoted to the Catalans and anxious for their well-being', and suggested that the Diputats would be well advised to take steps to find and bring to justice the murderers of Santa Coloma, in order to prove their own innocence.[5]

Sessa and Híjar were more courageous, or more foolhardy, than the majority of their colleagues, but there were many Castilian nobles whose hatred of the favourite was such as to make them rejoice in his discomfitures, and who therefore felt no great sorrow at the course

---

[1] RAH: 11–10–5, leg. 6, fo. 123, Olivares to Cardenal Infante, 14 June 1640.

[2] AGS: GA, leg. 1328, Council of Aragon, 27 May 1640. Sessa is said to have been the author of a paper presented to the king in 1629 attacking the government of Olivares—'Your Majesty is not king, he is a person of whom the count takes special care, in order to enjoy the office of king for himself.' (AAE: Corresp. Espagne, no. 15, fos. 400–401 v.)

[3] Ramón Ezquerra, *La Conspiración del Duque de Híjar, 1648* (Madrid, 1934), p. 108. Pinós died in prison a few months later.

[4] See Pau Boquet to Consellers, 26 May, and Manlleu to Consellers, 2 June (AHB: CCO, 1639–40, fos. 253–4 and fo. 262).

[5] Manlleu to Diputats, 12 June 1640.

which events were taking in Catalonia. The ministers who filled the Councils and Juntas, however, were almost all the creatures of Olivares, or else felt it unwise for the time being to challenge his ascendancy. As a result, no breath of criticism ever reached the king. He knew only what his ministers told him, and inevitably, as the years passed, he had come to think as his ministers thought. The government at Madrid— king, favourite and Councils—was a closed ring. Isolated from the chill breezes of the outer air, it legislated in a vacuum, calling more meetings to draft more papers to be considered by more Juntas, until king and Conde Duque and Protonotario were weighed down by stacks of documents, and decisions had been changed, revoked, revised, until they had lost all meaning.

At this moment of crisis in the Monarchy's fortunes, it is instructive to watch Olivares and his colleagues at work. All the Conde Duque's earlier schemes for the rapid taking of decisions by a small policy-making Junta seem by now to have gone awry. Questions of importance were endlessly discussed by a vast number of ministers. When the news of Santa Coloma's death arrived, the Council of Aragon, consisting of six ministers—Cardinal Borja, the Protonotario and the regents Vico, Magarola, Bayetolá and Sisternes—met immediately and decided that however horrifying the news, there was nothing that could be done for the time being, 'because we have no means at our disposal for punishing such a terrible crime and correcting the ways of the province'.[1] In fact, as long as there was no available army in the peninsula, there was nothing that Madrid could do but watch and wait. This conclusion was communicated by the Protonotario to a Junta composed of members of the Consejo de Estado and the Junta de Ejecución, specially summoned by Olivares when the news arrived.

The special Junta consisted of fifteen ministers, and each of them spoke at some length.[2] Their views may be summarized as follows:

Pedro de Arce. A terrible and unprecedented affair. Agrees with Council of Aragon, with certain qualifications, at least until more information available.

Don Nicolás Cid. Dissimulation and further tolerance of the Catalans pointless. Time to consider punitive measures.

[1] ACA: CA, leg. 287, no. 7, consulta, 12 June 1640.
ACA: CA, leg. 287, no. 89, Consejo de Estado, 12 June 1640.

Protonotario. Dissimulation and further tolerance of the Catalans inevitable, until the season ripe for punishment. Therefore agrees with Council of Aragon (of which he was the leading member).

José González. Cardona to attempt to pacify the province; the general pardon to stand, making an exception for Santa Coloma's murderers.

Marquis of Castrofuerte. Since no troops are available and the French might intervene, agrees with González on allowing the general pardon to stand. Troops should be brought from Italy and recruited in Castile, and an army of 30,000 men be formed. Dissimulate for now, but have everything ready for exemplary punishment.

Count of Oñate. Necessary to think first of the pacification of the province rather than its punishment, because there is no army ready. Agrees that it would be a good idea to take steps in preparation for punishment of the Principality, but in such a way as not to antagonize it. Supports Council of Aragon.

Marquis of Santa Cruz. Pessimistic about pacification by gentle methods, but agrees with Oñate.

Count of Monterrey. The lack of troops compels the use of 'suave' measures, and therefore agrees with Council of Aragon; but an army should be raised.

Marquis of Mirabel. The same.

Marquis of los Balbases. There are two problems: the unrest of the Principality and the danger of an entry by the French. Without solving the first there is no way of dealing with the second, because 'our army is extremely small and disarrayed'. Therefore there is no alternative for the present to leniency. Of the three types of persons in Catalonia, the malefactors, the indifferent and the good, it is essential to remove the fear of the first two classes that they will be punished, and of the third that the king will change their laws and modify their privileges.

Duke of Villahermosa. Agrees with Council of Aragon and González.

Olivares. Confesses that he is not so courageous as to vote against all those who have advocated gentle measures, and therefore agrees with what they have proposed. Has no wish to be a prophet, but admits that he was going to express a totally different opinion....Cannot diverge from the views of so many, in the knowledge that Our Lord is instructing them. . . .

Cardinal Spínola. Agrees with Council of Aragon, but uncertain about a general pardon till more information received.

Inquisitor-General. Has previously supported a lenient policy, but now considers the situation to be so completely changed that such a policy is no longer suitable. Proposes a balance between the extremes of rigour and moderation. Suggests that the Inquisition should begin proceedings against 'persons who went against the king'.

Cardinal Borja (President of the Council of Aragon). Agrees with Council of Aragon. Considers that the sedition should be quietened by 'gentle and suave measures', because of the danger of movements by the French. The province to be pardoned and reassured that there is no intention of altering its constitutions in the Corts. If it sees an army being formed, it will only become exasperated. 'And although it is true that all his recommendations up to now have been quite the opposite, he has realized the risks and the disasters that might follow if conciliatory methods are not used', and has therefore changed his mind.

The king replied to the *consulta* at length, urging particularly the preparations advocated by Castrofuerte, and ending:

And as regards the proposal of Cardinal Borja; although I suspect that in the last resort it comes to the same thing as what everyone else says, the Council of Aragon should see it in full session, because it has recommended the opposite on so many occasions. . . . Although in practice, as I have said, it comes to the same thing.

The Council of Aragon duly met on 15 June, and advised that the Cardinal's proposal and the conclusions of the *consulta* did in fact come to the same thing—namely, that the first step was to pacify the province. It was not Borja's intention that insubordination should go unpunished. As for his suggestion that the Principality should be reassured as to the safety of its constitutions, this was not practicable at present because the reassurance would not be believed, and because it would be regarded as a sign of weakness.[1]

[1] ACA: CA, leg. 287, no. 88, consulta, 15 June 1640.

Was Olivares secretly annoyed or secretly relieved that the majority had voted against immediate action in Catalonia? Had Borja genuinely changed his mind or did he still in reality hold to the rigorous policies he had advocated in April and May? These are questions to which even the fullest accounts of the daily discussions of the Councils can provide no answer. Olivares was always determined that, however events should turn out, the record would show him to have been on the side of the angels. Borja felt himself deeply indebted to the king for favours received.[1] The extent of his obligations may well have swayed his judgments as President of the Council of Aragon, and his vote of 12 June was possibly a belated, if momentary, recognition of the mistakes he had made.

Whatever the innermost thoughts of those who sat at the council table, their decisions at this moment could make very little practical difference. Since they had no army to send to Catalonia, they could only wait, or, as Olivares put it, 'gain time'.[2] Their decisions in the week after Santa Coloma's death—numerous, conflicting, hesitant— were also largely irrelevant. The Junta agreed to the establishment in Aragon of a special Council for the 'pacification of Catalonia'.[3] It presumably began arrangements for the recruiting of new levies in Castile. Otherwise, there was nothing it could do but leave the direction of affairs to the duke of Cardona.

Unfortunately, there was very little either that Cardona could do. At the time of his reappointment as viceroy, he was in extremely bad health. On the evening the news reached him, Don Ramon Rubí de Marimón called on him,

and the poor man was so worn out by his illness that he had to rest, and was incapable of discussing business. They had bled him forty-two times that year to relieve the pain from his gout, which, in conjunction with other infirmities had given him a chill on the liver, and he was so consumptive that he could not stand upright.[4]

In spite of this, he accepted the appointment, and took his oath for the third time as viceroy of Catalonia on the morning of 19 June. Only six judges of the Audiència came out of hiding to accompany him.

[1] AGS: GA, leg. 1331, Borja in a paper of 13 Dec. 1640.
[2] ACA: CA, leg. 287, no. 133, Junta de Estado y Ejecución, 18 June 1640.
[3] AGS: GA, leg. 1328, Junta de Ejecución, 15 June 1640.
[4] Rubí, *Levantamiento*, fo. 115

Cardona's first task as viceroy was to intervene at Perpinyà, which had been the scene of terrible incidents in the past few days. Its experience of the troops had so shaken and angered the populace that on 4 June it rioted, simply because the town council had met, and it was automatically assumed that the meeting had been called to arrange for the billeting of more soldiers.[1] The riot so terrified the town councillors that when the soldiers in retreat from Catalonia appeared near Perpinyà on 11 June, they refused to admit them. For some days the troops waited outside the city walls, while the inhabitants fortified the town and called for help from the surrounding countryside and the Principality, 'and also, it is believed, from France'.[2] On 15 June, after the troops had been reduced to desperation by hunger, their commander, Geri de la Rena, gave his artillery orders to bombard the town. After an all-night bombardment and a brief engagement between the troops and the inhabitants, Perpinyà surrendered, but not before news of its plight had reached the outer world. An army of 4000 insurgents from the neighbouring region hastened to its relief, but withdrew when the troops came out to meet it. The troops themselves, for the moment out of danger, were billeted in and around Perpinyà, twelve or thirteen men to a house.[3] Half demolished by the bombardment, oppressed by hungry and vindictive soldiers, the capital of Rosselló was a crushed and ruined city.

When the news of the tragedy of Perpinyà reached Barcelona, the Consell de Cent voted to send five hundred men to its assistance, and the Braços recommended the Diputats to send another seven hundred.[4] On the following day, however, after taking his oath, Cardona had a long talk with the Diputats, in which it was agreed that he should go to Perpinyà himself, accompanied by Tamarit and by a Conseller of Barcelona. The party left Barcelona on 22 June, Cardona being the sole representative of the king as no member of the Audiència dared go with him. When the party reached Figueres, royal despatches arrived informing Cardona that a special council had been set up in Fraga to advise on Catalan affairs in conformity with the decision of the Junta de Ejecución on 15 June. The viceroy was much distressed by the news,

[1] *Mémoires de Pierre Pasqual*, p. 49.
[2] AGS: GA, leg. 1367, Don Felipe de Guevara to F. Ruiz de Contreras, 20 June 1640.
[3] ACA: CA, leg. 393, Bishop of Elna to Pedro de Villanueva, 20 June 1640.
[4] ACA: G, Dietari, 1638–41, part III, fo. 398.

since the creation of the council seemed to him to undermine his authority,[1] but in fact the council, which had scarcely yet been constructed, did nothing to interfere with his plans. These were to calm the Principality by punishing the guilty army commanders, and by getting the organs of the viceregal administration working once more.

For all his good intentions, Cardona was fighting a losing battle, and it is by no means certain that his illness left him with sufficient strength to grasp the complexity of the problems that faced him. He made one tactical blunder so surprising as to suggest that his two years of retirement had left him ill-informed about events and personalities in the Principality. The death of Don Francesc de Erill at the beginning of the year had left vacant the post of Canceller, which was always held by an ecclesiastic. Cardona recommended for the post none other than the officious and extremely unpopular bishop of Urgell.[2] The long-standing feud between the bishop and his canons had of late grown so bitter that Fontanella, acting for the chapter of Urgell, had drawn up in May for presentation to the Provincial Council of Tarragona a long form of protest against the bishop's extortions and exactions in his diocese.[3] It was therefore not in the least probable that a Diputació, two of whose members were canons of Urgell, and whose chief legal adviser was Fontanella, should take kindly to the idea of seeing Pau Duran as Canceller of Catalonia.

At this moment, however, the attitude of the Diputats was of secondary importance. For the present at least, they had ceased to be the masters. The change can be detected in the tone of their letters to their representatives in Madrid over the course of three months. In April and May their correspondence was full of expressions of despair at the tragic condition of the Principality, and was pervaded by a sense of utter helplessness. In the days immediately after the release of Tamarit, this note of despair was replaced by one of confidence as the peasants drove back the troops. This in turn gave way to deep anxiety as it dawned upon the Diputats that the movement in the countryside was something more than a simple movement of revenge against ill-disciplined soldiery.

[1] Rubí, fo. 115v.
[2] AGS: GA, leg. 1328, Junta de Ejecución, 28 June 1640.
[3] ACU: Cartes, 1630–40, *Copia de la súplica se dona a la provincia contra lo Bisbe Pau Duran.*

What causes us most concern now [they wrote on 12 June], is that the insurgents are roaming unrestrained through all this part of Catalonia from Barcelona to Vallès and Vic, where they have burnt and are burning many houses. ...It is well known that these excesses have been committed by people gathered together without a leader and without advice, guided only by their own passions—people who do not value their lives and have nothing to lose.[1]

The rebellion, which at first seemed to promise a providential liberation to the Principality from its oppressors, had already become an embarrassment to those who at the beginning had greeted it with enthusiasm. First it had turned on the troops; then on the ministers of the central administration, and finally on all those in authority—local officials and town councillors, indiscriminately bracketed as traitors. The ruling class of Catalonia—the nobles, the merchants, the lawyers, the wealthy burgesses—were becoming increasingly alarmed as they saw the volcano beginning to erupt beneath their feet. Barcelona itself, at the forefront of resistance when the struggle was purely fiscal, was now swept aside by those who dismissed its record of resistance with contempt. One night a man came to the house of Jaume Agramunt, secretary to the city council, and gave him two letters, one for the city and one for the Diputats, threatening to burn his country house and kill him if he failed to deliver them.[2] The letters were signed by the 'Captain-General of the Christian army',[3] and contained a fierce attack on the city of Barcelona for its failure to resist injustice. In highly emotional and rhetorical language, the city of Barcelona was accused of bringing down the wrath of God upon the Principality by its pusillanimity in the face of enemy pressure, and the rulers of Barcelona were compared unfavourably with their predecessors in the reign of John II. But Catalonia was a faithful land—the land in which the Holy Inquisition was first set up and in which the Holy Sacrament was most fervently adored—and, although the city of Barcelona might have forgotten God's cause, 'the rustic and the simple, moved by the Holy Spirit, have formed a great army called "the Christian army".' The

---

[1] ACA: G, LT, 1639–40, fos. 315–16, Diputats to ambassadors, 12 June 1640.

[2] ACA: G, LT, 1639–40, fos. 341–2, the same, 23 June 1640.

[3] ACA: CA, leg. 287, no. 9, letter from 'lo capità general del exèrcit christià', dated 19 June 1640. A Castilian translation of this letter is printed by Pujol y Camps in *MHE*, vol. XXI, pp. 52–5, with the comment that its presence in Madrid is proof of Olivares's excellent spy service in the Principality. It was in fact forwarded to the Court by the bishop of Lleida, with a covering note, and so was not discovered by a spy.

army's watchwords were 'Long live the Holy Catholic Faith and the King of Spain, and down with bad government!'; and although at present dispersed, it could gather rapidly under the command of its chosen Captain-General. Speaking for his men, the Captain-General claimed that it was the royal ministers in Catalonia, high and low, who had brought disaster upon it by their violation of its laws and liberties. 'They must all be punished, or removed from the Principality, as rotten branches from the tree.' There was no novelty in asking the king to replace and punish his ministers, for precedents were to be found in the reign of John II. And if Barcelona failed to take the lead, the Christian army would do so, using every method at its disposal to extirpate wicked ministers.

The identity of the 'Captain-General of the Christian army' is puzzling. The threatening letters sent to the towns during the last week of May had been signed by the so-called *mestre de camp cathalà*,[1] who is believed to have been a Majorcan. These new letters mark the appearance of a superior commander, to whose identity there are only the faintest clues. An anonymous document now in the Biblioteca Nacional of Madrid and dated 7 June 1640 reads:

At this time, the leaders of the rebels, of whom there were many...threatened new disasters...and chose as their leader the vilest of their number—one from the Galera Capitana of Spain, who escaped from prison when they freed the Diputado: a man of low birth and infamous ways, who was selected as being the most depraved of the lot. This man sent imperious orders to the towns, addressed like royal commands, to help with all necessary men and supplies...and signed himself Governor of the arms of Christ. But as the whole country blazed with the same fire, he was well and promptly supplied, although, in the enmity of the rival factions, he treated *cadell* villages more tyranically than the others because he was a follower of the *nyerros*....[2]

The rebel leader, then, was an escaped galley-slave and a *nyerro*. In his letter about the events of Corpus, Dr Vinyes refers to one escaped convict, Rafael Goday, and to his friend, Sebastià Estralau, 'leader of the rebels of Empordà'.[3] A Madrid newsletter reports that the rebels were led by 'Estraheque, a ruffian who had spent nine years as a galley-slave'.[4] Had the name got corrupted by the time it reached Madrid, and were Estralau and Estraheque one and the same man?

[1] See above, p. 430.   [2] *MHE*, vol. XXI, p. 52.   [3] See above, p. 450.

[4] Pellicer, 'Avisos', *Semanario Erudito*, vol. XXXI, p. 174. The Vicedirector of the Biblioteca Nacional has kindly checked the printed version against the manuscript for me, and tells me that there can be no doubt about the reading Estraheque.

The authorship of the letter also raises difficulties. The bishop of Lleida ascribed it to a man of considerable erudition, although he had got his history wrong.[1] Even if the erudition does not seem quite as remarkable as the bishop appears to think, the letter does not look quite like the unaided work of a galley-slave of 'low birth'. But the exact authorship of the letter is of less interest than its contents, which would not, in the bishop of Lleida's opinion, have any appeal for the educated classes but would greatly attract the populace. The religious slant of the argument may have been deliberately designed to appeal to the peasantry and lesser townspeople. A struggle against oppression in the name of the Holy Faith and of the liberties of Catalonia—this, at least nominally, was the cause for which they would be willing to lay down their lives.

The tide of popular revolution was flowing so fast in June of 1640 that the Diputats and the civic aristocracies of Catalonia were in imminent danger of being submerged. An anonymous informant wrote to Cardona from Barcelona early in July that the city found itself so 'threatened by the rest of the country that it has to go along with the others instead of their following it, as has been the custom up to now'. The Catalan nobility was similarly being terrorized. All the nobles and gentry were afraid of being branded as traitors and being told that they would be the first to die, 'and they can expect no help from their vassals, who are so tired of them that they will put up with them no longer'.[2]

It was as if the atrocities committed by the troops had raised the lid from a cauldron and revealed a seething populace beneath. All the suppressed anger and bitterness of the Catalan population, pent up for so many decades, were suddenly released in the summer of 1640 as the result of the intrusion of an alien element—the soldiery—into the life of the Principality. Here was a social revolution, beginning in the countryside and spreading to the more discontented elements in the towns. It seemed as though all the tensions that could be detected in the social life of the Principality over the last forty years had placed such a strain on the structure of Catalan society that at last it had given way. The hatred of the lesser peasantry and the landless for the wealthy

[1] ACA: CA, leg. 287, no. 9, Bishop of Lleida to King, 8 July 1640.
[2] ACA: CA, leg. 287, no. 29, letter of 13 July 1640 to Cardona.

peasant and the noble; the bitterness of the rural unemployed; the desire for revenge of the bandit element against those who had repressed it; the old feuds of town against country, of the poorer citizens against the municipal oligarchies, even the traditional feuds of *nyerros* and *cadells*—all these burst suddenly and explosively to life in Catalonia as government disappeared and the traditional forces of order showed themselves too confused and hesitant to act.

From all over Catalonia during the summer and autumn came the same stories of violence, murder and popular revolt. It is possible that the disorder would have been less if the proclamations issued by Santa Coloma in December 1639 offering large concessions over the apprenticeship laws and eligibility for municipal office had been more fully obeyed.[1] This would have taken the sting out of much of the discontent of the lower urban classes against the exclusive civic aristocracies. But in Barcelona itself they were only half obeyed, and it is doubtful whether much notice was taken of them in other towns of the Principality. In March 1640 the town councillors of Lleida had written to their syndic in Barcelona to discover what the city had done about the proclamations. He replied that many of those engaged in mechanical arts—cobblers, tailors, carpenters—who had been to Salces had in fact received their certificate of proficiency and had opened shops; but 'as regards the *artistes*, the notaries, barbers and apothecaries, nothing has been done. In fact, certain young men have tried to set up shop by virtue of the royal proclamations', but this had been prevented. A suit had then been filed in the Audiència, in which the College of Surgeons claimed that no one could set up on his own who had not first adhered to its own statutes and regulations, proved the purity of his ancestry and taken the examination in the customary manner. As a result 'no *artista* up to today has been admitted as a notary, apothecary, or surgeon, according to the terms of the proclamations'.[2] The guilds and corporations had thus shown themselves sufficiently strong to maintain their exclusive control over municipal life; the municipal oligarchies had retained their monopoly of office, and the millennium on which the excluded townspeople had pinned their hopes had failed to dawn.

[1] See above, p. 382.
[2] APL: R. 855, Domingo Calderó to Pahers of Lleida, 17 March 1640.

The disappointment of the lower classes in the towns over their failure to break the hold of the unpopular municipal oligarchies may well help to account for much of the urban unrest in the Principality during 1640. Their hopes had been raised only to be dashed again, and they saw in the breakdown of authority the opportunity for revenge. At Manresa, for example, 'wicked spirits among the worst sort of people (of whom there is never any lack in big towns) turned against certain rich and powerful citizens, calling them traitors to the land, and said that if the *segadors* came, they would burn down their houses....'. The form of their discontent was dictated in Manresa, as it must have been in many other towns, by traditional municipal politics, and by the feuds of *nyerros* and *cadells*. The *nyerros* of Manresa forced the municipal authorities to remove the staff of office from the *batlle*, Josep Malet, who was a *cadell*, and give it to Josep Milangels, a *nyerro*. 'This exasperated the *cadells* and both bands threatened to raise armed men from outside.' The town councillors were powerless to prevent the riots that ensued, for 'in both parties there are youths and other persons who have no desire for public peace and tranquillity'.[1]

The town of Vic, where the chief Conseller had been murdered at the end of May, was a scene of perpetual disorder during the summer. The house of Don Lluís Descallar was sacked in June by a mob led by two or three 'drunkards' whom Descallar had 'more or less saved from the gallows' and taken into his service for his own dubious ends. Among the principal agitators in Vic during that summer were a baker called Ricart; the prior of the Carmelites, who nominally preached against the riots but in reality tried to provoke them, and who sheltered in his house a great friend of the rebels—'as a result of which the devotion of the citizens for the Church began to cool'; and a priest from the Segarra, 'a man unworthy of his clerical status'.[2] The street of San Pere in Vic was traditionally the most turbulent, and it was here that the riots started, although the rioters were generally joined by armed outsiders whom they had called to their help.

The general pattern of disorder in the Principality resembled that in

---

[1] AHM: leg. 1089, Consellers of Manresa to Dr Maurici, 17 September 1640. Claris attempted to intervene in these disturbances, and ordered the arrest of Milangels, 'even if he is in sanctuary' (Claris to Don Pedro Aimerich, 28 September 1640, *MHE*, vol. xxi, p. 329). Does this perhaps suggest that Claris had affiliations with the *cadells*?

[2] Sanz, *Relació*, pp. 46–57.

Manresa and Vic: municipal riots, originating in the poorer quarters and inspired by social antagonisms and long-standing municipal feuds, coupled with incursions into the towns of armed bands from the countryside, drawing their recruits from among the rural labourers and the rural unemployed.

In Manresa, *nyerros*a gainst *cadells*....In Esparraguera, those in the upper town against those in the lower, again inspired by the feuds of *nyerros* and *cadells*. In Sarrià, the same. As for Barcelona, the people from the villages many times attacked the city gates...under the pretext of coming to kill traitors, saying that the citizens of Barcelona were traitors because they tried to stop them; and not being able to get a foothold in the city, they held up its provisions,—even the ice—and cut the water supply.[1]

Catalonia, convulsed by a great social upheaval, was falling victim to civil war.

The fact that this was a social convulsion placed the governing classes of Catalonia in a very delicate position. Their natural desire for the restoration of public order and the retention of their social authority naturally made them rally to Cardona in the work of pacification. Yet at the same time their own abhorrence of the policies of Madrid, and their fear of being branded as traitors by a rebellious populace, prevented them from giving Cardona full and unwavering support. They could not allow themselves to appear in the eyes of their own compatriots as half-hearted in their acceptance of a movement which had freed their country from Castilian oppression. If the rebels demanded punishment of the army commanders and of guilty ministers, they could do no less. As a result, they made certain minimum demands of the king. They could be content with nothing less than that all the troops should be withdrawn from the Principality; that all castles should be put under the control of Catalans; that all the members of the Audiència should be dismissed; that the constitutions should be punctiliously observed; and that the soldiers responsible for burning the churches should be punished, and the damage be made good.[2]

While these demands might help to safeguard them from the fury of the rebels, they could only appear outrageous to the ministers in

---

[1] Rubí, fos. 120v–121.

[2] Anonymous letter to Cardona, 13 July 1640. These demands are similar to those put forward by the Diputats in a written reply, dated 14 July, to Cardona's request for advice (ACA: G, Dietari, 1638–41, part III, fo. 418).

Madrid. How, for example, could Spain be saved from a French invasion, if no royal troops remained along the Catalan frontier? In the enthusiasm of the moment the Catalans replied that they would defend the frontier themselves. To those who had watched their efforts at Salces, this seemed singularly optimistic. But at this time of national euphoria, the Catalans treated facts and figures with an abandon worthy of Madrid. Did they not have 170,000 men between the ages of twenty and thirty-six, together with a further 700,000 women, children and men over thirty-six years of age? Could they not send 200,000 men to the front, and still find enough to work the fields? Did they not have sufficient gold and silver mines of their own to make them economically self-sufficient?[1] It was a nice irony that whereas in previous years the Principality had protested its poverty while Madrid exaggerated its wealth and resources, it was now the Catalans who exaggerated their own resources, in their determination to cut loose from Madrid.

Of all the Catalan demands, Cardona met only one. He arrested the two most unpopular army commanders, Geri de la Rena and Leonardo Moles. This, the first of the rebels' demands, was one on which he suffered no qualms, and which even the Court was reluctantly prepared to stomach.[2] But as soon as he tried to set about the restoration of the viceregal government, he ran into difficulties. The members of the Audiència refused to come out of hiding, since the Catalan authorities would not—and indeed could not—guarantee their safety. It soon became clear that any hope of full co-operation between viceroy and Diputats was likely to founder on this and other problems relating to the Audiència. Cardona suggested that one of its members, Dr Ramon Rubí, should undertake inquiries into the burning of the churches of Riudarenes and Montiró, but Tamarit replied that the Diputats were unable to agree, and asked for the appointment of a private lawyer.[3]

The Diputats' rejection of Rubí is highly significant, because his name is not one of those which appear on the list they had drawn up of ministers guilty of breaking the law.[4] In fact, they were rejecting him not because he was guilty of any specific offence, but simply because he was a member of the Audiència. For the first time a royal minister was

[1] Letter to Cardona of 13 July 1640.
[2] AGS: GA, leg. 1329, King to Cardona, 20 July 1640.
[3] ACA: CA, leg. 391, Cardona to King, 14 July 1640.
[4] ACA: G, Dietari, 1638–41, part III, fos. 414–15.

considered *persona non grata* merely by virtue of the fact that he *was* a royal minister. This itself marked a decisive change in the attitude of the Diputació. The change was probably inevitable. The rebels were demanding a complete renewal of the viceregal administration, and the Diputats could not afford to show themselves hesitant on so fundamental a point. But they were hardly likely to feel any scruples in bringing their demands into line with those of the rebels. Their own feud with the Audiència over the contraband, and perhaps also the personal enmity between Drs Fontanella and Vinyes,[1] had left them in a state of mind in which they were happy to see the downfall of the king's judges. If asked to justify their attitude, they had ready to hand the doctrine which Fontanella had devised in the course of the struggle over the *quints*—the doctrine that the Audiència had ceased to be an impartial body, and never produced decisions favourable to the Principality.[2] With the Diputats' repudiation of the existing Audiència in July 1640, Fontanella's thesis had come into its own. The break so long foreshadowed between the Catalan authorities and the supreme royal tribunal in the Principality was now an accomplished fact. The rejection of Rubí as a fit person to conduct an inquiry into the troubles, symbolized the dissolution of that tacit compact between king and Diputats which had formed the basis of Catalonia's government.

Cardona took the uncooperative attitude of the Diputats very much to heart. It 'shows Your Majesty the state that things are in, and how little Barcelona is doing to strengthen the authority of the ministers. It greatly distresses me to see how little I can do, however much I try.'[3] The viceroy was painfully aware that unless either Madrid or Barcelona changed its attitude, he had no hope of success. But mercifully he was to be spared the knowledge of how complete was his failure. His illness had grown steadily worse ever since his arrival at Perpinyà, and on 22 July he died. Catalonia, already without a viceregal administration,

---

[1] The paper prepared by the Diputats for presentation to Cardona on 14 July (Dietari, fo. 418) contained a strong attack on the person of Dr Vinyes, who 'before becoming a minister was a fierce defender of the constitutions of Catalonia and the rights of the fatherland, but after his appointment he advised in exactly the opposite sense, as can be seen from all his papers...'. This was probably inspired by Dr Fontanella. A few days earlier, Vinyes himself wrote from his hiding-place a letter in which he, in turn, attacked Fontanella (ACA: CA, leg. 393, Vinyes to ?, 7 July 1640).

[2] See above, p. 295.

[3] Cardona to King, 14 July 1640.

was once again without a viceroy, and the Diputats remained the sole figures of authority in a province swept by revolution.

Claris and his colleagues had to choose between trying to ride the revolution, and seeking peace with Olivares at the risk of seeing themselves overwhelmed by the forces of anarchy. Their own interests and inclinations, the advice of their friends, their reading of the state of the Principality and the intentions of Madrid, prompted them to choose the first of these two possible courses. In choosing, they launched Catalonia decisively on a revolutionary career. For the Catalan Revolution of 1640 was, in reality, not one revolution but two. The first was the spontaneous, unpremeditated social revolution of the poor against the rich, of the dispossessed against the possessors: the outcome of all those social discontents which had racked the Principality for so many decades. The second was the political revolution against Castilian domination: the outcome of the prolonged conflict of interests between the Principality of Catalonia and the Court of Spain, of which the remote origins can be traced far back into the sixteenth century, but which each year since the death of Philip II had rendered more acute. The leaders of the first revolution were nameless; the leaders of the second were the Diputats.

Although the Diputats were eventually to place their country under the protection of France, it would probably be true to say that neither they, nor the great mass of their fellow-citizens, seriously envisaged the termination of the Principality's allegiance to Philip IV, even as late as the summer of 1640. Even though more than a century of royal absenteeism had gradually weakened the patriarchal and personal ties between the king and his Catalan subjects, they still looked upon him as a father who—if once the just complaints of his children were allowed to reach his ears—would promptly act to right their wrongs and remove the cause of their distresses. If the rebel bands shouted 'Death to traitors!' they also shouted, with equal enthusiasm, 'Long live the king!'

The instinctive loyalty of the peasantry to a king they scarcely knew is not really very surprising. More surprising is the residue of trust which no less a person than Claris himself still seemed to place in the justice and mercy of the king. This was revealed in his handling of the affairs of his chapter of Urgell, whose feud with its bishop was reaching its climax just at the moment when the political relationship between

II   PAU CLARIS

DOM IOSEPH DE MARGARIT ET DE BIVRE, *Marquis*
d'Aguilar, Comte d'Offone, Vicomte de Cabrere et Bas, Baron de la
Ilacune; Seigneur du Chasteau d'Ampurda Maistre Rational de la
Maison et Cour de sa Majesté tres Chreshenne, Lieutenant General
en ses armées, et Gouuerneur de Catalogne.

III   DON JOSEP MARGARIT I BIURE

the Principality and the Court of Spain was foundering. At the end of July, Claris and his colleague in the Diputació, Jaume Ferran, wrote a joint letter to the Urgell chapter, urging it to

send a canon promptly to Madrid to give His Majesty (whom God preserve) full information on all the excesses committed by the bishop and his officials ...and to beseech His Majesty in his royal mercy to sequestrate the jurisdiction of the diocese of Urgell, and place there a royal official to administer it in a proper manner, or else to allow you to move the cathedral elsewhere....[1]

Here, then, at the very moment when the Diputació is rejecting the king's ministers as unsuited for the government of the Principality, the Diputat Eclesiàstic is simultaneously asking for the appointment of a royal official to administer his own diocese of Urgell. But this is not all. This letter, which expects the king of Spain to come to the help of the canons of Urgell in their struggle with the most 'royalist' of all the bishops in Catalonia, was written by a man who had almost certainly already begun treasonable negotiations with France. The exact date on which the Catalan Diputació first made contact with the French authorities has never been satisfactorily determined.[2] Richelieu had for some time shown a considerable interest in Catalan affairs; there were French spies in the Principality, of whom the most notorious was Father Ferrand, a monk at Montserrat; and there is a strong probability that certain informal contacts with the French had been made by Catalans associated with the Diputació as early as April 1640, when the Diputats had gone into hiding to escape arrest. Dr Rubí writes in his contemporary account:

The moment at which the Diputats began to treat with the French is much debated. Some say that it was years before. This view is held by those who claim to have secret information on the evils of the age, and they fail to realize that a corporation is incapable of secretly planning a rebellion years in advance. My own view is that the Diputats grew afraid when they saw the viceroy dead, and tried to find out what sort of help they could expect from France if His Majesty should attempt to punish the province, and the first person to enter France was Francesc Vilaplana, the cousin of the Diputat Eclesiàstic, Claris.[3]

[1] ACU: Cartes, Claris and Ferran to Chapter of Urgell, 23 July 1640.
[2] See Sanabre, *Acción de Francia*, pp. 91–4, for a discussion of this difficult problem. His reconstruction of the course of the negotiations is the most plausible and the best documented that has so far been accomplished.   [3] Rubí, fo. 121 v.

Recent investigations would suggest that Rubí dated the first contacts a little late. On 19 July the Diputats sent a secret letter to Tamarit at Perpinyà, instructing him for the safety of his own person to leave Perpinyà secretly and at all speed for Figueres or Ceret in the event of Cardona's death; and the Conseller of Barcelona received similar instructions.[1] This strongly suggests that discussions, informally and unofficially begun by Vilaplana some months earlier (probably with the connivance of Claris), had already before Cardona's death assumed a more formal character, and that the Diputats were afraid that their discovery might lead to the arrest of Tamarit and the Conseller.

How is Claris's apparently sincere expression of confidence in the good offices of the king of Spain in relation to the affairs of Urgell to be reconciled with his secret approaches to the king of France? The most plausible answer would probably be that Claris himself saw no contradiction in his behaviour: that he neither expected, nor wished for, a complete rupture with the Spanish Court, and that he still retained a deep residue of loyalty to his sovereign. On the other hand, it could legitimately be argued that he was playing a double game, and that the despatch of a canon of Urgell to Madrid would serve as a convenient smoke-screen to cover his negotiations with the French. Two contemporary writers imply that the break with Spain was the outcome of a conspiracy by Claris and a few other determined and discontented men. 'All the world knew', remarked a Catalan ecclesiastic, Dr Alegre, a few years later, 'that only Claris, Vergós, Tamarit, Fontanella and two other men out of favour, handed over the province to France.'[2] Assarino, the Italian historian of the Catalan Revolution, also ascribed it to a handful of disappointed seekers after office.[3] This view of the revolutionaries as conspirators motivated by private discontents is not without a certain foundation in fact, but as a complete explanation of their behaviour it is both crude and unsatisfying, since it precludes any of that sense of loss and bewilderment which usually accompanies a conflict of loyalties.

In trying to determine the motives which inspired Claris's conduct at this decisive moment, it is only fair to watch the unfolding panorama from his vantage-point in the Diputació. He saw his country devastated

[1] Sanabre, p. 93.
[2] BN: MS 2382, fos. 134–58, paper by Dr Alegre (1651), fo. 138.
[3] Assarino, p. 68.

by the barbarities of the troops, its houses pillaged and its churches burnt; he saw its treasured laws and privileges under persistent attack by the Court at Madrid over a long period of years; he saw justice overthrown, the royal authority abolished, and his countrymen in arms not only against the established government but against the whole order of society. As the supreme representative of the Catalan nation it was his duty to preserve and hand down to posterity the precious gift that had been temporarily placed in his keeping. Referring to the privileges of the cathedral chapter of Urgell, he had written six months before: 'Do not let us lose in our time what our forebears so bravely won.'[1] This was as relevant to the laws and privileges of the Principality as to those of his cathedral chapter. For his chapter was only a small-scale replica of that perfect community to which his highest allegiance lay: the Generalitat of Catalonia.

Where was he to turn for the salvation of this perfect community? To Madrid? The king, while just and magnanimous, was kept in ignorance of the grievances of his Catalan vassals by evil-intentioned counsellors, whose behaviour over the past twenty years had made it impossible to believe their promises. It was true that they had belatedly asked the Diputats for their advice on calming the Principality, but they had ignored the answer. The Diputats had made it clear that there was no hope of a return to normal conditions until all the troops had been withdrawn from Catalonia and the Comtats. The troops had not been withdrawn. Even worse, it seemed that they were to be re-inforced. At the end of June, the Principality was alarmed by rumours that the troops at present in south Catalonia and Rosselló were to be joined by many more from Aragon, and by a large contingent of English which had arrived at Corunna.[2] Since Madrid's policy was in fact to strengthen the troops on the frontier against a French attack, the rumour was not entirely without foundation.

The Principality's position naturally seemed desperate to Claris. A Castilian attack threatened it from without; civil war from within.

This is a time when the entire province is without justice [he wrote in his letter of 23 July to the canons of Urgell], because the duke of Cardona's life is drawing to a close and the royal ministers are in hiding. Therefore we must

---

[1] See above, p. 344.
[2] ACA: G, 909, Lletres secretes, 1605–74, Diputats to Manlleu, 30 June 1640.

conduct our affairs in the light of *raison d'état* (*raho de estat*) and prudence... occupying the posts that we do, we are in deep distress to see this province in imminent danger of destruction.

In these circumstances, '*raison d'état* and prudence' suggested the wisdom of making an approach to France. In Claris's eyes this neither constituted treason, nor a decisive rupture with the king of Spain. It was no more than a means of insuring the Principality against an unpleasant eventuality that might yet be averted.

There was always a possibility that French assistance would not be needed. The king might yet discover the truth; Olivares and the Protonotario might realize in time the error of their ways. It was even possible that there might be a change of regime. Such mystery surrounds any contacts that may have existed between the Catalans and the enemies of Olivares at Court, that it is impossible to say whether ideas were entertained at this moment in Barcelona of engineering a palace revolution at Madrid. The Castilian aristocracy as a whole was bitterly opposed to Olivares; the Castilian populace was discontented. The successful resistance of Catalonia to the demands of Madrid would greatly increase the chances of the Conde Duque's falling from power and it is difficult not to believe that there was at least some understanding between the Conde Duque's enemies and the Catalans. If there was no actual conspiracy against Olivares, there was certainly much pamphleteering, and perhaps something worse. In a meeting of ministers on 14 July, Olivares said that the various revolutionary manifestoes circulating in Catalonia had in fact been written not in the Principality but at Madrid. The Junta agreed on the need to clamp down on the circulation of seditious papers and pamphlets at Court, and appointed a special committee to examine those papers now in circulation and write an official reply.[1] Olivares had always shown himself alive to the possibilities of the pamphlet;[2] by the summer of 1640 he was no less alive to its dangers.

When Claris first began negotiations with France, he was acting well in advance of public opinion in the Principality. It is doubtful at this moment whether the majority of the Catalans would have counten-

---

[1] ACA: CA, leg. 287, no. 24, Junta de Ejecución, 14 July 1640.
[2] See José M.ª Jover, *1635. Historia de una polémica y semblanza de una generación* (Madrid, 1949), for the Conde Duque's propaganda machine.

anced or approved any form of understanding with the French. While they had no wish to have anything more to do with Castile, the idea of throwing themselves into the arms of the French, their traditional enemies, can only have been abhorrent to them. They were determined in July and August of 1640 to stand on their own feet; to prove themselves militarily and economically self-sufficient and capable of defending their frontier against the enemies of the king without having recourse to military aid from Castile.

The Catalans' eventual acceptance of a French alliance was not, therefore, the result of any deep affection for the French. The alliance was foisted upon them partly by the intransigent attitude of Madrid, which finally left them with no alternative, and partly by the skilful tactics of a small group of men who, for one reason or another, had committed themselves to dealings with the French at an early stage of the revolution, and were either unable or unwilling to pull back. In this sense, Dr Alegre was right in saying that 'only Claris, Vergós, Tamarit, Fontanella and two other men out of favour' handed over the province to France.

Since secret negotiations with France entailed obvious risks, it would be interesting to know what it was that made this handful of men, the self-appointed leaders of Catalonia's political revolution, willing to run them. It is at this point that their past histories assume a general importance. Assarino characterized them as 'disappointed'; Dr Alegre as 'out of favour'. For some of the revolutionary leaders, this description appears to be correct. Any list of those who played a prominent part in steering the Principality towards a French alliance should include the following names:

> Pau Claris ⎫ Diputats
> Francesc de Tamarit ⎬
> Dr Joan Pere Fontanella (assessor to the
>   Diputació) and his son, Josep Fontanella
> Francesc Joan de Vergós
> Dr Pere Joan Rossell
> Francesc de Vilaplana
> Don Ramon de Guimerà
> Don Felip de Sorribes
> Jeroni and Rafael Matali (brothers, Barcelona merchants)

Miquel Puigventós (Barcelona merchant)
Don Jacint Vilanova (frontier baron)
Don Aleix de Senmenat (frontier baron)
Dr Francesc Puig (canon of Tortosa)
Don Josep Margarit i Biure
Don Josep d'Ardena

Some of these men had certainly tried, and failed, to obtain offices and honours; others may possibly have tried, and in any event had no chance of success; still others were completely out of favour, after coming into conflict at some point in their careers with the representatives of the Crown.

At the head of the first group—those who had failed to obtain office—must stand the name of Dr Fontanella. His career, in contrast to that of Dr Vinyes, was one long record of failure to obtain a post in the Audiència.[1] 'He is a vain man, and he has sons whom he is anxious to accommodate with ecclesiastical pensions', wrote an agent of Madrid after the outbreak of the revolution, commenting on the possibility of winning over the rebel leaders by bribery.[2] Another member of this group was Don Ramon de Guimerà. Don Ramon was one of those nobles who had been involved in the activities of the bandits,[3] on the side of the *nyerros*, and then, like Bernardino de Marimón,[4] had attempted to curry favour at the time of the dispute over the new viceroy in 1622, by inducing a large bevy of gentlemen from his neighbourhood to go to Barcelona through heavy snows to vote in the interests of the king.[5] He was less fortunate than Marimón, for his loyal behaviour failed to win him office. He applied for the post of Procurador Reial of the Comtats but his application was unsuccessful. To some extent his character and reputation probably hindered his chances: he was described by royal officials as 'more than a little ill-behaved'.[6] This description does not seem to apply to another disappointed seeker after office and distinction, Don Aleix de Senmenat. As a boy he had actually been appointed a page to Philip III but fell ill,

[1] See above, p. 294.
[2] AGS: GA, leg. 1368, anonymous, very rough draft (in very poor condition), probably of December 1640, on the subject of possible mediation in Catalonia by the nuncio.
[3] ACA: CA, leg. 356, Almazán to King, 2 Aug. 1614.
[4] See above, p. 168.
[5] ACA: CA, leg. 370, petition of Guimerà, Dec. 1624.
[6] AHN: Consejos, lib. 1884, Council of Aragon, 19 Aug. 1626.

and was never able to take up his post.[1] He was anxious to serve the king, and anxious also for the distinction (and the revenues) that came with membership of one of the military orders. His application was favourably considered, but the abrupt termination of the Corts of 1626 prevented it from being successful.[2]

Of those who had no chance of obtaining office and honour, Claris himself may stand as a representative. As a canon of Urgell who was on the worst possible terms with his bishop, he had no hope of preferment so long as the present regime continued. The French, on the other hand, promised him the archbishopric of Tarragona.[3] It can never be known what part, if any, the hope of preferment played in Claris's calculations. All that can be said is that his personal dilemma was one common to many Catalans. For over a hundred years, the nobles, ecclesiastics and lawyers of Catalonia, who formed the Principality's natural governing class, had been starved of opportunities of employment and advancement. The scarcity of administrative and ecclesiastical posts in Catalonia, its lack of a resident Court, and the virtual exclusion of Catalans from offices outside the borders of their own country, had all helped to create a climate of discontent. The general sense of bitterness caused by the lack of opportunities was much increased by the feuds between individual families and by the realization that so much depended on the possession of effective influence in the right place at the right moment. Why, for instance, should a Marimón obtain office, and not a Guimerà? It can only have been because there was already a Marimón in the administration—the governor, Don Alexos de Marimón—ready to put in a word for his cousin at the right moment. As a result, offices in Catalonia had come to be the preserve of a few families, like the Marimóns and the Magarolas, and the rest were left out in the cold. In the majority of cases, disappointed expectations of office would scarcely have been sufficient to turn the victims towards revolution. But individual disappointments, and the general sense of frustration, help to explain the weakness of the ties that bound the Catalan governing class to the Court, and the consequent

[1] ACA: CA, leg. 369, Viceroy to King, 26 Aug. 1623. Illness, however, may not be the true explanation of his failure to become a royal page. The duke of Monteleón recommended that he should not be given the post in order to punish his father for criminal activities (ACA: CA, leg. 350, Monteleón to King, 19 Oct. 1609).

[2] ACA: CA, leg. 260, no. 50, *Apuntamientos*, 28 April 1626.

[3] J. Pellicer de Tovar, *Idea del Principado de Cataluña* (Antwerp, 1642), p. 552.

refusal of that class to fight for the preservation of the Castilian connection when the revolution occurred.

In addition to those who may have suffered disappointment, a significant number of the revolutionary leaders had experienced actual violence or humiliation at the hands of royal ministers. A warrant had been issued for the arrest of two of them, while at least six others had actually spent some time in gaol. Fontanella only escaped arrest at the time of the contraband controversy because he went into hiding. In August 1639 Santa Coloma had ordered the arrest of Guimerà for deserting the camp at Salces,[1] though Guimerà indignantly insisted that he had every intention of returning.[2] Of those who had seen the inside of a prison, Vergós and Tamarit had been gaoled in March 1640 on the orders of Madrid,[3] Vergós having already narrowly avoided arrest two years earlier in the contraband affair.[4] Rossell and Rafael Matali had been imprisoned in 1634 for the part they played in the struggle over the *quints*.[5] Margarit, who was to become governor of Catalonia under the French, had had a particularly chequered career. One of the more lawless of the Catalan barons, he and his father-in-law, Don Rafael de Biure, had found themselves in the common gaol, in company with sixteen of their vassals, after a number of skirmishes with their neighbours.[6] With the appointment of his friend and relative, Santa Coloma, to the viceroyalty of Catalonia, Margarit's prospects of a return to favour seemed much improved. But he was to be sadly disillusioned. One of his enemies was found murdered. Suspicion naturally fell on Margarit, and the new viceroy, anxious to show his impartiality, refused to accept his pleas that he was not implicated.[7] As a result, relations were broken off between the houses of Margarit and Queralt,[8] and Margarit found himself excluded from favour once more.

The most remarkable of all the previous careers of the revolutionaries is, however, that of Francesc de Vilaplana. Vilaplana was the younger

---

[1] See above, p. 370.
[2] ACA: G, caja 21, Don Francesc d'Erill to Santa Coloma, 18 Sept. 1639.
[3] See above, pp. 407–8.   [4] See above, p. 352.
[5] See above, p. 297.
[6] ACA: CA, leg. 503, petition of Don Rafael de Biure, 1632 (?).
[7] ACA: G, caja 4, Margarit to Santa Coloma, 19 March 1638.
[8] Sevillà, fo. 140. Sevillà, who was tutor to Margarit's sons, claims that Margarit was entirely innocent and that two ordinary highway robbers later confessed to the crime. He may well be right, but Margarit's reputation in the neighbourhood makes it easy to see why suspicion immediately fell on him.

son of one of the aristocratic families of Rosselló, which had settled in Perpinyà. He was also very closely connected by marriage to the family of Pau Claris, who referred to him as his nephew. In 1620, while still a boy, Vilaplana had climbed one night into the prison at Copons, where a friend of his was detained, and shot and killed the *batlle* in cold blood while he was asleep.[1] Since his brother Antoni de Vilaplana was implicated in the crime, his castle was demolished on Alcalá's orders. Francesc himself was saved from the death sentence by his good family connections and the fact that he was a minor, but he was condemned to perpetual exile in the castle of Peñón off the coast of Africa. 'This wicked *caballero* has such a propensity to murder,' wrote the bishop of Solsona, 'that if he is released and comes back to the Principality, he will go on killing anyone who has offended him.'[2] After some fourteen years in his African prison, Vilaplana had his sentence commuted to military service in Flanders.[3] On his way from Africa to Flanders he mysteriously disappeared in the area of Perpinyà. Santa Coloma, afraid that his presence would renew all the old feuds of the border country, ordered that he should be arrested or told to leave the country at once.[4] He was not arrested, nor did he leave the country; and the winter of 1638 and spring of 1639 found him engaged in an acrimonious quarrel with another frontier baron, Don Ramon Xammar.[5] At this moment Claris entered on the scene, and chose his nephew as *sargento mayor* of the *tercio* which had been raised by the Diputació for the Salces campaign. In November he made further use of the patronage of the Diputació to give him the post of controller of customs at Perpinyà, which allowed him almost unlimited opportunities to profit from the contraband trade with France.[6] Vilaplana's close relationship with the Diputat Eclesiàstic and his intimate knowledge of the border country, made him the ideal instrument for the opening of negotiations between the Diputació and France. It remained only for Vilaplana, 'on familiar terms with the *monsieurs* of Languedoc, and having already discovered that their reactions were favourable',[7] to

[1] ACA: CA, leg. 275, no. 19, Bishop of Solsona to King, 12 Feb. 1628.
[2] *Ibid.* [3] ACA: CA, leg. 385, Cardona to King, 13 Sept. 1634.
[4] ACA: Varias de Cancillería, R. 387, Santa Coloma to Don Cristóbal Gallart, 13 July 1638.
[5] ACA: G, caja 11, Torres to Santa Coloma, 3 Feb. 1639.
[6] ACA: G, LT, 1639–40, fos. 164–6, Diputats to Vilaplana, 29 Nov. 1639.
[7] Gaspar Sala, *Epítome de los principios y progresos de las guerras de Cataluña en los años 1640 y 1641* (Barcelona, 1641), cap. III (no page numbers).

receive from the Diputats, some time in July 1640, full authority to begin more formal discussions with the French.

Men like Vilaplana and Guimerà had little reason to love a regime which had humiliated and maltreated them. Yet it would be foolish, on the strength of a few dubious incidents in their careers, to adduce private grievances as the sole explanation of their conduct. Seventeenth-century Catalans showed themselves adept at equating private grievance with public wrong, without a trace of hypocrisy. Many of them cherished a passionate loyalty to their fatherland which their own misfortunes served only to strengthen. The part played by personal grievance in driving a man to take up arms against the established authority can very easily be overestimated, and the variety and complexity of each individual's character be correspondingly undervalued.

A record of the personal grievances of these men is useful only in so far as it may go some way towards explaining why they, in particular, should have taken the lead in organizing revolution. A Vilaplana had nothing to lose; a Margarit had much to gain. Between them stood others bold enough, angry enough, desperate enough, to exchange words for action. As a group, they possessed an influence out of all proportion to their number. The authority enjoyed by some of them in the civic life of Barcelona, the family connections and the personal friendships of the others, enabled them to build up a constantly increasing body of support throughout the Principality.

The first task was to steer the policies of Barcelona in the required direction. This required a majority both in the Consell de Cent, and among those members of the Braços who lived in Barcelona or sufficiently near it to attend regularly. The leaders of the revolution were well placed to win votes in the Consell de Cent, particularly among the 48 *ciutadans* and the 32 merchants, whose votes were all-important. Vergós, Josep Fontanella, Don Felip de Sorribes, Miquel Puigventós, and the two Matali brothers were all members of the Consell de Cent in 1640.[1] Other members who had close ties with the leaders included Dr Joan Francesc Rossell, father of Dr Pere Joan Rossell; Francesc Claris, brother of Pau Claris; Don Francesc Sorribes, brother of Don Felip de Sorribes; Pau Boquet, a member of the important Claris-Gaver-Boquet connection; Lleonard Serra, who had been arrested with

[1] AHB: Delibs., 1640, fo. 2, list of members of Consell de Cent.

Vergós, and doubtless several others whose family relationships and personal friendships have yet to be traced. These men formed an invaluable nucleus of support for Claris in the very heart of the city council. Unfortunately, the fact that the register of deliberations only gives the formal decisions of the Consell de Cent makes it impossible to discover who proposed a particular line of conduct on important occasions. All that remains of the original discussions is a small number of scrappy notes, but they are just full enough to show that the most active speakers in the Consell de Cent in 1640 were Vergós, Matali, Puigventós, and a *ciutadà*, Agustí Pexau.[1] It is Vergós in particular who seems to have dominated city politics at this moment. He was a member of the secret Junta set up by the Diputats to advise them on policy;[2] he was active in the *braç militar*, and served as a liaison between it and both the Consell de Cent and the Diputació;[3] 'although an idiot, and not in the least eloquent', he had become, as a result of his imprisonment, the 'oracle of the juntas'.[4]

It was possible to collect support in other parts of the Principality in much the same way as in Barcelona. The network of family relationships and ties of dependence which ran to and fro across the Principality provided a useful means of building up and manipulating majorities in town councils and cathedral chapters. The exact story of how this was done must necessarily remain obscure, since so much depends on unknown quantities, such as the local standing of individual families and the extent of the influence they could command. 'Don Joan de Peguera is the idol of Manresa and all that region.'[5] It would be natural to expect that Peguera's cousin, Claris, made good use of this influence. It is also probable that the revolutionary leaders exploited to the utmost the organization of the traditional Catalan factions. 'Jeroni Calders has great influence in Lleida because he is a member of the faction of the *cadells*, and almost all the gentry there belong to the same faction and are related to him.'[6] His support could therefore be of crucial importance.

Although faction-fights had already broken out in some towns, like

---

[1] AHB: Sótanos. Bosses Deliberacions, 1640.
[2] Sanabre, p. 92.
[3] ACA: G, R. 68, *Borrador* of proceedings of the *braç militar*, 1626–40.
[4] Tormé i Liori, p. 220.
[5] AGS: GA, leg. 1374, paper by Archdeacon of Barcelona, forwarded to Madrid by the marquis of los Vélez, 4 Feb. 1641.
[6] *Ibid.*

Manresa, it does not seem that the rivalry between *nyerros* and *cadells* had yet flared up sufficiently to preclude some measure of unity among the leaders of the revolution. In the days to come, when the French had gained control of the Principality and Fontanella enjoyed the dominant influence, the country would be run by the *cadells*;[1] but in 1640, in so far as it is possible to discover individual allegiances, both *nyerros* and *cadells* appear to have been represented among the leaders of the revolution. Vilanova and Guimerà were probably *nyerros*; Fontanella and Margarit were *cadells*. Among them they could command an efficient and highly organized body of support, extremely useful in the preparation of revolution.

It is in the Seu d'Urgell that the interplay of national and local politics is most obvious, and the ways in which revolution was forwarded are most easily observed. During the summer of 1640, the feud between the canons of Urgell and their bishop, Pau Duran, led to scenes of disorder similar to those in Vic or Manresa, but of greater moment in that two national figures, Claris and the bishop, were both involved, and the issues themselves assumed a national importance.

The latest round of disputes between the bishop and his canons had opened in December 1639 when the bishop ordered a visitation by his vicar-general of the parish church of Sant Miquel. This church was *infra claustra* and, in the view of the canons, there was neither authority nor precedent for an episcopal visitation.[2] Consequently, they barred the door against entry by the vicar-general. He tried to force his way in, and was attacked by four of the canons, Viver, Sansa, Rossell and Cesses, who managed to wrest from him the iron bar he was holding.[3] The vicar-general tried to retaliate by arresting Rossell, and was struck two or three times by Sansa. When he heard what had happened, the bishop embarked on a long struggle to bring the offenders to book and prevent them from entering the choir of the cathedral. Further causes of dispute arose in the new year, and the chapter also became involved in fresh controversy with the municipal authorities of Urgell. Fifty supporters of the canons were brought in from outside and housed in

[1] Rocabertí, *Presagios fatales*, pp. 14 and 21.
[2] ACU: Cartes, 1630–40, Claris to Chapter of Urgell, 20 Dec. 1639.
[3] A letter from the canons of Urgell to those of Girona, dated 7 Jan. 1640 (ACU: Cartes), and one from the bishop to Santa Coloma of 30 April 1640 (ACA: G, caja 30) suggest that the events occurred roughly as here described.

their lodgings and in the cathedral; and shooting followed.[1] The vice-roy, not unnaturally, was much disturbed by the disorders, and at-tempted to mediate between the bishop and the canons,[2] but without success. The canons sent to Barcelona as their representative in the negotiations, one of their number, Don Llorenç de Barutell. Barutell sought legal assistance from the two Fontanellas,[3] and it was presumably as a result of their discussions that the form of protest by the chapter against the bishop was drawn up for presentation to the Provincial Council in May.[4] Meanwhile, the bishop himself had not been idle. The air was thick with interdicts and excommunications, and it was the bishop who pressed hardest for proceedings against Claris at the time when Madrid was searching for a pretext to arrest him,[5] on the grounds that Claris was lending support to his fellow canons in their nefarious activities with armed ruffians.[6]

The failure to discover any incriminating evidence against Claris was a setback to the bishop, but he was determined to impose his authority. The hostility between the canons and the townsmen provided him with welcome allies, of whom he proceeded to make the most. The *batlle* and other municipal officials were called in to take action against delinquent clerics,[7] and the canons replied by summoning to their aid the notorious Baron Boquet, the most powerful bandit-noble in the region, and the governor of their estates.[8] Boquet entered the town with twenty-five armed men but thought it prudent to retire when he discovered the strength of the opposition. It was now the middle of July; the bishop himself was in Perpinyà with Cardona, working hard to secure the post of Canceller of Catalonia; the country was generally in an uproar, from which the Seu d'Urgell had so far escaped only because troops had not recently been billeted in its neighbourhood. The withdrawal of Boquet set the stage for the coming of civil war to the Seu.

On 15 July all seventeen canons suddenly disappeared from the town, and took refuge in a church half a league outside. At four o'clock on the morning of 20 July seventy or more armed men, led by Boquet and

---

[1] ACU: Cartes, 1630–40, Josep Montella to Pere Cardon, 10 April 1640.
[2] ACU: Cartes, 1630–40, Santa Coloma to Chapter of Urgell, 31 March 1640.
[3] ACU: Cartes, 1630–40, Barutell to Chapter of Urgell, 10 April 1640.
[4] See above, p. 459.   [5] See above, p. 408.
[6] ACU: Cartes, 1630–40, Barutell to Chapter of Urgell, 29 April 1640.
[7] ACV: Cartes, 1640–9, Chapter of Urgell to Chapter of Vic, 28 July 1640.
[8] ACA: CA, leg. 393, Vicar-General of Bishop of Urgell to King, 21 July 1640.

accompanied by Canons Viver and Rossell, broke into the city, seized the cathedral, and fortified themselves against a siege. 'We have laid in some small stocks of provisions, so our spirits are high', reported Canon Rossell exultantly from the cathedral to his colleagues waiting anxiously outside the town.[1] In the event, the provisions, while no doubt enjoyed, proved to be unnecessary. Negotiations opened between town and chapter, the town council was split,[2] and the canons, at least for a few days had won their way. But the counter-revolution was close at hand. By August, the townsmen had once again managed to expel Boquet and his men, but the war between town and chapter continued intermittently throughout the rest of 1640 and well into the new year, with the canons gradually gaining the upper hand.

When Claris and Ferran heard of the July disorders, they recommended an immediate appeal to the king.[3] Their sympathies naturally lay with their colleagues, and it was of vital importance to them that the bishop should not become Canceller.

If you do not succeed in settling this question satisfactorily, there will be new controversies every day, especially with the present prelate, who causes disturbances wherever he goes, as you well know, and at present has the faithful town of Perpinyà turned upside down. He is the greatest enemy that the Catalan nation has, and in spite of this he is doing everything possible to become Canceller of Catalonia.[4]

The struggle over ecclesiastical jurisdiction between canons and bishop thus merged into the wider struggle to keep the bishop out of the second most influential post in the Principality. The war between canons and townsmen was a miniature version of the civil war now raging in the Principality; the rebellion of the canons against their bishop a miniature version of the national rebellion against the ministers of the viceregal administration. In their rebellion, the canons and the revolutionary leaders were natural allies, to such a degree that the bishop of Urgell—admittedly a far from impartial witness—declared their aims to be the same.[5] While it is impossible to say how far French influence had penetrated the Urgell chapter before the summer of 1640, the

[1] ACU: Cartes, Canon Rossell to Canons of Urgell, 20 July 1640.
[2] AMU: Llibre de consells, 1615–57, fo. 320v.
[3] See above, p. 469.
[4] ACU: Cartes, Ferran and Claris to Chapter of Urgell, 23 July 1640.
[5] ACA: CA, leg. 393, Bishop of Urgell to King, 27 Aug. 1640.

canons received a preferential treatment in later years which suggests that the French were well aware of the value of their services. Barutell became Canceller; Ferran an Inquisitor; Villatorrent a preacher to the king of France, and almost all the others obtained lucrative offices of one kind or another.[1]

While the canons of Urgell, and Claris and his colleagues, together with their friends, relations and dependants, may reasonably be regarded as the active agents of revolution, this by no means implies that they imposed their views on a country unwilling to receive them. They were working in soil that had already been well prepared. Although Catalonia as a nation was traditionally, and violently, anti-French, at least a section of the population cannot have looked entirely askance at the prospect of a French alliance. Most barons in the border country had close personal ties with their French neighbours; many Barcelona merchants had commercial contacts with France; a large number of shopkeepers in the Principality were dependent on supplies of French goods, and Rosselló and Cerdanya could not survive without French trade. One of the most vigorous adherents in Rosselló of a French alliance was a certain Josep Escuder, a lawyer, who acted as agent to the countess of Quirra for the disposal of her Canet salt which was brought to Conflent for sale to the French.[2] There must have been many like him, whose commercial interests helped to determine their political allegiance.

Even more important in helping to swing the Principality towards a French alliance was the existence in Catalonia of a large population of French origin.[3] The great French immigration of the last hundred years was slowly transforming the racial composition of the Catalan population. In Barcelona, the census of French inhabitants of 1637 showed that 1297 heads of households in the city and its environs were of French origin.[4] With the average number of children in these households under two,[5] a coefficient of four people to a household would

---

[1] BN: MS 2382, fos. 134–58, paper by Dr Alegre. It comes as no surprise to discover (fo. 146) that the canons attempted in 1648 to restore the church in Catalonia to its primitive state by beginning an agitation to have all bishops elected by their chapters.

[2] AGS: Est., K. 1709, no. 89, Juan de Garay to Cristóbal Gallart, 3 Dec. 1640, and no. 7, consulta of Council of Aragon, 4 Feb. 1641.

[3] See above, p. 26.

[4] E. Moreu-Rey, *Els Immigrants Francesos a Barcelona* (Barcelona, 1959), p. 19.

[5] *Ibid.* p. 18.

suggest a French population in Barcelona of 5190—over 10 per cent of the entire population of the city. These French immigrants were employed in every kind of occupation—spinners, dyers, bakers, cobblers, agricultural labourers—but the largest group were servants. Claris had a French coachman; Tamarit, Calders, Dr Rubí, Dr Puig and many others all had French domestic servants.[1] Since these would have lived in the houses of their employers, the total French population of Barcelona must have been appreciably higher.

The French inhabitants of Catalonia were so numerous that it was worth their while to establish special French guilds and confraternities, of which there were more than thirty in the diocese of Barcelona alone.[2] There were, in consequence, strong nuclei of French in almost every Catalan town of importance, and it may well be that these confraternities provided happy hunting-grounds for Richelieu's agents. On the other hand, the majority of French inhabitants had been settled in Catalonia for upwards of thirty years before the revolution began.[3] Many of them had intermarried with Catalans and had been so successfully assimilated into Catalan life that they could be regarded as natives. During the war with France between 1635 and 1640 the Catalans were convinced that they were loyal to their adopted country. In March 1639, for example, Don Joan de Llupià wrote from Perpinyà protesting to Santa Coloma against the taxation of French inhabitants and the confiscation of their arms. He claimed that half the population of Perpinyà consisted of Frenchmen or sons of Frenchmen, 'and in the surrounding villages and countryside, three out of every four'. In the last forty years these settlers had always fought side by side with the Catalans against French attacks, and their loyalty was incontestable.[4]

It is possible to trace people of French extraction who showed themselves passionate devotees of the French alliance after the outbreak of the revolution. There was, for instance, the rector of Ribes in the diocese of Urgell, the son of a Frenchman, 'and one of the most disloyal vassals that Your Majesty has in Catalonia'.[5] But there seems no reason to question the general truth of Llupià's assertion about their loyalty in the

[1] Moreu-Rey, p. 18.
[2] Nadal and Giralt, 'Ensayo metodológico...', p. 272.
[3] Moreu-Rey, p. 24.
[4] ACA: G, caja 12, Don Joan de Llupià to Santa Coloma, 30 March 1639.
[5] Dr Alegre's paper, fo. 152.

period between 1635 and 1640. In spite of this, the fact that so large a proportion of the Catalan population was of French extraction ought not to be discounted in explaining the relative facility with which Catalonia exchanged its allegiance to the king of Spain for allegiance to the king of France. It has been estimated[1] that in the 1660's, the percentages of foreign inhabitants of the bishopric of Barcelona were:

French	13·7
Spaniards (all parts of the peninsula)	5·0

It was only from the eighteenth century that Castilians and Andalusians began emigrating in large numbers to Catalonia. If the surplus population of sixteenth-century Castile had been compelled to find its outlet in the Spanish peninsula rather than the New World, Catalonia would have acquired Castilian rather than French settlers, and Olivares's task in fusing the different provinces of the peninsula might have been made appreciably easier. As it was, the immigrants who established themselves in the Principality were people without any historical or racial traditions that might have predisposed them towards retention of the link with Castile. This was the real significance of the French immigration for the Catalan Revolution of 1640.

Although there was a strong element in Catalonia with French connections, its existence is not enough to account for the success of Claris and his colleagues in steering their nation into a French alliance. Claris was primarily successful in carrying his policies to a satisfactory conclusion because the attitude of Madrid left no visible alternative and because the Catalan ruling class was not prepared to stand in his way. This was the decisive element in the accomplishment of Catalonia's political revolution in 1640. Twenty-five years before, when anarchy threatened as a result of the activities of the bandits, the ruling class had rallied round Alburquerque, even though this meant an increase in royal authority in the Principality, and a corresponding diminution of the country's traditional liberties.[2] In 1640, when anarchy actually came, the ruling class was not inclined to accept a comparable reassertion of royal authority as the cure for its ills. This striking difference between the attitude of the Catalan oligarchy in 1615 and 1640 is a measure of the extent to which the policies of the government in

---

[1] Moreu-Rey, p. 30.   [2] See above, ch. v.

Madrid during the intervening period had succeeded in alienating the Catalan ruling class from the Court of Spain.

The policies of the Court between 1620 and 1640 had progressively lost it the adherence of every social group in Catalonia which had a stake in the maintenance of the existing order. The nobles had been alienated by Alcalá's contemptuous disregard for aristocratic privileges in his war on the bandits; by the appointment of non-Catalans to the command of the Catalan fortresses and to lucrative pensions charged to Catalan bishoprics; and by the persistent attempts of the Crown to make them serve in person or by proxy in the king's wars. There were those, like Don Felip de Sorribes,[1] whose status as feudatories of the Crown had exposed them to summary orders to serve in Italy and elsewhere. There were others like Margarit[2] who found forgotten feudal obligations suddenly revived. All were antagonized by the revival of the archaic usage of *Princeps Namque* in 1637, ordering them to take their vassals to the war at their own expense, and by the treatment they received at the hands of Santa Coloma during the Salces campaign. Upbraided by the viceroy and the king for their slackness and lack of interest in the war, they sent Don Diego de Rocabertí on a special mission to Madrid in the autumn of 1639 to establish their innocence. In the past, they complained, they had been held in much higher estimation than they were nowadays, when viceroys failed to distinguish between a noble and a common soldier.[3] A quarter of their number died at Salces, but the lavish *mercedes* they expected from a grateful king were few and far between. Starved of offices, deprived of honours, treated in a way that their ancestors would never have tolerated, the Catalan nobles and gentry saw no reason at the moment of crisis in the summer of 1640 to risk their lives for the sake of a king who had so singularly failed to appreciate their services.

The Catalan clergy had equal, or greater reason, to feel disgruntled. They had borne heavier, and far more regular taxation, than any other group in Catalan society. Cathedral chapters had found themselves saddled with Castilian bishops; non-Catalans, like the king's brother, the Cardenal Infante, had been preferred to Catalan abbeys.[4] Monas-

---

[1] ACA: CA, leg. 386, Don Felip de Sorribes to King, 18 March 1636. He refused on the pretext that his health was bad, his wealth negligible and his lawsuits onerous.
[2] ACA: CA, leg. 391, Tomàs Fontanet to Santa Coloma, 6 March 1639.
[3] ACA: CA, leg. 283, no. 106, consulta, 8 Nov. 1639.   [4] Sanabre, p. 18.

teries and convents had been exasperated by attempts to introduce the Tridentine reforms, which disturbed them in the enjoyment of their customary ways, and little by little reduced their traditional autonomy. Clergy and members of the religious orders alike discovered that the sole road to preferment was the road that passed through Madrid; that only a Pau Duran could become a bishop in Catalonia. In these circumstances it is hardly surprising to hear from the commander of the king's forces in Rosselló of

the licentiousness of the clergy and the religious in the convents of this diocese, all of whom have reached the last stages of sedition, for in the confessional and the pulpit they spend their entire time rousing the people and offering the rebels encouragement and advice, inducing the ignorant to believe that rebellion will win them the kingdom of heaven.[1]

Finally, even the civic aristocracies, which had welcomed Alburquerque's iron measures with undisguised relief twenty-five years earlier, had by now been cured of any desire to sell their birthright for a mess of pottage. Twenty years of persistent interference by royal officials in the affairs of the municipal corporations had seen to that. The city of Barcelona, and many lesser towns, had been exasperated by the efforts of the Crown to exact the payment of the *quints*. They had grown tired of being approached for a gift or a loan whenever the treasure fleet failed to arrive on time. They had seen their credit destroyed and their debts accumulate as royal ministers descended upon them to insist on the raising of more men and the sending of more supplies to Rosselló during the Salces campaign. The most dignified municipal officials had been driven to the indignity of taking refuge in churches in order to escape compulsory attendance at the camp. Their monopoly of office had been openly challenged by the royal proclamations, issued without the least regard for the niceties of a hierarchical system of government on which the survival of the established order of society depended. Then, in the spring of 1640, their towns had been subjected to the attentions of savage, undisciplined troops who had looted and killed and endlessly asked for more money. Their attempt to meet the king's demands had brought them only a further succession of still more insistent demands, and the hatred of the populace.

[1] AGS: Est., K. 1709, no. 40, Don Juan de Garay to King, 11 Oct. 1640.

For all these reasons, the more responsible members of Catalan society could not react to the challenge of social disorder as their fathers had reacted twenty-five years before. Too much had happened in the years between. Convinced by their experiences during those years that the Court intended to break their laws, destroy their liberties and reduce them to a legal and economic status comparable to that of Castile, they deliberately turned their backs on Madrid. It was unthinkable that they should unite with Castile for centuries to come.[1] This was the frame of mind to which the policies of Olivares had reduced the Catalan ruling class by the summer of 1640, and it was just at this moment that social revolution struck the Principality.

The coming of a social upheaval confronted the ruling class with a cruel dilemma. It was terrified by the mob, but could not appeal, as it had been wont to do, to the 'royal authority' for protection because the Crown no longer possessed any authority in Catalonia. Since the vice-regal government had ceased to exist, such an appeal could only be made direct to Madrid, and this was not something that could be done with any enthusiasm. It also entailed grave dangers at a time when the word 'traitor' was on everybody's lips. Unable to see any way in which, while remaining in Catalonia, they could both save their lives from the mob and retain their loyalty to their king, many nobles and gentry began discreetly to leave the Principality for Aragon and Valencia.[2] Those who stayed were frightened and confused. Suddenly cut adrift from their traditional moorings, they could see no haven from the violent storm that had overtaken them. But at the tiller stood Pau Claris and a little band, bent on making for the open sea rather than return to harbour. And on the shore, now fast receding, could be seen the heavy, hunched figure of the Conde Duque, transfixed by the sight of the battered vessel as it slowly disappeared over the horizon, apparently heading for France.

[1] Anonymous letter to Cardona of 13 July 1640.
[2] Pellicer, 'Avisos', p. 192.

CHAPTER XVII

CATALONIA AND PORTUGAL

In May, when the first reports of serious disorders in Catalonia were reaching Madrid, the English ambassador wrote home that he saw 'nothing in the business that is hard to settle'.[1] Two months later, when the disorders had taken on the semblance of a revolution, he wrote— not perhaps without a certain feeling of satisfaction—that 'it will be now a very hard matter to compose them without discomposing the king's authority, which might have been prevented if the business had been undertaken in time, as the Conde once told me in the matter of Scotland and as he gloried to have done in the late commotions of Portugal'.[2] The unfortunate Conde Duque had discovered, too late, that he had a Scotland of his own, and that the subjects of the king of Spain were no less rebellious than those of the king of England.

Since the murder of Santa Coloma, the Conde Duque's attitude had been one of mingled astonishment, horror and incomprehension.

In effect [he wrote to the Cardenal Infante in June] it is a general rebellion without a leader and without foreign provocation—the outcome of sheer exasperation with undisciplined soldiers, who have given no little pretext for it. I assure Your Highness that it has driven me to distraction...and I see us losing an army there which it has cost what Your Highness knows to gather together.[3]

For some time Olivares seems almost to have been walking around in a dream, incapable of understanding or evaluating the news that came from Catalonia. He was prepared to allow Cardona a free hand, but failed to appreciate that this was not of much value when Cardona was given no cards to play with it. He failed, or refused, to recognize that the Catalans would never return to obedience until their wrongs had been set right and their fears put to rest. Now that the troops had retreated to two confined areas in north and south Catalonia, he could

[1] PRO: SP, 94.41, fo. 319, Hopton to Windebank, 6/16 May 1640.
[2] PRO: SP, 94.42, fo. 10, Hopton to Cottington, 15/25 July 1640.
[3] RAH: 11–10–5, leg. 6, fo. 125, Olivares to Cardenal Infante, 24 June 1640.

not understand why the rebellion should continue, and why the news from Catalonia grew steadily worse when it should be getting better.

Olivares's bewilderment at the turn of events in Catalonia would seem to be confirmed by his complete failure to exploit the social dissensions in the Principality. The spread of anarchy might have been regarded as a heaven-sent opportunity for winning back the loyalty of a ruling class which had suddenly discovered the power of the mob. But the opportunity was not so much missed as ignored. This may partly be attributed to a lack of clear information in Madrid as to exactly what was happening in Catalonia; but it must also be ascribed to the rigidity of a government which had come to hold such definite views about all things Catalan that it had lost the ability to change course when the situation demanded it.

It was hopeless to expect to recover the allegiance of the Catalan ruling class without paying attention to its complaints. That these were numerous might have been seen from the endless series of embassies that had been sent to the Court by the Catalans during the past twenty years. Yet nothing was done to assure the Catalans that they would have less ground for complaint in the future than they had had in the past, although some people in Madrid were of the opinion that such an assurance offered the only hope of ending the revolution. Matías de Novoa, the courtier who used his diary as a safety-valve for all his feelings about Olivares, had some acid remarks to make.

Our Ruler, hesitant, and nearly swamped by the weight of affairs...went around asking how he could pacify Catalonia. If he were to ask me, I should answer that it could be done by leaving it alone; by not always harrying its inhabitants; by not inflicting on them every hour for a full nineteen years, Juntas and decrees and councils, and investigations into their estates and persons; by using temperate words and temperate actions, and treating them in a way that befits the vassals of so illustrious a prince.[1]

The duke of Sessa had a suggestion of more practical value for immediate purposes. In his view, the king should go to Barcelona almost unaccompanied, 'and thus show his confidence in that nation, as Charles V did to the Flemings'.[2]

The chronicler Pellicer, who reported Sessa's suggestion, added: 'in

[1] Novoa, *MHE*, vol. LXXX, p. 225.
[2] Pellicer, 'Avisos', *Semanario Erudito*, vol. XXXI, pp. 193–4.

my opinion it was not a bad idea'. But although it might at least have been worth considering, there is no evidence that it was ever mentioned at the council table. Indeed, there is no sign that any minister during June and July offered a single constructive suggestion for preserving Catalonia's allegiance to the king. While this inability to meet a new situation with new ideas can to some extent be explained by the poor quality of many of the ministers responsible for the government of the Spanish Monarchy, it can be fully understood only in the context of the relations between the Court and the Catalans during the preceding decades. The character of those relations had been determined by the particular policy adopted by Madrid many years earlier towards the various kingdoms of the Monarchy. A friend of the duchess of Cardona told her that he had read somewhere that there were only three ways in which a prince could make sure of a province of whose loyalty he was uncertain. 'The first, to go and live in it. The second, to destroy it; and the third, to leave it with its own laws and customs, governing it in its own fashion...and being content with this, without trying to extract any further advantage from it.'[1] Of these three lines of policy, Olivares had toyed with the first, but the number of provinces subject to the king of Spain made it impracticable; and he had rejected the third because the desperate military and financial position of the Spanish Crown would not allow it. As a result, he had been gradually man-œuvred into a position in which only the second policy—destruction—remained.

The outbreak of rebellion in Catalonia put the Conde Duque in a position where he had either to carry this policy to its logical conclusion of military conquest and the abolition of the Principality's most trea-sured liberties, or else execute a complete *volte-face*. This was presum-ably what Sessa and his friends would have liked, but unfortunately it involved a *volte-face* in much more than Madrid's Catalan policy alone. Olivares's original policy not only towards Catalonia but towards all the various provinces of the Spanish Monarchy had been dictated by the exhaustion of Castile's reserves of manpower and money. As long as war continued, he had no choice but to attempt to exploit the re-sources of the other provinces; and since they would naturally resist

---

[1] 'Cartas de algunos PP. de la Compañía de Jesus', *MHE*, vol. XVI, p. 72. Letter from Duchess of Cardona to her sons, 8 Nov. 1640.

exploitation by having recourse to their privileges and immunities, those privileges and immunities would have to be systematically disregarded until one by one they had been whittled away. If a pistol held at the Conde Duque's head now compelled him to treat Catalonia's liberties with deference, the other provinces could be expected to take the hint. Catalonia simply could not be treated in isolation. A radical change in Catalan policy must be accompanied by a radical change in Olivares's treatment of all the other provinces of the Monarchy, and this entailed financial and military sacrifices on a scale that the Crown could never stand. Already an Aragonese embassy was on the way to Madrid to request relief from quartering troops and to represent that a householder's obligations were limited to the provision of water, salt, light and a bed.[1] If Olivares withdrew the army from Catalonia and exempted the Principality from quartering troops, it would be hard to ignore appeals from other provinces for similar treatment. If these were allowed, the Union of Arms would become a dead letter, Castile would once again find itself sustaining the entire burden, and the Spanish Monarchy would collapse.

All these arguments naturally assumed the continuation of the war. But what if the war could be brought to an end? The most radical solution to the Conde Duque's troubles would obviously have been to cut his losses abroad, make peace with the French, or the Dutch, or both, and then have a free hand to settle Spain's internal problems. As early as March 1640 Olivares was prepared to make big concessions, including the virtual abandonment of the duke of Lorraine, for the sake of peace.[2] But peace negotiations with Richelieu had always foundered on the same problems: the length of the proposed truce and the refusal of the cardinal to abandon his Dutch allies or compel them to give up their conquests in Brazil.[3] And if Richelieu had been as anxious as Olivares for peace in the first years of the war, it was clear that by July 1640, after the revolt of the Catalans, his interest in an immediate peace settlement had sensibly diminished,[4] and that he now lacked any serious inducement to bring pressure to bear on the Dutch.

The Dutch, for their part, had no particular desire at this moment to end a war which had become progressively more successful. As early

[1] Pellicer, 'Avisos', pp. 191–2.   [2] See above, p. 402.
[3] Leman, *Richelieu et Olivarès*, p. 169.
[4] Cánovas, *Estudios del Reinado de Felipe IV*, vol. I, p. 441, note 1.

as 1629 Olivares had made moves for a truce with the United Provinces, and he redoubled his efforts after the Dutch capture of the Brazilian towns of Olinda and Recife in 1630.[1] But all attempts at negotiation broke down on the question of Brazil. By 1635 the Conde Duque was prepared to offer the Dutch Breda and 200,000 ducats, and agree to the closing of the Scheldt, if they would return Pernambuco. But the Dutch West India Company was in no mind to abandon its valuable new acquisition. After a difficult five years, its settlers had successfully established themselves in Pernambuco, and Prince John Maurice, Count of Nassau, who took up his post as captain-general of Dutch Brazil in January 1637, extended the Dutch hold over the north-eastern coastline for a further three hundred miles.[2] Olivares was determined to prevent them from consolidating their position. After years of preparation, a new Spanish-Portuguese armada finally set out from Lisbon in September 1638 to attempt the reconquest of Brazil, but after reaching Bahia early in 1639 it did nothing for nearly a year. Then, on 12 January 1640, its Portuguese commander, the count of la Torre, was brought to battle by a Dutch fleet under half the strength of his own, and, after four days of inconclusive fighting, he abandoned his attempt to attack Pernambuco and allowed his armada to disperse to the West Indies. Dutch command of the Brazilian seas was thus assured.[3]

That Olivares was anxious to prevent the Dutch from becoming permanently established in the western hemisphere was understandable. But the importance he attached to Brazil—an importance that made him insist on its restitution as an indispensable condition for peace—sprang also from motives of domestic policy. Brazil was a possession of the Portuguese Crown, and Portugal was, if anything, even less reconciled than Catalonia to its union with Castile. As his willingness to agree to the closing of the Scheldt indicated, the Conde Duque was prepared to sacrifice even the vital interests of Flanders, so long as Portuguese interests in Brazil were preserved. The permanent loss of Brazil would have an incalculable effect on Portugal, and this was a risk that the Conde Duque simply dared not run.

Once again, therefore, Olivares found his freedom of movement

[1] Boxer, *The Dutch in Brazil*, p. 45.
[2] C. R. Boxer, *Salvador de Sá and the Struggle for Brazil and Angola, 1602–1686* (London, 1952), p. 115.
[3] *Ibid.* pp. 119–20.

sharply impaired by the looseness of the constitutional structure which held the kingdoms of the Monarchy together. He could not make peace without offending the Portuguese; he could not continue the war without offending the Catalans; and, if he compromised with the Catalans, there was no knowing how Aragon, Valencia, and even Portugal itself, would react.

That was why the Conde Duque's 'lenient' policy lacked any real meaning. The price of real 'leniency' seemed too high for Madrid to pay. Moreover, not only could a successful Catalan challenge to royal authority prove dangerously infectious, but to abandon the Catalans even momentarily to their own devices would be to invite a French invasion which the Catalans on their own would never be able to resist. But while this explains the inability of the ministers in Madrid to exchange their old Catalan policy for a new, it does not fully explain their failure to make the most of such opportunities as remained to them. They might have exploited the king's personal prestige as the father of his subjects; they might have used favours and *mercedes* and all the resources of patronage to win over individual Catalans with a large following in the Principality; and they might have taken advantage of the social dissensions within Catalonia. By July of 1640 it is very probable that none of these measures would have been successful: the differences between Catalonia and the Court were now so great and so numerous that revolution could only have been averted by far-reaching concessions such as Madrid could not possibly have made. But at least they were worth examining, and apparently they were not examined. It is hard to resist the impression that the ministers had been so exasperated by twenty years of defiance by the Catalans that, at least subconsciously, they now greeted the opportunity for the use of force almost with relief. The persistent effort to hold themselves in check year after year as the Catalans persistently obstructed their designs had gradually told upon them. Always antipathetic to the Catalans and their liberties, and weary of displaying what seemed to them a heroic self-restraint, they watched the gradual deterioration of the Catalan situation with an alarm not untouched by a certain degree of perverse satisfaction.

Every fresh piece of bad news from the Principality was received during July as further proof of Catalonia's innate iniquity. That the royal ministers could not appear publicly in safety; that Barcelona and the other towns were reported to be laying in arms and working on their fortifications—all this was outrageous. By the time of Cardona's death, Olivares and his colleagues seem, perhaps without realizing it, to have closed their minds to the possibility of anything other than a solution by force. It was as if they were sitting waiting for confirmation that military intervention was the sole policy now open to them. The confirmation they so confidently expected was not long in coming.

With the virtual loss of Barcelona to the Crown, its place had been taken by Tortosa as the port from which troops were sent to Italy and provisions to the remnants of the army in Rosselló. At the beginning of July, when 300,000 ducats were on their way to Tortosa for the payment of the troops, and when the infantry were being assembled and reorganized in the surrounding country, the Tortosa populace began to be restive.[1] The town authorities took prompt action, and serious trouble was averted. But three weeks later a letter was received by the town councillors urging Tortosa to revolt because the troops arriving in the town were to be used against the Principality.[2] The meeting of the town council on 21 July to discuss the contents of this letter coincided with the arrival in Tortosa of a considerable quantity of powder to be stored in the castle. When the council was brought news of this, it sent a request to the *batlle general*, Don Lluís Monsuar, who was responsible for maintaining amicable relations between the town and the military, that the powder should be placed not in the castle but in the municipal stores. Monsuar refused on the grounds that the populace could be trusted, but he was wrong. As the powder was being brought to the castle, the populace rioted, seized the powder, took what it wanted and blew up the rest. The riot then took a familar course. Shouting 'Treachery!' and 'Long live the land!' the mob sacked the houses of a town councillor and of certain officials connected with the welfare of the infantry, and laid siege to the castle in which Monsuar had taken refuge. Don Pedro de Velasco, an Aragonese inspector of the army, was killed, but intervention by the Tortosa clergy saved the life of Monsuar and of the soldiers either stationed or convalescing in the town. With a gesture unique in the annals of the Catalan revolution, the leaders of the mob ordered the troops to leave the town for Valencia,

[1] AGS: GA, leg. 1329, Junta de Ejecución, 14 July 1640.
[2] ACA: CA, leg. 391, account of events in Tortosa by Don Lluís Monsuar.

and actually handed out a *real* to be divided between every three men who passed through the gates.

The viceroy of Valencia, in sending the news of the Tortosa disturbances to Madrid, suggested that they were caused by 'the fear that Your Majesty intended to introduce into their land both the laws of Castile and *vellón* coinage'—a long-standing fear in the Crown of Aragon and one which, unless it were laid, could well lead to revolt in Valencia and Aragon also.[1] Olivares dismissed this suggestion with the remark that Don Fernando de Borja, the viceroy of Valencia, was a 'man who makes a mystery of everything',[2] but he was in no mood to play down the gravity of the recent events in Tortosa. They were 'extremely serious, because at the very least they obstruct the passage of troops and deprive us of a good port; and they involve placing an extra burden on the innocent kingdoms....A serious affair, a very serious affair', which demanded a thorough reappraisal of policy.

The reappraisal was carried out on 31 July. Olivares represented to the Junta de Ejecución that the news from Catalonia grew worse every day, taking into account the fact that

not a single one of the lenient measures advocated by Your Majesty in your surpassing goodness has been of any use....Not only is there no sign of the province growing more peaceful, but the spirit of sedition is spreading, as can be seen from the Tortosa affair. Therefore I consider it absolutely necessary to decide whether the measures to be taken should be public or secret, although certain measures have already been taken with the greatest possible circumspection.[3]

The Conde Duque's assessment of the state of Catalonia and his suggestions for corrective measures were unanimously approved by his colleagues. Not all of them went quite as far as José González, who described his master's speech as inspired by the Holy Spirit,[4] but none had any fault to find. Pedro de Arce said that things had reached such a pass that 'it is essential to dissimulate no longer and to use rigorous measures, because gentle measures have been attempted by the Conde Duque ever since Corpus without any effect'. Even Balbases joined in the general chorus of approval. 'Even if this affair had not occurred at Tortosa, there were sufficient reasons before this' for a punitive action

[1] AGS: GA, leg. 1329, Junta de Ejecución, 27 July 1640.
[2] *Ibid.*   [3] AGS: GA, leg. 1329, Junta de Ejecución, 31 July 1640.
[4] AGS: GA, leg. 1329, Junta de Ejecución y Consejeros de Estado, 31 July 1640.

against the Catalans, 'although I confess that the thought of making war against a province of Spain appals me, especially with France so close'.

Although one or two other ministers hinted at the risk of intervention by the French, it was generally agreed that this was less of a danger than the repercussions of Catalonia's behaviour in other provinces if they saw the Catalans escape unpunished. 'For the peace and tranquillity of that province', the Junta decided, 'it is essential to hold Cortes, because what has to be done cannot be done without new laws, nor can things be properly managed without a Cortes.' In fact, Olivares was now determined to carry out the plans so often debated and so often discarded—to force the Union of Arms through the Catalan Corts under the threatening shadow of an army. But he can hardly have failed to regret that he had left it until so late. In 1635 he still had reserves of troops and the danger of effective French intervention was not so considerable. In 1640 the hazards were infinitely greater and an army was much less easily raised. Even if certain military preparations had already been made in Castile, it was no small matter to organize an army and have it ready to enter Catalonia in September, as the Junta required.

Olivares himself had few illusions as to what would happen if his plans miscarried.

If the action unanimously approved by the Council of Aragon and all the members of the Council of State and the entire Junta de Ejecución should go wrong [he wrote in what might almost be his Catalan testament], it is very possible that all the kingdoms of Spain will either be (if I dare say it) absolutely lost or else in such terrible danger, misery and tribulation that only a miracle can save them, and our affairs abroad in such a terrible state that we should have to abandon all our allies in order to make peace, however infamous.[1]

In spite of this, the risk must be taken, but Olivares's own words make it clear that his immediate intention was not that total abolition of Catalonia's laws and liberties with which Catalan historians have credited him.[2] The Principality was to be reduced to a state in which it

---

[1] AGS: GA, leg. 1329, paper by Olivares of 11 Aug. 1640.

[2] E.g. F. de Sagarra, *La Unitat Catalana en 1640* (Barcelona, 1931), p. 9. Further proof that Olivares only intended a limited alteration of the Catalan constitutions rather than their total abolition is provided by the fact that in September a special Junta was carefully examining all the constitutions put forward by the Catalans in the Corts of 1626 (AGS: GA, leg. 1330, Junta de Cortes, 18 Sept. 1640).

could be deprived '*only of those laws which specifically obstruct good govern-ment and the administration of justice, and which stand in the way of uniformity with the other kingdoms of the Crown*;[1] and secondly, of whatever pre-vents the billeting of an army in moderation, so long as it is necessary to have one there'. Even now he seems to have entertained faint hopes that military action might be avoided. He still thought that it might be possible to open the eyes of the Diputats:

I cannot in any way reject the possibilities of negotiation until the last possible moment; and I would even go so far as to agree that if a way could be found of billeting that army safely, even on moderate terms so long as there were no clashes, I would be willing to put up with everything else for the time being, and leave things in their present state until a better time. But to question whether the army is really necessary at a time when we are at war, and to attempt to shift it from disobedient and disloyal provinces on to those which are faithful and resigned—this is inconceivable, and cannot from any stand-point be right or reasonable.

Although the Conde Duque appears to have been much more alive to the risks he was running than were many of his colleagues who so enthusiastically supported his proposals, he still showed a surprising optimism. He looked upon the campaign as a fifteen-day affair. If the army entered Catalonia on 1 October, or even on the 15th, the French could not possibly have sufficient troops ready to intervene in strength. The assumption that the action would quickly be over tended to under-estimate the possibilities of Catalan resistance and to exaggerate the abilities of Spanish generals. The marquis of los Vélez, who was to command the army, was sadly lacking in military experience and repeatedly said that he would rather be a humble water-carrier than a soldier.[2] But the army itself, at least on paper, looked more than adequate. It was to consist of 1990 cavalry and 35,538 infantry, of whom 7000 were soldiers of the Cantabrian army, 18,000 members of the Castilian militia, and the remainder drawn from the various frontier fortresses.[3] This information inspired the Junta de Ejecución to rapturous applause of the Conde Duque:

[1] My italics.
[2] AGS: GA, leg. 1374, Junta Grande, 15 Feb. 1641. That such an unsuitable appointment can have been made must be taken as further evidence of the *falta de cabezas*—the lack of leaders—of which Olivares was always complaining.
[3] AGS: GA, leg. 1329, *Relación de lo que SM tiene resuelto para castigo de lo sucedido en Tortosa...*, 11 Aug. 1640.

The Junta must confess to Your Majesty that the role of the Conde has been as might have been expected of a person of his wisdom; and without doubt much is owed to his zeal and vigilance, for by night and day and at every hour he thinks of nothing but ways of furthering Your Majesty's service....The preparations are so far advanced that it seems impossible that so much could have been achieved in so short a time.[1]

While the government in Madrid hurried on with its preparations for the army to be sent against Catalonia, the Catalans themselves had not neglected certain obvious precautions. As soon as Cardona died, the rumour spread through Catalonia that if the new viceroy was a bishop, it could only mean that the king intended to use force against the Principality.[2] The bishop of Barcelona, Garcí Gil Manrique, was duly appointed viceroy at the end of July and took the oath of office on 3 August.[3] But to everybody except himself it was obvious that he was a cipher, and he was treated as such from the beginning. Ignoring the pleas of the bishop, the Principality continued to work hard at its defences. The Catalan towns were scrambling among themselves to obtain weapons and ammunition. A representative of Girona, on a mission to Barcelona to buy up to five hundred pieces of artillery managed to conclude a deal for six pieces just before the agent for Lleida had time to intervene.[4] Barcelona itself, as early as 9 July, had been sent a letter by Don Aleix de Senmenat offering to sell it between five hundred and a thousand muskets, to be delivered in August.[5] In view of Senmenat's connections as a frontier baron, it is to be presumed that these arms came from France.

The Diputats had a double object in encouraging the Catalan towns to press forward with their defences. Rumours of an intended invasion of the Principality by a royal army obviously made it necessary to prepare for any eventuality; but it was also essential for Claris's purposes that the Principality should be able to show itself capable of resisting invasion by the French without the need to appeal for outside help. This argument of Catalonia's military self-sufficiency was the most important of all those presented by the Diputats for the with-

[1] AGS: GA, leg. 1329, Junta de Ejecución, 11 Aug. 1640.
[2] Rubí, *Levantamiento*, fo. 117v.
[3] ACA: CA, leg. 288, no. 57, Bishop of Barcelona to King, 4 Aug. 1640.
[4] AMG: Corresp. 1640–9, Magi Pujol to Jurats of Girona, 28 July 1640.
[5] AHB: Delibs., 1640, letter from Senmenat between fos. 254 and 255.

32-2

drawal of the soldiers. It was very hard to demand convincingly that the king should remove all his troops from Catalan soil if the Catalans themselves were unable to bar a French entry into Spain. Therefore the Diputats must be able to prove to Olivares that Catalonia could raise an army of 30,000 or 40,000 men. They took this very seriously and wrote to the various towns asking for exact numbers of the men and munitions they could provide in the event of invasion.[1] But if the Diputats themselves really believed that the Principality could put and keep 40,000 men in the field, their belief was not shared by the ministers in Madrid. During July and August Olivares's conversations with the ambassadors of the Diputació always returned to the question of the 40,000 men. Where would they find the men? How could the Principality arm them and pay them?[2] The ambassadors answered as best they could, the intrepid Jeroni de Navel fighting a heroic rearguard action,[3] but it was hard to believe, on the record of the Principality during the past twelve months, that the figure of 40,000 was anything but arbitrary and unrealistic.

Even as the Diputats protested their ability to raise 40,000 armed men, they were seeking to strengthen their ties with France. After the death of Cardona, and the return of Tamarit to Barcelona, Don Aleix de Senmenat had arrived at Perpinyà on the pretext that he had come to get married.[4] While waiting for his dispensation to come through, he spent his time accumulating weapons for sale in Catalonia, but this was not his sole activity. Some time during the middle of August he seems to have taken over from Vilaplana the conduct of the secret negotiations with Espenan.[5] News of these negotiations reached the ears of Don Juan de Garay, the commander of the troops in Rosselló, and on 23 August he arrested Senmenat as he was about to leave Perpinyà. At the same time he arrested two or three other important figures suspected of associating with the French: Don Gabriel de Llupià, the son of Don Joan de Llupià, the most influential noble in Perpinyà; Canon Ros, a canon of Elna; Dr Subirà, assessor of the Capitania General, who played an ambiguous part in the contraband

[1] ACA: G, LT, 1640–1, fo. 24, Diputats to Consellers of Granollers, 22 Aug. 1640.
[2] AGS: GA, leg. 1329, Junta de Ejecución, 14 Aug. 1640.
[3] ACA: CA, leg. 286, no. 135, Junta of Council of Aragon, 1 Sept. 1640.
[4] AGS: GA, leg. 1329, Juan de Garay to Olivares, 29 Aug. 1640.
[5] Sanabre, *Acción de Francia*, pp. 93–4.

controversy; and Jacint Ams, a citizen of Perpinyà, well known in Rosselló and Barcelona for his commercial activities.[1] Ams had nominally been engaged in buying 2500 French sheep for the Barcelona meat market. When Garay only gave him a licence to import five hundred a week, he slipped into France and passed more than 5000 sheep into Spain by way of Conflent. Since his visit to France happened to coincide with the meeting between Espenan and Senmenat, Garay took the hint and decided to make sure of his person.[2]

The news of the arrests caused consternation in Barcelona. The Diputats at once summoned the Braços which sent a deputation to protest to the viceroy. He replied, quite truthfully, that he was not even aware of the arrests,[3] and wrote anxiously to Garay begging him not to provoke a complete break with the Catalans because this might entail the loss of the Principality and the ruin of Spain.[4] Everyone knew that the viceroy was quite without authority, and that the remedy could never come from him. 'The whole country is tired of putting up with such oppression and acts of violence by the soldiers', wrote the Diputats to Manlleu.[5] If anything was to be done, it was they alone who could do it, and they laid their plans accordingly.

A royal proclamation had been published in Madrid on 19 August announcing the king's intention to hold Cortes in Aragon and Valencia, 'and conclude those of Catalonia...restoring in that Principality the free exercise of justice, which has been violated and made impossible by certain wicked and seditious persons...'.[6] The Diputats decided to respond by summoning their own Corts. The plan was discussed by a special Junta of eighteen nominees of the Diputats and accepted by the Braços on 2 September.[7] The meeting was to be called for 10 September, and its purpose, neatly duplicating that of the official Corts as proclaimed by the king, was to 'restore justice' in the Principality. As a convocation of the Braços, its composition differed significantly from that of the ordinary Corts. Whereas the Corts consisted of single

---

[1] He is incorrectly described by Sanabre, p. 97, as a canon of Elna. His name was spelt indifferently Ams, Am or Ham.
[2] Garay to Olivares, 29 Aug. 1640.
[3] ACA: G, Dietari, 1638–41, part III, fos. 426–8.
[4] AGS: GA, leg. 1329, Viceroy to Garay, 27 Aug. 1640.
[5] ACA: G, LT, 1640–1, fos. 45–7, Diputats to Manlleu, 1 Sept. 1640.
[6] 'Jesuitas', *MHE*, vol. xv, p. 467.
[7] ACA: G, Dietari, 1638–41, part III, fo. 442.

representatives from towns and cathedral chapters, those eligible for a meeting of the Braços were far more numerous, and included all *ciutadans honrats* and all canons who could manage to come to Barcelona. Motions were proposed by the Diputat Eclesiàstic as president, and resolutions were approved by a majority vote. It is not clear whether there was any precedent for such a meeting, announced as it was by special proclamations throughout the Principality. The Diputats rather dubiously maintained that precedents did exist, but explained that, even if they did not, their action was fully justified by the needs of 'natural defence' and was therefore permitted by 'divine and human law'.[1] The irony of employing exactly the same justification as that used by Olivares for disregarding Catalonia's privileges may perhaps have escaped them.

The Diputats had two purposes in summoning the special Braços: to attempt to restore order in the Principality and, less explicitly, to secure approval for the measures taken by the Diputats in organizing resistance to Madrid. In effect, the Braços were to be presented with a *fait accompli.* As soon as the decision had been taken to summon them for 10 September, Vilaplana left Barcelona, crossed the frontier, and reopened the discussions with Espenan, so abruptly broken off by the arrest of Senmenat. On 7 September they signed an agreement of which one copy was sent to Claris at Barcelona, and another was sent to the king of France.[2] An informal alliance between the Principality and France had therefore already been arranged before the Estates actually met.

The Braços opened at three o'clock on the afternoon of 10 September. The meeting was attended on the opening day by thirty-four ecclesiastics, of whom four were abbots, and the rest canons, no bishops having accepted; 144 members of the *estament militar* and 70 of the *estament reial.*[3] Three hours were spent in the reading of a long paper presented by the Diputats, listing all the atrocities committed by the troops, and answering point by point the eight charges against the Catalans which had been drawn up in Madrid: the attack on the royal troops, the release of Tamarit, the burning of Monrodón, the murder of Dr Berart and of Santa Coloma, the persecution of the royal

[1] ACA: G, LT, 1640–1, fos. 131–3, Diputats to Manlleu, 29 Sept. 1640.
[2] Sanabre, p. 94.
[3] ACA: G, Dietari, 1638–41, part III, fo. 448.

ministers, the obstruction of government, and the fortification of the Principality without royal authorization.[1] After the reading was finished, the session was adjourned until 13 September to allow time for more delegates to arrive.[2]

The relatively small size of the gathering on the opening day was a matter for some concern, since it might give the impression to the outside world that many Catalans had doubts of the legality of the proceedings, or else were anxious not to implicate themselves too deeply in what might later be regarded as a treasonable conspiracy. On 12 September the Diputats decided that all those eligible to attend should be ordered to appear at Barcelona within six days, under threat of heavy penalties.[3] Even threats do not seem to have been very successful: the Braços, resumed on 13 September, were never very well attended. But the poor attendance finally worked to Claris's advantage. While delegates from distant parts of the Principality arrived late and in disorganized parties, those from Barcelona and its neighbourhood had already been in session for some days and provided a solid bloc on which Claris and his friends could depend in an emergency.[4] On the suggestion of the Diputats, the Braços agreed to the creation of a special Junta of thirty-six to take charge of all matters relating to the defence of the Principality.[5] This effectively transferred all real authority from the Braços to a hand-picked body of close supporters of the Diputats. At the same time Claris finally made sure of Barcelona's support. On 17 September the Consell de Cent voted that the Diputats should be asked to appoint a commander 'of any nationality' for the forces now being raised for the defence of Catalonia.[6] This was tantamount to formal approval by the city of Barcelona of the Diputats' policy in seeking a French alliance. With the establishment of a special Junta for war and the assurance of Barcelona's backing, the Diputats were safe. 'Take heart', they wrote to Vilaplana on the day of the Consell de Cent's vote. 'Things are going well.'[7]

The negotiations with France were now common knowledge. While

[1] This paper is printed in *MHE*, vol. xxi, doc. no. 229, along with many other documents relating to the Braços.
[2] AMG: Corresp., 1640–9, Rafael Vivet and Antoni Martí to Jurats of Girona, 11 Sept. 1640.
[3] Dietari, 1638–41, part III, fo. 457.
[4] Rubí, *Levantamiento*, fo. 128v.
[5] *MHE*, vol. xxi, doc. 233.   [6] *Ibid.* doc. 238.
[7] ACA: G, LT, 1640–1, fo. 85, Diputats to Vilaplana, 17 Sept. 1640.

the Junta of thirty-six set about appointing commanders and organizing the defences, Espenan and Vilaplana were each joined by men of higher category—Duplessis Besançon and Don Ramon de Guimerà—to carry the negotiations a stage further. On 24 September the four men met in the Capuchin convent in the town of Ceret, and Guimerà presented a document to the French plenipotentiaries on behalf of the Diputació. This contained a formal request for the favour of the king of France 'in the war with which the Principality is threatened by the ministers of Spain', and for the assistance of up to two thousand cavalry and six thousand infantry, together with arms and munitions.[1] Duplessis at once left with this petition for the Court of Saint Germain, to seek new instructions.[2]

Now that the Principality had officially asked for French help, and had promised 'perpetual brotherhood' with France in return, the Diputats had burnt their boats. Claris knew that there was no going back. This made his position during the next few weeks particularly delicate, for there was always a possibility that Madrid might suddenly reverse its policy and seek a negotiated instead of an imposed settlement with the Principality. There were, indeed, signs that this was happening. Olivares was in an extremely pessimistic frame of mind.

This year [he wrote in a long memorandum of mid-September on the events of 1640] can undoubtedly be considered the most unfortunate that this Monarchy has ever experienced...because never have such great preparations been made in all theatres of war, and yet the results have been far worse than could ever have been imagined....[3] And all this together must be regarded as far less disastrous than the rebellion and obduracy of Catalonia, for one cannot talk of success in an action against one's own vassals, in which all gain must be loss. We have been reduced to a new war inside Spain which is already costing millions, at a time when we are already in fearful straits.[4]

It was probably these considerations, together with the discovery that the Catalans were already in close touch with the French, that prompted the Conde Duque to summon Manlleu for a long interview on 18 September, in which he made a final bid for a peaceful settlement. After complaining of the Principality's behaviour in taking up arms,

[1] Sanabre, p. 99. [2] Sanabre, p. 101.
[3] In particular, the French had captured Arras in August.
[4] AHN: Est., leg. 674, *El Conde mi Señor sobre el estado en que han quedado las armas este año....*

'His Excellency offered to give a document signed by His Majesty's hand and personally guaranteed by His Majesty, that he would not abolish any of the privileges and constitutions, but would maintain them all...'.[1]

In the light of the Conde Duque's comments on the disastrous state of the Spanish Monarchy and the tragedy of the embroilment with Catalonia, this offer has the ring of sincerity. At the very least it may be interpreted as an effort to keep the door to negotiation open. Assarino, in his contemporary history, claims that Manlleu's letters reporting Olivares's willingness to negotiate were answered with a rejection by the Junta of thirty-six. The Braços considered the Junta's reply too extreme, but Claris had taken care to despatch it before the Braços saw it, so that it was too late for anything to be done.[2] It is impossible to determine the truth of this allegation, or of a further allegation that Claris employed a confidant to write letters from Madrid insisting that the Court would never show mercy to the Catalans.[3] In spite of this, the charge is not inherently improbable. Although Claris was very careful in his negotiations with France to avoid a complete break with the king of Spain, it was obvious that, rightly or wrongly, he had come to the conclusion that Olivares and the Protonotario could not be trusted, and there was no hope of a peaceful settlement so long as they remained in power. 'The Conde Duque and the Protonotario from 1626 until today have been the enemies of our nation, and have lost no occasion to show it.'[4] Even if they gave way before Catalan resistance this time, they would soon find another opportunity to oppress the Principality. It was therefore essential to reject their blandishments, and this was only possible if those Catalans who still hankered for a peaceful solution were made to realize that their hopes were vain. Hence the letters from the confidant in Madrid, and the fierce personal attacks on Olivares and the Protonotario which the Diputats were now busily sponsoring.

Although one waxed hot when the other waxed cold, there were certain curious similarities in the attitudes and policies of Claris and

---

[1] AMG: Corresp. 1640–9, copy of letter from Manlleu to Diputats, 22 Sept. 1640.
[2] Assarino, *Rivolutioni*, pp. 143–4.
[3] The story of the confidant is told by Assarino, p. 141, by Rubí, *Levantamiento*, fo. 125 v, and by Tormé i Liori, p. 243.
[4] Diputats to Manlleu, 22 Sept. 1640, *MHE*, vol. XXI, p. 114.

Olivares. Claris had no real desire for war against his king; Olivares had no real desire for war against the Principality. Each had gradually been driven into a position in which war seemed inescapable. For Olivares, the moment had come with the revolt of Tortosa at the end of July; for Claris, it had come with the formal commitment to France. Olivares in September might still hope to avert war, but his attitude to the Catalans remained unchanged and he still stood by the policies which had originally driven them to take up arms. It is a striking testimony to his ambivalent approach to Catalonia that in the very same paper in which he remarked that all gain was loss in a war with one's own vassals, he was also capable of envisaging the advantages of a successful campaign against the Catalans. 'Once things are settled, I take it that, with what Catalonia will be able to give, there will be sufficient Spaniards to send to Italy, Alsace or the Tyrol.'[1] Like a will-o'-the-wisp the Union of Arms continued to lure him on.

Half in anguish, half with relief, Olivares and Claris found themselves leading their countries into war, and each took elaborate steps to justify his action to the world at large. In addition to Madrid's formal accusations against the Principality,[2] elaborate papers justifying the behaviour of the government were being drafted by a battery of publicists and pamphleteers habitually employed by the Conde Duque on such occasions. All documents which might provide useful ammunition were handed to the government's leading propagandist, Guillén de la Carrera;[3] the result was a pamphlet which, after expatiating on the happy situation of Catalonia, 'the province which, of all those in Europe, has been least burdened in the present calamities', examined the various demands put forward by the Catalans and showed why they were impracticable or unreasonable.[4] Guillén was not alone. By the end of October, at least four other papers were circulating in Madrid justifying the policies of the government, all of them 'speaking of the Catalans with the delicacy which a father might use in speaking of a son, or a gallant of his mistress'.[5]

[1] Olivares's paper, AHN: Est., leg. 674.
[2] See above, pp. 502–3.
[3] AGS: GA, leg. 1329, note from Pedro de Villanueva to Guillén de la Carrera, 14 Aug. 1640.
[4] BC: Fullet Bonsoms 5426, *Papel del Sr. Don Alonso Guillén de la Carrera*.
[5] Pellicer, 'Avisos', p. 230. One at least of these, *Porqué? Paraqué?*, is in BC: Fullet Bonsoms 5427.

The Diputació showed an equal vigour, if less restraint, in its own defence. It summoned a special Junta of theologians which was able to produce numerous grave arguments from Aquinas, Suárez and others explaining why the Principality was fully entitled to take up arms in its own defence.[1] Less erudite, and more effective, was the famous *Proclamación Católica*, published in Barcelona in October,[2] 'in which in thirty-eight articles or paragraphs they represent to His Majesty the causes of their action, and conclude with the greatest effrontery ever displayed by vassals to their king, by maintaining that the Señor Conde Duque and the Señor Protonotario have destroyed the Monarchy'.[3] It was written by an Augustinian friar, Gaspar Sala.[4] From the time of the publication of the *Proclamación Católica*, Sala became the Catalan equivalent of Guillén de la Carrera. He was rewarded for his pains with the creation of a special chair of theology at Barcelona,[5] and eventually became abbot of Sant Cugat.

While the pamphlet warfare was being furiously waged, both sides were preparing for more serious hostilities. Here again, Claris and Olivares found themselves confronted with very similar problems. Each was afraid of treason and conspiracy. In Madrid, a warrant was issued for the arrest of a certain Don Bartolomé de Goicoechea, a wealthy and well-connected man, who had publicly said that the Catalans had done well to revolt, and the Castilians had done badly not to follow suit.[6] In Barcelona, the Braços agreed that a general oath of loyalty should be taken to the province, and that all who refused should be treated as 'traitors to the fatherland'.[7]

Both leaders encountered very serious difficulties in raising and equipping an army. The Diputació had no money, and it was essential to levy new taxes. An impost of 5 per cent was placed on the income of all ecclesiastics,[8] and elaborate plans were prepared for a general inquiry into private incomes throughout the Principality. This was to be very thorough. Those responsible were reminded that 'in Catalonia there are many houses both of peasants and others in which are living younger brothers and other persons who possess their own properties, many of

[1] *MHE*, vol. XXI, doc. 251.
[2] BC: Fullet Bonsoms 5229, *Proclamación Católica a la Magestad piadosa de Felipe el Grande*....
[3] Pellicer, 'Avisos', pp. 229–30.
[4] AHB: Delibs., 1640, fo. 349.   [5] *Ibid.* fo. 340.
[6] Pellicer, 'Avisos', p. 213.   [7] *MHE*, vol. XXI, doc. 242.
[8] AMG: Corresp., 1640–9, Claris to Jurats of Girona, 20 Sept. 1640.

them believed to be of considerable value'. They were also told not to neglect servants earning over 9 *lliures* a year.[1] In October the Junta of thirty-six decided to increase the *dret del general* by 4*d.* a pound on everything except cloths, which were already paying 10 per cent. It was estimated that this would increase its value by 12,000 *lliures* a year. It was also agreed to increase the *dret de la bolla* on silk goods by 1*s.* in the pound, making it equal to the tax already placed on woollen goods, and probably yielding a similar revenue of 16,000 *lliures* annually.[2] In the same month, the city of Barcelona augmented its revenues by appropriating the royal patrimony which had served as security for the city's loan to the king in 1632.[3]

The difficulties in raising money were nothing to those encountered in raising troops. The disorders in the towns and countryside had not abated during the autumn, in spite of the efforts of the Diputats, the nobility and town councillors to reimpose authority, and they were seriously interfering with the preparations for war. A proclamation issued by the Diputats on 24 October tells its own sad story.

It has come to our notice that in various parts of the Principality and Comtats many vagabonds have assembled, having neither house nor home, nor work nor livelihood, and are going around in gangs armed with *pedrenyals*, wandering through the towns, disturbing and interfering with the levying of troops for the garrisons, threatening the officials and other persons responsible for these levies, and seriously delaying military preparations....[4]

But recruiting was hampered not only by the wandering bands who resisted all authority and kept Catalonia in a state of constant uproar, but also by the general reluctance of the mass of the population to come forward for the defence of the fatherland. By the end of September, reports were coming into the Diputació from all parts of the Principality of the refusal of the population to undertake military service.[5] Early in October the Diputats found it necessary to set up a special tribunal to punish villages and individuals who refused to obey the orders for mobilisation. It was an exact repetition of the story of 1639,

[1] AMG: Corresp., 1640–9, paper sent by Girona syndics to Jurats of Girona.
[2] AMG: Corresp., 1640–9, resolution by Braços, 22 Oct. 1640.
[3] AHB: Delibs., 1640, fo. 340.
[4] AMG: Corresp., 1640–9, proclamation by Claris, 24 Oct. 1640.
[5] See Sanabre, pp. 105–6.

except that on this occasion the enemy were the Castilians, not the French, and the whips were being wielded by the ministers not of the Crown but of Catalonia's own Diputació. There could hardly have been more striking confirmation of the theme which runs right through Sanz's diary of events in Vic, that public spirit no longer existed, and that each thought only of himself. The gradual disintegration of Catalan society during the past few decades had brought in its train a moral collapse which ruined the chances of the Catalan revolution from the outset.

The failure of the Catalans to come forward in their own defence forced Claris to place more and more reliance on the French. Duplessis Besançon arrived in Barcelona from France on 20 October and received a great welcome from the Diputació. His first meeting with Claris was not, however, without a certain irony. Rather surprisingly, none of the Diputats understood French, and Duplessis was forced to address them in Castilian. Claris was obliged to answer in the same language, and prefaced his discourse with an expression of regret that he had to 'speak the language of a nation for which they all held an aversion'.[1] Discussions between Duplessis and the Diputats continued for a week, in an atmosphere that was not particularly cordial. The Diputats still hesitated to renounce their allegiance to Philip IV, and insisted, in the classic manner of revolutionaries, that their revolution was directed solely against the king's evil counsellors.[2] They also hesitated to give the French full facilities for disembarking troops, but agreed to allow French ships to use Catalan ports, and to pay for the upkeep of the three thousand men to be sent to the Principality by France. They were forced to agree to the despatch of nine hostages to France, as a guarantee of the safety of the French troops in Catalonia.

Claris could not feel particularly happy about the French conditions, but there was no other way of defending a province which was unwilling to defend itself, and at least he could be sure of French assistance. He might perhaps have felt more confidence had he known of the troubles of Olivares. The army for the invasion of Catalonia had been assembled with great difficulty, and did not present, in the eyes of the English ambassador, a very awe-inspiring spectacle. 'Though the Catalans be weak in comparison with the king, yet they will keep their strength together better, for the king's army consists of married men

---

[1] AAE: Corresp. Espagne, Sup. no. 3, fo. 198 v.   [2] Sanabre, p. 103.

who long to be at home, and of gentlemen, the most part whereof have hardly means to set themselves on horseback.... Some of them begin to absent themselves already.'[1] There is every indication that by the autumn of 1640 Olivares was faced with an acute crisis of manpower. His attempts to mobilize the Spanish nobility and gentry had proved a miserable failure: only some nine hundred to fourteen hundred of them had arrived to take part in the Catalan campaign, after many months of threats and inducements by the government.[2] The governors of provinces like Galicia were writing that it was utterly impossible for them to raise a single volunteer, and populations would flee at the sight of a recruiting sergeant.[3]

It was obvious that the resources of the Spanish Monarchy were now strained to the utmost. The English ambassador sensed the impending collapse: 'An ill success would put the affairs of this Crown in a worse case than were now fit for the state of Christendom, which begins already to be unequally balanced.'[4] The Conde Duque himself, seeing new and more terrible implications every day in the Catalan revolt, was in a state of anguish:

In the midst of all our troubles, the Catalan is the worst we have ever had, and my heart admits of no consolation that we are entering an action in which, if our army kills, it kills a vassal of His Majesty, and if they kill, they kill a vassal and a soldier.... Without reason or occasion they have thrown themselves into as complete a rebellion as Holland, for news has today arrived that they have signed an agreement with the French and placed themselves under the protection of that king....[5]

It might have been thought that, with the army of los Vélez in a highly precarious situation, and French military assistance to Catalonia now certain, the sooner the Principality could be invaded, the better. But Olivares still seems to have entertained hopes that the Catalans might yet see reason, although the bishop of Barcelona wrote to say that there was no hope of success in the duchess of Cardona's efforts at mediation, and the time for negotiation was past.[6] Perhaps because of

[1] PRO: SP, 94.42, fo. 40, Hopton to Windebank, 12/22 Sept. 1640.
[2] Domínguez Ortiz, 'La movilización de la nobleza castellana en 1640', *Anuario de Historia del Derecho Español*, vol. xxv (1955), p. 811.
[3] AGS: GA, leg. 1368, Marquis of Valparaíso to King, 18 Nov. 1640.
[4] PRO: SP, 94.42, fo. 51, Hopton to Windebank, 22 Sept./2 Oct. 1640 .
[5] RAH: 11–10–5, leg. 6, Olivares to Cardenal Infante, 10 Oct. 1640.
[6] ACA: CA, leg. 391, Bishop of Barcelona to King, 11 Oct. 1640.

Olivares's hopes of a negotiated settlement, and also because of the un-
preparedness of the army, all of October was wasted. It was only at the
end of the month that los Vélez reported that he had ordered the army
to move towards the Catalan frontier as a preliminary to its entry into
the province.[1]

Even now there were many delays. The viceroy of Aragon, the duke
of Nochera, wrote to Madrid that although the orders were promptly
given, it took time to have an army of 20,000 in marching order. The
artillery train had to be brought from Guipúzcoa to Aragon, and new
gun-carriages had to be provided for it in Zaragoza, where the necessary materials were not available and had to be brought from elsewhere.
Moreover, the inclement weather would affect the figures for the
conscripts, of whom every day there were less. Nochera used these
unpleasant facts as a pretext for one final effort to dissuade Madrid
from armed intervention. If the king were victorious, it would be
a bloody victory, and Catalonia would be ruined. If he lost, Aragon
and Navarre would be in danger. 'Since the province is holding
out for only two points—the withdrawal of the troops and merciful
treatment with a guarantee to maintain its *fueros*—the matter does
not appear impossible of settlement at the present time.... It is highly
dangerous to punish vassals when there is a powerful enemy next
door...'.[2]

Nochera's plea was dismissed by the Junta de Ejecución on the
grounds that he was insufficiently informed. Now that the army was
actually on the move, the Junta was once again in an intransigent mood.
Further attempts at negotiation through the duchess of Cardona would
only delay its progress until the coming of winter made campaigning
impossible. 'Having worked so hard to form an army, and being on
the point of plucking the fruit, this is not the time to stop.' Olivares
added as a personal postscript that 'no one was as anxious for a settlement as he'.[3] But the army continued its march.

On 23 November it entered Tortosa, where the marquis of los Vélez
took his oath as viceroy of Catalonia in succession to the despised and
forgotten bishop of Barcelona. On 27 November it began serious

[1] ACA: CA, leg. 233, no. 74, Los Vélez to ?, 25 Oct. 1640.
[2] Nochera to King, 6 Nov. 1640 (*MHE*, vol. xxi, doc. 370), and see Adolphe Coster,
Baltasar Gracián (Paris, 1913), pp. 42–4.
[3] AGS: GA, leg. 1331, Junta de Ejecución, 5 Nov. 1640.

military operations with the capture of Xerta, and on 8 December the main body of the army left Tortosa and started advancing northwards along the coastal route. Catalan resistance was weak and ineffectual, but even in these early days of the campaign, los Vélez did not display any marked capacity either as a commander or as a viceroy charged with a peculiarly delicate mission. His instructions had stipulated that as soon as the army entered Catalonia, all matters of government and administration should be left to native ministers, 'so as to prove that it is not my intention to alter their constitutions and privileges'.[1] It was quite clear from the tenor of these instructions that everything possible should be done to reassure the Catalans, and the royal proclamation issued by los Vélez on crossing into the Principality had expressly promised that the army would 'enter peaceably'.[2] In spite of this, the surrender of a Catalan defence force of some six hundred men at Cambrils on 15 December was followed by the massacre of the prisoners and the execution of their commanders. This was an act of disastrous folly. Until the massacre at Cambrils, the Catalans were surrendering with scarcely a struggle, and the campaign had proved little more than a leisurely military promenade. But the massacre confirmed all the Catalans' worst fears of Castilian intentions, and removed all possibilities of a rapid and relatively bloodless termination of the Catalan revolution.[3]

While the marquis of los Vélez was gingerly advancing into Catalonia, interest had suddenly shifted in Madrid from the east of the Iberian peninsula to the west. On 1 December the Portuguese rose in revolt against the king of Spain, and proclaimed the duke of Braganza as King John IV.

The revolt of Portugal, coming so soon after that of Catalonia, was at once closely connected with it, and inspired by similar discontents,[4] for Olivares's Portuguese policy had been an exact duplicate of his Catalan policy. When Philip IV succeeded to the Spanish throne, Portugal, like Catalonia, was producing no revenues for use outside its own territory, and both the Portuguese fleet and the garrisons on Portuguese soil had to be maintained at Castile's expense.[5] Similarly, the Castilians

---

[1] AGS: GA, leg. 1331, draft instructions, 7 Nov. 1640.
[2] *MHE*, vol. XXI, p. 284.   [3] Sanabre, pp. 115–16.
[4] There is no adequate history of the Portuguese revolution. The brief account that follows is based largely on a number of documents which I came across in the course of my researches on Catalonia.   [5] AGS: Hacienda, leg. 555, paper by the Count of Salazar, 2 Dec. 1618.

bore the brunt of the relief expeditions despatched during the next two decades to recover Portuguese Brazil from the Dutch.[1]

In order to ensure Portuguese participation in the enterprises of the Monarchy, Olivares decided to press on with the introduction into Portugal, as into Catalonia, of the Union of Arms. The first step was to secure more effective control of the government of Portugal and impose on the country a regular system of taxation. In 1634 Princess Margaret of Savoy was sent to govern the country, with the assistance of the marquis of la Puebla and other Castilian advisers. Although Castilians were thus introduced into the government of the country in a way that was not possible in Catalonia, their presence did not further Olivares's designs. Instead, their bickerings with each other and with their Portuguese colleagues reduced the government to impotence.[2]

Olivares was not much more fortunate in his attempt to introduce regular taxation. The instructions to the princess and the marquis of la Puebla included an order to establish a 'fixed revenue' of 500,000 *cruzados* a year for the country's defence and the recovery of its lost possessions.[3] The new taxes imposed for this purpose aroused considerable popular discontent in a country where the union with Castile had always been abhorrent to the mass of the population, and in 1637 they led to serious riots in Évora and other towns. Richelieu attempted to take advantage of these riots and make contact with the leaders,[4] but his hopes that they would lead to a general revolution were disappointed. Although the clergy abetted the popular movement, it had no chance of success without the support of Braganza and the participation of the nobility, and neither was willing to move.

The lack of aristocratic support for the rioters enabled Olivares to put down the movement without great difficulty, but the Évora riots seriously disturbed him. As in Catalonia, however, he reacted to resistance not by modifying his policies but by deciding to pursue them more vigorously, and the Junta for Portugal actually toyed for a moment with the idea of sending Santa Coloma to Lisbon in order to strengthen the administration.[5] Finally, the Conde Duque decided to

---

[1] Boxer, *The Dutch in Brazil*, p. 45.
[2] AGS: Est. (Portugal), leg. 4047, no. 96, consulta, 25 Jan. 1636.
[3] AGS: Est. (Portugal), leg. 4047, no. 103, Marquis of la Puebla to King, 13 Aug. 1636.
[4] I. S. Révah, *Le Cardinal de Richelieu et la Restauration du Portugal* (Lisbon, 1950), pp. 10 ff.
[5] AGS: Est., leg. 2660, Junta de Portugal, 12 June 1638.

summon to Madrid various influential Portuguese ecclesiastics and nobles to give their views on how the government of the country might be improved. From Olivares's own comments on Portugal at this moment, it is clear that the 'improvement' of Portugal's government meant its closer association with that of Castile. It was to be emphasized to the Portuguese delegates that 'for as many as sixty years Portugal has been separate and isolated from all the rest of the Monarchy, with little advantage to all the other kingdoms, which indeed have been forced to come to its help.... And it has refused to come into line with the rest of the Monarchy....'[1] The Conde Duque might have been writing of Catalonia.

The backslidings of the Portuguese only served to confirm Olivares's belief that they must be integrated into the Spanish Monarchy at the first possible opportunity. That this was his intention was by now public knowledge. In the summer of 1639 Pellicer wrote in one of his weekly newsletters from Madrid: 'It is reported that the union of the Portuguese Crown with that of Castile is proceeding fast...and that the archbishop of Évora will be appointed President of the Councils of Castile and Portugal. This is a great and difficult undertaking, in view of the natural antipathy of Castilians and Portuguese. Time will show whether it will be successful....'[2] In spite of the obvious popular resistance to the Union of Arms, Olivares pressed ahead in Portugal as in Catalonia. Everything suggests that in the year 1639–40 he was determined to make the Union a reality throughout the Spanish Monarchy. Even Peru was not exempt, and when the viceroy, the count of Chinchón, attempted to enforce the Union, he found himself faced with revolts in Potosí, Cuzco and Abancay.[3]

Revolts in Catalonia, revolts in Peru, smouldering discontent in Portugal...in each country where Olivares attempted to introduce the Union of Arms, the story was the same. And yet he persisted. His determination to go ahead with his plans in spite of storm signals from widely separated parts of his empire may well appear an act of blind folly. But the shortage of money, and particularly the shortage of troops, had become so serious that the Union of Arms seemed to offer to the hard-pressed ministers in Madrid their sole hope of salvation. In

[1] AGS: Est., leg. 2660, paper by Olivares, 1638.
[2] Pellicer, 'Avisos', p. 51, 19 July 1639.
[3] Pellicer, 'Avisos', pp. 117–18, 10 Jan. 1640.

the early spring of 1640 there was still a chance that the gamble might come off. The Catalans might yet be compelled under pressure to offer soldiers for the armies in Italy. In Portugal 6000 men had actually been raised for service abroad, and were on their way to Italy when the Catalan Revolution broke out. They were promptly incorporated into the army for the invasion of Catalonia, and los Vélez was given instructions to treat them with special care, because this was the first time that Portuguese had gone to fight in a territory other than their own. If all went well with them, it would make it easier to use Portuguese wherever they were required, and so 'bring about the union of all my subjects and vassals'.[1]

The Catalan Revolution had implications for Portugal which could not escape the Conde Duque. If the Catalans dared to revolt against the government, there was no guarantee that the Portuguese would not follow suit; and in the presence on Portuguese soil of the duke of Braganza, the obvious candidate for a vacant throne, the Portuguese possessed an asset denied the Catalans. The Conde Duque's policy had been to smother Braganza with kindness, as a preliminary to luring him away from his native land. The outbreak of the revolution in Catalonia made it vital to act quickly and get Braganza and as many Portuguese nobles as possible out of the country before it was too late. With what must have seemed a masterstroke of ingenuity, Olivares decided that all his problems could be solved by mobilizing the Portuguese nobility for the campaign in Catalonia. This would at once remove a potentially dangerous element from Portugal, and help to increase the size of an army which was seriously hampered by the shortage of troops.

Olivares's ingenious scheme in fact helped to precipitate the revolution it was intended to avoid. If Portugal was ever to throw off its allegiance to the king of Spain, it must do so while Braganza and the aristocracy were still in the country. Plans for revolution were laid during the autumn, probably with the connivance of Richelieu who is believed to have sent funds to the conspirators in Lisbon.[2] It is possible that some people outside Portugal were aware of what was afoot: the duke of Híjar, that strange harbinger of Spanish revolutions, claims to

[1] AGS: GA, leg. 1329, instructions to los Vélez, 18 Aug. 1640.
[2] Révah, p. 39.

have given the Conde Duque a warning of Portuguese intentions, together with the exact date of the rising, three months before it actually occurred.[1] But it hardly needed a Híjar to show that trouble was brewing in Portugal. In his newsletter for 16 October, Pellicer remarked that there was bad news from Portugal because the nobility were reported to have refused to obey the decree ordering their mobilization, and had threatened any of their number who left the country to join the royal army. Pellicer even reported the rumour that the king deliberately intended to remove the nobles from the country in order to have them out of the way and under closer control.[2]

If this was common gossip in Madrid, it is all the more remarkable that Olivares and his colleagues seem to have had not the slightest inkling of the danger that threatened them. After the Portuguese had revolted, the Conde Duque made an impassioned oration in the Junta de Ejecución, which included the extraordinary statement that the conspiracy had been kept so secret among the 170 Portuguese in the Court that 'there was not the slightest clue to the plot that was being hatched'.[3] It is hard to know whether Olivares was speaking the truth, or whether he had been so successful in convincing himself that a Portuguese revolt was impossible that he had dismissed all warnings as absurd, and was now seeking to exculpate himself for having failed to take preventive measures. Here again there was a curious parallel to the Conde Duque's handling of the Catalan problem. In both Catalonia and Portugal, he seems to have closed his eyes to what was happening, and to have persisted in his policies with an almost wilful obtuseness until the unpleasant truth was so starkly revealed that even he could no longer ignore it; and by that time there was nothing that could be done. There could be no better example of this than the decisions reached by the Conde Duque and his colleagues at a meeting of the Junta de Ejecución on 27 October, nearly a fortnight after Pellicer's newsletter had reported the disaffection of the Portuguese aristocracy. News had reached Madrid that Brazil was in urgent need of help. Pedro de Arce, the Protonotario and José Gonzalez all agreed that, if Castile helped Portugal recover Brazil, it was perfectly reasonable that Portugal should help

[1] See his letter of 14 May 1648 to Sor María, quoted in Francisco Silvela, *Cartas de la Venerable Madre Sor María de Agreda y del Señor Rey Don Felipe IV* (Madrid, 1885), vol. I, p. 46, note 1.
[2] Pellicer, 'Avisos', pp. 227–8.
[3] AGS: GA, leg. 1331, Junta de Ejecución, 23 Dec. 1640.

Castile recover Catalonia. Balbases insisted on the importance of recovering Brazil, but agreed that the situation inside Spain was even
more serious, and, as it affected 'all members of the Monarchy...it is
necessary that all should assist'. These words were the signal for Olivares
to launch out into another vigorous defence of his ideas on the unity
of the Monarchy. He praised the 'wisdom' of Balbases.

And ignorant and malicious assertions to the contrary have brought the
Monarchy to its present state. People say that Portugal has only to come to
the help of Portugal, Aragon to that of Aragon, whereas all these kingdoms
should come reciprocally to each other's assistance, for there is no trouble in
one that does not affect the other. The Catalan question is the first demanding
settlement because Catalonia is the head and heart of Spain, and these kingdoms, all being joined together, suffer the resulting humours, which make
their way to every part of the body. Then comes Brazil....But in the first
place, I must repeat that Portugal must come to our help in Catalonia, as it is
doing and should be striving to do, because on the outcome in Catalonia
depends our ability to go to the relief of Brazil....[1]

It was all so rational, so convincing. It was even possible to prove
statistically to the Portuguese that they would be the gainers. Castile
would be spending 800,000 ducats on the relief of Brazil, whereas
Portuguese expenditure on the Catalan campaign would not come to
120,000 ducats.[2] It never seems to have struck the Conde Duque and
his colleagues that the Portuguese might see matters in a different light.
And so, while Olivares went on passionately preaching his great
doctrine of the Union of Arms, Portugal revolted.

When the first news of trouble in Portugal reached Madrid, the
ministers found the reports difficult to believe,[3] and it only dawned
upon them by slow degrees that Portugal had ended its sixty-year
union with Castile with hardly a shot being fired. The existence of two
simultaneous revolutions inside the peninsula demanded a rapid and
searching reappraisal of Spain's entire foreign policy. Already, in a
paper written in the middle of November and submitted to his colleagues a month later, the Conde Duque had said that 'the Catalan
revolt has been the absolute ruin of all our affairs....I propose peace,
and more peace, and for this purpose full powers have been sent to our

[1] AGS: GA, leg. 1331, Junta de Ejecución, 27 Oct. 1640.
[2] AGS: GA, leg. 1331, Junta de Ejecución, 29 Nov. 1640.
[3] AGS: GA, leg. 1331, Junta de Ejecución, 7 Dec. 1640.

representatives in all areas.... We must pray to our Lord for a general peace, which, even if it is not good, nor even mediocre, is better than the most favourable war....'[1]

Realising that all his policies were foundering in the shipwreck of the Spanish Monarchy, Olivares made a pathetic attempt to absolve himself from blame: no one, he said,

had cleaner hands than he. His disinterestedness was proved by experience.... If it is contested that wars have occurred, he can prove to everyone's satisfaction that he is no soldier and was not responsible for them.... He desires and loves peace so much that he would throw himself at the feet of anybody who can bring it about, and would give all he had to see it concluded. But in the post he occupies he has to carry out the policies that have been agreed. If people were to look at all the papers relating to the wars, they would see that he never voted for any of them. For the Italian war, which has led to so many misfortunes, there were twelve votes, and he alone, by the grace of Our Lord did not vote.[2] As for the French war, look and see who voted for that; and look, too, and see who it was who proposed writing to the Pope to send a legate for the conclusion of an unconditional peace. He alone voted for this....[3]

The Conde Duque's humiliating and undignified outburst is the first sign that his personal position at the head of the Monarchy was no longer absolutely secure. The king still supported him unswervingly, but even the king was by now beginning to recognize that, although his favourite might be intelligent and able, he was, to say the least, very unfortunate. But the personal tragedy of the Conde Duque was only one facet of the greater tragedy that was overtaking the Spanish Monarchy. It was hard to know what he, or anyone else, could now do to stem the tide. Struck by the secrecy which had surrounded the activities of the Portuguese conspirators, and the habitual lack of secrecy which surrounded all the discussions of the Juntas in Madrid, Olivares ordered his colleagues to submit their opinions independently in writing. They can hardly have given him much encouragement. Balbases, practical as always, said that this was the time for 'major remedies' and proposed, in the first place, a settlement in Catalonia. Although the

---

[1] AGS: Est. (Flandes), leg. 2055, paper by Olivares enclosed in consulta of Consejo de Estado, 17 Dec. 1640.

[2] This refers to the Mantuan War of 1628–31. Olivares's remark may be literally correct, but the part he played in the outbreak of that war was, to say the least, ambiguous. See above, p. 262.

[3] AGS: GA, leg. 1331, Junta de Ejecución, 23 Dec. 1640.

army might in a few days be successful, he none the less advocated a settlement which would leave the Catalans content. He also suggested that it would be desirable to arrange a truce with the Dutch, 'seeing first if we have enough money to deal with Brazil, or, if this is impossible, with Portugal...'. The count of Castrillo, who had so often opposed the Conde Duque's Catalan policies, was even more outspoken. In his opinion, the revolt of Portugal made it necessary to come to terms with Catalonia at once, without waiting for the outcome of military operations.

We have the chance of a settlement because the Catalans are asking for one, and therefore I do not intend to discuss as to its being desirable or possible because nothing would be so disastrous as to remain at war with Catalonia and Portugal. We must, then, accept the best possible settlement. This will allow us to avoid dividing our army, which would be unsatisfactory for both areas, and would leave us with two wars, excluding any others that might break out in other parts of Spain. We must immediately send to Portugal all the forces we have in Catalonia, in order to stifle the blaze before it sets fire to more....And a truce or suspension of arms with the Dutch this winter would be of incomparable value.

The other councillors, Santa Cruz, Cardinal Spínola, and Villahermosa, all wrote in a similar vein. In the words of Santa Cruz: 'the most important thing of all is peace with the Catalans, without haggling over conditions, fully satisfying them that Your Majesty has forgiven them'.[1]

There did indeed at this moment seem to be a slight possibility of a settlement with the Catalans. The marquis of los Vélez was meeting very little opposition in his northward advance; Espenan was so discouraged by the inability and open refusal of the Catalans to resist, that on 22 December he reached a private agreement with los Vélez to withdraw all French troops from Catalonia, and on 24 December he surrendered Tarragona to the Spanish army.[2] On 23 December, ignorant of the favourable turn of events in Catalonia, the Junta Grande considered and approved a set of conditions drawn up by Olivares for presentation to the Principality. The Catalans on their side were to throw out the French and revoke all agreements with them; to offer token assistance against the Portuguese; to allow some 6000 to 8000

---

[1] AGS: GA, leg. 1331, secret *votos* of ministers, 13–16 Dec. 1640.
[2] Sanabre, pp. 116–20.

men to remain billeted in the Tortosa area, as a precaution against a French invasion, the billetings to be in conformity with the constitutions, if nothing better could be arranged; to give a *donativo* and to assist in the fortification of Perpinyà and the various fortresses. In return, the king would grant a general pardon for everyone except those responsible for the murder of Santa Coloma; he would punish guilty soldiers and members of the Audiència, and he would guarantee the maintenance of the constitutions in their present form.[1]

Even these conditions do not appear unduly generous, although the plight to which the Catalans were now reduced might perhaps compel their acceptance. But conditions such as these were still difficult enough for the ministers of the king of Spain to stomach. The sight of the greatest king in the world being reduced to treat with rebellious subjects was a humiliation such as they could never have anticipated. On hearing the news that Madrid had now agreed to a negotiated settlement with the Catalans, that old Castilian war-horse, the marquis of Villafranca, wrote Olivares a letter of burning indignation from Valencia. If, he declared, the Catalans were conciliated rather than punished, all the kingdoms of the Monarchy would revolt, as the Portuguese had already done. It was therefore quite impossible for him to agree to any settlement with the Catalans.[2]

Some members of the Junta Grande were shocked by the violent language of the marquis's letter, and the marquis of Mirabel thought it ought to be burnt, 'so that future ages will never know that such a proposal has been made to Your Majesty'. But Olivares considered such censures excessively harsh. 'His words read like the Gospel, and there are few who can discourse better than the marquis.' The king himself felt that, if Villafranca believed negotiation to be impossible, he could hardly have written better, and deserved thanks. 'But what has been agreed must not be altered, because I am the father, ready to welcome my son at whatever time he may return.'[3]

The prodigal, alas, had not yet awoken to the error of his ways. The news of the surrender of Tarragona, coming so soon after the massacre at Cambrils, caused a violent popular reaction in Barcelona. Treachery was in the air. When the news reached Barcelona on 24 December the

[1] AGS: GA, leg. 1331, Junta Grande, 23 Dec. 1640.
[2] AGS: GA, leg. 1374, Marquis of Villafranca to Olivares, 16 Jan. 1641.
[3] AGS: GA, leg. 1374, Junta Grande, 26 Jan. 1641.

mob ran wild. With a savagery surpassing that of Corpus, the mob, again joined by insurgents from outside the city, hunted down 'traitors', and murdered three members of the Audiència, Drs Gori, Puig and Ramon, who had escaped in the popular rising six months before.[1] The Diputats were forced to throw open the prisons; there were riots outside the town hall on 26 December, houses were set on fire, and the risings spread to villages all round Barcelona.[2] The English ambassador commented on the news:

In Barcelona there hath happened a great dissension between the magistrates and officers of justice, who would have come to an agreement with the king, and the people that would not....I do now begin to think that this madness of the common people (who are many, and the nobility and gentry few, not exceeding 600) will throw that Principality into the hands of the French.[3]

The Catalan ruling class was fatally split. It is probable that at this moment the majority would have favoured an acceptance of the king's conditions. But the power of the mob was great, and Claris and his colleagues were determined to fight to the end. Discovering with horror the treachery of Espenan, the Diputats sent urgent personal appeals to Richelieu to save them from disaster.[4] In response to these appeals, Duplessis Besançon, who was not far from Barcelona, returned to the city for secret conversations with Claris. It was clear that the French distrusted the Catalans and were not prepared to commit themselves to the full defence of the Principality until they could be sure that Catalonia had broken completely with the king of Spain, and had no intention of reopening negotiations with him. As a result of the discussions, Claris stated in a meeting of the Braços on 16 January that

M. Duplessis Besançon has presented the terms on which he is entitled by the Most Christian King to offer assistance for the preservation of this province. These terms stipulate that it shall place itself under his protection, and its government shall be organized in the form of a Republic, in accordance with the conditions to be agreed between the province and the Most Christian King.[5]

The rupture with Castile was complete. The dreams of Claris and his friends had come true; Catalonia was an independent republic. But

[1] Assarino, p. 164.   [2] Sanabre, p. 124.
[3] PRO: SP, 94.42, fo. 106, Hopton to Vane, 20/30 Jan. 1641.
[4] Sanabre, p. 129.   [5] Sanabre, p. 131.

it lasted for only a week. Although there was now less danger of a Catalan reconciliation with Castile, Duplessis was not fully satisfied by the proposed new form of government. An entirely republican government neither seemed feasible, nor did it guarantee a sufficiently close association with France. As the army of the marquis of los Vélez drew closer day by day to Barcelona, Claris was in no position to haggle over French conditions. On 23 January he explained to the Braços that the heavy expenses of war and the overwhelming difficulties of organization made the scheme for a republic impracticable. He therefore proposed that the Principality should place itself under the government of the king of France 'as in the time of Charlemagne, with a contract to observe our constitutions'.[1] Catalonia had exchanged one master for another.

Catalonia's surrender to France came just in time. A small Junta for war was established, with dictatorial powers, in which Duplessis played the preponderant role. He rapidly organized the defence of Barcelona, now threatened by the presence of the invading army. The Catalan-French defending force met the army of los Vélez on the hill of Montjuic outside the walls of Barcelona on 26 January. Los Vélez, with the fate of Spain resting on his shoulders, incomprehensibly allowed himself to be drawn into battle, and, after suffering serious but not disastrous casualties, still more incomprehensibly gave the order to retreat.[2] Barcelona was lost, and, with it, Olivares's last hope of restoring the Monarchy's fortunes.

[1] Sanabre, p. 134.

[2] Even this performance failed to terminate the singularly unsuccessful official career of the Marquis of los Vélez. He was later to be appointed viceroy of Sicily, where—dogged by misfortune to the end—he was caught up in the revolt of 1647, during the course of which he died.

CHAPTER XVIII

EPILOGUE

'This year can undoubtedly be considered the most unfortunate that this Monarchy has ever experienced. . . .'[1] Olivares's verdict still stands. The year 1640–1 seems in retrospect, as it seemed at the time, a crucial year in the history not only of the Spanish Monarchy but also of a Europe which had lived for so long beneath the shadow of its power. The events of the second half of the century were to confirm the English ambassador's belief that 'the greatness of this monarchy is near to an end'.[2] It may well be that, in the very different conditions of the later seventeenth century, Spain's greatness would anyhow have been eclipsed by a new French imperialism, able to call upon far greater reserves of native manpower, but in so far as the ending of Spain's hegemony can be dated to any particular moment, the great crisis of 1640–1 would seem to have been decisive.

This crisis was much more than the product of any one single event. It was, rather, the outcome of a series of sudden shocks administered to an organism already strained to breaking-point by structural weaknesses of long standing. It was a crisis of manpower and of money. It was a crisis of military and political leadership. It was a crisis of economic organization and constitutional structure, long envisaged and now, suddenly, a fact.

Duplessis Besançon, Richelieu's agent in Catalonia, saw in the Catalan Revolution the event that sprang the mine.

One can say without exaggeration that the consequences of this event were such that (apart from the revolt of Portugal, whose loss was so prejudicial not only to Spain's reputation but to the whole structure of its monarchy—and which would never have dared revolt without the Catalan example, since it was afraid of being rapidly overwhelmed if it engaged alone in so hazardous a dance) our affairs (which were not going well in Flanders, and still worse in Piedmont) suddenly began to prosper on all sides, even in Germany; for our enemy's forces, being retained in their own country and recalled from elsewhere to defend the sanctuary, were reduced to feebleness in all the other theatres of war. . . .[3]

---

[1] See above, p. 504. [2] PRO: SP, 94.42, fo. 192, Hopton to Vane, 26 July/4 Aug. 1641.
[3] AAE: Corresp. Espagne, Sup. no. 3, fos. 240v–241.

This analysis, however, fails to take into account the extent to which Spain's military position in Europe had already deteriorated before the Catalan revolt, as a result of the fall of Breisach and the battle of the Downs. It also suffers from being the verdict of a man professionally involved in the events in Catalonia, and with an obvious personal interest in making the most of their importance. Others were less impressed. It is a striking testimony to the disunity of Habsburg Spain that the correspondence of the *Casa de Contratación* (the House of Commerce) of Seville, which is always so sensitive to every passing event in the remotest regions of the Americas, contains not a single reference to Catalonia during those turbulent summer months of 1640.[1] Catalonia was Mediterranean Spain, a world away from the Atlantic Spain of Seville. Its fate remained a matter of indifference to Sevillan merchants with their eyes fixed on the Indies. Not so, however, the fate of Portugal, a vital part of Spain's Atlantic system. It was the Portuguese, not the Catalan, Revolution which alarmed the merchants, and deepened the great commercial depression of the Sevillan Atlantic; a depression that was rapidly corroding one of the principal foundations of Spanish power.

The collapse of the Spanish-American trading system, based on the port of Seville, was undoubtedly one of the most important constituent elements of the crisis of 1640.[2] Seville's shipping was in an advanced state of decay; its trade with America was dwindling; its merchants were demoralized by the high-handed fiscal policies of the Spanish Crown. It is significant that in 1640, the year of the revolutions, no silver fleet arrived at Seville.[3] The mounting crisis of Spain's Atlantic system therefore did much to reduce Olivares's chances of successfully meeting the challenge presented by Spain's military reverses and by the revolutions of Catalonia and Portugal. The Crown's resources were drastically diminished, its opportunities for obtaining credit sharply curtailed, just at the moment when credit was most needed; and, as always at moments of crisis, only Castile stood between the Crown and disaster. The consequences were immediately felt. In February 1641 Olivares again began tampering with the Castilian coinage. *Vellón*

[1] Chaunu, *Séville et l'Atlantique*, vol. VIII, 2, ii, pp. 1831–2.
[2] The character and significance of this crisis have for the first time been brought out by Pierre Chaunu, *op. cit.* vol. VIII, 2, ii, pp. 1793–1851.
[3] Domínguez Ortiz, *Política y Hacienda de Felipe IV*, p. 291.

prices shot up to dizzy heights, and the premium on silver in terms of *vellón* reached 200 per cent before a deflationary decree in September 1642 once more brought prices tumbling down.[1]

The crisis of the Spanish Atlantic therefore left Castile naked and defenceless, and it is arguable that the disruption of Seville's American trade itself rendered Spain's defeat inevitable; for what was Castile without the silver, and the markets, of the New World? But questions of timing remain paramount, and it is here that the Catalan Revolution played a crucial part.

Although France's allies had scored important successes between 1638 and 1640, France's own military showing had been singularly unimpressive. Nor had matters gone well at home. Richelieu, like Olivares, ruled a discontented land, and he had, in Languedoc, a Catalonia of his own. During the spring and summer of 1640 reports reached Barcelona of discontent in the South of France.[2] The inhabitants of Languedoc resented the policies of Paris as fiercely as the Catalans resented those of Madrid. A rising there, or in any other of France's disaffected provinces, would have been as grave an embarrassment to Richelieu as the Catalan revolt to Olivares, and it may have been the happy accident of Catalonia which saved Richelieu from finding himself in the Conde Duque's unenviable position before the year was out.

Once revolution had actually broken out in Catalonia, however, a new and decisive element was introduced into the Franco-Spanish struggle. One of the two protagonists now found itself involved in a costly and disastrous civil war at the very moment when it needed all its diminished reserves of money and manpower for campaigns abroad. By diverting men and supplies from foreign battlefronts the Catalan Revolution did much, as Duplessis Besançon suggested, to precipitate Spain's military collapse. At the same time, the Catalan example encouraged the Portuguese to break loose from the Spanish Crown, and, by so doing, proved that Catalonia was not quite so far removed from the world of the Atlantic as the Sevillan merchants believed. Military defeat, political revolution, and economic collapse, were thus subtly interrelated, even if, at the time, the relationship was not always plain. The Catalan and Portuguese revolutions, themselves the culmination

[1] *Ibid.* p. 262, and Hamilton, *American Treasure*, pp. 85–6.
[2] AGS: GA, leg. 1368, Bishop of Elna to Pedro de Villanueva, 30 May 1640.

of a series of circumstances deriving from the initial economic weakness of Castile and aggravated by the flaws in the political structure of the Monarchy, only served to place a further unbearable strain on an already tottering edifice. The year 1640, in effect, marked the disintegration of an entire economic and political system.

Amidst the ruins stood the sombre and forlorn figure of the Conde Duque. 'The little prosperity of those two great businesses', wrote the English ambassador of the Catalan and Portuguese revolutions, 'doth strangely afflict the Conde Duque de Olivares, in so much as his secretary Carnero hath said he believes it will either break his heart or drive him into a monastery.'[1] With a supreme effort he set himself to repair the disasters that had befallen the Monarchy during his years of power. The king still stood by him, but even the king was growing uneasy, and the state papers of 1641 and 1642 suggest that, spurred by persistent charges that important matters of state were being withheld from him,[2] Philip was intervening increasingly in government affairs.[3]

Deep as was the hatred of the Castilian populace for the Conde Duque, effective political action against him could only come from the ranks of the aristocracy. The Castilian nobles now seized every possible opportunity to show the king what they thought of his favourite. Indeed, the last years of the Conde Duque's rule were characterized by a virtual 'strike' of the grandees. Only a handful of nobles—mostly Olivares's friends and relations—now attended upon the king in public and private functions, and on Easter Day in the royal chapel the grandees' seats were entirely deserted except for that of the young count of Santa Coloma.[4] But while the nobles had abandoned the Court, they had not abandoned their intrigues. In the late summer of 1641 a plot was unearthed which led back to two great Andalusian nobles, the duke of Medina-Sidonia and the marquis of Ayamonte, both of them members of the Conde Duque's own house of Guzmán.

[1] PRO: SP, 94.42, fo. 113, Hopton to Secretary of State, 3/13 Feb. 1641.

[2] AGS: GA, leg. 1375, King on consulta of Junta Grande, 21 April 1641.

[3] The amount of time and attention which Philip IV devoted to affairs of state throughout his reign has, however, been greatly underestimated. He himself claimed to read all letters and *consultas* (Cánovas, *Estudios*, vol. I, pp. 237–8) and certainly the numerous comments in his own hand to be found on *consultas* even before the last years of Olivares, suggest that he was as confirmed a *papelista* as his grandfather. The principal difference was that his powers of decision were even less, and that he placed his confidence in a single man to an extent which Philip II would have found impossible.

[4] Marañón, *Olivares*, pp. 92–3.

Medina-Sidonia was the brother of the new queen of Portugal, and, although the conspirators' exact intentions are uncertain, the duke's confession suggests that plans were being hatched not only to remove the Conde Duque and to restore an aristocratic chamber to the Cortes of Castile, but also to follow Portugal's example and turn Andalusia into an independent kingdom.[1] The marquis of Villafranca's gloomy prophecy that the Catalan rising would be only the first of a whole series of revolts seemed about to be confirmed.

The conspiracy of Medina-Sidonia, his own cousin, stunned Olivares.

I have observed in the Conde these two months an extraordinary sadness [wrote the English ambassador] and an utter neglect of all things but those of Andalusia.... I hear it observed by some that converse with the Conde that he is so overlaid with care... that his judgement begins to break, and that he is so intent upon his own conservation as all he doth in those great affairs is rather for show to content the king's eye, than to the effect of his service.[2]

Although Medina-Sidonia's failure was a serious setback, the nobles still hoped to undeceive the king. Their opportunity came with the Catalan campaign of 1642. During much of 1641 a royal visit to the army in Aragon had been under discussion, only to be constantly deferred on one pretext or another. The king himself became irritated by the delays and, on meeting the Protonotario one day, is alleged to have snatched a *consulta* from his hands, torn it to pieces, and told him to speed up preparations for the visit to Aragon instead of seeking new pretexts for postponing it.[3] Eventually the king left Madrid on 26 April 1642, making his journey by slow stages to Zaragoza. Here he remained for six months, watching the fitting out of the army designed to recover Catalonia from the French. Olivares begged him that he should be allowed to lead this army in person, so that at least he might die with honour,[4] but the Junta de Ejecución, whose members knew their fate to be inextricably bound up with that of the Conde Duque, strongly advised against accepting this offer, 'for he is the *primum mobile* of Your Majesty's orders, and the day he leaves Your Majesty's

[1] BN: MS 6043, fos. 188–90, *Carta del papel que dió a SM el Duque de Medina Sidonia.*

[2] PRO: SP, 94.42, fos. 211–13, Hopton to Vane, 14/24 Sept. 1641.

[3] *Cartas de algunos PP. de la Compañía de Jesús, MHE,* vol. XVI, pp. 321–2. It is very difficult to separate fact from fiction in the story of the king's visit to Aragon. If Olivares was deliberately putting off the king's journey, there is no evidence of this from his own hand. The whole affair is examined in Marañón, *op. cit.* pp. 342–7.

[4] AGS: GA, leg. 1424, paper by Olivares, 2 Sept. 1642.

presence, his absence will be felt in the despatch of all the many affairs of the Monarchy...'.[1]

Indispensable as his presence may have been, nothing could alter the fact that his continuing tenure of power was being attended by an unbroken series of misfortunes. On 9 September Perpinyà surrendered to the French, and, with its fall, all Rosselló was lost. Still worse, the army which finally set out from Aragon under the command of Olivares's close friend the marquis of Leganés, was defeated on 7 October in its attempt to recapture Lleida, and lost five thousand men.[2]

With the French now encamped on the border of Aragon and with the Portuguese making daily incursions into Castile,[3] the king was compelled to recognize the magnitude of Olivares's failure. But could he find the resolution to dismiss the minister on whom he had so utterly depended for over twenty years? There was no shortage of people anxious to help him to reach a decision. Away in Madrid Olivares's enemies, like busy moles, were tunnelling away beneath the now shaky edifice of the Conde Duque's government. The tunnelling operations were led by the count of Castrillo, who had on so many occasions in the past criticized the Conde Duque's Catalan policies, and who had, rather surprisingly, been entrusted with the administration in Madrid while Olivares was away in Aragon. Castrillo was a member of the house of Haro, closely related to Olivares's house of Guzmán, and the Conde Duque presumably felt that he could rely on family loyalties. But Olivares had himself recently subjected these loyalties to a severe strain. In January 1642, no longer with any hope of legitimate children, the Conde Duque had legitimated a bastard son, Don Enrique Felípez de Guzmán, and in so doing had deprived his nephew, Don Luis de Haro, of his hopes of succession to Olivares's titles and estates.[4] The Haro family was naturally affronted by the spectacular rise of the upstart, and any lingering sentiments of loyalty to the Conde Duque disappeared.

It seems probable that Castrillo's plans were carefully laid by the time the king returned to Madrid in December. How much pressure he brought to bear on the king is not known, but on 17 January 1643 the Conde Duque received a note from his master giving him formal per-

---

[1] AGS: GA, leg. 1424, Junta de Ejecución, 17 Sept. 1642.
[2] Sanabre, *Acción de Francia*, pp. 211–12.
[3] AGS: GA, leg. 1422, Junta de Ejecución quedada en Madrid, 5 Oct. 1642.
[4] See Marañón, ch. xx, for this curious episode in the Conde Duque's career.

mission to retire from office. On 23 January he left Madrid for his house at Loeches, never again to return to the capital where he had reigned for twenty-two years. His stay at Loeches, however, was to be short. It was too close to Madrid for the comfort of his enemies, and the appearance of the *Nicandro*, a defence of Olivares's policies inspired by the Conde Duque himself, provided them with a pretext for moving him farther away. In June 1643 he was exiled to his sister's palace at Toro, and here, surrounded by his own little court, he lived out the last two years of his life. He was to die on 22 July 1645 under the shadow of madness:[1] 'a great man who knew how to make gigantic designs, but he lacked aptitude in the execution of them, and felicity in the outcome'.[2]

Olivares's fall from power followed less than two months after the death of his victorious rival, Cardinal Richelieu. For both France and Spain it was the end of an epoch. On the Conde Duque's disgrace, power was momentarily assumed by the king and then gradually slipped, as Castrillo had planned, into the hands of the Haro family. Olivares's disinherited nephew, Don Luis de Haro, became in fact, if not in name, the king's principal minister, and was careful to abandon, along with the title of favourite, several of the more unpopular features of his uncle's government.[3] Among the first signs of the changes at Court was the decline in the influence of the Protonotario. On 27 April 1643 a royal decree, after expressing complete satisfaction in the person of the Protonotario, announced the king's intention of 'removing him from my secretariat and from his post of councillor' of the Council of Aragon, on account of the 'lack of confidence shown in him by the Catalans' whose return to allegiance the king wished to hasten.[4] Villanueva was compensated for the loss of these offices by a place in the Council of the Indies, but it was clear that, with his patron gone, the days of his greatness were over. His enemies, however, were still not content. For some years he had been under suspicion of heresy on account of his close connections with the notorious convent of San Plácido,[5] but

---

[1] Marañón, *Olivares*, chs. XXIII–XXIX, gives a detailed account of his fall from power, exile and death.

[2] The seventeenth-century Sevillan chronicler, Ortiz de Zúñiga, *Anales...de Sevilla*, p. 705.

[3] The government of Don Luis de Haro, who remained in power until his death in 1661, has never been studied and would certainly repay investigation.

[4] AGS: Gracia y Justicia, leg. 266, copy of royal decree sent to Cardinal Borja.

[5] See above, p. 257.

he had been too powerful to touch. Now the evidence against him was remorselessly collected, and on 31 August 1644 he was arrested by the officers of the Inquisition.[1] After two years in gaol he was penanced by the Inquisition and required to abjure, and the rest of his life was devoted to an attempt to secure reversal of his sentence. He died at Zaragoza on 21 July 1653, but his case dragged on for another seven years, adding further elements of the bizarre to that strange and faintly sinister reputation which he had acquired during the years of his greatness at Court.

With the disappearance of both Olivares and Villanueva from the centre of affairs, life at Madrid became very different. Haro and his friends did all in their power to obliterate the memory of the nightmare years of the Olivares regime. As if by general agreement, the past twenty years were wiped from the slate, as if they had never been. The Juntas were abolished; the aristocracy returned to Court. And with infinite patience and a certain agility, Don Luis set about the formidable task of piecing together the broken fragments of the Spanish Monarchy.

The first essential requirement was to reduce Spain's commitments abroad. Until 1640 it had seemed that peace with France would be more easily obtained than peace with the Dutch, but the prospects were completely altered by the events of that year. The principal obstacle to peace with the Dutch had been the problem of Brazil, but this was now removed, since Brazil was Portuguese territory and therefore no longer of immediate concern to the Spanish Crown.[2] But while the Portuguese Revolution, by solving the problem of Brazil, had increased the possibilities of peace with the Dutch, the Catalan Revolution had considerably reduced the chances of peace with France. The French could hardly abandon allies to whom they had promised their protection,[3] and Spain could never make peace unless Catalonia were restored. If, as seemed likely, he could not obtain a general peace, Haro's best hope was therefore to attempt to divide the French and the Dutch, sign a separate treaty with the United Provinces, and then, with his commitments reduced, seek to reconquer the Principality of Catalonia, leaving the recovery of Portugal to a more auspicious time.

[1] Lea, *History of the Inquisition*, vol. II, pp. 140ff.
[2] See Fritz Dickmann, *Der Westfälische Frieden* (Münster, 1959), p. 261.
[3] Dickmann, p. 98.

Epilogue

When the delegates for a peace conference began arriving in the Westphalian towns of Münster and Osnabrück during 1644, Spain's representatives had only the weakest of hands to play. The downfall of the Conde Duque had not produced the expected miracle, and Spain's military position continued to deteriorate after the defeat of the infantry at Rocroi on 19 May 1643. Military reverses were to be followed by another financial crisis, culminating in a new state bankruptcy on 1 October 1647.[1] Overshadowing all this was a fresh movement of political unrest, which for a moment threatened the Monarchy with total disintegration. Exasperated by the endless stream of fiscal demands, both Sicily and Naples revolted in the summer of 1647.[2] Fortunately for Don Luis de Haro, the French failed to make the most of their opportunity and the usual social divisions enabled the Spanish authorities to quell the risings. But for a few agonizing months the very survival of the Monarchy hung in the balance, and the discovery in August 1648 of a plot by the duke of Híjar to make himself king of an independent Aragon with the help of Cardinal Mazarin,[3] vividly suggested what might have happened if the scales had tipped the other way.

Spain's principal delegate at Westphalia, the count of Peñaranda, was painfully aware of his country's weakness. His only consolation was the civil war now breaking out in France. If properly exploited, this might give him the chance to press for a general settlement. But Spain was so weakened by its own troubles that it was unable to turn to full account the new situation created by the beginning of the Fronde, and the opportunity for peace with France passed.[4] Instead, Peñaranda had to be content with pursuing separate negotiations with the Dutch. The United Provinces had been increasingly alarmed by the growing power of France, and Peñaranda played on their fears by revealing to them a secret offer made by Mazarin to exchange Catalonia for Flanders.[5] By 3 January 1648 the general terms of a separate Spanish-Dutch treaty had been agreed,[6] and these formed the basis of the Treaty

---

[1] Domínguez Ortiz, p. 103.

[2] See R. B. Merriman, *Six Contemporaneous Revolutions*. The Sicilian revolt, which is not one of Merriman's six, is discussed by H. G. Koenigsberger, 'The Revolt of Palermo in 1647', *The Cambridge Historical Journal*, vol. VIII (1946), pp. 129–44.

[3] See Ramón Ezquerra, *La Conspiración del Duque de Híjar*.

[4] Fraga Iribarne, *Don Diego de Saavedra*, pp. 588–90.

[5] *Ibid.* pp. 564–6. [6] *Ibid.* p. 591.

of Münster of 24 October 1648. By this treaty, the Dutch broke away from the French alliance, leaving France to continue its war against Spain on its own. In return, Spain recognized the United Provinces as a sovereign, independent state. The revolt of the Netherlands, begun eighty years before, had reached its triumphant conclusion.

At Münster, the Dutch induced the Spanish Habsburgs to renounce in perpetuity all their claims to sovereignty. Could the Catalans, more recent rebels, do the same? By 1648 the prospects did not seem very hopeful. The end of the long war with the United Provinces, and the release of Spain from its commitments in Germany, where the Emperor had signed his own peace with France, would obviously allow Philip IV to concentrate more of his forces on the Catalan front. And already the Principality's political, military and economic situation was such as to raise considerable doubts about its capacity for indefinite resistance.

If, from the very beginning of the revolution, the cards were stacked against the survival of Catalonia as an independent state, the Catalans themselves did much to ensure the failure of their experiment. This was partly because the nature of the experiment was itself unclear to most of them. Their revolution had been a revolution against the Court of Spain—against the government of the Conde Duque and exploitation by Castile. It is doubtful whether, before it began, the participants had in mind any more positive objective. Once the immediate aim of expelling the Spanish soldiery had been achieved, the logic of events suggested to Claris and his colleagues the possibility of transforming Catalonia into an independent republic, but there is no evidence that they had previously entertained any such idea.

'It is not for the sake of living in a confused Republic that they withdrew from a monarchy. They have never approved those forms of popular government in which the feet often dictate to the head, and the wicked lay down the law for the good.'[1] So wrote a Frenchman who shared the anti-republican sentiments of most of his contemporaries, but the words were written to justify the Principality's acceptance of French suzerainty, and there is at least a hint that, at the beginning of the revolt, Richelieu himself felt differently. According to Duplessis Besançon,

[1] (Charles Sorel), *La Deffence des Catalans* (Paris, 1642), p. 98.

Cardinal Richelieu, who foresaw the difficulties that acceptance [of the Catalan offer to place themselves under French suzerainty] might one day place in the way of peace, hesitated for long to recommend it to His Majesty. He often explained that it would have been of greater advantage to France if this province had been set up as a republic under French protection, both because it would probably have made greater efforts to preserve its liberty, and because it would in this way have saved France part of the expenditure that it was afterwards called upon to make. But in the end, *seeing that Catalonia was not capable of this form of government*, and that otherwise it might rapidly return to subjection to Spain....His Excellency was of the opinion that it was necessary to accept.[1]

If this accurately represents Richelieu's views, the Catalans may justifiably be accused of having let slip a great opportunity to turn the Principality into an independent state. When the Catalan Republic was actually proclaimed it lasted for only a week, and served as no more than a decent façade behind which the transfer of allegiance from Spain to France could be accomplished. This was a travesty of republican government, and one for which the Catalans themselves were responsible. The Principality's potentialities for lapsing into social confusion and anarchy, so often suggested in the history of the preceding forty years, had been fully realized in the six months' interlude between the outbreak of revolution and the acceptance of French suzerainty. Richelieu was right: 'Catalonia was not capable of this form of government.' It lacked the social cohesion and political unanimity on which a stable governmental system could alone be established.

One man might eventually have succeeded in ending the disorder and in giving the Principality the firm leadership it so badly needed: Pau Claris. But Claris died very suddenly on 27 February 1641, possibly poisoned by an agent of Madrid.[2] After his premature disappearance from the scene, there remained no Catalan with sufficient authority to impose himself on the nation and prevent it from consuming itself in internecine feuds. While the country's ruling class had more or less recovered control from the marauding bands which had roamed at will during the summer and autumn of 1640, the events of the revolution had only served to accentuate its own internal divisions; and in the

---

[1] AAE: Corresp. Espagne, Sup. no. 3, fos. 237v–238 (my italics).
[2] Sanabre, *Acción de Francia*, pp. 139–40.

years after 1640 those divisions were to be cynically exploited by both the French and the Castilians for their own political ends.

By its internal divisions, Catalonia destroyed itself. But the very success of the French and Spanish Courts in widening the rifts within Catalan society is itself an indication of the extent to which Catalonia had already ceased to be its own master. In the years before the revolution its geographical position between the two great powers had given it the initiative by enabling it to play off one against the other. But as soon as it proclaimed its allegiance to Louis XIII it forfeited this advantage. From this moment its freedom of movement was gone, and its destinies were likely to be decided not in Barcelona but in the Court of France.

The French could hardly be expected to show a purely altruistic interest in the well-being of the Catalans. Now that the revolution had given French troops a welcome entry into the Iberian peninsula, military considerations were bound to be uppermost in the minds of Richelieu and his successor. Richelieu's first objective must therefore be to ensure that the government of the Principality remained firmly under French control, so that his armies could advance into Aragon and Valencia without fear of being stabbed in the back by a sudden new reversal of allegiance on the part of the Catalans.

The agreement of 23 January 1641 by which Catalonia declared its allegiance to Louis XIII in return for France's military protection, gave Richelieu the freedom of action he required. French troops were able to occupy the Principality's strong-points, and one of Richelieu's most trusted agents, d'Argenson, was sent to Barcelona, nominally to superintend the activities of the army, but in practice to keep a general watch over the Principality's political and administrative affairs.[1] This was followed by the appointment of a French viceroy, and the concentration of the country's administration in the hands of a group of Catalans on whom the French felt themselves able to rely. Josep Fontanella, who had become the confidant of d'Argenson, was made Regent la Cancelleria, and the Principality's key central and local posts were entrusted to the friends of Fontanella and of his father, Joan Pere Fontanella, the new Conseller-en-Cap of Barcelona.[2] At the same time, the French showed themselves aware of the supreme importance of obtaining a commanding influence over the policies of the city of Barcelona and the Diputació

[1] Sanabre, pp. 148 ff.   [2] Sanabre, pp. 199–200.

such as Olivares and the Protonotario had failed to secure. This was achieved by the simple process of having the lists of candidates for office carefully scrutinized before the customary lottery, and removing the names of all those persons judged to be partisans of Spain.[1] In this way the Barcelona council and the Diputació were regularly packed by the friends of France.

Unfortunately, the system did not work quite so smoothly as the French had hoped, for they had reckoned without the personal and family antipathies within the Catalan ruling class. The concentration of power in the hands of the Fontanellas inevitably caused anger and discontent, and, as a result, the years after 1642 saw a widening rift among the partisans of the French alliance. One faction was captained by the Fontanellas and by Don Josep d'Ardena, commander of the Catalan cavalry, the other by Don Josep Margarit, the Governador of Catalonia; and the composition of the factions, which extended right through the Principality, may well have been determined by the traditional allegiances of *nyerros* and *cadells*.[2]

While France's allies were torn by quarrels and faction, they were also confronted by a growing body of partisans of Castile. Those who had from the first remained faithful to Philip IV were joined during the 1640's by a stream of recruits from the opposite camp. Some no doubt changed sides because they were disappointed of office and influence in the new administration; others because they felt that the fall of Olivares had effectively removed the country's principal enemy and that Philip IV without his favourite would treat his erring vassals with generosity. But the most cogent reason for disillusionment with France was the behaviour of the French themselves.

France had originally promised to maintain its own troops in the Principality and stipulated that the Catalans would be expected to provide only for their own battalion, but this promise was not kept. As might have been expected, pay was no more regular when it came from France than when it came from Castile, and Diputació and towns found themselves subjected to constant demands for money and supplies. Nor, in practice, did the population find much difference between the French troops and the Castilian troops whom they had so enthusiastically expelled; and French viceroys, with an army at their beck and call,

[1] Sanabre, p. 608. [2] Sanabre, p. 249.

disregarded the constitutions with a confidence such as the Castilian viceroys had never quite managed to achieve.

The French army was, to all intents and purposes, an army of occupation, whose presence became increasingly necessary as anti-French riots flared up in one part of the country after another, encouraged and organized by the supporters of Castile. The growing confidence of Philip IV's adherents contrasted sharply with the increasing demoralization of the partisans of France. Since Richelieu's death it had become obvious, even to the most fanatical of them, that France regarded Catalonia as one more pawn on the international chessboard, to be used at will for the advancement of French interests. Richelieu himself, having gained so much from the providential uprising of the Catalans, had always displayed a close interest in their affairs. Mazarin, on the other hand, was more concerned to intensify the war on the other fronts, especially in his native Italy, and so, from 1643, Catalonia was relegated to a relatively subordinate place in the over-all designs of France.[1]

The diminution of interest in Catalan affairs at the French Court was followed by an increasing number of reverses for French arms in the Principality. The great French victories of 1642—the conquest of Rosselló, the capture of Monzón, the defeat of Leganés outside Lleida—were not followed up in 1643. Instead, the French commanders, starved of money, found themselves being gradually forced on to the defensive as Philip IV's armies began their slow advance from Tarragona and from Aragon.[2] Weak as were the Spanish forces, they reached the outskirts of Lleida in July 1643, recaptured Monzón in December, and finally, in July 1644, recovered Lleida, where Philip IV took a solemn oath to observe the Catalan constitutions.

Mazarin reacted to these defeats by relieving La Mothe, the French viceroy, of his post in December 1644 and replacing him by a distinguished commander, the count of Harcourt. For a moment, Harcourt succeeded in infusing new life into the French cause, and in May 1645 at last achieved an objective dear to the hearts of both Richelieu and Mazarin: the capture of Roses. Roses was the strongest fortress in the Principality, and its continued retention by a Spanish garrison had long been a serious irritant to the French. With its capture they now

[1] Sanabre, p. 242.
[2] For the following brief summary of military operations in Catalonia, I have relied on Sanabre, *op. cit.*, who treats them in great detail.

consolidated their hold over northern Catalonia, and removed the danger that the lines of communication between the Principality and France might be cut. But Harcourt's further military activities were less successful. He laid siege to Lleida in May 1646, but the city defended itself bravely, and a Spanish relieving force heavily defeated his army at the end of November. The defeat at Lleida brought to an end Harcourt's Catalan career, and his successor, Condé, met with a similar failure in June 1647 in a fresh attempt to retake the city.

By the time of the Westphalian settlement of 1648 the French position in Catalonia was therefore visibly weakened. The Spanish garrisons in Tarragona and Lleida were becoming increasingly bold and vigorous in their sorties; many towns and villages were coming out in favour of the king of Spain, and France's supporters were divided and demoralized. Suspicions were growing that Mazarin had no real interest in the Principality's ultimate fate, and these suspicions were confirmed by his manœuvres at the peace conference.

While the mass of the country was being alienated by the activities of the French soldiery, the wealthy bourgeoisie was becoming increasingly resentful of France's growing economic predominance. Indeed, the exploitation of Catalonia by the French for their own military and political ends was accompanied by an undisguised economic exploitation which was well on the way to transforming the Principality into a French colony. Merchants from Languedoc and Provence followed the French armies into Catalonia, where great opportunities awaited them. The disruption of the Principality's commercial ties with Sicily and Sardinia had left it heavily dependent on the granaries of Languedoc. With French grain came also French manufactures—cloth and silk and munitions of war. As a result, the French mercantile community in Barcelona acquired a virtual monopoly of Catalan trade, and French merchants like Pierre Lagassa built up enormous fortunes at the expense of Catalan merchants who were now deprived of their traditional markets.[1]

France's grip on the Principality's economic life only served to underline the fundamental weakness of Catalonia's position. As long as it remained an economic, as well as a political, satellite of the French it

---

[1] E. Giralt, 'La colonia mercantil francesa de Barcelona', *Estudios de Historia Moderna*, vol. VI, pp. 222–6. Appendix IV of this article, which gives an admirably clear picture of French commercial domination, provides biographical notices of 140 French merchants in Barcelona.

could expect to have no say in determining its own future. The maintenance of political independence therefore ultimately depended on the Principality's ability to make itself economically viable, and this in turn demanded a radical reappraisal of the country's traditional commercial habits and a willingness to search for new markets in a world which no longer centred on the Mediterranean. One of the most important long-term consequences of the Catalan Revolution was that it did at last force the Catalans to undertake this reappraisal. When Josep Fontanella passed through The Hague in 1644, on his way to the conference at Münster, he sent a letter to Barcelona which showed that he at least appreciated the needs of the age:

My visit to this country may perhaps prove of value not only for my principal mission, but also for the encouragement of Catalan commerce, which is the only means of escaping from our present misery; for the Dutch at the beginning of the war were much poorer and more broken down than us, but in a short time by means of trade they have made themselves the richest and most powerful people in the world. Catalonia has much greater potentialities than this land.... With the help of well-informed persons I shall try to work in the coming peace treaties for recognition of the right of the Catalans to free trade with the Indies and the rest of the world.[1]

Catalonia's gradual release from its obsession with Mediterranean markets—a release which was the essential preliminary to its economic revival in the later seventeenth and early eighteenth centuries—may perhaps be dated from this moment in 1644 when Fontanella learnt, as so many of his contemporaries were learning, the lesson of the Dutch. But, in the circumstances of 1644, his words inevitably had a Utopian ring. The Principality at this moment presented a picture of growing economic distress, and there was little that could be done to alleviate it. Under the pressure of war finance, the Catalan currency, which had been stable for twenty years, began to go the way of the Castilian.[2]

[1] Quoted in Sanabre, pp. 354–5.
[2] The changing value of the gold coin known as the *escut doble* suggests the intensity of the inflation:

	Rating	Price relative		Rating	Price relative
1640	56 *sous*	100	1647	108 *sous*	193
1642	68	121	1649	148	265
1643	64	114	1650	180	320
1644	88	157	1651	240	430
1645	92	164	1652	320	571
1646	100	178			

[Usher, *Early History of Deposit Banking*, Table 38, p. 462.]

Epilogue

The rising tide of monetary disorder was only a part of the general economic crisis that was now overwhelming the Principality. Catalonia had become one more battleground in the Thirty Years War, and the oppressions and destruction wrought by armies on the march were comparable to those suffered by the German lands. Populations fled their homes; the fields were deserted. In 1642, after two years of war in the Camp de Tarragona, it was reported that in Reus, a town of one thousand houses, less than four hundred remained, and Tarragona itself had lost five thousand of its seven thousand inhabitants.[1]

In the wake of hunger and destruction came plague. The epidemic had struck Castile and Valencia in 1647, and then swept into Andalusia where it killed half the population of Seville. In April 1650 it made its first appearance in Catalonia, in the region of Tarragona and Tortosa. For a moment it seemed as if it might remain confined to south Catalonia and Aragon, but, during the first months of 1651, it flared up elsewhere in the Principality and then proceeded to ravage a country which had lived through eleven years of constant warfare and had suffered, during the past three or four, a severe shortage of corn. Mortality figures are not available, but it is thought that the Principality lost in this plague more inhabitants than at any time since the great epidemics of the late fourteenth century.[2]

The great plague of 1650–4 destroyed any lingering chances Catalonia may still have had of preserving its independence from the Spanish Crown. Since 1648 Mazarin had been preoccupied with the Fronde, and France's domestic difficulties inevitably reduced the effectiveness of its arms abroad. This was the obvious moment for Philip IV to make a supreme bid for the recovery of the Principality, torn as it was by civil war, ravaged by plague, and ruefully conscious that it had exchanged a hard taskmaster for a harder. By the beginning of 1651 the French position was everywhere crumbling. In July of that year the army of the marquis of Mortara, based on Lleida, joined forces with the Tarragona army under the command of Philip IV's bastard son, Don Juan José de Austria, and the combined armies advanced on Barcelona. They

---

[1] Sanabre, p. 615. The incredible toll that billeting could take is suggested by the figures collected by the Diputats in 1657 of the number of houses in various towns before and after the quartering of troops. In one town, Sant Celoni, losses were as high as 82% with only 35 houses remaining out of 200 (see note 75 of Nadal and Giralt, 'Ensayo metodológico').

[2] Nadal and Giralt, *La Population Catalane*, pp. 42–4.

were too weak, however, for an assault on the city, and for a long time the siege languished. In response to desperate appeals from the Consellers, Marshal La Mothe, once again viceroy of Catalonia, forced his way into the city with a cavalry contingent in April 1652, but was unable to get to it the supplies of food it so urgently needed. Blockaded by land and sea, the plague-stricken capital was gradually being starved into submission. Mazarin, for all his difficulties at home, was extremely anxious that Barcelona should not be lost, and ordered the French squadrons to sail to its relief. But they failed to break the Spanish blockade, and, with their failure, the city was doomed.

Unable to feed the populace, the Consellers appointed a representative on 1 October 1652 to treat with the Spaniards. On 3 October the Governador, Margarit, fled from the city by boat, accompanied by a handful of the more fervent adherents of France, and on the same day Marshal La Mothe officially informed the marquis of Mortara of his willingness to discuss the terms of surrender. Finally, on 11 October at nine o'clock in the morning, the Conseller-en-Cap, accompanied by many of the leading citizens, left the city in solemn procession for a formal meeting with Don Juan de Austria. After an exchange of courtesies he presented Don Juan with the city's request that the king of Spain would again take it under his protection and confirm all its liberties and privileges. The prince in reply offered a general pardon for all crimes committed since 1640, excluding from the amnesty only Don Josep Margarit, and gave the city permission to send an ambassador to Madrid to place its request before the king. Two days later, in accordance with the terms of surrender, Marshal La Mothe and Don Josep d'Ardena left Barcelona, followed by the French, Swiss and Catalan troops who had been defending the city. Then the Spanish forces marched in, led by Don Juan de Austria. After attending a *Te Deum* in the cathedral, he took up residence in the palace of the dukes of Cardona. The long siege of Barcelona had come to an end, and the city had returned to allegiance to its former Count, King Philip IV of Spain.[1]

The surrender of Barcelona on 13 October 1652 marked the virtual end of the Catalan Revolution begun twelve years before. Three months later, Philip IV conceded a general pardon and promised to preserve the

---

[1] For the surrender of Barcelona, see Sanabre, pp. 533–44.

Principality's constitutions.[1] Catalonia was thus reinstated as part of the Spanish Monarchy, enjoying the same laws and privileges as it had enjoyed at the time of the accession of Philip IV in 1621. Skilfully Don Juan de Austria, now viceroy of Catalonia, set about wooing the bourgeoisie and erasing the bitter memories of a long and bloody civil war. But the Principality's sufferings were not yet over. The French, urged on by Fontanella, Margarit and their fellow-exiles in Rosselló,[2] had not yet abandoned all hope of recovering Catalonia. Between 1653 and 1658 French troops made constant incursions into the Principality, capturing the Seu d'Urgell and Puigcerdà and consolidating their hold on Roses. Mazarin was determined to have good bargaining counters when the time came to make peace.

It was on 9 May 1659 that France and Spain ordered their respective commanders to suspend the hostilities which had begun in 1635.[3] Three months later the peace conference began. As a preliminary to the negotiations Spain had already renounced its rights to Rosselló, but, at the conference, the French delegates insisted that Rosselló included Conflent and Cerdanya, which should similarly be incorporated into the Crown of France. They eventually obtained some, but not all, of their demands. By the Peace of the Pyrenees, signed on 7 November 1659 and sealed with the marriage contract of Louis XIV to Philip IV's daughter, María Teresa, Spain ceded to France both Rosselló and Conflent; and, by later negotiations, a Spanish-French frontier in Cerdanya was agreed, with thirty-three villages of Cerdanya being awarded to France.[4] Peace had come at last, but, as part of its price, the new frontier between Catalonia and France was henceforth to be the southern chain of the Pyrenees, and the Catalan-speaking lands were divided for ever.

Catalonia had emerged from its revolution with its territory reduced but its privileges intact, a part once again of the Spanish Monarchy. If the preservation of its privileges could be accounted a significant success, the achievement could hardly compare with that of Portugal. The Portuguese Revolution, unlike the Catalan, ended in the country's permanent separation from Castile. After the Peace of the Pyrenees, Philip IV made desperate attempts to recover his rebellious kingdom, but his treasury was empty and his armies feeble. The crushing defeat of the

[1] Reglà, *Els Virreis de Catalunya*, p. 142.
[2] Sanabre, p. 549, puts the number of exiles at about 700.
[3] Sanabre, p. 587.　　　　　　　　　　[4] Sanabre, pp. 588–94.

Spanish army at Villaviciosa on 17 June 1665 proved the final blow, and the king died three months later in the knowledge that Portugal was lost to the Spanish Crown. On 13 February 1668 the Queen-Regent of Spain and her ministers accepted the inevitable, and formally recognized the country's independence.

The Portuguese thus joined the Dutch as the only permanently successful rebels against the Spanish Habsburgs in the best part of two centuries. The rarity of their achievement is itself a striking commentary on the powers of survival of an empire whose territories were so numerous, so widely scattered and, in some respects, so loosely attached to the central government, that its capacity for surmounting crises—particularly those of the 1640's—seems at times almost miraculous. To some extent, however, both Portugal's success and Catalonia's failure can help to explain the secret of its survival by exposing at once the limits of its weakness and the hidden sources of its unexpected strength.

Portugal began its revolution with certain outstanding advantages which Catalonia lacked. It had been united to the Crown of Castile within living memory, and national traditions had been fortified in the fifteenth and sixteenth centuries by the creation of an overseas empire at the very time when Catalonia's empire was becoming a thing of the past. It also had, in the duke of Braganza, a ready-made king, whose person proved to be a more effective symbol of national unity at home and of respectability abroad than the Catalan Diputació. Both Braganza and the Diputació could count on the lower clergy, whose support was essential for rallying the population to their cause; but it may perhaps be of some importance that, while the Portuguese and Brazilian Jesuits showed themselves fervent adherents of Braganza,[1] the Catalan Jesuits on the whole remained neutral and did not play a significant part in the revolt.[2]

The Portuguese and Catalan aristocracies were both discontented at the neglect of their interests by an absentee king. The upper bourgeoisie

[1] Boxer, *Salvador de Sá*, pp. 142–6.

[2] Miguel Batllori, S.I., 'Los Jesuitas y la guerra de Cataluña, 1640–59', *Boletín de la Real Academia de la Historia*, vol. CXLVI (1960), pp. 141–98. It is not clear why the Jesuits, who traditionally were defenders of the Spanish Monarchy, should have been favourable to Portuguese independence. H. and P. Chaunu, 'Autour de 1640: politiques et économiques atlantiques', *Annales: Economies, Sociétés, Civilisations* (1954), pp. 50–1, suggest that it may be because the Portuguese Jesuits had been expelled from Japan in 1640, partly as a result of the activities of Spanish Dominicans and Franciscans, and did not find in the king of Spain a helpful arbiter.

of both countries were also moved by similar grievances, for the city of Lisbon, like Barcelona, had been under constant pressure from Olivares to contribute to royal needs.[1] But in the character and attitude of the two bourgeoisies, and in the general nature of their response, there were significant differences which proved to be of great importance in determining the outcome of the revolutions. The Catalan bourgeoisie, while exasperated by Olivares's policies, broke with the king of Spain almost in spite of itself. An essentially provincial bourgeoisie, immured within its own corner of the Mediterranean world, it tended to see the political revolution as a possibly inevitable but none the less unwelcome disturbance to its traditional way of life; and its highest hope was that it should somehow be allowed to return as soon as possible to 'normal' conditions, suffering in the meantime the least possible inconvenience and danger.

The fact that the Portuguese bourgeoisie, unlike the Catalan, was not faced at the moment of political revolution with grave social upheaval, no doubt made it easier for it to accept the transition from the Spanish connection to independence. But, quite apart from this, Portugal's economic situation and its recent history helped to ensure a positive, and often enthusiastic, acceptance of the change, such as was not possible in Catalonia. Portugal belonged to a world which embraced Africa, America and the Far East, and this had done much to shape the development of the Portuguese mercantile community and to determine its political attitudes. If Portugal accepted without too much difficulty the union with Castile in 1580, one of the principal reasons for this may have been that it needed for its trade with the Far East a constant supply of silver which Castile's American possessions alone could provide.[2] The experiences of the decades after 1580 confirmed the economic advantages that came from being part of the Spanish Monarchy. Although Portugal's Far Eastern empire succumbed to the Dutch attack in the early seventeenth century, a second empire began to take shape, based on the sugar industry of Brazil;[3] and simultaneously Portuguese merchants made use of their privileged position to infiltrate into Castile's colonial possessions and into the American trade of Seville.[4]

---

[1] See Frédéric Mauro, *Le Portugal et l'Atlantique au XVIIe siècle* (Paris, 1960), pp. 468–9, for a list of Lisbon's contributions.

[2] Braudel, *La Méditerranée*, p. 1027, and Chaunu, *Séville et l'Atlantique*, vol. VIII, I, p. 261.

[3] Chaunu, 'Autour de 1640', p. 48.　　　　　[4] *Séville et l'Atlantique*, vol. IV, p. 570.

Beneficiaries of the dynamic economy of the Atlantic, Portuguese merchants thus operated in spheres far beyond the reach of their Catalan colleagues. They had close financial and commercial ties with the business communities of Amsterdam and northern Europe, and, in the reign of Philip IV, they were well represented at Court. It is symptomatic of the difference between the economic life of the two countries that there were no Catalan *asentistas* at the Spanish Court—no Duarte Fernández, no Manuel de Paz, both well-known figures in the world of international finance. The lack of figures of this calibre may have been one of the crucial weaknesses of Catalonia in the 1640's. While the role of the Lisbon business community in the winning and preserving of Portuguese independence is yet to be investigated, it seems probable that its connections with northern financial and mercantile interests prompted an active foreign concern in the preservation of independence, such as the Catalans lacked.[1]

If a mercantile community which supported union with Spain in 1580 turned away from it in 1640, this was because it felt that it no longer stood to gain anything from a continuing association. In the last two decades before the revolution, the Spaniards had shown themselves increasingly reluctant to share the wealth of their colonial possessions with the Portuguese interlopers.[2] Even more important, they had shown themselves incapable of defending Brazil, on which the prosperity of Portugal now primarily depended. Militarily, therefore, as well as economically, the union of the Crowns had lost its value. Revolution was a risk, but it was a risk that the Portuguese upper classes were now prepared to take, partly because of strong popular pressure from below, and partly because they hoped that it might in some way enable them to recover their most valuable overseas possession. Against all expectation their gamble succeeded. For some years after 1640 Brazil's fate hung in the balance, but the determination of the Portuguese to recover their Brazilian territories, and the general deterioration of the

---

[1] The nature of these connections is skilfully revealed in H. Kellenbenz, *Unternehmerkräfte im Hamburger Portugal- und Spanienhandel, 1590–1625* (Hamburg, 1954). The chapter devoted to the Portuguese *asentistas* in Domínguez Ortiz, *Política y Hacienda*, unfortunately does not discuss this question, although it shows that those Portuguese businessmen who were royal bankers remained faithful to the Spanish Crown after 1640. One Portuguese banker, Pedro de Baeza, was executed in Lisbon in 1641 for his complicity in a plot against John IV (AGS: GA, leg. 1400, Cardenal Infante to King, 7 Nov. 1641).

[2] Chaunu, 'Autour de 1640', p. 54.

Dutch West India Company's position after the departure of Prince John Maurice, eventually led to the expulsion of the Dutch.[1] Once Brazil was recovered, Portugal's chances of survival were immeasurably strengthened. In the sugar and slave trades the country possessed sources of wealth of which the Catalans could only dream. Enjoying, in addition, the protection of a France which was not too inconveniently close, and then the assistance of Restoration England, it was able to defy successfully, although not without moments of acute anxiety, the attacks of an enfeebled Spain.

The Portuguese Revolution succeeded primarily because the country's ruling class proved to be broadly united at the moment of decision,[2] seeing in national independence an opportunity to adopt new policies which might enable the country to realize its economic assets more effectively than was possible under continuing Spanish rule. The Catalan ruling class was not united, and in the 1640's the Principality lacked the economic opportunities which might have enabled it to steer a new course. If, as seemed probable, Catalonia's best hope for the future lay in securing a share of the American trade, this was more likely to be achieved by a continuation of the political association with Castile than by a total break. As a result, there was from the beginning of the revolution a fundamental incompatibility between the country's political aspirations and its real economic needs, such as was not to be found in Portugal.

If the revolt of Portugal confirmed Olivares's view that the principal weakness of the Spanish Monarchy was its lack of unity—its continuing failure to make its constituent provinces feel themselves equally privileged partners in a common cause—the outcome of the Catalan revolt showed that the Monarchy none the less possessed certain reserves of strength, whose existence Olivares himself may not have suspected. It seems somehow as if the very structure of the Monarchy compelled movements of discontent to flow in certain well-defined channels which ultimately ran themselves to ground. There was often, as in Catalonia

---

[1] See Boxer, *The Dutch in Brazil*, and W. J. Van Hoboken, 'The Dutch West India Company; the Political Background of its Rise and Decline', *Britain and the Netherlands*, ed. J. S. Bromley and E. H. Kossmann (London, 1960), pp. 41–61.

[2] There were, however, important exceptions. Some sections of the aristocracy, higher clergy and merchants 'remained attached to the dual monarchy and made several attempts to reunite the two countries' [V. M. Godinho, 'Portugal and her empire', *The New Cambridge Modern History*, vol. v, *The Age of Louis XIV* (Cambridge, 1961), p. 392.].

in 1640 or the Netherlands in 1566, a discontented governing class, which felt itself neglected by an absentee king, and slighted and affronted by his local agents. There was also a restless populace, afflicted by social, fiscal and economic discontents, and bitterly opposed to alien rule. Aristocratic and popular discontent, dangerous in themselves, were infinitely more dangerous when they converged. Yet the very moment of convergence, while in theory it represented the point of maximum danger to Habsburg rule, could also mark the turning of the tide. For, with the disappearance of royal authority, the upper classes would suddenly find themselves face to face with the mob, and the previous unity of the revolutionary movement tended to dissolve under the pressure of social antagonism. In the Netherlands failure was averted by the brilliant leadership of William of Orange and by the existence of a religious issue which helped to bind together rebels drawn from different social groups. Elsewhere, whether in Catalonia, Naples or Sicily, the upper classes took fright, and either retreated from revolution or held themselves aloof.

This was a common enough response anywhere in sixteenth and seventeenth-century Europe at times when social disorder threatened. But in the Habsburg dominions the character of provincial government may have helped to make it peculiarly inevitable. This government was always in the nature of a compromise between royal authority and local institutions, and the effectiveness of a viceregal administration depended on the maintenance of a delicate equilibrium between royal officials and the province's native governing class. While this class may often have bitterly reflected that it was hopelessly far away from the fountain-head of patronage, the very remoteness of Madrid was in some respects of considerable benefit to it. With Madrid so distant, provincial aristocracies inevitably retained considerable power and influence, and even when they came into conflict with the viceregal government they had innumerable methods of limiting the effectiveness of any measure liable to prejudice their interests. In such circumstances, the advantages of a total break with Madrid were greatly reduced, especially if such a break could only be achieved at the cost of a social upheaval. In this way, what seemed at first sight to be the greatest weakness of the Habsburg system of government—its need to obtain the acquiescence of the traditional governing class in the provinces, and its consequent commitment to the preservation of the existing social order—often proved to be its greatest source of strength, since the attractiveness of revolution was much diminished. In fact, it may have been precisely because the Spanish Monarchy was *not* centralized, uniform and closely integrated in the way Olivares desired, that it managed to survive for so long. The very looseness and flexibility of the system gave it a resilience which a more rigid structure would almost certainly have lacked.

There was, however, a price to be paid. The Catalan and Portuguese revolutions had shown that Madrid could retain the allegiance of the provinces only so long as it left their governing classes in peaceful possession of their traditional rights and institutions. This meant a renunciation by the Spanish Crown of further attempts at constitutional reform and fiscal innovation, and the consequent abandonment of all hopes of restoring Spanish power. In the political climate of the 1650's, the renunciation was easily made. No one wished to see a return to the days of the Conde Duque, and Philip IV, like the Catalans themselves, was satisfied with a restoration of the *status quo* which had existed before the age of Olivares. The old style of conciliar government, restored on Olivares's fall, reached its apogee in the reign of Philip's successor, Charles II. The second half of the seventeenth century was indeed for the Spanish Monarchy the golden age of provincial autonomy—an age of almost superstitious respect for regional rights and privileges by a Court too weak and too timid to protest.[1]

The soporific atmosphere of these years would hardly appear conducive to change, but yet, within the traditional framework of the Spanish Monarchy, Catalonia at least was showing unexpected signs of life. It seemed somehow as if the Revolution had administered a sudden salutary shock to Catalan society. The Principality, left to its own devices, now began to take the first halting steps towards economic renewal. Its textile industry benefited from the freedom of trade that came with the Peace of the Pyrenees; an increasing English and Dutch demand for Catalan spirits brought a new prosperity to the countryside; Catalan merchants turned to Cadiz and Lisbon in search of colonial produce;[2]

[1] See J. Vicens Vives, *Aproximación a la Historia de España* (2nd ed., Barcelona, 1960), p. 165. It is an indication of the influence enjoyed by the provinces at the Court that in 1694 Charles II conceded to the Consellers of Barcelona the right to remain covered in the royal presence, which the city had vainly claimed in 1632 (Soldevila, *Història de Catalunya*, vol. II, p. 370).

[2] See J. Vicens Vives, *Manual de Historia Económica de España* (Barcelona, 1959), p. 423.

and a new, more practical and industrious generation helped to efface the traditional image of the bandit, and put in its stead the image of the hard-working Catalan, the prosperous and successful man of affairs.[1]

While the Catalan economy began to revive, and Catalan society began to find a new stability, Castile plumbed the depths of political and economic degradation in the years around 1680. The contrast was obvious and painful. So also was the contrast between the inert corpse of the Spanish Monarchy and the vigorous governments of other European states, which were steadily extending their power at the expense of privileged groups and regions. The triumph of the Aragonese over the Castilian style of government, which was implicit in Philip IV's readiness to confirm the Catalan constitutions, prevented the ministers of Charles II from following in the steps of Louis XIV even if they had so wished. But how long could a Spanish Monarchy that was no more than a loose structure of semi-autonomous states headed by a prostrate Castile hope to survive in the new Europe of the later seventeenth century?

Sooner or later the old system was bound to be challenged once more, when a new ruler from a new dynasty returned to Olivares's theme that the king of Aragon and Valencia and the Count of Barcelona should also be king of Spain. The challenge came between 1705 and 1714. The Catalans, no doubt influenced by their experience of French rule between 1640 and 1652, came out in support of the Habsburg claimant against the new Bourbon dynasty. But now their adversary was stronger, and 1705 proved to be no 1640. Abandoned once again by its allies—on this occasion the English—the Principality was defeated, and this time there was no reprieve. The Crown of Aragon was systematically stripped of the privileges it had preserved for so long, and Catalonia became a mere region of the new Bourbon state.

In retrospect, therefore, the Catalan Revolution of 1640 had only succeeded in buying the Principality a little more time. It perpetuated for a further fifty years a form of government which had already begun to appear anachronistic by the third decade of the seventeenth century, and which, in the light of contemporary developments elsewhere in

---

[1] This image seems to date from the eighteenth century (Herrero García, *Ideas de los Españoles del Siglo XVII*, pp. 305–8), although as early as 1623 González Dávila refers to the Catalans as hard-working (*Teatro de las Grandezas de la Villa de Madrid*, p. 428). But this does not appear to have been a widely held opinion at that time.

Europe, seemed destined to eventual extinction. Like other insurrections of the sixteenth and seventeenth centuries, it would thus appear a typical revolt of the old order—a 'medieval' revolt against the new-style monarchy.

The political thought of the rebels would tend to confirm this interpretation. Most of the arguments used to defend the revolution were highly conventional, and indeed the majority of them had already been deployed in the great controversy of 1621–3 over the appointment of the viceroy, and merely required a little repolishing to be fit for use in 1640. There was no difficulty in proving that Philip IV had contravened the laws and liberties of the Principality and had thereby broken his sacred contract with his Catalan vassals. All that was needed was to set the renunciation of allegiance into its historical context—a task neatly accomplished by Martí i Viladamor.[1] Catalonia, according to Martí, had preserved its natural liberty since the founding of Spain by Tubal; the right of the Catalans to elect their own Prince was confirmed under the government both of the Goths and of Charlemagne, and had remained intact ever since. Later writers on the French side might claim a traditional French tutelage over the Principality dating from Charlemagne's reign,[2] but to the Catalans the substitution of Philip IV of Spain by Louis XIII of France was no more than the proper exercise of the Principality's privilege of choosing its own ruler.

A revolt organized by Estates, which justified themselves by the use of conventional contractual arguments based on historical precedent, naturally had about it a faded, anachronistic air in the circumstances of the sixteenth and seventeenth centuries. Yet, as the revolt of the Netherlands suggested, the medieval garb in which the rebels chose to attire themselves could sometimes be misleading. If the stock argument from the idea of contract continued to be used, this was because it remained a most effective weapon against the power of the Crown; and if resistance continued to be organized through the Estates, this was because they remained the obvious and most convenient organs of opposition.

Undoubtedly there was in the Catalan, as in the Dutch, revolt a strong 'medieval' element. The traditional orders of society were fighting to retain their traditional privileges. Yet, in the political pamphlets of the rebels, there are occasional glimpses of wider issues. Catalonia

---

[1] *Noticia Universal de Cataluña.*   [2] Sorel, *Deffence des Catalans*, p. 104.

was naturally the centre, but it was not always the boundary, of the pamphleteers' interests. Gaspar Sala, in his *Secrets Públichs*, expatiated on the inhumanity of the Castilians towards the American Indians;[1] and coming nearer home in his famous *Proclamación Católica*, he indignantly described the insulting treatment received at the hands of Olivares by certain of the Spanish grandees (including, with an irony of which he seems to have been quite unaware, the detested duke of Alcalá).[2]

Another pamphleteer, Josep Çarroca, went even further towards voicing the grievances not only of the Catalans but of Spaniards in general after twenty years of government by Olivares. Opening with a great tirade against the 'tyranny of a detestable minister', his pamphlet went on to list the misfortunes that had befallen the Spanish Monarchy under the Conde Duque's rule, and then examined and refuted his various political maxims. Çarroca's principal target was Olivares's alleged intention of establishing *una ley, un Rey, una moneda*, but, while his criticism of Olivares's plans for unity was clearly designed to attract the sympathy of the peripheral provinces of Spain, he was also careful to expatiate on the many sufferings of Castile.[3]

For all its Catalan slant, Çarroca's manifesto may be seen without too much exaggeration as the manifesto of all Spain against the Conde Duque's government. As such, it is something of a landmark in Spanish history, for here is the first attempt, however hesitant, to overthrow a government at Madrid by means of agitation from the periphery. The Catalans in 1640 were too weak to achieve this by their own efforts, but they had set a precedent which later generations were to follow. The polemics of a Sala or a Çarroca suggest that, for all the mismanagement of the Catalan Revolution, the generation of 1640 had a greater political awareness than that of 1615. Where the generation of 1615 consumed itself in banditry and family vendettas, that of 1640 at least directed its discontent into political channels and showed a certain skill in exploiting the international situation to further its own ends. And, in spite of all

[1] Ch. 2 (no page numbers). This argument, one source of the 'black legend', had, however, already been used in William the Silent's *Apology* (*Apologie ou défense de...Guillaume Prince d'Orange*, Leyden, 1581, p. 50).

[2] *Proclamación Católica*, pp. 131 ff.

[3] *Política del Comte de Olivares, Contrapolítica de Cataluña* (Barcelona, 1641). Significantly enough, the work is dedicated to the cathedral chapter of Urgell, 'which was the first chapter to come out gloriously in defence of the province's reputation...and which carried on notable and discreet intelligence with the frontier gentry'.

their private discontents, some of the Catalans of 1640 did show themselves capable of taking a wider, and less exclusively Catalan, view of events. They were aware that the government of the Spanish Monarchy had been grossly mismanaged; they were aware of the misery to which Castile had been reduced. Gaspar Sala, indeed, quoted in the opening pages of his *Secrets Públichs* the writings of the Castilian *arbitrista* Lisón y Biedma[1] to illustrate the lamentable economic condition of Castile, and warned his compatriots that a similar fate was in store for their country if Olivares's centralizing ambitions were achieved. The Catalan Revolution was thus an attempt, badly bungled but none the less sincere, to save Catalonia from the fate of Castile; and, in its widest interpretation, it was a blind and desperate movement of protest against the policies of a dynasty which had brought Spain to disaster.

At last, therefore, as a result of 1640, the Catalans were becoming aware of Spain: aware of Spain as a political community, degraded by the follies of its Habsburg rulers; aware also of Spain as an economic community facing the Atlantic, which Catalonia had for so long ignored. And, in this new awareness, the Principality was slowly beginning to emerge from the isolation in which it had been buried—partly through its own fault, partly through the fault of the Court—for over a hundred years.

There was about this awakening a certain tragic irony. The whole policy of the Conde Duque had been designed to make the various provinces of the Monarchy aware of each other and of their mutual obligations, and gradually to weld them into a single whole. Yet all his attempts to realize his ideal had ended in disaster. Perhaps his task in Catalonia would have been easier if Lerma's government had intervened in 1615, as Philip II intervened in Aragon in 1592. Perhaps Olivares himself should have intervened earlier in the Principality, and imposed his 'uniformity' upon it in 1626 or 1632 before he became involved in war with France. Given his foreign policy, the general lines of his domestic policy seem predetermined, and such mistakes as he made may primarily have been mistakes of timing; but his task was not made any easier by the failure of his predecessors to prepare the ground, nor by his own indifference to national susceptibilities at a time when Castile could no longer impose its will by the mere use of force.

[1] M. Lisón y Biedma, *Discursos y Apuntamientos* (Madrid, 1621).

But, paradoxically, the very failure of the Conde Duque was itself a preliminary to partial success. In self-defence Catalonia was driven to take an interest in the outer world, and to protest vigorously against a government which had come to be hated through the length and breadth of Spain. In 1640 it spoke, for one brief moment, for all the peninsula. It spoke for the nobles and peasants of Castile, as well as for the Aragonese and the Vizcayans, the Portuguese and the Valencians. For that brief moment it touched a common chord which Olivares had sought for so long and with so little success. During its revolution of 1640 Catalonia was brought to realize, however unwillingly, that it was part of Spain. But the events attending the outbreak of the revolution were not easily forgotten. Where community of interest urged, and still urges, the need to unite, the memories that survive the centuries serve only to divide. The revolt of the Catalans at once epitomized and foreshadowed the tragedy of Spain.

APPENDIX I

A NOTE ON COINAGE[1]

The Catalan coinage

Authorities:

Botet y Sisó, J.: *Les Monedes Catalanes* (3 vols., Barcelona, 1908–11).

Gil Farrés, Octavio: *Historia de la Moneda Española* (Madrid, 1959).

Salat, J.: *Tratado de las Monedas Labradas en el Principado de Cataluña* (2 vols., Barcelona, 1818).

Usher, Abbott Payson: *The Early History of Deposit Banking in Mediterranean Europe* (*Harvard Economic Studies*, vol. LXXV, Cambridge, Mass., 1943).

The Crown of Aragon, unlike Castile, was part of the *libra* system, and financial accounts were kept in pounds, shillings and pence:

$$1 \text{ } lliura \text{ } (ll.) = 20 \text{ } sous$$
$$1 \text{ } sou \text{ } (s.) = 12 \text{ } diners \text{ } (d.)$$

Prices, however, were sometimes quoted in Catalan *reals* (1 Catalan *real* = 2 *sous*, so that there were 10 *reals* to the Barcelona pound).

The following coins were minted by the Barcelona mint in the seventeenth century (up to 1640):

Gold (the value of these gold coins fluctuated during the monetary crisis of the first two decades of the century):

dobla de dos cares (double-ducat—the *excelente de la granada*). This coin came to be known as the *trentí*, because its value was 30 *reals*, i.e. 60s. By 1614 it had risen to 70s., but after 1618 it settled down at 66s., or 33 *reals*.

ducat (or *escut* or *mig trentí*): half a *trentí*.

florí (minted from 1614): half a *ducat*.

onzen (minted from 1618): a third of a *trentí*, and known as the *onzen* because it was worth 11 *reals*.

A. P. Usher (*Early History of Deposit Banking*, table 37, p. 457) gives the following figures for the metallic content of the pound at Barcelona, 1599–1618:

	Fine silver (gm)	Fine gold (gm)	Ratio silver to gold
To 6 Sept. 1599	31·00	2·94	10·5
6 Sept. 1599	31·00	2·32	13·4 [*cont.*

[1] I am much indebted to Mr P. Grierson of Gonville and Caius College, Cambridge, for his advice.

	Fine silver (gm)	Fine gold (gm)	Ratio silver to gold
8 Jan. 1603	31·00	2·47	12·5
11 July 1611	27·80 (?)	2·32	12·0 (?)
13 Jan. 1614	27·80 (?)	2·00	13·90
8 July 1617	27·10	2·00	13·55
6 Dec. 1617	27·60	2·00	13·80
21 Feb. 1618	27·60	2·11	13·1

Silver
          real (or *croat*) = 2 *sous*
          mig real = 1 *sou*
          sisé = 6 *diners*

Copper
          ardit = 2 *diners*
          menut = 1 *diner*

The Castilian coinage

Authorities:

Gil Farrés, *op. cit.*

Hamilton, Earl J.: *American Treasure and the Price Revolution in Spain, 1501–1650* (Harvard Economic Studies, vol. XLIII, Cambridge, Mass., 1934).

Mateu y Llopis, Felipe: *La Moneda Española* (Barcelona, 1946).

The Castilian money of account was the *maravedí*, corresponding to a small coin of *vellón*,[1] and figures of royal revenues were expressed either in *maravedís*, or, more commonly in the seventeenth century, in ducats (the gold *ducado* had been replaced by the *escudo* in the reign of Charles V, but continued to be used for reckoning). The relative values of the Castilian moneys mentioned in this book are as follows:

1 *ducado* = 375 *maravedís*
1 *escudo* = 400 *maravedís* (raised to 440 by a pragmatic of 23 November 1609, cf. Hamilton, *op. cit.* p. 65)
1 (Castilian) *real* = 34 *maravedís* (i.e. 11 *reales* to the ducat)

---

[1] 'Vellon was originally a mixture of silver and copper used for fractional coins. After the restoration of the silver content at the close of the fifteenth century, debasement during the sixteenth century gradually reduced vellon to pure copper' (Hamilton, *op. cit.* p. 46, n. 3).

A Note on Coinage

Conversion table for Castilian and Catalan currencies

Castilian	Catalan	Catalan	Castilian
1 *real*	2 *sous* (1 Catalan *real*)	1 *sou*	½ *real*
1 *ducado*	22 *sous* (11 Catalan *reals*)	1 *lliura*	10 *reales* (i.e. just under a ducat)
1 *escudo* (in Catalan, *escut*)	26 *sous*		

Extract from a discourse of 1626 on the Catalan coinage:[1] 'In France, for one *real* one can buy 60 things; in Rome, 50; in Rosselló and Cerdanya, 40; in Catalonia, Aragon and Valencia, 24; and in Castile no more than 17.'

[1] BC: Fullet Bonsoms 5382, *Discurs sobre la moneda de belló de Cathalunya.*

SOME CATALAN WAGES AND PRICES

Professor Hamilton was unable to include details of Catalan wages and prices in his *American Treasure and the Price Revolution in Spain* because he could find no good connected series in Barcelona.[1] There are, however, in ACA: *Monacales* two account books of the Augustinian convent of Sant Guillèm (San Guillermo) in Barcelona. This convent, which seems to have had eleven inmates, was founded in 1587. The first book (lib. 103) entitled *Libro del gasto del Colegio (Agustino) de San Guillermo de Barcelona* covers the period from 1588 to 1621, although the pages from 1607 to 1612 are missing. The second (lib. 101) runs from 1621 to 1642. Apart from the seven missing years, it is possible to extract from them a connected series of corn prices, which are charted below. They also provide some details of other prices, to which it has been possible to add one or two more from other sources. (These prices, taken from very few samples, are not necessarily representative, and are given purely for purposes of comparison.)

PRICES

Quantity		Date	Price		
Animals			Lliures	Sous	Diners
Chicken	—	1621 and 1635	–	2	–
Hen	—	1640	–	9	–
Mule	—	1597	30	–	–
Oxen	1 pair	1598	30	–	–
Oxen	1 pair	1638[2]	37	4	–
Sheep	—	1640[3]	2	–	–
Clothes					
Boy's hat	—	1621	–	2	–
Boy's suit (*vestido para el mozo*)		1621	1	16	–
		1625	2	5	–
		1633	2	17	–
		1634	1	4	–
		1634	2	7	–
Black habit (for Augustinian)		1626	11	10	–

[1] Hamilton, *op. cit.* p. 146, n. 1.
[2] J. Serra Vilaró, *Baronies de Pinós i Mataplana*, vol. II, p. 458.
[3] AHC: *Llibre de XXIV*, fo. 132.

Some Catalan Wages and Prices

	Quantity	Date	Price		
			Lliures	Sous	Diners
Shirt	—	1589–1635	–	16 to 1 *lliura*	
Shoes	1 pair	1587–1641	–	8	–
Fuel					
Coal	1 *carga*	1620's and 1630's	About 20–22 *sous*		
Miscellaneous					
A Bible ('for reading in the community')		1588	–	16	–
Paper	1 *mano* (25 sheets)	1625–1638	–	1–2 *sous*	
Wax (white)	1 pound	1620's and 1630's	About 8 *sous*		
Wool	1 pound	1633	–	1	6
A musket (good quality)		1639[1]	1	10	–
Wine	1 *carga* (without transport costs)	Maximum prices in *sous*			

1621	52		1632	72
1622	41		1633	85
1623	58		1635	78
1624	46		1636	90
1625	40		1637	92
1626	70		1638	124
1627	50		1639	104
1628	50		1640	90
1630	90		1641	94
1631	88			

(It is always possible that the remarkable increase in wine prices is accounted for by the purchase of a better quality wine, but there is no indication of this. Occasional purchases of claret are noted separately, and are not included in this list.) For corn prices, see graph on following page.

[1] AHC: *Consells* (1639), fo. 29v.

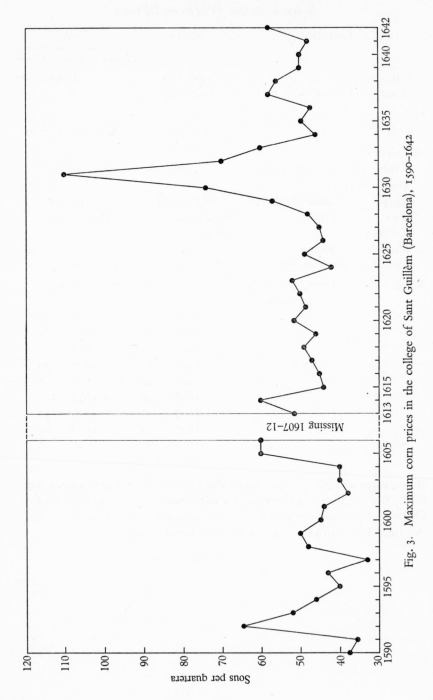

Fig. 3. Maximum corn prices in the college of Sant Guillèm (Barcelona), 1590–1642

Details of Catalan wages are as scanty as those of prices. Some random examples exist, however (of which a few are given on p. 60 above).

(1) *Manual labourers*

(*a*) Convent of Sant Guillèm, Barcelona

Carpenter	1 day	1588	4*s.* 2*d.*
		1596	6*s.*
		1635	8*s.*
Cook	1 week	1594	6*s.*
Houseboy	1 year	1636	4 *ll.* 16*s.*

(*b*) Manresa (municipal works)[1]

Carpenter	1 day	1622	6*s.*
Mason	1 day	1640	6*s.*
Building labourer	1 day	1640	4*s.*

(2) *Professional incomes*

Lawyer. A successful Barcelona lawyer, Dr Joan Magarola, made well over 1000 *lliures* a year from his practice in the late sixteenth century.[2]

Notary. A provincial notary, at Vilafranca del Penedès, earned the following from his notarial work:[3]

1621	302 *lliures*
1622	281 *lliures*
1623	235 *lliures* 12*s.* 6*d.*

(3) *Income from property*

Dr Antoni Magarola, a doctor of medicine, claimed that his property was sufficient for him to live as befitted a member of the *estament militar*, 'since it produces an annual income of more than 600 ducats' (*c.* 600 *lliures*).[4] If a reasonable income for a gentleman was something like 600 *lliures*, a noble would seem to have needed something in the region of 2000 *lliures* if he was to live as became his station,[5] but it is questionable how many Catalan nobles in fact possessed as much as this.

During the revolution, certain properties were confiscated by the French, and their value was listed in an undated paper entitled *Estat des confiscations*,

[1] AHM: leg. 965.
[2] ACA: CA, leg. 483, petition of Dr Magarola (1605?).
[3] Archivo Notarial, Vilafranca del Penedès, Pere Guasch, Manual 67, fo. 11. This reference was shown to me by Dr Emili Giralt.
[4] ACA: CA, leg. 488, petition of Antoni Magarola (1613?).
[5] ACA: CA, leg. 500, petition of Joan Francesc Brossa (1626).

now in AAE: Corresp. Espagne, Sup. no. 3, fos. 340–6. Although it is impossible to check the accuracy or completeness of the figures given, one or two of the examples may be of interest:

Property of Don Ramon Calders (former Governor of Catalonia):

The property consists of the village and domain of Pierola, and an estate near Martorell. Total annual value—860 *lliures*. Charges against it not known, but believed to be considerable.

Property of the Count of Vallfogona

		Lliures	s.	d.
(*a*) County of Vallfogona.	Total annual income	4,819	–	–
	Charges	1,077	10	–
		3,741	10	–
(*b*) Viscounty of Canet (including salt-mines worth 1201 *ll.* 16*s.* p.a.)		2,006	16	–
	Charges	444	10	–
		1,562	6	–
	Net value p.a.	5,303	16	–

Property of Don Guerau de Guardiola (formerly Lloctinent de Mestre Racional)

		Lliures	s.	d.
Property consists of houses, estates and ground-rents, to annual value of		643	15	6
	Charges	113	16	6
	Net value p.a.	529	19	–

Property of the Count of Santa Coloma

	Lliures	s.	d.
Annual income from county of Santa Coloma de Queralt and the barony of Pons	8,000	–	–
Village of Callar near Tarragona	1,800	–	–
A palace and two houses in Barcelona (occupied by French viceroy)	—	–	–
An estate and house in Badalona	100	–	–
Three houses in Barcelona, rented at	226	–	–
Various ground-rents	2,352	16	–
Total value (excluding the Tarragona property, too close to Spanish-occupied territory to be of profit)	10,678	16	–
Charges	1,800	–	–
Net value p.a.	8,878	16	–

Property of Francesc Frigola i Llordat, senyor of Maldà

	Lliures	s.	d.
Property consists of village of Maldà in Urgell, other ground-rents and an estate in Empurdà. Annual value	1,159	14	–
Charges	325	–	–
Net value p.a.	834	14	–

(4) Income from office

Municipal office

The salary of a Conseller of Barcelona from 1588 was 250 *lliures* p.a.[1] The town councillors (Pahers) of Cervera petitioned the king in 1626 for their salaries to be raised to 100 *lliures* p.a.[2] By contrast, the *cònsols* of Bagà, which was little more than a village, received a salary of 15 *lliures* p.a. between 1592 and 1648.[3]

Viceregal administration[4]

Viceroy	6000 ducats p.a.	Judges of the Audiència *c.* 1000 *lliures* p.a.
Governador	1460 *lliures* p.a.	
Canceller	1200 *lliures* p.a.	Local officials:

Veguers—from 50 to 200 *lliures* p.a.
Batlles—from 5 to 70 *lliures* p.a.

(5) Income and expenditure of a cathedral chapter

Printed below is a summary of the accounts of the cathedral chapter of the Seu d'Urgell for the two years 1 May 1640 to 30 April 1642, as given in ACU: *Balans de les entrades i eixides del capítol*. The full complement of the chapter was twenty-four canons.

Income (for two years)

	Lliures	sous	diners
Farm of the revenues of the chapter's properties:			
Terra alta	13,362	–	8
Cerdanya	3,966	4	–
Terra baixa	4,564	4	–
Revenues of marquisate of Camarasa	1,486	–	–
Arrears and payments of certain dues to the chapter	3,520	9	10
Censals of the *mensa capitular*	2,210	–	–
Other *censals* (annuities)	1,061	8	–
Sundry dues (e.g. lease of a mill)	476	–	–

[cont.

---

[1] F. Carreras y Candi, *Geografia General de Catalunya*, vol. on Catalunya, p. 729.
[2] AHC: *Llibre de XXIV*, fo. 16. [3] Serra Vilaró, *Baronies*, vol. II, p. 81.
[4] ACA: CA, leg. 373, memorandum on salaries, 1624.

	Lliures	sous	diners
Chapter's share of revenues from the property of Don Diego Alentorn, *senyor* of Seró, for 1640	231	19	7
Ditto from the town of Anglesola	86	13	9
Total income for two years	30,964	19	10

Expenditure (for two years)

The individual items of expenditure are too numerous and often too trivial to list.

	Lliures	sous	diners
The total expenditure for these two years was	28,755	11	4
Of this total, the largest individual item consisted of stipends, Easter offerings, etc., for the canons. Total for two years	13,425	3	5
Military expenditure (*socorro de guerra*) from 1 May 1640 to 30 April 1642 totalled	1,414	9	10
The *quarta* and *excusado* for 1640 totalled	261	7	8

Over the two years, therefore, the canons had a balance in hand of just over 2000 *lliures*, and annual income averaged 15,000 *lliures*. This income was about three times the value of the diocesan revenues—a disparity which may throw some light on the conflicts between the bishop and his chapter.

IMPORT AND EXPORT DUES

One of the most important sources of income of the Diputació was the so-called *dret de entrades i eixides* or *dret del General*. This was a tax levied on all Catalan imports and exports, with the exception of imported grain and other essential foodstuffs.[1] The standard rate of payment was 4*d*. in the pound, except on money taken from the country by private persons, which was liable to a higher duty—5 per cent from 1599.[2] The tax seems to have been collected in ports and at customs stations situated on the highways to Aragon, France and Valencia, and the collectors were entitled to keep 2*s*. in every pound they collected, with the exception of a small group of collectors who received a fixed salary.[3]

A detailed record of the yield of the tax was kept at the Diputació in a register known as the *Llibre de Values*. Many volumes have survived in the Archive of the Crown of Aragon, but have not, to my knowledge, ever been examined.

The registers group the collecting-posts together under the name of the principal customs station in the district, and classify them into three divisions:

(1) Barcelona

(2) *Levant*	Perpinyà	Puigcerdà		
	Mataró	Vic		
	Girona			
(3) *Ponent*	Balaguer	Seu d'Urgell	Tremp i Pallars	Lleida
	Tarragona	Tortosa	Montblanc	
	Cervera	Tàrrega	Falset	

Details are given of the sum collected at every customs station over a period of three months, and also of the totals from each group of posts over the course of the year. There are figures both for the total yield, and for the sum remaining after the deduction of the collectors' salaries.

Apart from the many numerical slips that may have been made at various stages of the proceedings, there are obvious difficulties in handling and interpreting these figures. Nothing is really known about the administration of the system; and, from the repeated statements in the ordinances of the Diputació it is clear that there was constant fraud. There is no distinction

---

[1] Details will be found in *Capítols dels Drets y Altres Coses del General del Principat de Cathalunya* (Barcelona, 1635), Capítols de Corts, 1481, fos. 2ff.

[2] *Ibid.* Capítols, 1599, fo. 70 (cap. XL).   [3] *Ibid.* fos. 123–5 (cap. LXXXVIII).

TABLE I

Year (July–June)	Barcelona Lliures	Remainder of Principality Lliures	Total Lliures
1596–7	25,000	19,000	44,000
1597–8	23,000	20,000	43,000
1598–9	31,000	33,000	64,000
1599–1602	Missing	Missing	—
1602–3	24,000	20,000	44,000
1603–4	16,000	16,000	32,000
1604–5	16,000	19,000	35,000
1605–6	12,000	16,000	28,000
1606–7	15,000	16,000	31,000
1607–8	13,000	15,000	28,000
1608–14	Missing	Missing	—
1614–15	19,000	17,000	36,000
1615–16	22,000	16,000	38,000
1616–17	26,000	17,000	43,000
1617–18	21,000	15,000	36,000
1618–19	22,000	17,000	39,000
1619–20	20,000	16,000	36,000
1620–1	20,000	17,000	37,000
1621–2	21,000	13,000	34,000
1622–3	22,000	17,000	39,000
1623–4	17,000	17,000	34,000
1624–5	12,000	13,000	25,000
1625–6	18,000	17,000	35,000
1626–7	21,000	19,000	40,000
1627–8	21,000	15,000	36,000
1628–9	17,000	10,000	(Totals for 1628–32
1629–30	18,000	8,000	not definitive as
1630–1	18,000	7,000	some figures
1631–2	19,000	5,000	missing)
1632–5	Missing	Missing	—
1635–6	14,000	10,000	24,000
1636–7	15,000	9,000	24,000

between levies on imports and those on exports, so that the figures cannot be used as a guide to the state of Catalan production. Moreover, the fact that the duty was also levied on the transit of money means that they cannot be used as a reliable guide to the total volume of trade.

The figures, therefore, can be said to show accurately only the total receipts from the tax, as reported by the collectors. This itself, however, is of some interest for the light it throws on the annual variations of one of the principal sources of wealth of the Generalitat. In addition, there is always a possibility that, for all their defects, they do give a very rough picture of fluctuations in Catalan commerce over a period of thirty years—a subject on which at present almost nothing is known. It may therefore be not entirely useless to print a summary of them.

Table 1 shows the total yield on *entrades i eixides* before deduction of salaries. These figures are taken from ACA: G, 85, nos. 21–9, and I have divided them into two sections: dues levied in Barcelona, and dues from the rest of the Principality (*Levant* and *Ponent*). Figures are given to the nearest thousand *lliures*, and the year runs in all cases from 1 July to 30 June.

TABLE 2

Lliures

1599–1602 (July–June)	158,000
1602–5	102,000
1605–8	82,000
1608–11	92,000
1611–14	95,000
1614–17	103,000
1617–20	101,000
1620–3	99,000
1623–6	81,000
1626–9	93,000

Table 2 shows the revenues from the *dret de entrades i eixides* by three-year periods (again from July to June), as supplied by another source—the statement of accounts of the Diputació drawn up for the Corts of 1632. (ACA: G, 147/2, Balans de les Generalitats de Catalunya.) As far as can be seen, these figures represent the sum actually entering the Diputació, i.e. the total yield *after* deduction of salaries. I have again rounded off figures to the nearest thousand.

ROYAL OFFICIALS CONNECTED WITH THE GOVERNMENT OF CATALONIA

There is no general list of the holders even of the more important offices in the Spanish Monarchy in the sixteenth and seventeenth centuries, and information about names and about dates of appointment is scanty and widely scattered. At this stage even a partial list of officials concerned in the government of one province of the Monarchy may possess a certain value, and it is here presented as a small contribution towards a general list which, it is to be hoped, will one day be constructed.

While this list attempts to cover appointments between 1598 and 1640, it has often been quite impossible to discover the names of officials in the reign of Philip III, and it is only from about 1621 that the list becomes in any way comprehensive.

A dotted line indicates that the official was still in office at the time of the outbreak of the Catalan Revolution of 1640. † indicates his death.

(1) MADRID

The Council of Aragon

The following were the members and principal officials of the Council of Aragon in July 1615:[1]

Vice-Chancellor	Don Andreu Roig
Treasurer-General	The count of Chinchón
Regents	Don Felipe Tallada
	Don Salvador Fontanet
	Martínez Boclin
	Lucas Pérez Manrique
Protonotary	Don Francisco Gassol
Fiscal advocate	Miguel Martínez del Villar
Secretaries	Agustín de Villanueva
	Domingo Ortiz
	Antonio Orlandés
	Juan Lorenzo de Villanueva

[1] ACA: CA, leg. 489, *Relación de lo que se dió a los Sres. y Ministros del Supremo Consejo de Aragón...*, 27 July 1615.

Royal Officials connected with the Government of Catalonia

Vice-Chancellor (*Vicecanciller*)

Don Andreu Roig (Catalan)	Before 1615–Winter 1622†
Don Pedro de Guzmán	21 July 1623–November 1623†
Garcí Pérez de Araziel	† October 1624 before taking oath

(Post in abeyance till 1646)

President (replacing Vice-Chancellor)

Marquis of Montesclaros	January 1628–9 October 1628†
Don Enrique Pimentel (Bishop of Cuenca)	17 October 1628–1632
Duke of Alburquerque	11 November 1632–18 July 1637†
Cardinal Borja	21 July 1637–......

Treasurer-General (*Tesorero General*)

Count of Chinchón	c. 1613–1626
Marquis of Montesclaros	30 December 1626–January 1628
Duke of Medina de las Torres	11 January 1628–......

Regents (*Regentes*)

(a) Aragonese

(1)		(2)	
Miguel Martínez del Villar	?–24 January 1625†	Lucas Pérez Manrique	?–1622
Miguel Pueyo	1625–1630	Baltasar Navarro de Arroyta	1623?–1633?
Matías de Bayetolá	1630–......	Miguel de Morlanes	1635–1638

(b) Valencian

(1)		(2)	
Francesc de Castellví	?–February 1638†	Francesc de León	1625–1630?
		Melcior Sisternes	1633–......

(c) Catalan

(1)		(2)	
Salvador Fontanet	?–February 1633†	Miquel de Salvà i de Vallseca	1621–13 November 1627†
		Dr Aguiló	†1628 before taking oath
		Dr Joan Magarola	1630–......

(d) Sardinian

Luis Blasco	1623?–1627?
Francisco de Vico	1627–......

Protonotary (Protonotario)

Francisco Gassol	?–13 May 1619 †
Jerónimo de Villanueva	1620–......

Secretary for Catalonia

Juan Lorenzo de Villanueva	?–17 October 1637 †
Pedro de Villanueva	1637–......

(II) CATALONIA

(1) *Viceroys of Catalonia*

Duke of Feria (Lorenzo Suárez de Figueroa)	November 1596–April 1602
Archbishop of Tarragona (Joan Terés)	April 1602–June 1603
Duke of Monteleón (Hector de Pignatelli)	July 1603–1610
Bishop of Tortosa (Pedro Manrique)	November 1610–August 1611
Marquis of Almazán (Francisco Hurtado de Mendoza)	September 1611–October 1615 †
Duke of Alburquerque (Francisco Fernández de la Cueva)	April 1616–April 1619
Duke of Alcalá (Fernando Afán de Ribera y Enríquez)	April 1619–September 1622
Bishop of Barcelona (Joan Sentís)	September 1622–March 1626
Bishop of Urgell (Luis Díaz Aux de Armendáriz)	May 1626–January 1627 †
Bishop of Solsona (Miguel Santos de San Pedro)	February 1627–May 1629
Duke of Feria (Gómez Suárez de Figueroa)	June 1629–November 1630
Duke of Cardona (Enrique de Aragón)	November 1630–May 1632
The Cardenal Infante (Fernando de Austria)	May 1632–April 1633
Duke of Cardona	April 1633–February 1638
Count of Santa Coloma (Dalmau de Queralt)	February 1638–June 1640 †
Duke of Cardona	June 1640–July 1640 †
Bishop of Barcelona (Garcí Gil Manrique)	August 1640–October 1640

Royal Officials connected with the Government of Catalonia

(2) Viceregal administration[1]

(a) Canceller

Dr Jaume d'Agullana	1605–1617 (?)†
Dr Antoni Carmona	July 1617–April 1621†
Don Pere Puigmarí	April 1621–August 1630
Dr Joan Magarola (never took up office because of appointment to Council of Aragon)	18 October 1630–6 September 1631
Don Francesc de Erill	9 September 1631–6 January 1640†

(b) Regent la Reial Cancelleria

Dr Jeroni Torner	?–October 1608†
Miquel de Salvà i de Vallseca	January 1609–1621 (appointed a Regent of Council of Aragon)
Dr Miquel Sala	June 1621–1639 (retired)
Dr Miquel Joan Magarola	August 1639–......

(c) Governador de Catalunya

Don Enric de Cardona	?–December 1602†
Don Joan de Queralt	1603–1611†
Don Jeroni d'Argensola	June 1611–December 1613
Don Alexos de Marimón	December 1613–September 1639†
Don Ramon de Calders i Ferran	13 September 1639–......

(d) Governador dels Comtats (Rosselló and Cerdanya)

Don Joan de Queralt	?–1603 (appointed Governor of Catalonia)
Don Jeroni d'Argensola	1603–1611 (appointed Governor of Catalonia)
Don Guillèm de Iborra	August 1611–1615†
Don Cristòfol Gallart	October 1615–......

(e) Lloctinent del Mestre Racional

Don Guerau de Guardiola	1613–......

(f) Batlle General

Count of Erill	?–1617
Don Lluís Monsuar	1617–......

[1] Names are given in Catalan.

(g) Regent la Tresoreria

Don Francesc d'Agullana   ?–August 1609†

Don Cristòfol Gallart   November 1609–1615 (appointed Governador dels Comtats)

Francesc Bru   1620–March 1626

Don Lluís Descallar   July 1627–March 1629

Don Ramon de Calders i Ferran   1629–1639 (appointed Governor of Catalonia)

Don Miquel Salvà i Vallgornera   1639–......

(h) Advocat fiscal patrimonial

Dr Hipòlit Muntaner   ?–1627†

Dr Cristòfol Fumàs   1627–1633

Dr Felip Vinyes   1634–......

(i) Procurador Reial dels Comtats

Don Gabriel de Llupià   ?–1623

Don Joan de Llupià   1623–......

(III) AUDIÈNCIA OF CATALONIA

(a) The Audiència in 1621 (ACA: CA, leg. 366)

1a *sala*
- Dr Josep Dalmau (retired)
- Dr Josep Ferrer
- Dr Jeroni Sanjust
- Dr Mijavila i Franquesa
- Dr Francesc Gamis
- Dr Hipòlit Muntaner

2a *sala*
- Dr Joan Gallego
- Dr Jeroni Astor
- Dr Pere Soler
- Dr Josep Roca
- Dr Baltasar Morell

3a *sala*
- Dr Francesc Bonet
- Dr Joan Magarola
- Dr Miquel Sala
- Dr Francesc Ferruz

Jutges de Cort
- Dr Miquel Rollan
- Dr Montserrat Ramon
- Dr Lluís Besturs

(b) The Audiència in 1640

1a *sala*

Dr Don Ramon Rubí de Marimón   Escaped to Madrid

Dr Gabriel Berart   Killed, 7 June 1640

Dr Lluís Ramon   Killed, 24 December 1640

Dr Felip Vinyes   Escaped to Madrid and made a Regent of the Council of Aragon

(One vacancy through the death of Dr Balaguer)

2a *sala*

Dr Miquel Carreras	Remained in Barcelona
Dr Jeroni Guerau	Killed trying to escape
Dr Don Bernat Pons	Escaped to Madrid
Dr Don Onofre d'Argensola	Died in hiding
Dr Benet Anglasell	Escaped to Madrid

3a *sala*

Dr Jaume Mir	Escaped to Madrid
Dr Francesc Corts	Escaped to Madrid
Dr Josep Massó	?
Dr Joan Baptista Gori	Killed, 24 December 1640

Jutges de Cort

Dr Rafael Puig	Killed, 24 December 1640
Dr Rafael Joli	Escaped to Madrid
Dr Don Guillèm Meca	Escaped to Madrid

GLOSSARY OF CASTILIAN AND CATALAN TERMS

In compiling this glossary I have drawn heavily on the glossary of technical and administrative terms provided by Abbott Payson Usher in *The Early History of Deposit Banking in Mediterranean Europe*.

Catalan words are printed in capital letters and Castilian words in italics.

ACTA DE CORT. A law which began its life as a royal decree or pragmatic, but which subsequently achieved the status of a CONSTITUCIÓ (q.v.) at the request of the CORTS (q.v.). Cf. CAPÍTOL DE CORT.

AGUTZIL. The equivalent of the Castilian *alguacil*. An official responsible for the maintenance of law and order, under the command of the GOVERNADOR (q.v.).

Alcabala. The tax on sales levied in Castile.

Arbitrista. Literally, a schemer or projector. The *arbitristas* in seventeenth-century Spain were the men who devised expedients and drew up schemes, whether sound or unsound, for the restoration of the royal finances and of the Castilian economy.

ARTISTA. An artisan, tradesman or skilled craftsman.

Asiento. A contract. The form of agreement made between the king and his bankers (*asentistas*) for the provision of money at a determined time and place under agreed conditions (see p. 260).

Atarazanas. See DRESSANES.

AUDIÈNCIA (*Audiencia*). The supreme tribunal in Catalonia, sitting in Barcelona. It was divided into three chambers (SALES, q.v.) and consisted of seventeen judges. Besides its judicial activities, it had also come to act as an advisory body to the Viceroy (see p. 86). Cf. CONSELL REIAL.

BATLLE. Bailiff. A local administrator appointed by king or lord, and entrusted with judicial as well as administrative duties, at the lowest level of jurisdiction.

BATLLIA GENERAL. The office in Barcelona, presided over by the BATLLE GENERAL, which was entrusted with the supervision of the Crown's patrimonial rights in the Principality. It acted as a court as well as an administrative office (see pp. 93–4).

BOLLA. See DRET DE LA BOLLA.

BRAÇ (plural BRAÇOS). Estate (sometimes called ESTAMENT). The three Estates of Catalonia consisted of clergy (BRAÇ ECLESIÀSTIC), nobility (BRAÇ MILITAR), and the representatives of the towns (BRAÇ REIAL). These three Estates were represented in the CORTS of Catalonia (q.v.), where they deliberated separately. Outside sessions of the CORTS, a meeting of the BRAÇOS could be summoned at short notice by the DIPUTATS (q.v.) to discuss matters of urgent interest and to give them advice and instructions. It would be attended by those representatives of the BRAÇ ECLESIÀSTIC and members of the BRAÇ MILITAR who were present in Barcelona at the time, and by the chief councillor of the city of Barcelona, who on this occasion spoke for the entire BRAÇ REIAL. The CORTS differed from the BRAÇOS in that they could be summoned only by the king, with due warning which allowed the attendance of members from distant parts of the Principality, and included representatives of thirty-one towns. Unlike the BRAÇOS they could (with royal assent) make laws.

CANCELLER. The Chancellor of Catalonia—a cleric presiding over the first chamber of the AUDIÈNCIA (see p. 85).

CAPÍTOL DE CORT. A law made in the CORTS at the request of the CORTS themselves, and accepted by the king with the words *Plau al senyor rei*—it pleases the king. Cf. CONSTITUCIÓ.

CAVALLER (*Caballero*). A knight, a member of the lesser aristocracy, as distinguished from a noble. Also sometimes known as a DONZELL or MILITAR.

CENS. A ground-rent.

CENSAL. An annuity or 'rente', which may apply (*a*) to a ground-rent, or (*b*) to interest from loans made to institutions and public corporations.

CIUTADÀ HONRAT. A distinguished citizen of Barcelona or of some other town. The highest civic rank, hereditary by nature, and originally conferred either by royal grant or by election by the existing group of distinguished citizens, theoretically in recompense for services rendered to the city.

COMTATS (*Condados*). The Counties of Rosselló and Cerdanya, united to the Principality of Catalonia.

Consejo de Aragón. The Council of Aragon, evolved out of the royal council of the medieval kings of Aragon. Now sitting in Madrid, it was entrusted with the affairs of Catalonia, Aragon, Valencia and Sardinia, and consisted (before Olivares's reforms) of a Treasurer-General, a Vice-Chancellor (*Vicecanciller* q.v.) and five Regents (*Regentes*).

Consejo de Estado. The Council of State, primarily, although not exclusively, concerned with external affairs. Nominally the most important Council in the Spanish Monarchy, although under Olivares it lost much of its powers to special Juntas, especially the *Junta de Ejecución* (q.v.).

Consejo de Hacienda. The Council of Finance. A council in Madrid—not in the first rank of the councils—entrusted with the administration of the royal finances.

CONSELL DE CENT. The Council of One Hundred, the city council of Barcelona, which met in the CASA DE LA CIUTAT, or town hall, of Barcelona to advise the CONSELLERS (q.v.) on matters of municipal government. For its composition see pp. 165–6.

CONSELLER-EN-CAP. The presiding officer of the executive council of Barcelona (the CONSELLERS, q.v.) and the principal representative of the city.

CONSELLERS. The five municipal councillors of Barcelona, holding office for one year, who formed the executive council of the city and were in charge of its government and the defence of its privileges.

CONSELL REIAL. Royal Council. An alternative name for the AUDIÈNCIA (q.v.)

CÒNSOL. A town councillor of Perpinyà or of a town in the Perpinyà region. See also JURAT and PAHER.

CONSTITUCIÓ. A statute or law, originally proposed either by the king or by the CORTS, but made jointly in the CORTS by both. (Cf. CAPÍTOL DE CORT.) The CONSTITUCIONS of Catalonia were the body of statutes by which the Principality was governed. They were compiled and printed in three volumes in 1588.

Consulta. A document drawn up by royal ministers, offering advice to the king.

CORTS (*Cortes*). The representative body, or parliament, of Catalonia, summoned by the king for the voting of subsidies and the passing of laws. Cf. BRAÇOS. The *Cortes* of Castile, summoned much more frequently than the Catalan CORTS, were less representative in that they consisted only of the representatives (*procuradores*) of eighteen towns—nobles and clergy no longer attending. Like the Catalan CORTS they were expected to vote subsidies, but, unlike them, they did not possess the right of legislation, since, in Castile, the power to make laws resided in the Crown. They could, however, present petitions, which, if accepted, became law.

CRIDA. An edict or proclamation issued by the viceroy of Catalonia.

DIPUTACIÓ. The deputation, or standing commission, of the CORTS of Catalonia, consisting of three DIPUTATS and three OIDORS (representing the three Estates), holding office for a term of three years and meeting in the palace of the GENERALITAT in Barcelona. The DIPUTATS were the supreme representatives of the Catalan nation, and were responsible for the defence of its laws and liberties, and for the collection of taxes, which were raised to meet the expenses of the DIPUTACIÓ and to pay for the subsidies granted to the king by the CORTS. Technically the DIPUTACIÓ DEL GENERAL DE CATALUNYA, it was often known as the GENERALITAT (q.v.).

DIPUTAT (*Diputado*). One of the three DIPUTATS DEL GENERAL, the Commissioners of the CORTS, who ran the DIPUTACIÓ (q.v.). See also OIDOR. There were also local DIPUTATS, entrusted with collecting the revenues of the GENERALITAT in the localities.

DISSENTIMENT. A statement of dissent which could be placed by a member of the CORTS and which, if accepted by his BRAÇ (q.v.), could slow down or halt the deliberations of the CORTS.

Donativo (DONATIU). A voluntary gift to the king, usually compulsory.

DONZELL. See CAVALLER.

DRESSANES (*Atarazanas*). The Barcelona dockyards, run by the DRESSANER (a Crown appointment).

DRET DE LA BOLLA. The tax on textiles levied by the DIPUTACIÓ. Its official title was DRET DE LA BOLLA DE PLOM I SEGELL DE CERA (the ball of lead and seal of wax).

DRET DE ENTRADES I EIXIDES. Tax on imports and exports, levied by the DIPUTACIÓ. Also known as the DRET DEL GENERAL (see Appendix III).

DRET DE LA NEU. A tax on the ice (literally 'snow') supplied to the city of Barcelona for refrigeration purposes, and brought either from Montseny or from the Pyrenees.

ESCUT. An *escudo* (see Appendix I on the Catalan coinage).

ESTAMENT. Estate (Cf. BRAÇ).

FADRISTERN. The younger brother in the Catalan family, who traditionally leaves home in search of a living (see pp. 38–40).

FOGATGE. By origin a tax on FOCS (hearths). The equivalent of a census of householders. The last general FOGATGE in the Principality of Catalonia before the eighteenth century took place in 1553 (see p. 26).

Fuero (*Fueros*). Originally a royal charter of rights and privileges granted— mainly in Castile—to a city or town in the course of the conquest of territories held by the Moors. *Fueros* was a word that appears to have been frequently applied in the seventeenth century to the laws and liberties of an entire state, like Aragon. This usage, although technically incorrect, was popularized by nineteenth-century historians, and has been adopted in this book, in certain contexts, for the sake of convenience.

GAVATX. The common Catalan term for a Frenchman. Also used as a term of abuse. The origin of the word is uncertain, but it may be derived from Gévaudan in France, a notoriously poor region from which came many immigrants into Spain (see Nadal and Giralt, *La Population Catalane*, p. 114, and the references there given).

GENERALITAT. The generality, or Estates, of Catalonia. The name was applied to the DIPUTACIÓ (q.v.), with which it eventually became synonymous.

GOVERNADOR. The Governor of Catalonia, the viceroy's deputy in the administration of the Principality. There was also a GOVERNADOR DELS COMTATS who resided at Perpinyà and was responsible for the government of Rosselló and Cerdanya.

GREMI (*Gremio*). A guild.

GREUGES. Complaints against royal abuses, made in the CORTS. The complaints were investigated by the JUTGES DE GREUGES, a special committee of

The Revolt of the Catalans

eighteen, of whom nine were represented by the king and nine by the
CORTS. The committee's report had to be examined by the king before the
CORTS adjourned or a subsidy was voted.

HABILITACIÓ. The inspection of credentials: the essential qualification for
administrative office or for a place in the CORTS.

HEREU. The heir, who inherits the bulk of the family property (see
pp. 36–9).

INSACULACIÓ. The system of balloting for public office in Catalonia, by
which names were placed in a bag or urn, and drawn by lot.

Junta de Ejecución. The most powerful administrative organ at Madrid in the
later years of Olivares's government. A small Junta consisting of Olivares
and other principal ministers, set up to avoid the delays and cumbersome
processes of government through the *Consejo de Estado* (q.v.).

JURAT. A town councillor of Girona or of a town in the Girona region. The
equivalent of a CONSELLER of Barcelona. See also CÒNSOL and PAHER.

LLOCTINENT. A lieutenant or deputy. LLOCTINENT GENERAL was an alternative
name for the viceroy of Catalonia.

LLOTJA (*Lonja*). Originally a public place or building in which merchants met
for commercial transactions. The LLOTJA of Barcelona was the centre of
Barcelona's commercial life, the bourse of registered merchants who
nominally controlled the city's trade.

MAS or MASIA. The peasant farmstead, run by the owner himself or by the
MASOVER (see p. 30).

MENESTRAL. A lesser craftsman. Extended in the sixteenth century to a class
of rural labourers.

Merced (plural *mercedes*). A reward or token of favour, granted by the king
to a vassal or vassals in return for a real or pretended service (*Servicio*, q.v.)
(see p. 41).

MER I MIXT IMPERI. The full civil and criminal jurisdiction enjoyed by some
Catalan barons in their domains (see p. 97).

MESTRE RACIONAL. A royal official responsible for seeing that royal rents and
dues in Catalonia were properly collected. By the seventeenth century
the post was hereditary in the family of the marquises of Aytona, and the
work was done by the LLOCTINENT DEL MESTRE RACIONAL, at the head of a
small office of accounting and investigation.

MILITAR. See CAVALLER and BRAÇ.

Millones. A tax collected in Castile from 1590, and periodically renewed by
the Castilian *Cortes*, on the sale of wine, oil and meat.

OBSERVANÇA. The constitution beginning DE OBSERVANÇA was one of the most
important of the Catalan constitutions. Decreed in 1481, it provided
methods for ensuring that the constitutions were observed by the king and
his officials (see p. 226).

OIDOR. One of the three officials known as the OIDORS DE COMPTES, responsible for examining the expenditure of the GENERALITAT, and forming with the three DIPUTATS the DIPUTACIÓ of Catalonia. The word OIDOR was also frequently used of a judge of the AUDIÈNCIA.

PAGÈS. A peasant. See REMENÇA.

PAHER. A town councillor of Lleida, or of a town in the Lleida region. See also JURAT and CÒNSOL.

PARAIRE. Technically a wool-dresser. Often a large-scale dealer in wool (see p. 55). Cf. TEIXIDOR.

PEDRENYAL. A firearm much favoured in seventeenth-century Catalonia, possessing a flintlock mechanism (see pp. 103-4).

PRAGMÀTICA. An ordinance made by the king outside the CORTS and having the force of law in so far as it did not conflict with the CONSTITUCIONS.

Procurador (Castilian or Catalan). An agent. The official appointed by a baron to govern his estates.

Protonotario. The Protonotary of the Council of Aragon—an office held from 1620 by Jerónimo de Villanueva, who was universally known simply as the Protonotario (see pp. 256-9).

PUBILLA. An heiress (see p. 37).

QUARTERA. A measure of grain, equal to 1·70 bushels. 1 QUARTÀ = $\frac{1}{12}$ QUARTERA.

QUINT (quinto). A fifth of the revenues of certain Catalan towns, claimed by the Crown.

REGALIA. A royal prerogative. The king's REGALIES were his fiscal and other rights, including certain judicial rights covering the more heinous crimes, which would be dealt with directly by the AUDIÈNCIA, instead of being first examined in local or baronial courts.

REMENÇA. The money payment by which a serf acquired his personal liberty. The PAGESOS DE REMENÇA were the fifteenth-century peasants who were subject to personal redemption.

SALA (plural SALES). A chamber. The principal room of a house. One of the three chambers in the AUDIÈNCIA.

SEGADOR. A harvester or reaper.

SENYOR (Señor). A lord. A Catalan baron was SENYOR of his village, and some barons were more frequently known by the title of their property than by their own name (e.g. Don Alexandre d'Alentorn was commonly called the SENYOR de Seró).

Servicio (SERVEI). Any service rendered to the king, financial or otherwise, and hence also used of a subsidy granted by the Cortes (see p. 41). Cf. also merced.

SÍNDIC. A syndic or agent, with limited powers to represent another person or corporation. The agents of cities and royal towns in the CORTS were known as SÍNDICS.

SOMETENT. A hue and cry. The armed contingent provided by towns and called out in emergencies. A SOMETENT GENERAL called the whole nation to arms.

SOTSVEGUER. Sub-vicar. The official in charge of a subdivision of a VEGUERIA (q.v.).

TAULA. Table or bench, and hence a bank. The TAULA DE CANVI (exchange) of Barcelona was the City Bank of Deposit.

TEIXIDOR. A weaver. Cf. PARAIRE.

Tercio. An infantry regiment, nominally of three thousand men, but by the seventeenth century considerably smaller.

TRACTADOR. A representative of one of the Estates in the CORTS, or of the king, whose duty it was to discuss affairs and bring about agreements between king and CORTS, and between the Estates themselves.

TRESORERIA. The pay office of the royal administration in Catalonia, presided over by the REGENT LA TRESORERIA (see p. 95).

VEGUER. Originally the vicar or local representative of the sovereign. The royal official in charge of one of the seventeen VEGUERIES—the administrative units into which Catalonia was divided. Cf. also SOTSVEGUER.

Vellón. Billon. Originally an alloy of copper and silver. In 1599 Philip III authorized for Castile a coinage of *vellón* of pure copper.

Vicecanciller. The Vice-Chancellor of the Council of Aragon, who acted as president of the Council. The post was allowed to lapse after 1623 (see pp. 255–6), but was revived after the fall of Olivares.

VICE-REGIA. A form of government whereby the Principality of Catalonia was ruled by the GOVERNADOR in the interim period before the king took his oath to observe the constitutions and appointed a viceroy.

Visita. The common procedure of inquiry in the dominions of the king of Spain into the conduct of royal officials. Carried out by a *visitador* appointed by the Crown, and technically done in secret, unlike the *residencia*, which was conducted in public at the end of an official's term of office. In accordance with a decision of the CORTS of 1599 there was supposed to be a *visita* of the royal administration in Catalonia every six years, but in fact it proved to be infrequent and irregular (see p. 89). The process of a *visita* was also used by the Catalans themselves for inquiry into the conduct of DIPUTATS and OIDORS at the end of their period of office.

APPENDIX VI

SOURCES

(I) MANUSCRIPT SOURCES

A: General
B: Barcelona City Archives and Libraries
C: Catalan Local Archives
D: Diaries and Contemporary Descriptions

A: GENERAL

It is a measure of the state of historiography of the reign of Philip IV that little or no reference has been made to the principal difficulty which confronts the historian of the reign who attempts to work from government documents. This difficulty is the distressing thinness of the documentation of the Councils whenever topics of major importance are approached. The explanation of this is probably to be found in Olivares's methods of government. His use of special Juntas removed many of the most important policy decisions from the Councils, and it is no doubt in the papers of the Juntas that the secrets of his government were buried. Unfortunately, the Conde Duque was given permission by the king to collect state papers relating to his period of office, and he is known to have taken a vast quantity of documents with him on his departure from Madrid in 1643. Against his wishes, his great library was dispersed after his death, and many, though apparently not all, of his papers eventually passed into the hands of the dukes of Alba. In 1794 and 1795 fires in the Alba Palacio de Buenavista destroyed the entire collection, with the single exception of volume 313.[1] For this reason it is unlikely that it will ever be possible to give to Olivares the kind of detailed study that has been given to Richelieu, and the account given in this book of Olivares's Catalan policy in 1639–40, inadequate as it is, may be the closest it is possible to get to any aspect of his policy. On the other hand, prophecies of this kind are notoriously dangerous and there is always a strong possibility that private Spanish archives and archives outside Spain will one day yield unexpected treasures. Dr Marañón, in the bibliography of his *Conde-Duque de Olivares*, gives a list of several of Olivares's letters and papers, some of which survive in contemporary copies scattered through the archives of Europe. I hope some day to be able to collect and edit the more important of these papers, many of which are likely to prove of outstanding interest to historians of the seventeenth century.

[1] Duque de Alba, *El Archivo de la Casa de Alba* (Madrid, 1953), p. 19.

Fortunately, the papers of the Council of Aragon have fared rather better than those of other Councils, although here also there are very large gaps. It is these papers, together with the *consultas* of the Junta de Ejecución for the year 1640, which have unexpectedly survived in the section entitled Guerra Antigua at Simancas, that provide the essential evidence for the discussion of Madrid's Catalan policy in this book. Many questions, however, remain to be answered, and unless or until new papers appear, this will not be possible. None the less, by a happy stroke of fortune much of the private correspondence received by Santa Coloma has found its way into the Archive of the Crown of Aragon, although this has happened for no other viceroy of Catalonia. These thirty-three boxes of correspondence, although containing much that is of little more than specifically military interest, have made it possible to complement the other, more official, papers for the crucial years 1639 and 1640, and to treat the immediate antecedents of the Catalan Revolution in greater detail than could otherwise have been done.

The following section lists the most important sources of general state papers and of diplomatic or other correspondence.

France

(a) Paris

    (i) Archives du Ministère des Affaires Étrangères (AAE)

Correspondance Politique, Espagne: 16; Supplément no. 3. (Valuable papers on the government of Catalonia, mostly prepared by or for Duplessis Besançon.)

    (ii) Bibliothèque Nationale (BN)

Baluze: 238. (Papers belonging to Dr Pujades, including a history of the plan for irrigating the plain of Urgell.)

Manuscrits Espagnols: 114–16. (Dr Sevillà's history of Catalonia since 1598. See section D.)

(b) Perpignan. Archives Départementales des Pyrénées-Orientales (ADP) Série B. 390. (Papers of 1639–40.)

Great Britain

(a) London

    (i) Archive of the Archbishopric of Westminster (AAW)

MS E. 2: Letter-book of Thomas Fitzherbert (Secretary to the duke of Feria, the viceroy of Catalonia from 1596 to 1602. The book includes one or two interesting letters of Feria on Catalan affairs and on the political situation in general.)

    (ii) British Museum (BM)

The British Museum contains an important, although diffuse, collection of Spanish manuscripts. (See Pascual de Gayangos, *Catalogue of the Manuscripts in the Spanish Language in the British Museum*, 4 vols., London 1875–95.) It is richer for the reign of Philip II than of his successors, but contains, among other documents of Philip IV's reign, some important papers by Olivares.

Additional MSS: 13,997 (papers on the Union of Arms); 14,007 (letters from Olivares to the Cardenal Infante); 25,686 (papers by Dr Francisco Ribas on the Catalan Corts of 1632); 25,688 (contains the *Nicandro*, the famous apologia for Olivares written after his fall from power); 25,689; 36,449 and 36,450 (letter-books of Sir Walter Aston, British Ambassador in Spain, 1620–5 and 1635–8).

Egerton MSS: 315; 338; 339 and 340 (papers of 1623–30 on the proposed Spanish trading companies); 347 (includes Olivares's great memorandum on government of 1624); 1820 (notebook of Sir Arthur Hopton, British agent in Spain, 1631–6); 2053 (papers by Olivares); 2082.

(iii) Public Record Office (PRO)

State Papers (Spain) 94.40, 41 and 42 (letters from Sir Arthur Hopton from the time of his return to Madrid in 1638).

(b) Oxford

Bodleian

MS Add. A. 137: *Relación del Levantamiento de Cataluña por Don Ramón Rubí de Marimón* ... 1642. (See section D.)

Rawlinson MSS: C. 799, *A Relation of Sundry Voyages and Journeys made by me, Robert Bargrave* (1654). (Includes a description of Barcelona and its commercial possibilities.)

Rawlinson MSS: D. 120, fos. 11–13, *An Incursion into Catalonia* (anon., 1648).

Spain

(i) Archivo de la Corona de Aragón, Barcelona (ACA)

Papers and registers are divided into several sections. (For the organization of the archive, see *Archivos de Barcelona. 1. Ciudad*, Guias de Archivos y Bibliotecas, Barcelona/Madrid 1952.) I have consulted the following:

Section 1. Archivo Real. Cancillería (Canc.)

Registros (R.): 3896 and 5515 (names of those attending the Corts of 1518 and 1626).

Registros (R.): 5214; 5526; 5527 (orders from viceroys to royal officials).

Procesos de Cortes 51 (official account of proceedings of Corts of 1626).

Varias de Cancillería: R. 332. (*Instrucciones públicas y secretas de SM. para el Duque de Segorbe y de Cardona*. October 1630. A volume of instructions for a new viceroy of Catalonia, of great interest.)

Varias de Cancillería: R. 387. (*Salida de Correspondencia del Conde de Santa Coloma*. Santa Coloma's orders to his officials, in such bad condition as to be almost useless.)

Section 2. Archivo Real. Patrimonio Regio

This section contains various books of the different financial departments of the viceregal administration in Catalonia, but I did not find them of any special use.

Section 3. Consejo Supremo de Aragon (CA)

An outstandingly valuable selection of papers of the Council of Aragon, beginning in the late sixteenth century and continuing right through the seventeenth. The section is divided into various subsections, including separate series for the secretariats of Aragon, Valencia and Catalonia. I have confined myself almost entirely to the Catalan secretariat, which again is divided into series, each following a more or less chronological order:

Legajos (leg.) 265–290: *consultas* of the Council of Aragon from the 1580's to 1640. An extremely useful, although unequal, series.

Legajos (leg.) 343–387: *cartas*. Largely consists of letters sent by the various viceroys of Catalonia to Madrid between about 1600 and 1640, interspersed with more *consultas* and various memoranda on Catalan affairs.

Legajos (leg.) 477–511: *memoriales*. Petitions addressed to the king, and again covering the years *c.* 1600–40. These petitions contain an immense amount of information of a personal nature, and provide unique material for a reconstruction of Catalan society in this period.

In addition, the following *legajos* contain much miscellaneous information that I have found useful, but scarcely lend themselves to classification: 1 and 2 (on the President and Treasurer-General of the Council of Aragon); 210; 224; 225; 226; 228; 230; 232; 233; 235; 260; 261 (papers on Corts of 1632).

Section 5. Generalidad de Cataluña (G)

Another important section, containing the documentation of the Diputació. I have consulted the following series:

Dietarios and *Deliberaciones*. Official reports of the proceedings of the Diputació. The fact that these are a purely impersonal record of the decisions reached by Diputats and Braços greatly diminishes their interest; and their value for this period, apart from the assistance they provide in establishing the chronology of events, is not very great. I have therefore consulted in detail only the volumes for 1614–17, 1620–3, 1626–9 and 1638–41.

Lletres Trameses (LT). Registers of letters sent by the Diputats. I have confined myself almost entirely to the volumes for 1638–9, 1639–40 and 1640–1. Unfortunately, very little of the correspondence received by the Diputació in this period has survived.

Registros (R.). R. 68: rough record of meetings of the *braç militar* (outside the Corts), covering, very erratically and incompletely, the years 1626–40. R. 1051–1053: records of the sessions of the *braç militar* in the

Sources

Corts of 1599. R. 1057–1058: records of the sessions of the *braç militar* in the Corts of 1626 and 1632. These volumes are extremely rough and incomplete, but, consisting as they do of notes taken during the course of the proceedings, they are of much greater interest than the official records kept in Latin in *Procesos de Cortes* 51 (section 1, *Cancillería*).

Miscellaneous volumes

14: *Consistori de Jurats de Virreys no haven jurat SM*. A collection, taken from the official records of the Diputació, of all the proceedings in the controversy over the appointment of the viceroy, 1621–3.

65/2: Records of the *Confraria de Sant Jordi* of Barcelona—the guild of the city aristocracy. Details of tournaments, etc.

78/4: *Llibre de Habilitacions*. Names of those eligible for posts in the Diputació.

85: nos. 20–9. *Llibre de values*. Registers of the revenues of the tax levied by the Generalitat, known as *entrades i eixides*.

114: *Dietari i Itinerari del Molt Ill. Sr. Francesc de Tamarit*. Record of the expedition of the Diputat Militar to the siege of Salces in 1639.

147: An attempted summary of the accounts of the Diputació, intended for presentation to the Corts of 1626. A hopeless muddle.

147/2: *Balans de les generalitats de Cathalunya per les corts del any 1632*. A rather fuller and clearer statement of accounts than the preceding volume.

909: *Lletres secretes*, 1605–74. Secret letters despatched by the Diputació. Useful, but not as secret as might have been hoped.

Boxes (cajas)

1–33: Boxes of correspondence between 1636 and 1640 addressed mainly to the count of Santa Coloma, each box containing letters for one or two months. Extremely valuable.

Section 6. Clero secular y regular

Monacales. Libros 45, 101, 103 (account-books of Barcelona convents).

(ii) Archivo General de Simancas (AGS)

A general guide to the resources of this magnificent collection is provided by Mariano Alcocer Martínez, *Archivo General de Simancas. Guia del Investigador* (Valladolid, 1923), and there are also printed catalogues to some of the sections. I have consulted the following sections:

(a) Cámara de Castilla

Legajo 2796. Documents relating to the career and trial of the duke of Lerma's Catalan favourite, Don Pedro Franqueza. Some interesting correspondence on Catalan affairs, and much revealing information on the state of the Crown's finances at the beginning of the reign of Philip III.

(b) Consejo y Juntas de Hacienda (Hacienda)

A remarkably rich series of *legajos* on the finances of the Spanish Monarchy, quite unexploited except for the recent study of Philip IV's finances by Professor Domínguez Ortiz, *Política y Hacienda de Felipe IV* (Madrid, 1960). I have examined a large number of *legajos* covering the period 1598–1640, and have found them invaluable for the light they throw on the financial problems of the Monarchy in these years (although they are less satisfactory for the later 1620's and the 1630's than for the earlier period). For the purposes of this book I have only quoted from them sporadically, and do not feel it necessary to provide here a list of all the *legajos* examined. It is to be hoped that the entire section will one day be systematically examined, and used as the basis for a general study of Spanish finances in the sixteenth and seventeenth centuries, along the lines of the studies by Professor Domínguez Ortiz and Dr Ramón Carande (*Carlos V y sus Banqueros*, vol. II, Madrid, 1949).

(c) Estado (España) (Est.)

Disappointingly thin for every aspect of Olivares's period of power, although there are a number of unknown and interesting papers by the Conde Duque himself, examining the Monarchy's situation and its prospects in the coming year. The contents of the *legajos* suggest the relative decline in the importance of the Consejo de Estado during the ministry of Olivares. In writing this book I have made most use of the following *legajos*: 255; 2640; 2645; 2646; 2651 (instructions for the Cardenal Infante); 2654; 2655–8 (papers on the proposed expedition to Catalonia in 1635); 2660 (important papers on Portugal); 2663; 4126; K. 1709; (Flandes) 2040, 2055; (Inglaterra) 2849; (Portugal) 4045, 4047.

(d) Guerra Antigua (GA)

Another enormous and extremely rich section, so far virtually unused and still uncatalogued for this period. This section should form the basis of any future study of the Spanish army and navy in the sixteenth and seventeenth centuries, although the variety of the documents it contains is likely to make it very difficult to use. While most of the material is strictly military, dealing with campaigns, munitions, personnel etc., the *legajos* for 1639 and 1640 contain invaluable documents of the Junta de Ejecución on Catalan affairs, which may have escaped Olivares's notice when he fell from power. Some of these documents were published by the nineteenth-century Catalan historian C. Pujol y Camps in the appendices to his edition of Parets's diary (*Memorial Histórico Español*, vols. xx–xxv). His selection of them was, however, curiously indiscriminate, perhaps because of the difficulty of discovering the contents of a large number of uncatalogued bundles of documents dealing with a wide variety of topics. It remains as difficult now as it was then to find one's way around these *legajos*, but the following have been of considerable use to me: 916; 1182 (the Leucata campaign); 1256 (June 1639); 1257 (July 1639); 1261 (October–December 1639); 1262 (August 1639); 1326 (January 1640); 1327 (March 1640); 1328 (May and June 1640); 1329 (July and August 1640); 1330 (September 1640); 1331 (October–December 1640, including *consultas* on the Portuguese revolt); 1336 (February 1640); 1354–1372 (correspondence of 1639–40, of which I have used 1354; 1355; 1358; 1361; 1364; 1366; 1367; 1368); 1374 (January–February 1641); 1375 (March and April 1641); 1376 (May, June and July 1641); 1377 (August and September 1641); 1378 (October–December 1641); 1379 (March 1641); 1422 (January, February, and June 1642); 1423 (March 1642); 1424 (April and September 1642); 1425 (July 1642).

(iii) Archivo Histórico Nacional, Madrid (AHN)

(a) Consejos suprimidos

Libros 1881–5: *consultas* of the Council of Aragon between 1621 and 1628 of varying degrees of importance and on a wide variety of subjects, especially the internal organization of the Council. There is a forty-year gap in the series, which begins again in the 1670's.

(b) Estado

Legajos 674; 860 (papers of great importance on the Catalan Corts of 1626 and 1632. A selection of these was printed in Manuel Danvila y Collado, *El Poder Civil en España*, Madrid, 1886, vol. VI, pp. 177–238). *Libros* 737 and 738 (*consultas* of the early years of Philip IV's reign, especially on the Union of Arms).

(c) Inquisición

Legajos 1594 and 2155 (papers of the Barcelona Inquisition, relating particularly to the limitations on its powers proposed by the Catalan Corts).

(iv) Biblioteca Nacional, Madrid (BN)

Sección de manuscritos. An important collection of manuscripts on a large variety of subjects. Copies of many of Olivares's best-known memoranda are to be found here, and there are many papers of general interest for the reigns of Philip III and IV. I have made use of the following MSS:

2358: *Respuesta a un papel del Duque de Alcalá en razón de las Cortes de Cataluña año 1626* (anonymous reply to a paper by the duke of Alcalá, written by someone with personal experience of the 1626 Corts).

2382: contains a printed paper by Dr Francesc Alegre, a canon of Urgell, on recent ecclesiastical events in Catalonia (1651).

3619: *Dietari de Sucesos de la Ciudad de Gerona.* A diary kept by Jeroni de Real, a leading citizen of Gerona, from 1637 (see section D).

6043: contains the confession of the duke of Medina-Sidonia (1641).

6745: contains a brief eye-witness account of the Catalan Corts of 1626.

(v) Real Academia de la Historia, Madrid (RAH)

G–43: *Anales de la Corona de Aragón en el Reinado de Felipe el Grande.* MS by Diego José Dormer.

11–10–5, *legajo* 6: copies of letters from Olivares to the Cardenal Infante between 1635 and 1641. These letters, together with others in the British Museum, are of the greatest interest and deserve publication.

11–13–5: letters from Olivares to the duke of Alcalá.

Salazar K–40: a book of *consultas* of the Council of Aragon, relating largely to the seventeenth century.

B: BARCELONA CITY ARCHIVES AND LIBRARIES

(See *Archivos de Barcelona*, 1, *Ciudad*)

(i) Academia de Buenas Letras (ABL)

I have used this collection only for the diary of Pujades (see below, section D).

(ii) Archivo Histórico de la Ciudad de Barcelona (AHB)

A fine collection of city records, some of which have been of the greatest use for the elucidation of the city's political behaviour in the reigns of Philip III and IV. I have confined myself exclusively to the section known as the *Fondo Municipal*, of which I have consulted the following series (see *Archivos de Barcelona*, pp. 43–4):

(*a*) Registros de Deliberaciones (Delibs.). Records of meetings of the Consell de Cent in 223 volumes, running from 1443 to 1774. These registers unfortunately suffer from the same defects as those of the Diputació. They are official proceedings veiled in a decent anonymity, recording only the decisions taken and not the way in which they were reached. This inevitably restricts their value, and I have used extensively only the volumes for 1626 and 1632 (which contain the proceedings of the sub-committee entrusted with the affairs of the Corts), and for 1638, 1639 and 1640.

(*c*) Lletres closes (LC). These are letters despatched by the city. I have consulted the volumes covering the years 1620–40.

(*e*) Cartes Comunes Originals (CCO). A magnificent collection of bound volumes of correspondence received by the city of Barcelona. The letters from the various special ambassadors sent by the city to the Court at different times have proved of exceptional value—more so than those of Barcelona's permanent agent in Madrid, Joan Grau, who discreetly tended to confine himself to generalities. I have been through all the volumes from 1600–40, together with one loose folder of seventeenth-century letters which were not bound in with the rest.

(*l*) Libro 57, *Matrícula dels antichs ciutadans honrats de Barcelona* (names of honorary citizens).

Corts 1626 and 1632. Rough registers of proceedings in the *braç reial* in the Corts.

Archivo Patrimonial. Papers relating to the estates of the Biure family.

(iii) Archivo de Protocolos (APB)

A remarkable collection of notarial records, classified under the names of notaries. A notary would keep different manuals for marriage contracts, wills, inventories, etc. There is in these manuals a vast amount of information which could prove of immense value to social and economic historians, although systematic exploitation would be difficult because of the lack of indexes in most of the manuals. I have run through the manuals of all the leading notaries between 1600 and 1640 in an attempt to work out some of the more important family relationships in the Catalan aristocracy and upper bourgeoisie and I have found some of the volumes of marriage contracts of great value for studying the structure of the Catalan family in the seventeenth century. The existence of these records would make it perfectly possible to study the fortunes of individual families over a long period, and it would, for instance, be revealing to study the rise in wealth and social prestige of a family which gets a son into the Audiència. It is greatly to be hoped that studies of this nature will one day be undertaken. Nor is there any need to confine these studies to inhabitants of Barcelona, since several towns (e.g. Girona) also have their own notarial archives containing records of a similar character. Some notarial records are written in Latin but the majority are in Catalan.

(iv) Biblioteca Central (BC)

Formerly the Biblioteca de Catalunya. It contains an important collection of MSS and of rare political pamphlets.

(*a*) *MSS*

501: fos. 157–71. Perot de Vilanova, *Memòries pera sempre*. (See section D.)

510: rough notes by Don Federic Despalau at end of volume entitled *Armas de algunas familias de Cataluña* by Bernat Mestre. (See section D.)

762: Albert de Tormé i Liori, *Miscellaneos* (sic) *históricos y políticos sobre la guerra de Cataluña desde el año 1639*. (See section D.)

979: fos. 66–70. *Diversos discursos sobre las cosas tocantes al servey de Deu, del Rey y bé comú de Catalunya*. Anonymous account of certain social and administrative grievances, probably drawn up in preparation for the Corts of 1626.

(b) *Fullets Bonsoms*

A remarkable collection of rare Catalan tracts and pamphlets made by Sr Bonsoms, invaluable for the study of seventeenth-century Catalonia and of the Revolution of 1640. An inventory exists. I have made use particularly of the following: 12; 15; 16; 5203 and 5204 (attack on the Catalans by the duke of Alcalá and a reply); 5211; 5229 (*Proclamación Católica*); 5382 (a discourse of 1626 on the Catalan coinage); 5394; 5404 (*Parer de Jaume Damians*, 1630. An important pamphlet on Catalan trade and industry); 5246 and 5247 (royalist tracts against the Catalan rebels); 9966 and 9967 (discussion of the merits of the Castilian and Catalan languages).

(v) Biblioteca de la Universidad de Barcelona (BUB)

The following MSS. have proved useful:

115: *Historia General del Principado de Cataluña...1598–1640*. Catalogued as the work of an eighteenth-century writer, Serra i Postius, it is in fact another copy of the contemporary history by Dr Sevillà, to be found in BN (Paris). (See section D.)

224: *Dietari de Miquel Parets*, vol. I. (See section D.)

975: *Dietari, 1627–30* (by Jeroni Pujades). (See section D.)

1189: *Verdad Defendida*...By Nofre de Selma i de Salavert (1632). An extravagant but entertaining and sometimes acute attack on Catalan social attitudes and behaviour, hitherto apparently unknown.

It has unfortunately been impossible to trace 21–4–3, catalogued as a collection of papers on Philip IV's visit to Catalonia in 1626, made by Dr Pujades. This might have been of very great value, and it is to be hoped that it will one day be rediscovered.

C: CATALAN LOCAL ARCHIVES[1]

(a) *Ecclesiastical*

On the whole, I have not made great use of ecclesiastical records. There is a great need for a study of the Catalan clergy and religious orders in the sixteenth and seventeenth centuries, and I believe that there is abundant documentation for such a study, although it is widely dispersed. I have largely confined myself to clerical records which impinge on the national scene, in the hope of discovering something about the political attitude of the clergy. For this purpose I have visited the following archives:

(i) Archivo Arzobispal de Tarragona (AAT)

Registers of sessions of the Provincial Council, of which I consulted nos. 24 (1602); 27 (1613); 32 (1635).

[1] Names of towns are given in their Castilian form.

(ii) Archivo Capitular de Tarragona (ACT)

Carteras 38; 39; 68. Correspondence received by the cathedral chapter between 1600 and 1640 (of limited value).

(iii) Archivo Capitular de la Seo de Urgel (ACU)

A disorganized but wonderfully rich archive, where I have found material of the greatest importance for the study of this turbulent cathedral chapter in the years before 1640, together with a number of unknown letters from Pau Claris. Most of this material comes from files of correspondence received by the chapter between 1600 and 1640 (labelled Cartes).

(iv) Archivo Capitular de Vich (ACV)

Cartas 1; 2; 3; 4. Correspondence covering the period 1580–1649. File 3 contains letters of great interest from the chapter's syndic at the Corts of 1626.

(b) Municipal

It is not easy to discover what municipal archives exist in Catalonia, especially after the destruction wrought by the Civil War, and how far they are likely to contain documents relating to the seventeenth century. I have therefore done a certain amount of travelling from town to town in the hope of tracking down surviving collections. While I have visited the major towns, with the exception of Igualada, Montblanch, Reus and Tortosa (in all of which there are municipal archives), the following should in no sense be taken as a comprehensive list:

Cervera (AHC)	Perpignan (AMP)
Gerona (AMG)	Seo de Urgel (AMU)
Lérida (APL)	Vich (AMV)
Manresa (AHM)	

I found nothing of value to me in the municipal archives of Camprodón (archive largely destroyed in 1835), Olot (although there is much here for the eighteenth-century historian), Santa Coloma de Queralt (documents almost entirely destroyed in the Civil War) or Tarragona (though this does contain some seventeenth-century material).

The town of Figueras in a petition of 1632 (ACA: CA, leg. 503) pronounced the following judgment: 'Experience has shown that archives of documents are more a matter of confusion than anything else.' Municipal archivists have performed wonders in reducing the confusion to order, often working under almost impossible conditions, and knowing that their labours are likely to receive little or no public recognition even in their home towns. They have almost everywhere received me with the greatest kindness, and have given me the freedom of their archives with a generosity such as an unknown foreign research student had no right to expect. I am deeply indebted to them.

Municipal documentation for the early seventeenth century usually consists of registers of municipal deliberations, copies of letters despatched by the town council, and files of correspondence it received (often classified as Cartes Rebudes, CR), together with fiscal and administrative records which I have only very cursorily examined. Generally, I have consulted the municipal registers only for the years 1639 and 1640, in an attempt to discover the impact of the Salces campaign, the billetings and the outbreak of the revolution in different parts of the Principality. On the other hand, I have, where possible, examined all the municipal correspondence between 1598 and 1640. In some towns, especially Cervera (which has perhaps the richest of all municipal archives for this particular period) this correspondence has often proved of the very greatest interest. Towns often sent special representatives to Barcelona, and even, occasionally, to Madrid, and they wrote back vivid accounts of the political situation and of the personalities they met. In particular, the letters of municipal syndics at the Corts of 1626 and 1632 provide much in the way both of information and of personal reactions which cannot be gleaned from official records. Since full references are given in the footnotes, I have not felt it necessary to list the files examined in each archive. It is very much to be hoped that the resources of Catalan local archives will be more systematically exploited for the writing of local histories in the years to come.

D: DIARIES AND CONTEMPORARY DESCRIPTIONS

Diaries and memoirs tend to be very rare in seventeenth-century Spain as compared with seventeenth-century England. In view of their rarity, it seems worthwhile to list separately records of this nature which have either come to light in the course of my researches, or which have not perhaps received the attention they deserved.

Despalau: rough notes at end of BC: MS 510 by Don Federic Despalau, covering a few of the political events of the last three decades of the sixteenth century. Of special interest for the introduction of the *excusado* into Catalonia in 1572, and for the Corts of 1599.

Guardia: diary of Joan Guardia of Corcó. The diary of a Catalan peasant, covering the middle decades of the seventeenth century. The original is in private hands, but a copy was shown me by Mossèn Junyent, the municipal and diocesan archivist of Vich. The diary consists of a series of year-by-year descriptions of the state of the weather and the crops. Of considerable interest for agrarian history, it deserves to be published.

Parets: *Dietari de Miquel Parets* (BC: MS 224). The Catalan version of a diary kept by Miquel Parets, a humble citizen of Barcelona, between 1626 and 1660, and published in a much less fresh and attractive Castilian version by Pujol y Camps (*MHE*, vols. xx–xxv). Apart from one or two eyewitness accounts, the diary is no more than a rather dull chronicle, redeemed neither by insight nor by inside information.

Pasqual: *Mémoires de Pierre Pasqual (1595–1644)*, ed. Paul Masnou (Perpignan, 1905). A moving record by a citizen of Perpignan of the misfortunes of his home town during a period of war and plague.

Pujades: *Dietari.* Incomparably the most important diary of this period to have come to light so far. Jeroni Pujades was a famous antiquarian and historian, author of the celebrated *Coronica Universal del Principat de Cathalunya*, of which the first part was published in 1609. While working in the library of the University of Barcelona, I came across an anonymous diary for 1627–30 (BUB: MS 975) which, from internal evidence, proved to have been written by Pujades. Other parts of Pujades's diary were known to exist in the Academia de Buenas Letras, and indeed had been used by Soler y Terol in his study of the bandit *Perot Roca Guinarda* (Manresa, 1909), but had otherwise been neglected. These three volumes turned out to be, if anything, even more interesting than the volume for 1627–30. Unfortunately, there is a ten-year gap in a decade where a diary would have been particularly interesting: 1610–20. The surviving parts of the diary are therefore as follows:

1 (1601–5), ABL; 2 (1606–10), ABL; 3 (1621–5), ABL; 4 (1627–30), BUB. In spite of the gaps, which may yet be filled, the diary fully deserves to be published in an annotated edition. Pujades explains that it began as a continuation of a diary begun by his father, Miquel Pujades, but that he felt that the beginning of a new century deserved a new volume. In his diary he notes down a certain amount of personal detail, but a large part of it is devoted to public events of one kind or another. Since he was well informed and possessed strong personal views, an extraordinarily lively picture emerges of Catalan life in the early seventeenth century. There are sharp and often mordant vignettes of public figures in the life of the Principality, and outspoken remarks about banditry, political and commercial events, and the rise of the low-born to wealth and titles (a phenomenon he incessantly deplores).

Real: *Dietari de Sucesos de la Ciudad de Gerona*, by Jeroni de Real (BN: MS 3619. Another, apparently slightly different version, in the municipal archive of Gerona). A diary, dating from 1637, kept by a leading citizen of Gerona, concentrating largely on events in the Gerona region. Valuable for the beginnings of the revolution. C. Pujol y Camps made use of this diary in his *Gerona en la Revolución de 1640* (Gerona, 1881).

Rubí: *Relación del Levantamiento de Cataluña por Don Ramón Rubí de Marimón …1642* (Bodleian MS Add. A. 137, fos. 74–157). Rubí was a member of the Audiència at the time of the revolution. His narrative starts with the end of the Salces campaign, and deals with the events of the revolutionary

year, ending with the dramatic story of his own escape from Catalonia.
I have come across no copy of this narrative (which is written in Castilian)
in the libraries of Barcelona or Madrid. While it is disappointingly uninformative on many of the things which someone in Rubí's position would
probably have known, it is none the less an extremely useful account of the
outbreak of the revolution, and throws light on certain points which in
other accounts remain obscure.

Sanz: *Relació breu dels sucessos, segonas intentions y locuras que an succehit y se son
fetas en la ciutat de Vich desdel any 1634 fins al del 1641 inclusive*, by Joan
Baptista Sanz. Published in *La Veu del Montserrat*, vol. xxv (1902). A
devastating account by an embittered citizen of Vich of the cowardice and
follies of his fellow-citizens, including a vivid narrative of the coming of
the revolution to Vich.

Sevillà: *Historia General del Principado de Cataluña. . .1598–1640*, by Dr Sevillà
(BUB: MS 115, and BN (Paris): MSS Espagnols 114-16). A contemporary history of the more important events in the Principality. Uneven,
erratic and often inaccurate, but containing some original anecdotes
together with personal information about leading Catalan figures. Pujol y
Camps made use of the Paris text.

Tormé i Liori: *Miscellaneos* (sic) *históricos y políticos sobre la guerra de Cataluña
desde el año 1639*, by Albert de Tormé i Liori (BC: MS 762). A verbose and
uninspired account of the origins of the revolution by a Catalan noble unsympathetic towards it. Some useful information. Used by Pujol y Camps.

Vilanova: *Memòries pera sempre* (BC: MS 501, fos. 157–71). Personal notes
of a Catalan gentleman, Perot de Vilanova, with some comments on
political events in the 1560's and 1570's. Particularly interesting for the
personal details.

(2) PRINTED WORKS

There is an admirable bibliography of works on Spanish history by B.
Sánchez Alonso, *Fuentes de la Historia Española e Hispano-Americana* (3 vols.,
3rd ed., Madrid, 1952), and since 1953 new books and articles on all aspects of
Spanish history have been listed, with critical comments, in a quarterly
publication, *Indice Histórico Español* (Barcelona). In view of the existence of
these bibliographical aids, I have felt it superfluous to provide a detailed list
of books consulted either for general Spanish history or for the history of
Catalonia. Full references will be found in the footnotes of my text to all
authorities directly cited. A few general comments, however, on Spanish and
Catalan history during the first half of the seventeenth century may be of
some interest.

(i) *Seventeenth-century Spain. General*

In spite of the impressive bibliography for the reigns of Philip III and IV,
general studies of major importance are very few indeed. The Spanish states-

man Antonio Cánovas del Castillo (1828–97) laid the foundations for all future work on the period in his *Historia de la Decadencia Española* (Madrid, 1854), *Bosquejo Histórico de la Casa de Austria* (Madrid, 1869), and *Estudios del Reinado de Felipe IV* (Madrid, 1888). Cánovas was the first man to break away from the harsh picture of a tyrannical Olivares drawn by nineteenth-century Spanish liberals, and his three works reveal in a most interesting way his gradual evolution towards a more sympathetic appreciation of Olivares as he himself grappled with Spain's problems. While he produced much new evidence, however, his own political career prevented him from undertaking a radical reappraisal of the period in depth.

Martin Hume, *The Court of Philip IV. Spain in Decadence* (1st ed., London, 1907; new ed., n.d., 1928?), remains the best-known general history of the reign. It is lively and entertaining, and makes good use of contemporary documents, but it is also superficial and inaccurate, and ought by now to have been superseded. Hume's taste for the picturesque tends to make him eschew the rigours of austere analysis.

Gregorio Marañón, *El Conde-Duque de Olivares* (Madrid, 1936; 3rd ed., 1952), is an important biography. Using a vast amount of new material, Dr Marañón, approaching his subject more from the point of view of a doctor and psychologist than of an historian, sought to analyse the character of the Conde Duque and the hidden springs of his passion for power. The result is stimulating, if not always convincing. The disjointed nature of the book reinforces the impression given by Dr Marañón's classification by sub-sections of the Conde Duque's principal characteristics, that he has taken Olivares to pieces but never quite managed to put him together again. The biography, however, is very valuable for the light it throws not only on the details of Olivares's career but also on his relations with his contemporaries. It is at its weakest in its study of the Conde Duque's political activities, which, in a book of over five hundred pages, rate only a single chapter of little more than twenty. There is an extremely full and useful bibliography.

(ii) *The Catalan Revolution*

Two important studies of the revolution were written by contemporaries: *Historia de los Movimientos, Separación y Guerra de Cataluña en Tiempo de Felipe IV* (Lisbon, 1645), by the Portuguese Francisco Manuel de Melo; and *Le Rivolutioni di Catalogna* (Bologna, 1648), by the Italian Luca Assarino. Melo, justly famed for his style, relies too much on his imagination and is not to be trusted (see the criticism by Celestino Pujol y Camps, *Melo y la Revolución de Cataluña en 1640*, Madrid, 1886). Assarino is more reliable, but provides no more than a straight narrative of the more outstanding events, probably based on the reports of Catalan exiles who fled to Italy.

Nineteenth-century general histories of Catalonia, of which the most important are V. Balaguer, *Historia de Cataluña y de la Corona de Aragón* (5 vols., Barcelona, 1860–3), and A. de Bofarull y Brocá, *Historia Crítica de Cataluña* (9 vols., Barcelona, 1876–8), tended to produce a stock picture of the revolution from a firmly nationalist standpoint, based primarily on tradition and on the records and pronouncements of the revolutionaries. This traditional picture was for the first time seriously challenged in the late nineteenth century by Celestino Pujol y Camps, particularly in his edition of Parets's chronicle (*MHE*, vols. xx–xxv), where he published a great many documents which suggested that there was another side to the story. Pujol's militant approach did not endear him to his contemporaries, and his methods laid him wide open to criticism. Instead, therefore, of laying the foundations for a new, and better documented, approach to the subject, his often embarrassing findings were dismissed or ignored. The traditional picture survived, as can be seen in two discourses given by Ferran de Sagarra in the *Ateneu Barcelonès* in 1930 and 1931, each of them bearing very revealing titles: *Les Lliçons de la Història. Catalunya en 1640*, and *La Unitat Catalana en 1640*. The general lines of the picture are also to be found in incomparably the best general history of Catalonia—Ferran Soldevila, *Història de Catalunya* (3 vols., Barcelona, 1935), of which a revised edition is in an advanced state of preparation.

Since the Spanish Civil War, the interest of the younger generation of Catalan historians has shifted away from political to social and economic history. This holds out promise of a great enrichment of Catalonia's attitude to its past, but their work is still only in its early stages and a vast amount remains to be done. For the time being, therefore, general Catalan history remains in a state of suspension. The only recent important contribution to the political history of the revolutionary period is José Sanabre, *La Acción de Francia en Cataluña en la pugna por la hegemonía de Europa (1640–1659)* (Barcelona, 1956), which stands on its own, outside any of the main currents of Catalan historical writing. It is a very meticulous narrative of events in Catalonia during the revolutionary years, based on prolonged investigations in French and Catalan archives. It will remain a standard source of information for the events of these years, although unfortunately it is defective in documentation from Castilian archives, and so tends to neglect developments in Madrid. My intention all along has been to produce an account of the circumstances attending the outbreak of the Catalan revolution, rather than of the revolution itself, and the publication of Mossèn Sanabre's important study has seemed to me to make it even less necessary to examine in detail the events of the years 1641–52. It also contains a very full bibliography of contemporary and modern works on the Catalan revolution, which precludes the necessity of printing another such bibliography here.

INDEX

Abancay (Peru), 514
Abbots
  in Corts, 218, 221, 242
  in Provincial Council of 1636, 321
  preferment of Cardenal Infante, 486
  of Sant Cugat, 149, 507
Absenteeism, royal
  and Crown of Aragon, 9, 12–13, 182, 202
  and Catalonia, 47, 74, 153, 157, 181–2, 468
Administration, of Spanish Monarchy, see Court; Monarchy
Administration, viceregal, in Catalonia, ch. IV, passim
  officials, list of (1598–1640), 568–71; viceroy, 79–83, and see Viceroyalty; Governador, 83, and see Governador; agutzils, 83, and see Agutzils; Audiència, 84–90, and see Audiència; local officials, 83–4, and see Local government
  justice, administration of, see Jurisdiction
  revenues of, 92–7, and see Revenue, royal (in Catalonia); financial departments, 93–6; salaries of officials, 72, 84, 93, 94, 96, 135, and see Appendix II (4); financial weakness of administration, 92, 94, 96–7, 107, 314
  effectiveness of, limited by Catalan constitutions, 78–9, 81–2, 101–2, 107, 295; by concessions in Corts of 1599, 102; Olivares's determination to avoid further concessions in Corts of 1626, 235, 236
  dependence of on support of Catalan ruling class, 102, 105, 438, 546–7, and see Ruling class; unpopularity in country at large, 87–9, 145, 377
  removal of to Girona (1635), 302, 304, 316–17; return to Barcelona (1637), 320
  and contraband controversy (1638), 338–41, 351–2
  collapse of in 1640, 433, 459, 467–8, 471, 488; demand for punishment and dismissal of ministers, 461, 465–7
  see also Audiència; Jurisdiction; Local government; Monarchy (in Catalonia); Office; Viceroyalty; Visita
Aerschot, duke of, 296
Africa, North, 53, 188
Agitators, 371, 422, 447
Agramunt, Jaume, secretary to Barcelona city council, 460

Agriculture
  in Castile, 183
  in Catalonia, 25, 28, 32, 56–8, 186; war devastation, 362, 368, 391
  see also Corn; Drought; Irrigation
Aguilar, count of, army commander, 392
Agutzils, 83, 289, and see Monrodón, Miquel Joan
Álamos de Barrientos, Baltasar, political theorist, 184, 191, 198
Alba, family of, 17
  3rd duke of (Fernando Álvarez de Toledo), 19
Albanell, Don Galcerán, tutor to Philip IV, 69, 200 n. 1
Alburquerque, 7th duke of (Francisco Fernández de la Cueva), viceroy of Catalonia, 278, 325 n. 3
  appointment and arrival in Catalonia, 110, 116–18
  and constitutions, 118–20, 128, 227
  restoration of order, 121–6, 221, 485
  and the towns, 122–3, 126–7, 140, 145–6, 237
  later policies towards Catalans, 301, 312–15 passim
Alcabala, 185, 189; see glossary
Alcalá, duke of (Fernando Afán de Ribera y Enríquez), viceroy of Catalonia, 224, 229, 290, 421
  character of, 127–8; and horrors of governing Catalonia, 147
  and Fontanella, 169
  antagonizes: aristocracy, 128, 147, 221, 486; Diputació, 128–30, 138, 147 (and see Galleys); towns, 138, 140, 144–7; Barcelona, 146–7
  reappointment of, 148–9, 152–3
  and Court of Madrid, 150–1, 154, 192
  threatens constitutions, 159, 187, 227, 250
  proposes Corts for constitutional reforms, 151, 223–4, 388
  memorandum against conclusion of Corts, 249, 259
  see also under Quints
Alegre, Dr, Catalan ecclesiastic, 470, 473
Alemany, Don Carles de, 100
Alemany, Dr Don Enric d', canon and sacristan of Vic, 231, 244, 289
Alentorn, Don Alexandre d', son of Don Nofre, 58, 76

Index

Index

Index

Barcelona (*cont.*)

finances

revenues, 96, 164, 333

list of services to king (1626–37), 333; loans for royal visits, 243, 267–8, 269, 272, 388, 508; gifts, 269, 303, 320–1, 333; refusal to lend 70,000 ducats (1639), 353–4, 359; loan to Diputació, 380

ceremonial and precedence, 54, 109, 164–5; cost of embassy to Madrid, 136 n. 4

privileges, 161, 269; concerning troops, 97, 164, 382, 403; right to be covered in royal presence (*cobertura*), 276–7, 547 n. 1; towns' objections to extent of city's privileges, 223, *and see under* Towns for Barcelona's relations with towns

in reign of Philip III

relations with Monteleón, 107; with Almazán, 108–9; and dearth of coins (1615), 114; approval of Alburquerque, 124; antagonized by Alcalá, 146–7

in reign of Philip IV

dispute over appointment of viceroy, 155–7, 160, 168, 170–7

and Corts of 1626, city's syndics in, 215–16, 218; royal entry, 217–18; city's anxiety for satisfactory conclusion, 232, 236; departure of king, 242, 243; despatch of Conseller with petitions for king, 243–5; petitions of 1626, 267, 303, 349

dispute with Perpinyà (1629), 265–6

dispute with Cardona over plague precautions (1631), 269–70, 272

dispute over privilege of remaining covered in royal presence (1632), 276–8, 281–5, 333, 547 n. 1; *dissentiment* placed in Corts of 1632, 278–85 *passim*

dispute over *quints*, see *Quints*; Navel sent to Madrid, 291–3, 295–6

removal of Audiència (1635), 299–302, 304, 316–19; return (1637), 320

embassy to prevent reappointment of Cardona (1636), 317; Cardona's return, 320

troops for Leucata (1637), 325; for defence, 334

Santa Coloma's attempts to reconcile city and Court (1638), 331, 332–4; explanation of city's intransigence, 335

and contraband dispute (1638), 349–51, 353–5

pragmatics of 1639 on French residents

and levy for fortifications, 352–4; Navel sent to Madrid, 354, 358–60

order for appropriation of *dret de la neu*, 353–4, 364

Salces campaign, troops for, 364, 381; obstructionist tactics, 378–9, 381–3; departure of Conseller-en-Cap for Salces, 382–3; return, 398

protests against behaviour of troops (1640), 398–400

suggested billeting of troops in, 403, 407

arrest of Serra, Vergós and Tamarit, 407–9, 416; embassy sent, 408–9; rebels enter and free prisoners, 428–30

Corpus day, 445–51; Olivares's refusal to see envoy, 452

assistance for Perpinyà, 458

and revolutionary leaders, 470, 478–9, 503; alienation from Crown, 487; preparations for war, 494–5, 499

riot of 24 December, 520–1

battle of Montjuic, 522

under the French, 534–5

besieged and recaptured by Spaniards (1651–2), 539–40

bank, 62–3, 380; *Taula de Canvi* (deposit bank), 62–3, 164, 450

casa de la ciutat (town hall), 156, 166

Customs House (*Duana*), affair of 1632, 292, 297, 298

dockyards (*Dressanes*), 61, 93, 161, 280; placing of Castilian arms on, 147

fortifications, 161, 213, 280, 494–5

Llotja, 161, 165, 359; decline of, 274–5

prisons, 147 n. 2, 319, 352, 359, 521; attacked by insurgents, 429–30

Santa Eulalia (patron saint of city), 216, 382

theatre, 69 n. 6, 162

Barcelona, diocese of, 27

bishops of; see Gil Manrique, *and* Sentís

cathedral of, 109, 216, 276–7, 428, 540

canons of, 131, 152, 291

Barutell, Don Llorenç de, canon of Urgell, 481, 483

Batlle(s), 83–4, 93, 98, 103; *see* glossary of Cadaqués, in clash with troops, 250

Batllia General, 93–6

Bayetolá, Matías de, Regent of the Council of Aragon, 317, 319, 376, 454

Bellafilla, Josep de, city councillor of Barcelona

in dispute over appointment of viceroy, 163, 167, 173, 175

as ambassador to Court, 164, 270, 272, 300

Benavides, Don Juan de, Inspector General of the Army, 445

Index

Index

Index

Currency
in Castile, 7; chronic monetary instability in seventeenth century, 62, 186; crisis of 1627–8, 261–2; of 1641–2, 524–5; vellón, 214, 261–2, 307, 358, 401, 524–5; of lower standard than Catalan, 61; fears of introduction into Crown of Aragon, 213–14, 496, 550
in Catalonia, 7, 140; disorders of 1599–1617, 61–4, 108, 114, 123; recoinage (1611), 63–4; inflation of 1640–52, 538–9; export of, 223, 564; municipal mints, 62; counterfeiting, 62, 64, 85, 100, 159
see also Appendix I
Customs
barriers, 7, 159, 203
dues, 129, 339–40, 348; *and see* Appendix III
dispute (1632), 292, 297, 298
Cuzco, 514

Dalmau, Francesc, *ciutadà honrat* of Barcelona, 303
Damians, Jaume, Barcelona merchant, 56, 238
Defence
imperial, problem of, 184, 190–2, 197 n. 2, 204–6, *and see* Union of Arms
of Catalonia, 82, 213, 237, 319; coastal, 129, 211; neglected state of defences, 97, 138, 150, *and see* Castles; compulsory levy for, 352–4, 361, 414; Catalan self-sufficiency for, 466, 473, 499–500. *See also under* Army
of Barcelona, 213, 280
the supreme law, 356, 361, 390, 401, 406, 502
Descallar, Don Lluís, noble of Vic, 464
Despuig, Cristòfol, writer, 13 n. 3, 72 n. 1, 322
Desvalls, Beltran, Conseller-en-Cap of Barcelona, 283
Díaz Aux de Armendáriz, Luis, bishop of Urgell, viceroy of Catalonia, 225, 259
Diputació, 7, 46, 130–8; composition, 46, 130–3; composition in 1638, 341–2; powers, 134, 152, 406; revival in 1638, 341, 348, 355; lawyers of, 149, 152, 156–7, 169, 348–53 *passim*, 459; offices in, 72, 132–5, 136, 137, 223, 239, 284; corruption, 129, 134; demands for reform, 136–7, 223, 240, 284, 359
finances, 230, 239, 249
revenues, 92, 134–6, 138, 239, 379–80; threatened seizure of, 408, 414–15; *dret del general*, 92, 134, 273–4, 339–40, 348, 508; *dret de la bolla*, 92, 129, 134, 508; duty for galleys, 129, 134–5, 379; reserve for subsidies, 92, 136, 239, 331;

increase in dues (1640), 507–8; expenditure, 135–6, 239, 359, 379; salaries 92, 96, 134–5, 359; celebrations, 136–7, 336, 359; embassies, 136, 379
relations
with viceroys, 137–8; duke of Feria orders arrests, 50–1, 87; Almazán, 108–9; Alburquerque, 120–1, 123; Alcalá, 128–9, 138, 147, *and see* Galleys; Santa Coloma: contraband dispute, 340–1, 347–53, 365, enmity with Diputats, 346–7, 364–6, 371, 378–80, 398–400, arrest of Tamarit, 408–9
with Audiència, 352, 466–7
with Madrid: arrests of 1569, 50–1; dispute over appointment of viceroy, 148–60 *passim*, 169–71; protests over troops, 330, 347; attitude to billeting, 394, 396–400, 404–6, 435; embassy of 1640, 405–6, 452–3, 500, 504–5; conditions for pacification, 435, 439, 465–6; final break, 468–72, 521–2
with Catalan ruling class, 101, 120–1, 160, 162–3; unpopularity in Principality at large, 101–2, 127, 137, 146, 211
with clergy, 288
with Barcelona, 151–2, 168–9, 349–55, 478–9, 503
with insurgents, 429, 435, 450, 459–60, 464–5; efforts to mobilize Principality, 499–500, 508–9; convocation of Braços (September 1640), 501–3
with France, 469–70, 477–8, 500–4, 509, 521–2, 534–5
Dissentiment, 220–1, 226–45 *passim*
placed by Barcelona (1632), 278–9, 283–5
see glossary
Dockyards (*dressanes*) of Barcelona, 61, 93, 161, 280, 291, 359
placing of arms of Castile on, 147
superintendent of, 168
Donativo
in Castile (1625), 208, 246, 260; (1632), 271
in Crown of Aragon, 208, 210, 319, 520
see glossary
Downs, battle of (1639), 402, 524
Dowries, 35, 36, 38, 71
Dressanes, *see* Dockyards
Drought, 25, 32, 56–8, 60, 273, 426
prayers for rain, 33, 50, 444–5
see Irrigation
Duplessis Besançon, Bernard, Richelieu's agent in Catalonia, 504, 509, 521–2
on Catalan character, 44 n. 2; on significance of Revolution, 523; on Catalan republic, 532–3

Index

Index

Index

Pujades *(cont.)*
(1625), 213; monastic reforms, 253, 258; Louis XIII, 254; San Plácido scandals, 257–8; loss of silver to Italy, 268
Pyrenees, 22, 23, 24, 541
Peace of the (1659), 541, 547

Queralt, Don Lluís de, son of count of Santa Coloma, 380, 448, 452, 526
Quintana, Josep, Diputat Reial, 342 n. 1
Quints, 93, 96, 144–7
Alcalá and, 144–7, 150, 192, 249
towns' attempts to secure royal renunciation in Corts of 1626, 222–3, 224, 232, 234, 236–7; in Corts of 1632, 276, 279
royal offer to cancel arrears (1626), 241; fresh proposal for exaction (1632), 281; unwillingness to consider wholesale renunciation (1640), 440
of Barcelona: Alcalá's proposal, 146–7, 150, 160; Diputats support city, 151–3; Osona's promise (1623), 176–8; influence on city's policy in 1626, 224, 236–7, 267; possible renewal of Crown's claim (1629–30), 268; struggle of 1634–5, 290–304 *passim*; the search for a compromise (1636–8), 318, 320, 331, 333, 341, 349
as a contribution to alienation of municipal oligarchies, 487
Quirra, countess of, 483

Ramon, Dr Josep, lawyer to duke of Cardona, 233
Ramon, Dr Lluís, judge of the Audiència, 368, 521
Reart, Francesc, priest of Perpinyà, 339
Recife, captured by Dutch (1630), 493
Reconquista, 3
Recruiting
in Castile, 185, 192, 306, 402
in Crown of Aragon, 206–7, 323
in Catalonia, 317–18, 324–5, 362
see also Princeps Namque
Regalia, 85, 87, 101, 350, 409
writ of, and Jeroni de Navel, 298, 302
see also glossary
Regent la Reial Cancelleria, 85, 121, 534
Regent la Tresoreria, 76, 95–6, 102
Regents (of Council of Aragon), 9, 121, 151, 230
alleged unreliability of, 255
and Union of Arms, 210–11, 213–14
individual recommendations on policy towards Catalonia, 265, 287
and see Fontanet, Salvador *and* Magarola, Joan

Reguer, Don Francesc, Barcelona tax-farmer, 129
Religious orders in Catalonia
foundations, 26; lands and jurisdiction, 97
representation in Diputació, 131
unruliness and low educational standards, 111, 252; attempted reforms, 252–3, 258, 486–7
and risings of 1640, 422, 427, 446–7, 464, 487
Republic, Catalan, 521–2, 532–3
ministerial suspicion of plans to establish, 280–1
Requesens, family of, 65
Requisitioning, 367–8, 376–8
Reus, 24, 426, 539
population, 27
Revenue, royal
in Castile, *see* Finance
in Catalonia, 92
annual income, 96
sources of income (*see also* Taxation): feudal aids (*coronatge*), 208; judicial, 96; papal concessions, 92–3, 238, *and see under* Church; royal patrimony, 94–5, 210, 314, 336, *and see* Patrimony; *quints*, 96, 144–5, *and see under* Quints; subsidies from Corts, 49 n. 4; gifts and loans from towns, *see under* Barcelona *and* Towns
revenue departments, 93–6
expenditure, 96–7
from America, *see* Silver
from other parts of Monarchy, 184–5, 189, 190–1, *and see* Taxation
Revolution, in Catalonia
fears of: (1615), 117; (1622–3), 155, 171–2; (1634), 289; (1640), 410–11
of 1640: Olivares's alleged instigation of, 200–1; as a social upheaval, 460, 462–5, 468, 521, 533; leaders of, 473–9, 483; leaders' break with Castile, 521–2; objectives, 532–3; theoretical justification, 549–51; end of, 540–1; significance of, 523–6; compared with Portuguese, 541–5
Ribas, Dr, 283, 295
Ribera de Sió, 56
Ribes, rector of, 484
Ricart, baker of Vic, 464
Richelieu, Cardinal
advent to power (1624), 212
unrest in France, 262, 305–6, 403, 525
desire for peace, 305, 492
war with Spain (1635), 306; campaign of 1638, 332; of 1639, 360, 369
and Catalonia, 469, 484, 532–4, 536
and Portugal, 513, 515

Index